Alonzo K. Parker.

Poughkeepsie, Jan. 1871

THE

LIFE OF JESUS CHRIST

IN ITS

HISTORICAL CONNEXION AND HISTORICAL DEVELOPEMENT.

BY

AUGUSTUS NEANDER.

TRANSLATED FROM THE

Fourth German Edition,

BY

JOHN M'CLINTOCK AND CHARLES E. BLUMENTHAL,
PROFESSORS IN DICKINSON COLLEGE.

NEW YORK:
HARPER & BROTHERS, PUBLISHERS,
329 & 331 PEARL STREET,
FRANKLIN SQUARE.
1870.

TO MY CHRISTIAN BRETHREN IN THE UNITED STATES OF AMERICA.

THE present age may be considered an epoch of transition in the developement of the kingdom of God; and, as such, it is full of signs. Among the most striking of them is a greater zeal for the spread of the Gospel and the Bible through all nations, combining many and various agencies for that work; as well as a closer union among all earnest Christians, seekers of salvation and truth, of all lands, however widely separated—a new Catholic Church, which, amid all the diversity of outward ecclesiastical forms, is preparing that unity of the spirit which has Christ for its foundation. Especially is it matter of rejoicing to see a growing spirit of fraternal union between the Christians of the Old World and those of the New; a land in which Christianity (the destined leaven for all the elements of humanity, how various soever) developes its activities under secular relations so entirely novel.

It was, therefore, very gratifying to me to learn that Professors M'CLINTOCK and BLUMENTHAL had determined to put this volume, the fruit of my earnest inquiries, before the transatlantic Christian public in an English dress. To see a wider sphere of influence opened for views which we ourselves (amid manifold struggles, yet guided, we trust, by the Divine Spirit) have recognized as true, and which, in our opinion, are fitted to make a way right on through the warring contradictions of error, cannot be otherwise than grateful to us. For truth is designed for all men: he who serves the truth works and strives for all men. The Lord has given to each his own *charisma*, and with it each must work for all. What is true and good, then, is no man's own; it comes from the Father of Lights, the Giver of every good gift, who lends it to us to be used for all. And what is true, must prove itself such by bearing the test of the general Christian consciousness.

But the pleasure with which I write these words is not unmingled with anxiety. To write a history of the greatest Life that has been manifested upon earth—that Life in which the Divine glory irradiated earthly existence—is indeed the greatest of human tasks. Yet the attempt is not presumptuous (as I have said in the preface to the German edition), if it be made upon the Gospel basis: every age witnesses new attempts of the kind. It is part of the means by which we are to appropriate to ourselves this highest life; to become more and more intimate with it; to bring it nearer and nearer to ourselves. Every peculiar age will feel itself compelled anew to take this Divine Life to itself through its own study of it, by means of science, animated by the Holy Spirit; to gain a closer living intimacy with it, by copying it. To eat His flesh and drink His blood (in the spiritual sense) is indeed the way to this intimacy; but science also has its part to do, and this work is its highest dignity. But yet, in view of the grandeur and importance of this greatest of tasks, in view of the difficulties that environ it, and our own incapacity to execute it adequately, we cannot see our work diffused into wider and more distant circles, without fear and trembling. We are fully conscious of the dimness that surrounds us, growing out of the errors and defects of an age just freeing itself from a distracting infidelity. May we soon receive a new outpouring of the Holy Ghost, again bestowing tongues of fire, so that the Lord's great works may be more worthily praised!

I have another, and a peculiar source of anxiety. This book has arisen (and it bears the marks of its origin) amid the intellectual struggles which yet agitate Germany, and constitute a preparatory crisis for the future. Those who are unacquainted with those struggles may, perhaps, take offence at finding not only many things in the book hard to understand, but also views at variance with old opinions in other countries yet undisturbed. The English churches (even those of the United States, where every thing moves more freely) have perhaps, on the whole, been but slightly disturbed by conflicting opinions of precisely the kind that find place among us. Had they to deal with the *life-questions* with which we have to do, they would be otherwise engaged than in vehement controversies about church order and other unessential points. It would be easier, *then*, for them to forget their minor differences, and rally under the one banner of the Cross against the common foe. Perhaps a nearer acquaintance with the religious condition of other lands may contribute to this end.

I am, notwithstanding, still afraid that some readers unacquainted with the progress of the German mind, which has de veloped new intellectual necessities even for those who seek the truth believingly, may take offence at some of the sentiments of this book. Especially will this be likely to happen with those who have not been accustomed to distinguish what is Divine from what is human in the Gospel record ; to discriminate its immutable essence from the changeful forms in which men have apprehended it ; in a word, with those who exchange the Divine *reality* for the frail support of traditional beliefs and ancient harmonies. I would lead no man into a trial which he could not endure ; I would willingly give offence to none, unless, indeed, it were to be a transitory offence, tending afterward to enlarge his Christian knowledge and confirm his faith. How far this may be the case, I am not sufficiently acquainted with the transatlantic Church to be a competent judge. Nor would I, on my own sole responsibility, have introduced this work (which arose, as I have said, among the struggles of our own country) to a foreign public: this I leave to the esteemed translators, hoping that their judgment of the condition of things there may be well founded.

But of this I am certain, that the fall of the old form of the doctrine of Inspiration, and, indeed, of many other doctrinal prejudices, will not only not involve the fall of the essence of the Gospel, but will cause it no detriment whatever. Nay, I believe that it will be more clearly and accurately understood ; that men will be better prepared to fight with and to conquer that inrushing infidelity against which the weapons of the old dogmatism must be powerless in *any* land ; and that from such a struggle a new theology, purified and renovated in the spirit of the Gospel, must arise. Everywhere we see the signs of a new creation ; the Lord will build himself, in science as well as in life, a new tabernacle in which to dwell ; and neither a stubborn adherence to antiquity, nor a profane appetite for novelty, can hinder this work of the Lord which is now preparing. May we never forget the words of the great apostle, "*Where the Spirit of the Lord is, there is Liberty.*" Whatever in this book rests upon that *one foundation* than which none other can be laid, will bear all the fires of the time ; let the wood, hay, and stubble which find place in all works of men, be burned up.

Perhaps the impulse* which the American mind has received

* Not, it is to be hoped, a one-sided, partisan tendency, as is justly remarked by Professor PORTER, whose article on "*Coleridge and his American Disciples,*" in the Bibliotheca Sacra for February, 1847, I have read with great interest.

from the profound Coleridge, who (like Schleiermacher among ourselves) has testified that Christianity is not so much a definite system of conceptions as a power of life, may have contributed, and may still further contribute, to prepare the way for a new tendency of scientific theology in your beloved country.

A. Neander.

Berlin, November 4 1847.

TRANSLATORS' PREFACE.

THE work, of which an English version is presented in this volume, appeared originally in 1837. It has already passed through four editions, from the last of which* this translation has been made.

It is well known that Dr. NEANDER has been engaged for many years in writing a "General History of the Christian Religion and Church," and that he has published separately an account of the "Planting and Training of the Early Christian Church by the Apostles." He would doubtless have felt himself constrained, at some period, to give a history of the life and ministry of the Divine Founder of the Church; and, indeed, he states as much in the preface to this work (page xxi.). The execution of this part of his task, however, would perhaps have been deferred until the completion of his General History, had not the "signs of the times" urged him to undertake it at once. Its immediate occasion was the publication, in 1835, of STRAUSS's "Life of Christ,"† a work which, as every one knows, created a great sensation, not merely in the theological circles of Germany, but also throughout Europe. A brief sketch of the state and progress of parties in Germany may be useful to readers not familiar with the literature of that country; and we here attempt it, only regretting our incapacity to give it fully and accurately.

Notwithstanding the *dread* with which German theology is regarded by many English and some American divines, it was not in German soil that the first seeds of infidelity in modern times took root. It was by the deistical writers of England, in the early part of the last century, that the authenticity of the sacred records was first openly assailed. The attacks of Toland, Chubb, Morgan, &c., were directed mainly against the credibility and sincerity of the sacred writers; and their blows were

* Das Leben Jesu Christi, in seinem geschichtlichen Zusammenhange und seiner geschichtlichen Entwickelung dargestellt von Dr. AUGUST NEANDER, vierte und verbesserte Auflage, Hamburg, bei Friedrich Perthes, 1845.

† Das Leben Jesu, Kritisch bearbeitet von Dr. DAVID FRIEDRICH STRAUSS. 2 Bde Tubingen, 1835, 4te Aufl., 1840.

aimed, avowedly, against the whole fabric of Christianity. It is needless to say that they failed, not merely in accomplishing their object, but in making any very strong or permanent impression on the English mind. Nor has an infidelity of exactly the same type ever obtained firm footing in Germany. The English Deism, first promulgated in the Wolfenbüttel fragments, set the German theologians at work upon the canon of Scripture, and upon Biblical literature in general, with a zeal and industry unknown before; and many of them pushed their inquiries with a freedom amounting to recklessness; but a direct and absolute denial of the authority of the word of God is a thing almost unknown among them. Still, professed theologians, of great talents and learning, and holding high official positions, adopted a theory (the so-called *Rationalism*) more dangerous than avowed infidelity, and succeeded, for a time, in diffusing its poison to a painful extent.

The declared aim of the Rationalists was to interpret the Bible on *rational* principles; that is to say, to find nothing in it beyond the scope of human reason. Not supposing its writers to be impostors, nor denying the record to be a legitimate source, in a certain sense, of religious instruction, they sought to free it of every thing *supernatural;* deeming it to be, not a direct Divine revelation, but a product of the human mind, aided, indeed, by Divine Providence, but in no extraordinary or miraculous way. The *miracles,* therefore, had to be explained away; and this was done in any mode that the ingenuity or *philosophy* of the expositor might suggest. Sometimes, for instance, they were no miracles at all, but simple natural facts; and all the old interpreters had misunderstood the writers. Sometimes, again, the *writers* of the sacred history misunderstood the facts, deeming them to be miraculous when they were not; *e. g.*, when Christ "healed the sick," he merely prescribed for them, as a kind physician, with skill and success; when he "raised the dead," he only restored men from a swoon or trance; when he "subdued the storm," there was simply a happy "coincidence," making a strong impression upon the minds of the disciples; when he fed the "five thousand," he only set an example of kindness and benevolence which the rich by-standers eagerly followed by opening their stores to feed the hungry multitude, &c., &c. But even this elastic exegesis, when stretched to its utmost capacity, would not explain every case: some parts of the narratives were stubbornly unyielding, and new methods were demanded. For men who had gone so far, it was easy to go farther; the text itself was not spared; this passage was doubtful, that was corrupt, a third was spurious. In short, "criticism," as this desperate kind of interpretation was called, was at last able to make any thing, and in a fair way to make *nothing*, out of the sacred records. But still the rationalist agreed with the orthodox supernaturalist in admitting that there was, at bottom, a basis of substantial truth in the records; and asserted that his efforts only tended to free the substantive verity from the envelopements of fable or perversion with which tradition had invested it. The admission was a fatal one. The absurdities to which the theory led could not long remain undetected. It was soon shown, and shown effectually, that this vaunted criticism was no criticism at all; that the objections which it offered to the Gospel history were as old as Porphyry, or, at least, as the English Deists, and had been refuted again and again; that the errors of interpretation into which the older expositors had fallen might be avoided without touching the truth and inspiration of the Evangelists; and, in a word, that there could be no medium between open infidelity and the admission of a supernatural revelation. During the first quarter of the present century the conflict was waged with ardour on both sides, but with increasing energy on the side of truth; and every year weakened the forces of rationalism. Still, the theological mind of Germany was to a considerable extent unsettled: its Tholucks and Hengstenbergs stood strong for orthodoxy; its Twesten and Nitszch applied the clearest logic to systematic theology; its Marheineche and Daub philosophized religiously; its Bretschneider and Hase upheld reason as the judge of revelation; while not a few maintained the old rationalism, though with less and less of conviction, or at least of boldness.

It was at this point that Strauss conceived the audacious idea of applying the *mythical* theory to the whole structure of the Evangelical history. All Germany has been more or less infected with the mytho-mania, since the new school of archæologers have gone so deeply into the heathen mythology. *A mythis omnis priscorum hominum cum historia tum philosophia procedit*, says Heyne: and Bauer asks, logically enough, "if the early history of every people is mythical why not the Hebrew?"* The mere application of this theory to the sacred records was by no means original with Strauss: he himself points out a number of instances in which

* Strauss, i., § 8.

Eichhorn, Gabler, Vater, &c., had made use of it. His claim is to have given a completeness to the theory, or rather to its application, which former interpreters had not dreamed of; and, to tell the truth, he has made no halting work of it. That Jesus lived; that he taught in Judea; that he gathered disciples, and so impressed them with his life and teaching as that they believed nim to be the Messiah; this is nearly the sum of historical truth contained in the Evangelists, according to Strauss. Yet he ascribes no fraudulent *designs* to the writers; his problem is, therefore, to account for the form in which the narratives appear; and this is the place for his theory to work. A Messiah was expected; certain notions were attached to the Messianic character and office; and with these Christ was invested by his followers. "Such and such a thing must happen to Messiah; Jesus was the Messiah; therefore such and such a thing must have happened to him." "The expectation of a Messiah had flourished in Israel long before the time of Christ; and at the time of his appearance it had ripened into full bloom; not an indefinite longing either, but an expectation defined by many prominent characteristics. Moses had promised (Deut., xviii., 15) 'a prophet like unto himself,' a passage applied, in Christ's time, to Messiah (Acts, iii., 22; vii., 37). The Messiah was to spring of David's line, and ascend his throne as a second David (Matt., xxii., 42; Luke, i., 32); and therefore he was looked for, in Christ's time, to be born in the little town of Bethlehem (John, vii., 42; Matt., ii., 5). In the old legends the most wonderful acts and destinies had been attributed to the prophets: could less be expected of the Messiah? Must not his life be illustrated by the most splendid and significant incidents from the lives of the prophets? Finally, the Messianic era, as a whole, was expected to be a period of signs and wonders. The eyes of the blind were to be opened; the deaf ears to be unstopped; the lame were to leap, &c. (Isa., xxxv., &c.). These expressions, part of which, at least, were purely figurative, came to be literally understood (Matt., xi., 5; Luke, vii., 21, *sqq.*); and thus, even before Christ's appearance, the image of Messiah was continually filling out with new features. And thus many of the legends respecting Jesus had not to be newly invented; they existed ready-made in the Messianic hopes of the people, derived chiefly from the Old Testament, and only needed to be transferred to Christ and adapted to his character and teachings."*

* Strauss, i., § 14.

These extracts contain the substance of Strauss's theory; his book is little more than an application of it to the individual parts of the history of Christ as given in the Evangelists. A few instances of his procedure will suffice. He finds the key to the *miraculous conception* in Matt., i., 22: "All this was done that it might be fulfilled which was spoken of the Lord by the prophet, saying,"* &c. "The birth of Jesus, it was said, must correspond to this passage; and what was to be, they concluded, really did occur, and so arose the myth." The account of the star of the Magians, and of their visit from the East, arose from a similar application of Numbers, xxiv., 17; Psa. lxxii., 10; Isa., lx., 1–6,† &c The temptation of Christ was suggested by the trials of Job: its separate features helped out by Exod., xxxiv., 28; Lev., xvi., 8, 10; Deut., ix., 9,‡ &c. The Transfiguration finds a starting-point in Exod., xxxiv., 29–35.§ So we might go through the book.

The appearance of the work, as we have said, produced a wonderful sensation in Germany; greater, by far, than its merits would seem to have authorized. It was the heaviest blow that unbelief had ever struck against Christianity; and the question was, what should be done? The Prussian government was disposed to utter its ban against the book; and many evangelical theologians deemed this the proper course to pursue in regard to it. But Dr. Neander deprecated such a procedure as calculated to give the work a spurious celebrity, and as wearing, at least, the aspect of a confession that it was unanswerable. He advised that it should be met, not by authority, but by argument, believing that the truth had nothing to fear in such a conflict. His counsel prevailed; and the event has shown that he was right. Replies to Strauss poured forth in a torrent; the Gospel histories were subjected to a closer criticism than ever; and to-day the public mind of Germany is nearer to an orthodox and evangelical view of their contents than it has been for almost a century.

Besides the general impulse given by Strauss to the study of the Four Gospels, he has done theology another good service. His book has given a deadly blow to *rationalism* properly so called. Its paltry criticism and beggarly interpretations of Scripture are nowhere more effectually dissected than in his investigations of the different parts of the history and of the expositions that have been given of it. In a word, he has driven rationalism out of the field to make way for his myths; and Neander, Eb-

* Strauss, i., § 29. † Ibid., § 36. ‡ Ibid., § 56. § Ibid., § 107.

rard, and others have exploded the myths; so that nothing remains but a return to the simple, truthful interpretations which, in the main, are given by the evangelical commentators.

But, it may be asked, why trouble ourselves with controversies of this kind here? We cannot help it. Strauss's book, at first, could not find a respectable publisher in England; and a garbled translation, containing its very worst features, was put out in a cheap form for the million. The same, or a similar abridgment, has been circulated to a considerable extent in this country. And within the last year a translation of the whole work, from the last German edition, has been published in London in three handsome volumes. That the soil of many minds is ready to receive its pestilent doctrines, both in that country and in our own, is too sadly true to be denied. The Westminster Review for April, 1847, contains an article on *Strauss* and *Parker* which talks about the Evangelists in the coolest strain of infidelity imaginable, and refers, with obvious complacency, to the signs of "unbelief or illumination" (it cares not which) that are at present so abundant in England.

To a certain extent, as we have remarked, Neander's Life of Christ has a polemic aim against Strauss. But this is a small part of its merits; indeed, but for the notes, an ordinary reader would not detect any such specific tendency. It unfolds the life of the Saviour from the record with great clearness and skill; it invests the outline, thus obtained, with the fresh colours of life, without resorting to forced constructions and vain imaginings; and, above all, it seeks, with child-like humility and reverence, to learn and exhibit the mind of the Spirit. The characteristic of spirituality, so strongly stamped upon all the works of this great writer, is especially prominent here. None, we think, can read the book without becoming not merely better acquainted with the *facts* of the life of Christ, but more anxious than ever to drink into its *spirit*.

At the same time, it is not to be concealed that Neander differs in his views on some points of doctrine, as well as of interpretation, from most Evangelical theologians. We wish to state distinctly that we do not hold ourselves responsible for these peculiarities of opinion. It was at one time our purpose to append notes to such passages as we deemed most objectionable; but after mature deliberation this intention was laid aside. It is hardly fair to criticise a man in his own pages, even if one is able to do it. The general spirit and tendency of the work cannot, we are sure, be otherwise than beneficial, or we should never have attempted to translate it. Its specific errors can be met and refuted elsewhere.

The noble candour of Neander in the letter which precedes this preface must disarm all severity. Let us remember, in our judgment of what may appear to us even grave errors of opinion in the book, that its author has fought for every step of ground that has been gained of late years by spiritual religion in Germany; and, while we lament the "dimness" which this great man confesses with such Christian-like humility, let us acknowledge the grandeur of his idea of the kingdom of God, and the earnestness of his devotion to it. His starting-point, and many of his paths, are different from ours; it must, therefore, gladden our hearts, and may, perhaps, confirm our faith, to see that he reaches, after all, the general results of Evangelical theology.

One word for the translation. We have tried to do our best; but we feel that we have *not* done very well. It is hard to translate German; and of all German that we have tried to put into intelligible English, Neander's is the hardest. We have not attempted a literal version (for we want the book to be read); nor, on the other hand, have we willingly gone into mere paraphrase. We have sought to seize the sense of the author, and to express it in our own tongue; but none can be better assured than ourselves that we have very often failed. Readers of the original work will see that we have taken some liberties with it which demand explanation. The division of the text into books, chapters, and sections will, we hope, make the work more intelligible and acceptable to English readers. In many of the author's paraphrases of Scripture passages we have substituted the words of the English version, where it could be done without affecting the sense; and many passages, also, to which he had merely alluded, are quoted at length. A few sentences have been transferred from the text to the notes; and a few passages of the notes, of purely polemical interest, which would have needed explanation to put them fairly before the American public, have been omitted. In all that we have done, we have endeavoured to comply with the spirit of Dr. Neander's wishes, as kindly communicated to us by himself.

January 5, 1848.

LIST OF DR. NEANDER'S WORKS.

Das Leben Jesu Christi, in seinem geschichtlichen Zusammenhange und seiner geschichtlichen Entwickelung: 1te Aufl., 1837; 4te Aufl., 1845 (The Life of Jesus Christ, in its Historical Connexion and Historical Developement: 1st ed., 1837; 4th ed., 1845).

Geschichte der Pflanzung und Leitung der Christlichen Kirche durch die Apostel: 1te Aufl., 1832; 4te Aufl., 1847 (History of the Planting and Training of the Christian Church by the Apostles: 1st ed., 1832; 4th ed., 1847).

Allgemeine Geschichte der Christlichen Religion und Kirche (General History of the Christian Religion and Church).

(a) Die drei ersten Jahrhunderte: 1te Aufl. in 3 Bänden; 2te Aufl. in 2 Bd., 1842–43. (The three first centuries: 1st edition in 3 volumes, 1825; 2d edition in 2 vols., 1842–43.)
(b) Das 4te–6te Jahrhundert: 1te Aufl. in drei Bänden, 1828; 2te Aufl. in 2 Bd., 1846–47. (Fourth to sixth century: 1st ed. in 3 vols., 1828; 2d in 2 vols., 1846–47.)
(c) 6te–8te, in 1 Bd. (Sixth to eighth, 1 vol.), 1834.
(d) 8te–11te, in 1 Bd. (Eighth to eleventh, 1 vol.), 1836.
(e) 11te–13te, in 2 Bänden. (Eleventh to thirteenth, 2 vols.), 1841 and 1845.

Ueber den Kaiser Julianus und sein Zeitalter (The Emperor Julian and his Times), 1812.

Genetische Entwickelung der vornehmsten Gnostischen Systeme (Genetical Developement of the principal Gnostic Systems), 1818.

Anti-Gnosticus. Geist des Tertullianus und Einleitung in dessen Schriften (Anti-Gnosticus. Genius of Tertullian and Introduction to his Writings), 1825.

Der heilige Chrysostomus und die Kirche in dessen Zeitalter, 2 Bd., 1820; 2te Aufl. 1te Bd., 1832 (Chrysostom and the Church in his Times, 2 vols., 1820; 2d ed. of 1st. vol., 1832).

Der heilige Bernhard und sein Zeitalter (Bernard and his Times), 1813.

Denkwürdigkeiten aus der Geschichte des Christenthums und des Christlichen Lebens: 1te Aufl. in 3 Bd., 1822; 3te Aufl. in 2 Bd., 1845–46 (Memorabilia from the History of Christianity and the Christian Life: 1st ed. 3 vols., 1822; 3d ed. 2 vols., 1845–46).

Kleine Gelegenheitschriften praktisch-Christlichen, vornehmlich exegetischen und historischen Inhalts, 3te Aufl., 1829 (Smaller Treatises, chiefly exegetical and historical, 3d ed., 1829).

Das Eine und das Mannichfältige des Christlichen Lebens; Eine Reihe kleiner Gelegenheitschriften, grössertentheils biographischen Inhalts (Series of smaller Treatises, chiefly biographical), 1840.

Das Princip der Reformation, oder Staupitz und Luther (The Principle of the Reformation; or Staupitz and Luther), 1840.

PREFACE

TO

THE FIRST EDITION.

In the Preface to my Representation of the Christian Religion and Church in the Apostolic Age, I assigned my reasons for the separate publication of that work, and stated its relations to my General History of the Church. It remained for me to treat of that which formed the ground of the manifestation and existence of the Apostolical Church itself, viz., the Life and Ministry of the Divine Founder of the Church; and I have, moreover, been urged from many quarters to execute this necessary portion of my work. I was made to pause in the former undertaking by the lofty sacredness of the subject and its many difficulties; how much more, then, in the latter! But the signs of the times (to which, as a historian of the Church, I could not but take heed), the uncertainty of human affairs, and the opportunity afforded by a pause in my General History, have overcome my scruples, and led me, trusting in God, to go on with this work.

Yet well may he hesitate who undertakes to write the life of Christ! "Who, indeed (as Herder finely answered Lavater), could venture, after *John*, to write the life of Christ?"* Who will not agree with Anna Maria von Schurmann, that such an attempt is "to paint the sun with charcoal: the life of a Christian is the best picture of the life of Christ?"†

Yet why should not history (though assured that its description must be far behind the reality) occupy itself with the highest manifestation that has appeared in humanity—a manifestation which sanctifies, but does not spurn, the labours of men? The artist, in-

* "*I* write the life of Christ—*I?* Never. The Evangelists have written it as it can and ought to be written. Let *us*, however, not *write* it, but *become* it?" (Beiträge zur näheren Kenntniss Lavater's, von Ulrich Hegener: Leips., 1836.) May the good Zurichers, who have lately shown themselves so worthy of their sires in their resistance to revolutionary violence and their enthusiasm for the faith (*dogma Christianum dogma populare*, Augustin. opus imperf. c. Julian, ii., 2), erect a Christian national memorial by an edition, as complete as possible. of Lavater's correspondence

† Cf. Reinhard, Plan Jesu, 1; Heubner's Anm.

spired by devotion, paints a picture of Christ without any aid from history, merely from intuition of the idea of Christ. But we *have* the lineaments of the historical Christ, in fragments at least; and there is wanting only insight into their connexion to frame them into a harmonious whole. We feel the necessity of calling up vividly before our minds, in our own stage of life and scientific progress, this realized Ideal, which belongs to all ages; and at particular epochs in the mutations of time this necessity is always felt anew. The image of Christ, not of yesterday nor to-day, ever renews its youth among men, and, as the world grows old, penetrates it with a heaven-tending youthful vigour. What PHOTIUS says of the various ideas of Christ among different nations may be applied to different periods of time, viz., "that each, by a new representation, must make itself familiar with the image of Christ." Obviously, however, the peculiarities of different periods must be distinguished. Some periods mark a new creation in the Christian Church and in humanity, as *already appeared;* others, by dissolution and crisis, *prepare* the way for it. Our age belongs to the latter class: we stand between the old world and a new one to be called into being by the ever old and ever new Gospel. For the fourth time Christianity is preparing a new epoch in the life of humanity. *Our* labors can only be preparatory to that new creation, when, after the regeneration of life and science, the great acts of God shall be proclaimed with new tongues of fire!*

But it may be questioned, also, whether it is possible, from the authorities in our hands, to exhibit a connected description of the life of CHRIST? Christian consciousness will be satisfied with nothing less than an intuition of Christ's life as a whole; and, therefore, science must undertake to free it from all alloy, and to found it on a substantial basis. It is by means of the Christian consciousness that we feel ourselves allied to all Christianity since the outpouring of the Holy Ghost—Christian consciousness, the living source from which every thing in life and science, which has really enriched the Church, has proceeded and must proceed; a far different thing from the changeful culture of the day, which, without it, must ever be ephemeral and transitory. To serve this last is the most wretched of servitudes. It is, indeed, time for a new beginning of Biblical criticism, of New Testament exegesis,

* Most keenly does the author feel (as did his late friend, *B. Jacobi,* who has left behind him a blessed and honoured memory) that his work bears the marks of its production in an age of crisis, of 'solation, of pain, and of throes.

of inquiries into the formation of the canon. There are great difficulties, indeed, especially in the chronology,* in the work which we have to do. But this, instead of deterring, must only stimulate us to greater efforts. We must only guard against relinquishing our hopes too hastily, and keep aloof from all prejudices either of antiquity or novelty; and then this undertaking may be one of the preparations, however trifling, for a new epoch in this part of history.

As for those who deny that our field is properly historical, and place it in a pre-historical and mythical region, I need say nothing here, as I have sought to refute them in the course of the work itself.

In regard to my relations to the various theological parties of the age, I must refer to the Preface to the first volume of my "Apostolic Age;" and to my letter to DEWAR, chaplain to the British Embassy in Hamburg. Whatever appears to me to be true, or most probable, after candid and earnest inquiry, with all reverence for the sacredness of the subject, I utter, without looking at consequences. Whoever has a good work to do must, as Luther says, let the devil's tongue run as it pleases. There are two opposite parties whom I cannot hope to please, viz., those who will forcibly make all things *new*, and fancy, in their folly, that they can shake the rock which ages could not undermine; and those who would retain, and forcibly reintroduce, even at the expense of all genuine love of truth, every thing that is old; nay, even the worn-out and the obsolete. I shall not please those hypercritics who subject the sacred writings to an arbitrary subtilty, at once superrational and sophistical; nor those, on the other hand, who believe that here all criticism—or at least all criticism on internal grounds—cometh of evil. Both these tendencies are alike at variance with a healthful sense for truth and conscientious devotion to it; both are alike inimical to genuine culture. There is need of criticism where any thing is communicated to us in the form of a historical tradition in written records; and I am sure that an impartial criticism, applied to the Scriptures, is not only consistent with that child-like faith without which there can be no Christianity or Christian theology,† but is necessary to a just

* Wherever I have not sure grounds for decision, I say "*perhaps*:" nor am I ashamed of it, unfashionable as "perhaps" is, nowadays, in matters of science. Would that our young votaries of science would lay to heart the excellent words of NIEBUHR, on the degrees of confidence, in the "Lebensnachrichten," ii., 208.

† But the theologian must have more than a merely critical mind and critical aims: he

acuteness* and profoundness of thought, as well as to that true consecration of mind which is so essential to theology. The child-like faith of the theologian who cannot violently rid himself of the critical element of his times or of human nature, is thus proved, as it were, in the fire of temptation; this is the *tentatio* (particularly in this age of scientific struggle) which must go along with *oratio* and *meditatio*, in the depths of the earnest and humble spirit. Without this priestly consecration, there can be no theology. It thrives best in the calmness of a soul consecrated to God. What grows amid the noisy bustle of the world and the empty babble of the age is not theology.

God reveals himself in his *word* as he does in his works. In both we see a self-*revealing*, self-*concealing* God, who makes himself known only to those who earnestly seek him;† in both we find stimulants to faith and occasions for unbelief; in both we find contradictions whose higher harmony is hidden except from him who gives up his whole mind in reverence; in both, in a word, it is the law of revelation that the *heart* of man should be tested in receiving it; and that, in the spiritual life as well as in the bodily, man must *eat his bread in the sweat of his brow.*

Berlin, July 18, 1837.

needs a spiritual mind, a deep acquaintance with divine things; and he must study the Scriptures with his *heart* as well as *head*, unless he wishes his theology to be robbed of its salt by his criticism.

* Not *too* sharp, so as to be notched.

† This is the pervading thought of Pascal (the sage for all centuries) in his *Pensées*, though blended with many errors of Catholicism and absolute Predestination. Great thanks are due to *Faugere* for the edition of this work (1844) in its original form.

PREFACE

TO

THE THIRD EDITION.

The reception of this work among the opposing theological parties of the age has been such as I anticipated in the Preface to the first edition. It is, therefore, the less necessary for me to vindicate myself against special accusations on any side. I am satisfied that the principles of my theological procedure are in the main correct, and that their claims will finally be justified. To answer the revilings or false inferences of fanatical prejudice on either hand, or to enter into purely personal controversy, forms no part of my purpose. Yet, in order to leave no room for doubt as to my own theological stand-point, it appears necessary that I should notice a few of the opinions that have been passed upon the work.

A review from the pen of Consistorial Counsellor Schulz has appeared in the *Allgemeine Darmstädtische Kirchenzeitung*, which opposes me merely by dictatorial decisions; and, by isolating various passages* of my work from their connexion, ascribes to me opinions which are foreign to my whole theological system What I say will not be disputed by any one who candidly examines that review and compares it with my work. I have called the attention of my readers in this edition to these perversions of my words; perversions in which Schulz shakes hands with men of a school directly opposite to his own. Were I not satisfied of his integrity, I should be under the necessity of calling them *dishonest* perversions; as the case is, I see in them only the prejudice of that *enthusiasm of reason* so admirably characterized by Jacobi in his remarks upon "Reason which is not Reason" (ii., 492). Of those who are enslaved by this enthusiasm, he says: "Their belief is always reason, nor can they recognize another's reason except in his belief. They inquire not how he feels, perceives, observes,

* The reviewer has been able to point out but *one* oversight—certainly no proof of careless haste in a work on such a subject. The mistake was one which might have happened to any one in an unlucky moment, which could not fail to be noticed by any one, and which, in fact, was noticed by myself as soon as I glanced again at the passage.

or infers, but only what his opinions are—whether they agree with their canon or not; and that decides the matter." This stand-point as surely generates a prejudice which precludes all just judgment of the opinions of others, and leads (though unconsciously) to falsehood, as does the enthusiasm for an absolute system of doctrines which lays down, as a standard, a definite number of articles of faith, or principles therewith connected, and makes this standard a criterion of every one's claim to Christianity. In the judgments formed of my work, as well as in many other matters of our time, these two sets of prejudices have led to similar results.

"What," inquires SCHULZ several times, "will the believers in creeds say to this?" Now, as to the opinion of this or that set of *men*, I am indifferent; it concerns me only to know how far my statements accord with *truth*, especially Christian truth. It is proper that I should say, however, that I go along with those who oppose "creed-believers" (to use SCHULZ's term) so far as this viz., that I could not subscribe to any of the existing symbols (except the Apostles' creed, which testifies to those fundamental facts of Christianity that are essential to the existence of the Christian Church) as an unconditional expression of my religious convictions.

I believe that our path lies, through the strifes and storms of the present time, to a new creation in the Church, when the same Holy Spirit* that works in the life of the Church, and produces all truly Christian creeds as expressions (defective, indeed, as all human representations of the Divine must be, and stamped with the varying culture of the time) of Christian truth, will produce a symbol adapted to the new stage of the Church's developement, if it become necessary that such an expression of the animating faith of the Church be given in a new literal form. But I go along with the theologians (so called creed-believers) in what I believe to be the fundamental principle of the Reformation and of the Evangelical Church; the doctrines, viz., of the corruption of human nature (not, however, excluding, but presupposing, an element of affinity for God [Gottverwandte] in human nature); and

* The Holy Spirit going out from faith in Christ, who was crucified for the sins of men, who truly rose from the dead and ascended to heaven; the Holy Spirit, which has proved itself the same since the first Christian Pentecost, at all times, among all people, learned or unlearned; not the changeful spirit of the times, which corresponds more nearly to what is called in the New Testament the spirit of the world, and whose manifestations stand opposed to those of the Holy Spirit.

of justification by faith in Jesus as the Redeemer. The essential part of the Evangelical Confession (the Augsburg Confession and its Apology), so far as it is an exposition of this doctrine, together with the unchangeable verities to which the Apostles' Creed bears witness, seem to me the irrefragable basis of the Evangelical Church; which, on this basis, *protests* against all popery whether the Roman or any other impure spirit of the age; against human statutes, no matter of what kind. Dr. SCHULZ reproaches me for speaking of the sinfulness of human nature. On the other hand, I cannot but be astonished that this truth, so clearly revealed in the Scriptures, nay, lying at their basis, and so plainly written upon every human heart, should be denied by any man. He wishes, moreover, that the terms "natural reason" and "self-righteousness" may hereafter not appear in my writings. In this respect I cannot possibly gratify him. These terms have a well-established right in the Evangelical Church; the conceptions which they express are closely connected with its fundamental principle; they are, moreover, firmly founded in Biblical Anthropology.* They are not the offshoot of a "new Evangelical" Theology, but of an old Evangelical faith. It is a mere pretended "enlightenment" (which, notwithstanding it may, by destroying, prepare the way for better things, is yet in its positive elements a source of darkness) that can object to those conceptions.

I have to thank Dr. HASE for the kindness with which he has spoken of my work in the *Jahrbücher für wissenschaftliche Kritik;* but it would take more space than a preface will allow to come to an understanding with him upon the points in Apologetics and Dogmatics on which he touches in his review. I can only remark, that a description of the life of Christ (although it *must* proceed from the Christian consciousness, which alone can afford a living intuition of it) does not necessarily demand for its foundation a complete and well-defined theory of the *person* of Christ. On the contrary, it would be one of the excellences of such a

* It is a trick of Jesuitism (which is by no means confined to one form, but often assumes the shape of the fanaticism of reason or understanding) to protest (in *form*) against the tendencies of the journal called the *Evangelische Kirchenzeitung*, while, in *fact*, the protest is not meant to bear against those tendencies—not against antiquated dogmas—but against the unchangeable fundamental truths of the Church of Christ; truths which *can* appear to be antiquated dogmas only to the shallow and superficial spirit of the times; a spirit as contracted as it is conceited. At the same time, it cannot be denied that the one-sidedness, the exaggerations and multiform sickliness of the tendencies referred to may have contributed to produce a reaction. We say this *sine ira et studio,* with a full sense of the sincere and earnest zeal, and the true Christian endeavours and results of those tendencies which find an organ in the *Kirchenzeitung*.

work, that various doctrinal tendencies (if supranaturalistic) could be satisfied with it. It must deal with *facts*, which are more weighty than men's conceptions, changeful as they are. All dogmatical theories except those which are willing to do violence to history must agree in acknowledging certain facts. What I have said of the human developement of the life of Christ harmonizes well with the consequent doctrine of a *status exinanitionis;* without this, in fact, the human life of Christ can have no reality. As to my views of the Ascension, I must adhere to them, until I can be convinced that without them the full import of Christ's *resurrection* can be asserted. Nor is it simply strength of faith that leads me to these results; from the beginning my religious life has been too much affected by the culture of this age to allow me to glory in such a faith—to compare myself with those men of child-like simplicity, those heroes whose Divine confidence is exalted above all doubt.* I have adopted them from consecutive reasoning upon the principles of the Christian faith. There is no middle ground here; unless, indeed, in order to avoid admitting a limit to all explanation, without, at the same time, affirming the opposite, we cover up the difficulty in phrases and formulas.

To all those who consider the Socratic *ignorance* as folly, and who have settled beforehand the highest questions—questions whose right answers the great MELANCTHON placed among the beatitudes of the intuition of a better life—my dogmatical system must appear weak and unsatisfactory.

In the reviewer of my work in the Halle *Literaturzeitung* (Church-counsellor SCHWARZ of Jena), I am happy to recognize a worthy man, who can acknowledge with congenial spirit, even amid differences of opinion, the work of an earnest mind and of serious study—a phenomenon every day becoming rarer in this age of selfish and excited party spirit. I am gratified, though not surprised, to find, from the beautiful notice of my book by Dr. LÜCKE, that that old and worthy friend agrees with me in all essential points.

To find ourselves at one in the recognition of certain truths with men whom we must admire and honour on many accounts, even though our convictions, on important subjects, may be opposed to each other, cannot be otherwise than gratifying. I have

* Truth before all things. I would not *seem* to be what I *am not*. This book, which could only have arisen in this age of strife and discord, is itself a mirror of the progress of my mind.

no sympathy with that narrowness of mind which refuses to do justice to the advocate, however able, of opinions which we ourselves must reject. That is an unworthy arrogance which, in its zealous defence of a holy cause (a cause which, above all others breathes humility, and teaches us more and more that all our knowledge is but fragmentary), deems itself authorized to look down haughtily upon its opponent, however superior in scientific ability; or even seeks to cover the weakness of its own arguments by what is intended, according to the sickly taste of the age, to pass for wit and humour.

I cannot, therefore, but rejoice to find that my treatment of the subject, with that of others engaged in the same controversy, has induced Dr. STRAUSS to soften down his mythical theory of the life of Christ in various points, and to acknowledge the truth of several results arrived at by my historical inquiries. In his public acknowledgment of this I recognize a candour and love of truth which is far more honourable than mere intellectual greatness. At the same time, I am grateful to him for the kindness with which he has spoken of me personally. A certain degree of harmony, then, may be attained by the application of those fundamental principles of historical criticism which all sound thinkers must acknowledge to be correct. Yet it is *only* a certain degree; it is easy to be understood how the harmony thus reached is interrupted by the wider differences which lie at the foundation of the subject.

The chief points of controversy turn upon *essential* differences of religious thought and feeling. These fundamental differences are clearly set forth by Dr. STRAUSS in the closing dissertation of his third edition, and in his essay on the Permanent and the Transitory (*das Bleibende und Vergängliche*) in Christianity. They are to be found chiefly in opposing views of the relation of God to the world, of the personality of spirit, of the relation between the here and the hereafter, and of the nature of sin. The controversy, to our mind, does not lie between an old and a new view of Christianity, but between Christianity and a human invention directly opposed to it. It is nothing less than a struggle between Christian Theism and a system of world- and self-deification. This system (by a *relative* historical necessity) had to unfold itself in theological and philosophical rationalism, in order to be overthrown by the power of Christian truth in the natural progress of life and thought. Symptoms of it can be detected in the sects of the Middle Ages, and in many of the manifestations that preceded the Reformation; and it would have broken forth at an earlier period, had not the Evangelical enthusiasm of the Reformation suppressed it for a time. We may apply here the words of MELANCTHON, uttered, with his deep historical insight, in a connexion akin to this: *Dogmatum semina, quæ longe graviora tumultus aliquando excitatura fuerant, nisi Lutherus exortus esset ac studia hominum alio traxisset* (Corpus Reformator., tom. i., f. 1083). Far be it from me to judge the heart of any man; in this regard each must be his own accuser. A man that knows he serves a truth above the range of the human mind knows, at the same time, how far below it he himself stands, and how high, on the other hand, others, whose individual culture modified by the spirit of the age may have laid them open to error, may in heart be raised above their error. Whoever has entered into the struggles of his age will be willing, at the same time that he judges himself, to be mild in his judgments of others, who, although they may have been further carried away by those same struggles, have preserved a seemly and becoming moderation. It is the *principle* alone that is in question, and *that* cannot be judged too strictly.

I conclude with the golden words of one of the greatest men of modern times in testimony of the truth, and in opposition, not only to the vain attempt to amalgamate Christianity with the principle of modern *mis*-culture, but also to the spirit which seeks to reduce all minds to one mode of doctrinal conception—to the stand-point which strives to make the piece-work of human knowledge absolute. "The man who does not hold Christ's earthly life, with all its miracles, to be as properly and really historical as any event in the sphere of history, and who does not receive all points of the Apostolic Creed with the fullest conviction, I do not conceive to be a Protestant Christian. And as for that Christianity which is such according to the fashion of the modern philosophers and Pantheists, without a personal GOD, without immortality, without an individuality of man, without historical faith—it may be a very ingenious and subtle *philosophy*, but it is no Christianity at all. Again and again have I said that I know not what to do with a metaphysical GOD; and that I will have no other but the GOD of the Bible, who is *heart* to *heart*. Whoever can reconcile the metaphysical God with the GOD of the Bible, may try it, and write symbolical books to suit all ages; but he who admits the absolute inexplicability of the main point, which can only be approached by asymptotes, will never grieve at the impossibility of possessing any *system* of religion."* May the man who, with rare world-historical insight, was able to explain the signs of the times, be heard of many!

Berlin, May 6, 1839.

* *Leben Niebuhr's,* Thl. ii., 344. We cannot be too grateful to the publishers for putting forth this treasure of sound feeling and profound truth.

PREFACE

TO

THE FOURTH EDITION.

I HAVE sought, in this fourth edition, to improve as far as I could, both the matter and form of the work; but do not deem it necessary to add any thing to what has been said in former prefaces upon my mode of treating the subject. I have thought it best, in spite of a desire to economize space, to republish those prefaces; adding here and there a remark called for by the relations of the times, which I should have otherwise put into a separate preface. Although I would willingly have buried in oblivion the unpleasant personal allusions (contained in the second preface) to a man whom I honour and esteem, I have considered it necessary to republish it, in view of the truths which it contains, and their bearing upon the times.

And now let my book, with the blessing of GOD, enter anew among the strifes of the age; standing in the midst of which, I shall not suffer myself to be shaken or perplexed by the "τὰ ἐν μέσῳ ἀμφοτέρωθεν κτείνεται."

A. NEANDER

Berlin, 3*d* *August,* **1845.**

CONTENTS.

INTRODUCTION.

CHAPTER I.

THE IDEA OF THE HISTORY OF CHRIST IN GENERAL.

CHAPTER II.

SOURCES OF THE HISTORY OF CHRIST.

BOOK I.

BIRTH AND CHILDHOOD OF JESUS.

CHAPTER I.

INTRODUCTION.

CHAPTER II.

THE MIRACULOUS CONCEPTION.

CHAPTER III.

THE BIRTH AND CHILDHOOD OF CHRIST.

BOOK II.

THE MENTAL CULTURE OF JESUS: HIS LIFE TO THE TIME OF HIS PUBLIC MINISTRY.

CHAPTER I.

JESUS NOT EDUCATED IN THE THEOLOGICAL SCHOOLS OF THE JEWS.

CHAPTER II.

THE LIFE OF JESUS TO THE OPENING OF HIS PUBLIC MINISTRY.

BOOK III.

PREPARATIVES TO THE PUBLIC MINISTRY OF CHRIST

PART I.

OBJECTIVE PREPARATION: MINISTRY OF JOHN THE BAPTIST

CHAPTER I.

RELATION OF THE BAPTIST TO THE JEWS.

CHAPTER II.

THE RELATION OF THE BAPTIST TO THE MESSIAH.

PART II.

SUBJECTIVE PREPARATION: THE TEMPTATION OF CHRIST.

CHAPTER I.

IMPORT OF THE INDIVIDUAL TEMPTATIONS.

CHAPTER II.

IMPORT OF THE TEMPTATION AS A WHOLE.

BOOK IV.

THE PUBLIC MINISTRY OF CHRIST ACCORDING TO ITS REAL CONNEXION.

PART I.

THE PLAN OF CHRIST.

CHAPTER I.

THE PLAN OF CHRIST IN GENERAL.

CHAPTER II.

THE PLAN OF CHRIST IN ITS RELATION TO THE OLD TESTAMENT IDEA OF THE KINGDOM OF GOD.

CHAPTER III.

NEW FORM OF THE IDEA OF THE PERSON OF THE THEOCRATIC KING.

PART II.

THE MEANS AND INSTRUMENTS OF CHRIST.

CHAPTER I.

THE MEANS OF CHRIST IN GENERAL.

CHAPTER II.

CHRIST'S MODE OF TEACHING IN REGARD TO ITS METHOD AND FORM.

A. ITS GENERAL PRINCIPLES.

B. CHRIST'S USE OF PARABLES.

C CHRIST'S USE OF ACCOMMODATION.

CHAPTER III.

CHOICE AND TRAINING OF THE APOSTLES AS TEACHERS.

CHAPTER IV.

THE CHURCH AND BAPTISM.

CHAPTER V.

THE MIRACLES OF CHRIST: THEIR CHARACTER AND OBJECTS.

A. THE OBJECTIVE CHARACTER OF MIRACLES.

B. THE MIRACLES OF CHRIST AS VIEWED BY HIS CONTEMPORARIES.

C. CHRIST'S OWN ESTIMATE OF HIS MIRACLES.

CHAPTER VI.

THE MIRACLES OF CHRIST CONSIDERED IN REGARD TO SUPERNATURAL AGENCY.

A. MIRACLES WROUGHT UPON HUMAN NATURE.

I. *The Healing of Diseases.*

BOOK V.

THE PUBLIC MINISTRY OF CHRIST ACCORDING TO ITS CHRONOLOGICAL CONNEXION.

INTRODUCTION.

ON THE DIFFERENCES BETWEEN THE SYNOPTICAL GOSPELS AND JOHN.

PART I.

FROM THE COMMENCEMENT OF CHRIST'S PUBLIC MINISTRY TO THE TRIUMPHAL ENTRY.

CHAPTER I.

JESUS AND JOHN THE BAPTIST. THE FIRST DISCIPLES.

CHAPTER II.

FIRST PUBLIC TEACHING OF CHRIST. CAPERNAUM.

CHAPTER III.

CHRIST AT CANA.

CHAPTER IV.

FIRST JOURNEY TO JERUSALEM TO ATTEND THE FEAST OF PASSOVER.

CHAPTER V.

JESUS AT ÆNON, NEAR SALIM.

CHAPTER VI.

RETURN THROUGH SAMARIA TO GALILEE: THE SAMARITAN WOMAN.

CHAPTER VII.

CHRIST'S FIRST GENERAL MINISTRY IN GALILEE.

CHAPTER VIII.

CHRIST'S SECOND JOURNEY TO JERUSALEM.

CHAPTER IX.

CHRIST'S SECOND COURSE OF EXTENDED LABOUR IN GALILEE.

The Sermon on the Mount.

Introduction.

CHAPTER X.

JESUS IN NORTH GALILEE, AND ON THE WAY TO CESAREA PHILIPPI.

CHAPTER XI.

CHRIST'S JOURNEY TO JERUSALEM TO ATTEND THE FEAST OF TABERNACLES.

CHAPTER XII.

RETURN FROM CAPERNAUM TO JERUSALEM THROUGH SAMARIA.

CHAPTER XIII.

CHRIST'S STAY AT JERUSALEM DURING THE FEAST OF DEDICATION.

CHAPTER XIV.

CHRIST IN PERÆA (BETHABARA).

CHAPTER XV.

CHRIST IN BETHANY.

CHAPTER XVI.

CHRIST IN EPHRAIM.

CHAPTER XVII.

CHRIST'S LAST PASSOVER JOURNEY TO JERUSALEM.

PART II.

FROM THE TRIUMPHAL ENTRY TO THE ASCENSION.

CHAPTER I.

FROM THE TRIUMPHAL ENTRY TO THE LAST SUPPER

CHAPTER II.

THE LAST SUPPER.

CHAPTER III.

CHRIST'S LAST DISCOURSES AT TABLE WITH THE DISCIPLES.

CHAPTER IV.

DISCOURSES OF CHRIST AFTER RISING FROM TABLE.

CHAPTER V.

GETHSEMANE.

CHAPTER VI.

THE TRIAL AND CONDEMNATION.

CHAPTER VII.

THE CRUCIFIXION.

CHAPTER VIII.

THE RESURRECTION.

CHAPTER IX.

THE ASCENSION.

INTRODUCTION.

CHAPTER I.

THE IDEA OF THE HISTORY OF CHRIST IN GENERAL.

§ 1. *The Indifference of Criticism rejected.*

IT has been often said that, in order to true inquiry, we must *take nothing for granted.** Of late this statement has been reiterated anew, with special reference to the exposition of the *Life of Christ.* At the outset of our work we refuse to meet such a demand. To comply with it is impracticable; the very attempt contradicts the sacred laws of our being. We *cannot* entirely free ourselves from presuppositions, which are born with our nature, and which attach to the fixed course of progress in which we ourselves are involved. They control our consciousness, whether we will or no; and the supposed freedom from them is, in fact, nothing else but the exchange of one set for another. Some of these prepossessions, springing from a higher necessity, founded in the moral order of the universe, and derived from the eternal laws† of the Creator, constitute the very ground and support of our nature. From such we *must* not free ourselves.

But we are ever in peril of exchanging these legitimate sovereigns of our spiritual being, against which nothing but arbitrary will can rebel, for the prepossessions of a self-created or traditional prejudice, which have no other than an arbitrary origin, and which rule by no better title than usurpation. But for this peril, the way of the *science* of life would be as safe as the way of life itself. Life moves on in the midst of such diversified and ever-commingling prepossessions, especially in our own time, which, torn by contrarieties (contrarieties, however, which subserve a higher wisdom by balancing each other), forms the period of transition to a new and better creation. On the one hand we behold efforts to bring the human mind again into bondage to the host of arbitrary prejudices which had long enough enslaved it; and

* [*Voraussetzungslosigkeit:* "freedom from presuppositions."]

† Of which, says Sophocles, beautifully,

ὧν ὄλυμπος
πατὴρ μόνος, οὐδέ νιν θνατὰ
φύσις ἀνέρων ἔτικτεν, ὀυδὲ
μάν ποτε λάθα κατακοιμάσει
μέγας ἐν. τούτοις θεὸς
οὐδὲ γηράσκει.

on the other, we see a justifiable protest against these prejudices running into the extreme of rejecting even those holy prepossessions which *ought* to rule our spiritual being, and which alone can offer it true freedom.

What, then, is the duty of Science? Must she dismiss all prepossessions, and work out her task by unassisted thought? Far from it. From nothing nothing comes; the Father of spirits alone is a *Creator*. Empty indeed is that enthusiasm which seeks only the mere sound of truth—abstract, formal truth.* This absolute abnegation of all prepossessions would free the soul from those holy ties by which alone it can connect itself with its source—the source of all truth—and comprehend it by means of its revelations in humanity. The created spirit cannot deny its dependence upon God, the only creative Spirit; and it is its obvious destination to apprehend the revelation of God in creation, in nature, and in history. So, the work of *science* can only be to distinguish the prepossessions which an inward necessity constrains us to recognize, from such as are purely voluntary. Indeed, the healthfulness of our spiritual life depends upon our ridding ourselves of the latter, and, at the same time, yielding in lowliness and singleness of heart to the former, as the law of the Creator, as the means by which light from heaven may be conveyed to our minds. All that the *intellect* has to do in regard to these last is to demonstrate their necessity, and to show that our being contradicts itself in rebelling against them.

§ 2. *The Truth, that Christ is* GOD-MAN, *presupposed.*

What, then, is the special presupposition with which we must approach the contemplation of the Life of Christ? It is one on which hangs the very being of the Christian as such; the existence of the Christian Church, and the nature of Christian consciousness.† It is

* It is one of Pascal's best thoughts, that "On se fait une idôle de la vérité même; car la vérité hors de la charité n'est pas Dieu; c'est son image, et une idôle, qu'il ne faut point aimer, ni adorer, et encore moins faut-il aimer ou adorer son contraire, qui est le mensonge."

† It was one of the *epoch-making* indications of SCHLEIERMACHER'S influence upon theology that he succeeded in stamping this phrase (Christian consciousness) as current, with the meaning that he assigned to it, in an age which (although some men, blind to the lessons of history, look back upon it longingly as the golden age of our nation) was guided only by the naked understanding, and destitute at once of faith and of true historical insight. He used it to denote Christianity as an undeniable. self-revealing power, entering into the life of humanity; an immediate, internal power in the spiritual world, from which went forth, and is ever going forth, the regeneration of the life of man, and which produces phenomena which can be explained in no other way. This phrase, and the thought which it expresses, are able to maintain their ground against that formalism of thought which is so hostile to every thing *immediate*, and wishes to substitute empty abstractions for the living powers that move the human race, as well as against that low and mean view of the world (impertinently obtrusive as it has been of late) which owns no power above those which build rail-ways and set steam-engines agoing. As the intuitive consciousness of God indicates to the human mind the existence, the omnipresent power and the self-revelation of

one at whose touch of power the dry bones of the old world sprung up in all the vigour of a new creation. It gave birth to all that culture (the *modern* as distinguished from the *ancient*) from which the Germanic nations received their peculiar intellectual life, and from which the emancipation of the mind, grown too strong for its bonds, was developed in the Reformation. It is the very root and ground of our modern civilization; and the latter, even in its attempts to separate from this root, must rest upon it: indeed, should such attempts succeed, it must dissolve into its original elements, and assume an entirely new form. It is, in a word, the belief that *Jesus Christ is the Son of God in a sense which cannot be predicated of any human being*,—the perfect image of the personal God in the form of that humanity that was estranged from him; that in him the source of the Divine life itself in humanity appeared; that by him the idea of humanity was realized

§ 3. *This presupposed Truth and the Historical Accounts mutually confirm and illustrate each other.*

But as man's higher nature can only reach its true destiny in Christian consciousness, from which the great First Truth just mentioned is inseparable, it is necessary that this first truth should be shown to be essential also to the *general* consciousness of man. That it is so can be proved from its harmony with the universal and essential prepossessions of human nature; but the exhibition of this proof belongs more properly to the department of Apologetics. It is shown to be a necessary and not a voluntary prepossession; first, because it satisfies a fundamental want of human nature, a want created by history, and foreshadowing its own fulfilment; and, secondly, because this view of Christ's person arose from the direct impression which his appearance among men made upon the eye-witnesses, and, through them, upon the whole human race. This image of Christ, which has always propagated itself in the consciousness of the Christian Church, originated in, and ever points back to, the revelation of Christ himself, without which, indeed, it could never have arisen. As man's limited intellect could never, without the aid of revelation, have originated the idea of God, so the image of Christ, of which we have spoken, could never have sprung from the consciousness of sinful humanity, but *must* be regarded as the reflection of the actual life of such a Christ. It is Christ's self-revelation, made, through all generations, in the fragments of his history that remain, and in the workings of his Spirit which inspires

a personal Deity, so does this "Christian consciousness" testify that Christ lived, and that he continues, by his Spirit, to operate upon mankind. The works of creation only reveal God to him who already has a consciousness of the Divine existence; for he who has not God within can find him nowhere. So it is only he who has a "Christian consciousness" that can recognize Christ in the fragments of tradition and the manifestations of history, or that can comprehend the history of Christ and his Church.

these fiagments, and enables us to recognize in them one complete whole.* It is a stream of the Divine Life which has spread abroad through all ages since the establishment of the Christian Church. And the peculiar mark of this *Divine Life* is precisely this, that it is grounded in a consciousness of absolute dependence upon Christ; that it *is* nothing else but a constant renewing after the image of Christ. But as we often find this stream darkened and troubled, we are necessarily led back to HIM, the well-spring from whom the full-flowing fountain of Divine Life gushes forth in all its purity; the Son of GOD, and the Redeemer of men. He who could with Divine confidence present himself as such to mankind, and call all men to come unto him to satisfy the cravings of their higher nature, must have had within himself the authority of an infallible consciousness.

Now if we can show that the Life of Christ, without the aid of the First Truth which forms the ground of our conception of it, must be unintelligible, while, on the contrary, with its assistance, we can frame the Life into a harmonious whole, then its claims will be established even in the exposition of the Life itself.† Nay, the idea of Christ

* STRAUSS, in his "Leben Jesu" (part ii., p. 719), has drawn a just distinction between the *abstract idea* of human perfection which is involved in our consciousness of sinfulness, and seems inseparable from our natural tendency to the idea of GOD, and the "actual (*concrete*) working out of the picture, with the traits of individual reality." In relation to this last he says, "Such a faultless picture could not be exhibited by a sinful man in a sinful age; but," adds he, "such an age, itself not free from these defects, would not be conscious of them; and if the picture is only *sketched*, and stands in need of much illustration, it may, even in a later and more clear-sighted age, willing to afford favorable illustrations, be regarded as faultless." In opposition to this, we have to say that the picture of the Life of Christ which has been handed down to us does *not* exhibit the spirit of that age, but a far higher Spirit, which, manifesting itself in the lineaments of the picture, exerted a regenerating influence not only in that age, but on all succeeding generations. The image of human perfection, concretely presented in the Life of Christ, stands in manifold contradiction to the tendencies of humanity in that period; no one of them, no combination of them, dead, as they were, could account for it. Whence, then, in that impure age, came such a picture (a picture which the age itself could not completely understand, of which the age could only now and then seize a congenial trait to make a caricature of), the contemplating of which raised the human race of that and following ages to a new developement of spiritual life? The study of this picture has given a new view of the destiny of humanity; a new conception of what the ideal of human virtue should be, and a new theory of morals: all which vanish, however, when we withdraw our gaze from its lineaments. The spirit of ethics, which had taken to itself only certain features of the picture broken from their connexion with the whole, and was corrupted by foreign elements that had bound themselves up with the Christian consciousness, was purified again in contemplating the unmutilated historical Prototype in the days of the Reformation. And whenever the spirit of the age cuts itself loose, either in the popular turn of thought or in the schools of philosophy, from this historical relation, it estranges itself also from the ethics of Christianity, and sets up a new and different ideal of perfection from that which the revelation of CHRIST has grounded in the consciousness of man.

So much for what *Strauss*, l. c., and *Baur* (Gnosis, p. 655), have said against *Schleiermacher*.

† Τὰς ὑποθέσεις ποιούμενος οὐκ ἀρχὰς, ἀλλὰ τῷ ὄντι ὑποθέσεις, οἷον ἐπιβάσεις τε καὶ ὁρμάς, as Plato says, in a different connexion, at the end of the sixth book of the *Repulic*.

which has come down to us through Christian consciousness (the chief element of which is the impress which He himself left upon the souls of the Apostles) will, by comparison with the living manifestation (*i. e.*, of Christ in his life), be more and more distinctly defined and developed in its separate features, and more and more freed from foreign elements.

So it is in considering the life of any man who has materially and beneficially affected the progress of the race, especially if the results of his labours have touched upon our own interests. We form in advance some idea of such a man, and are not disposed, from any doubtful acts of his that may be laid before us, to change our preconceived notion for an opposite one. But while this preconceived idea may be our guide in studying the life of such a man, the study itself will contribute to enlarge and rectify the individual lineaments of the picture.

But we must not lose sight of one important difference. In all other men there is a contrast between the ideal and the phenomenal. While in many of their traits we may discern the Divine principle which forms their individuality, the archetype of their manifestation in time, in others we see opposing elements, which go to make a mere caricature of that principle. We can obtain no clear view of the aim of the life of such men, unless we can seize upon the higher element which forms the individual character; just as an artist might depict accurately a man's organic features, and, for want of the peculiar intellectual expression, fail completely in giving the entire living physiognomy. But without a conception of the living whole we could not detect the separate features which mar the harmony of the picture. On the other side, again, if we contemplate the whole apart from the individual features, we shall only form an arbitrary ideal, not at all corresponding to the reality.

In Christ, however, the ideal and the phenomenal never contradict each other. All depends upon our viewing rightly together the separate features in their connexion with the higher unity of the whole. We *presuppose* this view of the whole, in order to a just conception of the parts, and to avoid regarding any necessary feature in the light of a caricature. This can the more easily be done, as the phenomena which we are here to contemplate stand alone, and can be compared with no other. And as, even in studying the life of an eminent man, we must commune with his spirit in order to obtain a complete view of his being, so we must yield ourselves up to the Spirit of Christ whom we acknowledge and adore as exalted above us, that He himself may show us his Divine image in the mirror of his Life, and teach us how to distinguish all prejudices of our own creating from the necessary laws of our being.

CHAPTER II.

SOURCES FOR THE HISTORY OF CHRIST.

§ 4. *Traditional Origin of the Synoptical Gospels.*

IN using the authorities, I shall follow the general rules of historical criticism, and seek the truth by comparing the individual accounts with themselves and with each other. A correct judgment of the nature of the authorities may be derived from thus examining them in detail.

The settled result of my investigations on this subject may be stated as follows: The historical remains, as well as the nature of the case, show that the writing of the Gospel history did not originate in any design to give a connected account of the life and public ministry of Christ as a whole, but rather grew out of a series of traditional accounts of separate scenes in his history. These accounts were partly transmitted by word of mouth, and partly laid down in written memoirs. The commission of the whole to writing naturally soon followed the spread of Christianity among the Greeks, a people much accustomed to writing. There can be no doubt that Paul made use of written memoirs of the life of Christ.* The objections of *Weisse* against this view are of no importance. Our first three Gospels resulted from the compilation of such separate materials, as Luke himself states in his introduction.† Matthew's Gospel, in its present form, was not the production of the apostle whose name it bears, but was founded on an account written by him in the Hebrew language, chiefly (but not wholly) for the purpose of presenting the discourses of Christ in a collective form.

§ 5. *Genuineness of John's Gospel.*

John's Gospel, which contains the only consecutive account of the labours of Christ, arose in a very different way. It could have emanated from none other than that "beloved disciple" upon whose soul the image of the Saviour had left its deepest impress. So far from this Gospel's having been written by a man of the second century (as some assert), we cannot even imagine a man existing in that century so little affected by the contrarieties of his times and so far exalted above them. Could an age involved in perpetual contradictions, an age of religious materialism, anthropomorphism, and one-sided intellectualism, have given birth to a production like this, which bears the stamp of none of these deformities?

* See my *Apostol. Geschichte*, 3d edit., p. 131.

† Luke, i. 1, 2.

How mighty must the man have been who, in *that* age, could produce from his own mind such an image of Christ as this? And this man, too, in a period almost destitute of eminent minds, remained in total obscurity! Was it necessary for the master-spirit, who felt in himself the capacity and the calling to accomplish the greatest achievement of his day, to resort to a pitiful trick to smuggle his ideas into circulation?

And then, too, while it is thought sufficient to say of the three other Gospels that they were compiled from undesigned fables, we are told that such a Gospel as this of John was the work of sheer invention, as lately *Dr. Baur* has confessed, with praiseworthy candour. Strange that a man, anxious for the credit of his inventions, should, in the chronology and topography of his Life of Christ, give the lie to the Church traditions of his time, instead of chiming in with them; stranger still, that, in spite of his bold contradiction of the opinions of his age in regard to the history, his fraud should be successful! In short, the more openly this criticism declares itself against the Gospel of John, the more palpably does it manifest its own wilful disregard of history.

§ 6. *Results of Criticism.*

A comparison of the representation of Christ derived from the traditions of the Apostolic Church, with that which the direct and personal knowledge of the beloved disciple affords to us, will not only aid our general conception of his image as a whole, but will also prove the identity of these two representations with each other, from their agreement as well in the separate features as in the general picture.

It must be regarded as one of the greatest boons which the purifying process of Protestant theology in Germany has conferred upon faith as well as science, that the old, mechanical view of Inspiration has been so generally abandoned. That doctrine, and the forced harmonies to which it led, demanded a clerk-like accuracy in the evangelical accounts, and could not admit even the slightest contradictions in them; but we are now no more compelled to have recourse to subtilties against which our sense of truth rebels. In studying the historical connexion of our Saviour's life and actions by the application of an unfettered criticism, we reach a deeper sense in many of his sayings than the bonds of the old dogmatism would have allowed. The inquiring reason need no longer find its free sense of truth opposed to faith; nor is reason bound to subjugate herself, not to faith, but to arbitrary dogmas and artificial hypotheses. The chasms in the Gospel history were unavoidable in the transmission of Divine truth through such lowly human means. The precious treasure has come to us in earthen vessels. But this only affords room for the exercise of our faith—

a faith whose root is to be found, not in science, not in demonstration, but in the humble and self-denying submission of our spirits. Our scientific views may be defective in many points; our knowledge itself may be but fragmentary; but our religious interests will find all that is necessary to attach them to Christ as the ground of salvation and the archetype of holiness.

BOOK I.

BIRTH AND CHILDHOOD

OF

JESUS.

BOOK I.

THE BIRTH AND CHILDHOOD OF JESUS.

CHAPTER I.

PRELIMINARY REMARKS.

§ 7. *Scantiness of our Information in regard to this Period of Christ's Life.—Nothing further really essential to the Interests of Religion.*

IN writing the life of any eminent man, we should not be likely to begin with a period when his character was fully developed and his world-historical importance recognized. On the contrary, we should study the *growth* of his being—seek for the bud which concealed the seed, and the powers that conspired to unfold it.

We cannot fail to have the same desire in studying that LIFE which far transcends every other, both in its own intrinsic excellence and in its bearing upon the history of the human race; but we are kept within very narrow limits on this point by the paucity of our materials, consisting, as they do, of fragmentary accounts, whose *literal* accuracy we have no right to presuppose. To exhibit these features in the life of Christ did not belong to the Apostolic mission, which was designed to meet religious rather than scientific wants; to relate the mighty acts of Christ, from the beginning of his ministry to the time of his ascension, rather than to show how, and under what conditions, his inner nature gradually manifested itself. It belongs to *science* to give a pragmatico genetical developement of the history; religious *faith* occupies itself only with the immediate facts themselves. We cannot expect this part of the history to give so accurate a detail as that which treats of Christ's public ministry and his redemptive acts; nor do the wants of faith require it.

§ 8. *Fundamentally opposite Modes of apprehending the Accounts.*

The problems offered to scientific inquiry at this point are, first, to distinguish the *objective* reality of the events from the *subjective* form in which they are apprehended in the accounts; and, secondly, to fill up, as far as may be, the chasms which necessarily arise in the history from

* I do not enter into the minute researches which are necessary to fix the exact date of Christ's birth.

its being composed of detached narratives. These problems nearly involve each other; for we must obtain a clear view of the events themselves, before we can solve the difficulties that arise in connecting them together. Of these, various views may be taken, different in themselves, yet each in harmony with the interests of religion.

But this cannot be said of *all* the different views which may be taken of the subject. The attempt might be made, for instance, to explain the life of Christ just as that of any eminent man, on the natural principles of human developement; rejecting, of course, the first truth of Christian belief in Christ as the Son of God and our Saviour. This theory, denying the supernatural element of Christianity, necessarily leads its advocates to consider every thing in the Gospel accounts which contradicts it as simply *mythical*. Thus, even in what may be called the *ante-historical* part of our work, we find arrayed against us those views which always reject the supernatural in the events of the life of Christ; although this is a dispute which cannot be settled empirically by inquiries into the separate accounts; for this very distinction of historical and non-historical presupposes a final decision between these opposing views made elsewhere. Thus, the Deistic and Pantheistic theories, which, although they arise from directly opposite modes of thought, agree perfectly in opposing supernaturalism, must deny, in the outset, what the supernatural-theistic views hold to be essential to the idea of a genuine world-redeeming Christ.

We must, then, in order to bring the individual features into harmony with our portraiture of Christ, form the latter definitely from a view of his whole life, and of the organism of that Christian consciousness which grows out of his impress left upon humanity, and manifests his perpetual revelation. In relation to the individual features of the history, it only remains to prove, by naked historical inquiry, that there is no sufficient ground, apart from the general prejudices of rationalism, to deny their historical basis; and to show that the origin of the accounts themselves cannot be explained without the actual occurrence of the events which they describe on the very ground where they arose

CHAPTER II.

THE MIRACULOUS CONCEPTION.

§ 9. *The Miraculous Conception demanded* à priori, *and confirmed* à posteriori.

IF, then, we conceive the manifestation of Christ to have been a supernatural communication of the Divine nature for the moral renewal of man, a new beginning in the chain of human progress; in one word, if we conceive it as a *miracle*, this conception itself, apart from any historical accounts, would lead us to form some notion of the *beginning* of his human life that would harmonize with it.

It is true, this human life of Christ took its appointed place in the course of historical events—nay, all history was arranged with reference to its incorporation; yet it entered into history, not as part of its offspring, but as a higher element. Whatever has its origin in the *natural* course of humanity must bear the stamp of humanity; must share in the sinfulness which stains it, and take part in the strifes which distract it. It was impossible, therefore, that the second Adam, the Divine progenitor of a new and heavenly race, could derive his origin from the first Adam in the ordinary course of nature, or could represent the type of the species, the people, or the family from which he sprung, as do the common children of men. We must conceive him, not as an individual representative of the type which descended from our first parents, but as the creative origin of a new type. And so our own idea of Christ compels us to admit that two factors, the one natural, the other supernatural, were coefficient in his entrance into human life; and this, too, although we may be unable, *à priori*, to state how that entrance was accomplished.

But at this point the historical accounts come to our aid, by testifying that what our theory of the case requires did, in fact, occur. The essential part of the history is found precisely in those features in which the idea and the reality harmonize; and we must not only hold fast these *essential* facts which are so important to the interests of religion, but carefully distinguish them from unimportant and accidental parts, which might, perhaps, be involved in obscurity or contradiction.

§ 10. *Mythical View of the Miraculous Conception.—No trace of it in the Narrative.—No such Mythus could have originated among the Jews.*

The accounts of Matthew and Luke agree in stating that the birth of Christ was the result of a direct creative act of God, and not of the ordinary laws of human generation. They who deny this must make one of two assumptions; either that all the accounts are absolute fables, or that *some* actual fact was the ground-work of the fabulous conception.

Those who adopt the former view tell us that, after Christ had made himself conspicuous by his great acts, men, struck with his extraordinary character, formed a theory of his birth to correspond with it. But this assumption is utterly irreconcilable with the simple and prosaic style in which Matthew tells the story of Joseph's perplexity at finding Mary pregnant before her time;* and the supposition that this prosaic narrative was the offspring of some previous mythical description, is out of all harmony with the character of the primitive Christian times. As for the second assumption, those who adopt it can assign no possible fact to explain the origin of the account, but one of so base a nature as utterly to shock every religious feeling, and every just notion of the overruling Providence of God. Had such an occurrence ever been deemed possible, the fanatical enemies of Christ would very soon have made use of it.† Both these assumptions failing, nothing remains but to admit that the birth of Christ was a phenomenon out of the ordinary course of nature.‡

Nor would such a *mythus* have been consistent with *Jewish* modes of thought. The Hindoo mind might have originated a fable of this character, though in a different form from that in which the account of the Evangelists is given; but the Jewish had totally different tendencies. Such a fable as the birth of the Messiah from a *virgin* could have arisen any where else easier than among the Jews; their doctrine of the Divine Unity, which placed an impassable gulf between God and the world; their high regard for the marriage relation, which led them to abhor unwedded life; and, above all, their full persuasion that the Messiah was to be an ordinary man, undistinguished by any thing supernatural, and not to be endowed with Divine power before the time of his solemn consecration to the Messiahship, all conspired to

* We cannot believe, notwithstanding what *Strauss* says on this point in his 3d edition, that a fable could *originally* be presented in so prosaic a garb as that of Matthew. Cases are not wanting, however, in which the substance of a mythus, after it had come to be received as history, has been given out in a prosaic form.

† They would have done so before Jewish malevolence employed the history of the miraculous conception to invent the fable which Celsus first made use of.—*Orig.*, i., 32. Had any such legends been in circulation before, we should find some trace of them in the Evangelists, who do not conceal the accusations that were made against Christ.

‡ *Schleiermacher*, whose reverence for sacred things forbade him to adopt the latter of these two suppositions, while his conscientious love of truth compelled him to admit the reality of the history, says, in comparing the statements of Matthew and Luke (*Critical Inquiries*, p. 47), "We may well leave the statement of Matthew in the judicious indefiniteness in which it is expressed; while the traditional basis of the poetical announcement in Luke rebukes those impious explanations which soil the veil they cannot lift." But, in sober truth, no one can admit the veracity of the history, and, at the same time, deny the miraculous conception, without falling into the very conclusion which Schleiermacher rejects with such pious indignation.

render such an invention impossible among them. The accounts of Isaac, Samson, and Samuel cannot be quoted as in point; these cases rather illustrate the Hebrew notion of the blessing of fruitfulness; and in them all the Divine power was shown, not in excluding the male, but in rendering the long-barren female fruitful, contrary to all human expectation. The conception of Christ would have been analogous to these, had Mary, after long barrenness, borne a son, or had Joseph been too old to expect offspring at the time.*

It was on this very account, viz., because the miraculous conception was foreign to the prevailing Jewish modes of thought,† that one sect of the Ebionites, who could not free themselves from their old prejudices, refused to admit the doctrine; and the section which contains the account is excluded from the Ebionitish recension of the Gospel to the Hebrews, which arose from the same source as our Matthew. As for the single obscure passage in Isa., vii., it could hardly have given

* E. g., in the apocryphal Gospel of James, ch. ix., it is stated, that when the priest was about to give Mary as a wife to the aged Joseph, the latter said, "I have sons and am old, while she is yet young; shall I not then become a mockery for the sons of Israel?"

† Professor *Weisse*, in his work, "Die Evangelische Geschichte" (The Gospel History, critically and philosophically treated, Leips., 1838), admits that the Jews could not have invented this *mythus*, but ascribes to it a *heathen* origin. How, in view of the relations that subsisted between early Christianity and heathenism, the pagan *mythus* of the sons of the gods could so soon have been transformed into a Christian one; and how the latter could have found its way into St. Matthew's Gospel, which unquestionably had a Jewish-Christian origin, are among the incomprehensibilities which abound in Prof. W.'s very intelligible work. He says, p. 178, that "as Paul found himself involuntarily compelled, in addressing the Athenians, to quote Greek poetry (*For we are also his offspring*, Acts, xvii., 28), so it is possible that the apostles to the heathen were led to adopt the pagan *mythus* of the sons of the gods, in order to make known to them the truth, that Christ is the Son of God, in a form suited to their way of thinking, and that their figurative language, literally understood, formed the starting-point for such a *mythus*." Things very heterogeneous are thrown together in this passage. What religious scruples need have hindered Paul from alluding to the consciousness of the Divine origin of the human race, which the Athenians themselves had expressed, and to the vague idea which they entertained of an unknown God? Nor was such an allusion likely to be misunderstood. How could a man, imbued with Jewish feelings in regard to the heathen mythology (feelings which his conversion to Christianity would by no means weaken), compare the birth of the Holy One—of the Messiah—with those pagan fables, whose impurity could inspire him with nothing but disgust? Weisse has transferred his own mode of contemplating the heathen myths to a people that would have revolted from it.

It is quite another thing when Weisse adduces the comparisons in which the early Christian apologists indulged. These men, themselves of heathen origin, were accustomed to the allegorical interpretations of the mythology, and it was natural for them to seek and occupy a position intermediate between their earlier and later views. But, so far from these comparisons having given rise to the accounts of the supernatural conception, it was the latter which caused the former. They wished to show to the heathen that this miraculous event was not altogether foreign to their own religious ideas, while they carefully guarded against the sensuous forms of thought involved in the myths; and, as they could *presuppose this event*, they had a right to employ the myths as they did, inasmuch as these poetical effusions of natural religion anticipated (though in sadly-distorted caricatures) the great truth of Christianity, that the union of the Divine with the human nature was brought about by a creative act of Omnipotence. The early apologists expressed this in their own way "*Satan invented these fables by imitating the truth.*"

rise to such a tradition among the people of Palestine, where, unquestionably, Matthew's Gospel originated.

§ 11. *Objections to the Narrative drawn from the subsequent Dispositions of Christ's Relatives, answered* (1) *from the nature of the case;* (2) *from the name* JESUS.

An objection to the credibility of the narrative has been raised on the ground that if such events had really preceded the birth of Christ, his own relatives would have been better disposed to recognize him as the Messiah. It is possible that the circumstances of his birth *did* raise their expectations to a lofty pitch; but as for thirty years no indications corresponding with ordinary views of the Messiah manifested themselves, their first impressions gradually wore away, only to be revived, however, by the great acts which Jesus performed after the opening of his public career. And as for Mary (in whom a doubt of this sort would appear still more strange, as she was directly cognizant of the miraculous features of the history), there is no proof whatever that she ever lost the memory of her visions, or relinquished the hopes they were so well calculated to raise. Her conduct at the marriage of Cana proves directly the reverse. She obviously expected a miracle from Christ immediately after the proclamation of his Messiahship by John the Baptist. The confirmation which John's Gospel, by its recital of this miracle, affords to the other evangelists is the more striking, as John himself gives no account of the events accompanying the birth of Christ.*

* (*a*) John's silence in regard to the miraculous conception is no proof that he was either ignorant of the accounts of that event or disbelieved them. His object was to testify to what he had himself seen and heard, and to declare how the glory of the Only begotten had been unveiled to him in contemplating Christ's manifestation on earth. But that he recognized the miraculous conception is evident from his emphatic declarations (in opposition to the ordinary Jewish idea of the Messiah), that the Divine and the human were originally united in the person of Christ, and that the LOGOS itself became flesh in him; while at the same time he avers that "*that which is born of the flesh is flesh.*" No man could hold these two ideas together without believing in the immediate agency of GOD in the generation of CHRIST (*b*) The objection that Jesus was known among the Jews as the son of Joseph and Mary, and that this fact was adduced against his claims, has been sufficiently met in the text; but it has been urged further that Christ himself, when this objection was brought against him (Matt., xiii., 55), did not allude to the miraculous conception. As to this, we need only say that it was far more likely and natural that Jesus should call men's attention to the proofs of his Divinity which were before their eyes in his daily acts, showing, at the same time, that the causes of their disbelief lay in themselves, rather than that he should dwell upon the circumstances which preceded his birth, the proof of which had to rest upon the testimony of Mary alone. (*c*) Nor is Paul's silence on this point proof of his not acknowledging it. It only shows that, for his religious sense, the sufferings and resurrection of Christ, the centre and support of the Christian system, stood out more prominently than the miraculous conception. In the passages in which he speaks of Christ's origin, he had a different object in view than to treat of this subject; *e. g.*, in Rom., ix., 5, "*Whose are the fathers, and of whom, as concerning the flesh, Christ came, who is over all, God blessed forever,*" and in Rom., i., 4, where he brings out prominently the

The name Jesus itself affords additional proof that his parents were ed by some extraordinary circumstances to expect that he would be the Messiah. Such names as *Theodorus, Theodoret, Dorotheus,* among the Greeks, were usually bestowed because the parents had obtained a son after long desire and expectation. As names were also given among the Jews with reference to their significancy, and as the name Jesus betokens "Him through whom Jehovah bestows salvation;" and, moreover, as the Messiah, the bearer of this salvation, was generally expected at the time, it must certainly appear probable to us that the name was given with reference to that expectation. Not that this conclusion *necessarily* follows, because the name *Jesus, Joshua,* was common among the Jews; but yet, compared with the accounts, it certainly affords confirmatory evidence.

§ 12. *Analogical Ideas among the Heathen.*

Moreover, inferences in *favour* of the accounts of the miraculous conception, as well as against them, may be obtained by comparing them with the ancient myths of other religions. The spirit of the pagan mythology could not have penetrated among the Jews, and therefore cannot be assigned to explain the similarity between the Christian and pagan views. We must seek that explanation rather in the relations that subsist between mythical *natural* religion and historical *revealed* religion; between the idea, forming, from the enslaved consciousness which it sways, an untrue actualization; and the idea, grounded in truth, and developing itself therefrom into clear and free consciousness.

The truth which the religious sense can recognize at the bottom of these myths, is the earnest desire, inseparable from man's spirit, for communion with God, for participation in the Divine nature as its true life—its anxious longing to pass the gulf which separates the God-derived soul from its original—its wish, even though unconscious, to secure that union with God which alone can renew human nature, and which Christianity shows us as a living reality. Nor can we be astonished to find the facts of Christianity thus anticipated in poetic forms (imbodying in imaginative creations the innate yet indistinct cravings of the spirit) in the mythical elements of the old religions, when we re-

two-fold manifestation of Christ, as the Son of David and as the Son of God, raised above all human and national relationships, as he revealed himself after the resurrection. If we could infer from such passages Paul's disbelief in the miracle, we can draw precisely the opposite conclusion from Gal., iv., 4; although, as the case is, we do not lay much stress upon the expression, "born of a woman." And if Paul could represent Jesus as the Son of God from heaven, as being without sin in the flesh (σάρξ), in which sin before had reigned, while at the same time he taught the propagation of sinfulness, from Adam down, it is likely that the supernatural generation of Jesus was so firmly established in the connexion of his own thoughts, that he felt the less necessity to give it individual prominence. We shall have occasion to make a similar remark hereafter in regard to the omission of the account of Christ's ascension as an individual event.

member that human nature itself, and all the forms of its developement, as well as the whole course of human history, were intended by God to find their full accomplishment in Christ. But the genius of Christianity is mistaken by those who despise the simplicity of the Gospel history, and contrast it with the poetry of religion. The opposition, apparently essential to the mere natural man, between poetry, transcending the limits of the actual, and the prose of common reality, is taken away by the manifestation of Christ, and *will* be done away wherever Christianity passes into flesh and blood. The peculiarity of Christian ethics is indeed founded upon this.

The characteristic difference between the religion of Theism and that of the old mythology lies in this one point: that in the evangelical histories the Divine power is represented as operating *immediately*, and not by the interposition of natural causes; while, in the mythical conceptions, the Divine causality is made coefficient with natural agencies; the Divine is brought down to the sphere of the natural, and its manifestation is thus physically explained.* Thus the Gospel histories, precisely as a just idea of Christ would lead us to presuppose, attribute to the creative agency of God alone the introduction of that new member of humanity through which the regeneration of the race is to be accomplished.

CHAPTER III.

THE BIRTH OF CHRIST.

§ 13. *The Birth of Christ in its Relations to the Jewish Theocracy.*

AS the entrance of Christ into the course of humanity was brought about by the co-working of supernatural with natural elements, so both these agencies conspired in *preparing the way* for that great event, the centre of all things, and the aim of all preceding history. So we interpret the relations of the Jews and heathens to the appearance of Christ. The *natural developement of the heathen* was destined, under the Divine guidance, to prepare them for receiving the new light which emanated from Jesus; and the history of the *Jewish people* was all preparatory to the appearance and ministry of Christ, who was to come forth out of their midst. This preparation was accomplished by means

* *Baumgarten-Crusius* has noticed this distinction in his Biblical Theology, p. 397; but *Strauss* denies it, and asserts that the expression υἱὸς Θεοῦ in Luke i., 35, is to be taken entirely in a physical sense. There is no such meaning in the passage; it predicates the terms "*the holy one,*" "*the Son of God,*" of Christ, on the ground of the special agency of the Holy Spirit in his birth. He who was conceived under such an agency *must* stand in a special relation to God. Not merely the Jewish mode of thinking on the subject, but also the fact that Jesus is designated both as the Son of David and the Son of God, exclude the physical interpretation.

of a chain of separate, but organically connected revelations, all tending toward the full revelation in HIM, whose whole life was itself to be the highest manifestation of GOD to man.

There was peculiar fitness in Christ's being born among the Jewish people. His life revealed the *kingdom of God*, which was to be set up over all men, and it properly commenced in a nation whose political life, always developed in a theocratic form, was a continual type of that kingdom. HE was the culminating point of this developement; in HIM the kingdom of God, no longer limited to this single people, was to show its true design, and, unfettered by physical or national restraints, to assert its authority over the whole human race. The particular typifies the universal; the earthly, the celestial; so David, the monarch who had raised the political theocracy of the Jews to the pinnacle of glory, typified that greater monarch in whom the kingdom of GOD was to display its glory. Not without reason, therefore, was it that Christ, the summit of the theocracy, sprang from the fallen line of royal David.*

§ 14. *The Miraculous Events that accompanied the Birth of Christ.*

The Divine purpose in the supernatural conception of Jesus could not have been accomplished without some providential forewarnings to his parents; nor could these intimations of the certainty of the approaching birth of the theocratic King have been given by ordinary, natural means. In the sphere of the greatest miracle of human history, the miracle which was to raise mankind to communion with Heaven, we do not wonder to see rays of light streaming from the invisible world, at other times so dark.

* However the discrepancies in the two genealogies of Christ may be explained, his descent from the race of David was admitted from the beginning, and the evangelists took it for granted as indisputable. How *Weisse* should deny this, as he does (p. 169), is unaccountable. His arguments can convince no one endowed with the slightest powers of observation, and need no answer. The only one which is at all plausible is that founded on Mark, xii., 35; and that depends upon the question whether Mark uses these words in their original application; a question which we shall hereafter have occasion to examine. Certainly, if they admit of more than one interpretation, we shall adopt any other sooner than that which comes into conflict with Paul, who assumed Christ's descent from David as certain. Could the apostles have embraced a notion which the Saviour himself had denounced as an invention of the scribes? There was nothing in Paul's turn of feeling or thought to incline him towards it, had it not been established on other grounds; on the contrary, the doctrine that Christ was *not* the Son of David, but the Son of God and the Lord of David, would have afforded him an excellent point of attack against Judaism. Although Luke's genealogy is not directly stated as following the line of Mary, yet it may have done so, and have only been improperly placed where it is. Justin Martyr (Dial. c. Tryph., f. 327) was acquainted with such a genealogy referring to Mary. Luke, i., 32–35, seems to show that Mary was of David's race. Her relationship to Elizabeth, the mother of John Baptist, does not prove the contrary; for members of the tribe of Levi were not restrained from inter marriage with other tribes; and Elizabeth, although of that tribe on the father's side, and herself the wife of a priest, might very well have sprung from the tribe of Judah on the mother's side.

From the very nature of the case, we can expect no full account of those extraordinary manifestations of which, naturally enough, Mary alone could testify.* But a mere *mythus*, destitute of historical truth, and only serving as the veil of an ideal truth, is a very different thing from what we are here stating, viz., that a lofty *history* may be imparted in a form which must have more than its mere literal force; and that events of a lofty character necessarily impart their higher tone to the language in which they are conveyed. In this latter case, we may harmlessly differ in our modes of arranging the materials, and of filling up the chasms of the history, so that we only hold fast the substantial facts which form its basis. The course of the events described in Matt., i., 18–25, may be arranged as follows: When Mary informed Joseph of the remarkable communication that had been made to her, he could not at once bring himself to believe it; which was not at all strange, considering its extraordinary character, and how little he was prepared for it. A struggle ensued in his feelings, and then occurred the night vision which brought his mind to a final decision.†

§ 15. *The Taxing.—Birth of Christ at Bethlehem*

By a remarkable interposition of Providence, interwoven, however, with the course of events in the world, was it brought about, that the promised King should be born in Bethlehem (as Micah the prophet had foretold), the very place where the house of David had its origin; while, at the same time, the lowly circumstances of his birth were in striking contrast with the inherent dignity and glory that were veiled in the new-born child.

The Emperor Augustus had ordered a general census of the Roman Empire, partly to obtain correct statistics of its resources,‡ and partly for purposes of taxation.§ As Judea was then a dependency of the empire, and Augustus probably intended to reduce it entirely to the

* Mary could only have been taught to expect the Saviour in a way harmonizing with her views at the time, and with the prevailing Jewish ideas of the Messiah, viz., that the Messiah should come of the line of David, to establish an everlasting kingdom among the Jews. But this was only a covering for the higher idea of the Redeemer, the founder of the eternal kingdom of God.

† We need be the less afraid of a free, unliteral interpretation when we find a difference in the subjective conception of these events by even the evangelists themselves, Matthew speaking only of dreams and visions, and Luke of objective phenomena, viz., the appearance of angels.

‡ This was not confined to the Roman *provinces*, but extended also to the *Socii.*—Tacit., Ann., i., xi.

§ Cassiodor., i., iii., ep. 52: *Augusti temporibus orbis Romanus agris divisus censuque descriptus, ut possessio sui nulli haberetur incerta, quam pro tributorum susciperet quantitatibus solvendam.* (Conf. *Savigny's* dissertation in the "Zeitschrift für die geschichtl. Rechtswissenschaft, Bd. vi., H. 3.) This language of the learned statesman shows that he followed older accounts rather than a Christian report drawn from Luke; and the expression of Tacitus confirms this conclusion. There is no ground, therefore, for the doubts started by *Strauss*, 3d ed., p. 257

state of a Roman province, he wished to secure similar statistics of that country, and ordered King Herod to take the census. In performing this duty, Herod followed the Jewish usage, viz., a division by tribes.* Joseph and Mary belonged to the tribe of David, and therefore had to repair to Bethlehem, the seat of that tribe. On account of the throng, they could find no shelter but a stable, and the new-born infant had to be laid in a manger.†

§ 16. *The Announcement to the Shepherds.*

It is in accordance with the analogy of history that great manifestations and epochs, designed to satisfy the spiritual wants of ages, should be anticipated by the prophetic yearnings of pure and susceptible hearts, inspired by a secret Divine consciousness. All great events that have introduced a new developement of human history have been preceded by unconscious or conscious prophecy. This may seem

* Luke's account of the matter is so prosaic and straightforward, that none but a prejudiced mind can find a trace of the *mythical* in it. Examine the Apocryphal Gospels, and you will see the difference between history and fable. And even if it could be shown that the census was incorrect, and that the gathering at Bethlehem was due to some other cause, no suspicion would thereby be cast upon the entire narration; the only reasonable conclusion would be, that Luke, or the writer from whom he copied, had fallen into an anachronism, or an erroneous combination of facts, in assigning the census as the cause of the gathering. Such an error could not affect in any way the interests of religion. Moreover, what right have we to demand of Luke so exact a knowledge of the history of his times, in things that did not materially concern his purpose? Such anachronisms, in things indifferent, are common to writers of all ages. But the account itself contains no marks of improbability. The emperor would naturally order Herod, whom he still recognized as king, to take the census, and Herod as naturally followed the Jewish usage in doing it. It was the policy of the emperor, at that time, to treat the Jews with kindness, and therefore he would naturally make the first attempt at a census as delicately as possible. How repugnant such a measure was to them is shown by Josephus's account of the tumults that arose on account of the census under *Quirinus*, twelve years afterward. Luke may have gone too far in extending (as his language seems to imply) the census over the whole empire; or, perhaps, in stating the *gradual* census of the whole empire as a *simultaneous* one. Perhaps he mistook this assessment for the census which occurred twelve years later, and on that account erroneously mentioned *Quirinus*. Nevertheless, Quirinus may have been actually present at this assessment, not, indeed, as governor of the province, but as imperial commissioner; for Josephus expressly says that he had held many other offices before he was Governor of Syria, at the time of the second census. I do not agree with any of the explanations, either ancient or modern, which attempt to make Luke's statement agree exactly with history; they all seem to me to be forced and unphilological, while the want of exactness in Luke is easily explained, and is of no manner of importance for the object which he had in view.

† The tradition in *Justin Martyr* (Dial. c. Tryph., 304, a), that they found shelter in a cave near the town, which had before been used for a cattle stall (*ἐν σπηλαίῳ τινὶ σύνεγγυς τῆς κώμης*), may be true, although we should not like to vouch for it. It is more likely that the prophecy in Isai., xxxiii., 16 (which Justin refers to in the Alexandrian version), was applied to this tradition after it arose, than that the tradition arose from the prophecy. At that time men were accustomed to find every where in the Old Testament predictions and types of Christ, whether warranted by the connexion or not. The tradition does not specify *such* a cave as the passage in Isaiah would lead one to expect, nor, indeed, does the passage seem distinctly to refer to the Messiah.

strange to such as ascribe to God the apathy of the Stoics, or who believe only in the cold, iron necessity of an immanent spirit of nature; but to none who believe in a personal, self-conscious Deity, a God of eternal love, who is nigh unto every man, and listens willingly to the secret sighs of longing souls, can it appear unworthy of such a Being to foreshadow great world-historical epochs by responding to such longings in special revelations.

Far more probable, then, would such manifestations be, in reference to the highest object of human longings, the greatest of all world historical phenomena; and so, at the time of Christ's coming, the people of Judea, guided by the prophecies of the Old Testament, yearned for the appearance of the Messiah with an anxiety only rendered more intense by the oppressions under which they groaned. This feeling would naturally be kept alive in Bethlehem, associated as the place was with recollections of the family of David, from which the Messiah was to come. So, even among the shepherds, who kept nightly watch over the flocks, were some who anxiously awaited the appearance of the Messiah. It is true, the account does not *say* that the shepherds thus longed for the Messiah. But we are justified by what followed in presupposing it as the ground for such a communication's being especially made to them; and it is not unlikely that these simple souls, untaught in the traditions of the scribes, and nourished by communion with God, amid the freedom of nature, in a solitude congenial to meditation and prayer, had formed a purer idea of the Messiah, from the necessities of their own hearts, than prevailed at that time among the Jews. A vision from Heaven conducted them on that night, so big with interest to man's salvation, to the place where the object of their desire was to be born.*

* Justly and beautifully says *Schleiermacher*, "There is something remarkable, some thing divine, in the satisfaction not seldom afforded in extraordinary times even to individual longings." We agree with this great teacher in thinking that this account came indirectly from the shepherds themselves, as it recites so particularly what occurred to themselves personally, and makes so little mention of what happened to the child after their arrival. The facts may be supposed to have been as follows: The faithful were anxious to preserve the minute features of the life of Jesus. (We cannot be persuaded by the assertions of modern Idealism that this feeling had no existence. We see every day how anxiously men look for individual traits in the childhood of great men.) Especially would any one who had the opportunity prosecute such researches in the remarkable place where Christ was born. Perhaps one of these inquirers there found one of the shepherds who had witnessed these events, and whose memory of them was vividly recalled after his conversion to Christianity. We cannot be sure that such a man would give with literal accuracy the words that he had heard; but, taking them as they stand, it is astonishing how free they are from the materialism which always tinged Jewish expression, and in how purely spiritual a way they describe the sublime transaction of which they treat. Whether we follow the received version or that of the Cod. Alex., we find the same thought expressed in the statement of the shepherds, viz., that "God is glorified in the Messiah, who brings peace and joy to the earth, and restores man again to the Divine favour."

§ 17. *The Sacrifice of Purification, and the Ransom of the First-born; their Weight as Proof against the Mythical Theory.*

The mass of the Jewish people, whose minds were darkened by their material and political views, entertained a totally false idea of the Messiah; but there were many at Jerusalem who longed for a purer salvation, and these, also, were to receive a sign that the object of their hopes had at last appeared.

Forty days after the birth of the infant Jesus his parents carried him to the temple at Jerusalem, in order to offer, according to their means, the prescribed sacrifice for the purification of Mary, and to pay the usual ransom for their first-born.* This appears strange, in view of the extraordinary circumstances that preceded and followed the birth of the child, which, one might suppose, would make it an exception to ordinary rules. The points which the Levitical law had in view seem not to have existed here: so remarkable a birth might have precluded the necessity of the Levitical purification. The ransom which had to be paid for other first-born sons, in view of their original obligation to the priesthood, could hardly be necessary in the case of an infant who was one day to occupy the summit of the Theocracy. It would be natural to suppose that Mary must have hesitated, and laid her scruples before the priests for decision before she could make up her mind to perform these ceremonies. But we cannot judge of such extraordinary events by common standards. Mary did not venture to speak freely in public of these wonderful things, or to anticipate the Divine purposes in any way; she left it to God to educate the child, which had been announced to her as the Messiah, so as to fit him for his calling, and, at the proper time, to authenticate his mission publicly and conspicuously.

Now a *mythus* generally endeavors to ennoble its subject, and to adapt the story to the idea.† If, then, the Gospel narrative were mythical, would it have invented, or even suffered to remain, a circumstance so foreign to the idea of the myth, and so little calculated to dignify it as the above? A *mythus* would have introduced an angel, or, at least, a vision, to hinder Mary from submitting the child to a ceremony so unworthy of its dignity; or the priests would have received an intimation

* Exod., xiii., 2, 12; Num., iii., 45; xviii., 15; Levit., xii., 2.

† The remarks of Strauss, l. c., p. 326, do not at all weaken what is here said. He adduces, also, the fact that Luke (iii., 21) states the baptism without mentioning John's previous refusal (Matt., iii., 14); but all the force of this lies in his presupposition that Luke's narrative is also mythical, which I deny. As to Gal., iv., 4, we of course believe that Christ strictly fulfilled the Mosaic law; but this fact, on Jewish principles, is no parallel to the other, viz., that Mary, under the circumstances of the miraculous birth, *needed* purification, and that the Messiah, who was destined for the highest station in the Theocracy *needed* a ransom from the obligation to the priesthood.

from heaven to bow before the infant, and prevent its being thus reduced to the level of ordinary children. Nothing of all this took place; but, instead of it, simply and unostentatiously, the high dignity and destiny of the child were revealed to *two* faithful souls.

§ 18. *Simeon's Prophetic Discourse.*

The aged and devout Simeon,* who had longed and prayed for the coming of Messiah's kingdom, had received the Divine assurance that he should not die without seeing the desire of his heart. Under a peculiarly vivid impulse of this presentiment, he entered the Temple just as the infant Jesus was brought in. The Divine glory irradiating the child's features harmonized with the longing of his inspired soul; he recognized the manifested Messiah, took the infant in his arms, and exclaimed, in a burst of inspired gratitude, "*Lord, now let thy servant depart in peace according to thy promise, for mine eyes have seen thy salvation which thou hast prepared before the face of all people, a light to enlighten the Gentiles, and the glory of thy people Israel.*"† Then, turning to Mary, he exclaimed, "*Behold, this child is set for the fall and rising again of many in Israel, and for a sign which shall be spoken against;‡ and a sword shall pierce through thine own soul also, that the thoughts of many hearts may be revealed.*"

Notice, now, the remarkable idea of the Messiah which these words convey; precisely such a one as we should expect from a longing *Jew*, of deep, spiritual piety. Although it cannot be said to contain really Christian elements, it is far above the ordinary conceptions of the times; and this not only confirms the truth of the narrative, but stamps the discourse as Simeon's own, and not a speech composed in his name.§ It is true, Simeon conceives the kingdom of Messiah as tending to glorify the Jewish people, but yet extends its blessings also over the heathen, and believes that the light of the knowledge of God

* We have no reason to suppose him to be the *Rabbi* Simeon, the father of Gamaliel, as no distinguishing mark of eminence is assigned to him.

† It is said in Luke, ii., 33, that "*Joseph and Mary marvelled*" at the words of Simeon Now it is strange that what he said should appear marvellous to the parents, who were already cognizant of so many wonderful events in the history of the child. But we are to remember that the first three Gospels do not contain connected histories, but compilations of separate memoirs; and, again, the writer of the narrative may have been so imbued with wonder at the extraordinary *whole*, as to transfer this feeling to his expression in detailing the separate *parts*, again and again. The narrative would have worn a very different aspect had Luke designed to compose a systematic work, with the parts accurately adjusted, instead of writing, as he did, with simple and straightforward candour.

‡ The results of Messiah's appearance among men depend upon their own spiritual dispositions: salvation for the believer, destruction for the unbeliever. Around his banner the hosts of the faithful gather; but infidels reject and fight against it. Salvation and doom are correlative ideas; all world-historical epochs are epochs of condemnation.

§ The accurate report of this discourse is accounted for by the supposition that the account came indirectly from Anna: not only the discourse, but the whole occurrence, must have made a deep impression upon her mind.

will illumine them also. Nor does he conceive Messiah's kingdom as triumphing at once by displays of miraculous power, but rather as developing itself after struggles with prevailing corruptions, and after a gradual purifying of the theocratic nation. The conflict with the corrupt part of the nation was to be severe before the Messiah could lead his faithful ones to victory. The foreboding of suffering to Mary, so indefinitely expressed, bears no mark of *post factum* invention. But the inspired idea of Messiah in the pious old man obviously connected the sufferings which he was to endure in his strife against the corrupt people with those which were foretold of him in Isaiah, liii.

The other devout one, to whom the destiny of the infant Jesus was revealed, was the aged Anna, who heard Simeon's words, shared in his joyful anticipations, and united in his song of thanksgiving.*

§ 19. *The Longing of the Heathen for a Saviour.—The Star of the Wise Men.*

Not only dwellers about Bethlehem, but also men from a far-distant land, imbued with the longing desires of which we have spoken, were led to the place where Christ was born by a sign suited to their peculiar mode of life, a fact which foreshadowed that the hopes of heathen as well as Jews, unconscious as well as conscious longings for a Saviour, were afterward to be gratified.† We have before remarked, that the *natural* developement of the heathen mind worked in the same direction as the movement of *revealed* religion among the Jews to prepare the way for Christ's appearance, which was the aim and end of all previous human history. There is something analogous to the law and the prophets (which, under revealed religion, led directly, and by an organically arranged connexion, to Christ), in the sporadic and detached revelations, which, here and there among the heathen, arose from the Divine consciousness implanted in humanity. As, under the Law, man's sense of its insufficiency to work out his justification was accompanied by the promise of One who should accomplish what the Law could never do, so, in the progress of the pagan mind under the law of nature, there arose a sense of the necessity of a new revelation from heaven, and a longing desire for a higher order of

* We agree with *Schleiermacher* in thinking it probable that the narrative came indirectly from Anna. She is far more minutely described in it than Simeon, although the latter and his discourse constitute the most important part of the account, while *her* words are not reported at all.

† If this narrative is to be considered as *mythical*, we must yet ascribe its origin to the same source which produced the Hebrew Gospel, viz., the Jewish-Christian congregations in Palestine—a likely origin, indeed, for a myth ascribing so great interest and importance to uncircumcised heathen! An extravagant exaggeration of the real occurrence was subsequently made, probably from a fragment of one of the recensions of the Hebrew Gospel (Ignat., Epist. ad Ephes., § 19): "The star sparkled brilliantly beyond all other stars; it was a strange and wonderful sight. The other stars, with the sun and moon, formed a choir around it, but its blaze outshone them all."

things. The notion of a Messiah, carried about by the Jews in their intercourse with different nations, every where found a point of contact with the religious sense of men; and thus natural and revealed religion worked into each other, as well as separately, in preparing the way for the appearance of Christ.*

Thus it happened that a few sages in Arabia (or in some part of the Parthian kingdom), who inquired for the course of human events in that of the stars, became convinced that a certain constellation or star† which they beheld was a token‡ of the birth of the great King who was expected to arise in the East. It is not necessary to suppose that an actual miracle was wrought in this case; the course of natural events, under Divine guidance, was made to lead to Christ, just as the general moral culture of the heathen, though under natural forms, was made to lead to the knowledge of the Saviour.

The Magi studied astrology, and in their study found a sign of Christ. If it offends us to find that God has used the errors of man to lead him to a knowledge of the great truths of salvation, as if thereby He had lent himself to sustain the False, then must we break in pieces the chain of human events, in which the True and the False, the Good and the Evil, are so inseparably linked, that the latter often serves for the point of transition to the former. Especially do we see this in the history of the spread of Christianity, where superstition often paves the way for faith. God condescends to the platforms of men in training them for belief in the Redeemer, and meets the aspirations of the truth-seeking soul even in its error!§ In the case of the wise men, a real truth, perhaps, lay at the bottom of the error; the truth, namely, that the greatest of all events, which was to produce the greatest revolution in humanity, is actually connected with the epochs of the mate-

* We do not insist upon *Tacit.*, Hist., 5, 13, and *Sueton.*, Vespasian, 4, who speak of a rumour spread over the whole East, of the approaching appearance of the great King, as it is yet doubtful whether these passages are not imitated from Josephus.

† It is necessary to distinguish what is objectively real in the narrative from what arises from the subjective stand-point of the author of our Matthew's Gospel, who certainly did not receive the account from an eye-witness. Not merely philological exegesis, but also historical criticism, are required for this; and if the result of such an inquiry be pronounced arbitrary, because it does not either affirm or reject the objective reality of *every thing* in the account, then must *all* historical criticism be pronounced arbitrary also, for it has no other mode of procedure in testing the accuracy of a narrative.

‡ Conf. Bishop *Munter's* treatise on the "Star of the Wise Men," and *Ideler's* Chronology, ii., 399. It is immaterial whether the sages were led to seek for the sign by a theory of their own, or by a traditional one.

§ *Hamann* strikingly says, "How often has God condescended, not merely to the feelings and thoughts of men, but even to their failings and their prejudices! But this very condescension (one of the highest marks of his love to man), which is exhibited every where in the Bible, affords subjects of derision to those weaklings who look into the word of God for displays of human wisdom, for the gratification of their pert and idle curiosity, or for the spirit of their own times or their own sect."—*Works*, i., 58.

nal universe, although the links of the chain may be hidden from our view.

In the narrative before us, we need not attach the same indisputable certainty to the details as to the general substance. That the Magians should be led, by their astrological researches, to a presentiment of the birth of the Saviour in Judea—that their own longings should impel them to journey to Jerusalem and do homage to the infant in whom lay veiled the mighty King—*this* is the lofty, the Divine element in the transaction, which no one who believes in a guiding, eternal love —no one who is conscious of the real import of a Redeemer—can fail to recognize.

We cannot vouch with equal positiveness for the accuracy of Matthew's statement of the means by which the sages learned, after their arrival in Jerusalem, that the chosen child was to be born in Bethlehem; but it matters little whether they were directed thither by Herod, or in some other way. At any rate, in so small a place as Bethlehem, they might easily have been guided to the exact place by providential means not out of the common way; for instance, by meeting with some of the shepherds, or other devout persons, who had taken part in the great event; and they, perhaps, described the whole as it appeared to them subjectively, when, after reaching the abode, they looked up at the starry heavens.

§ 20. *The Massacre of the Innocents and the Flight into Egypt.*

The account of the massacre of the infants at Bethlehem cannot appear incredible when we consider the character of the man to whom this act of blind and senseless cruelty, worthy of an insane tyrant, is ascribed.

It was that HEROD, whose crimes, committed in violation of every natural feeling, ever urged him on to new deeds of cruelty; whose path to the throne, and whose throne itself, were stained with human blood; whose vengeance against conspirators, not satiated with their own destruction, demanded that of their whole families;* whose rage was hot, up to the very hour of his death, against his nearest kindred; whose wife, Mariamne, and three sons, Alexander, Aristobulus, and Antipater, fell victims to his suspicions, the last just before his death; who, in a word, certainly deserved that the Emperor Augustus should have said of him, "*Herodis mallem porcus esse, quam filius.*"† It was that HEROD, who, at the close of a blood-stained life of seventy years goaded by the furies of an evil conscience, racked by a painful and incurable disease, waiting for death, but desiring life, raging against

* Joseph., Archæol., xv., viii., § 4.

† These words were applied, in the fifth century, by an anachronism of the pagan writer *Macrobius*, to the massacre of the infants at Bethlehem.—*Saturnal.*, ii., 4.

God and man, and maddened by the thought that the Jews, instead of bewailing his death, would rejoice over it as the greatest of blessings, commanded the worthies of the nation to be assembled in the circus, and issued a secret order* that, after his death, they should all be slain together, so that *their* kindred, at least, might have cause to weep for his death!† Can we deem the crime of sacrificing a few children to his rage and blind suspicion too atrocious for such a monster?

As we have no reason to question the narrative of the tyrant's attempts upon the life of the wonderful child whose birth had come to his ears, we can readily connect therewith the *flight into Egypt*. On the supposition that this flight actually took place, it was natural enough, especially with a view to obviate any objections which the issuing of the Messiah from a profane land might suggest to Jewish minds, for men to seek analogies between this occurrence and the history of Moses and the theocratic people; while, on the other hand, it would be absurd to suppose that a legend of the flight, without any historical basis, should have had its origin solely in the desire to find such analogies.

Thus, in the very beginning of the life of Him who was to save the world, we see a foreshadowing of what it was afterward to be. The believing souls, to whom the lofty import of that life was shown by Divine signs, saw in it the fulfilment of their longings; the power of the world, ever subservient to evil, raged against it, but, amid all dangers, the hand of God guided and brought it forth victorious.‡

§ 21. *The Return to Nazareth.*

Joseph and Mary remained but a short time with the child in Egypt. The death of Herod soon recalled them to Palestine, and they returned to their old place of abode, the little town of Nazareth,§ in Galilee.

* It was never executed.

† Josephus (Archæol., xvii., 6, 5) says of him: "Μέλαινα χολὴ αὐτὸν ᾕρει ἐπὶ πᾶσιν ἐξαγρια ἰνουσα." Even *Schlosser* admits (View of Ancient History and Civilization, iii., 1, p. 261 that the account of the massacre of the infants, viewed in this connexion, offers no im probability.

‡ Instead of seeing the expression of the idea in the facts, we might, with the idealistic ghost-seers, invert the order of things, and say that "the idea wrought itself into history in the popular traditions" (whose origin, by-the-way, it would be hard to explain after what has been said) "of the Christians." In that case we must consider every thing remarkable, every scintillation of Divinity in the lives of individual men, as absolutely fabulous. This were, indeed, to degrade and *atheize* all history and all life; and such is the necessary tendency of that criticism which rejects all immediate Divine influence.

§ It was formerly thought that Matthew and Luke contradicted each other here. Luke states that Nazareth was the home of Joseph and Mary, and that, having gone to Bethlehem for a special purpose (the taxing), they remained long enough to perform the necessary

§ 22. *Brothers and Sisters of Jesus; the Mention of them in the Gospel Narrative, Proof of its historical Character.*

Various scattered statements in the Evangelists lead us to conclude that Christ had younger brothers and sisters.* The religious principles of Joseph and Mary offered no hindrance to this; it harmonizes well with the Christian view of the sanctity of wedlock; nor is there any thing at variance with it in the authentic traditions of the apostolic age.

But had the miraculous conception been *mythical*, the idea of later-born children would have been abhorrent to the spirit which originated such a myth. In later times, indeed, this idea *did* appear abhorrent to some minds; but it still remains a mystery why the mythical spirit did not exercise its power in remodelling the historical elements.

It is worthy of note that Mark and John agree in stating that these brothers of the Saviour remained unbelievers during his stay on earth, a fact which illustrates the truthfulness of the history, since it by no means tended to glorify either Christ or his brothers, one of whom, at least (James), was in high repute among the Jewish Christians. It is not to be wondered at that *the prophet was without honour* among those who dwelt under the same roof, and saw him grow up under the same laws of ordinary human nature with themselves. True, this daily con-

ceremonies after the birth of the child, and then returned home. According to Matthew, *Bethlehem* appears to have been their settled place of abode, and they were only induced, by special considerations, to betake themselves to Nazareth after their return from Egypt. The apparent contradiction vanishes when we consider that the memoirs were collected and written independently of each other.

Luke may have received the account of the journey of Christ's parents to Bethlehem, without learning either their intention to remain there with the child, or the cause that led them to change that intention; while the author of the Greek text of Matthew may have adhered to the separate statements that were given to him, in ignorance of the special cause of the journey to Bethlehem. Both accounts may be equally true, and harmonize well with each other, although those who put them imperfectly together may not perceive the argument. Moreover, even in Matthew (xiii., 54) we find Nazareth named as Christ's "own country." There is no improbability in supposing that Joseph and Mary were induced, by the remarkable events which marked the birth of the child at Bethlehem, and by the revelation of his destiny that was vouchsafed to them, to fix their residence at the seat of the tribe of David, in the vicinity of the Holy City; but that fear of Archelaus, who emulated his father's cruelty and contempt of holy things, led them to change this purpose. This much is certain, that Matthew's statement of the apprehension which grew out of Archelaus's accession to the government agrees precisely with the testimony of history in regard to that prince, who, in the tenth year of his reign, was accused before Augustus of various crimes, and exiled to Vienna.—Joseph., xvii., xiii., 2.

* The word ἕως, in Matt., i., 25, in connexion with the statement that Jesus was Mary's first-born, leads us to infer Matthew's knowledge of children subsequently born to her (conf. *De Wette* on the passage), which we the more certainly conclude, as the same Evangelist mentions brothers and sisters of Jesus especially, together with his mother.—See Matt., xiii., 55. This view is the most natural in such passages as name them together, *e. g.*, Luke, viii., 21; Mark, iii., 31; John, ii., 12; vii., 3. It would be forced work indeed to suppose that in all these passages ἀδελφοί is placed for ἀνεψιοί.

tact afforded them many opportunities of beholding the Divinity that streamed through the veil of his flesh, yet it required a spiritual mind and a lively faith to recognize the revealed Son of God in the lowly garb of humanity. The impression of humanity made upon their *senses* day after day, and thus grown into a habit, could not be made to yield to the Divine manifestations, unless in longer time than was required for others; but when it *did* yield, and, after such long-continued opposition, they acknowledged their brother as the Son of God and the Messiah, they only became thereby the more trustworthy witnesses.

§ 23. *Consciousness of Messiahship in the Mind of Jesus.—Jesus among the Doctors.*

The extraordinary circumstances of the birth of Christ not only served as portents of the greatest event in the world's history, but also, perhaps, furnished *external* occasions for the developement, in the mind of Jesus, of the consciousness of his Messiahship. True, this developement, far from admitting of mechanical illustrations, required, above all, an inward light in the depths of the higher self-consciousness, the internal testimony of the Spirit; but such a testimony by no means precludes the agency of external impressions, acting as *suggestive* occasions. The inward Divine light and the revelation from outward events touch upon each other; and this connexion between the internal and the external belongs to the essence of purely human developement.*

Of the early history of Jesus we have only a single incident; but that incident strikingly illustrates the manner in which the consciousness of his Divine nature developed itself in the mind of the child. Jesus had attained his twelfth year, a period which was regarded among the Jews as the dividing line between childhood and youth, and at which regular religious instruction and the study of the Law were generally entered upon. For that reason, his parents, who were accustomed† to visit Jerusalem together‡ annually at the time of the Passover, took him with them then for the first time. When the feast was over, and they were setting out on their return, they missed their son; this, however, does not seem to have alarmed them, and perhaps he was accustomed to remain with certain kindred families or friends; indeed, we are told (Luke, ii., 44) that they expected to find him "in

* *Weisse* maintains (I cannot see on what grounds) that this view degrades the Divine element in the inner calling of Christ to a mechanical result of circumstances, p. 264.

† Luke (ii., 42) says, "*that they went to Jerusalem every year at the feast of the Pass over.*" This may mean either that Joseph attended yearly *no other* feast but this, which would imply that it was not the general custom in Galilee to attend the *three* chief feasts at Jerusalem, or that Mary used to accompany him to this feast only. In either case, it proves the peculiar eminence of the Passover.

‡ Mary accompanied her husband, although the Jewish law did not demand it.

the company," at the evening halt of the caravan. Disappointed in this expectation, they returned the next morning to Jerusalem, and on the following day found him in the synagogue of the Temple among the priests, who had been led by his questions into a conversation on points of faith.* His parents reproached him for the uneasiness he had caused them, and he replied, "*Why did you seek me? Did you not know that I must be about my Father's business?*" Now these words of Jesus contain no explanation, beyond his tender years,† of the relations which he sustained to the Father; they manifest simply the consciousness of a child, a depth, to be sure, but yet only a depth of presentiment.

We can draw various important inferences from this incident in the early life of Christ. At a tender age he studied the Old Testament, and obtained a better knowledge of its religious value by the light that was within him than any human instruction could have imparted. Nor was this beaming forth of an immediate consciousness of Divine things in the mind of the child, in advance of the developement of his powers of discursive reason, at all alien to the character and progress of human nature, but entirely in harmony with it. Nor need we wonder that the infinite riches of the hidden spiritual life of the child first manifested themselves to his consciousness, as if suggested by his conversation with the doctors, and that his direct intuitions of Divine truth, the flashes of spiritual light that emanated from him, amazed the masters in Israel. It not unfrequently happens, in our human life, that the questions of others are thus *suggestive* to great minds, and, like steel upon the flint, draw forth their inner light, at the same time revealing to their own souls the unknown treasures that lay in their hidden depths. But they give more than they receive; the outward suggestion only excites to action their creative energy; and men of reflective and receptive, rather than creative minds, by inciting the latter to know and develop their vast resources, may not only learn much from their utterance, but also diffuse the streams which gush with overflowing fulness from these abundant well-springs. And these remarks applying —in a sense in which they apply to no other—to that mind, lofty beyond all human comparison, whose creative thoughts are to fertilize

* How little of the *mythical* there is in this may be seen from the case of Josephus, who states of himself, that when he was fourteen years old the priests of the city met with him to put questions to him about the law.

† The addition of extravagant and fabulous colourings to historical elements may be seen in such instances as the following from Irenæus, on the childhood of Jesus, taken out of an apocryphal Gospel originating in Palestine: "When the teacher told the boy to pronounce *Aleph,* he did so. But when he told him to say *Beth,* the child replied, 'Tell me the meaning of *Aleph,* and then I will tell you what *Beth* is'" (an allusion to the mystical import of the letters, according to the Kabbala). There was any number of such apocryphal Gospels, as Irenæus says.

the spiritual life of man through all ages, and whose creative power sprang from its mysterious union with that Divine Word, which gave birth to all things, show us that His consciousness developed itself gradually, and in perfect accordance with the laws of human life, from that mysterious union which formed its ground.

And further—without in the least attempting to do away with the peculiar form of the *child's* spiritual life—we can recognize in this incident a dawning sense of his Divine mission in the mind of Jesus: a sense, however, not yet unfolded in the form in which the corruption of the world, objectively presented, alone could occasion its developement. The child found congenial occupation in the things of God: in the Temple he was at home. And, on the other hand, we see an opening consciousness of the peculiar relation in which he stood to the Father as the Son of God. We delight to find in the early lives of eminent men some glimpses of the future, some indications of their after greatness; so we gladly recognize, in the pregnant words of the child, a foreshadowing of what is afterward so fully revealed to us in the discourses of the completely manifested Christ, especially as they are given to us in John's Gospel.

BOOK II.

THE MENTAL CULTURE OF JESUS. HIS LIFE TO THE TIME OF HIS PUBLIC MINISTRY.

BOOK II.

THE MENTAL CULTURE OF JESUS. HIS LIFE TO THE TIME OF HIS PUBLIC MINISTRY.

CHAPTER I.

JESUS NOT EDUCATED IN THE THEOLOGICAL SCHOOLS OF THE JEWS.

WE have already seen that in the early progress of the mind of Christ every thing was original and direct, and that external occasions were needed only to bring out his inward self-activity. As we must suppose that his developement was subsequently continued in the same way, we come at once to the conclusion that His education for a teacher was not due to any of the theological schools then existing in Judea. But we can reach this conclusion also by comparing the peculiar tendencies of those schools with the aims of Christ, with his mode of life and instruction, and with the spirit which he diffused around him.

§ 24. *The Pharisees.*

In the outset, how unlike Christ was the legal spirit of *Pharisaism*, with its soul-crushing statutes, its dead theology of the letter, and its barren subtilties! Some few of the sect, endowed with a more earnest religious sense, and a more sincere love of truth than their fellows, could not resist the impression of Christ's Divine manifestation; but they came to him with a full knowledge of the difference between his mode of teaching and theirs, and not as to a teacher sprung from among themselves. They had first to overcome their surprise at his strange and extraordinary language, before they could enter into closer connexion with him. They had to renounce the wisdom of their schools, to disclaim their legal righteousness, and to attach themselves to Christ with the same sense of deficiency in themselves, and the same desire for what he alone could impart, as all other men.

§ 25. *The Sadducees.*

The spirit of the *Sadducees* presents a still more rugged contrast to the spirit of Christ. Their schools agreed in nothing but *denying;* their only bond of union was opposition to the Pharisees, against whom they strove to re-establish the original Hebraism, freed from the foreign elements which the Pharisaic statutes had mixed up with it. But an agreement in negation can be only an apparent one, if the negation rests upon an opposite *positive* principle. Thus certain negative doctrines, that agree with Protestantism in rejecting the authority and traditions of the Romish Church, separate themselves further from Protestantism than the Romish doctrine itself, by the affirmative principle on which they rest their denial, and by carrying that denial too far. The single positive principle of Sadduceeism was the one-sided prominence given by them to morality, which they separated from its necessary inward union with religion. But Christ's combat with the Pharisees arose out of the fullest interpenetration of the moral and religious elements. The Sadducees wished to cut off the progressive developement of Hebraism at an arbitrary point. They refused to recognize the growing consciousness of God, which, derived from the Mosaic institute, formed a substantial feature of Judaism, and hence could not comprehend the higher religious element from which, as a germ, under successive Divine revelations, the spiritual life of Judaism was to be gradually developed.* Rejecting all such growth as foreign and false, they held a subordinate and isolated point to be absolute and perpetual; adhering to the letter rather than the spirit. To the forced allegorizing of the Pharisees in interpreting the Scripture, they opposed a slavishly literal and narrow exegesis. But Christ, on the other hand, while he rejected the Pharisaic traditions, received into his doctrine all the riches of Divine knowledge which the progressive growth of Theism, up to the time of John the Baptist, had brought forth. His agreement, then, with the Sadducees, consisting, as it did, solely in opposition to Pharisaism, was merely negative and apparent.

Some have detected an affinity between the moral teaching of Christ and the Anti-*Eudæmonism* of the Sadducees, the principle,

* See below for the way in which Christ illustrated this to the Sadducees. As to the *Canon*, it cannot be actually proved that the Sadducees held it differently from other Jews. It is true, Josephus says (Archæol., xiii., x., 6) that they rejected every thing but the Mosaic law—*ἅπερ οὐκ ἀναγέγραπται ἐν τοῖς Μωϋσέως νόμοις*. But the Mosaic law is not here opposed to the rest of the Canon, but to oral traditions; and the only question was whether the Mosaic law *alone*, or in connexion with oral tradition, was to be held as authority for religious usages. The remaining books of the Old Testament were not in dispute, as no religious usages at all were derived from them. Still, it is not unlikely that the Sadducees went so far, in their opposition to Pharisaism, as to reject all doctrines that could not be shown to have a Mosaic origin, and to consider the Pentateuch as the sole, or, at least, the chief, source of religious truth. As we find such views of the Canon among the Jewish-Christian sects (Cf. the *Clementines*), we may infer that they previously existed among the Jews. They would hardly have denied Immortality and the Resurrection, if they had held the Prophets to be law in the same sense as the Pentateuch; although it is possible that they interpreted such passages of the Prophets in another way. The general terms in which Josephus speaks of the recognition of the Canon among the Jews (i., c. Apion, § 8) do not suffice to prove that there were no differences in this respect in the different sects.

namely, that man must do good for its own sake, without the hope of future recompense.* But here, again, Christianity agrees with Sadduceeism only in what it denies, not in what it affirms. The divine life of Christianity has no more affinity for that selfish Eudæmonism which seeks the good as means to an end, than for the spirit of Sadduceeism which denies the higher aims of moral action, and makes it altogether "of the earth, earthly." These opposite errors sprang from one common source, namely, the debasement of the spiritual life into worldliness, and therefore Christianity is alike antagonistic to them both, whether seen in the worldly admission of a future life by the Pharisees, or in its worldly rejection by the Sadducees. Yet in the doctrine of the former, it must be admitted, lay a germ of truth which only needed to be freed from selfish and sensual tendencies to show itself in its full spiritual import.†

§ 26. *The Essenes.*

The secrecy which the sect of the *Essenes* affected has given rise to many subtle and arbitrary hypotheses. Some have found in its ardent religious spirit ground for believing in a connexion between it and Christianity.‡ This argument, by proving too much, proves nothing; on the same principle we might show a connexion between Christianity and every form under which mysticism has appeared and reappeared in the history of religion. But there were other points of similarity between Essenism and Christianity, besides this mystic element which has its source in man's native religious tendencies. Essenism grew out of Judaism, and was pervaded by a moral belief in GOD, a spirit which was nourished and strengthened by habits of seclusion from the stir of life, of religious communion, and of quiet prayer and meditation. Other resemblances may be discovered between Essenism and the doctrine of Christ, or the forms of the first Christian communities; but they may be traced, like those just mentioned, to sources common to both, and therefore afford no proof of a real connexion between

* No reliance is to be placed in the Talmudic tradition in *Pirke Aboth*, i., 3, according to which the principle thus perverted to the denial of a future life came from Antigonus Ish Socho, or Simeon the Just. The prevalent orthodoxy was always inclined to ascribe error to the perversion of some orthodox doctrine.

† Dr. *von Cölln* arrives at the conclusion that "the moral philosophy of the Sadducees was better than that of the Pharisees, because the New Testament does not attack their moral principles, but only their denial of the Resurrection."—(Bibl. Theol., i., 450.) We do not admit the inference. This silence of the New Testament can be readily accounted for on the ground that Sadduceeism had few points in common with Christianity; and while it was necessary to guard men frequently against *Pharisaic* abuses of great truths (*e. g.*, of the truth that morality and religion are inseparable), the open contrast of Sadduceeism made such special controversy with its teachers unnecessary.

‡ First alluded to in an unpublished treatise of *J. G. Wachter, De Primordiis Christianæ Religionis, libri duo.* See, especially, Reinhard's Versuch über den Plan Jesu [Reinhard's *Plan of the Founder of Christianity*, translated by A. Kaufman, Andover].

them. A closer examination will demonstrate that the similarities were only apparent, while the differences were essential.

For instance, the Essenes prohibited *oaths*, and so did Christ. Here is a resemblance. But the former, confounding the spirit with the letter, made the prohibition—which grew out of their rule of absolute veracity and mutual confidence in each other—a positive law, unconditionally binding, not only within their own community, but in the general intercourse of life. Christ prohibited oaths, on the other hand, not by an enactment binding only from without, but by a law developing itself outwardly from the new spiritual life which he himself implanted in his followers. Paul knew that an asseveration, made for right ends, and in the spirit of Christ's command, was no violation of that command.

Again, the law of the Essenes prohibited *slavery*, and so was Christ's intended to subvert it. The sect agreed with the Saviour in seeing that all men alike bear the image of God, and that none can have the right, by holding their fellows as property, to degrade that image into a brute or a chattel. So far Essenism and Christianity agree; but see wherein they differ. The one was a formula for a small circle of devotees; the other was a system for the regeneration of mankind: the one made positive enactments, acting by pressure from without; the other implanted new moral principles, to work from within: the one put its law in force at once, and declared that no slave could be held in its communion; the other gave no direct command upon the subject. Yet the whole spirit of Christ's teaching tended to create in men's minds a *moral sense* of the evil of a relation so utterly subversive of all that is good in humanity, and thus to effect its entire abolition.

Let us take another apparent resemblance. The Essenes devoted themselves much to *healing the sick*, and so did Christ (and the gift of healing was imparted to the first congregations); but the agencies which they employed were essentially different. They made use of natural remedies, drawn from the vegetable and mineral kingdoms, and handed down the knowledge thereof in their books;* but the Saviour and his apostles wrought their cures by no intermediate agents, but by the direct operation of power from on high.† Even when Christ did make use of physical means, the results were always out of proportion to them.

Finally, let us compare the scope of Essenism, as a whole, with the aims of Christ's mission. Essenism, probably originating in a commingling of Judaism with the old Oriental‡ theosophy, manifested a

* Joseph., B. J., ii., viii., 6: ἔνθεν (*i. e.*, from old writings) αὐτοῖς πρὸς θεραπείαν παθῶν, ῥίζαι τε ἀλεξιτήριοι καὶ λίθων ἰδιότητες ἀνερευνῶνται.

† Cf. what is said further on, under the head of "The Miracles of Christ"

‡ Some modern writers prefer to derive Essenism from Alexandrian Platonism transplanted into Palestine, but I can find no proof that their view explains the general character

spirit at once monkish and schismatic.* How strong a contrast does such a system present to the active spirit of the Gospel, aiming only to implant holy feelings, and so to secure holy lives, seeking every where for needy souls, and, wherever the need appears, pouring forth its exhaustless treasures without stint! Such a spirit broke away at once the wall of separation between man and man, which the aristocratic and exclusive spiritual life of Essenism was ever striving to build up.

§ 27. *Supposed Influence of the Alexandrian-Jewish Doctrines.*

A few words in regard to the supposed influence of the doctrines of the Alexandrian Jews upon Christ's culture. Even admitting that these doctrines penetrated into Palestine, it can by no means be presupposed that they entered into Galilee, and especially into the narrow circle of the common people within which he was educated. The grounds on which some profess to find traces of such an influence in the discourses of Christ would serve as well to prove that Christianity derived its origin from Brama or Buddhu.†

§ 28. *Affinity of Christianity, as absolute Truth, for the various opposing Religious Systems.*

On the dissolution of Judaism, its elements, originally joined together in a living unity, necessarily produced various religious tendencies, which mutually opposed and excluded each other. In all these we can find something akin to the new creation of Christianity. And wherever Christianity appears for the first time, or reveals itself anew in its own glory, it must offer some points of affinity for the different opposing systems. The living, perfect truth has points of tangency for the one-sided forms of error; though we may not be thereby enabled to put together the perfect whole from the scattered and repellent fragments.

§ 29. *Christ's Teaching revealed from within, not received from without.*

Had the source of Christ's mighty power been merely a *doctrine*, it might have been received, or at least suggested, from abroad. But his

or the individual features of Essenism as well as that in the text. Moreover, I remain of the opinion that the doctrines of the *Therapeutæ* and the *Essenes* were allied, but independent religious tendencies.

* I can give no other translation than the following to the passage in Josephus (Archæol., xviii., 1, 5) which speaks of the Essenes. It will be seen that I take the word *εἰργόμενοι*, not in the *passive*, but in the *middle* sense. "They send, it is true, their offerings to the temple, but they bring no sacrifices, because they so greatly prefer their own way of purifying and sanctifying themselves; and, for fear of defilement by taking part with the rest of the people, they keep away from the common sanctuary, and make their sacrifices apart, surrounded only by the initiated."

† Cf. my Kirchengeschichte, 2d edit., Part I., for the relation between the Alexandrian theology and Christianity

power lay in the impression which his manifestation and life as the Incarnate God produced; and *this* could never have been derived from without.* The peculiar import of his doctrine, as such, consists in its relation to himself as a part of his self-revelation, an image of his unoriginated and inherent life; and this alone suffices to defy all attempts at external explanation.

§ 30. *The popular Sentiment in regard to Christ's Connexion with the Schools.*

Had Jesus been trained in the Jewish seminaries,† his opponents would, doubtless, have reproached him with the arrogance of setting up for master where he himself had been a pupil. But, on the contrary, we find that they censured him for attempting to explain the Scriptures without having enjoyed the advantages of the schools (John, vii., 15). His first appearance as a teacher in the synagogue at Nazareth caused even greater surprise, as he was known there, not as one learned in the Law, but rather as a carpenter's son, who had, perhaps, himself worked at his father's trade.‡ The general impression of his discourses every where was, that they contained totally different materials from those furnished by the theological schools (Matt., vii., 29).

* We recall here the profound sentiment of a prophetic German mind: "The pearl of Christianity is a life hidden in God, a truth in Christ the Mediator, a power which consists neither in words and forms, nor in dogmas and outward acts; it cannot, therefore, be valued by the common standards of logic or ethics."—*Hamann*, iv., 285.

† Dr. Paulus supposes that Christ, because he was called *Rabbi*, not only by his disciples, but by the distinguished Rabbi Nicodemus, and even by his enemies (John, vi., 25), obtained that title in the way usual among the Jews; and he intimates that Christ studied with the rabbis of the Essenes, and perhaps obtained the degree from them (Life of Christ, i., 1, 122). But when we remember that he stood at the head of a party which recognized his prophetic character, we can see why others, who did not recognize it, would yet call him *their* master, *e. g.*, Matt., xvii., 24; ὁ διδάσκαλος ὑμῶν. Nicodemus, however, did really acknowledge him as a Divine teacher; nor were those who addressed him as *Rabbi*, in John, vi., 25, by any means his enemies. This style of address, therefore, does not imply his possession of a title from a Jewish tribunal, but rather arose in the circle of followers that he gathered around him. As to the Essenes, it cannot be proved that they created *rabbis*, as did the Jewish synagogues; and if they did, such titles would hardly be recognized by the prevailing party, the Pharisees.

‡ It cannot be decided certainly that this was the case. There was a tradition in primitive Christian times to that effect; so Justin Martyr (*Dialog.*, c. *Tryph.*, 316) says: ταῦτα τὰ τεκτονικὰ ἔργα εἰργάζετο ἐν ἀνθρώποις ὤν, καὶ ζυγὰ, διὰ τούτων καὶ τὰ τῆς δικαιοσύνης σύμβολα διδάσκων καὶ ἐνέργη βίον. It may be that this, and the tradition, also, that Christ was destitute of personal beauty, were rather ideal than historical conceptions, framed to conform with his humble condition "in the form of a servant." Christ was not to come forth from a high position, but from a lowly workshop; as, according to the reproach of *Celsus*, his first followers were mechanics. But the report may have been true, and was, if the ordinary reading of Mark, vi., 3, be correct. Against this has been adduced the following passage in *Orig.*, *cont. Cels.*, vi., 36, viz.: ὅτι οὐδαμοῦ τῶν ἐν ταῖς ἐκκλησίαις φερομένων εὐαγγελίων τέκτων αὐτὸς ὁ Ἰησοῦς ἀναγέγραπται. The reading in Mark, vi., 3, may have been altered before the time of Origen, from a false pride that took offence at Christ's working as a common mechanic and a foolish desire to conciliate the pagans, who reproached Christians with this feature

CHAPTER II.

COURSE OF CHRIST'S LIFE UP TO THE OPENING OF HIS PUBLIC MINISTRY.

§ 31. *Growing Consciousness of His Messiahship in Christ.*

ALTHOUGH so many years of our Saviour's life are veiled in obscurity, we cannot believe that the full consciousness of a Divine call which he displayed in his later years was of sudden growth. If a great man accomplishes, within a very brief period, labours of paramount importance to the world, and which he himself regards as the task of his life, we must presume that the strength and energies of his previous years were concentrated into that limited period, and that the former only constituted a time of preparation for the latter.

Most of all must this be true of the labours of CHRIST, the greatest and most important that the world has known. We have the right to presume that HE who assumed as his task the salvation of the human race made his whole previous existence to bear upon this mighty labour. The idea of the Messiah, as Redeemer and King, streamed forth in Divine light, from the course of the theocracy and the scattered intimations of the Old Testament, in full extent and clearness, and in Divine light he recognized this Messiahship as his own; and this consciousness of GOD within him harmonized with the extraordinary phenomena that occurred at his birth.

But the *negative* side of the Messiahship, namely, its relation to *sin*. he could not learn from self-contemplation. He could not learn de-

in the life of their founder. *Fritzsche* founds an ineffectual argument on the following internal ground, viz.: "Christ's working at a trade would not have interfered with his appearing as a public teacher. The Jews had no contempt for artisans, and even the scribes sometimes supported themselves by mechanical toils." True, the *scribes* might occasionally work at trades without reproach, but to be *merely* a mechanic (and no scribe) was quite a different thing; so that the ensuing objection, "*How comes this carpenter to set up as our teacher?*" was quite in character, even among Jews. It does not follow because, afterward, only designations of *family* are given in the passage, that therefore the first designation was fixed upon him only as "the *son* of the carpenter;" for, certainly, the two ideas, "he himself is only a carpenter," and "his relations live among us as ordinary people," hang well together. They could utter, first, the most cutting contrast, "he is a *carpenter*, like the others, and he now will be a prophet," and then mention only his relations who were yet *living*, but not Joseph, who was already *dead*.

It is perfectly in accordance with the genius of Christianity (although not *necessarily* flowing from it), that the *Highest* should thus spring from an humble walk of life, and that the Divine glory should manifest itself at first to men in so lowly a form. The Redeemer thus ennobled human labour and the forms of common life; there was thenceforth to be no βάναυσον in the relations of human society. Thus began the influence of Christianity upon the civil and social relations of men—an influence which has gone on increasing from that day to this.

pravity by experience; yet, without this knowledge, although the idea of the Messiah as theocratic king might have been fully developed in his mind, an essential element of his relations to humanity would have remained foreign to him. But although his personal experience could not unfold this peculiar modification of the Messianic consciousness, many of its essential features were continually suggested by his intercourse with the outer world. There, in all the relations of life, he saw human depravity and its attendant wretchedness. The sight, and the sympathizing love which it awoke, made a profound impression upon his soul, and formed, at least, a basis for the consciousness of his own relation to it as Messiah.

We may assume, then, that when he reached his thirtieth year,* fully assured of his call to the Messiahship, he waited only for a sign from GOD to emerge from his obscurity and enter upon his work. This sign was to be given him by means of the last of GOD's witnesses under the old dispensation, whose calling it was to prepare the way for the new developement of the kingdom of GOD—by *John the Baptist,* the last representative of the prophetic spirit of the Old Testament, whose relation to CHRIST and his office we shall now more particularly examine.†

* The age at which the Levites entered on their office.—Numb., iv.

† A promising young theologian of Lübeck, *L. von Rohden,* has lately put forth an excellent treatise on this subject, well adapted for general circulation, entitled 'Johannes der Täufer, in seinem Leben und Wirken dargestellt."

BOOK III.

PREPARATIVES TO THE PUBLIC MINISTRY OF CHRIST

PART I. OBJECTIVE PREPARATION.—JOHN THE BAPTIST.

PART II. SUBJECTIVE PREPARATION.—THE TEMPTATION.

BOOK III.

PREPARATIVES TO THE PUBLIC MINISTRY OF CHRIST.

PART I.

OBJECTIVE PREPARATION. THE MINISTRY OF JOHN THE BAPTIST.

CHAPTER I.

THE CALLING OF THE BAPTIST, AND HIS RELATIONS TO THE JEWS.

§ 32. *How far the Baptist revived the Expectation of a Messiah.*

A PROCLAMATION of the approaching kingdom of God, involving the restoration of the sunken glory of the Theocracy, and the dawning of a brighter day upon God's oppressed ones, was essentially necessary as a preparation for Christ's public ministry.

But this was not all; it was equally necessary to announce Him who was called to the accomplishment of this great work. The expectation of the kingdom and the king should always have gone together; but we find that they did not actually do so. The prophecies of the general renewal were often distinct from those which foretold the agent chosen by God to accomplish it; and the hope of the former often existed in minds which had lost sight of the latter. A *Philo* proves this. The Greek and Alexandrian culture, and perhaps the combination of the two in the religious Realism of Palestine, may have tended to bring about this result. Be that as it may, it is essential for our purpose to keep the two ideas—the announcement of the kingdom and the proclamation of the Messiah—separate from each other.

Some suppose that John the Baptist was the first* to suggest the idea of a Messiah to the Jewish mind of that day. But certainly this idea, so thoroughly interwoven with the theocratic consciousness, could not have fallen into oblivion; nay, the sufferings of the people, their shame at being slaves to those whom they believed themselves destined to rule, and their desire for deliverance from this degrading bondage, must have constantly tended to bring it more and more vividly before them. It would be going too far, then, to say that this idea had been lost out of

* So *Schleiermacher* (Christliche Sittenlehre, p. 19) states that John's work was "to revive the forgotten idea of the Messiah."

the mind of that age, and that its revival was due to the efforts of a single individual. Much rather should we conceive that the spirit of the individual was stirred by an impulse from the spirit of the age. But while the general tendency of the popular mind prepared the way for John, his labours reacted mightily upon the spirit of the age, and formed, indeed, a new epoch in the hopes of men for the appearance of the Kingdom and of the Messiah. Christ himself makes this epoch the transition-period between the old and the new dispensations.*

It was essential, also, to this preparation for the Messiah, that the minds of the people should obtain a clear conception of the object to which their hopes were directed, and the means by which it was to be obtained, involving a more correct notion of the work and kingdom of Messiah, and of the moral requisites for participation therein. All this belonged to the calling of the Old-Testament order of prophets, of which John constituted the apex. We must look for the *peculiar* features of his position in the fact that he himself not only formed the point of transition to the new era, but was allowed to recognize and point out the Messiah, and to give the signal for the beginning of his public ministry.

§ 33. *Causes of Obscurity in the Accounts left us of the Baptist.—Sources: The Evangelists. Josephus.*

The difficulties and obscurities that remain in the accounts of this remarkable man seem to have arisen necessarily from the peculiar stand-point which he occupied. In a prophet or a forerunner, we must always distinguish between what he utters with clear self-consciousness, and what lies beyond the utterance, concealed even from himself, until a later period; between the fundamental idea, and the form, perhaps not wholly fitting, in which it veils itself. Opposite elements always meet each other in an epoch which constitutes the transition-point from one stage of developement to another; and we cannot look for a logical and connected mode of thinking in the representative of such an epoch. In some of his utterances we may find traces of the old period; in others, longings for the new; and in bringing them together, we may find different views which cannot always be made perfectly to harmonize.

The nature of the authorities to which we are confined makes it peculiarly difficult to come at the objective truth in regard to John the Baptist. On the one side we have the accounts of the *Evangelists*, given from the Christian stand-point, and for religious ends; and on the other that of *Josephus*,† which is purely historical in its character and aims.

* Matt., xi., 12. We shall have occasion to say more on this passage hereafter.
† [illegible] 1.

As to the first, it is very probable that John could be better understood in the light of Christianity than he understood himself and his mission. The aims of a preparatory and transition-period are always better comprehended after their accomplishment than before; so, truths which were veiled from John's apprehension stood clearly forth before the minds of the Evangelists. But this very fact may have caused the obscurity which we find in their accounts of the Baptist. We are very apt, in describing a lower point of view from a higher, to attribute to the former what belongs only to the latter. Any one who has passed through a subordinate and preparatory stage of thought to a higher one, will find it hard to keep the distinction between the two clearly before his consciousness: they blend themselves together in spite of him. So, perhaps, it may have happened that the distinctive differences between the stand-point of John and that of Christianity were lost sight of when the evangelical accounts were prepared, and that the Baptist was represented as nearer to Christianity than he really was. The likelihood of this result would be all the greater if the Christian writer had been himself a disciple of John; such a one, even though endowed with the sincerest love of truth, would naturally see more in the words of his old master than the latter himself, under his peculiar circumstances, could possibly have intended. After a prophecy has reached its fulfilment, it would be difficult, if not impossible, to reproduce the precise consciousness under which the prediction was uttered.

If, therefore, we find, on close inquiry, that the historical statements are somewhat obscured by subjective influences, our estimate of their veracity need be in no wise affected thereby. Such a result would not conflict in the least with the only tenable idea of Inspiration. The organs which the Holy Ghost illuminated and inspired to convey his truth to men retained their individual peculiarities, and remained within the sphere of the psychological laws of our being. Besides, Inspiration, both in its nature and its object, refers only to man's religious interests and to points connected with it. But *practical religion* requires only a knowledge of the truth itself; it needs not to understand the gradual genetic developement of the truth in the intellect, or to distinguish the various stages of its advance to distinct and perfect consciousness. On the other hand, these latter are precisely the aims towards which *scientific history* directs itself. It follows, therefore, that the interest of practical religion and that of scientific history may not always run in the same channel; and the latter must give place to the former, especially in points so vital as the direct impression which Christ made upon mankind. Frequent illustrations of this distinction are afforded by the interpretations of passages from the Old Testament given by the apostles.

In all our inquiries into the evangelical histories, we must keep in view the fact that they were written not to satisfy scientific, but religious wants; not to afford materials for systematic history, but to set forth the ground of human salvation in Christ and his kingdom. There was, indeed, *one* who could distinguish the different stages in the developement of revelation at a single piercing glance; but this one was HE in whom GOD and man were united. He himself told his Apostles that he had this power, and his words in regard to the stand-point of John the Baptist illustrate it. These words alone must form our guiding light.

It might be inferred, if what we have said be true, that the account of *Josephus*, which proceeds from a purely historical interest, should be preferred to that of the Evangelists. But it must not be forgotten that historical events can only be correctly understood when viewed from the stand-point of the province to which they belong; and so events that fall within the sphere of religion are only intelligible from a religious stand-point. And as John's import to the history of the world consists in the fact that he formed the dividing line between the two stages of developement in the kingdom of God, it cannot be fully understood except by an intuitive religious sense, capable of appreciating religious phenomena. Of such a religious sense Josephus was destitute. Now the religious sense can get along without the scientific; but the latter cannot do without the former, where the understanding of religious events is concerned; and hence the living peculiarities of John the Baptist vanished under the hands of Josephus, although he was able to apprehend John's character and appearance in their general features. To his religious deficiency must be added his habit of adapting himself to the taste and culture of the Greeks, a habit which could not but wear away his Jewish modes of thought and feeling. He saw in John only a man of moral ardour, who taught the truth to the Jews, rebuked their corruptions, and offered them, instead of their lustrations and outward righteousness, a symbol of inward spiritual purification in his water-baptism. With such a narrow view as this we could neither understand John's use of baptism, nor explain his public labours among such a people as the Jews. It is but a beggarly abstraction from the living individual elements which the Gospel accounts afford.

§ 34. *The Baptist's Mode of Life and Teaching in the Desert.*

We learn from Josephus* that many pious and earnest men among the Jews, disgusted with the corruptions of the times, retired, like the monks and hermits of Christianity at a later day, into wilderness spots,

* An example is afforded in the case of *Banus*, of whom Josephus, who was his disciple, gives an account in his autobiography, § 2: "ἐσθῆτι μὲν ἀπὸ δένδρων χρώμενον, τροφὴν δὲ την αὐτομάτως φυομένην προσφερόμενον, ψυχρῷ δὲ ὕδατι τὴν ἡμέραν καὶ τὴν νύκτα πολλάκις λουόμενον πρὸς ἁγνείαν."

and there, becoming teachers of Divine wisdom, collected disciples around them. Such a one was John. Consecrated from his birth, by a sign from heaven, to his Divine calling, he led a rigid and ascetic life from his very childhood. Had we nothing but Josephus's* account to guide us, we might suppose that John only differed from the other teachers of the desert in the fact that the spirit of his teaching was more practical, and tended to carry him out into a wider field of action. While *they* only revealed the truths of a higher life to such as sought them in their solitude, *he* felt constrained to go forth and raise his reproving voice aloud among the multitude, to condemn the Jews for their vices and their hypocrisy, and to call them, abandoning their false security and their debasing trust in outward works, to seek the genuine piety which comes from the heart. This part of John's ministry, viz., his work as a reformer, Josephus has brought out prominently; while he has entirely failed to notice the indelible stamp of the Baptist's labours left upon the history of the Theocracy.

John had retired to the desert region west of the Dead Sea, and there lived a life of abstinence and austerity, harmonizing well with his inward grief for the corruptions of his people. Like his type, Elias, he wore coarse garments, and satisfied his wants with a nourishment which nature offered in a species of locusts, sometimes used as food, and wild honey.†

§ 35. *John as Baptist and Preacher of Repentance.*

While John was thus sighing in solitude over the sins of a degenerate people, and praying that God would soon send the promised Deliverer, the assurance was vouchsafed to him from above that the Messiah should soon be revealed to him. He felt himself called to declare this assurance to the people, and to exhort them to prepare their souls for the approaching epoch. He abandoned the solitude of the desert for the banks of the Jordan,‡ gathered the people in hosts about him, and announced to them the coming appearance of both the Messiah and his kingdom, which ideas he never separated. He proclaimed to them that God would sift his people, and that the unworthy should be condemned and excluded from the Theocracy. He denounced as false and treacherous the prevailing idea that theocratic descent and the observance of outward ceremonies were the only

* Archæol., xviii., v. 2.

† In the Ebionitish recension of Matthew, we find the food of John described as μέλι ἄγριον, οὗ ἡ γεῦσις ἦν τοῦ μάννα, ὡς ἐγκρὶς ἐν ἐλαίῳ ("it had the taste of manna, as a cake baked in oil."—*Num.*, xi., 8). The simple statement of Matthew is here misrepresented, and even falsified. The ἀκρίδες (locusts) seemed to this writer food unworthy for John, and he makes ἐγκρίδες (cakes) out of them, and thus gets a chance of comparing John's food with manna.

‡ We follow the statement of Luke (iii., 2), which has the advantage in distinguishing from each other the periods in John's manifestation.

requisites for admittance into Messiah's kingdom, and exhorted all to true repentance as the one essential preparation. He made use of baptism as a symbol of preparatory consecration to the Messiah's kingdom, a course to which he might have been led by the lustrations common among the Jews, and by the intimations of prophecy, such as Mal., iii.; Zach., xiii.; Ezek., xxxvi., 25, even if the baptism of proselytes was not then extant among the Jews. Doubtless the Baptist stood in a special relation to those that flocked about him as followers; although, as preacher of repentance, as *the voice of one crying in the wilderness* (Isai., xl., 3), whose duty it was to prepare the way for the Messiah amid a people estranged from God, he held a general and common relation to all.

§ 36. *Relations of the Pharisees and Sadducees to the Baptist.*

We are naturally led here to inquire into the relations which John sustained to the different classes of the Jewish people. Was he, as preacher of repentance, only a man of the people, and did the Pharisees, the hierarchical party, manifest their jealous opposition from the very first, or did it arise by degrees at a later period? Of one thing we may be sure, from Matt., iii., 7, viz., that many Pharisees were to be found among the number that crowded about John and submitted to his baptism. Yet Christ, in one of his last discourses at Jerusalem (Matt., xxi., 32), drew a striking contrast between the publicans who believed in John's prophetic calling, and were led by him to repentance, and the Pharisees, who persevered in their self-sufficiency and unbelief. The words of Matt., xi., 16, seem also to indicate that the *general* spirit of the people was as hostile to John as it subsequently showed itself to Christ, and that only a few, open to the lessons of heavenly wisdom, admitted the Divine mission of the Baptist. So, also, in Luke, vii., 29, 30, the course of the people and the publicans, in following John and submitting to his baptism, is contrasted with the very opposite conduct of the Pharisees and lawyers, who "rejected the counsel of God against themselves."

Still, Matthew (iii., 7) states expressly, that "*many Pharisees and Sadducees came to John's baptism,*" and the form of the statement distinguishes these from the ordinary throng. It seems somewhat unhistorical that these sects, so opposite to each other, should be named together here, as well as in some other places in the Gospels; but an explanation is perhaps to be found in the fact that it was customary to name them together on the ground of their common hatred to Christianity. It appears improbable that men of the peculiar religious opinions of the Sadducees should have been attracted by the preacher of repentance, the forerunner of the Messiah; nor does John, in his severe sermon, make any special reference to that sect, an omission which could hardly have occurred had any of the sect so far departed from their ordinary habits as to listen to his preaching.* It does not follow, however, that the mention of the Pharisees is in the same predicament; on the contrary, the historical citation of the latter may have given rise to the unhistorical mention of the Sadducees. Nor does the fact that the Pharisees, at a later period, maintained an attitude of hostility towards John prove that they had opposed him from the beginning. His rigid asceticism and zeal for the Messiah were in entire harmony with the spirit of their sect; and they could listen with approval to his energetic reproofs and calls to repentance, so long as they were aimed only at the people and the publicans. So, in the Christian Church, ardent reformers and witnesses to the truth have been favoured even by the heads of the hierarchy, so long as they attacked only the common faults and vices of men. But the first assault upon the hierarchy itself roused all its hatred and its vengeance.

In the earlier period of John's preaching, then, there may have been nothing to excite the jealousy of the Pharisees. Moreover, it is not likely that all who bore the name of Pharisees were fully imbued with the spirit of the sect. Although the majority of them, intent only upon selfish and party aims, may have regarded John's ministry with an eye of suspicion, there were probably among them some earnest, upright men, upon whom his preaching could not fail to make an impression. These two thoughts may serve to reconcile Matt., iii., 7, with the other passages quoted, in which the hostility of the Pharisees is mentioned. Again, the expression of Christ in John, v., 35, seems to imply that the Pharisees received and approved John's prophecy of the coming Messiah, but did not allow his words to sink deep into their hearts or to operate upon their thoughts and inclinations. The severe sermon† reported by the Evangelists was certainly not adapted to such as came to John, penitent and broken-hearted, to obtain consolation and guidance; but rather to the haughty and arrogant Pharisee, who felt sure of his share in the Messiah's kingdom, appear when it might, without either repentance or forgiveness. It was these that he stigmatized as a "brood of vipers," and no sons of Abraham. It was these to whom he said, in tones of warning and reproof, "Who has told you that by simple baptism you shall escape God's coming judgment? Would you really escape it? Then repent, and do works meet for repentance. Trust not to your saying '*Abraham is our father;*' for I tell you that

* We cannot support the expression of Matthew by the statement of Josephus (xviii., I., 4), that the Sadducees were accustomed to accommodate their own convictions to the principles of the Pharisees, on account of the strong hold which the latter had upon the people. In this case, at least, no such accommodation was required, from the repute in which John was held among the Pharisees.

† Luke, iii., 7; Matt., iii., 7. Luke reports it as addressed to the people; Matthew to the Pharisees and Sadducees.

the developement of the kingdom is not confined to the race of Abraham; nay, from these very stones that lie upon the river bank, God can raise up his children."

In these last words he meant to tell them that if the Jews disgraced their Theocratic descent, God would remove his kingdom from them and impart it unto strangers. He ends by proclaiming that the Messiah would sift his people thoroughly, and exclude all that should be found unworthy. Such preaching must have been enough to imbitter and alienate the Pharisees, even if they had been before disposed to approve and favour the preacher.

§ 37. *Relations of John to the People, and to the narrower circle of his own Disciples.*

True penitents who came to the Baptist inquiring the way of life found in the severe ascetic a kind and condescending teacher. He gave them no vague and high-sounding words, but adapted his instructions with minute care to their special condition and circumstances. John resembled the austere preachers of repentance who sprung up in the Middle Ages in more than one respect; but especially in the two fold relation which he sustained, to the people generally, and to his disciples in particular. While the latter imitated his own ascetic piety in order to fit themselves for preachers of repentance, he did not demand of the former to abandon their ordinary line of life, even when it was one obnoxious to the prejudices of the Jews; the soldier was not required to leave the ranks, nor the tax-gatherer his office, but only to fulfil their respective duties with honesty and fidelity. All alike were commanded to do good; but only those whose occupations were sinful had to abandon them, and at his command many did so.*

§ 38. *John's Demands upon the People compared with those of Christ.—His humble Opinion of his own Calling.*

But how very moderate do John's requirements appear in comparison with those of Christ, who demanded at the very outset an absolute sacrifice of the will and the affections! This difference arose naturally, however, from the different positions which they occupied. John was fully conscious that the moral regeneration which was indispensable to admittance into the Messiah's kingdom could only be accomplished by a Divine principle of life; and, knowing that to impart this was beyond his power, he confined himself to a *preparatory* purification of the morals of the people. The great, the God-like feature of his character was his thorough understanding of himself and his calling. Filled as he was with enthusiasm, he yet felt that he was but the humble instrument of the Divine Spirit, called, not to *found* the new crea-

Matt., xxi., 32.

tion, but only to *proclaim* it; nor did the thronging of eager thousands to hang upon his lips, nor the enthusiastic love of his own immediate followers, ever ready to glorify their master, in the least degree blind his perceptions of duty, or raise him above his calling. Convinced that he was inspired of God to prepare, and not to create, he never pretended to work miracles, nor did his disciples, strongly as he impressed them, ever attribute miraculous powers to him.

CHAPTER II.

RELATION OF THE BAPTIST TO MESSIAH.

§ 39. *John's Explanation of his Relation to the Messiah. The Baptism by Water and by Fire.*

CAREFULLY, however, as John avoided exciting false expectations, they could hardly fail to arise at a period so full of foreboding and hope for the coming of Messiah, after time enough had elapsed for him to make a powerful impression upon the public mind as a preacher of repentance and proclaimer of a better future.* Many of those whom his preaching had so deeply moved became uneasy to ascertain his true relation to the Messiah; and as his language on the subject was always concise, and rather suggestive than explanatory, they were inclined to think that his real character was only kept in the back ground for the time, and would afterward be gradually unfolded. But when the Baptist saw that *men mused in their hearts whether he were the Christ or no*,† he resolved to define his relation to the Messiah explicitly and unmistakeably. *His* mission, he told them, was to baptize by water, as a symbol of the preparatory repentance which had to open the way for that renewal and purification of the nation by Divine power which was to be expected in the Messiah; the lofty one that was to follow, raised so far above himself, that he should be dignified by performing for him the most menial services. He it was that should *baptize them with the Holy Ghost and with fire;* that is to say, that as his (John's) followers were entirely immersed in the water, so the Messiah would immerse the souls of believers in the Holy Ghost, imparted by himself; so that it should thoroughly penetrate their being, and form within them a new principle of life. And this Spirit-baptism was to be accompanied by a *baptism of fire*.‡ Those who re-

* Paul's words (Acts, xiii., 25) lead us to infer that this took place first towards the end of John's career.

† Luke, iii., 15.

‡ Some think the "fire" is used as a symbol of the Holy Ghost, inasmuch as it is employed in other places in Scripture to denote Divine influences. In this view of the pas-

fused to be penetrated by the Spirit of the Divine life should be destroyed by the fire of the Divine judgments. The "sifting" by fire ever goes along with the advance of the Spirit, and consumes all who will not appropriate the latter. So John represents the Messiah as appearing with his "fan" in his hands, to purify the "threshing-floor" of his kingdom, to gather the worthy into the glorified congregation of God, and to cast out the unworthy and deliver them over to the Divine judgments.

§ 40. *John's Conception of Messiah's Kingdom.*

Let us inquire now upon what view of the calling and work of the Messiah, and of the nature of his kingdom, these expressions of the Baptist were founded. He contradicts the notion, so prevalent among the Jews, that all the descendants of Abraham who outwardly observed the religion of their fathers would be taken into the Messiah's kingdom, while his heavy judgments would fall upon the pagans alone. On the contrary, he maintains the necessity, for *all* who would enter that kingdom, of a moral new birth, which he sets forth to them by the Spirit-baptism; and proclaims, as a necessary preparation for this new birth, a consciousness of sin and longing to be free from it; all which is implied in the word μετάνοια, when stated as the necessary condition of obtaining the promised baptism of the Spirit. He expects this kingdom to be *visible;* but yet conceives it as purely spiritual, as a community filled and inspired by the Spirit of God, and existing, in communion of the Divine life, with the Messiah as its visible King; so that, what had not been the case before, the *idea* of the Theocracy and its manifestation should precisely correspond to each other. He has already a presentiment that the willing among the pagans will be incorporated into the kingdom in place of the unworthy Jews who shall be excluded. The appearance of Messiah will cause a sifting of the Theocratic people. This presupposes that he will not overturn all enemies and set up his kingdom at once by the miraculous power of God, but will manifest himself in such a form that those whose hearts are prepared for his coming will recognize him as Messiah, while those of ungodly minds will deny and oppose him. On the one hand, a community of the righteous will gather around him of their own accord; and, on the other, the enmity of the corrupt multitude will be called forth and organized. The Messiah must do battle with the universal corruption; and, after the strife has separated the wicked members of

sage, as the baptism by *water* symbolizes preparatory repentance, so that by *fire* symbolizes the transfiguring and purifying power of the Holy Spirit. Our own opinion is, however, that as judgment by fire is spoken of but a few verses after (Luke, iii., 17), it must be taken in the same sense here; and the *baptism by fire* referred to the sifting process immediately mentioned. Thus the fire is the symbol of the power which consumes every thing impure, in the same sense in which God is said to be "a consuming fire."

the Theocratic nation from the good, will come forth victorious, and glorify the purified people of God under his own reign.

§ 41. *John's Recognition of Jesus as the Messiah.*

(1.) Import of his Baptism of Jesus.—(2.) The Continuance of his Ministry.—(3.) Possible Wavering in his Conviction of Christ's Messiahship.—(4.) His Message from Prison.—(5.) Conduct of his Disciples towards Jesus.

As John's conception of the Messiah included his office in freeing the people of God from the power of evil, and imparting to them a new life in the life of God, it appears that he presupposed also the fulness of the Holy Ghost dwelling in him in such a way as that he could bestow it upon others. From the first germ of the idea of Messiah in the Prophets down to the time of Christianity itself, we find ever that a just and profound conception of his *office* involves in it a higher idea of his *person*. So, perhaps, John, although his expectation of a visible realization of the Theocracy shows him as yet upon Old Testament ground, may have at least touched upon the stand-point of Christianity. His position was very like that held by Simeon, and indeed, in general, by all those Jews who, in advance of the sentiments of the times, were inspired with earnest longings for the appearance of the Messiah, and thus stood upon the border-land between the two stages of the kingdom of God. And in John's representation of his own inferiority to him "that should come," and in his clear apprehension of the limits of his mission and his power—an apprehension that distinguished him from all other founders of preparatory epochs—we have an assurance that he will never imagine his preparatory stand-point to be a permanent one; and that, as he feels himself unworthy "to unloose the shoe-strings" of the lofty One that is to appear, so he will bow himself in the same humble reverence when He, whom his spiritual sense shall recognize as the expected one, shall appear in person before him.

We are fully aware of the objections that may be raised against these conclusions. It may be said, and truly, that one may do homage to an *idea*, whose general outlines are present to his intuition, but may be unfit to recognize the *realization* of the idea when presented before his eyes in all its features. The prejudices of his time and circumstances are sure to start up and hinder him from the recognition. But surely, in the case of John, the lowliness of mind and sobriety of judgment to which we have just referred give us ground to expect that he, at least, would so far surmount his peculiar prejudices as to recognize the admission of a higher element into the course of events —to recognize a stand-point even essentially different from his own; especially as he had himself pointed out beforehand the characteristics of such a difference. Yet we do not wish to deny that doubts may arise, in regard to the *fact* of John's recognition of Jesus as Messiah, in the minds of those who do not presuppose the unconditional credibility of the Gospels. Perhaps the remark above made, in reference to a possible commingling of the subjective and the objective in the Gospel accounts, may be applicable here. But before we proceed with our connected historical recital, we must seek sure historical footing, by inquiring into the grounds of the doubts referred to.

The following questions, perhaps, express these grounds: If John was really convinced of Christ's Messiahship, why did he continue his independent ministry, and not rather submit himself and all his followers as disciples to Christ? Why did he wait until after his imprisonment before sending to inquire of Jesus whether he were the Messiah, or men should look for another? Why, even after the Baptist's death, did his disciples preserve their separate existence as a sect? How happened it that, in a public proclamation of the Gospel (Acts, x., 37; xiii., 25), no stress is laid upon John's divinely inspired testimony concerning Christ—nay, it is not even quoted—while his exhortations to repentance and his announcement of the coming Messiah are dwelt upon as the preparation for Christ's public ministry? Do not these difficulties make it doubtful whether John really did, before the time of his imprisonment, recognize Christ's Messiahship? Or, is it not probable that the Christian view, which sees in Christ the ἐρχόμενος announced by John, was involuntarily attributed to the Baptist, and so the tradition grew up that he had personally recognized the Messiahship of Jesus, and introduced him into his public labours? In this case we should have to admit that he was first induced, while in prison, by what he heard of Christ, to recognize his calling—and that not only had this fact been transferred to an earlier period in his history, but too much made of it altogether.

Now it would be easy to overthrow this whole structure at once, by assuming the genuineness and authority of John's Gospel.* It is true, as has been before said, the disciple, after going beyond his Master, might have seen more in the previously uttered words of the latter than he himself had intended; but, at any rate, those words must at least have afforded *some* ground for the disciple's representation. If the above-mentioned doubts are well grounded, John's misrepresentation of what occurred between the Baptist and Christ is nothing short of wilful falsehood. The later Christian traditions, indeed, might have admitted such a transposition without the intent to deceive; but John was an *eye-witness.* We do not intend, however, to appeal to John's authority, but shall examine the matter on internal evidence, grounded on the nature of the case.

* John, i., 7, 15; iii., 32; v., 33.

(1.) Import of the Baptism of Jesus by John.

We first consider the baptism of Jesus by John. Those who carry their doubts of John's testimony farthest, dispute even the fact of this baptism. But this is absolutely groundless skepticism; for all the New Testament accounts, however else they may differ, presuppose the event as a fact. It would be impossible to account even for the origin of such a tradition, if the event itself did not originate it; the very application of John's baptism to the sinless Jesus must have caused difficulties to the Christian mind, which a peculiar line of thought alone could remove. But, admitting the fact, it cannot be supposed that Christ submitted to the baptism in the same sense, and for the same purpose, as others did; for we can find no possible connecting link between the sense of sin and the desire for purification and redemption felt by all ordinary applicants for the ordinance, and the consciousness of the sinless Redeemer. It was with this latter, unoriginated consciousness, however, that Jesus presented himself for baptism. But we cannot suppose that he did it in silence; such a course might have led the Baptist, if not otherwise enlightened, to suppose that he came forward in the same relation to the ordinance as other men. Its probability is diminished, too, in proportion to our idea of John's susceptibility for the disclosures which Christ might have made to him. We are led, therefore, by the internal necessity of the case, to suppose that, in administering the baptism, he received a higher light in regard to the relation which he himself sustained to Christ.

(2.) The Baptist's continuance in his Ministry of Preparation.

We must conclude, however, that if John did recognize Jesus as Messiah, he applied to him all his Old-Testament ideas of Messiah as the founder of a visible kingdom. With these views he would expect that Christ would bring about the *public* recognition of his office by his own Messianic labours, without the aid of *his* testimony. This expectation would naturally cause him to forbear any public testimony to Christ, and to content himself with directing only a few of the most susceptible of his disciples to the Saviour; but this would have been a merely private affair, forming no part of his open mission to the world. That mission remained always the same, viz., to prepare the way for the Messiah's kingdom, and to point to Him who was soon to reveal himself; *not* to anticipate his self-revelation, and to declare him to the people *by name* as the Messiah. This preparatory position of John had to continue until the time when the entrance of Jesus as Theocratic King, upon the establishment of his kingdom, gave the signal for all to range themselves under his banners. The Baptist, true to the position that had been assigned to him in the Theocratic developement, had to continue his labours until their termination, a termination which external circumstances were soon to bring about.* As, therefore, John's testimony was merely private, and never openly laid before the people; and, moreover, as its value depended entirely upon the recognition of John's own prophetic calling (a recognition by no means universal among the Jews), there is no difficulty in accounting for the fact that so little use was made of his testimony in the citation of proofs for Jesus's Messiahship by Peter and Paul, in the passages above referred to.†

(3.) Possible Wavering in John's Conviction of the Messiahship of Jesus.

Suppose, now, that John's faith *did* waver in his prison—that, in an unhappy hour, he was seized with doubts of Christ's Messiahship—would it follow that he had not before enjoyed and expressed with Divine confidence his conviction of the truth? Would the later doubt suffice to do away with the earlier and out-spoken certainty? Can the man who makes such an assertion have any idea of the nature and developement of religious conviction and knowledge—of the relation between the Divine, the supernatural, and the natural? It is true that scientific knowledge and conviction, logically obtained, can never be lost so long as the intellect remains unimpaired; but it is quite another thing with *religious* truths. These do not grow out of logic; but, presupposing certain spiritual tendencies and affections, they arise from an immediate contact of the soul with God, from a beam of God's light, penetrating the mind that is allied to him. The knowledge and the convictions which are drawn neither from natural reason nor from the knowledge of the world, but are always rebelled against by the latter until the whole spirit is penetrated by the Divine, can retain their vitality only by the same going forth of the higher life which gave them

* I am gratified to find that *Winer*, one of the most eminent investigators of Biblical literature, has given an intimation of the view which I have here fully carried out. See his "Biblisches Realwörterbuch," i., 692, 2d ed.

† Acts, x., 37; xiii., 25. Paul had much more occasion to quote John's testimony when preaching to his disciples at Ephesus (Acts, xix., 1–5). There is no ground for asserting positively that he did *not* quote it, although the passage does not state expressly that he *did;* for it remains doubtful whether the words τοῦτ' ἔστιν, of verse 4, are applied by *Paul* to the ἐρχόμενος announced by John, or were intended by him to be attributed to the Baptist. What is said of Apollos (Acts, xviii., 25: *he was instructed in the way of the Lord, knowing only the baptism of John*) cannot be understood nakedly of the pure, spiritual Messiahship This could only be the case if ὅδος τοῦ κυρίου (v. 25) were equivalent to Θεοῦ ὅδου (v. 26), and signified merely *the way revealed by God,* the right way of worshipping God. But this cannot be. The word κύριος must be taken in its specific, Christian sense, as applicable to Christ; an interpretation confirmed by what follows, viz.: *he taught diligently the things of the Lord,* which cannot refer to the doctrine of God, but to the proclamation of Jesus as Messiah. But if it could be fully proved that all these disciples of John knew as yet nothing of Jesus as the ἐρχόμενος announced by the Baptist, it would not affect our assertion at all; for we have already admitted that the latter only partially directed his followers to Christ as Messiah.

birth; only so far as the soul can maintain itself in the same atmosphere, and in the same tendency to the supernatural and the Divine. So one may, when in the full enjoyment of the higher life, when no vapours of earth dim his spiritual vision, have clear conception and conviction of religious truths, which may perplex him with obscurities at times when the earthly tendencies prevail. And thus we may explain the fluctuations and transitions in the developement of religious life, convictions and knowledge, of which the experience of Christians in all ages affords instances. It may be said that, although this explanation holds good of religious life in general, it cannot apply to an inspired prophet like John, or to the truths which he obtained from the light of a supernatural revelation. This objection would imply that a single objective revelation is the only source of Christian truth, which is not the case. The apprehension of such truths in every individual mind rests not merely upon this single objective ground, but also upon a repetition of the Divine manifestation to the mind itself. The difference between the inspired prophet and the ordinary Christian believer, in regard to the reception of God's truth, is not a difference in *kind*, but in degree. Christ declared that the least of Christians was greater than John; words that ill entitle us to draw such a line of distinction between the Baptist and living Christians of all ages as to apply another standard and another law to his religious life. It is true, there is a lifeless supernaturalism which views all Divine communications rather as *overlying* the mind than incorporating themselves with its natural psychological developement; and the opponents of revealed religion caricature this view to serve their purpose of subverting the doctrines they so bitterly hate. But notwithstanding, the doctrine of such Divine communication is perfectly in accordance with the facts of the Divine life as they are stated in the Scriptures; and we are compelled thereby to connect these manifestations with the natural growth of the mind in its receptive powers and spontaneous activity; to apply the general laws of the mind to the developement of whatever is communicated to it by a higher light.

As we have before remarked, John stood between two different stages of the developement of the Theocracy. It is, therefore, not unlikely that in times of the fullest religious inspiration, caused in his soul by Christ's revelations to him, he obtained views of the coming kingdom which he could not always hold fast, and his old ideas sometimes revived and even gained the ascendency. Although he had just conceptions of Messiah's kingdom in regard to its moral and religious ends, he was always inclined to connect worldly ideas with it. But the object of his hopes was not realized. He heard, indeed, a great deal about the miracles of Jesus, but saw him not at the head of his visible kingdom. The signal so long waited for was never given. Is it, therefore, matter of wonder if, in some hour of despondency, the worldly element in the Baptist's views became too strong, and perplexity and doubt arose within him?

(4.) The Message from Prison.

The inquiry which John sent to the Saviour from prison* shows that his doubts did not refer at all to the *superiority* of Christ, but to the question whether the mission of the latter was the Messiahship itself, or only a preparation for it. So great was his respect for the authority of Christ, that he expected the decisive answer to the question from his own lips. Neither the form of the question nor the Saviour's reply favour the supposition that John was led, simply by the reports of Christ's labours which had reached him in prison, to the thought that he might be the *ἐρχόμενος*. Had this been the case, Christ would have answered him as he did others in similar circumstances; he would not have warned him not to be perplexed or offended because his groundless expectations in regard to the Messiah were not fully realized in Christ's ministry, but, on the contrary, would have cherished a faith which could grow up in one who was languishing in prison, and unable to see with his own eyes the mighty works that were done, and would have encouraged him to yield himself fully up to the dawning conviction. The warning against *σκανδαλίζεσθαι* was precisely applicable to one who had once believed, but whose faith had wavered because his hopes were not fully fulfilled. The answer of Jesus, moreover, shows plainly in what expectations John was disappointed: they were, as we shall have occasion to show hereafter, such as grew out of his Old Testament stand-point, and attributed an outward character to the kingdom of God.

(5.) Conduct of John's Disciples towards Jesus.

It does not militate at all against our position, in regard to the Baptist's recognition of Christ, that many of his disciples did not join the Saviour at a later period; and even that a sect was formed from them hostile to Christianity. We have already seen that it was necessary for John to maintain his independent sphere of labour, and that his position naturally led him to direct only the more susceptible of his disciples to Jesus, and that too by degrees. These latter were probably such as had imbibed more of John's longing desire for "him that was to come," than of the austere and ascetic spirit of the sect. As to the rest, we have only to say that we have no right to judge the master by his scholars, or the scholars by their master. Men who hold a position preparatory and conducive to a higher one, often retain the peculiar and one-sided views of their old ground, and are even driven into an

* Matt., xi, 2, 3.

attitude of opposition to the new and the better. This seems to have been the case with John's disciples in relation to Christianity.

From this full investigation of the question, we cannot but conclude that there is no reason to doubt the historical veracity of the narrative. It is matter of *fact*, that John openly recognized Jesus as the Messiah when he baptized him. Having secured this firm historical basis, we proceed now, with the greater confidence, to inquire into the peculiar import of the baptism itself.

§ 42. *The Phenomena at the Baptism, and their Import.*

(1.) No Ecstatic Vision.—(2.) The Ebionitish View and its Opposite.—(3.) Develополement of the Notion of Baptism in New Testament.—(4.) The Baptism of Christ not a Rite of Purification.—(5.) But of Consecration to his Theocratic Reign.—(6.) John's previous Acquaintance with Christ.—(7.) Explanation of John, i., 31.—(8.) The Vision and the Voice; intended exclusively for the Baptist.

Two questions present themselves here: the bearing of the baptism upon John, and its bearing upon Christ. The first can easily be gathered from what has been said already, and from the concurrent accounts of the Evangelists. It is clear that John was to be enlightened, by a sign from heaven, in regard to the *person* who was to be the ἐρχόμενος whom he himself had unconsciously foretold. The second, however, is not so easy to answer. The accounts do not harmonize so well with each other on this point, nor are all men agreed in their opinions of the *person* of Christ; and these causes have given rise to several different solutions of the question.

The point to be settled is this: Was the Divine revelation made on this occasion intended, though in different relations, for both John and Christ; not merely to give the former certainty as to the person of Messiah, but to impart a firm consciousness of Messiahship to the latter? And did Jesus, thus for the first time obtaining this full consciousness, at the same moment receive the powers essential to his Messianic mission? Did what John's eyes beheld take place really and objectively, and the fulness of the Holy Ghost descend upon Jesus to fit him for his mighty work?

(1.) No Ecstatic Vision to be supposed in the case of Christ.

If we adopt this latter view, we must look at all the phenomena connected with the baptism, not as merely subjective conceptions, but as objective supernatural *facts*. It is true, we may imagine a symbolical vision to have been the medium of a Divine revelation common to Christ and John; but we must certainly be permitted to doubt the application of such a mode of revelation to Christ. It may be granted that the Prophets were sometimes, in ecstatic vision, carried beyond themselves and overwhelmed by a higher power: but in these instances there is an abrupt suddenness, an opposition of the human and the Divine; a leap, so to speak, in the developement of consciousness, which we could hardly imagine in connexion with the specific and distinctive nature of the person of Christ. Nor, in fact, is there a hint at such a possibility in the Gospel narratives.

(2.) Ebionitish Views of the Miracle at the Baptism, and its Opposite.

There are two opposite stand-points which agree in ascribing to the events of the baptism the greatest importance in reference to Christ's Messiahship. The first is that of the *Ebionites*, who deny Christ's specific Divinity. It is, that he not only received from without, at a definite period of his life, the consciousness of his Divine mission, but also the powers necessary to its accomplishment. The other view (proceeding, however, from firm believers in the divinity of Christ) supposes that the Divine Logos, in assuming the form of humanity, submitted, by this act of self-renunciation, to all the laws of human developement; and further, that when Christ passed from the sphere of private life to that of his public ministry, he was set apart and prepared for it as the prophets were; with this single element of superiority, viz., that he was endowed with the *fulness of the Holy Ghost.*

As for the first view, it is not only at variance with the whole character of Christ's manifestation, but also with all his own testimonies of himself. In all these there is manifested the consciousness of his own greatness, not as something acquired, but as unoriginated, and inseparable from his being. He does not speak like one who has become what he is by some sudden revolution. In short, this whole mode of thinking springs from an outward supernaturalism, which represents the Divine as antagonist to the human, and imposes it upon Christ from without; instead of considering his entire manifestation from the beginning as Divine and supernatural, of deriving every thing from this fundamental ground, and recognizing in it the aim of all the special revelations of the old dispensation. This is a continuation of the old Jewish view of the progress of the Theocracy: all is formed from without, instead of developing itself organically from within; the Divine is an abrupt exhibition of the supernatural. How opposite to this is the view which sees in the human, the form of manifestation under which the Divine nature has revealed itself from the beginning, and perceives, in this original and thorough interpenetration of the Divine and the human, the aim and the culmination of all miracles.

The second view above mentioned will appear the most simple and natural, if, instead of considering a Divine communication from with-but to have been made necessary by the self-renunciation of the *Logos* in assuming human form, we admit a gradual revelation (in accordance with the laws of human developement) of the Divine nature, potentially present, as the ground of the incarnate being, from the very first, and trace all that appears in the outward manifestation to the process of developement from within. In the lives of all other reformers, or founders of religions, whose call seems to have dated from a certain period of life, the birth-time, as it were, of their activity, it is impossible not to trace, in their later labours and in their own personal statements, some references to the earlier period when their call was un felt.* In the discourses of Christ, however there is not the most dis tant approach to such an allusion.

(3.) Different Steps in the New Testament Notion of the Baptism, up to that of John the Evangelist.

In the revelations of the New Testament, and in the process of the developement of Christianity which those revelations unfold, we can distinguish various steps, or stages, of progress from the Old Testament ideas to the New. Especially is this the case in regard to the person of Christ. The conception of Christ, as anointed with the fullness of the Holy Spirit, and superior to all other prophets, is akin to Old Testament ideas, and forms the point of transition to the New, which rest upon the manifestation of Christ. But it required a completely developed *Christian* consciousness to recognize, in his appearance on earth, the Divine glory as inherent in him from the beginning, and progressive only so far as its outward manifestation was concerned. These two views, however, by no means exclude each other; the one is rather the complement of the other, while both, at a different stage of developement, tend to one and the same definite aim. And the latter, or highest stage of Christian consciousness, we are naturally to look for in that beloved apostle who enjoyed the closest degree of intimacy with Christ, and was, on that account, best of all able to understand profoundly both his manifestation and his discourses. From John, too, we must expect the highest Christian view of the person of Christ. [The account of the principal event of the baptism is thus given in John's Gospel: "And John bare record, saying, *I saw the Spirit descending from heaven like a dove, and it abode upon him. And I knew him not; but he that sent me to baptize with water, the same said unto me, Upon whom thou shalt see the Spirit descending, and remaining on him, the same is he which baptizeth with the Holy Ghost. And I saw and bare record that this is the Son of* God."†] Now the fact thus stated, if in-

* As in *Luther* we see frequent references to the light which first broke upon his mind during his monastic life at Erfurth, an epoch of the utmost moment to his after-career as a reformer

† John, i., 32–34.

terpreted in an outward and material sense, and combined with the view of Christ which we mentioned a while ago as akin to the Jewish ideas, might easily give rise to the doctrine that Christ obtained at the baptism something which he had not possessed before.

Our conclusion is, that Christ was already sure of his Divine call to the Messiahship, and submitted himself, in the course of the Theocratic developement, to baptism, as a preparative and inaugural rite, from the hands of the man who was destined to conduct prophecy to its fulfilment, and to be the first to recognize, by light from heaven, the manifested Messiah.

(4.) The Baptism not a Rite of Purification.

The idea that Christ was baptized with a view to *purification* is absolutely untenable, no matter how the notion of purification may be modified. Akin to this idea, certainly, is the view held by some,* that he submitted to this act of self-humiliation in the same sense in which he humbled himself before God, as the One alone to be called good.† This view would suppose him conscious, not of actual sin, but of a dormant possibility of sin, inherent in his finite nature and his human organism, always restrained, however, by the steadfast firmness of his will, from passing into action. But if we suppose in Christ the abstract possibility to sin‡ which is inseparable from a created will, pure but not yet immutable—such a capability as we attribute to the first man before the fall—even this would not necessarily connect with itself a dormant, hidden sinfulness, involving in him a conscious need of purification in any sense whatever. Such a consciousness can grow only out of a sense of inherent moral defilement, by no means originally belonging to the conception of a created being, or of human nature. We cannot admit a dormant principle of sin as an essential element of the moral developement of man's original being. Sin is an act of free will, and cannot be derived from any other source, or explained in any other way.§ There is, then, in Christ's humbling himself, in his human capacity, before God, the only Good, no trace of that sense of need and want with which the sinner, conscious of guilt, bows himself before the Holy One. The act manifested only a sense, deeply grounded in his holy, sinless nature, of absolute dependence upon the Source of all good.

* *De Wette*, on Matt., iii., 16. Conf. his *Sittenlehre*, § 49, 50; and *Strauss*, too, after he had seen that the view formerly expressed by him was untenable (l. c., 432, 433).

† Matt., xix., 17.

‡ This is not the place to examine the old controversy whether Christ's sinlessness is to be regarded as a *posse non peccare* or a *non posse peccare*.

§ We cannot enter further into this subject here, but take pleasure in referring our readers to the late excellent work of *J. Müller*, viz., "Die Lehre von der Sünde," in which the subject is treated with remarkable depth and clearness. The new elucidations in the 2d edition, especially, evince a soundness of mind that is not more rare than excellent.

(5.) The Baptism of Christ a Rite of Consecration to his Theocratic Reign.

All difficulties are cleared away by considering John's baptism as a rite of preparation and consecration, first in its application to the members of the Theocratic kingdom, and secondly to its Founder and Sovereign. The repentance and the sense of sin which were essential preliminaries to the baptism of the former, could in no way belong to Him who, at the very moment when the rite was administered, revealed himself to the Baptist as the Messiah, the deliverer from sin. But while the import of the rite thus varied with the subjects to whom it was administered, there was, at bottom, a substantial element which they shared in common. In both it marked the commencement of a new course of life; but, in the members, this new life was to be received from without through communications from on high: while in Christ it was to consist of a gradual unfolding from within; in the former it was to be receptive; in the latter productive. In a word, the baptism of the members prepared them to *receive* pardon and salvation; that of Christ was his consecration to the work of *bestowing* those precious gifts.

(6.) Had John a previous Acquaintance with Christ?

If the Baptist had an earlier acquaintance with Jesus, he could not have failed, with his susceptible feelings, to receive a deeper impression of his divinity than other men. We cannot but infer, from Luke's* statement (chap. i.) of the relationship† between the two families, that

* The Apocryphal Gospels contain many fables in regard to Mary's descent from a priestly lineage, arising, perhaps, from the fact that the Messiah was to be both high-priest and king. (So in the second Testament of the Twelve Patriarchs, the Testament of Simeon, § 7: ἀναστήσει κύριος ἐκ τῶν Λευὶ ἀρχιερέα καὶ ἐκ τῶν Ἰούδα βασιλέα, both in the person of the Messiah.) There is nothing akin to these in Luke's account of the relationship between Mary and Elizabeth, the latter being of priestly lineage, which is only given *en passant*; the stress is laid upon the descent from *David's* line.

† Matthew's omission to mention this relationship and to give any reason for John's reluctance to baptize Christ, only proves his narrative to be more artless, and therefore more credible. The Ebionitish Gospel to the Hebrews shows far greater marks of design, and, indeed, of an alteration for a set purpose. It represents the miraculous appearances as preceding and causing John's conduct.—When John hears the voice from heaven, and sees the miraculous light, he inquires, *Who art thou?* A second voice is heard to reply, *This is my beloved Son, in whom I am well pleased.* John is thereby led to fall at his feet and cry, *Baptize thou me.* Christ, refusing him, says, *Suffer it.*—Here not only are the phenomena exaggerated, but the facts are remodelled to suit Ebionitish views, which denied the miraculous events at Christ's birth, and demanded that the sudden change by which he was called and fitted for the Messiahship at the moment of baptism should be made prominent by contrast with all that had gone before. They conceived, accordingly, that he *first* received the Holy Ghost when it descended upon him in the form of a dove, and that at that period he was endowed with a new dignity, and must offer new manifestations. His divine character was thus obtained in a sudden, magical way; and the two periods of his life, before and after that event, were brought into clear and sharp contrast: every thing that occurred at the baptism was deemed miraculous, while all the wonders of his previous

he had heard of the extraordinary circumstances attending the birth of Jesus. The Saviour "prayed" at the baptism (Luke, iii., 21). If we figure to ourselves his countenance, full of holy devotion and heavenly repose, as he stood in prayer, and its sudden association, in the mind of the Baptist, with all his recollections of the early history of Jesus, we cannot wonder that the humble man of God—all aware as he was that the Messiah was to be consecrated by his baptism—should have been overwhelmed, in that hour so pregnant with mighty interests, with a sense of his own comparative unworthiness, and cried, "*I have need to be baptized of thee, and comest thou to me?*"

(7.) Explanation of John, i., 31.

One of two things must be true: either John baptized Christ with sole and special reference to his Messianic mission, or with the same end in view as in his ordinary administration of the rite, involving in its subjects a consciousness of sin and need of repentance. Now it is clear that he did not take upon himself to decide to *what individual* the Messianic baptism was to be administered, nor was he willing to rest it upon any human testimony, but waited for the promised sign from heaven; and as for Jesus' receiving the rite in the *second* sense at his hands, his own religious sense must have rebelled against it. Nor is this contradicted by his words recorded in John, i., 31, "*And I knew him not; but that he should be made manifest to Israel, therefore am I come baptizing with water.*" John's refusal to baptize Christ did not

life were rejected; in short, his Divine and human nature were rudely torn asunder. We see in all this the effect of a one-sided theory in obscuring history, and detect in it also the germ of a tendency which led the way from Judaism to Gnosticism. So it was with the doctrines of Cerinthus and Basilides on the person of Christ, according to which Christ possessed, as man, the ἁμαρτητικόν of human nature (although it never became actual sin in him); and the Redeemer was not *Christ*, but the heavenly Spirit that descended upon him. Another instance of the way in which the general object of John's baptism (viz., purification and forgiveness) was brought to bear upon the doctrine of the person of Christ may be seen in the Gospel of the Nazarenes, translated by Jerome, in which the account runs, that when Christ was asked by his mother and brothers to go with them to John, in order to be baptized for the remission of sins, he replied, *quid peccavi, ut vadam et baptizer ab eo, nisi forte hoc ipsum quod dixi ignorantia est* ("unless I, who have not sinned, carry the germ of sin unconsciously within me"). (Hieron., b. iii., Dialog. adv. Pelag., ad init.). It is seen more strongly still in the κήρυγμα Πέτρου, according to which Christ made his confession of sin before the baptism, but was glorified after it. Thus we see two opposite tendencies conspiring to falsify history in the life of Christ. The one sought falsely to *glorify* his early life, and embellished his childhood with tales of marvel; the other sought to *degrade* his prior life as much as possible, in order to derive all that he afterward became from his Messianic inauguration. The relation of our Gospels to both these false and one-sided tendencies is a proof of their originality. I cannot suppose, with Dr. *Schneckenburger* (Studien der Evang. Geistlichkeit Würtemburgs, Bd. iv., s. 122), that Matthew's simple account of Christ's baptism was abridged from the Ebionitish narrative, which, as we have seen, gives evidence of a designedly false colouring. Nor can I agree with *Usteri* and *Bleek* (Stud. u. Krit., Bd. ii., s. 446, and 1833, s. 436), that the dialogue between John and Christ, which, according to the Ebionitish version, took place during the baptism, is inaccurately placed by Matthew before it.

necessarily involve (as we have already said) a knowledge of his Messianic dignity; and the words just quoted refer only to that dignity. He means to say with emphasis that his conviction of Christ's Messiahship is not of human, but of Divine origin. His previous expectations, founded upon his knowledge of the circumstances of Christ's birth, were held as nothing in comparison with the Divine testimony immediately vouchsafed to him.*

(8.) The Vision at the Baptism, and the Voice, intended exclusively for the Baptist.

When the Baptist thus drew back in reverence and awe, Christ encouraged him, saying, "*For the present*,† suffer it; for thus it becomes us (each from his own stand-point) to fulfil all that belongs to the order of GOD's kingdom." While Jesus prayed and was baptized, the reverence with which John gazed upon him was heightened into prophetic inspiration; and in this state he received the revelation of the Divine Spirit in the form of a symbolical vision; the heavens opened, and he saw a dove descend and hover over the head of Christ. In this he saw a sign of the permanent abode of the Holy Spirit in Jesus; not merely as a distinction from the inspired seers of the old dispensation, but also as the necessary condition to his bestowing the Divine life upon others. It indicated that the power of the Spirit in him was not a sudden and abrupt manifestation, as it was in the prophets, who felt its inspiration at certain times and by transitory impulses; but a continuous and unbroken operation of the Holy Ghost, the infinite fulness of the Divine life in human form. The quiet flight and the resting dove betokened no rushing torrent of inspiration, no sudden seizure of the Spirit, but a uniform unfolding of the life of GOD, the loftiness, yet the calm repose of a nature itself Divine, the indwelling of the Spirit *so* that

* It was the main object of John the Evangelist to bring out prominently the *Divine* testimony given to John the Baptist (as the latter pointed the former originally to Christ); the knowledge which the latter had derived from human sources was comparatively unimportant. In fact, he seems not to have thought any thing about it, and hence his words may imply that the Baptist had no previous acquaintaince at all with Christ; but such an interpretation of them is not necessary, considering the definite end which he had in view. Let an event be described by different eye-witnesses, and their accounts will present varieties and even contrasts, simply because each of them seizes strongly upon some one point, and leaves the rest comparatively in the back-ground. True, there are degrees in historical accuracy, and we must distinguish them. In this case, the one *certain* fact, involved in all the narratives, however they may differ in other respects, is, that the Baptist was led, by a revelation made to him at the time, to consecrate Jesus to the Messiahship by baptism. This fact must remain, even if the other discrepancies were irreconcilable. We always consider a thing stated in common by several variant historical narratives, to be more probably historically true.

† Showing that this relation between him and the Baptist was to be but momentary, and soon to be followed by a very different one. *De Wette's* remarks (Comm., 2d ed.) seem to me not very cogent. "Christ describes his baptism as πρέπον, and hence this view cannot be correct." But what made it πρέπον was the fact that it was but transitory and preparatory to the revelation of Christ in all his glory. The remark of Christ applied to the *now* and only to the *now*. The ἄρτι implies the contrast, which is not expressed.

he could impart it to others and fill them completely with it, not as a prophet, but as a Creator.

The higher and essential unity of the Divine and human,* as original and permanent in Christ, which formed the substance symbolized by the vision, was further and more distinctly indicated to John by the voice from heaven,† saying, "*This is my beloved Son, in whom I am well pleased.*" Words that cannot possibly be applicable, in their full meaning, to any mere man, but to Him alone in whom the perfect union of God and man was exhibited, and the *idea* of humanity completely realized. It was this union that made it possible for a holy God *to be well pleased* in man. John's Gospel, it is true, makes no mention of this voice; but it will be recollected that this evangelist does not relate the baptism (John, i., 29, 33), but cites John Baptist as *referring* to it at some later period. The subsequent testimony of the Baptist, thus recorded ("*I saw and bare record that this is the Son of God,*" v. 34), presupposes the heavenly voice which pointed out that Sonship. At all events, the voice expressed nothing different from the import of the vision; it was the *expression* of the idea which the vision itself involved.

We consider, then, that the vision and the voice contained a subjective revelation of the Holy Spirit, intended exclusively for the Baptist,‡

* We do not intend to say, by any means, that John comprehended this in the full sense which we, from the Christian stand-point, are able to give to it.

† Although the words of the voice, as given in our Gospels, contain at most only an *allusion* to Psalm ii., 7, we find that passage *fully* quoted in the Ebionitish *Evang. ad Hebræos.* The words are still better put together in the Nazarean Gospel of the Hebrews, used by Jerome: Factum est autem quum ascendisset Dominus de aqua, descendit fons omnis Spiritus Sancti et requievit super eum, et dixit illi; Fili mi, in omnibus prophetis expectabam te, ut venires et requiescerem in te. Tu es enim requies mea, tu es filius meus primogenitus, qui regnas in sempiternum (Hieron., l. iv., in Esaiam, c. xi., ed. Vallarsi, t. iv., p. 1, f. 156). Here a profound Christian sense is expressed: Christ is the aim of the whole Theocratic developement, and the partial revelations of the Old Testament were directed to him as the concentration of all Divinity; in him the Holy Ghost finds a permanent abode in humanity, a resting-place for which it strove in all its wanderings through these isolated, fragmentary revelations; he is the Son of the Holy Ghost, in so far as the fulness of the Holy Ghost is concentrated in him. But although a Christian sense is given, the historical facts are obviously coloured.

‡ We follow here especially the account of John, according to whom the Baptist testified only of what he had seen and heard. If this statement be presupposed as the original one, the rest could easily be derived from it. What the Baptist stated as a real fact for himself would readily assume an objective form when related by others. This original apprehension of the matter seems to appear also in Matthew (iii., 16), both from the heavenly voice being mentioned in indirect narration, and from the relation of εἶδε to αὐτόν; although the expression is not perfectly clear (conf. *Bleek*, Stud. u. Krit., 1833, s. 433, and *De Wette*, in loc.). A confirmation of the originality of Matthew's account may be obtained by comparing it with that in the Ebionitish Gospel. In this, first, the words are directly addressed to Christ, and Psalm ii., 7, fully quoted; then a sudden light illuminates the place, and the voice repeats anew, in an altogether objective way, the words that had been directed to Christ. In comparing our Evangelists with each other, and with the Ebionitish Gospel, we see how the simple historical statement passed, by various interpolations, into the Ebionitish form; and how a material alteration of the facts arose from a change of form,

to convince him thoroughly that He whose coming he had proclaimed, and whose way he had prepared, had really appeared. He was alone with Jesus; the latter needed no such revelation. What was granted to John was enough; he recognized, infallibly, the voice from heaven, and the revelation of the Spirit, by his inward sense; no outward sensible impression could give him more. For others the vision was not intended; it could benefit them only mediately through him, and in case they regarded him as a prophet.

After Jesus had thus, alone with John, submitted to his baptism, and received in it the sign for the commencement of his public Messianic ministry, he withdrew into solitude in order to prepare himself by prayer and meditation,* for the work on which he was about to enter. This brings us to inquire more closely into Christ's *subjective* preparation for his public labours.

through the addition of an imaginary and foreign dogmatic element. These accounts form the basis, also, of the view held by the sect called *Mandæans* (*Zabii*, disciples of John), who combined the elements of a sect of John's disciples opposed to Christianity, with Gnostic elements. But as their object was to glorify the Baptist rather than Christ, they further distorted and disfigured the original with new inventions. "The Spirit, called the *Messenger of Life*, in whose name John baptized, appears from a higher region, manifests still more extraordinary phenomena, submits to be baptized by John, and then transfigures him with celestial radiance. Jesus afterward comes hypocritically to be baptized by John, in order to draw away the people and corrupt his doctrine and baptism." (See Norberg's *Religionsbuch* of this sect.)

* The chronology of the Gospels by no means excludes such a time of preparation, although we cannot decide whether the "forty days" are to be taken literally, or only as a round number. John's Gospel, as we have said, does not relate the baptism in its chronological connexion (John, i., 19, presupposes the occurrence of the baptism); so that there is no difficulty in supposing a lapse of several weeks between the baptism and the first public appearance of Christ. The words in John, i., 29, may have been the greeting of the Baptist on first meeting Christ upon his reappearance. Nor does the retirement of Christ throw a shade upon the credibility of the narrative as matter of fact. It is entirely opposed to the *mythical* theory; for we do not see in it (as we should were it a *mythus*) any of the ideas of the people among whom Christianity originated; on the contrary, it displays a wisdom and circumspection in direct antagonism to the prevailing tendencies of the time. As St John's object was only to state those facts in Christ's life of which he had himself been eye-witness, his silence on the subject is easily accounted for.

PART II.

SUBJECTIVE PREPARATION. THE TEMPTATION

CHAPTER I.

IMPORT OF THE INDIVIDUAL TEMPTATIONS.

WHILE, on the one hand, we do not conceive that the individual features of the account of the Temptation are to be literally taken, the principles which triumph so gloriously in its course bear the evident stamp of that wisdom which every where shines forth from the life of Christ. Its veracity is undeniably confirmed by the period which it occupies between the baptism of Christ and his entrance on his public ministry; the silent, solitary preparation was a natural transition from the one to the other. We conclude, from both these considerations together, that the account contains not only an ideal, but also a historical truth, conveyed, however, under a symbolical form.*

The easiest part of our task is to ascertain the import of the several parts of the Temptation, and to this we now address ourselves. We shall find in them the principles which guided Jesus through his whole Messianic calling—principles directly opposed to the notions prevalent among the Jews in regard to the Messiah.

§ 43. *The Hunger.*

The first temptation was as follows:† After Jesus had fasted for a long time, he suffered the pangs of hunger. As no food was to be had in the desert, the suggestion was made to him, "If thou art really the Messiah, the Son of God, this need cannot embarrass thee. Thou canst help thyself readily by a miracle; thou canst change the stones of the desert into bread." Jesus rejected this challenge with the words,

* If we assign a symbolical character to the Temptation, it may be asked whether the *fasting*, which formed a ground-work for it, was not symbolical also. But the fasting is immediately connected with the obviously historical fact of Christ's retirement. We conceive it thus: Christ, musing upon the great work of his life, forgot the wants of the body. (Cf. John, iv., 34.) The mastery (and this we must presuppose) which his spirit had over the body prevented those wants from asserting their power for a long time; but when they did, it was only the more powerfully. It formed part of the trial and self-denial of Christ through his whole life, that, together with the consciousness that he was the Son of God, he combined the weakness and dependence of humanity. These affected the lesser powers of his soul, although they could never move his unchangingly holy will, and turn him to any selfish strivings.

† Matt., iv., 2–4.

'*Man shall not live by bread alone, but by every word that proceedeth out of the mouth of* God" (what is produced by God's creative word) To apprehend these words rightly, we must recall their original connexion in Deuteronomy (viii., 3), viz., that the Jews were fed in the wilderness with manna, in order to learn that the power of God could sustain human life by other means than ordinary food. They longed for the bread and flesh of Egypt, but were to be taught submission to the will of God, who was pleased to supply their wants with a different food. Applying this thought to Christ's circumstances, we interpret his reply to the tempter as follows: "Far be it from me to prescribe to God the mode in which he shall provide me sustenance. Rather will I trust his omnipotent creative power, which can find means to satisfy my hunger, even in the desert, though it may not be with man's usual food."

The principle involved in the reply was, that he had no wish to free himself from the sense of human weakness and dependence; that he would work no miracle for *that* purpose. He would work no miracle to satisfy his own will; no miracle where the momentary want might be supplied, though by natural means such as might offend the sensual appetite. In self-denial he would follow God, submitting to His will, and trusting that His mighty power would help in the time of need, in the way that His wisdom might see fit. On this same principle Christ acted when he suffered his apostles to satisfy their hunger with the corn which they had plucked, rather than do a miracle to provide them better food. On this same principle he acted when he gave himself to the Jewish officers sent to apprehend him,* rather than seek deliverance by a Divine interposition. Of the same kind, too, was his trial when he hung upon the cross, and they that passed by said, "*If he be the King of Israel, let him now come down from the cross, and we will believe him.*"†

§ 44. *The Pinnacle of the Temple.*

He was then taken to the pinnacle of the Temple, and the tempter said to him, "If thou be the Son of God, cast thyself down; thou art sure of aid by a miracle from God;" and quoted, literally, in application, the words of Psa. xci., 11, 12, "*The angels shall bear thee up in their hands, lest thou dash thy foot against a stone.*" But Christ arrays against him another passage, which defines the right application of the former: "*Thou shalt not tempt the Lord thy* God." (Deut., vi., 16.) As if he had said, "Thou must undertake nothing with a view to test God's omnipotence, as if to try whether he will work a miracle to save thee from a peril that might be avoided by natural means" (*i. e.*, by coming down from the battlement in the usual way).

* Matt., xxvi., 53. † Ib., xxvii., 42.

These words of Christ imply that the pious man can look for Divine aid at all times, provided he uses rightly the means which God affords him, and walks in the way which has been Divinely marked out for him by his calling and his circumstances: the Messiah was not, in gratuitous confidence of Divine assistance, to cast himself into a danger which common prudence might avoid. They involve the principle, that a miracle may not be wrought except for wise ends and with adequate motives; never, with no other aim than to display the power of working wonders, and to make a momentary, sensible impression, which, however powerful, could leave no religious effect, and, not penetrating beyond the region of the senses, must be but transient there. And on this principle Christ acted always, in not voluntarily exposing himself to peril; in employing wise and prudent means to escape the snares of his enemies; and going forth, with trust in God and submission to his will, to meet such dangers only as his Divine mission made necessary, and as he could not avoid without unfaithfulness to his calling. On this principle he acted when the Pharisees and the fleshly-minded multitude came to him and asked a miracle, and he refused them with, ["*there shall no sign be given to this wicked and adulterous generation but the sign of the Prophet Jonah.*"]*

§ 45. *Dominion.*

We do not take the third temptation as implying literally that Satan proposed to Christ to fall down and do him homage, as the price of a transfer of dominion over all the kingdoms of the world: no extraordinary degree of piety would have been necessary to rebuke such a proposal as this. We consider it as involving the two following points, which must be taken together, viz., (1) the establishment of Messiah's dominion as an outward kingdom, with worldly splendours; and (2) the worship of Satan in connexion with it, which, though not fully expressed, is implied in the act which he demands, and which Christ treats as equivalent to worshipping him. Herein was the temptation, that the Messiah should not develope his kingdom gradually, and in its pure spirituality from within, but should establish it at once, as an outward dominion; and that, although this could not be accomplished without the use of an evil agency, the end would sanctify the means.

We find here the principle, that to try to establish Messiah's kingdom as an outward, worldly dominion, is to wish to turn the kingdom of God into the kingdom of the devil; and to employ that fallen Intelligence which pervades all human sovereignties, only in a different form, to found the reign of Christ. And in rejecting the temptation, Christ condemned every mode of secularizing his kingdom, as well as all the devil-worship which must result from attempting that kingdom in a

* Matt. xii., 39.

world y form. We find here the principle, that GOD's work is to be accomplished purely as HIS work and by HIS power, without foreign aid; so that it shall all be only a share of the worship rendered to HIM alone.

And Christ's whole life illustrates this principle. How often was he urged, by the impatient longings and the worldly spirit of the people, to gratify their intense, long-cherished hopes, and establish his kingdom in a worldly form, before the *last* demand of the kind was made upon him, as he entered, in the midst of an enthusiastic host, the capital city of GOD's earthly reign; before his *last* refusal, expressed in his submission to those sufferings which resulted in the triumph of GOD's pure spiritual kingdom!

CHAPTER II.

IMPORT OF THE TEMPTATION AS A WHOLE.

§ 46 *Fundamental Idea.*

THE whole temptation taken together presents us one idea; a contrast, namely, between the founding of GOD's kingdom as pure, spiritual, and tried by many forms of self-denial in the slow developement ordained for it by its head; and the sudden establishment of that kingdom before men, as visible and earthly. This contrast forms the central point of the whole. All the temptations have regard to the created will as such; the *victory* presupposes that self-sacrifice of a will given up to GOD which determines the whole life. And as this self-sacrifice of the created will in Christ had to be tested in his life-long struggles with the Spirit of the world, which ever strove to obscure the idea of the kingdom of GOD and bring it down to its own level; so the free and conscious decision manifested in these three temptations, fully contrasting, as they did, the true and the false Messiahship, the unworldly and the secularized Theocracy, was made *before* his public ministry, which itself was but a continuation of the strife and the triumph.

§ 47. *The Temptation not an inward one, but the Work of Satan.*

We find, then, in the fa ts of the temptation the expression of that period that intervened between Christ's private life and his public ministry. These inward spiritual exercises bring out the self-determination which stamps itself upon all his subsequent outward actions. Yet we dare not suppose in him a *choice*, which, presupposing within him a point of tangency for evil, would involve the necessity of his comparing the evil with the good, and deciding between them. In the steadfast tendency of his inner life, rooted in submission to GOD, lay a decision which admitted of no such struggle. He had in common with human ity that natural weakness which may exist without selfishness, and the created will, mutable in its own nature; and only on this side was the struggle possible—such a struggle as man may have been liable to, before he gave *seduction* the power of *temptation* by his own actual sin. In all other respects, the outward seductions remained outward; they found no selfishness in him, as in other men, on which to seize, and thus become internal temptations, but, on the contrary, only aided in revealing the complete unity of the Divine and human, which formed the essence of his inner life.

Nor is it possible for us to imagine that these temptations originated *within;* to imagine that Christ, in contemplating the course of his future ministry, had an internal struggle to decide whether he should act according to his own will, or in self-denial and submission to the will of God. We have seen from the third temptation that, from the very beginning, he regarded the establishment of a worldly kingdom as inseparable from the worship of the devil; he could, therefore, have had no struggle to choose between such a kingdom, outward and worldly, and the true Messiah-kingdom, spiritual, and developed from within.

Even the purest man who has a great work to do for any age, must be affected more or less by the prevailing ideas and tendencies of that age. Unless he struggle against it, the spirit of the age will penetrate his own; his spiritual life and its products will be corrupted by the base admixture. Now the whole spirit of the age of Christ held that Messiah's kingdom was to be *of this world*, and even John Baptist could not free himself from this conception. There was nothing *within* Christ on which the sinful spirit of the age could seize; the Divine life within him had brought every thing temporal into harmony with itself; and, therefore, this tendency of the times to secularize the Theocratic idea could take no hold of him. But it was to press upon him from *without;* from the beginning this tendency threatened to corrupt the idea and the developement of the kingdom of God, and Christ's work had to be kept free from it; moreover, the nature of his own Messianic ministry could only be fully illustrated by contrast with this possible objective mode of action; to which, foreign as it was to his own spiritual tendencies, he was so frequently to be urged afterward by the prevailing spirit of the times.

But if, according to the doctrine of Christ,* the rebellion of a higher

* We must hereafter inquire whether this *is* Christ's doctrine, and only make here a preliminary remark or two. The arguments of the rationalists against the doctrine which teaches the existence of Satan are either directed against a false and arbitrary conception of that doctrine, or else go upon the presupposition that evil could only have originated under conditions such as those under which human existence has developed itself; that it has its ground in the organism of human nature, *e. g.*, in the opposition between reason and the

intelligence against GOD preceded the whole present history of the universe, in which Evil is one of the co-operating factors, and of which man's history is only a part; if that doctrine makes Satan the representative of the Evil which he first brought into *reality;* if, further, it lays down a connexion, concealed from the eye of man, between him and *all* evil; then, from this point of view, Christ's contest with the spirit of the world must appear to us a contest with Satan—the temptation, a temptation from Satan—continued afterward through his whole life, and renewed in every form of assault, until the final triumph was announced, "*It is finished.*" As the temptation could not have originated *in* Christ, he could only attribute it to that Spirit to which all opposition to GOD's kingdom, and every attempt to corrupt its pure developement, can finally be traced back. On the working out of Christ's plan depended the issue of the battle between the kingdom of GOD and the kingdom of the Evil One; and we cannot wonder, therefore, that this Spirit, ever so restlessly plotting against the Divine order, should have been active and alert at a time when, as in the case of the first man, an opening for temptation to the mutable created will was afforded to him.

Christ left to his disciples and the Church only a partial and symbolical account* of the facts of his inner life in this preparatory epoch; an account, however, adapted to their practical necessities, and serving to guard them against those seductions of the spirit of the world to which even the productions of the Divine spirit must yield, if they are ever allowed to become worldly.

propensities; that *human* developement must necessarily pass through it; but that we can not conceive of a steadfast tendency to evil in an intelligence endowed with the higher spiritual powers. Now it is precisely this view of evil which we most emphatically oppose, as directly contradictory to the essence of the Gospel and of a theistico-ethical view of the world; and, on the contrary, we hold fast, as the only doctrine which meets man's moral and religious interests, that doctrine which is the ground of the conception of Satan, and according to which evil is represented as the rebellion of a created will against the Divine law, as an act of free-will not otherwise to be explained, and the intelligence as determined by the will. I am pleased to find my convictions expressed in few words by an eminent divine of our own time, Dr. *Nitzsch,* in his excellent *System der Christlichen Lehre,* 2d ed., p. 152. They are further developed by *Twesten,* in his *Dogmatik.* The same fundamental idea is given in the work of *Julius Mnller,* already mentioned (*Lehre von der Sünde*).

* We can apply here Dr. *Nitzsch's* remark in reference to the Biblical account of the Fall (*Christl. Lehre,* § 106, s. 144, anm. 1, 2te. Aufl.): "The history of the temptation, in this form, is not a *real,* but a *true* history."

BOOK IV.

THE PUBLIC MINISTRY OF CHRIST

IN ITS

REAL CONNEXION.

PART I. THE PLAN OF CHRIST.

PART II. THE MEANS AND INSTRUMENTS OF CHRIST.

BOOK IV.

THE PUBLIC MINISTRY OF CHRIST IN ITS REAL CONNEXION.*

PART I.

THE PLAN OF CHRIST.

CHAPTER I.

A. THE PLAN OF CHRIST'S MINISTRY IN GENERAL.

§ 48. *Had Christ a conscious Plan?*

IT is most natural for us, in treating of CHRIST's public ministry, to speak first of the *plan* which lay at the foundation of it. First of all, however, the question comes up, whether he *had* any such plan at all.†

The greatest achievements of great men in behalf of humanity have not been accomplished by plans previously arranged and digested; on the contrary, such men have generally been unconscious instruments, working out GOD's purposes, at least in the beginning, before the fruits of their labours have become obvious to their own eyes. They served the plan of GOD's providence for the progress of his kingdom among men, by giving themselves up enthusiastically to the ideas which the Spirit of GOD had imparted to them. Not unfrequently has a false historical view ascribed to such labours, after their results became known, a plan which had nothing to do with their developement. Nay, these mighty men were able to do their great deeds precisely because a higher than human wisdom formed the plan of their labours and prepared the way for them. The work was greater than the workmen; they had no presentiments of the results that were to follow from the toils to which they felt themselves impelled. So was it with LUTHER,

* To promote unity of view, I deem it best, especially as much of the chronological order must remain uncertain, to treat and divide Christ's public ministry, *first*, according to its substantial connexion, and, *secondly*, according to its chronological connexion.

† We use the phrase "plan of Jesus," inasmuch as we compare his mode of action with that of other world-historical men, in order to bring out the characteristic features which distinguish him. The exposition which follows will show that I agree with the apt remarks of my worthy friend, Dr. *Ullmann*, made in his beautiful treatise on the "*Sündenlosigkeit Jesu*" (Sinlessness of Jesus), p. 71, and that his censures there of those who use the above-mentioned phrase do not apply to me. [See Ullmann's Treatise, translated by Edwards and Park, in the "Selections from German Literature."]

when he kindled the spark which set half Europe in a blaze, and commenced the sacred flame which refined the Christian Church.

Were we at liberty to compare the work of CHRIST with these creations wrought through human agencies, we should need to guard ourselves against determining the plan of his ministry from its results. We might then suppose that he was inspired with enthusiasm for an idea, whose compass and consequences the limits of his circumstances and his times prevented him from fully apprehending. We might also distinguish between the idea, as made the guide and the aim of his actions by himself, and the more comprehensive Divine plan, to which, by his voluntary and thorough devotion to GOD, he served as the organ. And it would rather glorify than disparage him to show, by thus comparing him with other men who had wrought as GOD's instruments to accomplish HIS vast designs, that GOD had accomplished through him even greater things than he had himself intended.

But we are allowed to make no such comparison. The life of CHRIST presented a realized ideal of human culture such as man's nature can never attain unto, let his developement reach what point it may. He described the future effects of the truth which he revealed in a way that no man could comprehend at the time, and which centuries of history have only been contributing to illustrate. Nor was the progress of the *future* more clear to his vision than the steps in the history of the *past*, as is shown by his own statements of the relation which he sustained to the old dispensation. Facts, which it required the course of ages to make clear, lay open to his eye; and history has both explained and verified the laws which he pointed out for the progress of his kingdom. He could not, therefore, have held the same relation to the plan for whose accomplishment his labours were directed, as men who were mere instruments of GOD, however great. He resembled them, it is true, in the fact that his labours were ordered according to no plan of human contrivance, but to one laid down by GOD for the developement of humanity; but he differed from them in this, that HE understood the full compass of GOD's plan, and had freely made it his own; that it was the plan of his own mind, clearly standing forth in his consciousness when he commenced his labours. The account of his temptation, rightly understood, shows all this.

With this, also, are rebutted those views which consider Christ as having recognized the idea of his ministry only through the cloudy atmosphere of Judaism; and those which represent his plan as having been essentially altered from time to time, as circumstances contradicted his first expectations and gave him clearer notions. They are further refuted by the entire harmony which subsists between Christ's own expressions in regard to his plan, as uttered in the two different epochs of his history.

§ 49. *Connexion with the Old Testament Theocracy.*

The object of Christ was, as he himself often describes it, to establish the kingdom of God among men; not, as we have shown, after a plan of man's devising, but after one laid down by God; not only in the general developement of the human race, but also, and specially, in the developement of the Jewish nation, and in the revelations of the old dispensation. We must, therefore, look back upon the Old Testament foundations of the kingdom of God, before we can correctly understand the plan of Christ as set forth in his acts and words. The one prepared the way for the other. In the former it was outward and confined to the narrow community of the Jewish people, in the form of a state founded and governed by Divine authority; in the latter it was to be universal, all-embracing, a communion, springing out of the consciousness of God, intended to be the principle of life and union for all mankind. In the former, the Divine law, ordering from without all the relations of state and people, governed the nation through organs appointed by God and inspired by his Spirit, viz., priests, kings, and prophets. But this idea could not be realized; *the kingdom of God could not be founded from without.* It needed first a proper material; and this could not be found in human nature, estranged from God by sin. The history of the Jewish nation was designed to bring this contradiction out into clear consciousness; and to awaken a more and more vivid anxiety for its removal, and for the re-establishment and glorification of the Theocracy. So the revelations of God pointed more and more directly to Him, the Messiah, under whose dominion the Divine kingdom was to be exalted, and the worship of Jehovah to be acknowledged and to triumph even among the nations so long estranged from him.

§ 50. *Christ's Steadfast Consciousness of his Messiahship.*

And Jesus knew and testified to his Messiahship from the beginning, from his first public appearance until his last declaration, made before the high-priests in the very face of death; although he did not always proclaim it with equal openness, especially when there was risk of popular commotions from false and temporal conceptions of the Messiah on the part of the people; but rather gradually led them, from the acknowledgment of his prophetic character (by which, indeed, they were bound to believe in his words), to recognize him as the Messiah, a Prophet also, but in the *highest* sense.

In this respect there is no contradiction whatever between the Synoptical Gospels* and John. They all agree in stating that Jesus spoke and acted from the beginning in consciousness of his Messiahship; and

* Matthew, Mark, and Luke.

also that, as circumstances demanded, he was sometimes more and sometimes less explicit* in regard to it. Nor is John silent† about the fluctuations and divisions of opinion (easily explained on psychological grounds), even among the more favourably disposed portions of the multitude: nay, he tells us that some of the Apostles were slow to believe, and wavered in their faith. All this, however, does nothing to prove similar fluctuations in Christ's conviction of his Messiahship. According to Matthew, Jesus commenced his ministry, like John the Baptist, by summoning men to repentance, as a preparation for the coming kingdom of God. But this by no means implies that his intention and his announcement, at the beginning, were the same as those of the Baptist. It was necessary for him to take this starting-point, as he joined his ministry upon John's proclamation, and upon the desire for the manifestation of the kingdom of God which it had awakened, in order to purify this desire and direct it to its object, the real founder of the kingdom. It was essential to awaken and preserve in the minds of the people a sense of the necessity of repentance as a condition of participation in the kingdom, and the first starting-point for a clear idea of its nature. After this general summons had gone before, Jesus could prove, by the impression of his own works, that the kingdom had really been manifested through him (Matt., xii., 28; Luke, xvii., 21). The proclamation of the approaching kingdom and the announcement of Jesus as its founder and central-point, were closely connected together; but sometimes the one was announced more prominently, and sometimes the other, as circumstances might demand. Compare the Sermon on the Mount with the discourses of Christ as recorded in John's Gospel.

§ 51. *No alterations of Christ's Plan.*

It may be imagined, however, that although Christ was conscious, from the beginning, of his calling to realize the idea of the kingdom of God, the plan of his work may have been modified from time to time according to the varying results which depended upon the vacillating temper of the public mind; that at first, perhaps, he hoped to find the greater part of the Jewish nation ready to receive him; and designed, under this supposition, to separate the incorrigible from the better part, and collect the latter into a Theocratic community under his government; and that he expected that the kingdom of God, once seated firmly in this way, would, by the might of its prevailing spirit of Divine life, by degrees transform all other nations into the same kingdom. In

* John, viii., 25; x., 24.

† John, vii., 40; Matt., xvi., 14; John, vii., 12. The less hostile portion of the people agreed, at first, only in believing that Christ had good intentions and was no seducer of the people.

fact, what an incalculable influence might a nation, thoroughly imbued with the spirit of Christianity and illustrating Christianity in all its relations, exert toward the moral regeneration of the rest of mankind! A light indeed would it be, not hid under a bushel, but throwing its beams on all sides into the surrounding darkness: the salt and the leaven, truly, of all mankind. And some,* in fact, assert that Christ cherished these hopes when he first appeared in public. Hence, say they, the joyous feeling with which he announced the "acceptable year" in the synagogue at Nazareth;† hence his purpose, manifested in the Sermon on the Mount, to give to the people new Theocratic statutes in accordance with his higher stand-point; hence his promise to the apostles that they should govern, under him, the new Theocratic community;‡ hence, too, his last lamentation over Jerusalem, that he had so often tried to save the nation which ought to have submitted to his guidance. All which, they say, presupposes a belief on his part that the results might have been different had the people listened to his voice, and that he expected more of them to listen to him; that the aim of his ministry was altered when he found the resistance more stubborn and general than he had supposed; and that, from the course of events themselves, he learned, in the light of the Divine Spirit, that the plan for the establishment of the kingdom of God which the Divine counsels had formed, was such, that he himself must submit to the power of his enemies, and rise victorious from his sufferings; while the kingdom itself was only to advance by slow degrees, and after many combats, to its final triumph.

Yet, after all, these reasonings are only specious, not solid. Even the most important of them rather opposes than sustains the theory they are adduced to support. It is true, there is such a thing as a holy enthusiasm for a Divine idea, which is blind to all difficulties, or deems that it can gain an easy victory. Such, however, was not the enthusiasm of Christ for his Divine work; on the contrary, he combined with it a discretion which fully comprehended the opposition he must encounter from the prevailing opinions and feelings of the times. He was far from trusting to the momentary impulses under which the people, excited by his words and actions, sought to join themselves to him. He readily distinguished, with that searching glance that pierced the depths of men's hearts, the few who came to him, drawn of the Father and following an inward consciousness of God, from those who sought him with carnal feelings, to obtain that which he came not to bestow. How did he check the ardour of his disciples, when he rebuked the false self-confidence inspired by a transient enthusiasm, and reminded them of their weakness! There was no extravagance in his demands upon

* *De Wette* and *Hase*. *Paulus* also, with some modifications.

† Luke, iv., 17, seq.

‡ Matt., xix., 28.

men; nothing exaggerated in his hopes of the future. Every where we see not only a conscious possession of the Divine power to overcome the world, which he was to impart to humanity, but also of the obstacles it should meet with from the old nature in which the principle of sin was yet active. This was the spirit which passed over from him to the Apostles, and which constituted the peculiar essence of Christian ethics. CHRIST, while as yet surrounded only by a handful of faithful followers, describes the renewing power which the seed that he had sown would exert on the life of humanity; yet, brilliant as the prospect is, his eyes are not dazzled by it; he sees, at the same time, how impurity will mix itself with the work of GOD, and how clouds will obscure it. Could HE whose quick glance thus saw the depths of men's hearts, and took in at once the present and the future, who knew so well the corrupt carnality of the Jewish nation before he entered on his public ministry, so far deceive himself as to suppose that he could *suddenly* transform the larger part of such a nation into a true people of GOD? HE that searched men's hearts and knew what was in man could not be ignorant that his severest battles were to be fought with the prevalent depravity of men; and in connexion with these struggles, how natural was it for him to look forward to the death which he should suffer in the faithful performance of his calling! Even at an early date he intimated the violent death by which he was to be torn from the happy fellowship of his disciples, leaving them behind him in tears and sorrow.*

His temptation, the historical truth and import of which we have shown, makes it clear that he had decided, before he commenced his public labours, not to establish the kingdom of GOD in a mere outward way by miraculous power. And this is further shown by his assigning, in the first epoch of his ministry, to John the Baptist, whom he called the first among the prophets, a subordinate place in relation to the new era of religion; for this could only have been done in view of John's inability fully to comprehend the essential feature of this new era, viz., the spiritual developement of the kingdom of GOD from within. And

* Matt., ix., 15. *Hase* says, indeed, that these words do not imply necessarily an approaching violent death, but might be uttered in view of the common lot of mortals. But, in the first place, Jesus, if he applied to himself the Old Testament idea of the Messiah, could not believe that he would be torn by natural death from the Theocratic community which he should found among the Jews, and thus leave it to the direction of others; but must expect (if he hoped to found an external Theocracy) always to remain present as Theocratic king. (This applies, also, to what *Hase* says (2d edit. of his *Leben Jesu*, p. 89), in opposition to his previously expressed views.) Again, it would be strange indeed for a man of thirty to express himself to older men, in reference to the common end of mortals, in such language as the following: "*Now* is your time for festal joy; for when your friend shall be removed, it will be time for fasting and sorrow." The whole connexion of the passage shows that Jesus did not expect to part from them under happy circumstances, but amid many conflicts and sufferings.

again, in reference to John he said, "*Blessed is he, whosoever shall not be offended in me;*" evidently presupposing that John's Old Testament views would be offended at the new era; a presupposition which refers to the new spiritual growth of the Divine kingdom. It is, therefore, undeniable that from the beginning Christ aimed at this *new* developement of that kingdom.

We find further proof of this in all the *parables* which treat of the progress of his kingdom, and the effects of his truth upon human nature, viz., the parables of the mustard seed, of the leaven, of the fire which he had come to kindle upon earth, all which were designed to illustrate the distinction between the Old Testament form of the Theocracy and that of Christ; to illustrate a developement which was not at *once* to exhibit an external stately fabric; but to commence with apparently small beginnings, and yet ever to propagate itself by a mighty power working outwardly from within; and to regenerate all things, and thus appropriate them to itself. All these parables presuppose the renewal of human nature by a new and pervading principle of spiritual life; and imply that the kingdom of God cannot be visibly realized among men until they become subjects of this renewal. To the same effect was Christ's saying (which we shall further examine hereafter), "*neither do men put new wine into old skins, else the skins break and the wine runneth out.*" He who uttered such truths, involving a steadfast and connected system of thought, *could* not have set out with the purpose of establishing an outward kingdom, and have afterward been induced by circumstances to change his plan in so short a time. What an immense revolution in his mental habits and course of thinking must a few months have produced, on such a supposition! It would be, indeed, a gross misapprehension of the precepts given in the *Sermon on the Mount* to interpret them literally as laws laid down for an outward Theocratic kingdom. Such an interpretation would involve the possibility of a struggle between Good and Evil in the kingdom of God; such as can never take place in Messiah's reign, if it be realized according to its idea. The form of a *state* cannot be thought of in connexion with this kingdom; a state presupposes a relation to transgression; an outward law, the forms of judicature, the administration of justice are essential to its organization. But all these can have no place in the *perfect* kingdom of Christ; a community whose whole principle of life is love. Laws intended for the *free* mind lose their import when their observance is compelled by external penalties of any kind whatever. More of this view hereafter, when we come to treat especially of the Sermon on the Mount.

Nor is a change in Christ's *feelings* to be in any wise admitted. The *year of joy* [the *acceptable* year, Luke, iv., 19] did not refer to the happy results which he hoped to attain, but to the blessed contents of the announcement with which he commenced his labours; the substance of the message itself was joyful, whether the dispositions of the people would make it a source of joy to them, or not. And even on his first proclamation at Nazareth, the hostility of the carnally-minded multitude could have enabled him to prognosticate the general temper with which the whole people would receive him. It follows by no means, from the wo which he uttered over his loved Jerusalem (Luke, xiii., 34, 35), that he had hoped at first to find acceptance with the entire nation, and to make Jerusalem the real seat of his Theocratic government. Yet, although he could not save the nation as a whole, he offered his warnings to the whole, leaving it to the issue to decide who were willing to hear his voice.

§ 52. *Two-fold bearing of the Kingdom of God—an inward, spiritual Power, and a world-renewing Power.*

There are two sides to the conception of the kingdom of God, as Christ viewed it; in reference to its ideal and its real elements, which must be contemplated in their connexion with each other. The discourses of Christ will be found every where to contradict a one-sided view of either of these elements.

The kingdom of God was indeed first to be exhibited as a communion of men bound together by the same spirit, inspired by the same consciousness of God; and this communion was to find its central point in Christ, its Redeemer and King. As he himself ordered and directed all things in the first congregation of his disciples, so he was subsequently to inspire, rule, and cultivate this community of men by his law and by his Spirit. The revelation of the Spirit, shared by all its members, was all that was to distinguish it from the world, so called in the New Testament, that is, the common mass of mankind, as alienated from God.

But as this community was gradually to prevail even over the mass of mankind through the power of the indwelling Spirit, it was not always to remain entirely inward and hidden, but to send forth, continually more and more, a renewing influence; to be the *salt*, the *leaven* of humanity, the *city set upon a hill*, the *candle* which, once lighted, should never be extinguished. And Christ was gradually, through this community, his organ and his royal dwelling-place, to establish his kingdom as a *real* one, more and more widely among men, and subdue the world to his dominion. In *this* sense were those who shared in his communion to obtain and exercise, even upon earth, a real world-dominion. It is the aim and end of history, that Christianity shall more and more become the world-governing principle. In fine, the end of this developement appears to be (though not, indeed, simply as its *natural* result) a complete realization of the Divine kingdom which Christ established in its outward manifestation, fully answering to its idea; a perfect world-dominion of CHRIST and of his organs; a world purified and transformed, to become the seat of His universal empire.

So did Christ intend, in a true sense, and in various relations, to describe himself as King, and his organs as partakers in his dominion of the world. It was, indeed, in a *real* sense that he spoke of his KINGDOM, to be manifested on earth. And as he was to build up this kingdom on the foundations laid down in the Old Testament, and to realize the plan of GOD therein prefigured, he could rightfully apply to himself the figures of the Old Testament in regard to the progress of the Theocracy, in order to bring the truths which they veiled clearly out before the consciousness of men.* Although his disciples at first took these figures in the letter, still, under the influence of Christ's intercourse and teaching, they could not long stop there. And not only his direct instructions, but the manner in which he opposed the idea of his spiritual and inward kingdom to the carnal notions of the Jews, contributed to give his followers the key to the right interpretation of these types and shadows.

In thus comparing Christ's discourses with each other, and in the unity of purpose which a contemplation of his *whole* life makes manifest, we find a guard for all after ages, against carnal misconceptions of his individual discourses, or of separate features of his life.† In general, when we find in the accounts of any world-historical man such a unity of the creative mind, we are willing, if individual features come up in apparent contradiction to the general tenor, to believe that he was misunderstood by incapable contemporaries; or, if this cannot be safely asserted, because the contradictory features are inseparable from others that bear his unmistakable impress, we endeavour, by comparing his manifestations, to find that higher unity in which even the unmanageable points may find their rightful place. Utterly unhistorical, indeed, is that perverted principle of historical exegesis which teaches that an original, creative mind, a spirit far above his times, is to be comprehended from the prevailing opinions of his age and nation; and which presupposes, in fact, that all these opinions are his own.‡

* Some suppose that every thing in Christ's discourses, as reported by Matthew and Luke, in reference to this real Theocratic element, is to be ascribed to the Jewish views that obscured the truth as uttered by Christ, and caused it to be reported incorrectly That this is not the case is obvious from Paul's plain references to such expressions of Christ's, *e.g.*, 1 Cor., vi., 2.

† We shall speak more particularly of this when we come to treat of the mode in which Christ trained his apostles.

‡ Conf. what *Schleiermacher* says (Hermeneutik, s. 20) of "historical interpretation," and also (s. 82) of the "Analogy of Faith."

CHAPTER II.

THE PLAN OF CHRIST IN ITS RELATION TO THE OLD TESTAMENT IDEA OF THE KINGDOM OF GOD.

The question now arises, in what relation the new form of the kingdom of God, according to Christ's plan, stood to the Old Testament form thereof; a question which we shall have to answer from the intimations afforded by Christ himself. Indeed, it has already been answered by our remarks upon his idea of the kingdom as developing itself from within; but as the subject has its difficulties, and especially as some have tried to prove that Christ spoke and acted at different times from opposite points of view, we must examine it more closely.

§ 53. *Christ's Observance of the Jewish Worship and Law.*

No question can arise as to Christ's intention to extend his kingdom abroad among the pagan nations; the Messianic predictions of the Old Testament had already intimated the general diffusion of the worship of Jehovah; and John the Baptist had hinted at the possible transfer of the kingdom of God from the Jews to the heathen, in case the former should prove to be unworthy of it. And what was afterward novel to the apostles was, not that the pagans should be converted and received into the fellowship of the Messiah, but that they should be received without accepting the Mosaic law. It was against the latter view, and not the former, that even the strictest Judaizers objected. It was to refute this that the Ebionites appealed to Christ's strict observance of the law, and to his saying, in the Sermon on the Mount, that he "*came not to destroy, but to fulfil the law*," and that "not one jot or tittle of the law should pass away."

We must not oppose this doctrine by quoting Christ's declarations that the essence of religion must be found in the soul, and that outward things could neither cleanse nor sanctify mankind;* for even in the light of the Old Testament it was known that piety of heart was indispensable to a true fulfilment of the law. Christ himself appealed to a passage in the Old Testament (Hos., vi., 6) in proof of this; and even the well-disposed scribe (Mark, xii., 33) admitted it. Still, the necessity of an outward observance of the law might be maintained by those who deemed inward purity essential to its value.†

Viewing the relation of Christ's doctrine to the legal stand-point only

* Such as Matt., xv., 11; Mark, vii., 15.

† Even Philo, from the stand-point of his religious idealism, held the necessity of a strict observance of the ritual law, believing that it facilitated the understanding of the *spiritual* sense of the law. He asserted this against the idealists, who adhered absolutely to the letter, in his treatise "*De Migratione Abraami.*"

on this side, we might conceive it to have stood as follows: Directing his attention only to the necessity of proper dispositions in order to piety, he held, as of fundamental importance, that nothing in religion not springing from genuinely pious feelings could be of any avail; and, holding fast to this, did not investigate further the question of the continued authority of the ceremonial law. Satisfied with saving what was most essential, he permitted the other to stand as inviolable in its Divine authority. Such a course would have been eminently proper in Christ, if we regard him as nothing more than a genuine reformer Every attempt at true reformation must have, not a negative, but a positive point of departure; must start with some truth which it fully and necessarily recognizes.

The view which we have just set forth is not invalidated by Christ's denunciations of the Pharisees for their arbitrary statutes and burdensome additions to the law.* In all these he contrasted the law, rightly and spiritually understood, with their false traditions and interpretations. As for actual violation of the law, he could never be justly accused of it; even Paul, who so strenuously resisted the continued obligation of the law, declares that Christ submitted to it.†

§ 54. *His Manifestation greater than the "Temple."*

But a comparison of Matt., xii., 6–8, with Mark, ii., 28, will suggest to us something more than a mere assault upon the statutes of the Pharisees. In the first passage he begins with his opponents upon their own ground. "You yourselves admit that the priests who serve the Temple on the Sabbath must break the literal Sabbatical law in view of the higher duties of the Temple service." Then he continues, "*But I say unto you, there is something here greater than the Temple.*"‡ In these, as in many of Christ's words, there is more than meets the ear.§ When we remember the sanctity of the Temple in Jewish eyes, as the seat of the Shekinah, as the only place where God could ever be worshipped, we can conceive the weight of Christ's declaration that *his* manifestation was something greater than the Temple, and was to introduce

* Matt., xxiii. † Gal., iv., 4.

‡ I prefer *Lachmann's* reading (μεῖζον) both on internal and external grounds. I cannot, however, believe, with *De Wette*, that the passage refers to Christ's Messianic calling alone; but rather to his *whole manifestation*, of which his ministry as Messiah formed part. Similar expressions of Christ refer to his whole appearance, *e. g.*, Matt., xii., 8, speaks of his *person*. Conf. Luke, xi., 30.

§ Justly says Dr. *von Cölln* (Ideen üb. d. inneren Zusammenhang der Glaubenseinigung und Glaubensreinigung in der evangel. Kirche, *Leips.*, 1824, s. 10): "Every religious student of the Scriptures, however he may be satisfied with the sense that he has obtained from them by the aids of philosophy and history, must be constrained to acknowledge that the simplest words of the Saviour contain a depth and fulness of meaning which he can never boast of having mastered." These holy words, containing the germ of an unending developement, could only be understood in the Spirit (as by the Apostles); and they who had not received this Spirit, like the Judaizers, who adhered to the letter, could not but misunderstand them.

a revelation of the glory of God, and a mode of Divine worship to which the Temple-service was entirely subordinate. We may infer Christ's conclusion to have been, "If the priests have been freed from the literal observance of the Sabbath law because of their relation to the Temple, heretofore the highest seat of worship, how much more must my disciples be freed from the letter of that law by their relation to that which is greater than the Temple! (Their intercourse with *Him* was something greater than Temple-worship.) They have plucked the corn on the Sabbath, it is true, but they have done it that they might not be disturbed in their communion with the Son of Man, and in reliance upon his authority. They are free from guilt, then, for the *Son of Man is Lord even of the Sabbath.*" He thus laid the foundation for that true, spiritual worship to which the Temple-service was to give way.

Of the same character were those words of Jesus which taught a STEPHEN that Christ would destroy the Temple and remove its ritual-worship. (Acts, vi., 14.) Whether he learned this from the words recorded in John, ii., 19, or from some others, we leave for the present undecided. The doctrine of PAUL in regard to the relation between the Law and the Gospel was only an extension of the truth first uttered by Stephen. This doctrine could not have originated in Paul, without a point of departure for it in the instructions of Christ himself; still less, if those instructions had been in direct contradiction to it.

Christ's declaration, "*My yoke is easy and my burden light*" (Matt., xi., 30), was designed, indeed, primarily, to contrast his manner of teaching and leading men with that of the Pharisees; but it certainly meant far more. It contrasted his plan of salvation with legalism generally, of which Pharisaism was only the apex. Paul's doctrine on the subject is nothing but a developement of the intimation contained in these words.*

§ 55. *The Conversation with the Samaritan Woman.*

We have thus far confined ourselves to Christ's declarations as given

* *Schleiermacher* (in his *Hermeneutik*, s. 82) very aptly applies the oft-abused comparison between Christ and Socrates to illustrate the relation between the apostolic doctrines, especially those of Paul, and the immediate teachings of Christ. He justly remarks, that while there was a *similarity* in the fact that the teachings of Socrates were not written down by himself, but transmitted through his disciples, who marked them with their own individuality without at all obliterating the Socratic ground-colours, the substantial *difference* lay in this, that the affinity of the Apostles was closer than that of the followers of Socrates, "because the power of unity which emanated from Christ was in itself greater, and acted so powerfully upon those Apostles who, like Paul, had marked individual peculiarities, that they appealed, in their teachings, exclusively to Christ. Although Paul first brought out the idea of the conversion of the heathen into perfect clearness before the Apostles, yet he advocated it in no other power than that of Christ. Had not the idea been contained in Christ's teaching, the other Apostles would not have recognized Paul as a Christian, much less an Apostle" The same remark may be applied to many other important doctrines.

by Matthew, Mark, and Luke, avoiding John, because the credibility of his reports of Christ's discourses has been more disputed. But, having shown the tendency of Christ's doctrine of the Law from the first Gospels *alone*, we are surely now entitled to appeal to his conversation with the woman of Samaria (John, iv., 7–30), in which he set forth the Christian view, that religion was no more to be confined to any one place. In fact, the discourse involves no doctrine which cannot be found in Christ's declarations elsewhere recorded. Perfectly accordant with his declaration to the hostile Pharisees who clamoured so loudly for the ritual law—"*the manifestation of the Son of Man is greater than the Temple; and he is Lord of the Sabbath*"—was his answer to a woman (ignorant, to be sure, and destitute of a spiritual sense of the Divine, but yet free from prejudice, and susceptible of receiving instruction from him, because she believed him to be a prophet), when she inquired as to the right place to worship God: "The time is coming when the worship of God will be confined to no visible temple; for *the hour cometh, and now is, when the true worshippers shall worship the Father in spirit and in truth.*" This declaration could only have been founded on the fact that something *greater than the Temple* had appeared among men.

§ 56. *The "Destroying" and "Fulfilling" of the Law.*

But although we infer that Paul's doctrine of the disjunction of Christianity from the Mosaic law was derived, mediately at least, from Christ's own words, we must admit that the Judaizing Christians, unfit as they were, from their Jewish stand-point, fully to apprehend his teaching, might have found some support for their peculiar opinions both in his words and in his actions. Take, for instance, the passage, "*Think not that I am come to destroy the Law and the Prophets; I am not come to destroy, but to fulfil.*"* Their Jewish views might interpret this to mean that he did not intend to abrogate the ceremonial part of the law, but to bring about a strict observance of it. Nor shall we apply here the distinction between the moral and the ritual law; neither the connexion of the passage nor the stand-point of the Old Testament would justify this. Certainly, as he used the terms *Law* and *Prophets* to denote the two great divisions of the Old Testament, and declared he would not destroy either, he must have had in view the *entire* law; it was the law, as a *whole*, that he came not to destroy, but to fulfil.

We need only to understand correctly what kind of "destroying" it is which Christ disclaims. It is a "destroying" which excludes "fulfilling;" a destroying which is not at the same time a fulfilling. The general positive clause, "*I am come to fulfil,*" is used as proof of the special and negative clause, "*I am not come to destroy the Law and the Prophets;*" nor are we to make the former a special one, by seeking

* Matt. v 17

an object for it in the preceding words. On the contrary, the general proposition, "*I am come to fulfil*," which holds good of Christ's entire labours, is, in this case, specially applied to his relation to the Old Testament. Christ's activity is in no sense a destroying and negative, but in every respect a fulfilling and creative agency. For instance, by that agency human nature is to lose none of its *essential* features; but only to be freed from the bonds and defects which sin has imposed upon it, so that its *ideal*, as originally designed by the Creator, may become the *real*. This is *fulfilling;* but yet it must be accompanied by the *destroying* of whatever opposes it. We apply the same principle to Christ's relation to the Mosaic law. The Mosaic Institute, as the fundamental law of the *special* Theocracy exhibited in the Jewish nation, was a veil, a limited form, in which the will of GOD, the eternal law of the Theocracy, was appropriately impressed upon the men of that time. But the *general* and eternal Theocratic law could not find its free developement and fulfilment in the form of an outward State law. The law (in its whole extent I mean, including what is called in a narrower sense the moral, as well as the ritual law) aimed to realize the will of GOD, to present the true δικαιοσύνη under the relations above defined. But what the law, in its whole extent, aimed at, is *accomplished* through Christ; the veil is rent, the bonds are loosed by the liberating Spirit, and the law reaches its before unattainable fulfilment. This fulfilment, indeed, involves the removal of all obstructions; but this destroying process cannot be called *destroying*, as it is an essential condition, and a negative element, of the fulfilment itself. So the fulfilment of prophecy in the manifestation and labours of Christ necessarily involved the destruction of the prophetic veil and covering of the Messianic idea.*

The Ebionites, adhering only to the letter, misunderstood Christ's declarations on this subject; but Paul, viewing them in their true spirit and universal bearing, obtained those views on the relation of the Law and the Gospel which he presents in such passages as Rom., iii., 31: viii., 3, 4.

§ 57. *The Interpolation in Luke*, vi., 4. (Cod. Cant.)

There is a traditional account of another remarkable saying of Christ in regard to the observance of the Sabbath,† viz., that on a certain occasion, seeing a man at work on the Sabbath, he said to him, "*Happy art thou if thou knowest what thou art doing; but if thou dost not know, thou art accursed, and a transgressor of the law.*" We must not leave this unnoticed, for as other words of Christ which did not find place in

* We shall see hereafter how this interpretation of Christ's words is verified in the whole train of thought in the Sermon on the Mount.

† In the *Cod. Cant.* (Cod. Bezæ), this passage immediately follows Luke, vi., 4: "τῇ αὐτῇ ἡμέρᾳ θεασάμενός τινα ἐργαζόμενον τῷ σαββάτῳ εἶπεν αὐτῷ· ἄνθρωπε, εἰ μὲν οἶδας τί ποιεῖς, μακάριος εἶ· εἰ δὲ μὴ οἶδας, ἐπικατάρατος καὶ παραβάτης εἶ τοῦ νόμου."

the canonical Gospels were handed down by tradition,* so it is *possible* that an event of the character here related may have been preserved in some collection of evangelical traditions (*e.g.*, an apocryphal Gospel or some other), and may have been afterward transferred to Luke, vi., 4, as having an affinity with the context there. There is nothing in the words themselves which Christ might not have uttered under certain circumstances; for their import is a sentiment which he always made prominent; viz., that all depends upon the *spirit* in which one acts. The force of the passage is, "Happy is he who has arrived at the conviction that God must be worshipped, not at special times and places, but in spirit and in truth; and who feels himself free from the Old Testament Sabbatical law. But he who, while acknowledging that law, allows himself to be induced by outward motives to labour on the Sabbath, is a guilty man; the law is in force for *him*, and, by violating his conscience for the sake of an external good, he pronounces his own condemnation."

It is quite a different question, however, whether this narrative does not bear internal marks of improbability; whether, under the specified circumstances, Christ would have spoken as he is reported to have done. First, it is hardly possible to imagine that any one, at that day, among the Jews of Palestine, would have ventured to labour on the Sabbath. Again, it is hard to believe that Christ would have pronounced such labour in any wise *good*, unless it were performed in the discharge of a special duty. Such a procedure, more than any other, would have laid him open to the reproach of contemning the law. He looked upon the law as having been a divinely ordained part of the developement of God's kingdom, and as, therefore, necessary, until the period when the *new* form of that kingdom should go into operation. Only in the progress of this new form was the abrogation of the law to follow from the consciousness of redemption through Christ; and then, indeed, its *destruction* would be one with its fulfilment; and until that point of progress arrived, Christ himself set the example of a conscientious observance of the law. He opposed the Pharisaic statutes, indeed, but it was because they took the law in its letter, not in its spirit, and surrounded its observance with difficulties. He made it a fundamental point, that all true obedience must spring from piety and love; but still it was obedience to the *law*. He gave therefore, as we have seen, *intimations* only of that higher period in which the law was to be done away; intimations, moreover, which could only be understood through his own Spirit, after his work upon earth was done. Hence he certainly could have pronounced no action good in which man's will allowed itself to anticipate God's order, especially an action, grounded on motives understood by nobody, which might have injuriously affected

* Acts, xx., 35.

the religious convictions of others. Paul lays down quite a contrary rule in 1 Cor., viii. Nor did Christ himself act in such a way in other cases.

There is, then, very poor authority for this passage, either internal or external. Its invention was probably suggested by the words of Paul in Rom., xiv., 22, 23, and affords a very good illustration of the difference between mere individual inventions and the genuine historical traditions of the Evangelists.

We close our survey of Christ's sayings in regard to his relations to the Old Testament with a remark directly suggested by it, from which the weightiest consequences may be deduced.

The manner in which he contrasted the Old Testament with its fulfilment, the New, and elevated the least of Christians above all the prophets, shows how clearly he distinguished the kernel from its perishable shell, the Divine idea from its temporary veil, the truth which lay in germ in the Old Testament, from the contracted form in which it presented itself to Old Testament minds. Applying this general principle to individual cases as they arise, we may learn how to interpret, in Christ's own sense, the figures which he employed to illustrate his Messianic world-dominion. In this way some of the results at which we have already arrived may find further confirmation.

CHAPTER III.

NEW FORM OF THE IDEA OF THE PERSON OF THE THEOCRATIC KING.

§ 58. *The Names* Son of God *and* Son of Man.

OUR conception of the *person* of the Messiah, as Theocratic King, is closely connected with that which we may entertain of the kingdom of God itself, and of its process of developement. In reference to both, Jesus joined himself indeed to the existing Jewish conceptions, but, at the same time, infused into them a new spirit and a higher regenerating element.

Both of the names which he applied to himself—*Son of God* and *Son of Man*—are to be found among the designations of the Messiah in the Old Testament; but he used them in a far higher sense than was current among the Jews. He obviously employed them antithetically: they contain correlative ideas, and cannot be thoroughly understood apart from their reciprocal relation. It is clear from Matt., xvi., 16; xxvi., 63; John, i., 50, and from all that is known of the current theo logical language of the Jews at that time, that the name "*Son of God*" was the most common designation of Messiah, as the best adapted to denote his highest dignity, that of Theocratic King. The name "*Son of Man*" involves, indeed, an allusion to the description of the Messiah in Dan., vii. (further illustrated in Christ's last words before the high-priests, Matt., xxvi., 64); but it is certain that this name was not among the more usual or best known titles of Messiah. This may explain why,* when Jesus on a certain occasion had stated a fact in regard to himself as Son of Man [viz., his approaching death] which did not accord with prevailing ideas, that his hearers began to doubt whether he did not mean to designate by that title some other person than the Messiah. It is used by none of the apostles for that purpose; and, indeed, nowhere in the New Testament, except in the discourses of Christ and in that of Stephen (Acts, vii., 56); and in this last case it is probable, as *Olshausen* justly remarks, that Stephen had an immediate and vivid intuition of Jesus, as he had seen him in his human form.

§ 59. *Import of the Title* Son of Man, *as used by Christ himself.—Rejection of Alexandrian and other Analogies.*

Christ must, therefore, have had special reasons for adopting, with an obvious predilection, the less known Messianic title. Even if we were to grant that he used it more frequently because of its less obvious application, in order, at first, to lead the Jews gradually to recognize him as Messiah; still we should not have a sufficient explanation of his employing it so generally and so emphatically.† We find a better reason for it in Christ's conscious relation to the human race; a relation which stirred the very depths of his heart. He called himself the "Son of Man" because he had appeared as a man; because he belonged to mankind; because he had done such great things even for *human* nature (Matt., ix., 8); because he was to glorify that nature; because he was himself the realized ideal of humanity.‡

* John, xii., 34.

† I must differ here from *Scholten, Lücke, Von Cöln* (Bibl. Dogm., ii., 16), and *Strauss* (Leben Jesu); and agree with *Schleiermacher, Tholuck, Olshausen,* and *Kling* (Stud. u. Krit, 1836, i., 137). Justly says *Schleiermacher* of the title "Son of Man," "Christ would not have adopted it had he not been conscious of a complete participation in human nature. Its application would have been pointless, however, had he not used it in a sense inapplicable to other men; and it was pregnant with reference to the distinctive differences between him and them" (Dogmatik, ii., 91, 3d. ed). Certainly there is manifest, in the often-repeated expressions, sayings, and proverbs uttered by Christ, more the impression of an original and creative mind than a mere appropriation of what might have been given to his hand by his age and nation. It is one of the merits of the great man whose words we have just quoted, that he vindicated this truth in many ways in opposition to a shallow theology. The unclean spirit which he banished is now endeavouring, with seven others worse than himself, to take possession of this age, in which endeavour, please God, he will not succeed.

‡ Conf. Matt., xii., 8; John, i., 52; iii., 13; v., 27; vi., 53. The force of the first passage in John (i., 52) is, that Christ would glorify humanity by restoring its fellowship with celes

We certainly cannot find in Christ's use of the title any trace of the Alexandrian Theologoumenon of the archetype of humanity in the *Logos*, of *Philo's* distinction between the idea of humanity and its manifestation (or the Cabbalistic *Adam Cadmon*); notwithstanding it was not by accident that so many *ideal* elements, formed from a commingling of Judaism and Hellenism, were given as points of departure to the *realism* of Christianity; although this last was grounded on the highest fact in history.

So, too, the fundamental idea of the title "Son of Man" is, perhaps, allied to that involved in the Jewish designation of Messiah as the "second Adam;" but it is clear that Christ was not led by the latter fact to employ it. Much rather do we suppose that the name, although used by the prophets, received its loftier and more profound significance from Christ's own Divine and human consciousness, independent of all other sources. It would have been the height of arrogance in any man to assume such a relation to humanity, to style himself absolutely MAN. But He, to whom it was natural thus to style himself, indicated thereby his elevation above all other sons of men—the Son of God in the Son of Man.

The two titles, "Son of GOD" and "Son of Man," therefore, bear evidently a reciprocal relation to each other. And we conclude that as Christ used the one to designate his human personality, so he employed the other to point out his Divine; and that as he attached a sense far more profound than was common to the former title, so he ascribed a deeper meaning than was usual to the latter.

§ 60. *Import of the Title* SON OF GOD.

(1.) John's Sense of the Title accordant with that of the other Evangelists.

We are indebted to John's Gospel, more than to either of the others,

tial powers. The second (iii., 13) imports that he reveals his Divine being in human nature, and lives in heaven as man. The third (v., 27), that as man he will judge the human race. The fourth (vi., 53), that we must thoroughly take to ourselves and be penetrated by the flesh and blood (*i. e.*, the pure humanity, the form of which he assumed to reveal the Divine) of him who can be called *man* in a sense that can be predicated of no other, and who himself has incarnated the Divinity. (On the passage from Matt., see p. 89.) In Matt., ix., 8, there is in the statement that the entire human nature is glorified in Christ, an intimation of what is expressed in the title "Son of Man" in Christ's sense of it.

It is remarkable, that while this emphatic title of the Son of Man appears in the discourses of Christ both in the synoptical Gospels and John, that its deeper sense, although not to be mistaken in some of the passages in the former, is far more vividly expressed in John. Yet if it were the case (as has been said) that John, following the prevalent opinion, designed to represent Jesus as the Logos appearing in humanity, and, leaving the human nature in the back-ground, to present the Divine conspicuously, he could not have used this title so frequently. There is no trace of Alexandrianism in John, nor can his preference for the expression be attributed to his individual peculiarities, for there is nothing of the kind in his Epistles. The only individual peculiarity that we can detect in John, in this respect, is his susceptibility to impression from certain emphatic expressions especially such as relate to the person of Christ.

for those expressions of Christ which relate especially to the indwelling within him of the Divine essence. It does not, however (as some suppose), follow from this that John, consciously or unconsciously, remodelled the discourses of Christ according to the Alexandrian theology. The fact may be explained on entirely other grounds, *e. g.*, his more intimate connexion with Christ, and the peculiar profoundness of his mind; moreover, the discourses recorded by him are longer and more consecutively didactic and controversial than those given by the other Evangelists. The impartiality, too, with which he sets forth the pure humanity of Christ is sufficient to prove the groundlessness of such a reproach.

If we can only find individual expressions in the other Evangelists which involve the idea of the "Son of God" in John's sense, we shall have proved satisfactorily that the latter was derived immediately from Christ himself. Now Matt., xi., 27, "*No man knoweth the Son but the Father, neither knoweth any man the Father save the Son,*" is just such a passage. It intimates precisely such a mysterious relation between the Father and the Son as John more fully sets forth as imparted to him by the revelation of Christ. So, also, the question propounded by Christ to the Pharisees, "*What think ye of the Christ? whose Son is he?*" could have had no other object than to lead them to conceive Messiah as the Son of God in a higher sense than they were accustomed to. Again, the heathen centurion (Matt., viii., 5), who deemed his roof unworthy of Christ, and begged him, without approaching his abode, to heal the sick servant by a word, certainly considered him as a superior being who had ministering spirits at command. He evidently did not form his idea of Christ from the common Jewish conceptions of the Messiah; on the contrary, his explanation (verse 9) of the impression which he had received (either from the accounts of others, or from personal observation of Christ's person and labours) is perfectly in keeping with his character and notions while as yet a pagan.* But Christ (who always rejected any honours that were ascribed to him from erroneous views†) not only did not correct the centurion, but held his faith up as a model.

In a word, the whole image of Christ presented in the synoptical Gospels exhibits a majesty far transcending human nature, and utterly irreconcilable with Ebionitish conceptions. A manifestation so extraordinary presupposes an inward essence such as that which John's Gospel fully unfolds to us.

(2.) And confirmed by Paul's.

Nor could the origin of *Paul's* doctrine of the person of Christ be

* The whole account bears the inimitable stamp of historical truth.

† Luke, xi., 27; xviii., 19.

explained, unless Christ himself had given statements corresponding to those recorded in John's Gospel. So, too, the various theological tendencies that developed themselves after the apostolic age presuppose a turn of thought intermediate between that especially exhibited in Matthew and that of Paul. Precisely such an intermediate point was occupied by John.*

* Lücke has justly remarked upon the difference between the classic, creative tendencies of the apostolic times, and the later imitations of them. The dividing line between the former and the latter is distinctly marked. The later developement of Christian doctrine presupposes the different apostolic types of doctrine, and among them that of John. It is, therefore, utterly unhistorical to seek the origin of such a Gospel as John's in later Church developements (as some attempt to do). The latter are utterly destitute of the harmonious unity of Christian spiritual elements that distinguishes the former

PART II.

THE MEANS AND INSTRUMENTS OF CHRIST.

CHAPTER I.

A. THE MEANS OF CHRIST IN GENERAL.

§ 61. *Christ a Spiritual Teacher.*

AS the kingdom which Christ came to establish was a spiritual one, intended to develope itself outwardly from within, so the means which he employed in its foundation were entirely of a spiritual nature. In his declaration before Pilate,* after he had (1) disclaimed any purpose of setting up an earthly kingdom, affirming at the same time (2) that he was ***King*** in a certain sense, he added (3) that *he came into the world to testify of the truth.* These three propositions, taken together, set forth his purpose to found his kingdom, not by worldly means, but by the testimony of the truth. But he testified of the truth by his whole life, by his words and works, comprising the entire self-revelation of Him who could say, "*I am the Truth.*"

Inasmuch, therefore, as he himself designates the testimony of the truth as his means of founding his kingdom; inasmuch, also, as he appeared first as PROPHET, in order to lead those who recognized him as such to recognize him also as Messiah and Theocratic King, we must treat of his work as Prophet, or of his exercise of the office of DIVINE TEACHER, as the instrument by which he laid the ground-work of his reign among men.

§ 62. *Different Theatres of Christ's Labours as Teacher.*

Christ exercised his office as teacher in two distinct theatres, Galilee and Jerusalem; and his mode of teaching varied accordingly. That carnal mania for miracles (directly contrasted by Paul† with the Greek pride of reason) which infected the Jews every where, whether in Galilee or Jerusalem, and added presumption to their narrow-mindedness, proved, indeed, in both places, the greatest hindrance to their reception of the words of Christ. This common Jewish feature of opposition to the spirit of Christ justified the Apostle John, when he was reviewing the past in its great outlines, in embracing not only the dominant Pharisaic party at Jerusalem, but also the hosts of Galilee, under the general conception of Ἰουδαῖοι.‡

* John, xviii., 33-38. † 1 Cor., i., 22. ‡ See John's Gospel, *passim*.

Yet as the people of Galilee were of a more simple turn of mind, and were less subject to the influence of Pharisaism than those of Jerusalem, they must naturally have been more susceptible to his instructions. But a prophet is not wont to be held in honour in his own country; nor was the narrow-minded, carnal supranaturalism of the Galileans likely to recognize in the son of the carpenter of Nazareth the man sent of God. It was not until the displays of his power in the metropolis of the Theocracy had revealed him in a higher light, that he found a better reception on his return to the villages of Galilee.*

It was partly, then, in Jerusalem, where the Jews gathered together from all the world at the Passover, and partly in Galilee, where he spoke to the people, clustered in more or less numerous groups about him, especially as he walked along the shores of Genesareth, that the scene of his labours as a public teacher lay.

§ 63. *Choice and Training of the Apostles to be subordinate Teachers.*

Those who had no ear to hear the teachings of Christ fell off one by one, and left around him a narrow and abiding circle of susceptible souls, who were gradually more and more attracted by him, and more and more deeply imbued with his spirit. A closer [the closest] circle still was formed of his constant companions, the Apostles. As the seed which he sowed was received and developed so differently in the soils of different minds, and as the import of his teaching could not be thoroughly comprehended until his work upon earth was finished, there was danger that the confused traditions of the multitude would hand down to posterity a very imperfect image of himself and his doctrines, and that the necessary instrument for the foundation of the kingdom of God, viz., the propagation of the truth, would be wanting.

It might be supposed that Christ could have best guarded against this result by transmitting his doctrine to all after ages in a form written by himself. And had He, in whom the Divine and the human were combined in unbroken harmony, intended to do this, he could not but have given to the Church the perfect *contents* of his doctrine in a perfect *form.* Well was it, however, for the course of developement which God intended for his kingdom, that what could be done was not done. The truth of God was not to be presented in a fixed and absolute form, but in manifold and peculiar representations, designed to complete each other, and which, bearing the stamp at once of God's inspiration and man's imperfection, were to be developed by the activity of free minds, in free and lively appropriation of what God had given by his Spirit. This will appear yet more plainly hereafter, from the principles of Christ's mode of instruction, as set forth by himself. At present we content ourselves with one single remark. Christ's declaration, "*It is*

* John, iv., 44, 45.

the Spirit that quickeneth; the flesh profiteth nothing,"* and his emphatic rejection of an act of worship that, without thought of the Spirit, deified only his outward form,† may serve to guard all after ages against that tendency to deify the *form* which is so fatal a bar against all recognition of the *essence*. What could have contributed more to produce such a tendency than a written document from Christ's own hand?

Since, therefore, Christ intended to leave no such fixed rule of doctrine for all ages, written by himself, it was the more necessary for him to select organs capable of transmitting to posterity a correct image of himself and his teaching. Such organs were the apostles, and their training constituted no unimportant part of his work as a teacher.

CHAPTER II.

CHRIST'S MODE OF TEACHING IN REGARD TO ITS METHOD AND FORM.

A. GENERAL PRINCIPLES.

§ 64. *His mode of Teaching adapted to the Stand-point of his Hearers.*

WE shall first seek, in the intimations of Christ himself, for the principles of his mode of teaching, and the grounds on which he adopted it.

Such an intimation may be found in Matt., xiii., 52. After he had uttered and expounded several parables in regard to the kingdom of GOD, and had been assured by the apostles that they understood him, he continued: "From the example I have given you, in thus making hidden truths clear by means of parables, ye may learn that *every scribe who is instructed into the kingdom of Heaven is like a householder, who bringeth forth out of his treasure things new and old.*" As a householder shows his visitors his jewels; exhibits, in pleasing alternation, the modern and the antique, and leads them from the common to the rare, so must the teacher of Divine truth, in the new manifestation of the kingdom of GOD, bring out of his treasures of knowledge truths old and new, and gradually lead his hearers from the old and usual to the new and unaccustomed. Utterly unlike the rabbins, with their obstinate and slavish adherence to the letter, the teachers of the new epoch were to adapt themselves freely to the circumstances of their hearers, and, in consequence, to present the truth under manifold varieties of form. In a word, Christ himself, as a teacher, was the model for his disciples.

As the passage above quoted referred primarily to the *parabolic* mode of teaching which Christ had just employed, we find in it an im-

* John, vi., 63. † Luke, xi., 27.

portant reason for the frequent use which he made of figures and similitudes. It was, namely, in order to bring new and higher truths vividly before the minds of his hearers, by means of illustrations drawn from objects familiar to them in common life and nature.

But the passage can be applied also to many other features of his mode of teaching; for instance, to his habit of leading his hearers, step by step, from the stand-point of the Old Testament to that of the New; adapting himself to the old representations and the Jewish modes of thought and speech derived from them (especially those which referred to Messiah's kingdom), and thus imparting the new spirit under the ancient and accustomed forms. All his *accommodation* to forms finds its explanation here.

§ 65. *His Teaching presented Seeds and Stimulants of Thought.*

Again, he told his disciples (John, xvi., 25) that up to that time he had veiled the truth in parables, but that the time was approaching when he should declare plainly and openly all that he had to tell them of his Father. He thus taught them that they would be enabled, at a later period, by the aid of the illuminating Spirit, to develope from his discourses the hidden truths which they enfolded. It must, therefore, by no means surprise us to find that the full import of most of his words was not comprehended by his contemporaries: such a result, indeed, was just what we might expect. He would not have been "Son of God" and "Son of Man," had not his words, like his works, with all their adaptation to the circumstances of the times, contained some things that were inexplicable; had they not borne concealed within them the germ of an infinite developement, reserved for future ages to unfold. It is *this* feature (and all the Evangelists concur in their representations of it) which distinguishes Christ from all other teachers of men. Advance as they may, they can never reach him; their only task need be, by taking Him more and more into their life and thought, to learn better how to bring forth the treasures that lie concealed in him.*

The form of his expressions, whether he uttered parables, proverbs, maxims, or apparent paradoxes, was intended to spur men's minds to profounder thought, to awaken the Divine consciousness within, and so teach them to *understand* that which at first served only as a mental stimulus. It was designed to impress indelibly upon the memory of his hearers truths perhaps as yet not fully intelligible, but which would grow clear as the Divine life was formed within them, and become an ever-increasing source of spiritual light. His doctrine was not to be

* *Schleiermacher* says beautifully (Christliche Sittenlehre, p. 72), that all our progress [in Divine knowledge] must consist solely in more correctly understanding and more completely appropriating to ourselves that which is in Christ.

propagated as a lifeless stock of tradition, but to be received as a living Spirit by willing minds, and brought out into full consciousness, according to its import, by free spiritual activity. Its individual parts, too, were only to be apprehended in their first proportions, in the complete connexion of that higher consciousness which He was to call forth in man. The form of teaching which repelled the stupid, and passed unheeded and misunderstood by the unholy, roused susceptible minds to deeper thought, and rewarded their inquiries by the discovery of ever-increasing treasures.

§ 66. *Its Results dependent upon the Spirit of the Hearers.*

But the attainment of this end depended upon the susceptibility of the hearers. So far as they hungered for true spiritual food, so far as the parable stimulated them to deeper thought, and so far only, it revealed new riches. Those with whom this was really the case were accustomed to wait until the throng had left their Master, or, gathering round him in a narrow circle, in some retired spot, to seek clearer light on points which the parable had left obscure. The scene described in Mark, iv., 10, shows us that *others besides the twelve apostles* were named among those who remained behind to ask him questions after the crowd had dispersed. Not only did such questions afford the Saviour an opportunity of imparting more thorough instruction, but those who felt constrained to offer them were thereby drawn into closer fellowship with him. He became better acquainted with the souls that were longing for salvation.

The greater number, however, in their stupidity, did not trouble themselves to penetrate the shell in order to reach the kernel. Yet they must at least have perceived that they had *understood nothing;* they could not learn separate phrases from Christ (as they might from other religious teachers) and *think* they comprehended them, while they did not. And so, in proportion to the susceptibility of his hearers, the parables of Christ revealed sacred things to some and veiled them from others, who were destined, through their own fault, to remain in darkness. The pearls, as he himself said, were not to be cast before swine. Thus, like those "hard sayings"* which were to some the "words of Life," and to others an insupportable "offence," the parables served to sift and purge the throng of Christ's hearers.

A single example will bring this vividly before us. On a certain occasion, when Christ had pronounced a parable, and the multitude had departed, the earnest seekers after truth gathered about him to ask its interpretation.† He expressed his gratification at their eagerness to

* John, vi., 60. † Luke, viii., 10; Mark, iv., 11.

learn the true sense of his words, and said: "*Unto you it is given* to know the mysteries of the kingdom of God, but to others in parables* [without the explanations that are given to susceptible minds], that they may see with their eyes, and yet not see; that they may hear with their ears, and yet not hear." There is here expressed a moral necessity, a judgment of God, that those who were destitute of the right will (on which all depends, and without which the Divine "drawing" is in vain), could understand nothing of the things of the Lord which they saw and heard. So long as they remained as they were, the whole life of Christ, according to the same general law, remained to them an inexplicable parable.† It is worthy of remark, that "*the others,*" with whom Luke contrasts the inquiring disciples, are styled by Mark (iv., 11) "*those that are without.*" The simplest way to interpret this phrase is to apply it to those who did not enter to ask a solution of what they had not understood; it may mean those who were outside of the narrower fellowship around Christ; but in either sense the result is the same.‡

"The mystery," in the passage above quoted, is something hidden from men of worldly minds; incomprehensible to them, and to all who are excluded, by their spirit and disposition, from the kingdom of God. And this is the case with *all* truths that relate to that kingdom, however simple and clear they may seem to those whose inner life has made them at home in it.

After Christ had explained the parable to his disciples, he took oc

* *I. e.*, they followed the inward "drawing of God (John, vi., 44, 45), and thence became susceptible of Divine impressions.

† According to Mark and Luke, the disciples asked of Christ the *meaning* of the parable; according to Matthew (xiii., 10), they inquired *why* he spoke to the multitude in parables. In Luke there is only an allusion to Isai., vi., 9; in Matthew the passage is cited in full. In both respects the statement in Mark and Luke seems to be the more simple and original. The apostles had more reason to ask the meaning of the parables than to find out Christ's motive for uttering them; yet as Christ, in reply, *did* state that motive, it was perhaps implied in the question. The full quotation of the passage in Isaiah was a natural change, and accorded with Matthew's habit. The connexion is well preserved in Matthew, and the difference between his statement and the others is merely formal; nor is there the slightest ground to suppose that the author of Matthew simply worked out Mark's account or some other which lay before him. It goes on naturally thus: in answer to the question *why* he spoke to the multitude in parables, Christ replied (v. 11), that it was not given to them, as to the disciples, to know the mysteries of the kingdom of God; the *reason*, founded in their moral dispositions, is stated in v. 12; and then, in v. 13, the Divine sentence, that "on account of their stupidity he spoke to them only in parables." There is nothing inconsistent here, nor is any arbitrary procedure attributed to Christ; for, in fact, the parables served to *veil* as well as to *reveal;* and they did the one or the other, according to the moral disposition of those that heard them.

‡ Whatever may have been the original expression of Christ in this passage, the fact that Luke speaks of "mysteries" in the plural, and Mark of "mystery" in the singular, contributes, at any rate, to its elucidation. We have here another proof that the germs of Paul's teaching are to be found in the discourses of Christ: this passage contains Paul's whole doctrine of the relation of the natural mind to the knowledge of Divine things; *e. g.* 1 Cor., ii., 14.

casion, from this particular case, to impress upon them the general lesson that every thing depended on the spirit in which they received his words. He came not (he told them) to hide his light, but to enlighten the darkness of men. It was his calling to be the Light of the world (Mark, iv., 21). (He spoke in order to *reveal* the truth, not to hide it.) The truth which he had obscurely intimated was to unfold itself for the instruction of all mankind (v. 22; cf. John, xvi., 25). Yet the organs who were destined to unfold it must have "*hearing ears*" (v. 23). And he proceeds (v. 24), "*Take heed, therefore, what ye hear* (be not like the stupid multitude, who perceive only the outward word); *and unto you that hear shall more be given* (my revelations to you will increase in proportion to the susceptibility with which you appropriate the truths which I have intimated)." And he concludes with the general law,* "Whosoever has—in reality *has*—whosoever has made to himself a *living* possession of the truths which he has heard, to him shall more be ever given. But he that has received it only as something *dead* and outward, shall lose even that which he seems to have, but really has not."† His knowledge, unspiritual and dead, will turn out to be worthless—the shell without the kernel.

Some have supposed that these words (v. 25) were merely a proverb of common life, of which Christ made a higher application. But the proofs that have been offered‡ in favour of the existence of such a proverb are by no means to the point; and, in fact, it would be hardly true applied to temporal possessions, for the poor man can increase his small store by industry and prudence; and the rich, without those qualities, may soon lose his heaped-up treasures. The saying is fully true only in an ethical sense; it speaks of moral, and not material possessions. Applied, however, as a proverb, it must refer, not to mere possession, but to property held as such, and can only mean that he who holds property, as his *own*, will not keep it as dead capital, but gain more with it; while he, on the other hand, who does not know how to use what he has, will lose it. Thus understood, the words are not only fully applicable to the special case before us, but also to manifold relations in the sphere of moral life.

The apostles had as yet, in their intercourse with their Master, received but *little;* but that little was imprinted on their hearts. They did not, like the multitude, receive the word only by the hearing of the ear, but made it thoroughly and spiritually their own. And thus was laid within them the foundation of Christian progress.

* Mark, iv., 25; Luke, viii., 18; Matt., xiii., 12.

† I must hold *ὃ δοκεῖ ἔχειν* to be the true reading of Luke, viii., 18, in spite of what *De Wette* says to the contrary.

‡ Conf. *Wetstein* on Matt., xiii., 12

§ 67. *His Mode of Teaching corresponds to the General Law of Developement of the Kingdom of God.*

It was, then, according to Christ's own words, a peculiar aim and law of his teaching, to awaken a sense for Divine things in the human mind, and to make further communications in proportion to the degree of living appropriation that might be made of what was given. And this corresponds with the general laws established by Christ for the developement of the kingdom of God. It is his law, that choice must be made, by the free determination of the will, between God and the world, before the susceptibility for Divine things (which may exist even in the as yet fettered soul, if it incline towards God), and the emotions of love* for the Divine which springs from that susceptibility, can arise in the human heart. The heart tends to the point from whence it seeks its treasure (its highest good).† The sense for the Divine, the inward light, *must* shine. If worldly tendencies extinguish it, the darkness must be total. Christ's words, Christ's manifestation, can find no entrance. The Divine light streams forth in vain if the light-perceiving eye of the soul is darkened.‡ The parable of the sower vividly sets forth the necessity of a susceptible soil, before the seed of the Word can germinate and bring forth fruit. And so he constantly assured the carnal Jews that they could not understand him in their existing state of mind. He who will not follow the Divine "drawing" (revealed in his dawning consciousness of God) can never attain to faith in Christ, and must feel himself repelled from his words. The carnal mind can find nothing in him.§ The *form* of his language (so he told those who took offence at it‖) appeared incomprehensible, because its *import*, the truth of God, could not be apprehended by souls estranged from Him. The form and the substance were alike paradoxical to them. The uncongenial soul found his mode of speaking strange and foreign; it is foreign no more when the spirit, through its newly-roused sense for the Divine, yields itself up to the higher Spirit. The *words* can be understood only by those who have a sympathy for the spirit and the substance.

Thus, then, the other Evangelists agree with John in regard to the fundamental principles of Christ's mode of teaching.

* *Pascal* (Art de Persuader), "qu'il faut aimer les choses divines, pour les connaitre. Beautifully said.

† Matt., vi., 21.

‡ Luke, xii., 34; Matt., vi., 22.

§ John, vi., 44.

‖ John, viii., 33, 44. In v. 43, λαλία expresses the *mode* of speaking. The *substance* is expressed by λόγος. See *Lücke's* excellent remarks on the passage.

B. CHRIST'S USE OF PARABLES.

§ 68 *Idea of the Parable.—Distinction between Parable, Fable, and Mythus.*

Without doubt the form of Christ's communications was in some degree determined by the mental peculiarities of the people among whom he laboured, viz., the Jews and Orientals. We may find in this *one* reason for his use of parables; and we must esteem it as a mark of his freedom of mind and creative originality, that he so adapted to his own purposes a form of instruction that was especially current among the Jews. But yet his whole method of teaching, as we have already set it forth, would have led him, independently of his relations to the people around him, to adopt this mode of communicating truth. Not inaptly has one of the old writers compared the parables of Christ's discourses to the parabolic character of his whole manifestation, representing, as it did, the supernatural in a natural form.*

We may define the parables as representations through which the truths pertaining to the kingdom of God are vividly exhibited by means of special relations of common life, taken either from nature or the world of mankind. A general truth is set forth under the likeness of a particular fact, or a continuous narrative, commonly derived from the lower sphere of life; the operations of nature, and the qualities of inferior animals, or the acts of men in their mutual relations with each other, being assumed as the basis of the representation. Those parables which are derived entirely from the sphere of nature are grounded on the typical relations that exist† between Nature and Spirit. So, in the vine and its branches, Christ finds a type of the relation between himself and those who are members of his body. He is the *true* Vine The law whose *reality* finds place in the spiritual life is only imaged and typified in nature.

Even though the *fable* be so defined as to be included in the parable, as the species is comprehended in the genus, still the latter, especially as Christ employs it, has always its own distinctive characteristics. The parable is allied to the fable, as used by Æsop, so far forth as both differ from the *Mythus* (an unconscious invention), by employing statements of fact, not pretended to be historical, merely as coverings for the exhibition of a general truth; the latter only being presented to the mind of the hearer or reader as real. But the parable is distinguished from the fable by this, that in the latter, qualities or acts of

* Διότι καὶ ὁ κύριος οὐκ ὢν κοσμικὸς, ὡς κοσμικὸς εἰς ἀνθρώπους ἦλθεν. Strom., vi., 677.

† "It can readily be shown that the parables, as used by Christ, had the significance of their types. Nature, as she has disclosed herself to the mind of man, must in them bear witness of Spirit." *Steffens* (Religionsphilosophie, i., 146). And so *Schelling*, on the relation between Nature and History, "They are to each other parable and interpretation." (Philos. Schriften, 1809, 457.)

a higher class of beings may be attributed to a lower (*e.g.*, those of men to brutes); while in the former, the lower sphere is kept perfectly distinct from the higher one which it serves to illustrate. The beings and powers thus introduced always follow the law of their nature, but their acts, according to this law, are used to figure those of a higher race. The fable cannot be true according to its form, *e. g.*, when brutes are introduced thinking, speaking, and acting like men; but the representations of the parable always correspond to the facts of nature, or the occurrences of civil and domestic life, and remind the hearer of events and phenomena within his own experience. The mere introduction of brutes, as personal agents, in the fable, is not sufficient to distinguish it from the parable, which may make use of the same contrivance; as, for instance, indeed, Christ employs the *sheep* in one of his parables. The great distinction here, also, lies in what has already been remarked; brutes introduced in the parable act according to the law of their nature, and the two spheres of nature and the kingdom of GOD are carefully separated from each other. Hence the reciprocal relations of brutes to each other are not made use of, as these could furnish no appropriate image of the relation between man and the kingdom of God. And as the lower animals are, by an impulse of their nature, attached to man as a being of a higher order, Divine, as it were, in comparison to themselves, and destined to rule over them, the relations between man and this inferior race may serve very well to illustrate the still higher relations of the former to the kingdom of GOD and the Saviour. Thus, for instance, Christ employs the connexion of *sheep* and the *shepherd* to give a vivid image of the relations of human souls to their Divine guide.

There is ground for this distinction between parable and fable, both in the *form* and in the *substance*. In the form, because the parable intends that the objects of nature and the occurrences of every-day life shall be associated with higher truths, and thus not only illustrate them, but preserve them constantly in the memory. In the substance, because, although single acts of domestic or social virtue might find points of likeness in the qualities of the lower animals (not morality in general, for this, like religion, is too lofty to be thus illustrated), the dignity of the sphere of Divine life would be essentially lowered by transferring it to a class of beings entirely destitute of corresponding qualities.

§ 69. *Order in which the Parables were Delivered.—Their Perfection.—Mode of Interpreting them.*

We find many parables placed together in Matthew, xiii.; and the question naturally arises whether it is probable that Christ uttered so many at one and the same time. We can readily conceive that he should use various parables in succession in order to present the same truth or several closely related truths, in different forms; this variety would tend to excite attention, to present the one truth more clearly by such various illustration, to put the one subject before the beholder's eye more steadily, in many points of view, and thus to imprint it indelibly upon his memory. But it is not to be supposed that Christ delivered a succession of parables different both in form and matter, or, if somewhat alike in form, different in scope and design; for this could only have confused the minds of his hearers, and thus frustrated the very purpose of this mode of instruction.

It will be easy to gather what is necessary to the *perfection* of the parable, from what we have said of its nature. In the first place, the fact selected from the lower sphere of life should be perfectly adapted, in its own nature, to give a vivid representation of the higher truth; and, secondly, the individual traits of the lower fact itself should be clearly exhibited according to nature. Hence, in order to understand the parables correctly, we must endeavour to seize upon the single truth which the parabolic dress is designed to illustrate, and refer all the rest to this. The separate features, which serve to give roundness and distinctness to the picture of the lower fact, may aid us in obtaining a more many-sided view of the one truth, the higher sphere corresponding to the lower in more respects than one (*e. g.*, the parables of the *shepherd* and the *sower*); but we must never seek the perfection of the parables of Christ in giving significancy, apart from the proper point of comparison, to the parts of the narrative which were merely intended to complete it; for this, by diverting the mind from the one truth to a variety of particulars, can only embarrass instead of assisting it, and must thus frustrate the very aim of the parable itself. Such a procedure would open a wide field for arbitrary interpretation, and could not fail to lead the hearer astray.

The separate parables will be treated in their proper connexions in the course of the narrative.

§ 70. *Christ's Teaching not confined to Parables, but conveyed also in longer Discourses.*

It followed, not only from Christ's chosen mode of teaching, but also from his relations to the new spiritual creation whose seeds he implanted in the hearts of his disciples, that he used pithy and sententious sayings and aphorisms instead of lengthened exhibitions of doctrine. They were intended to be retained in ever vivid recollection, and, notwithstanding their separation, to contain the germs of an organically connected system of moral and religious truth. The interpreter and the historian find the difficulty of placing these in their proper relations and occasions increased by the fact that the accounts of the first three

Evangelists arrange and present them in different connexions of thought. The Church, however, has lost nothing by this; it only establishes the doctrine that the truths uttered by Christ admit of manifold apprehension and application. Yet there is no ground for the assumption that Christ taught *only* by means of parables and aphorisms. The supposition, in itself, is sufficiently improbable, that he never employed longer and more connected forms of discourse for the instruction of the circles of disciples who had received impressions from him and gathered themselves about his person; and, besides, an example of this kind (recorded by the first three Evangelists) is to be found in the *Sermon on the Mount.* We shall hereafter inquire more closely into the system of Christian truth contained in that discourse.

§ 71. *John's Gospel contains chiefly connected and profound Discourses; and Why?*

We must here consider the difference between the form of Christ's expositions as given by the *first three* Evangelists, and as recorded by *John.* Some recent writers have found an irreconcilable opposition between them both of form and substance; and have concluded therefrom either that John, in reproducing the discourses of Christ from memory, involuntarily blended his own subjective views with them, and thus presented doctrines which a real disciple could not at the time have apprehended; or that some one else at a later period, and not John, was the author of this Gospel. They contrast the thoroughly practical bearing of the Sermon on the Mount with (what they call) the mystical character of the discourses recorded by John. They find every thing in the former simple and intelligible, while the latter abounds in paradoxes, and seems to study obscurity. Moreover, the latter is almost destitute of parables; a form of eloquence not only national, but also characteristic of Christ, judging from his discourses as given in the other Gospels.

But let any one only yield himself to the impression of the Sermon on the Mount, and then ask himself whether it be probable that a mind of the loftiness, depth, and power which that discourse evinces, could have employed only *one* mode of teaching? A mind which swayed not only simple and practical souls, but also so profoundly speculative an intellect as that of Paul, could not but have scattered the elements of such a tendency from the very first. We cannot but infer, from the irresistible power which Christianity exerted upon minds so diversely constituted and cultivated, that the sources of that power lay combined*

* We should believe this even if we were to admit *Weisse's* view, viz., that the basis of this Gospel was a collection of the λόγια τοῦ κυρίου made by John, and afterward wrought by another hand into the form of a historical narrative. But Weisse's critical processes seem to me to be entirely arbitrary. John's Gospel is altogether (with the exception of a

in Him whose self-revelation was the origin of Christianity itself. Moreover, the other Gospels are not wanting in apparently paradoxical expressions akin to the peculiar tone of John's Gospel, *e. g.*, "*Let the dead bury their dead.*"* Nor will an attentive observer find in John alone expressions of Christ intended to increase, instead of to remove the offence which carnal minds took at his doctrine. We repeat, again, that the words and acts of the true Christ *could* not have been free from paradoxes; and from this, indeed, it may have been that the Pharisees were led to report that he had lost his senses.

Still, it is true, that such passages are given by John much more abundantly than the other Evangelists. But there is nothing in his Gospel purely metaphysical or unpractical; none of the spirit of the Alexandrian-Jewish theology; but every where a direct bearing upon the inner life, the Divine communion which Christ came to establish. Its form would have been altogether different had it been composed, as some suppose, in the second century, to support the Alexandrian doctrine of the Logos, as will be plain to any one who takes the trouble to compare it with the writings of that age that have come down to us The discourses given in the first three Gospels, mostly composed of separate maxims, precepts, and parables, all in the popular forms of speech, were better fitted to be handed down by tradition than the more profound discussions which have been recorded by the beloved disciple who hung with fond affection upon the lips of Jesus, treasured his revelations in a congenial mind, and poured them forth to fill up the gaps of the popular narrative. And although it is true that the image of Christ given to us in this Gospel is the reflection of Christ's impression upon John's peculiar mind and feelings, it is to be remembered that these very peculiarities were obtained by his intercourse with, and vivid apprehension of, Christ himself. His susceptible nature appropriated Christ's life, and incorporated it with his own.

§ 72. *The Parable of the Shepherd, in John, compared with the Parables in the other Gospels.*

Parables, as we have said, are peculiarly fitted for oral tradition. We

few passages which are suspicious both on external and internal grounds) a work of one texture, not admitting of critical decomposition. In Matthew, not only internal signs, but also historical traditions, when considered without prejudice, seem to distinguish the original and fundamental composition from the later revision of the work. On the other hand, the author in whom we first find the tradition referred to (Papias, Euseb., iii., 39) makes mention of no such thing in regard to John's Gospel. He must have known the fact, had it been so, living as he did in Asia Minor. Some adduce Papias's silence about John's Gospel as a testimony against its genuineness; but his object, most likely, was to give in formation in regard to those parts of the narrative whose origin was not so well known in that part of the country; whereas John's Gospel was fresh in every one's memory there.

* Had this expression occurred in John, it might have been cited as a specimen of "Alex andrian mysticism."

need not wonder, therefore, that they are more abundant in the first three Gospels, which were composed of such traditions, than in John; and, moreover, the latter, presupposing them to be known, may have had, in his peculiar turn of mind, and in the object for which he wrote his Gospel, sufficient reasons for omitting them. Yet the discourses of Christ, as given by him, are marked by the very peculiarity that gives rise to the use of parables, viz., the illustration of the Spiritual and the Divine, by images taken from common life.

But real parables are not entirely wanting in John's Gospel. The illustration of the *shepherd and the sheep* (ch. 10) has all the essential features of the parable, and John himself applies that name to it (ver. 6). Here, as in other parables, we find a religious truth vividly represented by a similitude taken from the sphere of nature. As, for instance, in the parable of the *sower*, Christ is likened to the husbandman, the Divine word to the seed, and the various degrees of susceptibility for the word in men's souls to the variously productive soils in which the seed is planted; so, in this similitude, the relation of souls to Christ is compared with that of sheep to the shepherd; and the self-seeking teacher, who offers himself, on his own authority and for a bad purpose, as a guide of men, is likened to a thief who does not enter the sheep-fold by the door, but climbs over the wall. *Strauss* has remarked that this parable differs from those of the Synoptical Gospels in this, that it does not give a historical narrative, with beginning, middle, and end, of a fact actually *once* taking place, but makes use simply of what is *commonly* seen to happen. But even this feature cannot be said to be *essential* to all the synoptical parables, but only to those in which a specific occurrence in human intercourse is assumed to illustrate a spiritual truth;* for in those, on the other hand, which are not taken from social and civil life, but from the sphere of man's intercourse with *nature*, the one especial fact given is nothing but a specimen of what *commonly* takes place; and the form of the statement could be entirely changed in this respect, without at all affecting its substance. Of this the parable of the *sower* is an example, and, indeed, those of the *leaven* and the *mustard seed* also. So, too, John's parable of the shepherd and the sheep might be stated in the form of a fact once occurring, without losing a particle of its individuality.

* Even were the name *parables* (as a distinct form of similitudes) restricted to representations of this class, such a distinction would not destroy the analogy between Christ's discourses in John and those in the other Gospels, founded on their use, in common, of the same mode of vividly exhibiting spiritual truths.

C CHRIST'S USE OF ACCOMMODATION.

§ 73. *Necessity of Accommodation.*

We must mention Christ's adaptation of his instruction to the capacity of his hearers, as one of the peculiar features of his mode of teaching. Without such accommodation, indeed, there can be no such thing as instruction. The teacher *must* begin upon a ground common to his pupils, with principles presupposed as known to them, in order to extend the sphere of their knowledge to further truths. He must lower himself to them, in order to raise them to himself. As the true and the false are commingled in their conceptions, he must seize upon the true as his point of departure, in order to disengage it from the encumbering false. So to the child the man becomes a child, and explains the truth in a form adapted to its age, by making use of its childish conceptions as a veil for it.

In accordance with this principle, every revelation of God, having for its object the *training of mankind for the Divine life* (and we must never forget that this was the *sole* aim of Christianity, as well as of the preparatory institutions which preceded it), has made use of this law of *accommodation*, in order to present the Divine to the consciousness of men in forms adapted to their respective stand-points. And as Christ by no means intended, as we have before remarked, to impart a complete system of doctrine as a mere dead tradition; but rather to stimulate men's minds to a living appropriation and developement of the truth which he revealed, by means of the powers with which God had endowed them; it was the more necessary for him to adapt his instruction to the capacities of those who heard him. His teaching by parables, in which the familiar affairs of every-day life were made the veil and vehicle of unknown and higher truths, was an instance of accommodation. The pedagogic principle of joining the old with the new, of making the old new and the new old, and of deriving the new from the old, is fully illustrated in the saying of Christ before referred to, viz., that the teacher, instructed in the kingdom of Heaven, is like "*a householder, who bringeth forth out of his treasure things new and old.*" To this principle, constantly employed by Christ in his teaching, we must ascribe the extraordinary influence of Christianity upon human culture from the very beginning. But, just as the "*form of a servant*" hindered many eyes from seeing the Son of God in the Son of Man, so the Divine, which adapted itself to human infirmities by veiling its heavenly grandeur, was often concealed by the very veil which it had assumed.

§ 74. *Distinction between Positive* (Material) *and Negative* (Formal) *Accommodation; the latter necessary, the former inadmissible.*

We must carefully separate false from true accommodation; there is a broad distinction between a negative accommodation of the *form* and a positive one of the *substance.* The teacher who adopts the latter will confirm his hearers in an error, in order to gain their confidence, and to infuse into their minds, even by means of error, some important truth. But the laws of morality do not admit that "the end sanctifies the means;" nor can the establishment of error ever be a just means of propagating truth. And it is as impolitic as it is immoral; for error, as well as truth, contains within itself a fructifying germ, and no one can predict what fruit it will produce. He who makes use of it renounces at once the character of a teacher of truth; no man will trust him, and he can therefore exert a spiritual influence upon none. There is no criterion for distinguishing the truth of his aims from the falsehood of his means. Such an accommodation as this was utterly repugnant to the holy nature of Him who called himself THE TRUTH; and there is no trace of it to be found in his teachings.

It is quite a different thing with the *negative* and *formal* accommodation. As Christ's sole calling as a teacher was to implant the fundamental truths of the kingdom of GOD in the human consciousness, he could not stop by the way to battle with errors utterly unconnected with his object, and remote from the interests of religion and morality. Thus he made use of common terms and expressions without entering into an examination of all the false notions that might be attached to them. He called diseases, for instance, by the names in common use; but we should not be justified in concluding that he thereby stamped with his Divine authority the ordinary notions of their origin, as implied in the names. Nor does his citation of the books of the Old Testament by the accustomed titles imply any sanction on his part of the prevalent opinions in regard to their authors. We must never forget that his words, as he himself has told us, *are Spirit and Life;* and that no scribe of the old Rabbinical school, no slave to the *letter,* can rightly comprehend and apply them.

Nor did he make use of *positive* accommodation in seizing, as he did, upon those religious conceptions of the times which concealed the germ of truth under material forms. It was not his aim to preserve the mere shell, the outward form, but to disengage the inner truth from its covering, and bring it out into free and pure developement. This he could only effect by causing men to change their whole carnal mode of thinking, of which the material form of representation, just referred to, was only one of the results. These remarks apply especially to the use which he made of the common outward images of the

Messianic world-dominion; which he certainly would not have employed, if they had not contained a substantive truth in regard to the developement of the kingdom of God from the Old Testament standpoint.* To attack these material ideas directly, and present the pure, spiritual truth as a ready-made system, would have been fruitless; it was only from the deeper ground in which the erroneous tendencies were imbedded that they could be successfully overthrown. And Christ, taking the truth that lay in the outward form as his point of departure, attacked the *root* of all the separate errors; the selfish, carnal mind, the longing for worldly rank and rewards; and implanted, on the other hand, the purely spiritual ideas of the Divine kingdom, as seeds from which, in due time, a free reaction against the material tendency would spontaneously arise.

Of the same character was the use which Christ made of figurative analogies like that in Matt., xii., 43,† et seq. In such cases the figurative representation was employed, like the parable, to exhibit an idea vividly to the minds of his hearers, while, at the same time, its connexion was such that he could not possibly be misunderstood.

§ 75. *Christ's Application of Passages from the Old Testament.*

What we have said in regard to Christ's habit of taking up a concealed truth is especially applicable to his use of quotations from the Old Testament, which enveloped, as it were, and contained the germ of truths which he was fully to unfold and develope. In this point of view, he derived, from the Old Testament, truths which, though not contained in the letter of its words, were involved in its spirit and fundamental import. The higher spirit, which appeared in its unlimited fulness in Christ, was predominant in the Old Testament; all the preparatory revelations of that spirit had Christ for their aim; the Theocratic idea, which formed the central-point both of the Scriptures and the Jewish nation, had found no fulfilment, but looked to the future for its realization. Christ was perfectly justified, therefore, in so interpreting the Old Testament as to bring out clearly its hidden intimations and germs of truth, and to unfold from the covering of the letter the profounder sense of the Spirit. We shall have occasion to illustrate this more fully in our exposition of Christ's didactic and polemic use of the Old Testament. Paul's interpretation of the Old Testament was of precisely the same character; with this difference only, that Christ was better able to distinguish the different stages of the Theocratic developement, pointing, as they all did, to his manifestation.

* See p. 86 and 87.

† We shall have occasion to speak of this passage more fully in another connexion.

CHAPTER III.

CHRIST'S CHOICE AND TRAINING OF THE APOSTLES.

§ 76 *Christ's Relation to the Twelve.—Significance of the Number Twelve.—The Name Apostle.*

WE have before remarked, that among the most important means employed by Christ in founding the kingdom of God was the training of certain *organs;* not only to replace his personal labours as a teacher (which were limited to so very brief a period), but also to propagate a true image of his person, his manifestation, his Spirit, and his truth. Here arises the question, whether Christ intentionally selected twelve men for this purpose, and took the individuals thus chosen into closer communion with himself, or whether this intimate relationship arose out of a gradual separation of the more susceptible disciples from the mass, who formed by degrees a narrower and more permanent circle about his person; whether, in a word, the choice of the twelve was made once for all, by a definite purpose, or arose simply from the nature of the case.* Some adopt the latter notion, with a view to answer objections against the wisdom of Christ's selection; such, for instance, as that he chose several insignificant men, who accomplished nothing of importance, and omitted others who were afterward signally eminent and useful; that he must either have been deceived in admitting Judas into the number,† or else (what is entirely out of keeping with his character) must have made him an Apostle with a full consciousness of his inevitable destiny, in order to lead him on to his destruction. It is urged, moreover, against the probability of Christ himself having conferred the name of *Apostles* upon these men especially, that others, (*e.g.*, Paul), who laboured in proclaiming the Gospel at a later period, received that designation.

This question would be at once decided, if we could consider the *Sermon on the Mount* as an ordination discourse for the Apostles; but this view, as we shall hereafter show, is untenable. But there are passages‡ which speak expressly of the choosing of the twelve; and, even without attaching undue weight to these, there are other and sufficient grounds for believing that such a choice was actually made. Christ himself tells the Apostles (John, xv., 16) that they had not chosen him, but that he had chosen *them*, as his own peculiar organs, which would not have been true if they had first separated, of their own

* See the arguments for this view in *Schleiermacher on Luke*, p. 88.

† Celsus thought to disparage Christ by telling that he was betrayed by one of his disciples. (Orig., c. Cels., ii., § 12.)

‡ Luke, vi., 13; Mark, iii., 13, 14.

accord, from the rest of the multitude, and chosen him for their Master and guide, in a narrower sense than others.

Nor is the number *twelve* destitute of significance. Without seeking any sacred, mystical meaning in the number, we can well see in it a reference to the number of the tribes of Israel. The particular, Jewish Theocracy was a type of the universal and eternal kingdom of God; and Christ first designated himself as head of that kingdom in the Jewish national form. The twelve were to lead the kingdom as his organs.* Their superiority to all others, who should also act as organs of the Holy Spirit testifying within them of the Redeemer (the common calling of *all believers*), consisted in this, that they received a direct and personal impression of the words and works of Christ, and could thus testify of what they had *seen and heard.* This personal testimony of eye-witnesses is expressly distinguished by Christ (John, xv., 27) from the objective testimony of the Holy Spirit; which, indeed, animated them, but could also bear witness through other organs. Hence, when one of the twelve was lost, the Apostles deemed it necessary to replace him, and thus fill up the number originally instituted by Christ.†

The more general application of the name *Apostle* in the Apostolic age is no proof that Christ did not originally use it in the narrower sense. The Apostolic mind was under no such painful subserviency to the *letter* as to avoid the use of a name in a sense suggested by the name itself, simply because Christ had used it in a more contracted signification. The term ἀπόστολοι (שְׁלִיחִין) denoted persons sent out by Christ to proclaim the kingdom of God; and it was quite natural, as all who preached the Gospel were considered as sent out by him, that all who laboured in proclaiming it in a wide sphere should receive the same designation.‡ Although *Paul* used the term in its wider meaning, he yet considered the narrower sense to be the original one,§ and justified his application of the latter to himself only on the ground of the direct and immediate call which he had received from Christ.||

§ 77. *Choice of the Apostles.—Of Judas Iscariot.*

There are a few examples on record of Christ's drawing and attaching to himself disciples who exhibited to his piercing eye the qualities necessary for his service. Probably this procedure was the same in the cases not recorded. The wisdom of Christ, moreover, leads us to conclude that the cultivation of these agents, on whose fitness so much de-

* Matt., xix., 28; Luke, xxii., 30. *Ye also shall sit upon twelve thrones, judging the twelve tribes of Israel.*

† Acts, i., 21.

‡ The questions whether Christ chose twelve men as his special organs, and whether he himself gave them the name *Apostles*, are entirely distinct. There is no good reason to doubt the latter.

§ 1 Cor., xv., 7.

|| 1 Cor., ix. 1; xv., 9

pended, was an object of his special care and attention. Although we have not sufficient information to decide, in the case of each Apostle, why he especially was admitted into the number of the twelve, yet such examples as Peter and John, men of most striking character, who show us how the most marked features of human nature receive and tinge Christianity, illustrate the profound wisdom of Christ, and the penetrating glance with which he could detect the concealed plant in the insignificant germ. Yet we are not bound, in order to vindicate Christ's wisdom, to conclude that *all* the Apostles were alike men of mark, alike capable of great achievements. It was enough for the fulfilment of their calling that they loved him truly, that they followed him with child-like confidence, and gave themselves wholly up to the guidance of his Spirit; for thus they would be enabled to testify of him, and to exhibit his image in truth and purity. It was enough that among the number there were a few men of pre-eminently powerful character, on whom the rest might lean for support. It sufficed, nay, it was even advantageous, for the developement of the Church, that the Apostles, as a whole, left their accounts of the history of Christ *without* the peculiar stamp of individual character, since there was only one *John* among them capable of giving a vivid image of the life of the Saviour in harmonious unity. And it is, therefore, not at all wonderful that men appeared in the later period of the Apostolic Church who accomplished greater things than even some of the Apostles.

As for Judas Iscariot, it by no means follows from the passages which say that Christ *knew him from the beginning*, that he knew him as an enemy and a traitor; nor does the awful contrast between his Apostolic calling and his final fate show that Christ was wholly deceived in him. Judas may have at first embraced the proclamation of the kingdom of God with ardent feelings, although with expectations of a selfish and worldly stamp; which, indeed, was the case with others of the Apostles. He may have loved Christ sincerely so long as he hoped to find in him the fulfilment of his carnal desires. Christ may have seen in him capacities which, animated by pure intentions, might have made him a particularly useful instrument in spreading the kingdom of God. At the same time, he doubtless perceived in him, as in the rest of the Apostles, the impure influence of the worldly and selfish element, yet he may have hoped (to do for him what he certainly did for the others, viz.) to remove it by the enlightening and purifying effects of his personal intercourse; a result, however, which, we freely admit, depended upon the *free self-determination* of Judas, and could, therefore, be unerringly known to none but the Omniscient. And even when Judas, deceived in his carnal and selfish hopes, felt his affection for Christ passing into hatred, the love of the Saviour, hoping all things, though he saw the rising root of evil, may have induced him to strive the more earnestly to attract the wanderer to himself, in order to save him from impending ruin.*

§ 78. *The Apostles Uneducated Men.*

It may appear strange that Christ should have selected, as his chosen organs, men so untaught and unsusceptible in Divine things, and should have laboured, in opposition to their worldly tendencies, to fit them for their office; especially when men of learned cultivation in Jewish theology were at hand, more than one of whom had attached themselves sincerely to him. But we are justified in presupposing that he acted thus according to a special decision of his own wisdom, as he himself testifies (Matt., xi., 25): "*I thank thee, O Father, because thou hast hid these things from the wise and prudent, and hast revealed them unto babes.*" Precisely because these men, destitute of all higher learning, attached themselves to him like children, and obeyed even his slightest hints, were they best fitted to receive his Spirit with child-like devotion and confidence, and to propagate the revelations which he made to them. Every thing in them was to be the growth of the new creation through Christ's Spirit; and men who had received a complete culture elsewhere would have been ill adapted for this. They were trammelled, it is true, by their carnal conceptions of Divine things; but this was counterbalanced by their anxiety to learn, and their child-like submission to Christ as Master and guide; while, on the other hand, insurmountable obstacles would have been presented in the want of such submission—in the stubborn adherence to preconceived views of men who had been trained and cultivated before. Moreover, this reverential submission to Christ on the part of the disciples, in their daily intercourse with him, tended surely and constantly to refine and spiritualize their mode of thinking. His image, received into their inner life, exerted a steady and overruling influence. In the mode in which the new revelations were embraced and developed, we recognize the *general law*, according to which truths beyond the scope of human reason are imparted to it from higher sources, to be afterward appropriated and elaborated as its own. They were first received and unfolded by men who had no previous education to enable them to work out independently that which was given them; and only at a later period was a PAUL added to the Apostles—a man capable, from his systematic mental cultivation, of elaborating and unfolding, by his own power of thought, yet under the guidance of the same Spirit of Christ, the material of Divine revelation that was bestowed upon him. The fact, too, that a people like the Jews, and not the Greeks, were first the chosen organ for the propagation of revealed religion, is an illustration

* See, hereafter, more on the character and fate of Judas.

of the same law. Here we find the source of the ever-renewed struggle betwen Revelation, which demands a humble reception of its gifts, and Reason, which will recognize nothing that is not wrought out, or, at least, remodelled, in its own laboratory.

Still Christ could not have deemed the period of two or three years sufficient to prepare these untrained disciples, according to his mind, for teachers of men. Nor could he have foretold, with such confidence, the success of such men in propagating his truth for the salvation and training of men, for the victorious founding of the kingdom of GOD in all ages, had he not been conscious of powers higher than had been granted to any other teacher among men, which justified him in making such predictions.

§ 79. *Two Stages in the Dependence of the Apostles upon Christ.*

From the very beginning the Apostles stood to Christ in a relation of complete dependence and submission, but we must distinguish in this two different forms and periods. In the first, their dependence was more outward and unconscious; in the last, it was more inward, and thoroughly understood by themselves. From the beginning, they gave themselves up, with reverent confidence, to the will of Christ as their supreme law, inspired by the conviction that what he commanded was right; yet without a clear apprehension either of his will or word, and without the ability to harmonize their will with his by free consciousness and self-determination. But, during this stage of outward dependence, they were to be trained to apprehend his will (or, what is the same thing, the will of GOD revealed and fulfilled by him); to incorporate it with their own spiritual tendencies; in a word, to make it their own. Christ himself pointed out this two-fold relation, when he said to them, in view of his approaching death, in reference to their dawning consciousness of the necessity of his suffering in order to establish the Divine kingdom: "*Henceforth I call you not servants; for the servant knoweth not what his Lord doeth: but I have called you friends; for all things that I have heard of my Father I have made known unto you. Ye have not chosen me, but I have chosen you, and ordained you, that ye should go and bring forth fruit, and that your fruit should remain; that whatsoever ye shall ask of the Father in my name, he may give it you.*"* The servant follows the will of his master not as his own, but another's, without understanding its aim; but *friendship* is a harmony of souls and sympathy of intentions. The ultimate aim of all Christ's training of the Apostles was to raise them from the first stand-point to the second.

* John, xv., 15, 16. So, v. 14, "*Ye are my friends, if ye do whatsoever I command you.*" Their efforts to perform his will perfectly proved that they had made it their own.

§ 80. *Christ's peculiar Method of training the Apostles.*

The words of Christ recorded in Luke, v., 33; Matt., ix., 14,* throw a distinct light upon his peculiar method of training the Apostles. When reproached because he imposed no strict spiritual discipline, no fasting or outward exercises upon his disciples, but suffered them to mingle in society freely, like other men, he justified his course by stating (in effect) that "fasting, then imposed upon them, would have been an unnatural and foreign disturbance of the festal joy of their intercourse with him, the object of all their longings. But when the sorrow of separation should follow the hours of joy, fasting would be in harmony both with their inward feelings and their outward life. As no good could come of patching old garments with new cloth, or putting new wine into old skins, so it was not his purpose to impose the exercises of spiritual life, fasting, and the like, by an outward law, upon his yet untrained disciples, but rather, by a gradual change of their whole inward nature, to make them vessels fit for the indwelling of the higher life. When they had become such, all the essential manifestations of that indwelling life would spontaneously reveal themselves; no outward command would then be needed."

Here we see the principle on which Christ acted in the *intellectual*, as well as in the moral and religious training of the Apostles. As he would not lay external restraints, by the letter of outward laws, upon natures as yet undisciplined, so it was not his purpose to impart the dead letter of a ready-made and fragmentary knowledge to minds whose worldly modes of thought disabled them from apprehending it. He aimed rather to implant the germ, to give the initial impulse of a total intellectual renovation, by which men might be enabled to grasp, with a new spirit, the new truths of the kingdom of GOD. In every relation he determined not to "patch the old garment, or put new wine into old bottles." And this principle, thus fully illustrated by Christ's training of his Apostles, is, in fact, the *universal* law of growth in the genuine Christian life.

* More on these passages hereafter, in their proper connexion in the narrative.

CHAPTER IV.

THE CHURCH AND BAPTISM.

§ 81. *Founding of the Church.—Its Objects.*

CLOSELY connected with the questions just discussed is that of the *founding of the Church;* for the Apostles were the organs through whom the religious community which originated in Christ was to be handed down to after ages, the connecting links that were to unite it with its Founder. A clear conception of the idea of the Church, in comparison with what we have said of the plan of Christ, will make it obvious that he *intended* to establish the Church, and *himself* laid its foundation.

By the CHURCH we understand a union of men arising from the fellowship (communion) of religious life; a union essentially independent of, and different from, all other forms of human association. It was a fundamental element of the formation of this union, that religion was no longer to be inseparably bound up, either as principal or subordinate, with the political and national relations of men, but that it should develope itself, by its own inherent energy, as a principle of culture and union; superior, in its very essence, to all human powers. This involved both the power and the duty to create an independent community, and that community is THE CHURCH.

And Christianity is proved to be the aim and object of all human progress, not only by the craving for redemption, which no man can deny, in human nature, but also by the very idea of such a community as the Church, which overthrows all natural barriers, and binds mankind together by a union founded on the common alliance of their nature to GOD. The spirit of humanity, feeling itself confined by the limits which the opposing interests of nations impose upon it, demands a communion that shall overleap these barriers, and lay its foundations only in the consciousness, common to all men, of their relation to the Highest—a relation transcending the world and nature. Apart from Christianity, indeed, we could not conceive the idea of such a communion; but now that Christianity has freed Reason from the old-world bonds that hindered its developement, and unfolded for it a higher self-consciousness, there can be no *science* of human nature that does not reckon this communion as the aim of human progress, that does not assign to the Church its proper place in the universal moral organism of humanity. SCHLEIERMACHER has done this in his "Philosophical Ethics," and has thus found, in the Church, the point of departure for Christian morals. And so every system of ethics must do which is not willing to fall in the rear of human progress, and to be guilty of cruelly mutilating the nature of man. Nay, the minds of the sages who sought to break through the limits of the ancient world yearned for this idea long before its realization in Christianity. ZENO,* the founder of the Stoa, proclaimed it as the highest of human aims, that "men should not be separated by cities, states, and laws, but that all should be considered fellow-citizens, and partakers of one life, and that the whole world, like a united flock, should be governed by one common law."† Plutarch, who quotes these words, was probably right in saying that "Zeno had some phantom of a dream before him when he wrote;"‡ for how could an idea, so far transcending the spirit of antiquity, be realized in its sphere? Such a communion could only be brought about, at that time, by the destruction of the separate organization of nations, to the detriment of their natural and individual progress; and the very event in which Plutarch thought he saw its fulfilment, viz., the commingling of the nations by Alexander's§ conquests, carried the germ of self-destruction within it. A total revolution of the ancient world necessarily had to precede the realizing of this idea. Mankind had to be freed from the power of sin, and the disjunctive and repulsive agency of sin, before there could be any place for this Divine communion of life, which overleaps, without destroying, the natural divisions of nations. And this is the realization of the idea of the CHURCH.

Now as this revolution could only be brought about by Him who was at once Son of GOD and Son of Man, so HE, when he recognized himself as the Saviour and King bestowed upon mankind, was fully conscious, also, of his power to realize this idea. It is clear, from what we have said of the Plan of Christ, that the results which were to flow in after ages from the indwelling power of the Word proclaimed and sent forth by him to regenerate and unite mankind, lay fully revealed before his all-surveying glance. He knew that it contained the elements of a spiritual community that would burst asunder the confining forms of the Jewish Theocracy, and take all mankind into its wide embrace.

§ 82. *Name of the Church.—Its Form traced back to Christ himself.*

But even if it be admitted that Christ *intended to found a Church*, the further (but less important) question arises, whether the name,

* In his work, *περὶ πολιτείας.*

† *Ἵνα μὴ κατὰ πόλεις, μηδὲ κατὰ δήμους οἰκῶμεν, ἰδιόις ἕκαστοι διωρισμένοι δικαίοις, ἀλλὰ πάντας ἀνθρώπους ἡγώμεθα δημότας καὶ πολίτας, εἷς δὲ βίος ᾖ καὶ κόσμος ὥσπερ ἀγέλης συννόμου νομῷ κοινῷ συντρεφομένης.* Plut. in Alex., i., c. vi.

‡ *Τοῦτο Ζήνων μὲν ἔγραψεν ὥσπερ ὄναρ ἢ εἴδωλον ευνομίας φιλοσόφου καὶ πολιτείας ἀνατυπωσάμενος*

§ To whom he applies what can only be said of Christ: *κοινὸς ἥκειν θεόθεν ἁρμοστὴς καὶ διαλλακτὴς τῶν ὅλων νομίζων.*

ἐκκλησία, which has been stamped upon it, had its origin with himself. There is no ground for doubting even this (as some have done), and thereby casting suspicion upon passages like Matt., xvi., 18, in which he is reported to have used the term. The name corresponds to the Hebrew קָהָל, in connexion with הָאֱלֹהִים, יְהוָֹה, יִשְׂרָאֵל, which expressed the old Theocratic national community; and so was transferred to the new congregation of God, which was to emerge from the ancient covering. This communion in itself, indeed, is nothing but the form in which Christ has established the kingdom of God upon earth, and in which he intends it shall develope itself until its full consummation.

But it must not, therefore, be concluded that this community was ever to realize itself in the form of a *State*.* The name, borrowed from an earthly kingdom, is, on one side, entirely symbolical, and was immediately taken from the form in which the idea of the Divine community was represented by the Jewish nation. But the *essential* difference between the Jewish and the Christian stand-point consists in this, that in the latter the political element is wholly discarded. Excluding all other relations that belong to the essence of a state, the only *real* feature expressed by the symbolical name is the *monarchical* principle; and that, too, in a sense that cannot be applied to any temporal state, without subverting its organism, and making it a horde of slaves under the arbitrary will of a despot. The fundamental principle of the Christian community is, that there shall be no other subordination than that of its members to God and Christ, and that *this* shall be absolute; while, in regard to each other, they are to be upon the footing of complete equality. Christ himself drew a striking contrast between his own community and all political organizations in this respect.†

But even though it be admitted that Christ intended to found a visible Church, and gave the first impulse to a movement that was afterward to propagate itself, it does not necessarily follow that he himself directly established such a separate community, and made the arrangements and preparations that naturally belonged to it.

It may be said that the outward fabric of the visible Church could not be erected until that which constituted its true essence, viz., the life of the invisible Church, which as yet lay only in the germ, should be more fully unfolded—until the higher life had obtained in the disciples a more substantial and self-dependent form, a state of things presupposed in a community whose manifold members were recipro

* See this inference drawn by *Rothe*, in his work "Uber die Anfänge der Christlichen Kirche und ihrer Verfassung," p. 89.

† Luke, xxii., 25, 26

cally to affect each other. So, too, it may be said* that one of the specific differences between Christ and other founders of religions was, that, as he did not impart a complete and sharply-defined system of *doctrines* to his Apostles, but left it to their human activity, under the guidance of the Divine Spirit, to form such a system from the elements which he bestowed,† so, also, he founded no outwardly complete and accurately defined religious community, with a fixed form of government, usages, and rules of worship; but, after implanting the Divine germ of this community, left it also to human agency, guided by the same Holy Spirit, to develope the *forms* which it should assume under the varying relations of human society. According to this view, only the fructifying *elements* were given by Christ, and all the rest was left to human developement proper, animated by the Divine principle of life.

According to this view, the only defined community which Christ established was that of the Apostles, who, as bearers and organs of his Spirit, formed the sole prototype of the Church, which only grew up at a later period from the seed which Christ had sown. He did not wish to establish an exclusive school or sect, but to draw all men to himself. In this view, further, it would be necessary to suppose that he had, at that time, fixed no rite of initiation into his narrower fellowship; that such passages as John, iii., 22; Matt., xxviii., 19, arose only from the attempts of a later period to ascribe the origin of baptism directly to Christ; and that baptism, with confession of the name of Christ, was introduced by the Apostles subsequently‡ to the formation of a separate Christian congregation, as a sign of membership therein. And the high estimate§ which was put upon the rite may be ascribed, not to its having been instituted by Christ, but to the extraordinary phenomena of inspiration which were wont to attend it.

We agree fully with the fundamental principle of the view just recited. Christ only prepared the way for the foundation of the Church, according to its inner essence and its outward form; as he gave no complete doctrinal system, so he erected no Church fabric that was to stand through all time; his work was rather to implant in humanity the *new spirit*, which was to adapt to itself such outward

* As is asserted by *Weisse* (p. 387, seq.; 406, seq.), whose views and proofs we shall examine in another place.

† It is not without good ground, therefore, that we do not devote a separate section of this work to a systematic exposition of the *doctrines* of Christ, but content ourselves, both here and in the Apostolic age, with pointing out, in his words, the fundamental principles which were afterward expanded by the Apostles.

‡ *Weisse* thinks that the first trace of the institution is to be found in Acts, ii., 38.

§ The ecclesiastical import of baptism would remain untouched, even if it were granted that the symbol was first instituted by the Apostles at the time of the bestowing of the Holy Spirit, which the rite symbolized; for, even in that case, we must consider them as Christ's organs, and acting out his will.

forms as would meet the wants of human progress in successive ages. But, while we cordially go thus far, we do not find ourselves warranted, either by history or by the idea of such a community, in granting so wide a latitude as the theory demands to a principle so just in itself.

The gradual and natural formation of the circle of disciples about Christ is no reason for believing that he did not found a Church. His manifestation to men of different degrees of susceptibility caused, indeed, a sifting process, which soon separated the congregation of believers from the mass that rejected Christ; but the natural way in which this result was brought about is no argument against the *establishment* of the Church at that time, more than against its existence at *any* time; for, in fact, in a certain sense this is always the case. The relations of *Christ* to the world typified, in every respect, what were afterward to be the relations of *Christianity* to the world. We find the name of *disciples* applied with a wider signification than that of *Apostles;* and why may we not consider the bands of these, scattered through different parts of Palestine, and especially those who, apart from the Apostles, formed the constant retinue of Christ, as constituting the first nucleus of the Church?

§ 83. *Later Institution of Baptism as an Initiatory Rite.*

As for *Baptism,* we certainly do not find, either in the nature of the case or in the historical accounts, any ground for assuming that Christ himself, during his stay upon earth, instituted it as a symbol of consecration. As long as he could, *in person,* admit believers into communion with himself, no substituted symbol was necessary; and, besides, the Holy Spirit, which constitutes the essence of Christian baptism, and specifically distinguishes it from that of John, had not as yet been manifested. The element of *preparation* was sufficiently indicated by John's baptism, and therefore Christ (in the prophetic words which have been preserved to us in Acts, i., 5) contrasted that preparatory rite with the spiritual baptism which he himself was soon to impart to his disciples. The Apostles, however (quite naturally, in view of the ground which they occupied), were unwilling that John alone should baptize, and applied the rite, as the Messianic symbol of inauguration which Christ himself had recognized, in order to separate from the rest such as admitted the Divine calling of Jesus, and attached themselves to him.* We cannot infer from this, however, that there existed at the time a definite rule for the application of baptism. Yet, although Christ did not command, he *permitted* it, as fitted to form a point of transition from John's to Christian baptism.

But when he was about to withdraw his personal presence from his disciples, it became necessary to substitute a symbol in its place

* John, iv., 2.

His sufferings and resurrection, the fundamental *facts* from which the new creation, through the Holy Spirit, was to spring, had necessarily to take place before the institution of Christian baptism proper; for that baptism implies an appropriation of the fruit of his sufferings, a fellowship in his resurrection, and a participation of that life, in communion with Him, which is above the world and death. The full import of baptism could not be realized until the process which began with Christ's death and resurrection had reached its consummation; until the exaltation had followed the resurrection, and the glorified Redeemer had displayed his triumphant power in the outpouring of the Holy Ghost. The same effects which flowed to mankind in general from these facts, and the process which rested upon them, were to be repeated in every individual case of baptism.

CHAPTER V.

THE MIRACLES OF CHRIST.

§ 84. *Connexion of Christ's Miracles with his Mode of Teaching.*

WE have before remarked that what most distinguished the Teaching of Christ was, that it was his *self-revelation*, and in this view it embraces both his Words and Works. His MIRACLES, then, must be spoken of in connexion with his mode of Teaching. Although they are not to be sundered from their connexion with his whole self-revelation, yet, as an especially prominent feature of it, they served the highest purpose, in a certain sense, in vividly exhibiting the nature of Christ, as Son of GOD and Son of Man. They have also an additional claim to be mentioned in this connexion, as they served as a basis and support of his labours as a teacher, as a preparatory means of leading from sensible phenomena to Divine things, and of rendering souls, as yet bound to the world of sense, susceptible of his higher Spiritual influences.

In regard to the Miracles, three distinct inquiries present themselves: (I.) What was their real objective character and relation to the universe, and the Divine government thereof? (II.) In what view, and with what impressions, did the contemporaries of Christ receive them? (III.) What decision did Christ himself pronounce as to their nature, their value, and the ends he sought to accomplish by them?

(A.) THE OBJECTIVE CHARACTER OF MIRACLES.

§ 85. *Negative Element of the Miracle.—Its Insufficiency.*

We must distinguish in the Miracle a *negative* and a *positive* element. The former consists simply in this, that a certain event, either in the world of nature or man, is inexplicable by any known laws or powers. Events, however, thus simply inexplicable,* and even acknowledged to be so, are not *miracles*, unless they bear upon *religious* interests. Many will admit certain facts to be inexplicable by any known laws, and at the same time refuse to grant them a miraculous or supernatural character. Some are led, by an unprejudiced admission of the facts, to acknowledge, without any regard whatever to religion, that they transcend the limits of existing science, and content themselves with that acknowledgment; leaving it to the progress of natural philosophy or psychology to discover the laws, as yet unknown, that will explain the mysterious phenomena. Or, if the narrative of facts be such as to preclude even the possibility of such subsequent discovery and solution, they seek an explanation in ascribing chasms and deficiencies to the account, and withhold, for the time at least, their judgment upon the facts themselves; while a spur is given to inquiry and research, in order, if possible, by some process of combination or conjecture, to fill up the existing gaps of the narrative.

Even an *objective* (real) deviation from ordinary phenomena may be admitted by those who refuse to admit of miracles, in the religious sense of the term. That is, indeed, a narrow and ignorant skepticism which measures every thing by the stiff standard of known laws, and passes sentence at once upon every fact, no matter how well attested, which transcends those laws; but a more profound and scientific philosophy knows that there are powers yet undiscovered, which will explain many apparent anomalies. With such minds we can more readily come to an understanding in regard to the historical truth of a narrative of extraordinary events. No unprejudiced reader of history can deny the occurrence of inexplicable phenomena in all past ages; and even those of magnetism, ill-defined as they are as yet, have taught us not to decide so promptly against every thing that goes beyond our knowledge of the powers of nature.

Yet we must not suppose that all this gains any thing directly to the cause of religion, within whose sphere alone the conception of the miracle is a *reality*. It leaves us still in the domain of nature and of natural agencies. It is not upon this road, therefore, that we can lead men to recognize the supernatural and the Divine; to admit the powers of heaven as manifesting themselves upon earth. Miracles belong to a region of holiness and freedom, to which neither experience, nor observation, nor scientific discovery can lead. There is no bridge between this domain and that of natural phenomena. Only by means of our inward affinity for this spiritual kingdom, only by hearing and obeying, in the stillness of the soul, the voice of God within us, can we

* A *prodigium*, or τέρας, but no σημεῖον, distinguishing these words according to their original import.

reach those lofty regions. If there be obstacles in our way, no science can remove them.

In fact, the mode of thinking to which we have referred, instead of necessarily leading to *Theism* (the only *religious* stand-point; for religion demands something supramundane, and *must* enter the sphere of another world), is perfectly consistent with the *Pantheistic* view of the world, and may be used to confirm it. It is not the results of experience which fix our point of view; but the latter, independently assumed on other grounds, gives character to all our judgments of the former. Nay, by applying natural laws to religious phenomena, one may view new religions simply as proceeding from the laws of the developement of the universe, in order to form new epochs in the history of the world, and thence consider the founders of such religions as organs of the soul of the world, concentrating in them the hidden powers of nature. This was the view of Pomponatius, who thought that in this way, while denying every thing *supernatural*, he could admit many of what others call miracles. It is true, there are some of the miracles of the Bible which, on the face of them, admit of no such explanation, but one who holds such views will find no great difficulty in doubting every account of miraculous events which cannot be made to harmonize with them; as Pomponatius did, who could not with sincerity, after an utter denial of the supernatural, abandon his ground simply because some of the miracles could not be explained by it.

§ 86. *Positive Element.—Teleological Aim of Miracles.*

Miracles, then, are entirely different from results of the *powers of nature intensified*. The question of their character cannot be decided on the ground either of Deism or Pantheism (opposed as these theories are to each other; the one incorrectly separating the idea of God from that of the world, the other as incorrectly blending the two together), but only in regard to the Final causes of the government of God, considered as an Omniscient and Omnipotent personal Being. We might dispute with these theories in reference to isolated *facts*, on historical and exegetical grounds; but the question of *miracles*, as such, rises into a very different sphere, and no agreement on separate points would bring us nearer to an adjustment.

The *positive* element, which must be added to the negative one, already spoken of, in order to constitute any inexplicable phenomenon a miracle, is, that the Divine power in the phenomenon itself shall reveal it to our religious consciousness as a *distinctive sign* of a new Divine communication, transcending the natural progress and powers of humanity, and designed to raise it to a position higher than its originally created powers could have reached. That higher position to which the Divine revelations, *accompanied by miracles as distinctive signs,* were destined to elevate mankind, is the character originally stamped by God upon human nature, which was lost by sin. Man violently sundered his union with God, his true element of life, in which the Supernatural and the Natural were in perfect harmony: it was necessary, therefore, that the former should reveal itself in opposition to the latter—that Miracles should be opposed to Nature—in order that Nature might be brought back to her original harmony with God. But miracles, considered as signs of the Divinity revealed in the world of sense, cannot, as such, be considered apart from their connexion with the whole revelation of God. Their essential nature is to be discovered, not by viewing them as isolated exhibitions of Divine power, but as elements of his revelation as a whole, in the harmony of his inseparable attributes, the Holy Love and Wisdom appearing as much as the Omnipotence. It is this which stamps Divinity upon such phenomena, and attracts all souls that are allied to God. Thus the negative element of miracles is only a finger-post to the positive; the inexplicable character of the event leads us to the new revelation, which it accompanies, of that same Almighty love which gave birth to the laws of the visible world, and which, in ordinary times, veils its operations behind them.

§ 87. *Relation of Miracles to the Course of Nature.*

Omnipotence is *always* as directly operative in nature as it was at the creation; but *we* can only detect its workings by means of the law of cause and effect in the material world. Under this veil of natural laws, religious faith always discovers the Divine causality, and the religious mind, although it may, indeed, contemplate natural phenomena from different points of view, and may distinguish between *free* and *necessary* causalities in nature, will always trace them back to the immediate agency of Almighty love. Just so in miracles, we do not see the Divine agency *immediately*, but in a veil, as it were; the Divine causality does not appear in them as coefficient with natural causes, and therefore cannot be an object of external perception, but reveals itself only to Faith. But the miracle, by displaying phenomena out of the ordinary connexion of cause and effect, manifests the interference of a higher power, and points out a higher connexion, in which even the chain of phenomena in the visible world must be taken up.

Miracles, then, present themselves to us as links in that great chain of manifestations whose object is to restore man to his lost communion with God, and to impart to him a life, not derived from any created causality, but immediately from God. As here new and higher powers enter into the sphere of humanity, there must be novel effects resulting from them, which cannot be explained apart from the accompanying revelation, but point out to the religious consciousness their self-revealing cause. Such effects are the miracles, which, from the considerations we have mentioned, lay claim, even as inexplicable phenomena simply, to a religious interest. And although, from their very nature, they transcend the ordinary law of cause and effect, they do not contradict it, inasmuch as nature has been so ordered by Divine wisdom as to admit higher and creative agencies into her sphere; and it is perfectly *natural* that such powers, once admitted, should produce effects beyond the scope of ordinary causes.* In the Divine plan of the universe (of whose fulfilment the connexion of causes in the visible world manifests only *one side*), miracles stand in relations of reciprocal harmony to events occurring in accordance with natural laws. From the chain of causes involved in that great plan, indeed, no events, natural or supernatural, are excluded; both circles of phenomena belong to the realization of the Divine idea.

§ 88. *Relation of the individual Miracles to the highest Miracle, the Manifestation of Christ.*

In the miracles nature is shown to be related, like history, to the one highest aim of God's holy love, namely, the redemption of the human race to the communion of the Divine life, or, what is the same thing, the establishment of His kingdom among men. Nature was destined to reveal and glorify God; but it can only do this in connexion with rational beings, together with whom it forms the *world* as a whole. Now the communion of rational beings, working together with conscious freedom to reveal and glorify God, is nothing else but the kingdom of God; and as the unity which is to exhibit the world as a whole can only be complete when nature has been fully appropriated for the revelation of that kingdom, it follows that the realization of the latter is the aim of the whole creation—of both nature and history.

The manifestation of Christ, the founder of the kingdom of God, the bestower upon mankind of that Divine life which constitutes the essence of the kingdom, was the highest miracle, the central-point of all miracles, and required other and analogous phenomena to precede and follow it. But as the re-establishment of the original harmony between the natural and the Divine (which coincides with the completion of the Divine kingdom) was the final aim of redemption, so, when the Divine life, the essential principle of the miracle itself, which is purely and in its essence supernatural, was incorporated with the natural progress of humanity by the manifestation of Christ, it followed that thenceforward, in all ages, it should operate within the forms and laws of human nature.

* The Schoolmen of the 13th century rightly distinguished the *potentia activa* from the *potentia passiva*, in regard to the relation of the supernatural to the natural.

§ 89. *Relation of Miracles to History*

The relation of miracles to history is perhaps sufficiently obvious from what has been said. Every theory of history that proceeds from the stand-point of natural reason, admitting nothing superior to itself, must, from its very point of departure, reject the idea of miracles. It must seek to include and explain all events by one and the same pragmatical connexion of causes, and can therefore find no place for miracles. Even if it be desirous to examine the acts of Christ without prejudice, it can only, from its peculiar stand-point, manifest such freedom by representing truthfully, according to the accounts that remain, how Christ himself wished these phenomena to be regarded, and what impression they made upon his contemporaries.

But this holds good of only a very limited and arbitrary idea of history, one which barricades itself by its own prejudices against all higher views. The conception of the miracle, as such, is in no way repugnant to a really scientific theory of history; and as it is the task of the latter to study the proper character of every fact and phenomenon, the import of miracles, *as* miracles, is one of its necessary problems. The manifestation of Christ, indeed, can only be rightly understood when it is conceived as being originally Divine and supra-historical, and as having *become* historical; and Christianity can only be explained as a supernatural principle, destined to impart to history a new tendency and direction. In this connexion the individual miracles, preceding, accompanying, and following the manifestation of Christ, appear entirely in accordance with nature. As for history itself, when it does not refer to Christianity and the kingdom of God as the object of all human progress, it appears but as a lawless play of forces moving hither and thither, rising and falling, without aim and without unity. Christianity alone shows us that it has both. But in order to comprehend Christianity, and, through it, History, reason must receive the higher light of faith, without which the eye of the mind must remain blind to the operations and revelation of the Divinity in the course of human progress.*

(B.) THE MIRACLES OF CHRIST AS SUBJECTIVELY VIEWED BY HIS CONTEMPORARIES.

§ 90. *Miracles deemed an essential Sign of Messiahship.*

It is evident from many passages in the Gospel narrative that miracles were essentially necessary, as signs of the Messianic calling. Had Christ, therefore, wrought no miracles, his contemporaries could

* My view of the miracles agrees with what *Twesten* has said in the Introduction to his "Dogmatik;" and I am gratified to find a similar agreement, also, in his second volume, pt. i., p. 170, seq.

not have believed in his Messiahship; nor could he himself have been thoroughly and permanently convinced of it, had he not both been conscious of power to perform them, and put that power into exercise. John the Baptist was satisfied, from his own inability to achieve such works, that *he* was not endowed with the Messianic fulness of the Spirit; and it is obvious, from his receiving Christ's miracles as a proof of his Messiahship, that he expected such signs of the indwelling fulness of Divine power in the true Messiah.

Nor can it be proved (as some suppose) that it was common among the Jews to spread rumours of miracles wrought by men whose deeds had made them objects of popular veneration, as was subsequently the case in the Middle Ages, where we find miraculous powers ascribed to such men even during their lifetime. There is a great difference in the relations of the two periods. The Middle Age was the period of a *new creation*, developed from the new principle of life which Christianity (even alloyed as it was with Jewish elements) introduced among the uncultivated nations. It was a period of youthful freshness, enthusiasm, and poetry. The men of that time, through their lively faith in the Divine power of Christianity, as ever present and ever active, kept their connexion with the miracles that attended its first appearance unbroken, and figured and imitated them by their youthful and inventive power of imagination.* But while such was the relation between the Middle Age and the period of Christ's appearance, there was no similar relation between the latter and the Old Testament age. Christ did not manifest himself at a period of new creation through influences previously wrought into the life of the people by Judaism, but at a time when Judaism itself was decaying and dying; the revelations and mighty works of Divine power lay buried in a far-distant antiquity; and there was a vast chasm, visible to all eyes, between the lofty, holy age of Prophecy, and that weak and lifeless time. After the voice of prophecy was hushed, God was said to reveal himself only by occasional utterances; such, for instance, as the *Bath Col*,† a miraculous sound from heaven; or by words of men, interpreted as omens. Scarcely any tales of wonder were told but such as referred to the *Exorcists*,‡ who were skilled in the deceptive arts of jugglery, and were said to do many marvellous things. In short, it is sufficiently proved that miracles were deemed no ordinary occurrences among the Jews,§

* The miraculous tales of the excited Middle Age may be explained from the co-working of various influences, but this is not the place to enter into the subject.

† The Bath Col may be explained on the ground that a heavenly voice was supposed to be heard in a period of devotion, or that words accidentally spoken by one person had a peculiar subjective meaning for another, like the *tolle lege* of Augustine.

‡ Joseph., Archæol., viii., 2, 4.

§ Josephus says, with reference to miracles, "*τὰ παράλογα καὶ μείζω τῆς ἐλπίδος τοῖς ὁμοίοις πιστοῦται πράγμασιν.*"—Archæol., x., 2, 1.

by the fact that they were expected to be *distinctive* signs of the Messiah, and that they were not ascribed even to John the Baptist, notwithstanding his great deeds and the honour in which he was held as a prophet.

(C.) CHRIST'S OWN ESTIMATE OF HIS MIRACLES.

§ 91. *Apparent Discrepancies, and Mode of Removing them.*

There are apparent contradictions in the several explanations given by Christ of his miracles, and by following them out separately we might arrive at different views of the estimate which he himself placed upon them. But in order to bring perfect harmony out of these apparent contradictions, it is only necessary to distinguish the different points of view in which the miracles present themselves. It has been already said, that miracles can be correctly understood, not when viewed as isolated facts, but in connexion with the whole circle of Divine revelation. Those of Christ, especially, are intelligible only when considered as results of his self-revelation, or, as St. John expresses it, as *the manifestation of his glory*. They demand, therefore, to be so conceived in connexion as to exhibit vividly his whole image in each of these *separate* manifestations; and, on the other hand, the same considerations point out, as the highest aim of miracles, the revelation of Christ's glory in the *whole* of his personal manifestation.

(1.) Christ's Object in working Miracles two-fold.

In their *formal* import miracles are σημεῖα, signs, designed to point from objects of sense to God; powers which, by producing results inexplicable by ordinary agencies, are intended to lead minds yet under the bonds of sense, and unfitted for an immediate spiritual revelation, to yearn after and acknowledge a higher power. But as they were designed to show forth the *whole revealed Christ*, and as the Divine attributes, in the totality of which the image of God was realized in him, cannot be isolated from each other, so no separate manifestation of *power* could proceed from him, not at the same time exhibiting all the other attributes belonging to the Divine image. It is clear, therefore, that although miracles, in relation to nature, are especially manifestations of Power, they could not be performed except in cases where the other attributes, the Wisdom and the holy Love, were brought into requisition. For the same reason, too, we cannot conceive Christ's miracles as *epideictic*, *i. e.*, wrought for no other purpose than to display his power over the laws of nature. In them, as in all his other actions, the end which he had in view is shown by the given circumstances in each case.

Accordingly, we distinguish a two-fold object of his miracles, the first a *material* one, *i. e.*, the meeting of some immediate emergency, of some want of man's earthly life, which his love urged him to satisfy; the other and higher one to point himself out to the persons whose earthly necessities were thus relieved, as the *One* alone capable of satisfying their higher and essential spiritual wants; to raise them from this single exhibition of his glory in the individual miracle to a vivid apprehension of the glory of his entire nature. Nor was this last and higher aim of the miracle confined to the persons immediately concerned; it was to be to all others a *sign*, that they might believe in Jesus as the Son of God.

(2.) A Susceptibility to receive Impressions from the Miracles presupposed.

But all external influences designed to produce an impression such as we have stated demand a susceptible soil in the minds of those who are to receive them. The revelation of Christ by his works, no more than by his words, could produce a Divine impression without an inward susceptibility of Divine influences. The consciousness of God must exist in the soul, though dormant. The Divine revelation must find some point of contact in human nature before religious faith can spring up; there is no compulsory influence from without by which the unsusceptible soul can be driven to faith by an irresistible necessity.

So, when a carnal, worldly mind is the prevailing tendency, outward phenomena, however extraordinary, pass by, and make no impression. The mighty power of the *will* cannot be subdued by any external force. The worldly spirit makes every thing which touches it worldly too. Encompassed by Divine powers, it remains closed against them, in its earthly inclinations, thoughts, and feelings. The mind, thus perverted, cheats itself by denying all miracles, because to acknowledge them would oppose its fleshly interests, and contradict the system of delusion to which it is a slave. It calls the powers of sophistry to aid its self-deception, by converting every thing which could tend to undeceive it into a means of deeper delusion; like those Pharisees who, when compelled to acknowledge works beyond explanation by ordinary agencies, referred them to the powers of darkness rather than of light, in order to escape an admission which they were determined to evade. So he who *totally* rejects the supernatural has already decided upon all separate cases, and a miracle wrought before his very eyes would not be recognized as such. He might admit the *fact* as extraordinary, but would involuntarily seek some other explanation. A mode of thinking that controls the mind cannot be shaken by any power acting *wholly* from without. Such is the might of the free will, which proves its freedom even by its self-created bondage.

Or if miracles do impress the fleshly mind for a moment by the flash of gratification or astonishment which they afford, the impression, made merely upon the senses, is but transitory; for it lacks the point of contact in the soul which alone can make it permanent. How quickly are sensible impressions, even the strongest, forgotten when other and contrary ones follow them! And here we find one of the reasons why Christ refused the demand for miracles merely as proofs of his wonder-working power. For those, he said, whose perverted minds could not be roused to repentance by Moses and the prophets, would *not be persuaded though one rose from the dead.*

How grossly ignorant, then, of human nature must the Deists of the 17th century have been, who plead in opposition to the reality of Christ's miracles, the comparatively little effect which they produced!*

We shall find, therefore, Christ's own statements in regard to his miracles to harmonize perfectly with each other, if we properly distinguish the various classes of human character in their religious and moral relations to miracles, and the different relations and tendencies of the miracles themselves.

§ 92. *The Sign of the Prophet Jonah.*

Christ's declaration, in answer to a demand for a miraculous attestation of his Messiahship, that "*no sign shall be given to this generation but the sign of the Prophet Jonah,*" has been thought by some to indicate either that he wrought no miracles at all, or that he did not mean to employ them as proofs of his Divine calling. The passage preceding that declaration of itself is enough to refute this; for he had just appealed to the healing of a demoniac as proof of the Divine character of his power,† and to the fact that the kingdom of God was victoriously introduced among men by him‡ as a testimony that his ministry was Divine. But we can refute it by simply showing the only sense which the words could have conveyed, in the connexion in which they were used.

The works of Jesus had made a great impression, very much to the discomfort of those whose mode of thinking and party interests made it necessary for them to oppose him. They naturally sought to counteract this impression; to dispute the evidence of the facts which confirmed his ministry as Divine. While the most base and hostile, com-

* Like that strange enthusiast, *Daniel Müller*, who appeared in Nassau in the transition period between mysticism and rationalism, and in whom these two tendencies joined hands. From the extreme of mystic supernaturalism he passed over to the skeptical conclusions of our modern critics. In his treatise against *Lessing* he says, "It is impossible that there should have been a Christ 1700 years ago, who literally wrought such wonders as these. Had any man, by his mere word, caused the blind to see and the lame to walk, given health to the leper and strength to the palsied, fed thousands with a few loaves, and even raised the dead, all men must have esteemed him Divine, all men must have followed him. Only imagine what you yourself would have thought of such a man; and human nature is the same in all ages. And with so many followers, the scribes and Pharisees could not have killed him."—*Ilgen's Zeitschrift*, 1834, p. 257.

† Luke, xi., 20.

‡ Luke, xi., 22

pelled to admit the superhuman powers of Christ, attributed them to the kingdom of darkness, there were others who did not dare to utter such an accusation, but asked a sign of a different character, an objective testimony from God himself in favor of Christ and his ministry, which could not deceive; a visible celestial phenomenon, for instance, or a voice from heaven, clearly and unequivocally authenticating him as a messenger from God. In answer, then, to those who asked a Divine sign apart from his whole manifestation, a sign for that which was of itself the greatest of all signs, Christ appeals to that loftiest of signs, his own appearance as the God-Man, which included within itself all his miracles as separate, individual manifestations.* To this (he told them)—viz., that "The manifestation of the Son of Man was greater than that of Jonah or of Solomon"—belonged all those works of his which no other could perform; every thing was to be referred to that manifestation as the highest in the history of humanity. Had these words been spoken by any other, they would have convicted him of sacrilegious self-exaltation.

§ 93. "*Destroy this Temple,*" *&c.*

Similar to this was Christ's reply at the Passover, which he first kept in Jerusalem, to those who, unable to comprehend an act of holy zeal, asked him to prove his calling as a reformer by a miracle—"*Destroy this temple, and in three days I will raise it up.*" Instead of working a miracle, uncalled for by the circumstances, for their idle satisfaction, he pointed them to a sign that was to come, a great, world-historical sign, which may have been either his resurrection, that was to seal the conclusion of his ministry on earth, and bring about the triumph of his kingdom, in spite of the machinations of his foes, who hoped to destroy his work by putting him to death; or the creation, as the end and aim of his whole manifestation, of the new, spiritual, and eternal Temple of his kingdom among men, after the visible Temple should have been destroyed by their own guilt.

§ 94. *Christ's Distinction between the material Element of Miracles and their essential Object.*—John, vi., 26.

Christ himself distinguishes the *material* part of the miracle, *i. e.*, its effect in satisfying a momentary want, and its *formal* part, as a sign to point from objects of sense to God, and to accredit himself as capable of

* We cannot but be surprised at the remark of *De Wette*, Comm. on Matt., 2d ed., p. 132: "If Jesus had wished to express this thought, he would have uttered nonsense—*No sign shall be given to them, but still given.*" Christ said that to those who were not satisfied by his whole manifestation, as a sign, no other separate sign would be given; how could any thing be a sign for them to whom the highest sign was none? The words, however, do wear that air of paradox which we often find in the discourses of Christ

satisfying all higher spiritual wants. To those who embraced the miracles in this latter sense, properly as σημεῖα, he freely communicated himself; and, on the other hand, he must more and more have alienated himself from those who attached themselves to him only from a momentary interest of the former kind. He, therefore, reproached those who eagerly sought him after the feeding of the five thousand, by saying that they did not seek him because they "*had seen the miracles*" (*i. e.*, as signs to lead them to something higher), but simply because their human wants had been satisfied—"*Ye did eat of the loaves and were filled.*" The light of his works (he told them) was not sufficient to lead them to believe on him, inasmuch as they lacked—what was essential to faith—a sense for the Divine. The gratification of their natural senses was all they sought. In the spirit in which they were, faith was impossible; their preponderating worldliness of mind, subjugating the better tendencies of their nature, left room for no sense of higher wants, and prevented them from feeling the inward "*drawing of the Father.*"*

§ 95. *Christ appealed to the Miracles as Testimonies;* John, xv., 24.—*Three different Stages of Faith.*

Although Christ appeals (in John's Gospel) to the miracles as testimonies of his works, we are not to understand him as appealing to them simply as displays of power, for the grounds already stated. Yet he does, in more than one instance, declare them to be signs, in the world of sense, of a higher power, designed to lead minds as yet unsusceptible of direct spiritual impressions, to acknowledge such influences. "*If I had not done among them the works which none other man did, they had not had sin.*"†

In viewing the miracles thus as means of awakening and strengthening faith, we must distinguish different stand-points in the developement of faith. On the lowest stage stood those who, instead of being drawn by an undeniable want of their spiritual nature, inspired by the power of God working *within* them, had to be attracted by a feeling of physical want, and by impressions made upon their *outward* senses. Yet, like his heavenly Father, whose providence leads men to spiritual things even by means of their physical necessities, Christ condescended to this human weakness, sighing, at the same time, that such means should be indispensable to turn men's eyes to that which lies nearest to their spiritual being. "*Except ye see signs and wonders, ye will not believe.*"‡

A higher stage was occupied by those who were, indeed, led to seek the Messiah by a sense of spiritual need, but whose religious feelings were debased by the admixture of various sensuous elements. As these

* John, vi., 36, 44. † John, xv., 24. ‡ John, iv., 48

were yet in some degree in bondage to sense, and sought the Saviour without perfectly apprehending him as the object of their search, they had to be led to know him by miracles suited to their condition. Such was the case with the Apostles generally, before their religious feelings were purified by continued personal intercourse with Christ. He condescended to this condition, in order to lead men from it to a higher stage of religious life; but yet represented it as subordinate to that purer stage in which they should receive the whole impression of his person, and obtain a full intuition of the mode in which God dwelt and wrought in Him. Jesus said unto Nathanael, "*Because I said I saw thee under the fig-tree, believest thou? Thou shalt see greater things than these. Hereafter ye shall see heaven open, and the angels of God ascending and descending upon the Son of Man.*"*

A far loftier stage of faith was that which, proceeding from an inward living fountain, did not wait for miracles to call it forth, but went before and expected them as natural manifestations of the already acknowledged God. Such a presupposed faith, instead of being summoned by the miracles, rather summoned them, as did the pagan centurion whom Christ offered to the Jews as a model: "*I have not found so great faith, no, not in Israel.*"†

It appears, therefore, that Christ considered that to be the highest stage of religious developement in which faith arose, not from the sensible evidence of miracles, but from an immediate Divine impression finding a point of contact in the soul itself—from a direct experience of that wherein alone the soul could fully satisfy its wants; such a faith as testifies to previous motions of the Divine life in the soul. We have an illustration in Peter, who expressed his profound sense of the blessings that had flowed to him from fellowship with Christ, in his acknowledgment, "*Thou art the Christ, the Son of the living God.* And *Jesus said unto him, Blessed art thou, Simon Barjona, for flesh and blood hath not revealed it unto thee, but my Father which is in heaven.*"‡ This acknowledgment itself might have been made by Peter at an earlier period; but the *way* in which he made it at that critical moment, and the feeling which inspired it, showed that he had obtained a new intuition of Christ as the Son of God. It was for *this* that Christ called him "blessed," because the drawing of the Father had led him to the Son, and the Father had revealed himself to him in the Son. Peter made this confession, at that time, in opposition to others,§ who, although they had a dawning consciousness of Christ's higher nature, did not yet recognize him as the Son of God. The spirit in which he made it is illustrated by a similar confession made by him in view of the defection of many who had been led by "the revelation of flesh and blood" to be-

* John, i., 50, 51.

† Matt., viii., 10.

‡ Matt., xvi., 16, 17.

§ Matt., xvi., 14.

lieve in Jesus, and had afterward abandoned him,* for the very reason that their faith had so low an origin: "*Lord, to whom shall we go? Thou hast the words of eternal life. And we believe, and we are sure that thou art that Christ, the Son of the living God.*"†

And so, when *Thomas* doubted, Christ condescended to give him a visible proof of his resurrection;‡ but at the same time he declared that that was a higher faith which needed no such support, but rested, with undoubting confidence, upon the inward experience of Divine manifestations. "*Blessed are they that have not seen and yet have believed.*"

§ 96. *The Communication of the Divine Life the highest Miracle.*—John, xiv., 12.

Finally, the words of Christ himself assure us that the communication of the life of God to men was the greatest of all miracles, the essence and the aim of all; and, further, that it was to be the standing miracle of all after ages. "*He that believeth on me, the works that I do shall he do also, and greater works than these shall he do, because I go to my Father. And whatsoever ye shall ask in my name, that will I do, that the Father may be glorified in the Son.*" The power of diffusing the Divine life, which had been confined to him alone, was, by means of his glorification, to be extended to others, and to assume in them a peculiar self-subsisting form—the miracle which was to be wrought among all men, and in all time, by the preaching of the Gospel. ["*He shall send you another Comforter, that he may abide with you forever, even the Spirit of Truth.*"]

CHAPTER VI.

THE MIRACLES OF CHRIST CONSIDERED IN REGARD TO SUPERNATURAL AGENCY.

§ 97. *Transition from the Natural to the Supernatural in the Miracles.*

IT has been asserted in modern times, that in order to receive miracles at all, we must conceive them as directly and abruptly opposed to nature, and admit no intermediate agencies whatever. But we cannot be confined to this alternative by men who wish to caricature the views which we maintain. Abrupt contrasts may be set up in abstract theories; but in real life we do not find them. There are always intermediate agencies and points of transition. And why should this not be the case in the opposition between the natural and the supernatural? We think that we have already shown that the higher unity of the Divine plan of the world embraces miracles as well as the ordinary de-

* John, vi., 66 † John, vi., 69. ‡ John, xx., 27.

velopement of nature. We hold ourselves justified, therefore, in distinguishing, with regard to the *marvellous* part of the miracles, certain steps of transition from the natural to the supernatural. Not that we can separate these gradations so nicely as to constitute a division of the miracles thereby; but we can trace an important harmony with the universal laws of the Divine government of the world in the fact that here, too, there are no sudden leaps, but a gradual transition by intermediate steps throughout.

Looking at all the miracles, there are some in regard to which it may be doubted whether they belong to the class of natural or supernatural events; on the other side, there are some in which the creative power is exhibited in the highest degree, and which bear no analogy whatever to the results of natural causes. Between these extreme classes, there are many miraculous works in which the supernatural can be made vividly obvious by means of natural analogies. To these last belong most of the miracles which Christ wrought upon *human* nature; while those wrought upon the *material* world, rejecting all natural analogies, may be ranged under the second extreme class above mentioned. The latter are very few in comparison with the former, and far less intimately connected with Christ's peculiar calling.

A. CHRIST'S MIRACLES WROUGHT UPON HUMAN NATURE.

I. The Healing of Diseases.

§ 98. *The Spiritual Agencies employed.—Faith demanded for the Cure*

Those works of redeeming love which Christ wrought upon the human body, the healing of diseases, and the like, displayed the peculiar feature of his whole ministry. The ailments of the body are closely connected with those of the soul;* and even if, in individual cases, this cannot be proved, yet in the whole progress of human developement there is always a causal connexion between *sin* and *evil;* between the disorganization of the spirit through sin, and all forms of bodily disorder. There was a beautiful connexion, therefore, between Christ's work in healing the latter, and his proper calling to remove the fundamental disease of human nature, and to restore its original harmony, disturbed by sin.

Some of these diseases, also, arose purely from moral causes, and could be thoroughly cured only by moral and spiritual remedies. Little as we know of the connexion between the mind and the body,

* It is remarkable that great plagues often spread over the earth precisely at the same time with general *crises* in the intellectual or moral world; *e. g.*, the plague at Athens and the Peloponnesian war: the plagues under the Antonines and under Decius; the *labes inguinaria* at the end of the 6th century; the *ignis sacer* in the 11th; the *black* death in the 14th, &c. That great man, *Niebuhr*, whose letters contain so many golden truths, alluded to this coincidence in another connexion.—*Leben*, ii., 167

we know enough to make it in some degree clear to us how an extraordinary Divine impression might produce remarkable effects in the bodily organism.

We do not mean, however, by this remark, to bring all such influences down (as some have done) into the sphere of the purely subjective. It is true that a natural power, highly intensified, might produce effects closely resembling the supernatural; it is true that the imagination, strongly stimulated and exalted, often works strange wonders; but we have to do here only with effects which *must* be attributed to higher causes, which must be due to an objective Divine agency. In the cases to which we refer (as, indeed, in all cases), the objective and subjective factors could co-operate; the Divine influence of Christ upon the soul, and, through it, upon the bodily organism, could work together with the susceptibility to impression, the *receptivity* (so to speak), on the part of man. Hence it was that Christ demanded a special Faith as a necessary condition of his healing agency; indeed, we can find no instance of his working a miracle where a hostile tendency of mind prevailed.

We can conceive of bodily cures thus wrought by means of spiritual influences more readily than any others; and they correspond precisely with the laws which Christ's operations have never ceased to follow. But we cannot bring all the instances of healing which he wrought under this class; some of them were wrought at a distance, and offer no point of departure of this kind. And as we are compelled to admit, in some of the miracles, immediate operations upon *material* nature, we are the less authorized to deny that such direct influences were exerted upon the bodily organism.

§ 99. *Use of Physical Agencies in the Cure of Diseases.*

Christ employed his miraculous power in various modes of operation. He operated by his immediate presence, by the power of that Divine will which exercised its influence through his word and his whole manifestation; and this in the very cases in which we might admit a bodily cure by the use of physical agencies. Sometimes, indeed, there was besides a material application, *e.g.*, the contact of the hand. In other cases he made use of material substances, and even of such as were thought to be possessed of healing virtues, as, in blindness, of saliva,* water,† and anointing with oil.

But in these cases the means were too disproportionate to the results, for us to imagine that they were naturally capable of producing them; and as Christ did not *always* employ them, there is no room to suppose that they were necessary as vehicles of his healing power—a supposition which brings the miracles too far down into the sphere of

* *Plin.*, Hist Natur., xxviii., 7.

† Mark, viii.; John, ix.

merely physical agencies. We must rather presuppose that as Christ in his teaching, &c., took up the forms in common use among men to work out something higher from them, so he allowed his powers of healing to exhibit themselves in the use of these ordinary means in a symbolical way. He may have designed thereby to bestow some peculiar lessons of instruction.

The cures wrought at a distance do not admit of this material connecting link; but the operations of Christ's will could overstep all the barriers of space.

§ 100. *The Relation between Sin and Physical Evil.—Jewish Idea of Punitive Justice.—Christ's Doctrine on the Subject.*

We must now examine Christ's miracles of healing in their *moral* aspects, and in their connexion with his ministry as Redeemer. If it can be shown that all those disturbances of the bodily organism, which we call diseases, have their origin in *Sin*, as the source of all discord in human nature, we may infer that there is a close connexion between these miracles and his proper calling; and that, in healing the diseases *produced* by sin, by means of his influence upon the essential nature of the disturbed organism, he displayed himself also as the Redeemer from sin. In many cases, also, we may find the physical and the moral cure reciprocally operating upon each other.

The question first occurs, In what relation does Christ himself place disease to sin? This question is connected with the broader one, In what relation to sin does he place physical evil in general? In Luke, v., 20, and John, v., 14, he seems to assign a special connexion between sin and certain diseases as its punishments; but other expressions of his appear to contradict such a connexion. To solve this difficulty, we must not only distinguish the different aims of these several expressions, but also discriminate between the true and the false in the modes of thinking prevalent among the Jews.

The doctrine that sin is guilt, and that the Divine holiness reveals itself in opposition to sin, as punitive justice, is one of the characteristics of the religion of the Old Testament in its relations to the various shapes of natural religion. Punitive justice displays itself in the established connexion between sin and evil, in consequence of which the sinful will that rebels in act against the Divine law must be compelled, through suffering, actually to acknowledge that law, and to humble itself before its majesty. According to this view of the world, which subordinates the *natural* to the *moral*, all evil is to be attributed to sin; it shows itself to the soul estranged from God as belonging to, and connected with sin; the consciousness that sin is opposed to the Divine order of nature is developed by sufferings; and thus sin appears, even to the sinner, to be deserving of punishment. All history proves that the consequences of bad actions, as well as of good ones, operate for generations; all history testifies that "*God is a jealous God, visiting the iniquities of the fathers upon the children to the third and fourth generation.*" We can see this especially in the *crises* of the history of nations, by tracing them to their preparatory causes. The history of the Jewish nation, particularly, was designed to exhibit this universal law in miniature, but with striking distinctness.

To this conception of the punitive justice of God, as displaying itself in the progress of history and in the course of generations, a contracted Theodicy had joined itself, which arrogantly assumed to apply the universal law to special cases.* The book of Job had already refuted this contracted view; and Christ himself opposed it; taking, however, the basis of truth which was found in the Old Testament, purifying it from foreign admixtures of error, and giving it a fuller developement.†

The doctrine of punitive justice was in no degree impugned by the new and lofty prominence which Christ gave to the Redeeming *love* of God; on the contrary, the latter doctrine presupposed the former, but at the same time gave it peculiar modifications. And as Christ teaches us that all human events are subservient to the manifestation of redeeming love, the highest aim of God's moral government, it follows that the connexion between sin and physical evil, ordained by Divine justice, must serve the same great end. The *universal* evil introduced by sin is so distributed in *detail* as to aid in preparing the soil of men's hearts to receive and appropriate redemption and salvation, and in further purifying the hearts of those who have already become partakers of the Divine life.

There are two passages in which Christ contradicts, in the one negatively and in the other positively, the contracted view of punitive justice, before referred to.

The *negative* contradiction is given in Luke, xiii., 2, 4: "*Suppose ye that these Galileans were sinners above all the Galileans, because they suffered such things? I tell you, nay; but except ye repent, ye shall all likewise perish. Or those eighteen, upon whom the tower in Siloam fell, and slew them, think ye that they were sinners above all men that dwelt in Jerusalem?*" In this passage Christ teaches that the evil that befel the *individuals* did not necessarily measure their individual guilt, but that their particular sufferings were to be traced back to the *general* guilt of the nation.

* The fact that this view was maintained by the carnally-disposed, and that the later Jewish history often apparently reversed the connexion between sin and evil, piety and happiness, gave rise, subsequently, to an Ebionitish reaction, which maintained that in this world, belonging as it does to Satan, the wicked have possession of the goods of this life, while poverty and pain must be the lot of the pious; and that this state of things will only be compensated in the Millennium, or in the life to come. Christ's truth opposes both these false views.

† Luke, xiii., 4.

The *positive* contradiction is found in John, ix., 2, 3 : "*Master, who did sin, this man or his parents, that he was born blind?* Jesus answered, *Neither hath this man sinned, nor his parents; but that the works of God should be made manifest in him.*" Here he rebukes the presupposition that the calamity of the individual sufferer was to be referred to sins committed by his ancestors, and brings out, in strong contrast with it, that Almighty love which shows itself even by so distributing physical evil as to train men for salvation.*

We interpret, in accordance with this view, the explanations which Christ gave in several cases of a relation between disease and sin, and between healing and the pardon of sin. He referred either to the *general* connexion, through which all evil was intended to call forth the consciousness of sin; or to a closer connexion, in individual cases, between a given misfortune and a specific sin. The relation between the bodily cure and the pardon of sin was still closer.†

II. Demoniacal Possession.

The connexion, of which we have spoken, between sin and evil, must be especially predicated of those forms of disease which, view them as we may, exhibited a moral wreck, not only of the individual sufferers, but of the age in which they lived; and which admitted no means of perfect cure except moral influences. We mean the *psychical* diseases, the sufferings of the so-called Demoniacs.

§ 101. *Two Theories of the Affliction: (a) Possession by Evil Spirits: (b) Insanity.—Analogous Phenomena in other Times.*

There are two points of view, opposed to each other, but yet, perhaps, admitting of an intermediate ground, in which we may contemplate these forms of disease; they may have originated either (*a*) from internal causes in the soul itself, or (*b*) from causes entirely outward and supernatural. Those who adopt the first view confine their attention to the characteristic symptoms as reported, and compare them with the very similar ailments, the diseases of the mind and of the nervous system, which not only existed in that age, but have appeared at all subsequent periods.‡ Those who strictly adopt the latter view adhere closely to the letter of the narrative, and make no attempt to distinguish what is *objective* in it from what is *subjective;* but see in the miserable demoniacs only passive instruments of evil spirits.

If, in accordance with this view, we admit no intermediate agency, but ascribe the phenomena immediately to evil spirits, the cures must be directly attributed to Christ's dominion over the powers of the other

* We shall examine this explanation again in its proper place in the narrative.

† Matt., ix., 2–5.

‡ Similar diseases, occurring in the first centuries, were explained in this way by the physicians.—Orig., in Matt., xiii., § 6.

world; thus strikingly showing his supernatural control over a supernatural cause of disease. And, on the other hand, if we class these phenomena with diseases of the mind in general, and consider the supposed indwelling of evil spirits only as a symptom grounded on natural causes, we shall more readily be able to conceive how a disease arising entirely, or, at least, chiefly from a psychical cause, could be cured by a purely psychical agency. Nor would this in the least degree deny, or even detract from, the miraculous character of Christ's acts; for to restore a raving maniac to reason by a look or a word was surely beyond all natural psychological influence, and presupposed powers transcending all ordinary agencies. It is true, we find analogous cases in later times, in which great things were wrought by immediate Divine impressions, and by devout prayer in the name of Christ.*

Not only at the time of Christ's appearance, but also in the centuries immediately following,† many forms of disease like those called demoniacal in the New Testament were spread abroad; and we may infer that the same cause was at work in both periods.

§ 102. *Connexion of the Phenomena with the State of the Times.—Conceptions of the Jews in regard to them: of the Demoniacs themselves.*

The diseases of the mind in every age bear the stamp, to some degree, of the prevailing tendencies and ideas of the times; and those to which we refer reflected the peculiar and predominant features of the Jewish mind of that age. The wretched demoniacs seemed to be hurried onward by a strange and hostile power that subjugated their intellectual and moral being, and whose chief characteristic, as displayed in their paroxysms, was a wild and savage destructiveness. The Jews explained these phenomena according to their own notions, and especially by the general opinion that man was surrounded on every side by the operations of evil spirits, who were the authors of both moral and physical evil.‡ And as a fierce destructiveness was considered to

* We must not take the spirit of an age of materialism or rationalism as a rule for judging of all phenomena of the ψυχή, which veils within itself the *Infinite*; which is capable of such manifold excitement; and whose various powers are alternately dormant and active —now one prevailing, and now another. An age may be destitute of certain phenomena and experiences, because it has no organs for developing them; and this would prove nothing against their reality.

Although I can hardly think it possible that the view given in the text, taken in connexion with the general principles of this book, can be misunderstood, yet, in order to guard against a possible misinterpretation, I deem it best to add, that it was far from my intention to do away with the distinction between the natural and the supernatural, or to trace the latter entirely to the developement of powers inherent in the ψυχή. I wished only to point out the organ, the point of contact, in the ψυχή, for supernatural communications and influences; to show that it is *itself* supernatural in its hidden essence, which looks forward to be unfolded hereafter in the higher world to which it is allied.

† As seen in the Fathers, and in Lucian's *Philopseudes*.

‡ Some have attributed the prevalence of this opinion to an admixture of Persian reli

be characteristic of these spirits, the condition of the demoniacs was ascribed to their being *possessed* by one or more of them.*

The diseased persons themselves involuntarily conceived of their own experience according to the prevalent opinion, and their expressions, literally taken, contributed to confirm it. Every thing irrational which suggested itself to them appeared to their consciousness as the work and the will of the indwelling evil spirit. They conceived themselves, in fact, as possessed of two natures, viz., their real proper being (the true *I*), and the evil spirit which subjugated the other; and thus it happened that they spoke in the person of the evil spirit, with which they felt themselves blended into one, even in instincts and propensities utterly repugnant to their true nature. The sense of inward discord and distraction might rise to such a height as to induce the belief that they were possessed by a number of spirits, to whom they were compelled to lend their utterance.

We may find a reason for the remarkable prevalence of such phenomena at that time, not only among the Jews, but also throughout the Roman Empire, in the character of the age itself. It was an age of spiritual and physical distress, of manifold and violent disruptions; such as characterize those critical epochs in the history of the world at which, from the dissolution of all existing things, a new creation is about to unfold itself. The sway of Demonism was a sign of the approaching dissolution of the Old World.† Its phenomena—symptoms of the universally felt discord—were among the signs of the times which pointed to the coming of the Redeemer, who was to change that discord into harmony. The insatiable craving of want is always a precursor of the approaching supply.

§ 103. *Accommodation of the two extreme Theories.*

If now the question be asked whether these phenomena are to be considered as wholly natural or as supernatural, we answer, that these two extreme views may be more or less abruptly opposed to each other. On

gious doctrines; but it had a far deeper ground in the religious spirit of the age. It arose from the sense of *discord* which penetrated the whole mind of that time, and which was reflected in the doctrine of Dualism, then so extensively prevailing.

* We agree with *Strauss*, that, according to the Jewish mode of thinking, the interference of evil spirits must be really supposed, and that the views of Josephus (B. J., vii., 6, 3: τὰ γὰρ καλούμενα δαιμόνια πονηρῶν ἐστιν ἀνθρώπων πνέυματα, τοῖς ζῶσιν εἰσδυόμενα) were modified by his Greek culture. At a later period, when Oriental influences were more felt, the idea of demons, as spirits allied to matter, or as hypostatic emanations from the ὕλη, was common even among the educated Hellenists.

† *Schelling's* remark on this subject, in his "Philosophical Inquiries into the Nature of Human Freedom," is worthy of note: "The time is coming when all this splendour will be dissolved; when the existing body of this fair world will fall to pieces, and chaos come again. But before the final wreck, the all-pervading powers assume the nature of evil spirits; the very powers which in the sounder time were the protecting spirits of life, become, as dissolution draws on, agents of mischief and destruction.

the one hand, we may ascribe the *origin* of the disease to natural causes, and judge of the symptoms accordingly, without excluding the operation of the other concealed cause; the question whether such a cause existed or not can be by no means decided merely by the symptoms.

Christ teaches that all wickedness, and all evil in its connexion with wickedness, must be traced back to a higher cause—to a Spirit* that first rebelled against God, to an Original Sin, which gave birth to the first germ of wickedness. As he lays down a certain connexion between the various stages of the kingdom of God, so he assigns a simi-

* If it could be proved that Christ had only taken up the doctrine of the existence of Satan by way of *formal* accommodation (p. 114), the question of the demoniacs would be at once decided. It cannot be denied that in many of his expressions we might substitute, for *Satan*, the objective notion of *evil*, without at all affecting the thought. We might, indeed, admit that he used the doctrine (borrowed from the circle of popular ideas) merely as a figurative covering for *evil*, if *he himself* had any where intimated that he did not intend thereby to confirm the view of the origin of evil which the popular notion involved; just as we showed *from his own words* that, in transferring the popular figures to his Messianic kingdom, he *did* distinguish between the substantial truth and its formal covering. But this is by no means the case here. There is not a vestige of evidence in his conversations with his disciples to show that he did *not* intend to establish the doctrine that *a higher intelligence, estranged from God, was the original source of evil.* Neither can we class this question (as some do) among those which have no bearing on the interests of religion, and which Christ's mission did not require him to interfere with; our conception of evil will be very different if we confine it to human nature, from what it would be, if we admit its existence also in spirits of a higher order.

In John, viii., 44, Christ gives a perfectly defined conception of Satan; he designates him as "the Spirit alienated from truth and goodness (for, according to John's usage, ἀλήθεια involves both the *true* and the *good*); in whom falsehood and wickedness have become a second nature; who can find no abiding-place in the truth." The revelation of truth which the spirits were to receive from communion with the Father of Spirits passes by him unheeded; he cannot receive and hold it fast, because he has no organ to embrace it, no susceptibility for its impressions. Christ tells the Pharisees that they, serving the Spirit of Lies, and living in communion with him, showed themselves, by the spirit which their actions manifested, to be children of Satan, rather than of Abraham and God. *Schleiermacher's* attempt to prove (Works, iii., § 45, p. 214) that even in this passage the idea of a personal Satan is untenable, is by no means successful. "This passage," says he, "can not be interpreted throughout on the theory of the reality of the devil, without either opposing the devil to God in the Manichæan sense, or else calling Christ the *Son of God* in the same extended signification in which the Pharisees are called *Sons of the Devil.*" The argument is unsuccessful, we say, because the proper point of comparison would be, *not* the sense in which *Christ* can be called the Son of God, but the sense in which *pious men* could be so called; and in a comparison it is not necessary that all the relations should be adequate, but only those which are common to the point of comparison itself.

Nor can we admit that Christ, in making use of the current doctrine as a covering for his own, added nothing new to it. It is true that he made no disclosures on the subject to satisfy the speculative curiosity of science, but here, as elsewhere, made his communications only to meet practical wants. It is, however, precisely in the region of practical religion that the doctrine of the personality of Satan was newly modified by its connexion with the doctrine of Jesus, as the author of salvation. As for the passages in which "evil" might be substituted for "Satan," it is enough to say, that after the existence of such an intelligence, the first rebel against God, had been given as a fact, it was natural to employ him as the representative of evil in general. We may use "Satan" as a symbol for wickedness in general, without implying any thing against the doctrine of his personal existence. See p. 74

lar connexion between all the manifestations of the powers of evil. It is thus, in perfect accordance with the teaching of Christ, that we ascribe those fearful disturbances of the corporeal, spiritual organism (in which the might of the principle of sin in human nature and the moral degeneracy of that nature are so strikingly exhibited), to the general kingdom of the Evil One.

On the other hand, in admitting the higher and concealed cause, we need not necessarily conceive it as operating in a magical way, without any preparation. A preparation, a point of contact in the pyschological developement, is by no means excluded by such an admission, but, as is the case in all influences wrought upon man's inner nature, rather presupposed. In every instance we both can and ought to distinguish the symptoms of these diseases (as stated in the narrative) which arose from the hidden cause, from those which might have originated in the current opinions of the times, or in the peculiar psychological condition of the sufferers themselves. In either case we shall have to ascribe the radical cure, which Christ alone could accomplish, to the operation of his Spirit upon the evil principle in the man himself.

§ 104. *Christ's Explanations of Demonism purely Spiritual.—His Accommodation to the Conceptions of the Demoniacs.*

It is important to inquire whether Christ assigned, in express words, any definite view of the origin of these diseases, or established any view by taking it as a point of departure. That he did not *dispute* the current opinion, does not prove that he participated in it; this would have been one of those errors, not affecting the interests of religion, which his mission did not require him to correct. Apart from its moral ground, it belongs to the domain of science, which is left to its own independent developement—to natural philosophy, psychology, or medicine; sciences entirely foreign to the sphere of Christ's immediate calling as a teacher, although they might derive fruitful germs of truth from it. It was his peculiar office only to reveal to men the moral ground of both general and special evil, and thus to convince them that its thorough cure could be effected only by influences wrought upon the principle of moral corruption in which it originated. In order to this, the doctrine that these diseases were caused by indwelling evil spirits could be made use of as a point of departure, especially as the truth of the idea of a kingdom of Satan, in its moral sense, was presupposed.

In regard to Christ's accommodation to the conceptions which the demoniacs themselves had of their own condition, our remarks in another place (p. 114) in reference to the distinction between *formal* and *material* accommodation are not fully applicable. The law of veracity, in the intercourse of beings in possession of reason, does not hold good where the essential conditions of rational intercourse are done away. In such cases, language obeys its natural laws only in proportion as the use of reason itself is re-established.

There lay a profound truth at the bottom of the demoniac's consciousness that his feelings, inclinations, and words did not spring from his rational, God-allied nature (his true *I*), but from a foreign power belonging to the kingdom of the devil, which had subjugated the former. And this truth offered the necessary point of contact for the operation of Christ's spiritual influence to aid the soul, which longed to be delivered from its distraction and freed from its ignominious bondage. In the mind of the demoniac, the fundamental truth was inseparable from the *form* in which he conceived it; it was, therefore, necessary to seize upon the latter, in order to develope the former.

§ 105. *Difference between Christ's Healing of the Demoniacs and the Operations of the Jewish Exorcists.*

The so-called *Exorcists* were at that time practising among the Jews their pretended art of expelling demons; an art which they affected to derive from Solomon.* The means which they employed were certain herbs, fumigations, and forms of conjuration. They probably possessed a dexterous legerdemain, and perhaps by natural agencies, aided by the imagination, could produce powerful effects for the moment, the cases of obvious failure being forgotten in those of apparent success. Had Christ produced only similar effects, their very commonness would have made them unimpressive. The moral and spiritual influences of Christ, proceeding from his immediate Divine power, were of a totally different character from these juggling tricks.

An excellent illustration of this is afforded in the account of the cure of the deaf and dumb demoniac, in Luke, xi., 14; Matt., xii., 22. Even the most hostile Pharisees could not deny that in this instance something was done which could not be explained by natural causes; and to obviate the impression which it made upon the multitude, and to prevent them from acknowledging the Divinity of Christ, they accused him, contrary to their own convictions, of being in league with the ruler of evil spirits, and of working his wonders by powers derived from that dark source. Christ points out the contradiction involved in their assertion, and showed that such works could be wrought only by the power of God, which alone could free the human soul from the dominion of the evil spirit. He designates this individual case as a sign

* Joseph., Archæol., viii., 2, § 5. Josephus appeals to a remarkable proof of this fact, which one of these exorcists had given before Vespasian in presence of part of the Roman army. See the Greek Testament of Solomon (written at a later period) in Dr. *Fleck*' "Theologische Reisefrüchte," iii., 113.

that the kingdom of God, before which the powers of darkness must flee away, had manifested itself. He gives them to understand that the original source of evil in mankind and in men had first to be re moved, before its particular effects could be subdued. And from this it necessarily followed (he showed) that every casting out of evil spirits, every healing of demoniacs, which was not founded upon a victory over the original evil power, was only an apparent exorcism, and must be followed by a worse reaction. Thus the ordinary exorcists, who apparently produced the same effects as Christ, in reality did the very opposite. The evil was banished only to return with increased power.

He that does not work in communion with Christ, and by the power of the same Spirit, will, in producing effects *apparently* the same, bring about totally different results. He advances the kingdom of the devil, and not the kingdom of God.

The case of the Gadarene* who was restored from raving madness to a sound mind by the Divine power of Christ, and who was so drawn to the Saviour that he wished to remain always with him, shows that the radical cure of the demoniacs consisted in this, that they who were freed from the evil spirit were drawn to the Spirit of God which had delivered them. Such a condition was perhaps to many the crisis of a higher life. In this way Mary Magdalene appears to have been brought into the narrower circle of Christ's disciples.†

The silence of John's Gospel in regard to Christ's healing of demo niacs may be ascribed to the fact that the disease was more common in Galilee than in Jerusalem.

III. The Raising of the Dead.

§ 106. *Different Views on these Miracles.*

The position to be assigned to the miracle of the *raising of the dead* will depend upon the view which we take of the real condition of those said to be raised. Some suppose that they were not absolutely dead in the physiological sense, but that there was an intermission of the powers of life, presenting symptoms resembling death; and those who adopt this view of the case consider the miracle to differ only in *degree* from that of healing the sick.

But if the accounts are taken literally, and we suppose a *real* death, the miracle was *specifically* different from that of healing, and, in fact, constituted the very culminating point of supernatural agency. Yet, even to awaken the dormant powers of life, and kindle up again the expiring flame, would certainly have been a *miracle*, demanding for its accomplishment a Divine power in Christ.

A precise account of the symptoms, and a knowledge of physiology,

* Mark, v., 1. Luke, viii., 26.

† Mark, xvi., 9.

would be necessary to give us the elements for a decision of this question, in the absence of any testimony from Christ's own mouth to decide it. In regard to Christ's own words, it is a fair question whether he meant to distinguish closely between apparent and real death, or whether he made use of the term "death" only in accordance with the popular usage.

If it be presupposed that the dead were restored to earthly life after having entered into another form of existence—into connexion with another world—the idea of resurrection would be dismal; but we have no right to form such a presupposition in our blank ignorance of the laws under which the new form of consciousness developes itself in the soul after separation from the body.*

B. CHRIST'S MIRACLES WROUGHT UPON MATERIAL NATURE.

§ 107. *These exhibit Supernatural Power most obviously.*

We pass now to a consideration of the miracles which Christ wrought upon *material* nature, in which the supernatural exhibits itself in the highest possible degree, as an intermediate psychical agency is, by the very nature of the case, excluded.

Apart from individual cases, it is certain that a power of controlling nature is one of the marked features of the image of Christ given to us in the evangelical tradition. He had fully impressed men's minds with a belief of this. And in deciding upon the individual cases themselves, every thing depends upon the conception of Christ's character as a *whole*, with which we set out. Were such a narrative of the acts of an ordinary man handed down to us, even though we might be unable to separate the actual course of fact from the subjective dress given to it in the account, we should yet be inclined to suppose that the man had wrought *some* mighty influences upon the minds of his contemporaries, and that they had involuntarily transferred these to nature, which is so often made the mirror of what passes in the mind of man.

But if we set out in our investigation of the Gospel narrative with a just idea of the specific difference between Christ and any, even the greatest, of mere men; if we set out with a full intuition of the *God-Man*, we shall find no difficulty whatever in believing that he operated upon the most secret powers of nature as no other could have done, and, by the might of his Divinity, controlled nature in a way which finds no parallel among men.

* See hereafter on the resurrection of the "Widow's Son," and of "Lazarus."

BOOK V.

THE PUBLIC MINISTRY OF CHRIST

ACCORDING TO ITS

CHRONOLOGICAL CONNEXION.

PART I. FROM THE COMMENCEMENT OF HIS MINISTRY TO THE TRIUMPHAL ENTRY.

PART II. FROM THE TRIUMPHAL ENTRY TO THE ASCENSION

BOOK V.

THE PUBLIC MINISTRY OF CHRIST ACCORDING TO ITS CHRONOLOGICAL CONNEXION.

INTRODUCTION.

ON THE DIFFERENCES BETWEEN THE SYNOPTICAL GOSPELS AND JOHN.

IN comparing the first three Gospels with John, we find several discrepancies in regard both to the *chronology* of the narrative and to the *theatre* of Christ's labours.

§ 108. *Differences of Chronology.*

Matthew, Mark, and Luke include but *one* feast of the Passover within the period of Christ's public ministry, while John's narrative embraces *three or four.* It may be enough to say in regard to this, that the former Gospels do not confine themselves to a chronological arrangement, and therefore we are entitled to draw no conclusion from the fact that the Passover is mentioned in them but once, and that towards the close of Christ's career upon earth. The facts narrated may have extended through several years, and yet the mention of the Passover feasts may have been omitted, as other chronological marks have been.

There is nothing in the first three Gospels to contradict the theory that Christ's ministry lasted for several years. Even in Luke himself* there is a passing remark which necessarily presupposes the occurrence of one Passover in the *midst* of that ministry. There is nothing, then, to invalidate John's account, which mentions the occurrence of several

§ 109. *Differences as to the Theatre of Christ's Labours.*

According to the synoptical Gospels, *Galilee* was the chief theatre of Christ's labours, and he only transferred them to Jerusalem when he was going to meet his approaching death.

We must here more minutely examine the question before lightly

* Luke, vi., 1 the *σάββατον δευτερόπρωτον*, in connexion with the "ripe ears of corn."

touched upon (p. 99). Did Christ purposely confine his labours chiefly to Galilee in hope of finding more ready access to the hearts of its simpler-minded inhabitants, who were less in bondage to the traditions of the Pharisees than the people of Jerusalem? or was it because he was less exposed there to the "snares" of the Pharisees, and could, therefore, hope to exercise his labours more uninterruptedly, and for a longer period? Did he wait until he had laid the foundation of his work so firmly that it would endure, and propagate itself after his death, before he determined to go and meet the perils that awaited him at the seat of the priesthood? Did he only make up his mind to go, in spite of the dangers which he foresaw would environ him, in order to avoid the reproach of distrusting the Divinity of his own cause, and thereby giving occasion of perplexity to his disciples?

If these questions are answered in the affirmative, we should have to suppose that the tradition which John followed in his Gospel did not give correctly the original relations of Christ's labours. It was utterly inconsistent with a wish on his part to be recognized as Messiah, for him to conceal himself so long in a corner of Galilee, and to hold back, for so long a time, his testimony to his Divine calling before the face of the people and the priests at Jerusalem. It would have been a stumbling-block, indeed, for one who professed to acknowledge the old Mosaic religious ideas in all their holiness, to refrain, during the whole course of his public labours, from visiting the Temple at one of the chief feasts of the Jews.

§ 110. *Proof that Christ frequently exercised his Ministry in Judea and Jerusalem.*

It is every way accordant, indeed, with internal probability, that Jesus should have expected to find easier access to the simple-minded Galilean peasants than to the rich, the haughty, and the learned at Jerusalem. But it is altogether improbable to suppose that he would subject himself to the reproach of despising the ancient and holy institutions* of the Jews, by absenting himself from the gatherings of the devout at their chief feasts;† and it would have been strange if he had neglected the opportunity of extending his labours that was afforded by

* In the Talmudical treatise "*Chagigah,*" c. ii., none (among adults) but the deaf, the sick, the insane, and the very aged, are exempted from the obligation to attend the principal feasts at Jerusalem. Of course, this law could not apply to the Jews of distant countries, who were only required to send annually a deputation to the Temple, with sacrifices, and with the money arising from the price of the first fruits. Conf. *Philo,* Legat. ad Cajum, §§ 23, 31.

† Luke, ii., 41, shows that the devout of Galilee felt themselves bound to journey to Jerusalem at least at the Passover; the passage even speaks of the journey of a *woman,* on whom the law imposed no such obligation. We cannot (with *Strauss*) find any proof even in Matthew that absence from the festivals was held of no account among the Jewish-Christians.

the general coming together of Jews from all countries at those festivals.

And how unwise would it have been in him to defer the commencement of his labours in the Theocratic capital until the precise period when his ministry in Galilee must have drawn upon him the hatred and the fears of the prevailing Pharisaic party of Jerusalem, when he must have foreseen, too, that he would be overcome by them!

As to his putting off his journey to Jerusalem until the Apostles were sufficiently prepared to carry on the work without his personal presence, surely the Apostles knew as yet too little of his doctrines to render such a course consistent even with *human* foresight.

Moreover, the fanatical hatred of Christ which was manifested by the Pharisaical party can only be explained upon the ground that he had excited their opposition by a previous ministry, of some duration, in the city of Jerusalem itself. Nor are there wanting, even in the first three Gospels, intimations to the same effect, *e. g.*, Matt., iv., 25; xv., 1, in which the scribes and Pharisees of *Jerusalem* are spoken of as gathering round Jesus in *Galilee* and asking him entangling questions. It may have been the case, either that, *after* his labours in Jerusalem had drawn their hatred upon him, they followed, and watched him suspiciously, even in Galilee; or that some of the events that originally happened in the city were, in the course of tradition, intermingled and confused with those which occurred in Galilee. Again, the earnest exclamation of Christ, recorded in Luke, xiii., 34; Matt., xxiii., 37, distinctly implies that he had *often* endeavoured, *by his personal teaching in Jerusalem*, to rouse the people to repentance and conversion, that they might be saved from the ruin then impending over them. The words, "*children of Jerusalem*," although they might apply to the whole nation, must, in this exclamation, which is specifically addressed to the "*city which killed the prophets*," be taken as referring directly to the inhabitants of that city.

The account of Christ's relations with the family of Lazarus, given in Luke (x., 38–42), coincides in spirit with John's statement (xi., 5) of the intimate affection with which the Saviour regarded them; and the intimacy must have been formed during a prolonged stay in Jerusalem. The fact, too, that several distinguished men of that city (*e. g.*, Joseph of Arimathea, as we are told by the first Evangelists) had attached themselves to Christ, affords us the same conclusion. Nor can we fail to trace, in Luke's account (ix., 51–62) of his last journey to Jerusalem, some confusion, arising from a blending together, in the narrative, of events that had occurred on a former journey.

And, again, can it be imagined that Christ omitted to make use of his miraculous powers* *precisely* in Jerusalem, where the best opportunities

* This difficulty, indeed, is avoided in Matthew's Gospel, for it is there stated (xxi., 14).

of employing them for the relief of human suffering would have been afforded? Would there not, moreover, have been some trace of this in the mode of his reception at Jerusalem, similar, probably, to what occurred on his first labours at Nazareth? Would not his labours there have been very different from what the synoptical Gospels report them, if they had been his first efforts in the city?

Thus there are many things in the first three Gospels themselves which indicate and presuppose the accuracy of John's narrative. The latter is, besides, entirely consistent with itself, both in its chronology, and in its accounts of the several journeys of Christ to the Feasts.

Finally, those who infer from the synoptical Gospels that Christ made but *one* journey, must ascribe to the author of John's Gospel a fabrication, wilfully invented, to serve his own purpose. But the man who could do this could never have written such a Gospel. Moreover, were it a fiction, still, if intended to be believed, it would have been more accommodated to the popular tradition. No one individual could have remodelled the entire tradition after an invented plan of his own, contradicting all others.

But, on the other hand, by following John, we do not charge any falsification upon the three other Evangelists: we can easily conceive how the separate traditions, of which those Gospels were made up, may have been so put together, without any intention to deceive, as apparently to represent Christ as making one Passover journey. From the account of the appearances of Christ after the resurrection given by Matthew, we may see how easily such obscurities crept into the circle of Galilean traditions. Luke agrees with John in assigning Jerusalem as the scene of those appearances; yet, from reading Matthew alone, we might infer that they all took place in Galilee.*

quite indefinitely, however, that "he healed the lame and the blind in the Temple." It is impossible not to see that the historical connexion is lost in this passage of Matthew; we can gather it correctly only from John's Gospel.

* A favourable light is thrown upon the genuineness and credibility of John's Gospel by the fact that it alone contains a closely connected and chronological account of Christ's public ministry.

PART I.

FROM THE COMMENCEMENT OF CHRIST'S PUBLIC MINISTRY TO THE TRIUMPHAL ENTRY.

CHAPTER I.

JESUS AND JOHN THE BAPTIST.—THE FIRST DISCIPLES.

WE resume the thread of our historical narrative at the point where it was broken off.*

On issuing from the solitude in which he had prepared himself for his public labours, Jesus again sought the prophetic man who had given him the Divine signal for their commencement, and had consecrated him to his holy calling. Not, indeed, in order to form a close connexion with him, for John had to remain true to his office as Forerunner, and to continue his ministry in that capacity, until the Messiah should lay the foundation of his visible kingdom with miraculous power, and, by securing general acknowledgment, should indicate to the Forerunner, also, that he should submit himself, with all others, to the Theocratic King. But in the circle of Galilean disciples that had gathered around John, full of longing aspirations, Jesus might expect to find some suitable to be taken into fellowship with himself and trained to become his organs. The sphere of John's ministry was calculated to offer the best point of transition to Christ's independent labours.

§ 111. *Message of the Sanhedrim to John at Bethabara.*

Meanwhile John, with his disciples, had been traversing both shores of the Jordan; and just at that time he was on the east side of the river, in Perea, at Bethany, or Bethabara.† The Jewish Sanhedrim, the highest ecclesiastical authority, had at first quietly suffered him to go on preaching repentance. But when his followers and influence increased to such an extent that men were even inclined to look upon him as the Messiah, that high tribunal thought it best to send a deputation‡ to obtain from his own lips an explanation of the calling in which he laboured.

John did not at once give as positive a statement as was desired, but

* Page 69.

† Two different names given to the same place at different times, both having the same meaning, "a place of ships," "a place for crossing in ships" (a ferry). See *Lücke* on John, i 28; *Winer's* "Biblisches Realwörterbuch," i., 196, 2d ed.

‡ John, i. 19 seq.

satisfied himself with giving a negative to the popular idea which had probably caused the deputation to be sent ["*I am not the Christ*"]. But as he accompanied this denial with no further explanation in regard to himself, the messengers were compelled to press him with further questions. They naturally asked him, then, whether he wished to be considered as one of the great personages who were looked for as precursors of Messiah; presupposing that only in this sense he could assume a Divine calling to baptize. John continued to give curt replies, just enough to meet each separate question. Although in a spiritual sense he was the *Elias* who was to precede Messiah, he denied that he was so (*i. e.*, in the carnal sense in which they put the question and would understand the answer). He described himself only in general terms, not liable to perversion, as the *one* through whom the voice of God called upon the nation to repent and prepare for a new and glorious revelation that was at hand. Humbling himself, as the bearer merely of a prefigurative baptism, he pointed to the mightier One who should baptize with the *Spirit*, who already stood, unrecognized, in their midst. His remark, "*ye* know him not," was doubtless founded upon the fact (which he did not utter) that *he* knew him, as he had before been revealed at his baptism.

These answers to the deputation are less clear and full than those which the Baptist gave for the warning and instruction of individuals, as recorded in the first Gospels. As the ruling powers had little favour for John, he had good reason to suspect the intentions with which the Sanhedrim had sent their messengers. Hence the brevity and reserve with which he answered them.

§ 112. *John points to Jesus as the Suffering Messiah, and testifies to his Higher Dignity.*

On the day after John had thus (officially, as it were) pointed Christ out as having already appeared among the people, though unrecognized by them, the Saviour came forth from his seclusion, and showed himself in the midst of John's disciples.* The Baptist, beholding his approach, exclaimed, "*Behold the Lamb of God, that taketh away the sin of the world.*" The image of the Holy One, suffering for his people, and bearing their sins (Isa., liii.), stood before his soul as he uttered these words. As we have already seen, John believed that the Messiah would have to go through a struggle with the corrupt part of the people; and he readily joined to this belief the idea of a Messiah *suffering* for the sins of the people, and triumphing through suffering. The intuition to which he gave utterance was simultaneous with the appearance before his eyes of Christ's person, so gentle, so calm, and

* John, i., 29.

so meek;* and his conception of the idea of Messiah, in a prophetic spirit, reached its very acme. Yet we cannot define precisely the meaning which John himself attached to the words; for we cannot suppose in him a doctrinal conception of their import such as a fully Christian mind would have.† His was a prophetic intuition, bordering indeed on Christianity, but yet, perhaps, commingled with wholly heterogeneous elements.

After John had thus designated the character of Jesus, to whom he wished to direct his disciples, he repeats anew the testimony which he had before publicly given "of him that was to follow" (although probably not given, in the first instance, with the same confidence as to the *person*), and applies it, in stronger terms, to Christ—"*This is he of whom I said, After me cometh a man that is preferred before me, for he was before me.*"‡ ("Who has taken a higher place than I, according to his nature.")

* Hence the appropriateness of the figure of the *lamb* rather than of any other animal used in the offerings. What we say is enough to indicate the grounds on which we differ from other interpretations of this passage. Conf. *Lücke*, in loc.

† We do not suppose, therefore, that the Baptist had before his mind the full sense which the Evangelist, from his Christian stand-point, connected with the words. It cannot be known with certainty but that the former used the word עַם, which the latter translated κόσμος. From a mind like the Evangelist's we could hardly expect so fine a distinction between the *objective* and *subjective* to be distinctly marked in his statement of the words of another. He perhaps involuntarily blended them. He revered the memory of the Baptist, his spiritual guide; these words of the Baptist had greatly tended to develope his inner life, and had led him to Christ; it was, therefore, all the easier for him to attribute to them a higher Christian sense than the Baptist had when he uttered them. The interpretation which he gave to them may also thus have reacted upon the form in which they were impressed upon his memory. This view does not in the least impugn the veracity of the narrative, or tend to show that John was not its author. The whole tone of the Baptist's words is consistent with his character and habits. Moreover, as we have before remarked (p. 54), the kingdom of God, as spreading among the *heathen* nations, had opened partially to his view; he may, therefore, in the passage under discussion, have had reference to *mankind*, rather than to the Jewish world.

‡ John, i., 30. These obscurely prophetic words were the Baptist's own, and not put into his mouth by the Evangelist. But this only makes their explanation more difficult. According to the usage of the Greek, and of language generally, the *before* of place and time may express, figuratively, precedence of *dignity;* and, in this usage, ἔμπροσθέν μου γέγονεν is easily interpreted, "*although* (in the order of *time*) *he comes after me*, yet (in the order of *dignity*) *he was before me*." In the full certainty of prophetic intuition, the Baptist describes this as already realized. It is harder to interpret πρῶτός μου ἦν. Referring the words "he was before me" to the *pre-existence* of Christ, they would imply that his dignity as Messiah was to grow out of his pre-existing Divine nature. Nor could it, in this case, be said that the Evangelist had involuntarily modified the language of the Baptist by an infusion of his own Christian ideas; for, in the mind of the latter, the higher conception of the *person* of the Messiah, as well as of his work and kingdom, may have been developed from a profoundly spiritual interpretation of the prophecies of the Old Testament. This much, indeed, is implied in his partial statements (recorded by the other Evangelists) in regard to the peculiar indwelling of the Holy Ghost in the Messiah; although it does not follow that the Baptist was fully conscious of this. It remains a question, whether it would not be more in accordance with the simple conception of the Baptist to take πρῶτος as referring, not to *pre-existence*, but to priority of *nature*, which interpretation I have fol

§ 113. *John and Andrew, Disciples of John, attach themselves to Jesus.—Gradual Attraction of others.*

These words of the Baptist were listened to by two Galilean youths, who stood in the circle of his disciples—JOHN and ANDREW. It was about four o'clock in the afternoon, when, obeying the hint of the Baptist, they followed Jesus; refraining, however, in reverence, from disturbing his meditations. The Saviour, noticing them, turned kindly and asked what they desired. Even then they did not venture to express their longing to be honoured with his friendship; but only timidly inquired where he dwelt. Anticipating their request, he kindly invited them to visit him. The few hours that remained before evening were spent in his society. This was their first impression of Christ: he left it to work in their hearts. Thus was it also with SIMON (John, i., 42), in whom Christ discerned in a moment the yet dormant spirit of the *Man of Rock*. And those whose first impressions were thus received pointed Christ out to their fellows; and thus arose the *first* circle of disciples, which accompanied him from Peræa back to Galilee.*

CHAPTER II.

COMMENCEMENT OF CHRIST'S PUBLIC TEACHING.

§ 114. *The Miraculous Draught of Fishes.—Effect of the Miracle on Peter.*

ON his return to Galilee Christ at once began his labours as a teacher; not, however, in the synagogues, but in instructing the groups that gathered around him. He betook himself first, not to Nazareth, his native place, where he could least hope to be received as a prophet (the carnal mind looks only at the outward appearance), but to the little town of Capernaum. The young men who had accompanied him from Peræa were from the neighbourhood of Capernaum

lowed in the text. This involves no tautology; the "*becoming* greater" is derived from the "*being* greater." The word ἦν is used, and not ἐστί, to indicate that the "priority of essence" preceded "the priority of dignity," which was not obtained by Christ, in its manifestation, until a later period. It is an *oxymoron:* "he *was* that, which he has *become.*" Thus interpreted, the passage corresponds to what John says of Christ in another form, in Matt., iii., 11. If this view be adopted, we must remember to distinguish between the sense in which the Baptist uttered the words and that which the Evangelist, from his higher Christian consciousness, attributes to them.

* John, i., 42–47. It is apparent from John's statement alone that Christ did not take these young disciples, who were afterward to be his organs, immediately into close fellowship, but left them for a while to themselves. John gives us no further account of the forming of the Apostolic community; he presupposes many things, which we must endeavour to fill up by comparing the synoptical Gospels.

and Bethsaida; and he only waited for a suitable opportunity to take them into closer communion. Such an opportunity was the following:

One day, as he was walking upon the western shore of the Sea of Genesareth, an increasing throng of eager listeners collected about him. Some fishermen who had toiled all night and brought up nothing but empty nets, had left their vessels fastened near the shore. Jesus asked Simon, to whom one of the fishing-boats belonged, to push it out a little way from the shore, that he might stand on board, and thus address the people to better advantage.* On finishing his discourse, he turned to Peter, who doubtless was anew struck with the power of his words, and told him to cast his net into the deep. Although he had toiled all night in vain, he obeyed the Master at a word. This full confidence of Peter shows that he had already been impressed to some extent, at least, with the Divinity of Christ.† An impression of the most powerful character, however, must have been made upon him (as a fisherman) by the wonderful result of this once letting down of his net, after the vain attempts of the long night before. The manifestation of the Divine power to him in the exercise of *his own trade* was characteristic of the Divine operations generally in the history of Christianity; he was thus led from the Carnal to the Spiritual.‡ All his previous impressions were revived and deepened by this sudden exhibition of the power of a word from Christ, and the Saviour appeared so exalted that he felt himself unworthy to be near him ["*Depart from me, for I am a sinful man, O Lord!*"]§ The Divine power appears

* A comparison of Luke, v., with Matt., iv., 18, will vindicate the correctness of this representation. Here we have two independent statements: that in Matthew an abbreviated one, while Luke's is the vivid and circumstantial account of an eye-witness. The words of Christ to Peter, as given by Matthew (iv., 19), "*I will make you fishers of men,*" seem to presuppose an event such as the miraculous draught of fishes; but Matthew presents them as entirely isolated, while Luke gives the occasion of them very graphically. None but those abstractionists who must measure all phenomena, however infinite in variety, upon the Procrustean bed of their own logical formulas, will see in this account the stamp of a legendary story. It has all the freshness of life and reality about it. Whoever is well read in the history of the diffusion of Christianity in all ages will be able to recall many analogous cases. *Schleiermacher* (Comm. on Luke, *in loc.*, or "Werke," ii., 53), in his remarks on this case, showed with what nice tact he could distinguish *history* from *legend.* Honour to the memory of that great man, whose profoundly logical mind humbled itself, in pure love of Truth, before the power of History!

† It also confirms the account in John's Gospel. The connexion of the narrative which I have given abundantly shows that Matthew's account is not irreconcilable with Luke's, or both with John's, as some suppose. I do not mean to say, however, that the connexion thus made by comparing *all* the accounts was present to the minds of the writers *severally,* for in that case, doubtless, the form of their narratives would have been different from what it is now. Such discrepancies can surprise no man who has attempted to gather a connected narrative of any kind from several distinct accounts.

‡ Those who believe in a Divine teleological government of the world, in a Providence which makes Nature subserve the progress of the kingdom of God, must regard this event as one of those in which the border line between the natural and supernatural is hard to be distinguished, and which form the point of transition from the former to the latter.

§ On account of this peculiar relation between Christ and Peter, we can hardly suppose

fearful, in its holiness, to the sinner who is conscious of his sinfulness it fills him with consternation; he shrinks back from it with trembling Infinite, indeed, in view of the law, must the chasm appear between the sinner and the Divinely exalted Holy One.*

Christ seized upon this impression, and, glorifying the Physical into the Spiritual, by his prophetic explanation of the phenomenon, said to Peter [*Fear not; from henceforth thou shalt catch men*]: "Shrink not back in fear. Take confidence in me. Attach thyself henceforth *wholly* to me. Thou shalt see greater proofs of my power than this. In fellowship with me thou shalt achieve greater miracles. From henceforth thy net shall catch men."

The same impression, also, caused Andrew, James, and John† to join themselves from thenceforth more closely to Jesus.

§ 115. *The Calling of Nathanael.*

In the case of a JOHN, the full impression of Christ's personality, first received, prepared the depths of his youthful soul for sudden and

(although much may be said in favour of it) that this event occurred after he had known Christ for some time, or after he had been a witness of his first public labours at Jerusalem so, also, we cannot, for the same reason, place it after the wedding at Cana; although this last is more probable than the other, since we cannot say certainly what impressions the occurrences at Cana made, at first, upon the disciples. The view which we have followed in the text seems to be contradicted by the connexion between John, i., 43, and 46; but there is no real contradiction. The calling of Nathanael (John, i., 46) and that of Philip (i., 43) are not necessarily connected in place and time. John mentions an *intended* return to Galilee (v. 43), but says nothing about the journey itself; he may have been induced, by the mention of Bethsaida, to place the theatre of the account in that region. (See *Bleek*, Stud. u. Krit., 1833, ii.) The late *B. Jacobi* (in the same periodical, 1838, iv., 852) adduces against this view John's accuracy, in this passage, in mentioning time and place. It is not clear, however, that John meant to give, in each case in the chapter, the time and place exactly. His exactness extends only to the events which served to lead *John's disciples* to Christ; and it is not at all evident that Nathanael belonged to that number. The way in which Philip describes the Messiah to him, saying nothing of the Baptist's testimony, rather shows the contrary. Moreover, the opposite view would prove that Nathanael was first found in Galilee.

* The truth of this individual trait, as narrated of Peter, is confirmed by the subsequent developement of his character. The consciousness of his sinfulness and distance from the perfectly Holy One must, indeed, have remained; and his sense of the loftiness of Christ could be diminished by no degree of intimacy with him. But there was this great difference between the two periods of his religious life, that in the latter, as he imbibed more and more the spirit of communion with Christ, he felt himself no more repelled as a sinner from Him in whom the source of Divine life for men was revealed, but attracted to him, not merely by his own spiritual affinities, but by his personal experience, that HE "*had the words of eternal life.*" The *redeeming* power of the Divine One was more and more fully revealed to him; the Divinity appeared to him no more as a merely *outward*, but as an inward power. The central source of all the individual rays of Divinity shone forth upon his consciousness, and the separate rays of themselves, therefore, appeared in a new light.

† Luke says (v. 10) that James and John, the sons of Zebedee, were "partners with Simon;" they were, therefore, eye-witnesses of that event, and received the same impression from it. In Matthew's statement (iv., 21) they were with their father, in another vessel, "mending their nets." This agrees well enough with Luke, since he likewise mentions two vessels, and—not, indeed, the mending, but—the washing of the much-used nets.

separate impressions of the Divinity of Jesus, which soon brought him to a complete decision. But the narrow prejudices of a NATHANAEL had to be overcome by a separate supernatural sign before he could receive the impression of Christ's manifestation and nature as a whole. When Philip first announced to him that Jesus of *Nazareth* was the Messiah, he expressed both surprise and incredulity that any thing so high should come forth from a corner like Galilee. Instead of discussing the point, Philip appeals to his own experience, and tells him to "come and see." Nathanael's prejudice was not strong enough to prevent his compliance, or to hinder him from being convinced by facts. Christ sees and esteems his love of truth, and receives him with the words, "*Behold an Israelite indeed, in whom there is no guile*" (a true and honest-hearted member of the Theocratic nation). The candid youth is surprised to find himself known by a stranger. He expresses his astonishment, and Christ increases the impression made upon his feelings, by a more striking proof still of his supernatural knowledge, telling him that his glance, piercing the barriers of space, had rested on him before Philip called him as he stood "under the fig-tree" (this probably had some reference to the thoughts which occupied his mind under the fig-tree). His prejudices are readily removed [he acknowledged Christ as "*Son of God and King of Israel*"]; Christ admits that he is in the first stage of faith,* but tells him that his faith must develope itself from this beginning, and advance to a higher aim (John, i., 50, 51). A faith thus resting on a single manifestation might easily be perplexed by some other single o[illegible], that might not meet its expectations. That is a genuine faith (according to Christ) which carries itself to the very central-point of revelation, seizes the intuition of Divinity in its immediate nature and manifestation as a whole, and obtains, through immediate contact with the Divine in the Spirit, a stand-point which doubt can never reach. Nathanael was to see "greater things" than this isolated ray of the supernatural. He was to see the "*heavens opened upon the Son of Man,*" into whose intimacy he was about to enter, and "*Angels of God ascending and descending*" upon him. He was to learn Christ in his true relation to the developement of humanity, as Him through whom human nature was to be glorified; through whom the locked-up heavens were again to be opened; the communion with heaven and earth restored; to whom and from whom all the powers of heaven were to flow. Such was to be his Divine glory in its *full* manifestation; all other signs were but individual tokens of it.

* See p. 138.

CHAPTER III.

JESUS AT CANA.

§ 116. *The Change of Water into Wine.—Character and Import of the Miracle.—Little Impression made upon the People.*

THREE days after Christ had thus set forth the mode in which he from that time should reveal himself, he displayed, at a wedding in CANA,* the fulness of "the power of heaven" streaming forth from him self, which was to transfigure, as he had said, both nature and humanity. The wine provided for the occasion gave out, and Mary requested her Son to supply the lack by employing the powers that were at his command. Having recognized him as Messiah, she necessarily expected him to work miracles, and this expectation was increased by the impression which he had made in the short time that had elapsed after his consecration to the Messianic mission. She looked impatiently for the hour when he should reveal himself in his glory, as Messiah, before the eyes of all men.

But Christ, although he held all purely human feelings sacred, yet demanded that "man should deny father and mother" when the cause of GOD required it. He had now to apply this principle to his own mother, and, conscious of his Divine character and calling, to rebuke the request thus made to him, and the feelings which prompted it. "*What have I to do with thee? mine hour is not yet come;*" as if he had said, "Our wishes lie apart. My Divine powers cannot be made subservient to earthly aims and motives. My acts obey a higher plan and loftier laws, in accordance with which each of them has its appointed time. As yet, the moment for revealing myself in my Messianic dignity, by miracles apparent to all eyes, has not arrived."

Christ intended, as he here intimates, to come forth *gradually* from his obscurity. He had no idea of displaying his glory, as Mary wished, at once. Still, as she might have been accustomed to take from his words and look more than he uttered, she probably understood that her wish would be met, so far as the fact was concerned, though from a point of view totally different from her own. And so it was; the thing was done, but in no very striking way, nor in a way calculated to reveal his Messianic glory *to all eyes.*

As for the *character of the miracle* itself, we cannot place it, as some do, among the highest of Christ's miraculous acts. We conceive it

* It is to be remarked that Nathanael was "the son of Tholmai," *i. e.* Bartholomew, of Cana, which fact may confirm our view of the order of the events.

thus: He brought out of water, by his creative energy, a substance (wine), which is naturally the joint product of the growth of the vine, and of human labour, water being only one of the co-operating factors; and thus substituted his creative power for various natural and artificial processes. But we are not justified in inferring that the water was changed into *manufactured wine;* but that, by his direct agency, he imparted to it powers capable of producing the same effects; that he *intensified* (so to speak) the powers of water into those of wine.* Indeed, this latter view of the miracle conforms better to its spiritual import than the former.†

It is not a sufficient explanation of the *final cause* and moral bearing‡ of the miracle to say that Christ intended, by thus exhibiting his glory, to incite and confirm a faith in his calling. We must seek its import rather by contemplating it in reference to his moral self-revelation as a whole; by inquiring how the peculiar Spirit of Christ was reflected and illustrated in this single act.

While in retirement, he had resembled, in the austerity of his life, the ascetic preacher of repentance, John the Baptist. *Now*, however, in the very beginning of his public labours, no longer in solitude, but mingling in the social life of men, he enters into all human interests, shares all human feelings, and thus at once presents a contrast to the severe legalism of John. In the joyous circle of a wedding, he performs his first miracle to gratify a social want. Thus he sanctifies connexions, feelings, joys, that are purely human, by his personal presence, and by unfolding his Divine powers in such a circle and on such an occasion. In this view the miracle gives the spirit of Christian Ethics, whose task it is to apply to all human relations the image of Christ as

* I would be pleased to believe, if I could, that the view here taken had as old ecclesiastical authority as the late *Baumgarten-Crusius* supposes he has found for it, in the ancient hymn "De Epiphania Domini" (*Daniel*, Thesaurus Hymnologicus, i., p. 19): "Vel hydriis plenis aqua vini *saporem* infuderis." But the word *saporem* can hardly be made emphatic. In the sense of the hymn, the words "vini saporem infundere" probably mean nothing more than "in vinum mutare."

† Compare, as analogies, the *mineral springs*, in which, by natural processes, new powers are given to water; and the ancient accounts of springs which sent forth waters like wine—intoxicating waters: "Πολλαχοῦ δ' εἰσὶ κρῆναι αἱ μὲν ποτιμώτεραι καὶ οἰνωδέστεραι, ὡς ἡ περὶ Παφλαγονίαν, πρὸς ἣν φασι τοὺς ἐγχωρίους ὑποπίνειν προσιόντας."—*Athenæus*, Deip., ii., § 17, 18. Of another water says *Theopompus*, "τοὺς πίνοντας αὐτὸ μεθύσκεσθαι, καθὰ καὶ τοὺς τὸν οἶνον."

‡ The supposition that John's Gospel was written by some one of Alexandrian education, with a tendency to Gnosticism, is refuted by this narrative. Such a man would never have assigned such an object and such a scene for Christ's first miracle. Such a one could not have invented and put into the mouth of the "ruler of the feast" the clumsy jest which he uttered (John, ii., 9), (although we do not (as some do) lay stress upon it, and infer that the guests were nearly drunk). Any one writing a history of Christ apologetically, and with a view to exalt his character according to the tendency of those times, would rather have altered and adorned a true narrative of such facts (if such existed) than have invented a false one bearing against his object; or, if he had some *symbolical* meaning in his view, he would certainly have stated it.

stamped upon his self-revealed life. But it has a further and a great symbolical import: Christ employed water, one of the commonest supports of life, as the vehicle of a higher power: so it is the peculiarity of Christ's Spirit and labours, the peculiarity of the work of Christianity *not* to destroy what is natural, but to ennoble and transfigure it; to enable it, as the organ of Divine powers, to produce effects beyond its original capacities. To energize the power of Water into that of Wine is, indeed, in every sense, the peculiar office of Christianity.

This first stay of Christ in Galilee after his inauguration as Messiah was attended with important results in the training of the narrower circle of his disciples: but he does not appear, in that short time, to have made any lasting impression upon the people. There were few so ingenuous in their prepossessions as a Nathanael; the prejudices of many against the "son of the carpenter at Nazareth" could not be removed until they had obtained a vivid impression of his public labours at the feast of the Passover in the metropolis. Even in this beginning of his labours in Galilee, he had probably found occasion to apply the Jewish proverb, "*a prophet hath no honour in his own country*."*

CHAPTER IV.

FIRST JOURNEY TO JERUSALEM TO ATTEND THE FEAST OF THE PASSOVER.

§ 117. *The Purifying of the Temple.*

DURING the feast of the Passover Jesus appeared at Jerusalem in his prophetic calling, and accredited it by miracles.† On visiting the Temple, he found its worship disturbed by disorders which desecrated the holy place—a picture of the general secularization of the Theocracy.‡

* John, iv., 44: doubtless referring to this period; a supposition which the use of γάρ renders probable. Thus interpreted, we should have John's testimony that Christ had already sought to appear as a teacher in Galilee.

† Although the purifying of the Temple doubtless belongs to an early period of Christ's teaching, it is by no means clear, from John's account, that Christ had not taught and wrought miracles before; indeed, the manner in which the priests addressed him rather shows the contrary.

‡ Here a difficulty arises: the cleansing of the Temple is placed by John at the *beginning* of Christ's ministry, during his first stay at Jerusalem; by the other Evangelists at the *end* of his labours, during his last stay there. Unless the same event took place *twice*, and in the very same way (which is hardly probable), either John or the others must have deviated from the chronological order. It may appear more probable that an act implying so great power over the priests, and the throng of buyers and sellers, was done after his last triumphal entry, when the people were, for the moment, enthusiastic in his favour, than

For the convenience of the Jews from a distance who wished to offer sacrifices, booths had been erected in the Temple-court, in which every thing necessary for the purpose was kept for sale, and money-changers were also allowed to take their stand there; but, as might have been expected from the existing corruption of the Jewish people, many foul abuses had grown up. The merchants and brokers made every thing subservient to their avarice, and their noisy huckstering was a great disturbance to the worship of the Temple.

It was Christ's calling to combat the corruptions of the secularized Theocracy, and to predict the judgments of God against them. And as the general desecration of all that was holy was imaged in these profane doings at the Temple, he first manifested against them his holy anger. Threatening the traders with a scourge of small cords, he drove them out of the Temple; and said to those who sold doves, "*Take these things hence; make not my Father's house a house of merchandise.*"*

These words are not only applicable to the special case, but also contain a severe reproof of that carnal tendency which debases God's house into a merchant's exchange. The lifting up of the scourge could not have been in token of physical force, for—apart from Christ's character—what was one man against so many? It could only be a symbolical sign—a sign of the judgments of God that were so soon to fall upon those who had corrupted the Theocracy.†

There was no miracle, in the proper sense, wrought here, but a proof of the confident Divine power with which he influenced the minds of men; an example of the direct impression of Divinity, of the power of the manifestation of the Holy One as a punisher, in rousing the slumbering conscience. *Origen*, who found many difficulties in this narrative,‡ and was inclined to regard it as ideal and symbolical, thought

at the beginning of his labours. On the other hand, he would have had more occasion, after his triumphal entry, to avoid every thing that could occasion public disturbance, or wear the appearance of employing earthly power. As for the *difficulty* of the thing at his opening ministry, no one can say *what* influences the immediate power of God might produce upon the minds and feelings of men. It is certainly less easy to account for such an anachronism in *John*, whose account is all of a piece, and accurate in chronological order, than in the other Evangelists; the latter might naturally connect a fact like this, well adapted to oral tradition, with the *last* entry, which was the only one mentioned in the circle of accounts which they compiled. According to John (ii., 18), the Jews put the question, "*What sign showest thou us?*" &c.; in Luke, xx., 2, the Sanhedrim ask, "*By what authority doest thou these things?*" &c. It might be supposed that this last question suggested the statement of the event which gave rise to it, if it were certain (as, indeed, it is not) that in the passage in Luke it has this special reference to the act, and not a reference to Christ's teaching in general at that time.

* John, at most, *alludes* to Isa., lvi., 7; Jer., vii., 11: but the other Gospels give direct citations. This is another proof of the originality of John's narrative.

† How absurd would it be to attribute the *invention* of such an incident as this to a man of Alexandrian culture! Its utter repugnance to Alexandrian views is shown by the fact that Origen considered it one of the greatest objections to the credibility of the narrative.

‡ T. ix., in Joann.

that if it were to be received as history* the miracle would be greater than the change of water into wine, or, indeed, any other of Christ's deeds; as in this case he would not have had to act upon inert and lifeless matter, but upon living beings capable of resistance. But, on the contrary, no miracle, in the proper sense, was wrought, precisely because Christ had to operate upon *men*, endowed, it is true, with a will capable of resisting, but also with susceptibilities that had to yield to the moral and religious force of an immediate Divine impression, and with conscience, that slumbering consciousness of GOD which man can never wholly abnegate, and which may be roused by a commanding holy power, in a way that is not to be calculated. There are many things in history that must be regarded as *myths* by minds that judge only by the standard of every-day reality.

§ 118. *The Saying of Christ, "Destroy this Temple," &c.—Additional Exposition of it given by John.*

Some of the priests asked Christ by what signs he could prove his authority to act thus. He gave them an answer, at once reproof and prophecy, "*Destroy this temple, and in three days I will raise it up.*"

The most natural and apparent interpretation of these words, according to the circumstances under which they were uttered, laying no particular stress upon the specification of "*three days,*" would be the following: "*When you, by your ungodliness, which desecrates all that is holy, have brought about the destruction of the Temple, then will I build it up again;*" alluding (according to the mode of conception every where prevalent in the New Testament) to the relation between Christianity and Judaism. The kingdom of GOD had a common basis in both; the new spiritual Temple which Christ is to erect among men is, therefore, represented as the Temple at Jerusalem, rebuilt after its destruction; the latter being a symbol of the destruction of the entire Jewish worship, which was identified with the Temple itself. The Temple and the kingdom of GOD are identical in Judaism and in Christianity:† *there*, in a form particular and typical; *here*, in a form corresponding to its essence, and intended for all men and all ages. As Christ is conscious that the desecrated and ruined Temple will be raised up by him in greater splendour, he acts upon this consciousness, as reformer of the old Temple, in the very beginning of those labours which are to lay the foundation of the new and spiritual one.

But what a glance into futurity was required in him thus to foretell

* Origin, however, exaggerated the throng that Christ had to expel into *thousands*. John, more simply than the other Evangelists, speaks only of the expulsion of the *sellers*; they, of the *buyers* also.

† Just as the "House of God" (Heb., iii., 2–6) is made the same in both dispensations; as the later one fulfills the law of the older. I cannot see any force in *Kling's* objections (Stud. u. Krit., 1836, i., 127). The καινόν is already implied in the ἐγείρειν.

not only the ruin of the Temple by the guilt of the Jews—the dissolution of their worship being necessarily identified therewith—but also the erection of the spiritual Edifice that was to take its place; to predict in himself the mightiest achievement in the history of humanity, at a time when but a few apparently insignificant men had joined him, and even they had but a distant dawning idea of what he intended to accomplish! So vast a meaning was involved in those dark words—dark, as all prophecies are dark! An analogous meaning was contained in his expression on another occasion, "*Here is something greater than the Temple;*"* showing, perhaps, that he was accustomed thus to point from the temporary Temple to the higher one which had already appeared, and which would still further reveal itself in the course of his labours.

Among the accusations brought against Christ by the false witnesses, at a later period, was this, that he had said, "*I am able to destroy the Temple of God, and to build it in three days.*"† Some may suppose that the editor of our Greek Matthew may have been ignorant of the occasion and the true sense on which the words were uttered by Christ, and therefore attributed them *entirely* to the invention of the witnesses. It is likely, however, that the testimony was called *false* by Matthew, because the witnesses perverted, and put a false construction on Christ's real words; he had not said that "*he* would destroy the Temple," but (what is very different) that its destruction would be brought about by the guilt of the Jews. The priests might very naturally have falsely reported the words, in order to put a sense upon them that would not bear against themselves so closely, and which, at the same time, would appear more obnoxious to the people. In Mark, xiv., 58, the words are still more perverted by the false witnesses: "*I will destroy this Temple that is made with hands, and within three days I will build another.*"‡ Not that *they* understood Christ that he would build a spiritual temple instead of the visible one; but, probably, that he could, after destroying the latter, replace it in greater glory by magic (after the visionary representations of the Chiliasts), or cause one to descend from heaven. Even one of the thieves on the cross malevolently quoted these words against Christ. All this shows that, whatever amazement the words excited, they had made a great and general impression.§

* See above, p. 89. † Matt., xxvi., 61.

‡ Mark observes (xiv., 59): "*But neither so did their witness agree together.*"

§ It is a special confirmation of John's Gospel that he alone gives the natural occasion for the utterance of these words by Christ, and their original form. *Strauss*, however, thinks that the original form of the expression was that put into Stephen's mouth by his accusers, Acts, vi., 14; and that the "*three days*" were added subsequently, with reference to the resurrection. But these are *not* Stephen's words, nor is it even attributed to him that he quoted *Christ's*, but only that he uttered a thought of his own, perhaps derived from them. At any rate, the mention of the "three days" would have been unsuited to

The faithfulness of John is strikingly shown by the way in which he distinguishes his own interpretation of these words of Christ from the words themselves.* Christ, in uttering them (according to John's explanation), pointed to his own body [referring to the resurrection].

Although this does not appear to bear so directly upon the aim of Christ at the time, and upon the question of the Jews, as the view given above, it yet may involve the following deeper import, viz.: "The Temple at Jerusalem is only a temporary place consecrated to God; but Christ, in his human nature, shall build up the everlasting Temple of God for man. The former shall be destroyed, and not rebuilt; but the body of Christ, the temple of the indwelling Divine Nature, shall rise triumphant out of death."†

The first interpretation seems to us more simple, and to connect itself more naturally with Christ's intention; but the latter has the advantage in giving a more intelligible bearing to the "three days."‡

the thought ascribed to Stephen. The interpolation of the words "three days" is more improbable, as neither Matthew nor Mark explain them at all; on the contrary, it is much more likely that the *presence* of the words led to their being applied subsequently to the resurrection, than that the resurrection itself led to their interpolation.

* It may be disputed whether John's interpretation is intended to give the exact sense in which Christ used the words [or only accommodated them to the resurrection, as is perhaps implied in the 22d verse, "*when, therefore, he was risen from the dead, his disciples remembered that he had said this unto them*"]. An instance of such accommodation, of words uttered by Christ, in a sense different from the original one, is found in John, xviii., 9; although, in this case, John must have known that he applied them differently, and was glad to find them admit such application. John's authority, in regard to the sense of the words of the Master whom he followed so devoutly, and whose sayings he preserved so faithfully, is necessarily of great weight; still, in the explanation of special expressions [as to their original import], the natural relations and connexions might compel us to deviate from him. Nor would this at all conflict with Inspiration, rightly understood, which would only require that the explanation given by the Evangelist should be true in itself, although the words might not be applied with Christ's original meaning. He would none the less be the proclaimer of the *whole truth* made known to him by the illumination of the Holy Ghost. The mention of the "*three days*" (which cannot, indeed, be easily explained, except by the resurrection) might have led the author of this Gospel, who always dwelt with peculiar fondness upon every thing that concerned the person of Christ, at once to think of his resurrection. The interpretation given by the Evangelist is a further proof against the theory that this Gospel had a later Hellenistic or Alexandrian origin. It would have accorded much better with the taste of that school to apply Christ's words, in the grand prophetic bearing, to the building of the spiritual Temple (the *ναὸς πνευματικός*, in place of the *ναὸς αἰσθητός*) than to the resurrection of his body.

† I agree with *Kling's* (l. c.) refutation of certain modern objections to John's explanation, and also with his view of the impossibility of connecting the two interpretations together.

‡ Many passages have been quoted by others to prove that "*three days*" must necessarily mean a time of short duration, but I am not yet convinced of it. In general, it means "a round number," and we must learn from the context whether a longer or shorter period is intended. In this case the contrast with the length of time taken to build the Temple justifies us in assuming that a short period is meant. The new spiritual Temple, the progressive developement of the new spiritual kingdom of God, did in fact immediately follow the overthrow of the old form of the Theocracy.

§ 119. *Interview of Christ with Nicodemus.*

(1.) Disposition of the People and Pharisees towards Christ.—Dispositions of Nicodemus.

Many of the people were attracted to Christ during this his first stay at Jerusalem. And although the prevailing Pharisaic party looked upon him with an eye of suspicion, they could not openly oppose him, as he had not as yet arrayed himself against their statutes and traditions, but directed his blows against abuses which no one dared to defend. And even of the Pharisees it cannot be supposed that *all* were hypocrites, governed only by selfish motives; doubtless there were many whose piety, however debased by the errors of their entire system, was yet sincere.* Such could not remain without Divine impressions from the words and works of Christ.

A specimen of this better class was NICODEMUS.† To him, especially, the miracles of Jesus appeared to be works transcending all merely human power, and undeniable signs of a Divine calling. Beyond this general impression, however, he had no clear views of Christ's person or mission; and his desire to obtain more definite information was the greater, because he had participated in the expectations awakened by John the Baptist, in regard to the approaching reign of Messiah. Recognizing Christ as a prophet, he determined to apply to him personally, and came to him by *night*, to avoid strengthening the suspicions of his colleagues in the Sanhedrim, probably already aroused against him.

We may presuppose that he shared in the ordinary Jewish conceptions of the Messianic kingdom, and expected it soon to be founded in visible and earthly glory; although he may have had, at the same time,

* It is probable, in the nature of things, that although the Pharisees, scribes, and chief men, as a whole, were ill-disposed to Christ, there were among them individual susceptible minds. In the first Gospels we find *Joseph of Arimathea;* in Matt., ix., 18, *a ruler;* in Mark, xii., 28, *a scribe,* manifesting an interest in his Divine calling, and from these we may infer the existence of other cases. There is no ground, therefore, for *Strauss's* assertion that the case of Nicodemus is improbable. Utterly unhistorical, too, is his assertion (i., 633) that the accounts of rich and chief men coming secretly to Christ (and so of Nicodemus) were invented at a later period, to remove the reproach brought against the primitive Christians, "that none but the poor and illiterate attached themselves to Jesus." Instead of being a "reproach," it was the pride and glory of the primitive Church that the new creation of Christianity began among the poor; that the wise of this world were put to shame by the ignorant. There was no inducement, then, for such inventions. Moreover, this mode of thinking pervades the whole of John's Gospel; he that could represent Jesus as unfolding his highest truths to a poor woman could not have been tempted to *invent* a conversation between him and a distinguished scribe.

† *Strauss* strains hard to give a symbolical and mythical meaning to this common Jewish name, נַקְדִּימוֹן. There is no trace in the early Christian history of mythical persons thus originating from mere fancy, without any historical point of departure. Only at a later period was the history of really eminent men exaggerated by (voluntary or involuntary) invention into fables; *e. g.*, *Simon Magus* was thus made mythical.

some more worthy and spiritual ideas in regard to it. He considered himself sure, as a rigidly pious Jew and Pharisee, of a share in that kingdom. and was only anxious to be informed as to the approaching manifestation of Messiah.

Addressing Christ as an enlightened teacher, accredited from God by miracles, he expected to obtain from his lips a further account of his calling and of his relation to the Messianic kingdom. But instead of entering upon this, Christ purposely gives an answer especially adapted to the moral and religious wants of Nicodemus, and all of like mind.* The truth which he uttered was not only new and strange to Nicodemus, but also fundamentally opposed to his whole system: "*Except a man be born again,*† *he cannot see the kingdom of God*"

(2.) The New Birth.

Uprooting the notion that any particular line of birth or descent can entitle men to a share in God's kingdom, Christ points out an *inward* condition, necessary for all men alike, a title which no man can secure by his own power. His answer to Nicodemus presupposes that all men are alike destitute of the Divine life. It was directed as well against the arrogant self-righteousness of the Pharisees as against the contracted *externalizing* of the kingdom of God in Jewish particular ism. It involves also (although we are not sure, from the form of the expression, that Christ intended precisely this) that a faith like that of Nicodemus was insufficient; springing, as it did, from isolated miracles, and not from inward experience, or an internal awakening of the Divine life. Certainly it hit the only point from which Nicodemus could and must proceed in order to change his mode of conceiving the Messianic kingdom. Even if he at first still expected it to appear as an outward one, he must have had a higher and nobler moral conception of it. He doubtless took Christ's words "cannot *see* the kingdom" to mean "cannot share in the visible kingdom;" while Christ meant an inward spiritual "*entering into*" that kingdom which was first to be founded, as a spiritual one, in the hearts of men.‡

* An answer, too, entirely characteristic of Jesus, and which would not have occurred to one *inventing* this dialogue.

† Or "*from above;*" but I cannot prefer this reading, even after *Lücke's* arguments. "Born *again*" corresponds with "*becoming like children*" (Matt., xviii., 3); with παλιγγενεσία (Matt., xix., 28); compared with the λουτρὸν παλιγγενεσίας of Paul. We infer that this mode of expression belonged to the peculiar type of Christ's teaching, as it agrees, also, with his expressions (recorded in the first three Gospels) in regard to his operations upon human nature.

‡ The idea of a "new birth" was not unknown to the Greek and Roman mind, although its true import is only revealed in the light which Christianity lends to self-scrutiny. The *non emendari, sed transfigurari* of Seneca (Ep. ad Lucil., vi.), which is rather a rhetorical expression any how, applies to a gradual amendment of character by lopping off separate vices, and not to a radical change of nature. As the Christian new birth is the beginning of a process in human nature, which is to go on until the consummation of the kingdom of

The mere figure of a *new birth*, in itself, would have been nothing so unusual or unintelligible to Nicodemus; he could have understood it well enough if applied, for instance, to the case of a heathen submitting himself to circumcision and the observance of other Jewish usages.* But what startled him was the altogether novel application which Christ made of the figure; not to a change of external relations, as in the case above supposed, but to a totally different change, of which the learned scribe had not the glimmering of an idea. He knew not what to think of such an answer to his question, and no wonder; a dead, contracted, arrogant scribe-theology is always amazed at the mysteries of inward, spiritual experience. This first direct impression, perhaps, did not allow him, at the moment, to distinguish between the *figure* and the *thing*, and he asked, "*How can a man be born when he is old?*"

(3.) The Birth of Water and of the Spirit.

But Christ confirms what he had said, and explains it further: "*Verily, except a man be born of water and of the Spirit, he cannot enter into the kingdom of God.*"† He thus describes more exactly the *active* principle (the creative agent) of the new birth, the *Divine Spirit*, which implants a new Divine life in those who give themselves up to it; pro ducing a moral change, a reversion of the universal tendency of man, as the offspring of a race tainted by sin.

So much is clear. But what shall we say of the "*water?*"‡ We in

God, the new birth in individuals preparing the way for the new birth of a glorified world; so the *Stoic* doctrine speaks of a περιοδικὴ παλιγγενεσία τῶν ὅλων, ἀναστοιχείωσις. But this is connected with the pantheistic conception of a cycle of alternate destructions and renewals of the world, utterly opposed to the teleological point of view in Christianity. Ὁ τεσσαρακοντούτης, ἐὰν νοῦν ὁποσονοῦν ἔχῃ, πάντα τὰ γεγονότα καὶ τὰ ἐσόμενα ἑώρακε κατὰ τὸ ὁμοειδές.—(*Anton. Monol.*, xi., 1.) "He who lives only forty years and observes well, has experienced every thing which occurs in the whole eternity of this ever-renewed process."

* *Strauss* thinks (p. 701) that the way in which Paul uses the expression "*a new creation*" (2 Cor., v., 17; Gal., vi., 15), without explaining it, implies that it was in common use in Judaism. We do not agree with him, but rather see in such expressions the new *dialect* created by Christianity, which Paul's readers might be supposed to understand. If *Strauss's* view were correct, we should expect such antitheses in Paul as the following: "Circumcision cannot develope a new creation in the heathen, but leaves all in its old condition; a new creation can only grow out from within, through faith."

† How different the words of Christ, in their original simplicity, were from the later dress given to them, may be seen by comparing John, iii., 5, with the Clementines, Hom., xi., § 26: "ἐὰν μὴ ἀναγεννηθῆτε ὕδατι ζῶντι εἰς ὄνομα πατρὸς, υἱοῦ, ἁγίου πνεύματος," &c. It is immaterial whether this passage was borrowed from John's Gospel immediately, or from some tradition.

‡ It is said, by some, that the hand of a later writer is to be traced here, who planned this conversation, half fiction, half truth, upon the basis, perhaps, of an earlier narrative, and added "birth by water" to "birth by spirit," in order to give additional authority to baptism in the Church. But this theory is contradicted by the fact that baptism is only incidentally mentioned by John; that he nowhere expressly ascribes its institution to Christ, and nowhere says any thing of the baptism of the Apostles. A writer influenced by an ecclesiastical intent, and permitting himself to remodel the history of Christ from such a

fer from the fact that Christ says nothing more of "water," but proceeds to explain the operations of the "Spirit," that the former was only a point of departure to lead to the latter. It was the baptism of the Spirit, the "birth of the Spirit" into a new Divine life, that was unknown to Nicodemus; whereas John's baptism might have already made him acquainted with water as a symbol of inward purification, pointing to a higher purification of soul, to be wrought by the Messiah, and aiding in its comprehension.

After this preparation, Christ sets forth the general principle on which his previous declarations to Nicodemus were founded, viz., the total opposition between the *natural* life—the life of all those who continue to live according to nature simply—and the *new* life which God imparts [" *That which is born of the flesh is flesh, and that which is born of the Spirit is Spirit*"]. But as this "birth of the Spirit" was still strange to Nicodemus, Christ made use of a sensible image to bring it more vividly before him. "As none can set bounds or limits to the wind, as one hears and feels its blast, but can not track it to its source or to its aim; so it is with the breath of God's Spirit in those who have experienced the new birth. There is something in the interior life not to be explained or comprehended, which reveals itself only in its operations, and can be known only by experience; it is a life which no one can trace backward to its origin, or forward to its end."

The light begins to dawn upon Nicodemus. But to his mind, yet in bondage to a legal Judaism, prone to conceive all Divine things in an outward sense, and to keep God and man too far apart, the fact asserted by Christ seems marvellous; and he exclaims in amazement, "*How can this be?*" Jesus seizes upon this exclamation to humble the pride of the learned theologian, to convince him of his want of insight into Divine things, and to make him feel the need of further illumination. "You, a teacher of Israel, and this, without which all religion is a dead thing, not known to you! And if you believe me not when I speak of a mere matter of fact, which every man upon earth may test by his own experience,* how will you believe when I proclaim truths beyond the circle of man's experience and transcending the limits of his reason; when I tell you the hidden and unfathomable counsels of God for human salvation!"

motive, would not have made these omissions. It might even be said, with more plausibility, that *John* had been led to connect baptism and regeneration together, and had attributed this combination to Christ. We have no right, because of a mere difficulty, to charge such a thing, even though involuntary, upon the faithful disciple. The whole turn of John's feelings, the *mystic* element (in its good sense) that predominated in his mind, would alone have prevented him from making any *outward* thing prominent that was not made so in the original words of Christ.

* A Jewish believer could understand this, from its analogy to separate impulses of the Divine life experienced under Judaism.

(4.) Jesus intimates his own Sufferings.

This introduction prepares us to expect something *totally* opposed to the ordinary conceptions of the Jewish scribes. It would have been quite inappropriate if Christ had merely been about to speak of the ex altation of Messiah, for that idea was familiar enough; or even if he had been about to apply that exaltation personally to himself as Messiah; for this claim could not appear very marvellous to Nicodemus, who was already inclined to recognize him as a prophet. But nothing could have been more startling to Jewish modes of thought, or even to the mind of Nicodemus, who was still in bondage to the outward letter, than an intimation that Messiah was not to appear in earthly splendour, but was to found the salvation of mankind upon the basis of *his own sufferings*.* This was indeed, and ever, the stumbling-block of the Jews.

But Christ did not announce this truth, so strange to Nicodemus, plainly and in full breadth. Employing a well-known figure from the Old Testament, he compared the lifting up of the Son of Man with the serpent that was raised in the wilderness† before the eyes of all the people; and, having thus intimated the truth to the scribe by a simile drawn from his own familiar studies, he left it to be further developed by his own thoughts. The brazen serpent may have appeared to the fathers a paradoxical cure for the serpent's bite; and such a paradox is the salvation of the world through a suffering Messiah. The very strangeness of the comparison must have stimulated the mind of Nicodemus.‡

CHAPTER V.

JESUS AT ÆNON, NEAR SALIM.

WE cannot fix with certainty the length of Christ's first stay in Jerusalem after the beginning of his public ministry. But it is

* See p. 83, 84.

† Conf. the explanation of *Jacobi*. (Stud. u. Krit., 1825, pt. i.)

‡ The words of Christ end with ver. 15, we think. Nicodemus had the goad in his mind, enough to wake him out of his spiritual slumber, and urge him to deeper thought upon the truth, partly clear and partly obscure, to which he had listened. In the nature of the case, therefore, Jesus would not be likely to add any thing further. The verses, 16–21, have al together the air of a commentary added by the Evangelist, from the fullness of his heart and experience. He has seen the working of the Gospel, and the judgments, too, which attend its preaching, and he records them. John's Gospel is a *selection* from the history of the Gospel, made with a definite purpose; he begins it with a reflection, and he frequently interrupts the narrative with a course of reflection, as appears to us to be the case in the passage under consideration. Verse 16 takes up and repeats Christ's closing words in

certain that he went directly thence to *Ænon*,* near Salim (Salumias), a part of the country which was, at that time, the theatre of John the Baptist's labours. Here he probably spent most of the time from the Passover to the late harvest. He may have had two objects in this, viz., to continue the training of his disciples more uninterruptedly, and also to make use of the connecting link which the ministry of John the Baptist afforded. The reason for the continuance of the latter's separate labours has already been mentioned.†

§ 120. *Jealousy of John's Disciples.—Final Testimony of the Baptist. —His Imprisonment.*

The rapid growth of Christ's sphere of labour excited the jealousy of many of John's disciples, who would hear of no other master but their own, and who had not imbibed enough of his spirit to know that *he* was to give way before the higher one. They had seen that Christ obtained his first disciples by John's testimony in his favour. Having no desire themselves to go beyond John's teaching, they did not strive to understand that testimony fully, and deemed it unreasonable that Christ, who owed his first followers to the recommendation of their own master, should exalt himself above the latter. But when they mentioned their surprise to John, he answered them, "Do not wonder at this; it had to be so. No man can usurp what Heaven has not granted him. (No man's labours can transcend the limit appointed by God. Christ's influence proclaims the Divinity of his calling. Men would not join him, if God did not give them, in him, what I could never bestow.)" He then calls them to witness that he had never announced *himself* to them as Messiah, but always, and only, as the Forerunner: *"I said I am not the Christ, but that I am sent before him."*

It is to be observed (and it confirms what we have said of the historical position of the Baptist) that he does not here appeal to his private declarations as to Christ's Messiahship, made to individual susceptible disciples, but only to his continuous public testimony. The jealous

verse 15, and *explains* them, as the γάρ obviously shows. The marks of a change in the speaker seem to me very evident. It appears to be characteristic of John not to mark such transitions very distinctly; although, of course, he could never intend to intermix his own words with those of the Saviour.

* עֵינָן, a name derived from עַיִן (*"a place abounding in water"*), John, iii., 23. Eusebius (*Onomastikon*) says that such a place was still pointed out, eight Roman miles south of Scythopolis, near Salim and the Jordan. (Hieron., Opp., ed. Vallars, iii., 163; *Rosenmüller*, Handb. d. Biblisch. Alterth., ii., 2, 133; *Robinson's* Palestine, iii., 322.) This suits the place described in John, as Christ goes thence to Samaria. If it appear strange that the *Baptist* should go to Samaria, it is to be remarked that the place belonged, as a border town, to Judea; and the Baptist may have found it necessary, in order to avoid persecution, to betake himself to this out-of-the-way corner. Perhaps, also, with his more liberal tendency of mind, he had no scruples about abiding on the borders of Samaria.

† Page 57.

spirits, therefore, may never have had, from the lips of their master, any such special direction to Christ.

But he added, "My goal is reached; my joy is fulfilled. I have led the Bride (the Theocratic congregation) to the Bridegroom (the Messiah), to whom she belongs, who alone can fulfil her hopes. He must increase, but I must decrease."*

In uttering these words the Baptist probably had a presentiment that the end of his career was at hand. When he returned to the other side of the river, Herod Antipas, who ruled in Peræa, succeeded in laying hold of him. The rigid censor of morals, who had no respect for persons where the holy law of God was concerned, had offended the tetrarch;† and, by order of the latter, he was conveyed as a prisoner to the border fortress of Machærus.‡

* John, iii., 30. Thus far the words bear the stamp of the Baptist, their meaning being figuratively intimated rather than expressed. But those which follow (31–36) are totally different. The Evangelist, having in his own Christian experience so rich a commentary upon the words of his former Master, feels bound to apply it in explaining them. The relation of the Baptist to Christ sets aside all that has been said, in later times, about some imaginary person's having invented this scene and tacked it on to John's Gospel. Had such a one, as *Strauss* thinks, made the fiction in order to oppose the disciples of the Baptist (who kept aloof from Christianity) by the authority of their own master, he would have gone much further; it would have been just as easy, and far more effective, to invent a dialogue between Christ and the Baptist himself. The apocryphal writings of that period, manufactured to favour certain religious ideas, were not wont to confine their inventions within such narrow limits.

† Josephus differs from the Gospels (Matt., xiv., 3–5; Mark, vi., 17–20; Luke, iii., 19–20) as to Herod's reasons for this act; according to the latter, it was done because John had reproved him for carrying off and marrying his brother Philip's wife; according to the former, the tetrarch was induced by fear of political disturbances. "*Δείσας τὸ ἐπὶ τοσόνδε πιθανὸν αὐτοῦ τοῖς ἀνθρώποις μὴ ἐπὶ ἀποστάσει τινὶ φέροι· πάντα γὰρ ἐώκεσαν συμβουλῇ τῇ ἐκείνου πράξοντες, πολὺ κρεῖττον ἡγεῖται, πρίν τι νεώτερον ἐξ αὐτοῦ γενέσθαι, προλαβὼν ἀναίρειν ἢ μεταβολῆς γενομένης εἰς τὰ πράγματα ἐμπεσὼν μετανοεῖν.*"—(Archæol., xviii., v., § 2.) Now the character of the Evangelists, as historians, would not be affected, if we admit that they followed the popular report, even though incorrect, as the matter had no connexion with their immediate object. But the difficulty is cleared up, and a better insight into the nature of the case obtained, by the supposition that Josephus gave the *ostensible*, and the Evangelists the *real* and secret reason that impelled Herod. As the Baptist did not claim to be Messiah, and exhorted the people to fidelity in the several relations of life, Herod could have had no political fears except such, indeed, as might arise from John's honest boldness in reproving his sins. It is a further proof of his personal hatred to John, that he not only imprisoned, but *killed* him. History affords many instances in which faithful witnesses to the truth have fallen victims to the craft of priests or women, and often of the two combined.

‡ Supposing that John appeared in public about six months before Christ, and that he was imprisoned about the same length of time after Christ's first Passover, his whole public ministry lasted for about a year.

CHAPTER VI.

JESUS RETURNS THROUGH SAMARIA TO GALILEE.—THE SAMARITAN WOMAN. (John, iv.)

THE Pharisaic party became more suspicious of Jesus than they had been of the rigid preacher of repentance, when it was found that his ministry was beginning to attract still greater attention than John's had done. He determined, therefore, to leave that part of the country.* Galilee offered a safe abode; and, besides, a good spiritual soil for his instructions would probably be found there, as deep impressions had been made upon the minds of many Galileans attending the Passover, by his public labours at Jerusalem. He took the shortest road—three days' journey—to Galilee, through Samaria; and made use of the opportunity to scatter seeds for the future among the people of that country, who were then longing for new revelations, and among whom no political perversions of the Messianic idea were to be found, as among the Jews.

§ 121. *Impressions made upon the Samaritan Woman.*

In the mean time the summer months, and part of autumn, had passed away. It was in seed time, which lasted from the middle of October to the middle of December, that Jesus arrived in the fertile plain of *Sichem.* Fatigued with travelling, he stopped to refresh himself about midday† at the well of Jacob. He was alone, for he had sent his disciples into the city to buy provisions; not without the intention, probably, to elevate them above the Jewish prejudice which regarded the Samaritans as unclean. While he sits by the well-side, a poor woman from the neighbouring city comes‡ to draw fresh water. He asked her for water to quench his thirst, and embraced the occasion (as he always embraced every moment and opportunity to fulfil his Divine calling) to plant in her soul the seeds of Divine truth.§

* Here is the occasion of Matthew's statement, Matt., iv., 12. But as the first three Gospels only speak expressly of Christ's *last* journey (see p. 155), no distinction is made between his stay in Galilee *before* and *after* his first journey. Hence arose the mistake as to the time of John's imprisonment, to correct which error in the tradition probably John, iii., 24, was intended.

† That traveling could be continued until twelve o'clock shows that it must have been late in autumn.

‡ This, too, could not have been done at that hour in summer.

§ Here is another refutation of the theory that assigned an Alexandrian origin to this Gospel. A man trained in that school would have been as little disposed as a Jewish theologian of Palestine to represent Jesus as conversing with a poor woman and displaying to her the prospect of a new future of religious developement! But it was perfectly in keeping with the character of Him who thanked God that "what had been hidden from

Adapting his mode of teaching to her condition and culture, he made use of a natural figure, offered by the occasion [" *If thou knewest the gift of God, and who it is that saith unto thee, ' Give me to drink,' thou wouldst have asked of him, and he would have given thee living water*"].

The figure was admirably adapted to awaken in her as yet unspiritual mind a longing for the precious possession thus intimated, before she could apprehend the nature of the possession itself [" *Whosoever drinketh of the water that I shall give him shall never thirst: it shall be in him a well of water springing up into everlasting life*"]. How joyfully must she have heard of water, ever fresh and flowing, which one could always carry with him, and never need thirst or be weary with constant travelling the dusty road to draw! And so, under this figure, Christ pictured forth for her the Divine life which he had come to impart, which alone can quench the thirst of the soul, and is, for all who receive it, an endless stream of life flowing onward into eternity!

After thus exciting in her mind a desire for the miraculous water, of which she could as yet form no just conception, he breaks off without giving her further explanations of what, at that time, she could not be made to understand. He turns the conversation, first, to make her look *within*, as self-knowledge alone can prepare us rightly to apprehend Divine things; and, secondly, to satisfy her that he was a prophet by showing an acquaintance with parts of her private history of which, as a stranger, he could have known nothing.*

§ 122. *Christ's Decision between the Worship of the Jews and that of the Samaritans.*

Struck with his insight of her secret history, the woman recognized him as a prophet. She must, in consequence, have supposed that a higher sense lay hid in what he had uttered, enigmatical as it yet appeared to her, and she laid it up in her mind. It was natural, also, for her to question him further, as a prophet, on religious subjects, and thus elicit from him new instruction. And what question so likely to occur, or fraught with deeper interest to her, than that which formed

the wise had been revealed unto babes," and who had come to break down all barriers that separated men, and to glorify human nature even in the form of woman!

* It has been made a question whether Christ, at the moment when he requested the woman to call "her *husband*" (John, iv., 16), had the full and supernatural knowledge of her real circumstances, and only spoke thus to her *in order* to test her disposition, and induce her to speak of her course of life with candour; or whether he had *not* that knowledge at the moment, and really wished her husband to come, in order to open a communication with the Samaritans; so that the final turn of the conversation was different from what he had expected. We are not acquainted with the laws under which the beams of supernatural knowledge broke forth from the soul of Christ, nor with the relation between external *occasions* and the internal developement of his higher knowledge. And therefore we cannot say whether the woman's explanation, that " she had no husband," excited the streaming forth of the Divine light within him or not.

the bone of contention between the Jews and Samaritans, and which was suggested to her by the very spot on which they stood, Mount Gerizim itself towering up just at hand [" *Our fathers worshipped in this mountain, and ye say that in Jerusalem is the place where men ought to worship*"].

The answer of Christ has a two-fold reference: one to the existing stage of the Theocracy, thus answering the spirit of the woman's question; the other alluding to the higher stage of the Theocratic developement which he himself was about to introduce.

In regard to the first, he decides (v. 22) in favour of the Jews. "The Samaritans are ignorant of the true worship of God, because they reject the prophets, the several stages of revelation that have prepared the way for that which is the aim of all, the manifestation of the Redeemer; the Jews, on the other hand, do worship God intelligently,* since they *have* recognized his successive revelations, and are thus fitted to be the medium through which salvation may come forth for men; to lead to which salvation is the end and aim of all God's revelations. Jerusalem, meanwhile, had to be the seat of worship, because from Jerusalem the Redemption, which was to raise worship to a higher sphere, was to spring up."

§ 123. *The Worship of God in Spirit and in Truth.*

Christ thus showed that the worship at Jerusalem was only preferred in view of the salvation that was to come forth there, and that the superiority would cease at the time of its coming forth. He had, then, to describe that higher era before which the question in dispute between Jews and Samaritans would wholly cease: " *The hour cometh, and now is, when the true worshippers shall worship the Father in spirit and in truth, for the Father seeketh such to worship him: God is Spirit, and they who worship him must worship him in spirit and in truth.*" To the worship of God as previously conceived—the sensuous, external worship, confined to special times and a fixed place—Christ opposes a worship limited by neither, but proceeding from the Spirit, and embracing the whole being. The true worship of God, as Spirit, can only spring from Divine affinities in the Spirit.

And such worship can only be "Worship in the Truth;" the two are inseparable; the Truth must be taken up into the life of the Spirit before it can utter spiritual worship—Truth, the Divine element of life, the link that binds the world of spirits to God, their original. As worship in spirit is opposed to that which is confined wholly, or chiefly, to isolated outward acts, so worship in the Truth is opposed to that which

* This, of course, is only said *objectively*, with reference to the stand-point of the Jewish nation; *subjectively*, applied to individuals, it would only be true of those who correspond in spirit to the definition that follows.

adheres to sensuous types and images that only veil the truth. And this true spiritual worship can only flow from those who are in communion of life with God, as Father.

Christ used the words, "the time cometh, *and is now*," because the true, spiritual worship was realized, in its perfection, in himself; and because he had planted seeds in the hearts of his disciples, from which it was to develope itself in them, and through them in all mankind.

§ 124. *The Spiritual Worship.—Its Bearing upon Practical Life.*

Christ uttered here no merely theoretical truth, bearing only upon *knowledge*, but one eminently *practical*, and including in itself the whole work which he was to accomplish in humanity. The sages of both the East and the West had long known that all true worship must be spiritual; but they believed it impossible to extend such worship beyond the narrow circle of thoughtful and spiritually contemplative minds; nor did they even know rightly how to realize it for themselves. They sought in Knowledge what could only spring from Life, and was in this way to become, not the privilege of a favoured few, but the common good of all men.

On the other hand, Christ not only gave the true Idea, but realized it. As Redeemer of men, he placed them in a relation to God, through which the tendency to true and spiritual worship is imparted to their whole life. He made the Truth which he revealed the source of life for men; and by its means, as spirits allied to God, they worship him in Truth. Only in proportion as men partake of the Divine life, by appropriating Christ's revealed truth, can they succeed in worshipping God in spirit and in truth.

The knowledge of God as Spirit was by no means communicated to men ready made and complete. It was to develope itself in the reflective consciousness only from true worship of God, rooted in the life; here, and here only, were men to learn* the full import of the words, "God is Spirit."†

How has the lofty truth, the world-historical import, of this saying of Christ been lost sight of by those who have taken it as an isolated expression, apart from its connexion with Christian Theism and with the whole Divine process for the developement of Christian life, by those abstract, naked, one-sidedly intellectual Deists and Pantheists

* The history of religious opinions in the first three centuries affords most vivid proof of this. E. g.: "πᾶν πνεῦμα, εἰ ἁπλούστερον ἐκλαμβάνομεν, σῶμα τυγχάνον." (Orig. in Joann., t xiii., § 22.)

† This great truth, rightly understood, was closely connected with the moral and religious wants of the Samaritans, as represented by the woman. The natural order of this conversation, the simplicity and depth of Christ's words—so free from the diffuseness characteristic of intentional imitation—is a strong proof of its originality.

who have dreamed that *they* could incorporate them into their discordant systems by their spiritual *Fetichism*, which substitutes the deification of an *Idea* for the spiritual, truthful adoration of God as Spirit! The aristocracy of education, the one-sided *intellectualism* of the ancient world, was uprooted by Christ when he uttered this grand truth to an uneducated woman, who belonged to an ignorant and uncultivated people: *For all men alike, the Highest must spring from life* [and not from culture].

§ 125. *Christ's Glances at the future Progress of his Kingdom, and at his own Death.*

After Christ had made himself known as *Messiah* to the Samaritan woman, she hastened joyfully to the city to tell the strange things that had happened to her. Her countrymen came out in throngs at her call. In the mean time, however, the disciples had returned, and found their Master just closing his conversation with the woman; and, although both surprised and curious, they asked no questions about the occasion or subject of the conversation.

But they wondered that he did not touch the provisions they had brought. His corporeal wants are forgotten in the higher thoughts that occupy him; the work of his life is before him, the planting of the seeds of Divine truth in a human soul, and through it in many others, even beyond the limits of the Jewish people. The Samaritan woman is an exponent of this new progress of the kingdom of God. Her countrymen are approaching; the seed is already germinating. He replies, therefore, to his disciples, "*I have meat to eat which ye know not of.* (The nourishment of the body is forgotten in that of the *Spirit.*) *My meat is to do the will of him that sent me, and to finish his work* (to sow the seed for the general diffusion of the kingdom of God among men)."

He then illustrates the work of God, which he had just begun among the Samaritans, by a similitude* from the face of Nature before them. Glancing, on the one side, at the peasants scattered over the fertile valley, busily sowing their seed, and, on the other, at the Samaritans, thronging from the town in answer to the woman's call, he says to the disciples, "Are ye not wont to say, at this season of the year, '*There are yet four months, and then cometh harvest?*'† So it is, indeed, in the natural, but not in the spiritual world. The seed is *just* sown, and already the harvest appears. '*Lift up your eyes*' (pointing to the approaching Samaritans), '*and see how the fields are already whitening to the harvest.*'"

* This similitude is of the same character with Christ's parables given in the first three Gospels in general, and especially with those taken from sowing seed, &c.; a sign of the common character that pervaded all his discourses.

† A proverb taken from the climate and farming of that part of the country.

A profound glance into the soul of Christ and the secret connexion of his thoughts is now opened to us.* He cannot utter this prediction of the glorious harvest that is to follow the seed which he has sown, without the mournful, though pleasant, thought that he shall not live to see its gathering. He must leave the earth before the harvest-home; nay, his death itself is to prepare the way for it. So he tells his disciples that *they* shall reap what he had sowed; but that he shall rejoice with them [" *That both he that soweth and he that reapeth may rejoice together. I sent you to reap that whereon ye bestowed no labour*"].† Distant intimations like this were the only announcements of his approaching death that Christ made at this early period of his ministry.‡

§ 126. *Subsequent State of the Samaritans.*

At the earnest request of the Samaritans, who were deeply impressed with his appearance and his words, Christ remained two days with them before continuing his journey to Galilee. We have no information as to the immediate fruit of these his first labours among that people; perhaps it was the source of that religious awakening among them which is recorded in the Acts (viii., 14). If this be so, the seed sown by Christ, rich and fruitful as it was in the short time of his stay, was not afterward carefully cultivated until the Apostles went to Samaria; many foreign elements had crept in, and enthusiasts and fâlse prophets had led the people astray. The pure manifestation of Divinity was followed by a paltry caricature. The unsophisticated Samaritans believed in Christ, from the Divine power of his words and his appearance, without any miracle; but at a later period, when their minds had been debauched by magical arts and legerdemain, the most striking miracles were requisite to restore them.

CHAPTER VII.

CHRIST'S FIRST GENERAL MINISTRY IN GALILEE.

§ 127. *Christ heals the Nobleman's Son.—Chooses Capernaum for his Abode.—Healing of Peter's Wife's Mother.*

ON his arrival in Galilee Jesus went again to Cana. (John, iv., 46.) While there, there came to him a man belonging to the court

* A mark of truth, not of fiction.

† There is no ground whatever to refer John, iv., 37, 38 (as *Strauss* does) especially to the later ministry of the Apostles in Samaria. The prediction which they contain is just like those in Matt., x., 26; Luke, xii., 3; and in the parables hereafter examined (p. 188–190). Any one putting these words into Christ's mouth, in order to point to the labours of the Apostles in Samaria as having been preceded by Christ's, would have been less reserved and delicate about it by far.

‡ Luke, v., 35.

(βασιλικὸς) of Herod Antipas, and begged him to go down to Capernaum and cure his son, who was dangerously ill. Distress drove this man to Christ; although he might (if he had chosen), perhaps, have received Divine impressions before. He probably was, at first, among the number of those who verified the proverb in regard to Christ, "a prophet is without honour in his own country." The Samaritans believed, because of their *inward* wants, and of the inward power of Divinity; the faith of the Galileans had to be roused by visible miracles and material blessings. To this must we refer the words of reproof uttered by Christ before he granted the man's prayer: "*Except ye see signs and wonders, ye will not believe.*"*

Having, by the miracle wrought in this case, produced a new and favourable impression upon the public mind at Capernaum, he chose that place as the seat of his ministry. Here he taught in the synagogue, and healed the sick. It happened on a certain Sabbath, that when he left the synagogue he went, attended by his disciples, to the house in which Peter lived, with his mother-in-law, who lay ill at the time of a fever.† Jesus healed her, at once and fully, so that she was able to attend to her household duties and detain her guests for the Sabbath-day's dinner.‡ As Christ spent the day in the house (the rumour having probably been spread that he would soon leave the town), sick persons were brought in from all sides; not, however, until after sunset, to avoid breaking the law of the Sabbath. On the next day the people strove to prevent his departure, but he told them, "*I must preach the kingdom of God to other cities also, for therefore am I sent.*"

§ 128. *Christ appears in the Synagogue at Nazareth.—His Life is Endangered.* (Luke, iv., 16–30.)

From Capernaum Christ went to Nazareth, but the fame of his great deeds at the former place had gone before him. All eyes were turned upon him when he appeared in the synagogue on the Sabbath; *they* had known him as a very different person from what fame now proclaimed him to be. He took the scroll of the prophets that was handed to him, and, Divinely guided, opened it at Isaiah, lxi., 1. We may infer from the words of this passage that he proclaimed the arrival of the prophetical Jubilee, and declared himself to be the promised one that was to open the eyes of the blind, and to bring liberty to those who languished in the bondage of sin and Satan.

But his hearers were unconscious of their spiritual bondage, and longed for no deliverance; they knew not of their blindness, and asked not to be healed. Engrossed in the affairs of life, they were conscious

* See p. 138.

† Luke, iv., 38; Matt., viii., 14; Mark, i., 29.

‡ *Joseph.*, De Vita Sua., § 54: "ἕκτη ὥρα, καθ' ἣν τοῖς σάββασιν ἀριστοποιεῖσθαι νόμιμόν ἐστιν ἡμῖν."

of no higher wants, and, therefore, although his words made an impression, it was only upon the surface. Their astonishment that a man whom they had known from childhood should speak such words of power was soon followed by the doubt, "How comes it that such a man should do such great things?" Incapable of appreciating the heavenly gifts which Christ offered, they wished him (in their hearts, if not with their lips) to work wonders there as he had done at Capernaum.

We have seen already* that the fundamental principles on which Christ acted forbade him to accept a challenge of this sort. He could do nothing for those who insisted on seeing in order to believe. Slaves to the outward seeming, and destitute of a spiritual sense, they would have been satisfied with nothing he might do; and he refused them with a rebuke that pointed to the ground of their offence and unbelief: "*Ye will surely say unto me this proverb, 'Physician, heal thyself;' whatsoever we have heard done in Capernaum, do also here in thy country.*" He then quoted, with special reference to Nazareth, the proverb which he had, on another occasion, applied to the whole of Galilee, "A prophet is without honour in his own country;"† and illustrated, by examples from the Old Testament (in opposition to their contracted arrogance), the truth that the grace of God, in the distribution and application of miraculous gifts, acts *freely;* so that they could not *extort* a miracle by their challenge, if it was the will of God that none should be wrought. He came by no means to heal *all* the Jewish nation.

At this rebuke the wrath of the scribes and of the rude multitude was enkindled against him,‡ and the protecting hand of God alone saved him from the death which threatened him.

This rejection of Christ at Nazareth, due mainly to the disposition of the chief men, is worthy of note as a type of the rejection which

* See p. 136.

† The Nazarenes represent the character of the whole Jewish people. The doctrine which Christ arrayed against them—that God's grace is not imparted according to any human standard—contains the germ of Paul's ninth chapter to the Romans, which meets similar Jewish demands.

‡ Luke's account of this is very graphic, but very brief; many other things may have occurred to stir up the anger of the people. But when we remember the fame that had preceded his coming, the striking exordium with which he opened his speech (addressed, however, only to susceptible souls), and, finally, that, instead of complying with their request, he refused and rebuked them at the same time, we may readily conceive why they should be angry at the "son of the carpenter," now coming forward with the pretensions of a prophet. Their excited selfishness now took the garb of zeal against a false prophet. According to Luke's account, Christ wrought no miracle here, and this accords with the words he uttered; the less detailed statements of the other Evangelists (Matt., xiii., 58; Mark, vi., 5) imply that he wrought a *few*. In this last case, it might be supposed that he did not leave the town immediately after the synagogue service, and that, meanwhile, something occurred to excite the people. It is probable, however, that we must consider Luke's statement the most definite, both in view of the general principles on which Christ wrought his mighty works, and also of the special relation in which he stood to the Nazarenes.

awaited him at the hands of the leaders of the whole nation from the same cause.

§ 129. *The Parable of the Sower.*—Christ's Explanation of the Parable to the smaller Circle of his Disciples.*

The time intervening between Christ's return to Galilee in November, and his journey to Jerusalem to attend the feast of the Passover in the following March or April, was spent in scattering the seeds of the kingdom more widely among the people of that country. Probably many of the events recorded by the first three Evangelists belong to this period.

Perhaps, also, it was during this period that he took occasion, as he walked by the shores of Genesareth, to offer Divine truth to the gathered crowds around him, in the form of a parable suggested by the labours of the peasants who were sowing their fields around. He exhibited vividly to their minds, under the figure of the seed, the object of his proclamation, the dispositions of mind with which it must be received in order to accomplish that object, and the hindrances with which it is wont to meet in human nature.

It is not to be supposed that Christ uttered this parable (which refers solely to the operations of the word proclaimed by him) as an isolated speech; indeed, it is distinctly intimated (Mark, iv., 2) that an exhortation or warning to his hearers preceded it.

He divides his hearers into two principal classes, (I.) those in whom the word received is unfruitful, and (II.) those in whom it brings forth fruit. In the first class, again, he distinguishes (*a*) the totally unsusceptible, and (*b*) those to whom the word, indeed, finds access, but yet brings forth no fruit. Of these last, again, there are two subdivisions.

I. The Unfruitful Hearers.

(*a.*) *The totally Unsusceptible.*

The seed, which does not penetrate the earth at all, but remains upon the surface, and is trodden or devoured by birds, corresponds to the relation of the Divine word to the wholly worldly, who, utterly unsusceptible, reject the truth without ever comprehending it at all.

(*b.*) *The partially Susceptible.*

(1.) *The Stony-ground Hearers.*—Under the figure of the stony ground, in which the seed shoots up quickly, but withers as soon, for want of earth and moisture, he depicts that lively but shallow susceptibility of spirit which grasps the truth eagerly, but receives no deep impressions, and yields as quickly to the reaction of worldly temptations as it had yielded to the Divine word. Faith must prove itself in strife

* Matt., xiii., 1-9; Mark, iv., 1-9; Luke, viii., 4-8.

against the world without, as well as within; but the mind just described never appropriates the truth in such a way as to obtain power to resist.

(2.) *The Word Choked among Thorns.*—The seed which germinates and takes root, but is stifled by the thorns that shoot up with it, figures the mind in which the impure elements of worldly desire develope themselves along with the higher life, and at last become strong enough to crush it, so that the received truth is utterly lost.

II. The Fruitful Hearers.

When seed is sown into good ground, it is variously productive according to the fertility of the soil. So the fruitfulness of Divine truth, when once appropriated, depends upon the degree in which it penetrates the whole interior life and all the powers of the spirit, stamping itself upon the truth-inspired course of life.

With what perfect simplicity are the profoundest truths in regard to the growth of religious life unfolded in this parable! So vivid an impression was made upon a woman in the throng, that she exclaimed, "*Blessed is the womb that bare thee, and the breast that gave thee suck.*"* But Christ rejected this external veneration, and said, as if with prophetic warning against that tendency to fix religious feeling upon the *outward*, which in later times so sadly disfigured true Christianity, "*No, rather blessed are they that hear the word of God and keep it;*" with obvious reference to the parable, which illustrated the faithful reception and use of the Divine word.

After the dispersion of the multitude, the smaller circle of disciples gathered about Christ and asked a further explanation of the parable.† He told them that to them it should remain no longer a parable;‡ *they* might clearly apprehend the truth which was only offered in a veil to the stupid multitude. After unfolding its import, he taught them that the truth *then* veiled in parables was to become a light for all mankind; that they were to train themselves to be his organs in diffusing it; but that, in order to this, they must ever grow in the knowledge of his truth by a faithful employment of the means that he had given them. "*No man, when he hath lighted a candle, covereth it with a vessel, or putteth it under a bench; but setteth it on a candlestick, that they which enter in may see the light.* (So, also, the truth, destined to be a light for all mankind, must not be concealed, but diffuse its light on all that seek to enter the kingdom of God.) *For there is nothing hid that shall not be known and come abroad.* (And he adds warningly to his disciples),

* Luke, xi., 27. We shall give our reasons, further on, in placing these words in this connexion. † Matt., xiii., 18–23; Mark, iv., 10–25; Luke, viii., 9–18. ‡ Cf. p. 105

Take heed, therefore, how ye hear; for whosoever hath, to him shall be given; and whosoever hath not, from him shall be taken even that which he SEEMETH *to have.* (Every thing depends upon the spirit in which the truth is received and put to use.)"

§ 130. *Parable of the various Kinds of Fish in the Net.**—*Of the Wheat and the Tares.*†

Marvellous was the spirit-glance with which Christ surveyed not only the process by which the higher life which he had introduced into humanity was to develope itself, according to its own inherent laws, but also the manifold corruptions and hindrances that awaited it. The parables in which he illustrated the hindrances and obstacles of the truth were also derived from the sphere of nature and of life immediately around him—the toils of the fishermen in the Sea of Genesareth, and of the husbandmen in the fertile fields about its shores.

He had to teach his disciples that not *all* who joined him were fitted to be genuine followers, and that the spurious and the true should be intermixed in his visible kingdom, until that final process of decision which God had reserved to himself. To convey this truth, he compares the kingdom of God, in the process of its developement on earth (which corresponds to the visible Church as distinguished from the invisible), to a net cast into the sea, in which fish of all kinds, good and worthless, are caught, and which are only assorted after the net has been drawn to the shore.

It was, perhaps, an expression of surprise on the part of his disciples, at the long forbearance of Christ toward some whom they deemed unworthy—and certainly there was *one* such in the immediate circle of his followers—that gave him occasion to utter the parable of the "*Wheat and the Tares.*" Its object was to warn them (and the leaders of the Church in all ages) against arbitrarily and impatiently anticipating the Divine wisdom, which guides all the threads of the Church's progress to one aim; against attempting to distinguish the spurious from the genuine members before that final sifting of the kingdom which God himself will make; to teach them that men have no means of making such decisions unerringly, and might cut off, as false, some who were, or might become, true subjects of the kingdom.

The chief point in the parable is, that while the genuine seed germinates and brings forth fruit, the bastard seed is also sown among it, and both shooting up together, the bastard wheat, from its likeness to the true, cannot well be discriminated until harvest, when its real nature is manifested. The other point of comparison is the impatience of the servants, who wish to pull up the tares at once.

* Matt., xiii., 47.

† Matt., xiii., 24.

It is a question whether the individual trait that the tares were sown by the enemy "*while men slept*" had any special prominence. If so, it contains an exhortation to the leaders of the Church to be watchful; implying that carelessness and indifference on their part may admit false members among the true. But no such exhortation is afterward expressed, and, moreover, the whole plan of the parable presupposes that these spurious admixtures will *necessarily* take place in the progress of the kingdom; that no care or foresight can prevent them. We must, therefore, consider this trait as belonging to the colouring rather than the substance of the parable.

§ 131. *Christ subdues a Storm on the Sea.—Character of the Act as a Miracle.—Its moral Significance.*

The disciples had many opportunities, on the Sea of Genesareth, of contrasting their own spiritual feebleness with the calmness of the Saviour's soul; an experience that was useful, not only at the time, but as a preparation for their own subsequent calling.

On one occasion,* sailing from the western to the eastern shore of the sea, in a vessel with a number of his disciples and others, he sunk into sleep, probably worn out with his previous labours in supplying the physical as well as spiritual necessities of the people. While he was asleep, a storm arose, so violent as to threaten the destruction of the vessel. The disciples, full of consternation, and always accustomed to seek his aid in distress, now roused him from sleep. In a few short words he commands the winds and the waves to "be still," and is obeyed; a calm is spread over the face of nature. He mildly rebukes the disciples: "*Where is your faith?* what sort of trust in God is this, which can so easily be shaken?"

Not only the disciples, but the other persons in the ship, were deeply impressed by this miracle. One of the strangers† (for the *disciples* had seen too many of his wonders to ask such a question) exclaimed. "What kind of man is this, that even the elements obey him."

The question has been started whether this occurrence cannot be explained from the subjective apprehension of the men themselves, *e. g.*, as follows. When Jesus awoke, and spoke calmly to them, his composure quieted their perturbed minds. A calm in the elements ensued; and they transferred the impression made upon their minds to Nature. Interpreting the few words uttered by Christ in this way, they involuntarily altered them a shade in repeating them afterward.

* Luke, viii., 22–25; Matt., viii., 23–27; Mark, iv., 36–41. The connexion of this history with that of the Gadarene in the text of the Evangelists is a proof of historical reality, no causal ground of such a connexion exists.

† The expression οἱ ἄνθρωποι, in Matt., indicates that these persons were not disciples.

Now, even if this theory were admitted, it would leave the Divine image of Christ untouched in its sublimity. He that, on awaking suddenly from sleep, could impress men's minds with such a belief, by a word and a glance, must have been the Son of GOD.

But the theory *cannot* be admitted. Christ must have known that the observers looked upon his words as the *cause* of the calm that ensued, and would not have employed a deceit to confirm their faith in his sovereignty, which, resting upon the foundations of truth, needed no such props as this. He would rather have taken occasion, from such a misunderstanding (had it occurred), to convey a useful lesson to his future Apostles. He would have told them, probably, that his work was, not to subdue the storms and waves of nature, but of men's souls; that to souls full of his peace and joy no powers of the world could bring terror.

In short, our interpretation of the event will depend upon the general view of the person of Christ with which we set out. Were an achievement like this attributed to a *saint*, we should be entitled to give it such an interpretation as the above; but it is ascribed to *Jesus, the Son of* GOD, who revealed, in the history which we have of his life, powers adequate to such a deed.

The moral design of the miracle was, partly, to impress his sovereignty upon the minds of certain persons who had before seen no exhibitions of it; and, partly, to confirm the faith of the Apostles in his power to subjugate nature, and make her operations tributary to the kingdom of God. And this sensible miracle was an image of that higher spiritual one which Christ works in all ages, in speaking peace to the soul amid all the tempests of life, and in bringing to obedience all the raging powers that oppose the progress of his kingdom.

§ 132. *The Gadarene Demoniac.* — Christ's Treatment of him after the Cure.—Inferences from it.*

Christ landed on the eastern shore, near the town of *Gadara*. Many pagans probably resided in that vicinity, as herds of swine abounded. A demoniac,† who could not possibly be kept chained in his raging paroxysms, but constantly broke his fetters and eluded his guardians, was wandering about near the landing-place. He believed himself inhabited and hurried hither and thither by a host of evil spirits. Driven naked from the haunts of men by the direful powers, he sought a dreary refuge amid the grave-stones and old tombs‡ of the wilderness.

* Matt., viii., 28; Mark, v., 1–20; Luke, viii., 26–39. *Two* demoniacs are mentioned by Matthew, perhaps because the demoniac speaks in the plural number. † Cf. p. 145.

‡ These are still to be found among the ruins of *Om-Keis*, probably the ancient *Gadara*. (Cf. Burckhardt, i., 426; Gesenius, Anmerkungen, 538; Robinson, iii., 535.) Origen must have been mistaken (t. vi. in Joann., § 24) in saying that *Gadara* could not be the spot.

Probably attracted by the noise of the landing, the demoniac ran to meet the passengers as they disembarked; having probably, also, heard of the fame of Jesus, which had spread from the western to the eastern shore of the lake. From what we can learn, we should judge that the man was a heathen, who had, however, dwelt much among the Jews, and therefore confounded Jewish and pagan notions together in his disturbed consciousness. So he probably addressed Jesus as "the son of the highest God," rather in a pagan than Jewish sense.* The appearance of Christ (probably combined with what he had previously heard) affected him profoundly; the warring powers within him—as was generally the case when Christ's Divinity came in contact with demoniacs—partly urged him toward the Saviour, and partly held him back; attracted as he was, he could not bear the presence of Jesus. There is something in him which resists and dreads the Divine power. Losing his proper identity in that of the evil spirits that possess him, he personates them, and recognizing, with terror, the Son of God as the future Judge, he exclaims, in anguish, "What hast thou to do with us, thou Son of the Highest? (What would the Heavenly, so near us?) Why hast thou come hither before the time (before the final doom), to make us feel thy power, and torment us?"†

Christ's first procedure is not such as to imply that he has to do with evil spirits. He directs his words to the *man*, seeks to get his attention and draw him into conversation, so as to prepare the way for further influences. As a beginning, he asks the man his *name*. But the demoniac, still blending his own identity with that of the evil spirits, answers, "*Legion;*" it is a whole legion of evil spirits that dwell in him. He then reiterates, in their person, the prayer that Christ would not cast them into Hades before their time; and perceiving a herd of swine feeding at a distance, the unclean spirits are associated with the unclean beasts in his perturbed thoughts. He then beseeches Christ that, if the spirits are compelled to leave the *man*, they may be permitted to enter the *swine*, under the notion that they cannot exist except as united to material bodies.

There is a gap here in our connexion of the facts. Did Christ *really* participate in the opinions of the demoniac, or was it only subsequently inferred,‡ from the fact that the swine rushed down, that Christ had

because there is neither lake nor precipice near; he probably looked for the theatre of the event in the immediate vicinity of the town, which by no means follows, necessarily from the narrative.

* Cf. the words of the heathen woman, Acts, xvi. 17.

† The original form of these words is probably that given by Matthew. Every thing leads us to conclude that the demoniac, impressed by the person of Christ, addressed him first.

‡ Strikingly as this graphic narrative bears the marks of truth, this is still its obscure point. Some have attempted to clear it up by the supposition that the demoniac threw himself upon the herd after Christ spoke to him. But this is inconsistent with the facts

allowed the evil spirits to take possession of them? It is certain, at any rate, that they *did* cast themselves over the precipice into the sea, as if driven by an invisible power, and that many of them perished.

One thing is very clear, a man in such a state could not have been cured by Christ's merely humouring his whims, and by a single coincidence like that of the herd's throwing themselves over the precipice. Nay, he could not have made the request that he did, nor have believed that the evil spirits had abandoned him at Christ's command, had not Christ, by the power of his spirit, made a mighty impression upon him before. What followed shows, however, more clearly that Christ used higher influences to restore his shattered soul to its pristine soundness.

Although no detailed account is left of what immediately followed, we may yet conclude, from the result, that many things occurred between Christ and the demoniac after the preparatory work above related. His heart had been made susceptible of farther spiritual influences. The presence and words of Christ produced additional effects, as we find the man sitting clothed, and in his right mind, at the feet of Jesus, listening to him with eager devotion. So moved is he, that he wishes to attach himself to Christ and follow him every where.

But Christ (who had reserved for a subsequent period the conversion of the heathen) tells the restored man to "*go home to his friends.*"* We see in this, as in many other examples, how Christ's conduct varied with circumstances, and how carefully we should guard against deducing general principles from his procedure in isolated cases. While he calls upon some to leave home and family to follow him, he bids this man to follow first the purely human feelings which had been reinstated in their natural rights within him; to return, sane and calm, to the family which he had abandoned as a maniac; and to glorify God among them, by telling them how Christ had wrought the mighty change, and giving them a living proof of it in his own person. He tells some on whom he had wrought miracles not to say too much about what he had done; but *this* one he commands to publish every

It is not probable that a paroxysm like this could have seized him after the impression which Christ had made upon him. Moreover, this explanation affords no ground for the notion of the demoniac that the spirits had abandoned him for the swine, but would rather convince him of the continuance of their power over him. In order to believe the former, he must have stood as a quiet spectator while the herd was violently driven into the sea by an invisible power. The analogy of the notions of the time favours this. In the reference to Josephus, before made (p. 150), the exorcist bids the demon leave the sufferer and enter a vessel of water that stood by; and his obedience is proved by the fall of the vessel of *its own accord*. So the swine must have rushed down of their own accord, to afford any proof that the devils had left the man and entered them. Finally, an attack of the swine, on the part of the demoniac, could have been no matter of surprise to the swineherds. (Matt., viii., 37.)

* Mark, v. 1

where among his friends what great things God had wrought for him. In this case it was *heathens* (not Jews) that were concerned.

The way in which Christ gave peace and harmony to this distracted and lacerated soul affords an image of the whole work of redemption. The first emotion of the uncultivated and (chiefly) heathen people around was *fear;* not the feeling then best adapted to render them susceptible of his teaching. But the simple story of the restored man's experience was adapted to lead them to contemplate Christ, no longer on the side of his power, but of his love and holiness.*

§ 133. *Christ Returns to the west side of Genesareth.—Healing of the Issue of Blood.*†

When Christ returned to the western shore of the lake, he found a multitude of people awaiting his arrival. One of the rulers of the synagogue, named *Jairus,* whose daughter of twelve years‡ lay so ill that her death was hourly expected, pressed through the throng to the Saviour, and besought him to go to his house. He arose to grant the sorrowing father's prayer, but the crowd detained them.

A woman who had suffered with an issue for twelve years, and had sought aid in vain from physicians, approached him through the press from behind. She did not venture to address him directly, but having formed the idea in her own way, she thought that a sort of magical healing power streamed forth from his person, and that she might be relieved of her malady simply by touching his garment. Her believing confidence, although blended with erroneous conceptions, was not disappointed.

Christ felt that some one had touched his robe,§ and inquired who it was. Peter, forward as usual, spoke for the disciples, and said (very candidly, doubtless, as he probably did not observe the woman's movement), "How canst thou be surprised, in the midst of such a throng, that the people approach and touch thee!" But Christ repeated his question, and the woman, who had not before ventured a word, expecting to be discovered, fell trembling at his feet, and pro-

* The narrative does not say whether this foundation of Divine knowledge was ever built upon among them.

† Matt., ix., 18–26; Mark, v., 21; Luke, viii., 40.

‡ *Strauss* says that this age of "*twelve*" was a mere fiction, in imitation of the twelve years of the issue of blood. There is not a shadow of reason to suppose that Luke's statements are not literally correct in both instances; but even if they were not, if a round number only is meant, and the one period modelled after the other, the veracity of the narrative would be in nowise impeached.

§ Luke's account could have been given by none but an eye-witness in such lively and minute detail; *e. g.*, Christ's question, Peter's answer, the repetition of the question, etc. Moreover, Luke makes the cure immediate upon the touching of the garment; in Matthew it follows the words of Christ in the usual way. Luke's eye-witness had the conception of the mode of cure that the woman herself had, and so interpreted Christ's words (viii., 46).

claimed before all what had happened to her. Jesus, kindly encouraging the trembling heart, said to her, "*Be of good cheer, thy faith hath saved thee; go in peace.*"*

§ 134. *Raising of Jairus's Daughter.—And of the Widow's Son at Nain.*

In the mean time a message came from the house of Jairus that his daughter was dead, and that, as nothing could be done, the Master need be troubled no further.† But Christ, not hindered by the news, said to the father, "*Be not afraid; only believe, and she shall be made whole.*"

What right had he to hold out this hope to the parent, and in what sense did he do it? Did he know, from the reported symptoms, that the death was only apparent, and that he was going to cure a fainting-fit by remedies in his possession? Had this been the case, he surely would have guarded against exciting hopes that might be disappointed; he would have said, in words, that his expectations were founded only on the supposition that the girl was in a trance; and as natural signs alone could give no unerring certainty of cure, he would, in mere prudence, have spoken conditionally, telling the father, perhaps, to trust in GOD, but yet, at the same time, to resign himself to the Divine will. In a word, he could only have spoken *as he did*, from a Divine confidence that he could, by the power of GOD within him, restore life to the *dead* body.

At the door of the house the mother comes to meet them. A throng of curious persons at the door desire to enter, but he admits only the parents, with three of his most intimate disciples. In the chamber of death he finds already gathered the minstrels and mourners. "*Weep not,*" said he to them; "*she is not dead, but sleepeth.*"

These words might have been used, it is true, if he meant (as some suppose) to state her condition according to the symptoms, and to make this a ground of consolation; as if he had said, "she is only in a trance resembling sleep." But they were equally appropriate, if, with-

* The narrative does not decide whether the approach of the woman was known to Christ, and he healed her intentionally, or whether the cure was a Divine operation, independently of him (a *physical* cause being laid out of the case), caused by the woman's faith, and thus serving to glorify her trust in Christ.

† The discrepancy between Luke's account (viii., 49) and Matthew's (ix., 18, seq.) has been made a ground of objection. It has been supposed that the second message is a mere filling up of Luke's. A similar discrepancy, as to the sending of a message, occurs in the case of the centurion, Matt., viii., 5–10; Luke, vii., 6. Grant that the two cases were entirely alike, it would not follow that there had been an intentional invention. But the dissimilarity of the two is greater than their similarity. In both cases, indeed, the message is, that Christ *need not come;* but the reason assigned in the one is, *that he can help without coming,* and in the other, that it is *too late for him to help at all.* What, then, is unlikely in either? especially as Luke's statements, derived from eye-witnesses, are full, while those of Matthew are abridged reports.

out any reference to natural symptoms and consequences, he meant only to say that this condition would be, *for her*, only sleep, as he was able to raise her out of it. The character in which Christ acted, as well as the whole connexion of the narrative, compel the conclusion that he spoke with reference to the *result* rather than to the *nature* of the condition in which the maiden lay; even though the circumstances might make it probable that this condition was a trance.

[*"And he put them all out."*] In stillness must such a work be wrought!

When the noisy mourners were gone, and he was alone with the few that had accompanied him into the chamber of death, he spoke to the maiden the life-inspiring words. He then "charged them to tell no man what had been done." It has been said that he did this to prevent their giving him the *false* reputation of having done a miracle in the case; false, because he had restored the maiden, in an entirely natural way, from a death that was only apparent. Had this been the case, he certainly would have explained himself more definitely. He would have told them, in that case, *how* to report the matter; not that they should not report it at all. But he could not have wished that the event should be otherwise regarded than as a work of Divine power; and the prohibition was doubtless made in view of circumstances, especially in view of the dispositions of the people.

To this period of Christ's ministry, probably, belongs also a miracle akin to the raising of Jairus's daughter, which is reported only by Luke.*

On a journey, accompanied by his disciples, and by many others who had joined him on the road, he arrives before the little town of *Nain*,† in the vicinity of Mount Tabor, and not far from the well-known Endor. Near the gate he meets a funeral procession; and in the sad line a widow, mourning for her only son. In compassion‡ to her grief, he

* Luke, vii., 11.

† Now a little village, *Nein*, inhabited by a few families.—*Robinson*, iii., 460 [Am. ed., iii., 218, 226].

‡ *Olshausen* thinks that, although Christ only made his compassion for the *mother* prominent in this miracle, he still had regard to the salvation of the *son*; for, as he well remarks, the life of one human being cannot be used merely as means for another's peace or welfare. But, although we cannot decide that Christ had reference at the time to the *manner* in which the youth's resurrection would tend to his personal welfare, he must have been satisfied that, in the wisdom of GOD, it was destined to secure it. As the organ of GOD, he must have been conscious of a harmony between—not merely his whole manifestation, but also—all his individual actions and the Divine plan for the government of the world. A physician may save a man's life by natural means without knowing, at the time, what use the man will make of it; but, if he is a believer, he must be satisfied that God would not allow it, if the restoration were not for the best, in regard to his individual well-being. The same *relation* would subsist if the means employed were supernatural.

exclaims, "*Weep not.*" Had he not been conscious of power to remove the cause of grief, by giving back her son, he would have tried to soothe her sorrow, instead of exciting a vain hope, only to plunge her deeper into anguish.

§ 135. *Doubts of John the Baptist in his Imprisonment.*—His Message to Christ, and its Result.—Christ's Testimony concerning Him.—His view of the relation between the Old and New Dispensations.*

John the Baptist had now languished in prison for several months in the fortress Machœrus. He was not wholly interdicted from intercourse with his disciples; for the fear of political disturbance from him was, as we have seen,† the ostensible, not the real, reason of his imprisonment.

In the testimony which he gave to Christ, just before his imprisonment,‡ he had declared his expectation that he would soon be obscured by the public manifestation of Jesus as Messiah, and by his recognition at the hands of the worthy members of the Theocratic nation. What he heard in prison of Christ's mighty works only made him look more impatiently for the founding of his visible Messianic kingdom. The delay of this event might very naturally cause doubts to spring up in his mind.§ But as his faith in the Divine calling of Jesus remained unshaken, he looked for a definite decision of the question from his own lips, and sent two of his disciples with the inquiry, "*Art thou He that should come, or do we look for another?*"||

In this reply Christ gives them, as proof of his Messiahship, the miracles that he had wrought, both upon matter and spirit.¶ He first combines the two classes, applying the material as a type or image of the spiritual; and then makes the spiritual especially prominent. "*The blind receive their sight*" (both physical and spiritual), "*the lame walk,** the lepers are cleansed, the deaf hear, the dead are raised,†† the poor have the Gospel preached unto them.*"‡‡

* Matt., xi., 2–15; Luke, vii., 19–30. † Cf. p. 179. ‡ Cf. p. 178. § Cf. p. 58.

|| We have before shown that this presupposes rather than contradicts the previous baptism and recognition of Jesus by the Baptist. It illustrates, however, the method in which the synoptical Gospels were compiled: the author of this statement, if he had known of that previous recognition, could hardly have failed to notice it.

¶ It by no means follows, from the narrative, that Christ wrought all these miracles in presence of John's messengers. They could hear of them any where, and see their effects. Nor is a chronological connexion between the resurrection of the widow's son and this message of John's to be inferred from the juxtaposition in which Luke places them; he may have been led to this by Christ's mention of "the raising of the dead."

** There is an obvious allusion here to Isa., xxxv., 5; lxi., 1; yet it is not absolutely necessary so to consider it. Nor are we bound to square the words of Christ by the quotation, and to infer that all which deviates from it has been added by another hand. A close connexion is obvious in the text.

†† This is to be understood especially of spiritual death and resurrection, a sense which joins better to the following clause, since it is precisely by the "preaching of the Gospel" that the spiritually dead are raised.

‡‡ The word "poor" may be taken in the spiritual as well as the natural sense here.

Thus he presents himself as the Messiah, selecting the sphere of his labours among the poor in goods and in spirit, displaying his relieving and redeeming power to those who feel their need of it; the self-revealing, yet self-concealing Messiah, who does not offer himself as Theocratic king visibly before men's senses, as the Jews expected—an expectation which perplexed even the Baptist's own mind. And, therefore, he closes with the pregnant words of warning, "*And blessed is he whosoever shall not be offended in me.*" (Happy is he who is satisfied, by these signs, to admit my Messiahship, and who is not offended because it does not precisely meet his expectations.)

After the disciples of John had departed, Jesus said to the multitude around him, "*What went ye out into the wilderness** *to see? A reed shaken with the wind* on the shore of Jordan?" To see a fickle, changeful man, the sport of outward influences? (He thus intends to represent John as a prophet, faithful and true to his convictions, and to vindicate him from any charge of instability on the ground that this question, sent by his disciples, was in conflict with his earlier testimonies.) "But perhaps ye went out to see a man in soft and splendid garments? Such men ye find not in deserts, but in the palaces of kings." A striking contrast between the preacher of repentance, the austere censor of morals, and the luxurious courtiers who wait upon the smiles of princes.†

After these negative traits, Christ designates the stand-point of John positively. He calls him a "prophet," and "more than a prophet," and points him out as the Forerunner, the preacher of repentance predicted in Malachi (iii., 1), who was to go before, in the spirit of Elias, and prepare the way for the Messiah. He declares that none, in all time before, had held a higher position in the developement of the kingdom of God than John; that none had enjoyed a higher degree of religious illumination.‡ Yet, said he, the least in the manifested king-

both, indeed, are connected, as it is among the poor in worldly goods that most of the spiritually poor are to be found, *i. e.*, such as feel their inward wants and crave a supply for them.

* It is *possible* that these words had no higher meaning, and were only used to impress the single thought negatively, thus: "Ye must have gone to the *wilderness* to seek something more than the wilderness itself could afford to you." But as all that follows refers antithetically to John, we infer that these words also had such a reference.

† Unless the words have this meaning, they appear to have none; with it, they imply that John's conduct had given occasion for such comparisons; and perhaps this may have contributed to his imprisonment.

‡ We cannot, in Matt., xi., 11, supply προφήτης after μείζων; the last clause of the verse forbids it. It probably was not in Christ's original words; and if it be not a gloss in Luke (vii., 28), it is only an explanatory addition in the statement itself. The "superiority" does not refer to subjective moral worth, in which, certainly, Christ could not intend to place the "least" in the Christian Church above this man of God; but refers to advantages for apprehending the nature and progress of the kingdom of God. It is in this sense that the

dom of God (*i. e.*, in the Church founded by Christ as Redeemer), the least among truly enlightened Christians is greater than John.

These words have a double importance, as they define not only Christ's view of the stand-point of John the Baptist, but also of the Old Dispensation in general, in regard to Christianity.

In regard to the first, we must distinguish wherein John was behind Christianity, and wherein he towered above the prophets. He was behind Christianity, because he was yet prejudiced by his conception of the Theocracy as external; because he did not clearly know that Messiah was to found his kingdom by *sufferings*, and not by miraculously triumphing over his foes; because he did not conceive that this kingdom was to show itself from the first, not in visible appearing, but as a Divine power, to develope itself spiritually from within outward, and thus gradually to overcome and take possession of the world. The least among those who understand the nature and process of developement of the Divine kingdom, in connexion with Christ's redemption, is in this respect greater than the Baptist, who stood upon the dividing line of the two spiritual eras. But John was above the prophets (and Christ so declared), because he conceived of the Messiah and his kingdom in a higher and more spiritual sense than they had done, and because he directly pointed men to Christ, and recognized Him as the manifested Messiah.

In regard to the second, viz., the relation of the Old Dispensation in general to Christianity, the fact that Christ places the Baptist *above* the prophets, who were the very culminating-point of the Old Covenant, and yet so far *below* the members of the new developement of the kingdom, exhibits in the most striking way possible his view of the distance between the old preparatory Testament and the New. The authority of Christ himself, therefore, is contradicted by those who expect to find the truth revealed by *him*, already developed in the Old Testament. If in *John* we are to distinguish the fundamental truth which he held, and which pointed to the New Testament, from the limited and sensuous *form* in which he held it, much more, according to Christ's words, are we bound to do this in the Old Testament generally, and in its Messianic elements especially. Following this intimation, we must, in studying the prophets, discriminate the historical from the ideal sense, the conscious from the unconscious prophecies.

The testimony which Christ added in regard to the *effects* of John's labours corresponds precisely with the above view of his stand-point.

greatest of the old, preparatory stage were less than the least of the new. Since the *prophets*, who form the point of transition between the two dispensations, occupied the highest stand-point in the religious developement of antiquity, the sense of the passage is the same, with or without the word προφήτης.

"*From the days of John the Baptist until now** *the kingdom of heaven suffereth violence, and the violent take it by force.*"† (That is, "the longing for the kingdom, excited by John's preaching, has spread among men; they press forward, striving to secure it, and those who strive with their whole souls obtain a share in it.") "*And if ye will receive it, this is Elias, which was for to come.*" (John is the Elias who was to come to prepare the way for Messiah—if you will only understand it—spiritually, not corporeally.)

§ 136. *Christ shows the Relation of his Contemporaries to the Baptist and to Himself.*‡—*The Easy Yoke and the Light Burden.—Jewish Legalism contrasted with Christian Liberty.*

The discourse which Christ continued to the groups around him is especially important as unfolding the relation in which he stood to the Jews.

"*They are like children sitting in the market-place, and saying, We have piped unto you, and ye have not danced; we have mourned unto you, and ye have not wept.*" The merry music and the mournful are alike displeasing; they will neither dance nor be sad. So it was with John and the Son of Man on the one hand, to the people of that time on the other. The ascetic of the desert, preaching repentance with fasting and austerity, was laughed at as a madman; the Son of Man, mingling in the intercourse of men, and sharing in their human joys, was "*a glutton and a wine-bibber.*" Yet "*Wisdom was justified of her children,*" was recognized by those who really belonged to her. (While the multitude, sunk in worldly-mindedness and self-conceit, and deaf to the voice of Divine wisdom, took offence, for opposite reasons, at both these messengers of God, the humble and susceptible disciples of the wisdom of God, on the other hand, could understand the different standpoints of John and Jesus, and appreciate the reasons for their different modes of life and action.)

* These words (Matt., xi., 12) obviously presuppose that John's labours had ceased, and, of course, that he had lost his liberty. This is enough to refute the hypothesis of *Schleiermacher,* that he sent the message *before* his imprisonment. The whole tenor of the passage implies that John's era was at an end. It has also been inferred from the words ἀπὸ τῶν ἡμερῶν Ἰωάννου, that the passage was a later interpolation, improperly put into Christ's mouth. If this were true, it would only affect the *form,* not the *substance* of the passage, and we should have to follow Luke, xvi., 16 (where, however, the words are obviously out of place). But it is not true.

† These words are expressly chosen to denote the earnest will, the struggle, and the entire devotion of soul which are requisite to enter into the kingdom of heaven. All the powers of the spirit, its submission, its efforts, are necessary at *all* times, to secure the kingdom amid the reactions of the natural man, the carnal mind, its selfishness, its worldliness of spirit; but at *that* time it was especially the worldly notions of the Messiahship that had to be struggled against. The nature of the case shows that βιάζειν is to be thus figuratively taken; the *usus loquendi* does not contradict it; and it suits the natural connexion of the passage.

‡ Matt., xi., 17

The discourse concluded with an exhortation to the gathered multitude, in which Christ, with the greatest tenderness, invited the susceptible souls among them (the children of Wisdom) to "*come unto him*"* and find, in his fellowship, a supply for all their wants. He contrasts himself, as the Redeemer of "*heavy-laden*" souls, with the rigid teachers of the law, who, while they burdened men's consciences with their multiplied statutes, imparted no power to perform them, and repelled, in haughtiness, the conscience-stricken sinner, instead of affording him peace and consolation. The contrast, perhaps, was intended to apply not only to the Pharisees, but to the Baptist, who also occupied the stand-point of the law.

The "friend of publicans and sinners" thus invites all who feel their wretchedness to enter his communion; and announces himself as the "meek and lowly" one, repelling none because of their misery, condescending to the necessities of all, taking off the load from the weary soul instead of imposing new burdens, and giving them joy and rest in his fellowship. He makes no extravagant, impracticable demands. *Obedience*, indeed ("the easy *yoke*"), he does require; but an obedience which (although it embraces more than the righteousness of the law) is easy and pleasant, flowing spontaneously from the Divine life within, and rendered in the spirit of love. "Come unto me (says he), all ye that labour and are heavy laden (all that sigh under the legal yoke and the sense of sin, like the '*poor in spirit*' of the Sermon on the Mount), and I will free you from your burdens, and give you the peace for which you sigh. Enter the fellowship of my disciples, and you will find me no hard master, but a kind and gentle one; you shall obtain rest for your souls, for my yoke is mild, and the burden which I shall lay upon you, light."†

Our inference, from Christ's own words, in respect to the relation in which he stood at that time to the Jewish people, is: That the *majority* of them were dissatisfied with him, as they had before been with the Baptist; but that a smaller number of those who had recognized the Divine calling of John, acknowledged also that of Christ, and passed over, in submission to the guidance of Divine wisdom, from the former to the latter.

It is clear that a strong opposition was already formed against Christ, and the chief point on which it supported itself was precisely that which distinguished the stand-point of the Saviour from that of the

* These incomparable words, preserved for us by Matthew alone (xi., 28–30), fitly conclude the discourse; the interposed passage (20–27) was probably taken from some other of Christ's addresses by the editor of our Matthew (see hereafter), and placed here because of its affinity to the context.

† Here is the germ of Paul's entire doctrine, not only of the contrast between *law* and *Gospel*, but also of the Gospel itself as a νόμος πίστεως, πνεύματος.

Old Testament, and also from the peculiar one of John the Baptist. It was the spirit of liberty with which, in Christianity, the Divine life takes hold of and appropriates to itself the relations of the world and society, in contrast with the spirit of ascetic opposition to the world. The Jews could see nothing of the holy prophet in a man who shared with his disciples in the pleasures of social life, and sanctified them by his presence; in a man who did not hesitate to partake of the entertainments of publicans and sinners. Striking, indeed, must have been the contrast between the comparatively unrestrained mode of life adopted by Christ's disciples, and the austere asceticism of the pupils whom the Baptist was training to be preachers of repentance, or of the neophytes of the Pharisaic schools. No schools of spiritual life, indeed, before that time, had trained their pupils as Christ did his. We can easily imagine the amazement of the Pharisees!

§ 137. *Christ's Conversation with the Pharisees in regard to the Mode of Life indulged by his Disciples.*—The Morality of Fasting.*

It is not strange, therefore, that on a certain occasion the Pharisees came to Christ, and expressed their surprise at the free and social mode of life in which he indulged his disciples. They did not confine their appeal to the example of their own school, but intentionally added that of the Baptist's disciples, believing that the latter would be the more to their purpose, as Christ had recognized John for an enlightened teacher.

It may be asked whether the Pharisees, in putting this question, sought only for instruction, and wished to obtain from Christ himself the principles on which a course so inexplicable to them was founded, or whether they meant to reproach him personally for sitting at the banquets of publicans and sinners, and only made use of their question about the disciples for a crafty blind to their attack? The gentle and instructive tone of Christ's reply seems (although it certainly is not proof) to favour the first view.† Would he have said so much to justify his conduct, without a word in reproof of their question, if he had to deal with crafty opponents utterly unsusceptible of instruction?‡

* Matt., ix., 11–17; Mark, ii., 15–22; Luke, v., 33–39.

† The collocation of Luke, v., 33 and 34, if it be the original chronological order, opposes this view. In that case, after Christ had caused the question of the Pharisees to recoil upon themselves, they returned with it in a more concealed form. But it is probable [that different classes of Pharisees were concerned in the two cases], and that, this distinction being lost sight of, the occurrence in question was connected with one of the real machinations of that party in general against Christ.

‡ We follow Luke, v., 33; Mark, ii., 18, which have more internal probability than Matt., ix., 14. It is, indeed, possible that those disciples of John who adhered only one-sidedly to the views of their master may have taken offence, and expressed it, just as the Pharisees did. Probably, too, at a later period, there grew up a gradual opposition between the Christians and part of John's disciples; and the Jewish sect of ἡμεροβαπτισταί may have been no other than these (*Hegesipp.* in Euseb., iv., 22. Cf. the *Clementines,*

Be that as it may, some of them came to him with the question, "*Why do the disciples of John fast often, and make prayers,* and likewise those of the Pharisees; but thine eat and drink?*" Christ replies: "Can you make the companions of the bridegroom fast while the bridegroom is yet with them? Does fasting harmonize with the festal joy of a wedding? The time of fasting, indeed, will come of its own accord, when the bridegroom is gone, and the festal days are over."

So privations, suited to the time of mourning, would have been out of keeping with the joyous life in common of the disciples and their Lord—with those happy days when the object of their desire was yet present in their midst. Fasting would have been as foreign to their state of mind—as outward and as forced—as to the guests at a wedding. But as the days of the feast are followed by others when fasting is in place; so, when the joy of happy intercourse with Christ shall give place to mourning at separation from Him who is their all in all, in those sad days, indeed, the disciples will need no outward bidding to fast. Their mode of life will naturally change with their state of feeling; fasting will then be but the spontaneous token of their souls' grief.

Taken in this sense, it is clear that the words could not have been intended to apply to the *whole life* of the disciples after Christ should have been removed from them. The sad feelings here described were not intended to be permanent; the transitory pain of personal separation was to be followed by a more perfect joy in the consciousness of *spiritual* communion with Christ. Applying the passage, then, to this transition period of grief, we infer from it, as the rule of Christian ethics in regard to fasting, that it is neither enjoined nor recommended,

Hom., ii., 23, Ἰωάννης ἡμεροβαπτιστής.) But it is by no means as probable that they joined themselves with the Pharisees, their bitter enemies; they could have had no tendency to associate with men whom they could consider as having had a hand, at least, in the sacrifice of their master. The fact that the scribes had quoted the example of John's disciples may easily have passed into the report that the latter had come to Christ with the same question. This view is adopted, also, by *Schleiermacher*. *De Wette's* objections are sufficiently refuted by what has been said.

* *De Wette* considers the mention of "prayer" (Luke, v., 33) as out of place, and argues from it that Luke had departed from the original tradition. But certainly it was natural enough for the Pharisees thus to characterize the (to them) strikingly worldly life of the disciples; for the former made a show of sanctity, not only by fasting, but by repeated prayers; and, moreover, John had prescribed a *form* of prayer for his disciples (Luke, xi., 1), which Christ as yet had not done. As the words "*eating and drinking*" are used in the question to designate the profane and carnal life, so "*fasting and prayer*" denote its opposite—the strict spiritual life. Now, had the word "prayers" originally existed in the passage, and been afterward *lost* in transmission, we might easily account for it: because it might be thought that Christ's reply does not allude to "prayer," that such a depreciation of prayer (mistakenly imagined) would be a stumbling-block, and, besides, contradictory to Christ's own teaching in other places. But to account for its *interpolation* is quite a different matter. As for Christ's not alluding to prayer in his reply, he had no call to do it; it was the spirit of outward and ascetic piety, as a whole, that he rebukes.

but only justified, as the natural expression of certain states of feeling analogous to those of the disciples in the time of sadness referred to; *e. g.*, the sense of separation from Christ, which may precede an experience of the most blissful communion with Him. In such states of the interior life, all outward signs of peace and joy, all participation in social intercourse and pleasure are unnatural and repugnant; although, when Christ is present in the soul, these social joys are sanctified and transfigured by the inward communion with Him. The interior life and the outward expression should be in entire harmony with each other. Another glance at this subject, however, after examining what follows, will afford us another view of it.

§ 138. *The Parable of the New Patch on the Old Garment, and of the New Wine in Old Bottles.**

Christ added another illustration in the form of a parable. "*No man putteth a piece of a new garment upon an old; if otherwise, then both the new maketh a rent, and the piece that was taken out of the new agreeth not with the old. And no man putteth new wine into old bottles* (skins), *else the new wine will burst the bottles and be spilled, and the bottles shall perish. But new wine must be put into new bottles, and both are preserved.*"

The old nature cannot be renewed by the imposition from without of the exercises of fasting and prayer; no outward and compulsory asceticism can change it. Individual points of character are significant only so far as they are connected with the tendency of the whole life: a reformation in *these*, indeed, may be enforced, and the stamp and spirit of the life remain unchanged. A fragment of the higher spiritual life, thus broken off from its living connexion (destroyed in the fracture), and forced upon the nature of the old man, would not *really* improve it; but, on the other hand, by its utter want of adaptation, would worsen the rent in the old nature—would tear it rudely away from its natural course of developement. A mere renewal from without is at best an artificial, hypocritical thing. The new cloth is torn, and a patch laid upon the old that does not fit it. The new wine is lost, and the old skins perish.†

* Matt., ix., 16; Mark, ii., 21; Luke, v., 36.

† We deviate from the ordinary interpretation of this parable. Our explanation is not only adapted to the preceding context (Luke, v., 33–35), but also fits the minute details of the comparison, which the one commonly given does not. According to the latter, the substance of the parable is, that the outward religious exercises of Judaism are not adapted to the higher stage, Christianity, for which the disciples were training. But Christ admits (verse 35) that fasting may be a good thing at the right time; which, he said, had not then come, but *would* come. Instead of taking up this point, and unfolding it in the parable in another aspect, as one might expect, the common interpretation introduces a new and entirely different thought, viz., that such exercises were unsuitable (not to their condition at *that* time, but) to Christianity at *any* time. Again, one would naturally think, from v. 34

The premature imposition, therefore, of such exercises upon the disciples, instead of developing the new life within them, would have hindered it by mutilating and crippling what they had.* Separate branches of the spiritual life, apart from their connexion with the whole, cannot be grafted upon the stem of the old nature; that nature must be renewed from within in order to become a vessel of the Spirit. (In the case of the Apostles, the way was prepared for this by their personal intercourse with the Saviour.) The *whole* garment had to be new; the wine required new bottles. The new Spirit had of itself to create a new form of life.

Glancing back from this point to the words before spoken on fasting, we may refer them to the privations that lay before the Apostles in their course of duty—privations which they would joyously go to meet under the impulse of the new Spirit that was to animate them.

But although no outward impulses (no patches upon the old garment) might be needed when the interior life should freely guide, it might yet naturally be the case that "*No man, having also drank old wine, straightway desireth new; for, he saith, the old is better.*"† The disciples had to be weaned gradually from the old life and trained for the new—a law applicable in all ages of the Church, and which, if faithfully observed, might have saved her from many errors in Christian life and morals.‡

This example affords another illustration of the truth that individual

35, that the "*new* wine" and the "*new* cloth" of the parable were intended to represent the fasting, &c., of which Christ was speaking, viz., *that* fasting which the Apostles were to practice at a later period. But the usual interpretation, on the other hand, supposes fasting to be something *defective in itself*, and as belonging to that form of life which is represented by the "*old* garment." The sense thus obtained contains a thought not true in itself; for, in the case of the Apostles, the new wine of Christianity *was* put into the old bottle of Judaism, and was intended to break it to pieces. If the prescribed fasting was to be disregarded by the Apostles as belonging to Jewish legalism, so also, on the same principle, the *whole* Jewish legalism would have to be done away by them, as foreign to the new spirit introduced by Christ.

It is remarkable that this obviously false interpretation should have kept so long in the back-ground the true one developed by *Chrysostom*, Hom. in Matt., xxx., § 4. Independently of my exposition, *Wilke* has recently declared himself (in his *Urevangelisten*) in favour of the view here given. *De Wette* styles it "forced," but how the term can apply to an interpretation so accurately fitting the details of the parable, I cannot imagine. I should be very glad to see the attention of interpreters directed to the views which I have set forth.

* *Sincerum est nisi vas, quodcunque infundis, acescit.*

† It is a proof of the originality and faithfulness of Luke's narrative, that this passage, so indubitably stamped with originality, and yet so closely connected with the context, is recorded by him alone.

‡ Pope *Innocent* III. understood and applied this passage correctly, in reference to the establishment of a mission in Prussia: "Cum veteres uteres vix novum vinum contineant." *Epp.*, l. xv., 148.

parts of Christ's teaching cannot be rightly understood apart from their connexion with his whole system of truth.

§ 139. *Forms of Prayer.—The Lord's Prayer; its Occasion and Import.**—*Encouragements to Prayer; God gives no Stone for Bread.*

We take up now a subject akin to that of which we have just treated, without implying (what, indeed, is of no importance) a chronological connexion between them.

We have seen that one thing which surprised the Pharisees was that Christ did not lay stress upon outward prayers. He had not, like John the Baptist, prescribed forms of prayer for his disciples. In this respect, as well as others, their religious life was to develope itself from within. From intercourse with Christ, and intuition of his life, they were to learn how to pray. The mind which he imparted was to make prayer indispensable to them, and to teach them how to pray aright.

On a certain occasion, the desire arose in their hearts, from beholding him pray, to be able to pray as he did; and one of them asked, "*Lord, teach us how to pray, as John also taught his disciples.*"†

Christ replied that they were not, in their prayers, to use "many words," and to repeat details to God, who knew all their wants before they could be uttered. And then, in a prayer framed in the spirit of this injunction, he gave them a vivid illustration of the nature of Christian prayer, as referring to the one thing needful, and incorporating every thing else with that. As prayer is no isolated thing in Christianity, but springs from the ground of the whole spiritual life, so *this* prayer, which forms a complete and organic whole, comprehends within itself the entire peculiar essence of Christianity.

"*Our Father who art in Heaven.*"‡ The form of the invocation

* Luke, xi.

† We follow Luke, xi. The passage in Matt., vi., 7–16, appears foreign to the original organism of the Sermon on the Mount, in which prayer, fasting, &c., were treated especially in *contrast with the hypocrisy of the Pharisees.* As that longer discourse was made a repertory for Christ's sayings, in which they were arranged according to their affinities, so perhaps it was with this. We may certainly conclude that Christ would not have sketched such a prayer for the disciples without a *special occasion* for it; for the wish to lay down forms of prayer was, as we have seen, remote from his spirit and object. But we cannot think it possible [with some] that Christ uttered this prayer as appropriate for himself, and that the disciples adopted it for that reason; it had no fitness to his position: *he*, at least, could not have prayed for the pardon of his sins. The occasion given by Luke was a very appropriate one; the form was drawn out by Christ at the request of the disciples. It was probable, moreover, from the nature of the case, that Christ, who did not wish to prescribe standing forms of prayer, would make use of such an occasion to explain further the nature of prayer itself [as he does in Luke, xi., 5–13]. In the Sermon on the Mount, also (Matt., vii., 7), a passage similar [to Luke, xi., 9] is found; and Matt., vi., 7, perhaps contains the beginning of Christ's reply to his disciples' request on the subject.

‡ In the shorter form of the prayer given in Luke, the words ἡμῶν and "ὁ ἐν τοῖς οὐρανοῖς

corresponds to the nature of the Christian stand-point; *our Father* because Christ has made us his children. We address God thus, not as individuals, but, in the fellowship of Christ, as members of a community which He has placed in this relation to the common Father. Side by side with this consciousness of communion as *children* goes that of our distance as *creatures;* the God that dwells in his children is the *God above the world* (so that Christianity is equally far from Pantheism and Deism). "Our Father—*in heaven*"—that the soul may soar in prayer from earth to heaven, with the living and abiding consciousness that earth and heaven are no more kept asunder. To this, indeed, the substance of the whole prayer tends.

"*Hallowed be thy name; thy kingdom come; thy will be done on earth as it is done in heaven.*" While the Christian, dwelling on earth, *where sin reigns,* prays to the Father *in heaven,* he longs that earth may be completely reconciled to heaven, and become wholly an organ of its revelations. And this is nothing else but THE COMING OF THE KINGDOM OF GOD, to which, as the centre of all Christian life, and the object of all Christian desire, the three positive prayers first given directly refer. The special prayer, "*Thy kingdom come,*" is guarded against the possibly carnal and worldly interpretation (to which the disciples were at that time inclined) by the one which precedes ("*Hallowed be thy name*"), and the one which follows ("*Thy will be done*"). The Holy One is to be acknowledged and worshipped by all, according to His holy nature and His holy name;* not by a nakedly abstract knowledge and confession thereof, but by a life allied to Him. This "hallowing" of the name of God implies the "coming of his kingdom," and this last is further developed in the prayer that "his will may be realized on earth, as it is in the communion of perfect spirits." The kingdom *will* have come when the will of men is made perfectly at one with the will of God, and to accomplish this is the very aim of the atonement. Among all rational intelligences, the one common essence of the kingdom of God is the doing his will, and thus hallowing his name.

"*Give us, day by day, our daily bread.*" The positive prayers for the supply of Divine wants are followed by one (and only one) for the supply of human wants; in regard to which, also, the disciple of Christ must cherish an abiding consciousness of dependence on the Heavenly Father. It is not the tendency of Christianity to stifle or suppress the wants of our earthly nature, but to hallow them by referring them to

are omitted. It is probable that the original form of the prayer is that given by Matthew. Luke is more accurate in giving the chronological and historical connexion of Christ's discourses, but Matthew gives the discourses themselves more in full.

* In Hebrew and Hellenistic usage, the *name* expresses the outward self-revelation of the *thing;* the image of the thing, as such, or in some defined relation. Where the Occidentalist would use the *idea,* the Orientalist, in his vividly intuitive language, puts the *name.* The sense then is, "God is to be hallowed as God the common Father."

GOD; at the same time keeping them in their proper sphere of subordination to the higher interests of the soul.

"*And forgive us our sins, for we also forgive every one that is indebted to us.*" The first *negative* prayers correspond to the first positive ones Conscious of a manifold sinfulness, which, so long as it remains, hinders the full developement of the kingdom of GOD within them, the disciples of Christ pray for *forgiveness of past sins*, originating in the reaction of the old evil nature. But they cannot pray for this, with conscious need of pardon, without a disposition, at the same time, to forgive the wrongs which others have done to themselves; only thus can their prayer be sincere, only thus can they expect it to be answered. The Christian's constant sense of the need of GOD's pardoning grace for himself necessarily gives tone to his conduct towards his fellows.

"*And lead us not into temptation, but deliver us from evil.*" The prayer for pardon of past sins is followed by one for deliverance in the future. The word "temptation" has a two-fold meaning in Scripture, expressing either *outward* trials of Christian faith and virtue, or an *inward* point of contact for outward incitements, caused by the strife of the sinful principle with the life of GOD in the soul; and the question may be asked, which of the two—the objective or subjective temptation—is referred to in the prayer. Certainly Christ could not have intended that his disciples should pray for exemption from external conflicts and sufferings; for these are inseparable from the calling of soldiers of the kingdom in this world, and essential for the confirmation of Christian faith and virtue, and for culture in the Christian life; and He himself told them that such trials would become the salt of their interior life. But, on the other hand, the prayer cannot be confined to purely subjective temptations; for Christ could not have presupposed that GOD would do any thing so contradictory to His own holiness as to lead men into temptation in *this* sense. A combination of the two appears to be the true idea of the prayer: "Lead us not into such situations as will form for us, in our weakness, incitements to sin;" thus laying it down as a rule of life for Christians not to put themselves, self-confidently, in such situations, but to avoid them as far as duty will allow. But every thing depends upon deliverance from the *internal* incitement to sin; and hence, necessarily, the concluding clause of the petition, "Deliver us from inward temptation by the power of the Evil One." Confiding, in the struggle with evil, upon the power of GOD, we need not fear such outward temptations as are unavoidable.

Thus the prayer accurately defines the relation of the Christian to GOD. The disciple of Christ, ever called to struggle against evil, which finds a point of contact in his inward nature, cannot fight this battle in his own strength, but always stands in need of the assistance of the Holy Spirit. The prayer holds the fundamental truths of Christian faith before the religious consciousness, in their essential connexion with each other—God, revealed in Christ, who redeems man, formed after his image, yet estranged from him by sin; who imparts to him that Divine life which is to be led on by him to its consummation through manifold strifes against the Power of Evil.

It appears, therefore, that Christ did not intend by "the Lord's Prayer" to prescribe a standing form of prayer to his disciples, but to set vividly before their minds the peculiar nature of Christian prayer, in opposition to heathen; and, accordingly, he followed it up by urging them to present their wants to their Heavenly Father with the most undoubting confidence (Luke, xi., 5–13). By a comparison drawn from the ordinary relations of life, he teaches that if our prayers should not appear to be immediately answered, we must only persevere the more earnestly (v. 5–8); and then impresses the thought that God cannot deny the anxious longings of his children (9, 10).

Here, also, the internal character of Christian prayer is strongly contrasted with the pagan outward conception of the exercise. Even the "*seeking*," the longing of the soul, that turns with a deep sense of need to God, is prayer already; indeed, there is no *Christian* prayer without such a feeling. The comparison that follows (v. 11–13) glances (like the Lord's Prayer) from the relation of child and parent on earth to that of the children of God to their Father in heaven—a comparison opposed, in the highest conceivable degrees, to all Pantheistical and Deistical notions of the relations between God and creation. "*If a son shall ask bread of any of you that is a father, will he give him a stone* (in shape resembling the loaf)? *or, if he ask a fish, will he give him a serpent? or, if he ask an egg, will he offer a scorpion?* And how should your Heavenly Father,* of whose perfect love all human affection is but a darkened image, mock the necessities of his children by withholding from their longing hearts the Holy Ghost, which alone can satisfy the hunger of their spirits?" Here, again, as in the Lord's Prayer, the main objects of Christian prayer are shown to be *spiritual;* the giving of the Holy Ghost, the one chief good of the Christian, includes all other gifts.†

* The words "*πατὴρ ὁ ἐξ οὐρανοῦ*," Luke, xi., 13, plainly point to the invocation in the Lord's Prayer.

† Cf. the indefinite *ἀγαθά*, in Matt., vii., 11, generalized from the *δόματα ἀγαθά* in the first clause of the verse. The "Holy Ghost" answers definitely to the point of comparison the nourishment of the soul, as bread is to the body.

§ 140. *Christ forgives the Magdalen at the House of Simon the Pharisee.*—The reciprocal action of Love and Faith in the Forgiveness of Sins.*

It was Christ's free mode of life with his disciples, his intercourse with classes of people despised by the Pharisees, his seeking the society even of the degraded, in order to save them, which first drew upon him the assaults of that haughty and conceited sect.

On one occasion he was invited to dine with one of the Pharisees, named Simon, a man certainly incapable of appreciating the Saviour Either from his natural temper, or from his peculiar disposition towards Christ, he gave him but a cool reception. While the Saviour was there, a woman came in who had previously led a notoriously vicious life, but who now, convinced of sin and groaning under it, sought consolation from Christ, from whom she had doubtless previously received Divine impressions. She threw herself at his feet, moistened them with her tears, wiped them with her hair, and anointed them with ointment. With what power must He have attracted the burdened soul, when a woman, goaded by conscience, could come to him with so sure a hope of obtaining balm for her wounded heart!

The Pharisee was astonished that He should have any thing to do with her. "Were this man," thought he, "possessed of the prophet's glance, piercing the thoughts of men, he could not be so deceived." Christ, noticing his amazement, gave an explanation of the principle on which he acted, that must have shamed and humbled Simon; contrasting his cold hospitality with the heartfelt love which the woman, though oppressed with grief and sin, had manifested for him. Looking at the disposition of the heart, he prefers the woman—guilty, indeed, before, but, even for that reason, now longing the more earnestly for salvation, and penetrated with holy love—to the cold, haughty, self-righteous Pharisee, who, with all his outward show of observing the law, was destitute of quickening love, the essential principle of a genuine Divine life. "*Her sins*," said he, "*which are many, are all forgiven, for she loved much; but to whom little is forgiven, he loveth little.*"

It is love, according to Jesus, which gives to religion and morality their true import. The *faith* of the woman proved itself genuine, because it sprang from, and begat love; the love from the faith, the faith from the love. Her grief for her sins was founded in her love to the Holy God, to whom, conscious of her estrangement, she now felt herself drawn. Her desire for salvation led her to Jesus; her love aided her in finding a Saviour in him; with warm love she embraced him as such, even *before* he pronounced the pardon of her sins. Therefore

* Luke, vii., 36, seq.

Christ said *of* her, "Her many sins are forgiven, because she has loved much;" and *to* her, "*Thy faith hath saved thee, go in peace;*" thus exhibiting the reciprocal relations of the two—the faith proving itself true by the love. The Pharisee, whose feelings were ossified, bound up in the mechanism of the outward law, was especially lacking in the love which could lead to faith; and therefore, in speaking to *him*, the woman's love, and not her faith, was made prominent by Christ.

The very vices of the woman made her conviction more profound, her desire for salvation more ardent, her love for the Redeemer, who pronounced her sins forgiven, more deep and heartfelt. But she had not, even in the midst of her transgressions, been further removed from the true, inward holiness that springs from the Divine life, than was the Pharisee in his best estate. He separated himself from God as effectually, by that unfeeling selfishness which often coexists with what is called morality, and with a conspicuous sanctity of good works, as if he had yielded, like the woman, to the power of evil passions. He was none the better because his colder nature offered no salient points for such temptations. Christ's standard of morality was different from that which the world, deceived by appearances, is wont to apply. The Pharisee had succeeded in avoiding these glaring sins, and in keeping a fair show of obedience to the law; but all this only propped up his self-deceiving *egotism*, which delighted in the illusion of self-righteousness. In such a man, the sense of alienation from God, the conscious ness of sin, as an abyss between him and the Holy One, without which there can be no true repentance, could find no place.

Nay, the abject woman, in her course of vice, may have been nearer to the kingdom than the haughty and self-righteous man; even then, there may have been a spark of love, stifled, indeed, by sensuality, but still existing in her heart, which needed only the touch of a higher power to kindle into flame. In her case, what was in itself bad may have been a means of good; good, however, which certainly might have been arrived at by another road. The pangs of repentance made her susceptible of Divine impressions, the Divine love that met her kindled the spark in her own heart; and she rose, by the living faith of love, above the Pharisee, who, in his arrogant selfishness, was hardened against Divine impressions, and did not recognize the love of God, even when he saw it manifested.*

* The simplicity of this narrative, and the stamp of Christ's spirit which it bears, are sufficient proofs of its originality and truth. But I find no ground for believing it to be identical with the anointing of Christ by Mary at Bethany, which also, according to Matt. (xxvi., 6), occurred in the house of a Simon. The resemblances are accidental; such things could occur again and again amid Oriental customs. That a woman, in order to show her reverential love for the Saviour, might serve him like a slave, wash his feet, not with water, but with the costliest material in her possession, &c.; all this could easily have occurred twice and both times, too, in the house of a man named Simon, which was a very common

§ 141. *Matthew the Publican called from the Custom-house.—Familiar Intercourse of Christ with the Publicans at the Banquet.—The Pharisees blame the Disciples, and Christ justifies them.—"The Sick need the Physician."*

What surprise and offence must the Pharisees have felt when they saw Christ admit even a *publican* into the immediate circle of his disciples.*

As he was walking one day along the shore of the lake,† he saw a publican sitting in his toll-booth, named MATTHEW; a man who had doubtless, like Peter, received many impressions from Christ before, and was thereby prepared to renounce the world at his bidding. Jesus, with a voice that could not be resisted, said unto him, "*Follow me.*" Matthew understood the call, and did not hesitate to follow, at any cost, Him who had so powerfully attracted his heart. He left his business, rejoicing that Christ was willing to take him into his closer fellowship. This decisive event was celebrated by a great entertainment,‡ intended also, perhaps, as a farewell feast to his old business associates.

name among the Jews; although it is possible that the name may have been transferred from the one account to the other. But while the resemblances are accidental, the *differences* are substantial. In the one the woman is an awakened sinner; in the other, one who had always led a devout life, and was, at the time, seized with additional gratitude at the saving of a beloved brother's life. In the one, the different relations in which a self-righteous Pharisee and an awakened sinner stand to Christ, who rejects no repentant sinner, are set forth; in the other, a heartfelt love, which knows no measure, is contrasted with the common mind, incapable of comprehending such love. In the one it is Christ that is blamed and justified; in the other, the woman.

* There are discrepancies in the narrative of the calling of Matthew, not, however, affecting the credibility of the account, which comes from several independent sources, and bears no marks of exaggeration. In Matthew's Gospel, ix., 9, the person here spoken of is called *Matthew*, and in x., 3, *Matthew the publican* is mentioned among the Apostles; but in Luke, v., 27; Mark, ii., 14, he is called *Levi*. Mark appears to be more definite than the others, calling him the *son of Alpheus*, which does not look like a fanciful designation. The difficulty might be overcome by supposing (what was not uncommon among the Jews) that the same man was designated in the one case by the name, in the other by the surname. An objection to this (though not decisive) is the fact that in the list of Apostles given in Matt., x., 3, he is called merely *Matthew the publican*, with no surname, and in the lists given by Mark and Luke, *Matthew*, simply, with no surname; and, further, that an old tradition existed, which discriminated Matthew and Levi, and named the latter, in addition, among the prominent heralds of the Gospel. (Heracleon, in Clem. Alex., Strom., l. iv., c. xi.) On this ground we might admit, with *Sieffert*, that the names of two persons, *i. e.*, of the *Apostle* Matthew, and some other who had been admitted, at least, among the Seventy, had been confounded together. But as Matthew himself was the original source of the materials of the Gospel which bears his name (materials arranged, perhaps, by another hand), we cannot attribute the confusion to this Gospel. It is, at the same time, possible that the giver of the feast (Luke, v., 29), Levi, was another rich publican, a friend of the publican Matthew, who afterward also attached himself to Jesus; especially as nothing is said in Matt., ix., 10, about a great feast being given at the house of Matthew; and that thus the name of Matthew, whose call to the ministry occasioned the feast, and that of Levi, the host, in whose life it made an epoch, and who afterward became known as a preacher of the Gospel, were confounded together.

† Mark, ii., 13.

‡ Luke, v., 29.

Christ, in whose honour the entertainment was given, did not disdain this token of grateful love, but took his place at the feast with a set of men who were regarded as the scum of the people, but to whom his saving influences were to be brought nigh.

Shortly after, some of the Pharisees took the disciples to task for their free and (as they thought) unspiritual mode of life, in eating and drinking with degraded sinners and tax-gatherers. It is evident that the attack was intended for Christ, though they hesitated, as yet, to assault him openly. He, therefore, took the matter up personally, and justified his conduct by saying, "*They that are whole need not a physician, but they that are sick.*" Indicating that he sought, rather than avoided, degraded sinners, because they, precisely, stood most in need of his healing aid, and were most likely, from a sense of need, to receive it willingly.

But he certainly did not mean to say tha he came to save *only* those who were sunken in vice. He was far, also, from meaning, that though all have need of him, all have not the *same* need of him; that any were excluded from the number of the "sick," who needed him as a "physician." But he taught that as he had come as a physician for the sick, he could help only those who, as sick persons, sought healing at his hands. He sought the tax-gatherers rather than the Pharisees, because the latter, deeming themselves spiritually sound, had no disposition to receive that which he came to impart. Undoubtedly, he did not mean to grant that they were sound, or less diseased than the publicans.

Indeed, he pointed out their peculiar disease by saying to them, "*Go ye, and learn what that meaneth, 'I will have mercy, and not sacrifice.'*"* On the one hand, by this quotation, he pointed out the feeling that inspired his own conduct, the love which is the fulfilling of the law; and, on the other, he indicated their fundamental error of making religion an outward thing, while they totally lacked the soul of genuine piety. This was to convince them that they themselves were sick and needed the physician. Dropping the figure, he gave them the same thought in plain terms: "*I came not to call the righteous, but sinners to repentance.*"

§ 141. *Christ's different Modes of Reply to those who questioned his Conduct in consorting with Sinners.—The Value of a Soul.—Parable of the Prodigal Son.—Of the Pharisee and the Publican.*

There is a difference in *one* respect in Christ's replies at differen times to those who found fault with his kindness to publicans and de graded sinners. In some cases he stopped short after vividly exhibiting

† Matt., ix., 13; Hos., vi., 6.

the mercy of God to all truly repentant sinners; in others, he not only justified his own conduct, but took the offensive against those who had attacked him, and showed them their own deficiencies in true righteousness, and their inferiority to the sincerely repentant publicans. The former course was probably taken with those who were more sincerely striving after righteousness, and who took offence at him on purer grounds. It is necessary to note this distinction in order to apprehend Christ's words rightly, and to derive, from comparing his discourses together, a connected system of doctrine.

Under the first class may be placed the parables which are recorded in the fifteenth chapter of Luke. In verses 3–10 we have a vivid illustration of the value which God attaches to the salvation of *one* soul, shown by the great joy which the repentance of a sinner causes in a world of spirits, allied in their sympathies to Him. This is the one point which is to be made prominent and emphatic in interpreting the passage; we should err in pressing the separate points of comparison further.

To the same class, also, belongs the parable of the *Prodigal Son.* The elder son, who remains at home and serves his father faithfully, represents a Pharisee† of the better class, who sincerely strives to keep the law and is free from glaring sins, but still occupies a strictly legal stand-point. The younger son represents one who seeks his highest good in the world, throws off the restraints of the law, and gives full play to his passions. But experience shows him the emptiness of such a life; estranged from God, he becomes conscious of wretchedness, and returns, sincerely penitent, to seek forgiveness in the Father's love.

Christ does not go far, in this parable, in illustrating the deficiencies of the Pharisee. His legal righteousness goes without specific rebuke, but his envy (v. 28) and his want of love ("the fulfilling of the law") show clearly the emptiness of his morality. It may have been the Saviour's intention to lead the person here represented to discover, of himself, his total want of the substance of religion.

The one chief point of the parable is to illustrate, under the figure of relations drawn from human life, the manner in which the paternal love of God meets the vilest of sinners when he returns sincerely penitent. How strikingly does this picture of the Father's love, ever ready to pardon sin, rebuke not merely the *Jewish* exclusiveness, but all those limitations of God's purposes for the salvation of the human race,

* Luke, xv., 11–32.

† This must be the case, on the supposition that Luke, xv., 2, expresses the precise occasion of this parable, but we cannot positively assert this. It is possible that one of the disciples who had not fully imbibed the spirit of Christ may have given the occasion for it

whether before or after Christ, which the arbitrary creeds of men have attributed to the Divine decrees! The parable clearly implies that the love of the Father contemplates the salvation of *all* his fallen children, among all generations of men. Yet it by no means excludes, although it does not expressly declare, the necessity of the mediatorial work of Christ; we must not expect to find the whole circle of Christian doctrine in every parable. Indeed, the mediation of Christ itself is the precise way in which the paternal love of God goes out to meet and welcome all his fallen children when they return in repentance. The parable images the condition of fallen man in general, as well as of that class of gross sinners to which, from the occasion on which Christ uttered it, it necessarily gives special prominence.

The line of distinction between the Pharisee and the publican is still more closely drawn in the parable contained in Luke, xviii., 9–14.* The publican humbles himself before God, deeply sensible of sin, and only seeking forgiveness, and is therefore represented as having the dispositions necessary for pardon and justification. The Pharisee, trusting in his supposed righteousness, exalts himself above the notorious sinner, and is therefore destitute of the conditions of pardon, though he needs it as much as the other. Christ himself deduces from the example this general truth: "*Every one that exalteth himself shall be abased, and he that humbleth himself shall be exalted.*" That is, he who sets up great pretensions before God on account of his self-acquired virtue or wisdom, will be disappointed; his arrogant assumption of a worth which is nothing but vileness will exclude him from that true dignity which the grace of God alone can bestow; which dignity *will* be bestowed, on the other hand, upon the sinner who truly humbles himself before God from a conscious sense of moral unworthiness.

In this parable we find the germ of Paul's doctrine; even of some of his weighty expressions on this subject. The doctrine is the same as that which Christ taught in pronouncing the "poor in spirit" blessed.

* This parable is one (cf. p. 107) in which a truth relating to the kingdom of God is illustrated by an assumed fact; but the fact is one taken from the *same* sphere of life as that which it intended to depict. Moreover, the relation which must exist, in all time, between the self-righteous saint *by works* and the humbly penitent sinner is illustrated by an example such as once constantly occurred in real life—in Pharisees and publicans.

CHAPTER VIII.

CHRIST'S SECOND JOURNEY TO JERUSALEM.*

§ 143. *The Miracle at the Pool of Bethesda.—The Words of Christ in the Temple to the Man that was healed.* (John, v., 1–14.)

CHRIST, having spent the winter in Galilee, was called again to Jerusalem by the feast of the Passover. His stay in the city at that feast forms a marked period in his history; for a cure wrought upon a certain Sabbath in that time was the occasion, if not the cause, of a more violent display of the opposition of the Pharisees than had yet been made against him.

A certain spring at Jerusalem was believed by the people to possess remarkable healing powers at particular seasons, when its waters were moved by (what they supposed to be) a supernatural cause.† It is un-

* John, v., 1. The chronology of the life of Christ depends a good deal upon the question whether the feast mentioned John, v., 1, was or was not the Passover. The indefiniteness of the word "feast" in this passage, and the mention of the Passover itself in John, vi., 4, might lead us to infer that the feast of *Purim* was meant, which occurred a few weeks before the Passover; but every thing else is against this inference. The Purim feast did not require of the pious Jew ἀναβαίνειν εἰς Ἱεροσόλυμα; had this feast, therefore, been in question, we might expect in John, v., 1, a statement of Christ's reason for going up to it, instead of waiting for the Passover. The most ancient interpretation favours the Passover (Iren., ii., 22), which feast was attended by most of the foreign Jews, and required the ἀναβαίνειν. The omission of the definite article in the text is not so important as some suppose. The text says ἦν ἑορτή—"*it was feast*"—further defined by ἀνέβη, showing that the *chief feast* is intended. Even in German [or English] we might say, loosely, "*it was feast*," omitting the article, as in the Greek. It is unlikely, too, that Christ, who had already roused the prejudices of the Pharisees against him, should have gone to the *Purim* feast, where he would have had to contend with them alone in Jerusalem, instead of continuing his labours undisturbed in Galilee until Passover. John's omission to say more of Christ's ministry up to the time of the next Passover (vi., 4) may be accounted for on the ground that it was not his purpose to recount his labours in Galilee, which were preserved in the circle of the ordinary traditions. The two first verses of chap. v. show how summary his account is. Only in chap. vii., 1, is an occasion offered for assigning the reason for Christ's stay in Galilee; we can the more readily account for the surprise of the brothers (vii., 3, seq.) if he spent the *whole year and a half* in Galilee.

† Against the credibility of this account, *Bretschneider* and *Strauss* adduce the silence of Josephus and the Rabbins in regard to such a healing spring; but this argument—like every *argumentum e silentio*, unsupported by special circumstances—is destitute of force. These very authorities tell us that there were many mineral springs in Palestine. *Eusebius*, in his work, "περὶ τῶν τοπικῶν ὀνομάτων τῶν ἐν τῇ θείᾳ γραφῇ, (Onomasticon), says, under the word "Βηζαθὰ"—"καὶ νῦν δείκνυται ἐν ταῖς αὐτόθι λίμναις διδύμοις, ὧν ἑκατέρα μὲν ἐκ τῶν κατ' ἔτος ὑετῶν πληροῦται, θάτερα δὲ παραδόξως πεφοινιγμένον δείκνυσι τὸ ὕδωρ, ἴχνος, ὥς φασι, φέρουσα τῶν πάλαι καθαιρομένων ἱερείων, παρ' ὃ καὶ προβατικὴ καλεῖται διὰ τὰ θύματα." (Hieron., Opp., ed. Vallars., tom. iii., pt. i., p. 181.) The old tradition, that the waters had become "red," from the washing of the sacrifices in them in old times, leads to the conclusion that it contained peculiar components. The legend of the angel (in v. 4, which, according to the best criticism, does not belong to John, but is a later gloss) could not have arisen unless the spring and its phenomena really existed. *Robinson* (Palestine, ii., 137, 156) thinks that he found

important whether this belief was an old one, or was called forth at a later period by actual occurrences, of which, as was common, too much was made. The healing-spring itself, or the covered colonnade connected with it, was called *Bethesda** ("place of mercy").

At this fountain Christ found, on the Sabbath day, a man who had been lame for thirty-eight years, and had long waited for the moving of the waters in hope of relief, but had never been able to avail himself of it for want of a kind hand to help him into the water at the auspicious moment. It is probable that many pressed to the spring in haste to catch the passing instant when its healing powers were active. But the sick man was to find help from a far different source. [*Jesus saith unto him, Arise, take up thy bed and walk, and immediately the man was made whole.*]

The restored man lost sight of the Saviour in the throng, but afterward Christ found him in the Temple, where he had probably first gone in order to thank God for his recovery. The favourable moment was seized by the Saviour to direct his mind from the healing of his body to that of his soul. His words, "*Sin no more, lest a worse thing come unto thee,*" may be considered either as implying that the sickness, in this particular case, was caused by sin, or as referring to the general connexion between sin and physical evil, in virtue of which the latter is a memorial of the former as its source. In either view they were intended to remind him of his spiritual necessities, and to point out the only way in which they could be relieved.

§ 144. *The Pharisees accuse Christ of Sabbath-breaking and Blasphemy.—His Justification.* (John, v., 10, 17–19.)

This occurrence gave the Pharisees the first occasion (so far as we know) to accuse Christ of breaking the Sabbath and of blaspheming against God. The first accusation was made in their contracted sense of the Sabbatical law, and of its violation; the latter arose from their legal Monotheism, and their narrow idea of the Messianic office.

In his justification, Christ struck at the root of the first error, viz., the carnal notion that the sanctity of the Sabbath was founded solely upon God's resting after the work of creation, as if his creative labours were then commenced and ended; and points out, on the other hand, the ever-continuing activity of God as the ground of all being—*my Father worketh hitherto, and I work.** ("As He never ceases to work,

in the irregular movement of the water in the "Fountain of the Virgin" phenomena similar to those recorded of the Pool of Bethesda, and contributing to explain them.

‡ חֶסֶד and בֵּית.

* John, v., 17. This is not out of place, nor borrowed from Philo, as some suppose, nor a mere metaphysical proposition, but one belonging immediately to the religious conscious

so do I work unceasingly for the salvation of men.") He rejects the narrow limits which their contracted view of the law of the Sabbath would assign to his healing labours, which were to go on uninterruptedly. Nor did he lower his tone in regard to the relations which he sustained to his Heavenly Father because his opponents charged him with claiming, by his words, Divine dignity and authority. On the contrary, he strengthened his assertions, taking care only to guard against their being perverted into a depreciation of the Father's dignity, by declaring that he laboured in unity with the Father, and in dependence upon him. "*The Son*," said he, "*can do nothing of himself, but what he seeth the Father do.*" (He would have to deny himself as the Son of God, before he could act contrary to the will and example of the Father.)

§ 145. *The Discourse continued: Christ intimates his future greater Works.—His Judgment, and the Resurrection.* (John, v., 20–29.)

Christ proceeds to declare (v. 20) that the Father *will show him greater works than these*, *i. e.*, than reviving the dead limbs of the paralytic. And what were these "greater works?" Without doubt, *that* work which Christ always describes as his greatest—as the aim of his whole life—the awakening, namely, of Divine life in the spiritually dead humanity; a work which nothing but the creative efficiency of God could accomplish. "*That ye may marvel;*" for those who then would not recognize the Son of God in the humble garb of the Son of Man would indeed, at a later period, be amazed to see works (wrought by one whom they believed to be dead) which must be acknowledged to be *great* in their moral effects, even if their intrinsic nature could not be understood.

He describes these greater works more exactly, and points out, at the same time, the perfect power which he would have to do them in the words: "*For as the Father raiseth up the dead, and quickeneth them, even so the Son quickeneth whom he will.*" The raising to *life* is as real in the latter clause as in the former. It depends upon His will, indeed; but his is no arbitrary will; and it follows that submission to his will is requisite before man can receive this Divine life. This, like that other passage—*the wind bloweth where it listeth*—breaks down the barriers within which Judaism inclosed the Theocracy and the Messianic calling.

And because it depends upon the Son to give light to whom He

ness. It is said, moreover, that Christ's transition (in verses 17, 19, seq.) from the Sabbath controversy to an exposition of his higher dignity is out of keeping with his character and mode of teaching, as exhibited in the first three Gospels. What would be said, then, if a transition like that recorded in Matthew, xii., 6, were recorded in John's Gospel?

will the whole judgment of mankind is intrusted to his hands. "*For the Father judgeth no man, but hath committed all judgment unto the Son.*" The negative is joined to the positive. The judgment is brought about by men's bearing towards Him from whom alone they can receive life: "*That all men should honour the Son, even as also they honour the Father.*" He that will not recognize the Divine mission of the Son dishonours the Father that sent him.

The truth thus enunciated in general terms, Christ presented still more vividly, by applying it to his work then beginning, and which was to be carried on through all ages, until the final judgment and the consummation of the kingdom of God. "*He that heareth my word, and believeth on him that sent me, hath everlasting life, and shall not come into judgment, but is passed from death into life* (the true, everlasting, Divine life). *The hour is coming, and now is, when the* (spiritually) *dead shall hear the voice of the Son of God, and they that hear shall live; for as the Father hath* (the Source of Divine) *life in himself, so hath he given to the Son to have* (Divine) *life in himself.* (If the Source of life, which is in God, had not been communicated to the human nature in him, then communion with him could not communicate the Divine life to others.) *And hath given him authority to execute judgment also, because he is the Son of Man* (as *man* he is to judge men)."

His hearers, who saw him before their eyes in human form, were startled, doubtless, by these declarations. They looked for Messiah to establish a *visible* kingdom, with unearthly splendours, expecting it to be attended by an outward judgment; and Christ's announcement of a *spiritual* agency, that was to be coeval with the world's history, was beyond their apprehension. He referred them, therefore, to the final aim of the course which he was laying out for the human race, the final Messianic work of the Judgment and the general Resurrection; a work in itself, indeed, more familiar to them, but which, as ascribed to *him*, must have still more raised their wonder. "*Marvel not at this; for the hour is coming in which all that are in the graves shall hear his voice, and shall come forth: they that have done good, to the resurrection of life; and they that have done evil, unto the resurrection of damnation.*"

§ 146. *The Discourse continued: Christ Appeals to the Testimony of his Works.* (John, v., 30–37.)

Having thus unfolded his whole Messianic agency, embracing both the present and the future, Christ returns (v. 30) to the general proposition with which he had commenced (in v. 19). As he had applied his unity of action with the Father to his whole course, so now he applies it specifically to his *judgment*, which must, therefore, be just and true: "*I can of mine own self do nothing; as I hear, I judge, and my judgment is just.*"

His decision against his opponents must, therefore, be just and true also. They need not say (he told them) that *his* testimony was not trustworthy, because given of himself (v. 31). It was another that bore witness of him, whose testimony he knew to be unimpeachable (v. 32). He did not allude to John, whose light, which had been to them, as to children, a source of transitory* pleasure, they had not followed to the point whither it ought to have guided them; he did not allude to John's, nor, indeed, to any man's testimony, but to a greater, viz., the *works* themselves, which the Father had given him to accomplish, and which formed the objective testimony to the Divinity of his labours: "*The same works that I do, bear witness of me that the Father hath sent me; and the Father himself, which hath sent me, hath borne witness of me*"† (v. 36, 37).

§ 147. *The Discourse continued: Incapacity of the Jews to Understand the Testimony of God as given in the Scriptures.* (John, v., 37–47.)

It was precisely through the works, Christ told them, that the Father had testified to him. "But," continued he, in effect, "it is no wonder that you ask another testimony of me, seeing that you are destitute of the spiritual capacity which is necessary to perceive *this* one. It cannot be perceived with the senses;‡ you have never heard with your ears the voice of the Father, nor seen with your eyes his form. God does not reveal himself to the fleshly sense; and in you no other sense is developed. And for this reason, too, you cannot understand the

* The words of John, v., 35, imply that the ministry of the Baptist belonged to the past, and they may have been spoken after his death; although the only *necessary* inference is, that he had ceased his public labours.

† I cannot agree with those who (like *Lücke*, Comm. John, v., 37) refer the first clause of verse 37 to the testimony of the Father, as given in the Old Testament. The connexion demands a climax. But how could the testimony of God in the *Scriptures* be more direct than in the *Divine agency of Christ* itself? There could be no revelation more direct or powerful than this. The *present* tense ("the works *bear* witness") is used in verse 36, because Christ's agency was still going on, and to continue. But because part of it was already past, and a subject of contemplation, the *perfect* tense is used in verse 37 ("the Father *hath borne* witness"). The 37th verse looks back to the 36th, the ὁ πέμψας με referring to the ὅτι ὁ πατήρ με ἀπέσταλκε. The climax consists in the transfer of what has been said of the *works*, as testifying of God, to *God himself*, as testifying through the works. Then Christ shows why the Jews do not perceive this testimony, but always demand new proofs. They ask a testimony that can be heard and perceived by the carnal senses; and there is none such to be had. God reveals himself only in a spiritual way, to the indwelling Sense for the Divine. This last they have not; and the revelation of the Old Testament has always been to them a dead letter; the word of God has not penetrated their inner being. To this very naturally follows verse 39, "*Ye search the Scriptures, for in them ye think ye have eternal life;*" which life only Christ can impart. In opposition to the most recent commentators, I must think this the true connexion of the passage.

‡ We may remember how the Jews were inclined to look for *Theophanies* (visible appearances of the Deity).

testimony of the Scriptures. The word of God, which you ought to have received *within you* from the Scriptures, dwells not *in* you; it has remained for you simply outward. Hence your 'searching of the Scriptures' is a lifeless thing. Thinking that, in the letter of the word, you have eternal life, you will not come unto Him who alone imparts that life, and to whom the Scriptures were only intended to lead; your dispositions and mine are directly contrary. I am concerned only for the honour of God; you for your own. With such a disposition, you cannot possibly believe in me. If another should come, in feeling like yourselves, and seek, in his own name, to lord it among you, *him* you will receive.* Moses himself, for whose honour you are zealous, but whose law you violate whenever it clashes with your selfish interests, will appear as your accuser. Did you truly believe Moses—not according to the letter merely, but also to the spirit—you would also believe in me."†

Had the Pharisees been truly sincere in observing the law, the law would have been to them a παιδαγωγὸς εἰς Χριστόν (*a schoolmaster to lead to Christ*), and they would have discovered the element of prophecy even in the Pentateuch itself. Their adherence to the letter made them blind to the Messiah; but their carnal mind caused their adherence to the letter. Justly, then, could Christ say to them, "*Ye* strive for the honour of Moses, yet, in fact, you seek your own honour more than his, and, therefore, do not believe him; how, then, can you believe *my* words, which must appear altogether strange and new?"

From this time the ruling Pharisaic party persecuted Christ as a most dangerous enemy, who exposed their sentiments with a power of truth not to be controverted. "Sabbath-breaking and blasphemy" were the pretexts on which they sought his condemnation.

CHAPTER IX.

SECOND COURSE OF EXTENDED LABOURS IN GALILEE.

SUCH was the affiliation of parties throughout Judea, that the opposition which the Pharisees stirred up against Christ at Jerusalem, soon made itself felt throughout the country. A new epoch of his ministry therefore began.

* Cf. the predictions, in the synoptical Gospels, of false prophets that should deceive the people.

† For Moses' highest calling was to prepare the way for Messiah. Both by the whole stage which he occupied in the developement of the Divine kingdom, and by individual prophetic intimations (like Deut., xviii., 15; Gen., iii., 15, in their spiritual meaning), he had pointed out the Messiah.

The charge of heresy and blasphemy having spread into Galilee, Christ was led to unfold, in a connected discourse, the relation which existed between the old stand-point of the law and the new era of the kingdom of God introduced by himself. His exposition was adapted to the capacities of his hearers at the time, and, therefore, did not include the circle of truths which was afterward to be revealed, through the Holy Spirit, in the progress of the kingdom. This discourse was the

SERMON ON THE MOUNT.

Introduction.

§ 148. (1.) *Place and Circumstances of the Delivery of the Sermon,* (2.) *Its Subject-matter, viz.: the Kingdom of God as the Aim of the Old Dispensation;* (3.) *The Two Editions, viz.: Matthew's and Luke's;* (4.) *Its Pervading Rebuke of Carnal Conceptions of the Messiahship.*

(1.)

In the course of the summer, as Jesus was returning from one of his extensive preaching-tours in Galilee, multitudes followed him, attracted by his words and works. Toward evening they came near Capernaum and a few of the company hastened thither in advance, while the greater number remained, in order to enter the city in company with the Master. The multitude stopped at the foot of a mountain near the town; but Jesus, seeking solitude, went higher up the ascent. The next morning he took his place upon the declivity of the mountain, and, drawing his twelve disciples into a narrower circle about him,* delivered the discourse. It was intended for all such as felt drawn to follow him; to teach them what they had to expect, and what would be expected of them, in becoming his disciples; and to expose the false representations that had been made upon both these points.

(2.)

The connected system of truths unfolded in the discourse was intended to exhibit to the people the kingdom of God as the aim of the Old Dispensation; as the consummation for which that dispensation prepared the way. The Sermon on the Mount, therefore, forms the point of transition from the Law to the Gospel; Christianity is exhibited in it as Judaism spiritualized and transfigured. The idea of the *kingdom* of God is the prominent one; the person of the Theocratic *king* is subordinate thereto. The discourse is made up of many sen-

* If Luke, vi., 13, is intended to recite the *choosing* of the Apostles, it is clear that it is done only incidentally, and not in chronological connexion. Luke does not say that the discourse was specially directed to the Apostles, nor is there a trace of internal evidence to that effect. The discourses of Christ that *were* specially intended to teach the Apostles the duties of their calling have a very different tone.

tentious passages, calculated, separately, to impress the memory of the hearers, and remain as fruitful germs in their hearts; but, on the other hand, bound together as parts of an organic whole. This was admirably adapted to preserve the discourse, in its essential features, uncorrupted in transmission.

(3.)

Accordingly, we find the two editions (Matt., v., vi., vii.; and Luke, vi., 20–29), each giving the body of the discourse, with beginning, middle, and end; although they certainly originated in different traditions and from different hearers.

Comparing the two copies, we find Matthew's to be more full, as well as more accurate in the details; it also gives obvious indications of its Hebrew origin. But the original document of Matthew passed through the hands of the Greek editor, who has inserted other expressions of Christ allied to those in the organic connexion of the discourse, but spoken on other occasions. Assuming that what is common to Matthew and Luke forms the body of the sermon, we have a standard for deciding what passages do, and what do not, belong to it as a connected whole.

(4.)

There runs through the whole discourse, implied where it is not directly expressed, a rebuke of the carnal tendency of the Jewish mind, as displayed in its notions of the Messianic kingdom, and of the requisites for participating therein; the latter, indeed, depending entirely upon the former. It was most important to convince men that meetness for the kingdom depended not upon alliance to the Jewish stem, but upon alliance of the heart to God. Their mode of thinking had to be modified accordingly. A *direct* attack upon the usual conceptions of the nature and manifestation of the kingdom would have been repelled by those who were unprepared for it; but to show what dispositions of *heart* it required, was to strike at the root of error. In his mode of expression, indeed, Christ adhered to the Jewish forms (*e. g.*, in stating the beatitudes); but his words were carefully adapted and varied, so as to guard against sensuous interpretations. The truth was clearly to be seen through the veil.

I. The Beatitudes.

§ 149. *Moral Requisites for Entering the Kingdom of God:* (1.) *Poverty of Spirit;* (2.) *Meekness;* (3.) *Hungering and Thirsting after Righteousness.*

(1.)

Glancing at the poor, who probably comprised most of his congregation, Christ says, "*Blessed are the poor in spirit, for theirs is the kingdom of heaven.* Happy are they who feel the spiritual wretchedness of the Theocratic nation; who long after the true riches of the kingdom; who have not stifled the higher cravings of their souls by worldly delights, by confidence in their Jewish descent, by the pride of Pharisaic righteousness and wisdom; but are conscious of their spiritual poverty, of their lack of the true riches of the Spirit and the kingdom."* Such are they to whom the kingdom of God belongs; "*theirs*," says Christ, "*is the kingdom of heaven;*" as, in certain respects, a present possession.

(2.)

As the pride of the Pharisee is joined with sternness, so poverty of spirit is attended by *meekness and humility.* In the Sermon, "*blessed are the poor in spirit*" is followed by† "*blessed are the meek, for they shall inherit the earth.*" A remarkable contrast: Dominion is promised to that precise disposition of heart which is most averse to it. A contrast, too, which serves to point out the peculiar *kind* of world-dominion promised, as distinguished from the prevailing Jewish ideas on the subject. According to the latter, the sceptre of the Messianic reign over the heathen nations was to be a sceptre of iron; according to the former, the "*gentle-spirited*" are to obtain possession of the earth.

It is true, the expression, "shall inherit the earth," is included (like the other beatitudes) in the more general one, "theirs is the kingdom of heaven;" it is doubtless true, also, that the phrase was not uncommon among the Jews; but we are not, therefore, obliged to conclude that the thought involved in it is only the general one of "the blessedness of the kingdom of God." The expression has a significance of its own. The "inheritance of the earth" is that world-dominion which Christians, as organs of the Spirit of Christ, are ever more and more to obtain, as the kingdom of God shall win increasing sway over

* "Poverty of spirit" includes all that we have here expressed. *De Wette* (in *Heidelb. Studien*, vol. iii., pt. 2, in his *Comment. de morte Jesu Christi expiatoria*, in his *Christliche Littenlehre*, pt. i., p. 246, and in his *Commentary*, in loc.) has done much to develope the idea genetically. He has rightly called attention to the derivation of the phrase from the Old Testament views. "The humble citizen of the fallen Theocracy, deeply feeling the misery of the Theocratic nation, bruised in spirit, and hoping only in God, is '*poor in spirit*,' in contrast with the haughty blasphemer, who has no such feeling: עָנָו, אֶבְיוֹן, in contrast with רָשָׁע; Isa., lxi., 1" Applying this spiritually, with reference to the inner life we naturally infer that the πτωχοὶ τῷ πνεύματι are "those who feel their want of that which alone can satisfy and enrich the Spirit," and so all the rest that we have intimated. The difference in these explanations—easily harmonized—consists only in the reference of the idea to its genetic historical developement in the one, and to the objective Christian meaning, which holds good for all ages. Conf. *James* (i., 9, 10), whose epistle accords in many points with the Sermon on the Mount, and follows its stand-point in the developement of Christianity.

† In the order of the Beatitudes, I follow the text of *Lachmann*, which gives them in a connexion not only logical, but corresponding with their aim as instruction.

mankind and the relations of society, until, in its final consummation, the whole earth shall own its dominion; and the Power which is to gain this world-dominion is MEEKNESS; the quiet might of gentleness it is with which GOD's kingdom is to subjugate the world.

(3.)

Christ, then, further developes the characteristics of poverty of spirit in the beatitude: "*Blessed are they that mourn* (that are conscious of inward woe), *for they shall be comforted.*" That this mourning is not grief for mere outward afflictions, appears from the next: "*Blessed are they which do hunger and thirst after righteousness, for they shall be filled*" (shall find their wants supplied in the communion of the kingdom of GOD).

§ 150. *Moral Result of Entering the Kingdom of God, viz.: The "Pure in Heart see God."*

The preceding beatitudes point out the moral requisites for *entering into* the kingdom of GOD; but it must not be inferred that they are demanded *only* on entrance into it, and no longer. Rather, as our appropriation of the kingdom can never be a finished act while we remain on earth, must its moral requisites continue, nay, continually grow in strength. We can discern already, in their connexion, the peculiar essence of Christianity. The Christian is conscious of no moral or spiritual ability of his own, needing only to be rightly applied to gain the wished-for end; on the contrary, he feels that he has, of *himself*, nothing but want and weakness, insufficiency and wretchedness. Already Christ announces redemption as his own peculiar work.

Presupposing, then, that those who are endowed with these requisites will enter his kingdom, satisfy their spiritual need, and share in his saving power, Christ describes them, in consequence, as "*pure in heart*" (pure, however, not according to the standard of *legal* piety). And to those who possess this purity he promises that "*they shall see God.*" They shall have *perfect* communion with Him, and that complete and intuitive knowledge of his nature which, founded in such communion, forms the bliss of everlasting life.

This promise refers, it is true, to that full communion with GOD which shall be realized in eternal life, or in the consummation of the kingdom of God only. But this by no means excludes its application to *that* participation in the kingdom which begins during our earthly life; just as the preceding promises were to be gradually and progressively fulfilled until their consummation. The prominent connexion of thought is, that the *knowledge* of Divine things must spring from the *life*, from that purity of heart which fits men for communion with GOD that in our life on earth we are to be prepared, by purification of heart, for complete Divine knowledge. For the rest, this promise leads over to those which relate to the future everlasting life (the consummation of the kingdom).

§ 151. *Moral Relations of the Members of the Kingdom to their Fellow men:* viz., *They are "Peace-makers," and "Persecuted."*

Christ next describes certain relations in which the members of his kingdom stand to others. Inspired by love and meekness, they seek *peace* with all men. But as they serve a holy kingdom, and do battle with the prevalent wickedness of men, they cannot escape *persecutions.* Here, again, Christ dissipates the hopes with which the Jews, expecting a Messiah, are wont to flatter themselves. Instead of promising to his followers a kingdom of earthly glory and prosperity, he predicts for them manifold persecutions, such as the prophets of old had suffered for the cause of God.

They shall suffer "for *righteousness*" sake; but he then passes over, from the *general* idea of the kingdom (righteousness—holiness) to his own person: "*Blessed are ye when men shall revile you,* &c., *for* MY *sake.*" Their very relations to *Him* were to draw upon them all manner of slanders and calumnies; thus presupposing that the prevailing Jewish opinions would be opposed by his disciples.*

The accompanying beatitudes are also full of meaning. "Blessed are the peace-makers, *for they shall be called*† *the children of God,*" that is, shall be invested with the dignity and the rights of children of God. This promise refers partly to the present life, and partly, in its highest meaning, to the future.‡ "Blessed are they which are persecuted, *for theirs is the kingdom of heaven.*" . . . "*For great is your reward in heaven.*"

The "reward" may be understood, even apart from what Christ has said elsewhere, from the connexion of this discourse itself.§ The first beatitudes show that *we* have no claim to the kingdom but our humble wants and susceptible hearts; the idea of *merit,* therefore, claiming a reward as its due, is wholly out of the question. The reward is a gracious gift. But when grace has admitted us into the kingdom, our par-

* This agrees very well with the point of time to which we have referred the Sermon on the Mount, *i. e.,* the period when the Pharisees began to persecute Christ and his disciples. Moreover, his foresight at that time of the hatred he would excite, and the persecutions his followers would suffer, combined with the fact that throughout the discourse there is not the slightest hint of a purpose to triumph over his foes by an overwhelming miraculous power—nay, that the whole spirit of the discourse is opposed to such a purpose—agrees very well with his anticipating, at the time, that he should die in fulfilling his calling.

† The name is the outward sign of the thing—its manifestation and confirmation.

‡ Indicated in κληθήσονται, especially.

§ Cf. *De Wette's* excellent remarks on Matt., v., 12.

ticipation in its "blessedness" depends upon our bearing in the struggles to which our membership in the kingdom exposes us on earth. The "reward," therefore, designates the relation between the Divine gifts and our subjective worth; the gifts are proportioned to the work which the members of the kingdom, as such, have to do.* It is obvious, then, that no external reward is meant—no acting with a view to such—for these ideas are foreign to the nature of the kingdom of God itself.

What, then, is the "reward?" It is, that the wants of our higher nature shall be satisfied; that we shall enjoy perfect communion with God, and, in consequence, perfect knowledge of him; that we shall have, and exercise, the perfect privilege of sons of God. It is nothing but the *perfect* realization of what is implied in "the kingdom," "the children of God," "the Divine life." In our struggles for the kingdom, we must direct our eye to the goal of the consummation; must feel that we struggle for no vain ideal. The two expressions "reward *in heaven*," and "inherit the *earth*," mutually illustrate each other; the latter is to be a *spiritual*, and not a carnal, Jewish, world-dominion; the former does not betoken a *locality*, but a perfected communion of life with God, *i. e.*, a Divine life brought to perfection.

II. Influence of the Members of the Kingdom of God in Renewing the World.

§ 152. *The Disciples of Christ the "Light" and "Salt" of the Earth.*

Christ then points out to his disciples the regenerating influence which the qualities before described must exert when exhibited to the world. His followers are "*the light of the world*," which, where it exists, cannot be hid, but must shine forth. They are to become "*the salt*" of mankind. As salt preserves from decay and corruption every thing to which it is applied, so Christians are to incite mankind to live according to their high destiny; are to impart freshness to humanity, and to preserve it from the corruption into which it *naturally* passes, by the power of their higher principle of life. The course of the human race, apart from Christianity, is always downward; all its civilization ends in barbarism. It is for Christians to preserve the spiritual life of mankind fresh and undecayed.

But if *the salt lose its saltness*—becomes stale and worthless—*wherewith shall it be salted?* Wherewith shall the Divine life be preserved in those to whom Christianity, the source of the reanimating, freshening power, has been dead? In that case, those that should stand upon the highest point of human developement will sink to the lowest; *it is good for nothing, but to be cast out and trodden under foot of men*

* Cf. *Nitzch's* striking observations on the Divine Justice and Rewards, *System der* Christlichen Lehre, p. 115, 2d ed.

Christ knew that the new element of life which, through him, was given to humanity, had power to keep it ever fresh and living; but he knew also the impure influences to which it would be liable. These words of his declare the fate of Christianity, whenever it degenerates into dead forms and outward show. History affords the fullest and saddest commentary upon this prophetic passage.

III. The Law of Christian Life the Fulfilment of the Old Law.

§ 153. *Fulfilling of the Law and the Prophets:* (1.) *General View;* (2.) *Particular Exposition;* (3.) *Demand for a Higher Obedience than that of the Pharisees.* (Matt., v., 17–20.)

(1.)

After commanding his disciples to become the "salt" of the earth, and to "let their light so shine before men that they might see their good works, and glorify their Father in heaven," it remained for him to set vividly before them, by specific illustrations, the *mode* in which they were to let their light shine through their actions; which would distinguish them palpably from those who then passed for holy men among the Jews.

This gave him occasion to refute the charge spread abroad by the Pharisees, that he aimed to subvert the authority of the law. But, instead of confining himself to a mere *refutation,* he took a course conforming with the dignity of his character, and justified himself in a *positive* way, by unfolding the relation in which his New Creation stood to the stand-point of the Old Covenant. He incorporated this, moreover, very closely with the practical purpose of the whole discourse (v. 17, seq.). He characterizes the new law of life by distinct and separate traits. He proclaims the new law as the fulfilment of the old. For since the old law proceeds from the commandment "to love God above all things, and our neighbour as ourselves," it contains the eternal law of the kingdom of God; and only where love rules the whole life can we secure this object, which the whole religious law of the Old Testament aimed at, but could not realize. "*On these two commandments* (says Christ, Matt., xxii., 40) *hang all the law and the prophets,*" *i. e.*, the whole Old Testament. They could not be fulfilled from the Old Testament stand-point, because men needed, in order to fulfil them, a new life, proceeding from the spirit of love; and this Christ came to impart. He presupposes its existence in those for whom he communicates the new law.

Moreover, although the *everlasting* Theocratic law could be derived from the two commandments specified, yet its *spirit,* tied down to the stand-point of the political Theocracy, and cribbed in its contracted forms could not attain its free and full developement. But Christ, by freeing it from this bondage of forms, brought it into complete developement, not only in the consciousness, but in the practical life. In this respect, then, he fulfilled the law; and this was the object for which he appeared.*

(2.)

Christ begins, therefore, by saying, *Think not that I am come to destroy the law and the prophets; I am not come to destroy, but to fulfil.*† By this we are to understand the whole of the Old Testament religion; he came to annul neither of its chief divisions, as his *general* mission was (last clause of v. 17‡) "not to destroy, but to fulfil." He adds, in a still stronger averment (v. 18), that not one jot or tittle of the law should lose its validity, but that all have its fulfilment, until the consummation of the kingdom of God.§ This last will be the great "fulfilment," for which all previous stages of the kingdom were but preparatory.

Here, again, it is shown that, in this sense, "destroying" and "fulfilling" are correlative ideas. The consummation of the kingdom will be the "*fulfilling*" of all which was contained, in germ, in the prepara-

* Cf. p. 91, 92.

† *Gfrörer* asserts ("*Heilige Sage,*" ii., 84, seq.) that these words were not Christ's, but were more likely put into his mouth by the later Judaists in their controversies with Paul; an opinion adopted also by Dr. *Röeth* (*Epist. ad Hebr. non ad Hebræos, sed ad Christianos genere gentiles Scriptam esse,* Francof., 1836, p. 214). The former writer thinks that these striking words, had they existed, would have been used against Paul by the strenuous advocates of the continued validity of the Mosaic law; which, he infers, they did *not* do, from the silence of Paul's epistles on the subject. We are compelled directly to contradict this assertion; it is refuted sufficiently by the close connexion of the words with the current of thought in the context. Paul understood their import too well to find any embarrassment from them in his controversies with the Judaists. If they were quoted against him, he refuted the false use made of them by his developement of the whole doctrine, rather than by separate and detailed quotation, as was his custom in controversy.

‡ *De Wette,* in explaining the 17th verse, attempts to prove, from Matt., vii., 12, and xxii., 40, that the "law and prophets" were conceived, also, as the source of the *moral law,* and deems that the words are here to be taken only in that sense, with no reference at all to the prophetic element of the Old Testament. I cannot agree with him. Even the passages which he adduces do not refer exclusively to the *moral* contents of the Old Testament, but to the Old Testament in its whole nature and extent. Christ designates—as the end and aim to which the whole Old Testament tends—only the quintessence of the whole Theocracy, religious as well as moral, viz.: *the spirit of love;* as also the end and aim of Redemption is to make love the ruling principle of man's nature. *De Wette* argues that "no one of his hearers could have imagined that Christ wished to be received as Messiah in opposition to all the prophecies of *the Prophets;* so he speaks afterward only of the fulfilling of the *law.*" Now the question is, was Christ speaking against a misunderstanding of his disciples, or against an accusation of his enemies? If the latter, as we suppose, he had good call to prove that his ministry was opposed neither to the "law" nor to the "prophets," and that he would show himself to be Messiah by fulfilling both. His subsequently making one part (the law) particularly prominent is no proof that he had not both in his mind before. Moreover, even *De Wette* has to admit that the prophetic element is alluded to in v. 18. We infer, therefore, that both "law" and "prophets" are referred to from the beginning.

§ Cf. Tholuck on v. 18.

tory stand-point; it will, on the other hand, be the "*destroying*" of all that was, in *itself*, only preparatory. In pointing to this consummation of the kingdom of GOD as the final "fulfilling" of all, Christ at the same time fixes the final end for the fulfilment of all the promises connected with the beatitudes. Thus the connexion with the words spoken before is closely preserved.*

(3.)

Passing from the Old Testament in general to the "law" in particular, and applying to it the general proposition that he had advanced, Christ commands his disciples (v. 19, 20) to fulfil the law in a far higher sense than those did who were at that time considered patterns of righteousness. In proportion as each fulfilled the law was he to have a higher or a lower place in the developement of the kingdom (v. 19). The principle of life which they all possessed in common (the essential requisite for fulfilling *any* of the demands of the sermon) by no means precluded differences of *degree;* it might penetrate one more thoroughly than another, and display itself in a more (or less) complete fulfilling of the law. Christ illustrates the same doctrine in the parable of the Sower.

Such, then, and so superior is the fulfilling of the law which Christ requires of all who would belong to his kingdom: *Except your righteousness shall exceed the righteousness of the scribes and Pharisees, ye shall in no case enter into the kingdom of Heaven.*†

§ 154. "*Fulfilling of the Law*" *in the Higher Sense.—General Contrast between the Juridical and Moral Stand-points.*

In verses 22–48 Christ illustrates, in a number of special examples, the sense in which the law was, not "destroyed," but "fulfilled" through him; also the sense in which the members of his kingdom were to signalize themselves by zeal in fulfilling the law; and also (but here subordinately) the difference between *their* righteousness—answering to their position in the new developement of the Divine kingdom—and the seeming righteousness of the Pharisees.

In these illustrations he contrasts the *eternal* Theocratic law with the *political* Theocratic law; the absolute law with the particular law of Moses. Although the former lay at the foundation of the latter, it could not, in that limited and contracted system, unfold and display it

* By assuming this relation to the law and the prophets, Christ gave himself out as Messiah. How untenable, then, is *Strauss's* assertion that at that time Jesus had *not* decidedly presented himself as Messiah! We have shown that the passage is too closely bound up with the organism of the whole sermon to be considered an interpolation.

† The γάρ in verse 20 obviously introduces a confirmation of the preceding verse; and this opposes *Olshausen's* view of the connexion, although he has well marked the distinction between verses 19 and 20.

self; and it could not be fully developed until the shell, the restraining form, which had cribbed and confined the spirit, was broken and destroyed.* The opposition is between the law as bearing only upon the overt act, and the law as bearing upon the heart, and fulfilled in it; between the *juridical* and the *moral* stand-point.

We infer, then, as a rule in interpreting the following separate precepts, that *outward* acts are to be taken as vivid exhibitions of a required *inward disposition*, and are to be understood literally only when they are the necessary expression of such a state of heart.

§ 155. *Fulfilling of the Law in the Higher Sense.—Particular Examples, viz.*, (1.) *Murder;* (2.) *Adultery;* (3.) *Divorce;* (4.) *Perjury;* (5.) *Revenge;* (6.) *National Exclusiveness.*

(1.) The law condemns the *murderer* to death. But the Gospel sentences even him who is *angry*† with his brother. The passion which, when full-blown, causes murder, is punished in the bud of revengeful feeling, whether concealed in the heart or shown in abusive words‡ (v. 22).

* I agree with the Greek and Socinian interpreters in thinking that Christ means here not merely the Pharisaic interpretations of the law, but also the legal stand-point in general. This follows necessarily, (1) from the connexion as we have unfolded it; (2) from the fact that he quotes the commandments in their literal Old Testament form. (Even "*thou shalt hate thy enemy*" (v. 43), though not found literally in the commandment, is implied in the preceding positive commandment, as limited by the particular Theocratic stand point); (3) because ἐῤῥέθη τοῖς ἀρχαίοις (v. 33) cannot well be interpreted otherwise than "*it has been said to the men of old*" (the fathers, hence during the Mosaic promulgation of the law). Had Christ referred to the statutes of *the elders* (which would not agree so well with the whole form of the expression either), he would have used πρεσβυτέροις, as also *De Wette* acknowledges. *Tholuck's* argument, of an antithesis between ἀρχαίοις and ἐγώ is not to the point; the connexion does not require such an antithesis. The opposition is not in the *subject* of the commandment, but in its *conception*. Christ recognized the voice of God in the Old Testament, and Moses as sent of God; but he wished to oppose the *fulfilling* form of the new legislation to the *narrow* and deficient form of Old Testament legislation, which belonged to a temporary and preparatory epoch. Had Christ had the *subject* of the commandment in view, τοῖς ἀρχαίοις would naturally have preceded ἐῤῥέθη; while the present collocation of the words indicates that the opposition is instituted between what *was said* in earlier times and what *was then said* by him. The prominence that he assigns to the *Pharisaical* conception and application of the law connects very well with this opposition to the old law in general; for the Pharisees especially refused to admit the *spirit* to pass from the old law and find its fulfilment in the new, but adhered to the *letter* in a one-sided and exclusive way. Pharisaism, in a word, was the culmination of the old stand-point, adhering to the letter, and estranged from the spirit.

† I must agree with those who reject εἰκῆ (v. 22). Thus to lessen the force of the law certainly does not harmonize with the connexion.

‡ It seems to me that the words "ὃς δ' ἂν εἴπῃ τῷ ἀδελφῷ αὐτοῦ· ῥακά, ἔνοχος ἔσται τῷ συνεδρίῳ" should be taken away from this passage. Apart from these, the connexion is perfect and obvious. Κρίσις=*judgment, condemnation*, its common meaning in the New Testament, and so γέεννα, with another word. *Degrees* of violation of the Theocratic law nowhere appear in this connexion; on the contrary, it teaches that the *smallest* violation, as well as the *greatest*, involves a disposition of heart opposed to the kingdom of God, which demands *holiness* of heart. Reviling is purposely put side by side with murder, because the dispo

(2.) The law of the particular Theocracy condemns the *adulterer.* But the law of Christ condemns the germ of evil passion in the husband, as the source of adultery* (v. 27).

(3.) As Christ thus already considers marriage as the union, in part, of two persons of different sexes, he takes occasion to develope still further his opposition to the stand-point of the Mosaic law in regard to this relation.†

The Mosaic law, intended for a rude people, who were to be cultivated by degrees, allowed *divorce;* seeking to place some restraints, at least, upon unlimited wilfulness. Political legislation must adapt itself to the material on which it has to act.‡ But the law of Christ sets forth the moral idea of marriage in its full strictness, and demands that its communion of life shall be indissoluble. Nothing but the actual adultery of one of the parties can dissolve the tie, and leave the innocent one at liberty to marry.§

sition that inspires the former leads, when further expanded, to the latter; the reviler is a murderer before that bar which looks only at the heart. A gradation between *ῥακά* and *μωρός* violates both the aim and connexion of the discourse, and seems entirely unbecoming its dignity. Moreover, we should then have to look for a gradation in the punishment, which, again, is inconsistent with the connexion. The "*Sanhedrim*" brings us before the Jewish civil jurisdiction—the politico-Theocratical stand-point—the very thing to which Christ opposes himself throughout the discourse. And how is *γέεννα*, in that case, to be distinguished from *κρίσις*? In what relation does the mention of the *Sanhedrim* stand to *κρίσις* and *γέεννα*? Things entirely incompatible are here brought together. All attempts to solve the difficulty lead to forced and untenable interpretation. The fact that *ῥακά* means just the same thing as *μωρέ*, confirms the supposition that the clause in question was introduced by the Greek translator as another version of the following, and original, clause in Matthew's Hebrew.

* Verses 23–26 are among those expressions of Christ which we suppose to have been uttered elsewhere, and transferred to this connexion from their affinity of subject. (Cf. v 25, 26, with Luke, xii., 58, 59.) So of v. 29, 30; Christ is treating of the mere legislation, not of the element of self-discipline as such.

† Polygamy was not yet wholly forbidden among the Jews, as appears from *Josephus.* Speaking in reference to the polygamy of Herod, he says: *πάτριον γὰρ ἐν ταὐτῷ πλείοσιν ἡμῖν συνοικεῖν* (Archæol., xviii., 1, 2). And *Justin* casts up to the Jewish doctors that, even in his time, "*οἵτινες καὶ μέχρι νῦν καὶ τεσσάρας καὶ πέντε ἔχειν ὑμᾶς γυναῖκας ἕκαστον συγχωροῦσι*" (Dial., c. Tryph. Jud., ed. Colon., 363, E). Still we may infer that the Jewish schools in Christ's time recognized monogamy as the only lawful marriage, from his saying nothing expressly on the subject, while the precepts that he delivers presuppose it.

‡ The *σκληροκαρδία τοῦ λαοῦ.* Matt., xix., 8.

§ I cannot agree with those who would make this law an outward one by legislation, the discourse aims at the *heart,* and its precepts can be fulfilled in the life only from the heart. They hold good only for those who recognize Christ as their Lord from free conviction, and are led by his Spirit; and who, therefore, find in them only the outward expression of the inward Spirit. The state can no more realize these laws than it can make Christians or create holiness. *Its* laws must be adapted to the *σκληροκαρδία τοῦ λαοῦ.* The attempt to accomplish, by legislative sanction, what *redemption* alone can do, would create a sort of stunted, Chinese life, but nothing better. Precisely because the Sermon on the Mount is the *Magna Charta* of the kingdom of God, it is not fit for a *state* law. On the other hand, I differ from those who suppose that Christ alluded only to the then existing form of Jewish divorce, which did not require legal investigation and decision. The moral idea which Christ developed had a more than temporary bearing.

(4.) The Mosaic law prohibits *perjury*, and maintains the sanctity of oaths. But the law of Christ demands that *yes* and *no* shall take the place of all other confirmation. "*Whatsoever is more than these* cometh of evil,*" *i. e.*, testifies to a want of that disposition of heart which every member of his kingdom ought to possess; a want of that thorough truthfulness which makes every other affirmation superfluous, and of the mutual confidence that depends upon it.

(5.) The Mosaic law, moreover, corresponding to the civil law, admits of retaliation, like for like. But the law of Christ so completely shuts out the desire of revenge, that it creates in its subjects a disposition to suffer all injury rather than to return evil for evil (v. 39).

(6.) The old law enjoined the "love of one's neighbour;" but none were regarded as "neighbours" but members of the Theocratic community, and, therefore, the law implied "hatred" of the enemies of that community as enemies of the kingdom of God. The law of Christ, on the contrary, enjoins love without limit;† a love that takes into its wide embrace enemies and persecutors, yea, even those who, as enemies of the kingdom of God, persecute its members; a love which not only impels us to do them good, but is so absolutely exclusive of even the germ of hatred, as to urge us to *pray* for them. The children of God are to be, like their heavenly Father, perfect in love (v. 45,

* The formulas in v. 34, 35, 36 (not properly oaths, as they do not take God to witness) illustrate still more forcibly Christ's purpose to banish from his kingdom every affirmation but *yes* and *no*. Had he not mentioned them, his hearers might have thought that he referred only to the immediate invocation of Jehovah to witness, which all pious Jews sought to avoid, and instead of which these very formulas, which helped those that were disposed to gloss over a perjury, were, in fact, invented. This is enough to refute what *Göschel* says (*über den Eid*, Berlin, 1837, p. 118, 119), in order to prove that Christ's precept was not directed against oaths in general. There was no necessity that he should define the proper sense of an oath; every body understood it; but it would have been by no means so obvious to his hearers that he condemned also the common formulas, invented out of reverence for the Divine name (*Philo*, De Special. Legib., § 1). He condemns them especially for the reason that it is inconsistent with the condition of dependent creatures to appeal to the creature in confirming an averment. There remained nothing but the true oath—the appeal to Almighty God—and this, also, he forbade; *yes* and *no* were to suffice. *Göschel* says (p. 116), "As Christ came not to abolish, but to fulfil the law, the law of the oath was not to be abolished, but fulfilled." True; just as the law, "*Thou shalt not kill,*" is fulfilled by avoiding emotions of hatred; just as the law of the Sabbath is fulfilled in consecrating every day to God. So *yes* and *no* are bonds as sacred for the Christian as an oath to other men.

† The First Epistle to the Corinthians (as *Rückert* has remarked) contains many passages, the germs of which are to be found in the Sermon on the Mount. Cf. iv., 8–13; vi., 7; vii., 10. Paul may also have borrowed from it these words of Christ, which were preserved for us only by his means, Acts, xx., 35, "*It is more blessed to give than to receive.*" This saying expresses the *disposition* which, in Matt., v., 40–42, is set forth in outward acts; the very nature of love, happy in communicating. How beautifully does this saying reveal the whole heart of Christ, whose whole aim was to impart to others from the fulness of his heavenly riches!

48). And the perfect love of God does not exclude His enemies. How perfect, indeed, must His love be, to seek the redemption even of His enemies!

IV. True Religion contrasted with the Mock Piety of the Pharisees.

§ 156. (1.) *Alms, Prayer, Fasting;* (2.) *Rigid Judgment of Self, Mild Judgment of others;* (3.) *Test of Sincerity in Seeking after Righteousness.* (Matt., vi., 1–18; vii., 1–5.)

(1.)

After setting forth the opposition between legal and true holiness, Christ passes on to contrast the latter with the false spiritual tendencies at that time existing; to contrast that piety which attaches no importance either to its own works or to the show of them, with the mock religion of the Pharisees, which did every thing for show. It is the contrast, in a word, between *being* and *seeming;* and no words could express it more strikingly than "*when thou doest thine alms, let not thy left hand know what thy right hand doeth.* So far from doing good that others may see it, thou must not even think of it as *thy own* work; do it, in childish simplicity, from thy loving spirit, as if thou couldst not do otherwise." This principle Christ applies to three separate acts, in which the Pharisees were specially wont to make a pious display, viz.: *Alms, prayer, and fasting** (vi., 1–18).

(2.)

The sin which is next† condemned (vii., 1–5) springs from the same root as the one just mentioned. The Pharisees judged others severely, but were quite indulgent to themselves, and, indeed, never rightly *examined* themselves. He that knows what true righteousness is, and feels his own want of it, will be a rigid censor of his own life, but a mild and gentle judge of others. ["*And why beholdest thou the mote that is in thy brother's eye, but considerest not the beam that is in thine own? Thou hypocrite! first cast out the beam that is in thine own eye, and then shalt thou see clearly to cast the mote out of thy brother's.*"]

(3.)

The Saviour then‡ gives (vii., 12) a *criterion* to distinguish true from

* Since Christ *specifies* these three, in order to apply to them the general principle of v. 1 (τὴν δικαιοσύνην μὴ ποιεῖν ἔμπροσθεν τῶν ἀνθρώπων), we infer that it was foreign to his purpose to give an exposition of the nature of prayer here, which confirms our view that the "Lord's Prayer" is not here in its proper chronological connexion.

† Matt., vii., 1, stands in a close logical connexion with vi., 18, and the preceding verses; and is also given by Luke, proving that it belongs to the original body of the discourse, but vi., 19–34 [*not* given by Luke in this connexion] appears as obviously not so. So of 5–11, below.

‡ The οὖν in verse 12, as well as the course of thought, connect it with v. 5

Pharisaic righteousness. "Therefore, all things *whatsoever ye would that men should do unto you, do ye also unto them ; for this is the law and the prophets.*" (If you are striving sincerely after the essence of righteousness, you will place yourself in the condition of others, and act towards them as you would wish them, in such case, to have acted towards you.)

It was certainly not Christ's purpose here to set up a rule of morals contradictory to the whole spirit of the rest of the sermon, which places the seat of true morality in the *heart.* Mere outward action, according to this rule, might spring from diverse dispositions, *e. g.*, the mere prudence of selfishness might lead us to observe it, in order to get like for like. But, placing it in connexion with what has gone before, and making *love* the mainspring of our actions, the rule affords a touchstone of their character. And when our actions stand this test, Christ says that "*the law and the prophets* (*i. e.*, the life and essence of piety to which they point) *are fulfilled ;*" for, as he elsewhere says, "*love is the fulfilling of the law.*"

V. Exhortations and Warnings to the Children of the Kingdom.

§ 157. *Exhortation to Self-denial.—Caution against Seducers.* (Matt., vii., 13–24.)

Christ had now pointed out the moral requisites *for entrance* into his kingdom, and the moral qualities which must mark its members. He now warns them (v. 13) against the delusion of expecting to secure its blessings in any easier way than he had pointed out, or hoping to avoid struggle and self-denial ;* and cautions them against false teachers, who would lead them into such delusions, and draw them out of the right way. First, he gives a warning against such as shall falsely pretend to a Divine call as teachers and guides, inspired by self-seeking alone. "Wolves in sheep's clothing,† their evil fruits, proofs of their evil hearts, distinguish them from genuine prophets of God" (v. 15, 20). This warning was strikingly applicable at that time of out-breaking battle with the hierarchical and Pharisaic party.

The general proposition, that the state of the heart must be shown by the "fruits," is then applied to all believers (v. 21–23). Not every

* Matt., vii., 13–14, describe the *difficulties* of the way, and join closely to what precedes. The figure of the "gate," &c., is more aptly introduced in Luke, xiii., 24, 25, and it might be supposed that the author of the *Greek* Matthew had transferred the passage to this connexion from the actual one in which Christ uttered it. But so obvious a figure as the "gate" and the "way" may have been used repeatedly by Christ; and in these two places, moreover, there is a difference in its application. In Luke, the "gate" is to be entered before the Master has closed it; in Matt., it is "the wide gate and the broad way, which many see; the narrow gate and the narrow way, which few find." In the former the thought is, "that few are willing to undergo the necessary labours and struggles to enter the kingdom;" in the latter, "the majority deceive themselves as to the difficulties of the task," &c.

† Cf. John, x., 1–5.

one who honours Jesus as Messiah and Theocratic King, and makes a zealous confession thereof, is thereby fitted to share in the kingdom; the *heart* must be shown to accord with the confession, by a faithful performance of the will of God.* [" *Not every one that saith unto me, Lord, Lord, shall enter into the kingdom of heaven; but he that doeth the will of my Father which is in heaven.*"]

VI. True and False Disciples Contrasted.

§ 158. *Test of Discipleship.* (Matt., vii., 24–27.)

Christ concludes the whole discourse with a contrast between true and false disciples; between those who take care to apply to their life and practice the truths which he had laid down, and those who do not. He thus makes prominent, in the conclusion, the great truth announced in the beginning, and carried through the discourse, viz., that a right disposition of heart is essential in all things. According to their right application of his words his hearers were to judge themselves, and find their destiny described (v. 24–27). [" *Therefore, whosoever heareth these sayings of mine, and doeth them, I will liken him unto a wise man, which built his house upon a rock: and the rain descended, and the floods came, and the winds blew, and beat upon that house, and it fell not; for it was founded upon a rock. And every one that heareth these sayings of mine, and doeth them not, shall be likened unto a foolish man, which built his house upon the sand: and the rain descended, and the floods came, and the winds blew, and beat upon that house, and it fell; and great was the fall of it.*"]

These words of warning, at the end of the discourse, harmonize well with its beginning.

END OF THE SERMON ON THE MOUNT.

§ 159. *Healing of the Leper on the Road to Capernaum.*†

After Christ had concluded his deeply impressive discourse, he dismissed the multitude and came down from the mountain with his disciples. Hosts of people attended him to Capernaum. A leper, who had probably heard of his miracles, and learned that he would pass that way, had planted himself by the road-side. Full of faith, he threw himself at the Saviour's feet and said, " *Lord, if thou wilt, thou canst make me clean.*" After Christ had granted his petition, he bade him (as was his wont in such cases) first to do what the law—which He had come to "destroy" only by "fulfilling"—demanded,‡ viz., to

* Ch. vii., 24, connects closely with v. 21. On the relation of v. 22, 23, to the rest of the passage, we shall speak hereafter.

† Matt., viii., 1. I follow Matthew's account, which suits the chronology, in preference to Luke's (v. 12), which says nothing about the locality of the event. It was not customary, under the Mosaic law, for lepers to reside within the cities. Cf. *Joseph.*, c. Apion, i., xxxi.; Archæol., iii., 11, § 3.

‡ Levit., xiv., 1

show himself to the priests and offer the prescribed sacrifice, in order to readmission into the Theocratic community, from which he had been excluded as unclean.

§ 160. *Healing of the Heathen Centurion's Slave at Capernaum.*—The Deputation of Elders.—Faith of the Centurion.*

As soon as Christ arrived at Capernaum, his aid was sought in behalf of another sufferer. The elders of the synagogue came to him with a petition in the name of a centurion. He was a heathen; but, like many other heathens of that age, unsatisfied with the old and languishing popular religion, and impressed, by the moral and religious spirit of the Jewish Theism, he has been led to believe in JEHOVAH as the Almighty. Whether a *proselyte of the gate*† or not, he had proved his faith by building a Jewish synagogue at his own expense.

His love and care for a faithful slave‡ shows how his piety had influenced his character. During Christ's absence this slave became severely ill; and just when he was ready to die, the centurion heard, to his great joy, of the Saviour's return. Placing his only hopes in Him, he hastened to ask his assistance. But he had been accustomed to look upon the Jews *alone* as consecrated to the worship of the Most High; and Christ yet appeared to belong only to that people. He did not venture, therefore, as a heathen, to apply to him directly, but sought the mediation of the *elders*, whom he had laid under obligation.§

* Matt., viii., 5; Luke, vii., 2. The chronological agreement of the accounts, derived from separate sources, is proof of their veracity. We follow Luke's, as the more original.

† The relation in which he appears to stand to Judaism and the Jews would make it probable that he *was* a proselyte of the gate. But, on the other hand, if he had been, the Jewish elders would probably have mentioned it in their recommendation of him; he would have had the usual designation, σεβόμενος, φοβούμενος τὸν Θεόν.

‡ The word used in Matthew is παῖς, נַעַר; which may, indeed, mean *slave*, but seems to be intended by him for "*son*," as he uses the article throughout the narrative (ὁ παῖς). This, however, may be explained on the ground that either the centurion had but *one* slave, or that he valued this one particularly. If "*son*" were intended, it might be accounted for from the ambiguity of the word both in Hebrew and Greek; the high degree of love which the centurion displayed, also, was more likely to be felt for a son than a slave, and this may have led to the use of the word.

§ Luke's account, on its face, shows that it was taken from life; but *Strauss* (with whom *De Wette* agrees) thinks it bears the marks of a later hand, working over Matthew's purer and more original statement. According to *Strauss*, the humility with which the centurion *himself* addressed Christ (Matt., viii., 8) gave rise to the conclusion that a *heathen* who had had so low an opinion of himself could not possibly have applied to Christ except through *Jewish* mediation; and then it was necessary to *invent* such an embassy, in order to assign a proper motive for Christ's immediate compliance with the request of the heathen. Grant. for a moment, that it were in itself reasonable and in harmony with the simplicity of our Evangelists; still, we should expect such an interpolation rather in *Matthew*, whose narrative is supposed to be derived from a Palestine Jewish-Christian tradition, than in *Luke*, who belonged more to the type of Paul. True, the conduct of the centurion, as stated by Luke, is precisely suited to his character, as shown in his words recorded by Matthew; to his mode of thought in regard to the person of Christ and the relation between Jews and heathen. But must the very naturalness and probability of the statement itself be made a

The centurion heard that Christ, in compliance with the request of the elders, was approaching his house. But then the thought arose, "Hast thou not gone too far in asking the Son of God, who has spirits at his command, to come to thy house? Hast thou not lowered him, by presuming that his corporeal presence is necessary to the healing of thy slave? Could he not have employed one of his hosts of ministering spirits to accomplish it?" ["*Say in a word,* and my *servant shall be healed. For I, also . . . say unto one, 'Come,' and he cometh; and to another, 'Go,' and he goeth.*"*] Although his hesitation, doubtless, arose in part from his unwillingness, as a heathen, to summon the Saviour to his house, his words imply that it arose far more from his conscious unworthiness in comparison with Christ's greatness. He conceived Christ to be the Son of God in a sense natural to one who had, from paganism, become a believer in Theism.

The centurion illustrates a state of heart which, in all ages of Christianity, belongs to those who are susceptible of admitting and embracing Christ: the consciousness, namely, of His loftiness and our own unworthiness. *Here* was the deep import of his signs of faith; and here the ground of these striking words of Christ addressed to the attendant multitudes: "*I have not found so great faith, no, not in Israel.*" He had, indeed, found access to the people; he had, indeed, found faith, but not *such* faith as that of this pagan. The faith of the Jews, prejudiced by their peculiar notions of the Messiahship, could not, as yet, raise itself to a just intuition of the super-human greatness of Christ. But the pagan, viewing Christ as Lord of the World of Spirits, had reached a point which the Apostles themselves were only to attain at a later period. And here we have a sign that the true and high intuition of the person of Christ was to come rather from the stand-point of paganism than of Judaism.

§ 161. *Healing of the Deaf and Dumb Demoniac.—The Charge of a League with Beelzebub: a Visible Sign demanded.—The Charge refuted.*

The constantly increasing influence of Christ naturally heightened

ground to suspect it as an invention? As for Matthew's statement, that the centurion *himself* applied to Christ, it may naturally and easily be explained on the supposition of an abbreviation of the narrative, or obliteration of individual features of the occurrence.

* We cannot admit Dr. *Strauss's* assertion that the prayer sent by the elders (Luke. vii., 3) is inconsistent with the second message (v. 6), and that, therefore, the connexion which in Matthew is natural is unnatural in Luke. Had Luke's account been a *fiction,* instead of making the centurion take back his prayer sent by the elders, it would have given the prayer a different character from the beginning. Considering it as a narrative of *fact,* it bears precisely the stamp of real life: the centurion, at first, absorbed in his anxiety, sends for Christ to come to him; afterward, when he finds the fulfilment of his desire at hand, the sense of his unworthiness in comparison with the greatness of Christ becomes prominent, and with it a sense of the impropriety of his request.

the wrath of the Pharisees. A movement which they could not check was in progress against the spirit and the interests of their party. But a powerful impression, wrought by a single miracle, gave the signal for a new and more artful attack. This occasion was the healing a man of imbecile mind, or a melancholy idiot, who went about appearing neither to see nor to hear any thing that passed around him.* The people received the cure as a sign of Christ's Messianic power.

It was necessary for the Pharisees to remove this impression from their minds. But how was it to be done? The *fact* could neither be denied nor attributed to natural agencies. In this dilemma they had recourse to falsehood, and accused him of employing an evil magic, a belief in which still propagated itself among the traditions† of Jewish fanaticism. The Prince of Evil Spirits, they said, in order to secure favour among the people for the false prophet who was labouring for Satan's kingdom, had given him power to exorcise inferior spirits from men; thus sacrificing a less object for a greater.‡

Others, again, whose hostility to Christ and to truth was not so decided (although they were not susceptible of Divine impressions), only refused to acknowledge the miracle as a sufficient sign of Messiahship, and demanded an immediate token from God—a voice from heaven, or a celestial appearance.§

Christ first replied to the most decided opponents, and, to show the absurdity of their accusation, reasoned as follows: "It is a contradiction in terms to suppose that good can be directly wrought by evil;‖

* Luke, xi., 14; Matt., xii., 22. This view of the case is founded upon the fact that the man's *dumbness* is ascribed (which is not done in other cases) to his being possessed with demons, and his subsequent ability to *hear* and *speak* to their expulsion. Matthew adds *blindness*, which harmonizes well with our view. We infer from the impression produced by the miracle that the case differed from ordinary possessions. It is possible, however, that the case is confounded in Matthew with other cures of blind men; cf. Matt., ix., 27–34. This last passage, v. 32–34, seems to be but an abridged account of the very case under discussion.

† *Celsus* took a hint from these.

‡ Matt., xii., 24–26.

§ How strongly expectations of this kind were cherished by the Jews is shown by the fact that *Philo's* Hellenic-Alexandrian culture could not free him from them, although the expectation of a personal Messiah is not prominent in him. He believes that, when the purification of the scattered Jews is accomplished, they will be drawn together from all nations, by a celestial phenomenon, to one definite place: "ξεναγούμενοι πρός τινος θειοτέρας ἢ κατὰ φύσιν ἀνθρωπίνην ὄψεως, ἀδήλου μὲν ἑτέροις, μόνοις δὲ τοῖς ἀνασωζομένοις ἐμφανοῦς."—*De Execrat.*, § 9.

‖ There is, indeed, a sense in which the kingdom of evil is always at war with itself; but in evil, as *such*, as opposed to good, there is always a definite relative unity. If this unity was destroyed, if Satan were to accomplish the same good as that wrought by the power of God, it would be a *contradictio in adjecto*; the kingdom of evil would be *ipso facto* subverted. Evil may, and indeed must, *indirectly* subserve good; but it cannot *directly* do good so long as its nature, as evil, remains. A kingdom, or a family, may continue to exist as such, with an internal discord in its bosom that is the germ of its dissolution; but the *relative* unity must remain. This truth admitted the further application—which Christ did not express, but left to the Pharisees to make—that Satan could not seek that evil should be conquered by evil; that one should be freed *from* the power of the Evil One *by* the power of the Evil One. Could evil thus do the works of good, it would be no more evil." He then applies an *argumentum ad hominem* to the Pharisees [*If I by Beelzebub cast out devils, by whom do your sons cast them out? therefore shall they be your judges*]. If a charge of the sort, he tells them, were brought against their exorcists, they would soon pronounce it untenable. It follows, then, that this Divine act—the delivery of a human soul from the evil spirit that had crushed its self-conscious activity—was wrought by the power and Spirit of God alone.

"*But,*" he continues, "*if I cast out devils by the Spirit of God, then the kingdom of God is come unto you.*" This *single* victory proves that a power has come among men which is able to conquer evil—the power, namely, of the kingdom of God, which ever propagates itself in struggling with evil; the negative presupposes the positive. The similitude that follows illustrates the same truth: "*When a strong man, armed, keepeth his palace, his goods are in peace; but when a stronger than he shall come upon him, and overcome him, he taketh from him all his armour wherein he trusted, and divideth his spoils.*" So, had not the power of evil *itself* been subdued by a higher power, such individual manifestations of it as the evil spirit in the demoniac could not have been conquered.*

§ 162. *The Conjurations of the Jewish Exorcists.* (Luke, xi., 23–26.)

It followed, from the foregoing words of Christ in reply to the Pharisees, that all cures of demoniacs wrought on any other principles must be entirely apparent and deceptive.† It was of no avail to remove individual *symptoms* while the *cause*, viz., the dominion of the evil principle, remained unshaken. The very agency that removed the former for a time would only strengthen the latter, to break forth again with increased power.

Therefore, although Christ, speaking κατ' ἄνθρωπον, presupposed that the Jewish exorcists could heal demoniacs, he could not recognize their cures as genuine. So he says (Luke, xi., 23), "*Whosoever is not with me* (works not in communion with me in the power of the Holy Ghost) *is against me* (opposes in his works the kingdom of God); *and he that gathereth not with me* (does not, in communion with me

to secure access to the hearts of men for one whose whole nature and labours were opposed to the kingdom of evil. "Satan, casting out Satan," would be no more Satan. The difficulties, therefore, which *De Wette* finds in the passage are overcome. The truth of Christ's proposition does not lie upon the surface.

* Christ here indicates that the so-called demoniacal possessions were nothing else but individual phenomena of Satan's kingdom manifested among men.

† As a physician, who treats the symptoms of disease, but neglects the cause, strengthens the latter by the very medicines which palliate the former. A vivid illustration of the pregnant truth here unfolded by Christ in reference to the cures of the demoniacs.

gather souls for the kingdom) *scattereth abroad** (leads them astray, and thus *really* works for the kingdom of Satan, against which he *apparently* contends)." The exorcists pretended, in casting out devils, to fight against Satan; but in fact, by their arts of deceit, were striving against the kingdom of God. How cutting a contrast to the assertion of the Pharisees that devils might be cast out by the aid of Satan!

The same truth is illustrated in parabolic form in verses 24–26; unless a radical cure of the demoniac is made by the redeeming power of the Divine Spirit, his soul remains estranged from God, the apparently cured disease seizes it with new force, the ungodly spirit finds his old haunt—his former dwelling is completely prepared for his reception.†

* This text is put in the same connexion in Matt. (xii., 30). But the διὰ τοῦτο of v. 31 does not naturally join with v. 30; there is no such causal relation as is implied by the phrase, nor does it join any more closely with what follows; indeed, it appears rather to belong at the *end* of all the proofs adduced against the Pharisees. The right arrangement is doubtless that of Luke (xii., 23–26); and the more profound order of the thought, as Luke presents it, is not the work of chance, but a proof of the originality of the account. I must differ, therefore, from Professor *Elwert*, who, in his ingenious dissertation (*Stud. der Geistl. Würtem.*, ix., i., 1836), denies that Luke, xi., 23, has reference to the verses immediately preceding. Understanding the parable more in the sense of Matthew (although he admits Luke's originality also), he connects this passage with it, and considers it as directed against the indecision of the multitude, who, after moments of enthusiastic excitement in Christ's favour, suffered themselves to be so easily led astray. But we ought not to seek new combinations when the original connexion of a passage, lying before us, offers a good sense. Even apart from this, however, Prof. E.'s explanation does not suit the latter clause of v. 23 at all—"*He that gathereth not with me, scattereth*"—which is obviously not directed against an inward disposition, but outward acts; viz., acts which *pretend* to be done in favour of Christ's kingdom, but in reality operate against it. Prof. E. himself admits (p. 180) that the words quoted, if taken strictly in their connexion, do not favour his view; but thinks he is justified, by their approaching to the character of a *proverb*, in departing from the strict construction. There is no proof, however, that Christ made use here of an existing proverb; but this is immaterial to the interpretation of the passage. On the whole, my view corresponds with that of *Schleiermacher*, in loc. The relation of Luke, xi., 23, to ix., 50, will be examined in its place hereafter.

† Luke, xi., 24–25. In Matt., xii., 43–45, the passage is introduced in a different connexion, and must be differently interpreted; it was applied to illustrate the truth, viz., that *that* generation, refusing to obey the call to repentance, should therefore fall into worse and more incurable corruption. This corresponds perfectly to the sense of the parable, and the thought which it contains finds a rich and manifold illustration in history, both on a large and small scale; in all those cases, namely, in which a temporary and apparent reformation, without a radical cure of fundamental evil, has been followed by a stronger reaction. This application of the passage implies that signs of an apparent amendment had shown themselves in "that generation;" and, moreover, it requires that the passage itself should be referred to the impressions, great, but not permanent, which Christ's works, now and again, produced upon the multitude. But it is clear that the nearer and stricter application of the passage is that given in Luke, viz., to the apparent healing of the demoniacs. One thing is evident from Matthew's use of it, viz., that it was well understood from the beginning that the passage was not to be taken literally, but figuratively, which, indeed, is obvious enough from the whole form of discourse. It would have been contrary to all analogy for the men of that time, disposed as they were to take every thing in a literal sense, to attach a spiritual meaning to these words, if it had not been obvious that he spoke them entirely by way of parable. This is written—quite superfluously—solely

§ 163. *Blasphemy against the Holy Ghost and against the Son of Man.* (Matt., xii., 32.)

Christ, having thus shown to the Pharisees the emptiness of their charge, and the absurdity of the assumption which formed its basis, then assumed the offensive, and pointed out to them the *ground* of their coming to utter such a self-refuting accusation. It was because the disposition of their *hearts* ruled and swayed their decision; what aggravated their guilt was, that they suppressed the consciousness of God and of truth, to whose strivings in their minds their very accusation bore testimony. "Because you cannot really believe that I work with the power of the Spirit of Evil, but, on the other hand, could readily have satisfied yourselves that I could do such works only by the power of the Holy Ghost, *therefore,* I say unto you, it is *one* thing with those who stumble at the human form of my manifestation, and are unable to recognize the Son of God in the veil of flesh, with those who, through prejudice or ignorance, blaspheme the Son of Man because he does not appear, as they expected the Messiah would, in earthly splendour;* and quite *another* thing with *you,* who *will* not receive the revelation of the Holy Ghost that comes towards you, who suppress the conscious truth within you, declaring that to be the Evil Spirit's work which you feel yourselves impelled to recognize as the work of the Holy Ghost" (v. 31–33).

Where the root in the heart is not corrupted, where the sense of truth is not stifled—as in the case of those who blaspheme the Son of Man *not known as such*—there Christ finds a starting-point for repentance, and access for forgiveness. But where the Spirit of Lies has taken full possession, says he, there can be no room for repentance, and, consequently, no forgiveness. It is not clear, however, whether he meant to charge upon the very individuals in question this total suppression of truth and submission to the Spirit of Lies, thus utterly excluding *them* from repentance and pardon; or whether, by drawing this distinct line of demarcation, he wished to show them how precarious a footing they held, far from the first class, and near to the second. In fact, the Spirit of Lies, which permits no impressions of

against *Strauss;* for the sense in which Christ used the parable is plainly obvious from the connexion.

* There were some such among the Jews, led away by prejudice and ignorance, rather than by evil dispositions, to blaspheme what they did not understand. These were not beyond the reach of Divine impressions and convictions, if presented at more favourable periods. Many who then stumbled at the Son of Man in *the form of a servant* were afterward more readily led to believe by the operations of the Spirit proceeding from the *glorified* Son of Man. But what clearness and freedom of mind, what elevation above all personal influences, did Christ display in thus distinguishing, in the very heat of the battle, the different classes of his enemies! The distinction thus drawn by Christ is applicable to the different opponents of Christianity in all ages.

the Good and the True, held a high degree of dominion over these Pharisees.

Christ further told the Pharisees (in close connexion with his exposure of their evil disposition of heart) that, in their moral condition, they could not speak otherwise than they had done: "*O generation of vipers! how can ye, being evil, speak good things?*" Their decision upon his act bore the impress of their ungodly nature. "*For out of the abundance of the heart the mouth speaketh;*" and *therefore* it is—because the evil nature can express itself outwardly in words as well as deeds—that Christ attaches so much import to their words. The judgment of God, which looks only at the heart, will visit words no less than works: "*I say unto you, that every idle word that men shall speak, they shall give account thereof in the day of judgment; for by thy words thou shalt be justified, and by thy words shalt thou be condemned.*"*

§ 164. *Purpose of Christ's Relatives to confine him as a Lunatic.—He declares who are his Relatives in the Spiritual Sense.*†

While Christ was thus exposing the machinations of the Pharisees and the evil spirit that inspired them, he was informed that his mother and his brothers, who could not approach on account of the throng, were seeking him.‡ As the scene that was going on threatened bad results to the Pharisaic party by making a strong impression upon the people, the Pharisees had sought to break it up, by persuading his relatives that he had lost his senses.§ His severe discourses, doubtless, appeared to many a bigoted scribe as the words of a madman (John, x., 20), and the Pharisees probably made use of them in imposing upon his relatives. The apparent contrarieties in Christ's discourses and actions could only be harmonized by a complete and true intuition of

* This announcement was directly opposed to the Pharisees' doctrine, according to which morality was judged by the standard of *quantity*.

† Matt., xii., 46–50; Mark, iii., 31, seq.; Luke, viii., 19, seq.

‡ By ἔξω (in Matthew and Mark) we are, perhaps, to understand "*outside of the throng*," or, outside of an enclosure. It is not necessary (nor, indeed, suitable) to assume that the assembly was gathered in a house.

§ Mark, iii., 21. This does not look [as some would have it] like a wilful colouring, added to the facts by tradition, or by Mark himself; but rather indicates, as do slight characteristic touches in other passages given by Mark alone, that this Evangelist made use of authorities peculiarly his own. Such an *invention*, or perversion of tradition, would have been utterly inconsistent with the tone of thought and feeling generally prevalent in regard to Christ: who, in those days, would have believed that *Christ's own brothers* could listen to such a blasphemy against him! It has been supposed, again, that the statement in Mark originated in a misunderstanding of the accusation brought against Christ by the Pharisees; but this is impossible; who *could* suppose the accusation to mean that "he cast out devils, being himself a demoniac?" On the other hand, different members of the Pharisaic party, or the same persons with different objects in view, might have originated both slanders; at one moment charging him with the Satanic league, and at another with being a demoniac himself.

his personality; to his brothers he was always an enigma and a paradox, and they could, therefore, the more easily, in an unhappy moment, be perplexed by the crafty Pharisees.* It is difficult, however, to imagine that *Mary* could have been thus deceived; she may have followed them from anxiety of a different kind about her son.

But Christ, surrounded by a host of anxious seekers for salvation, heard the announcement undisturbed. To show, by this striking case, that blood relationship did not imply affinity for his Spirit, he asked, "*Who is my mother, and who are my brothers?*" Pointing to the seeking souls around him, and to his nearer *spiritual* kindred—the disciples—he said, "*Behold my mother and my brothers! For whosoever shall do the will of my Father which is in heaven, the same is my brother, and sister, and mother.*"†

§ 165. *The Demand of a Sign from Heaven answered only by the Sign of the Prophet Jonah.* (Luke, xi., 16, 29–36.)

We stated, on p. 240, that the less violent of Christ's opponents demanded of him "a sign from heaven." In answering these, he showed that their ungodly disposition of heart was at once the ground of their unbelief and the secret motive of their demand.

[*An evil and adulterous generation seeketh after a sign; and there shall no sign be given to it, but the sign of the Prophet Jonah. For as Jonah was a sign to the Ninevites, so, also, shall the Son of Man be to this generation.*] "In vain did they ask a new sign; *such* a one as they asked they should not obtain. No other sign should they have but that of the Prophet Jonah,‡ *i. e.*, the whole manifestation of Christ,§ by

* It is worthy of note that John (vii., 5–7) mentions, precisely with reference to this same point of time, that Christ's brothers did not believe in his Divine calling, but wished to put him to the proof; and that he then described them as belonging to the world.

† These words are given by Luke (viii., 21) in a different connexion; one in which, indeed, Christ might very well have uttered them, although the occasion for them does not appear so obvious as in Matthew and Mark. In connexion with the account of the healing of the deaf and dumb demoniac given by Luke, we have a different passage (xi., 27, 28) from the one now under discussion, but which yet contains something of a similar import, viz.: a contrast between a mere outward love of Christ's person and true reverence for him. This affinity of meaning may have caused the two passages to change places with each other. We presupposed this in our use of Luke, xi., 28, on p. 189. And the affinity of the two expressions may have also caused the two accounts in Matthew and Mark to be chronologically connected together.

‡ See above, p. 136.

§ In Matt., xii., 40, the reference is made to bear upon the *resurrection* of Christ, which is quite foreign to the original sense and connexion of the passage. It was Christ's whole manifestation, then developing itself *before the eyes of them that heard him,* that was in question; the resurrection was witnessed only by persons who were *already believers,* for whom it was a sign to reanimate their faith. For those who persisted in unbelief, *notwithstanding* the sign of his whole manifestation, the resurrection was a sign of reproof, a testimony that the work of God had triumphed over all their machinations. A special application of the type in this way would have drawn the attention of the hearers away

which the Jews were to be called to repent and escape the threatened judgment." He was to be a sign, shining for all mankind; and this candle, once lighted, *was not to be put in a secret place, neither under a bushel, but on a candlestick, that all who should enter the house might see the light* (v. 33). So was HE to be a light unto all men. But in order to receive the light, the *eye* must be sound. And what the eye is to the body, the inner light of Divine consciousness, originally implanted in our nature, is to the soul. Where this light has become darkness; where the Divinity in man, the consciousness of GOD, has been subjugated and stifled by the world, all that is within is full of darkness, and no light from without can illumine it. The *organ* wherewith to receive Divine revelations is wanting (v. 34–36).

Thus it was, because of the inner darkness of their souls, that these men could not understand "the sign" given by Christ's whole manifestation; and for this reason it was that, in spite of all the signs that lay before their eyes, they ever asked for more.

§ 166. *Discourse pronounced at a Feast against the Hypocrisy of the Pharisees and the Lawyers.* (Luke, xi., 37–52.)

While Christ was engaged in the conversation just referred to, a certain Pharisee, who did not display his hostile disposition so openly as the rest, but masked it under the garb of courtesy, came and invited him to breakfast, probably with a view to catch up something in his words or actions that might point a charge of heresy, or serve to cast suspicion upon him at a subsequent period.

In this spirit, he found it quite a matter of offence that Christ sat down to table without washing his hands. The Saviour took occasion from this to expose the hypocrisy of the sect; and availed himself, for the purpose, of illustrations drawn from the objects around him at the feast. "You Pharisees make the cups and dishes clean outside, but leave them full of dirt within. So you are careful to preserve an outward show of purity, but inwardly you are full of avarice and wickedness.* Ye fools, are not the inward and the outward, made by the

from the main point of comparison. For these reasons, we think the verse in question is a commentary by a later hand.

* It is a question whether Matt., xxiii., 25, or Luke, xi., 39, contains the original form of these words. In the latter, the second member of the illustration is wanting; Christ passes over from the illustration (the vessels) to the thing illustrated (the Pharisees). The two members are more complete in Matthew: "Ye make clean the outside of the cups and platters, but inwardly *they* are full of extortion and wickedness," *i. e.*, their contents were obtained by avarice and oppression. But neither is this precisely apt, nor does it seem likely that Christ would have reproached the Pharisee exactly in this form. In Luke the *last* member of the *illustration* (the cups are dirty within) and the *first* member of the *application* (ye are careful for outward purity) are wanting. In the above interpretation of Matthew we follow the reading ἀδικίας; it would not apply if we take that of the *lect. recept.*, viz., ἀκρασίας; which is not without good authority. This reading recommends itself

same Creator, inseparable? From *within* must true morality proceed; from the heart must the essence of piety be developed."

From this he takes occasion (v. 41–44) to expose the mock piety of the Pharisees, displayed in their satisfying themselves, not merely in religion, but also in morality, with outward and empty show.* They manifested their hypocrisy (v. 42) in giving "tithes" of the most trifling products (mint, cummin, &c.), and entirely neglecting the more essential duties of righteousness and love. Their vanity and haughtiness were shown (v. 43) in their claiming to lord it over every body. They were (v. 44), like tombs, so beautifully painted that no one would suppose them to be graves; but whose fair exterior concealed nothing but putrefaction.

At this point a *lawyer*† who was present asked Christ whether he

as the more difficult: it is easy to conceive, as *De Wette* remarks, how the others could have grown out of it.

* Luke, xi., 41, presents a difficulty. On any interpretation it seems to me that τὰ ἐνόντα corresponds to ἔσωθεν, as contrasted with ἔξωθεν, v. 39, and must therefore be applied to the *heart.* This being admitted, the only question is whether the words were or were not spoken ironically. If they were not, it must seem strange that Christ, whose design was to aim at *the disposition of the heart,* should have laid down any thing so easily perverted into *opus operatum.* It may be said that, in accordance with a mode of teaching which he frequently adopted, viz., to give a specific instead of a general precept,—to command an outward act, as a sign of the disposition, instead of enjoining the disposition itself; he here enjoins alms-giving as proof, in act, of the possession of that love which *imparts* to others. This appears to be confirmed by the verse following, in which justice and love are mentioned as virtues wholly neglected by the Pharisees; implying that their alms-giving, previously mentioned, being destitute of the proper disposition, was valueless. But, on the other hand, where Christ employs this mode of teaching, the peculiar *kind* of special injunction that he gives is always determined by the character of his hearers; and *alms-giving* would have been an inapt injunction to *Pharisees,* who, as we learn from the Sermon on the Mount, made great show and display thereof. Still, the injunction may have been given in view of the character of the *individual* Pharisees before him, who may have been known as avaricious men; and Christ may have known that to part with their money would be a test of love which they could not stand. If it be supposed that the words are not accurately reported, and that the special injunction is due to the *writer,* and not to Christ, still the connexion sufficiently guards even the writer from the charge of setting forth the *opus operatum.*

All difficulties would disappear if we could assume that Christ intended only to point out the prevailing spirit in which the Pharisees acted, and the sophisms with which they satisfied their consciences. "As to your inward parts, all you have to do is to give alms, and lo! all is clean for you!" (You think that alms-giving is to cleanse your life and atone for your sins.) Although this view does not appear perfectly simple and natural, I cannot share in the decisive sentence which modern writers, and even *De Wette,* have pronounced against it. It may be connected with verse 42, as follows: "You cannot with this mock piety satisfy the law of God, and escape his judgments; but *Woe unto you!*" He then adds another illustration—their "tithing of mint," &c., as corresponding to their kind of alms-giving; and contrasts both forms of hypocrisy (last clause of v. 42) with the true righteousness and love of which they were destitute.

† There appears to have been a marked distinction between these νομικοῖς and the Pharisees proper. They probably applied themselves more to the *Scriptures* than to the *traditions;* not, however, wholly rejecting the authority of the latter. (Perhaps they formed a transition sect to the later *Karaites.*) This might account for their expecting Christ to express himself more favourably of them than of the Pharisees, but did not save them

meant to apply these censures to the class to which he belonged, also From this the Saviour took occasion, in the remainder of the discourse (v. 45–52), to expose the crimes that were peculiar to the lawyers.

§ 167. *Christ Warns his Disciples against the Pharisees.—The Power of Divine Truth.* (Luke, xi., 52; xii., 3.)

It is probable that the conversation, commenced at the breakfast-table, was continued in the open air;* the irritated Pharisees interrogated him anew, seeking, by captious questions, to find some handle by which to gratify their malice and secure the vengeance which they hoped to wreak upon him. A multitude of other persons gathered; groups were formed around Christ; and the Pharisees finally withdrew. The Saviour then addressed himself to the immediate circle of his disciples, and gave them warnings and cautions, probably occasioned by the recent machinations of the Pharisees. "*Beware of the leaven of the Pharisees, which is hypocrisy;*" a leaven which impregnates all that comes from them, and poisons all who come in contact with them. They were to be on their guard; to trust no appearances; the hostile aim was there, even when carefully concealed. *All* their acts alike were poisoned by hypocrisy; against them all it would be necessary to watch.†

from his reproach. They could derive a lifeless and unspiritual system from the letter of the *Scriptures* as well as from traditions; could be as severe as the Pharisees in judging others, and as indulgent towards themselves. This distinction between the νομικοί and the others confirms the originality of Luke. *Strauss* and *De Wette* think that these interlocutions of other persons, giving occasion to new turns of the discourse—a sort of table-talk—belong merely to the peculiar dress which Luke gives to the account; but it appears to me on the contrary, that their apt adaptation to the several speakers is a strong proof of the originality of the narrative. They belong to the very character of table conversation; and their faithful and accurate transmission may be easily accounted for; they were probably again and again repeated, and finally, in aid of memory, committed to writing. Any argument against the verisimilitude of these accounts, drawn from the modern etiquette of the table, is totally out of place, and valueless.

* We see from Luke, xi., 53, compared with xii., 1, that the conversation was continued. The transition is not managed with the art that we should look for in a *fictitious* narrative; had Luke *invented* the dialogue, he would hardly have joined so awkwardly, without any connecting link, the table conversation with the discourse afterward delivered to the multitude. But our assertion that Luke, in describing the table-talk with what preceded and followed, has actually given us a real scene from the life of Christ, does not imply there is nothing in the statement that belongs in another place. Things are repeated here which we find often in both Matthew and Luke. The case was probably as follows: an original body of discourse, *e. g.*, the Sermon on the Mount, a conversation on some special occasion, at table or elsewhere, was handed down and written, subsequently, in particular memoirs. Other separate expressions, not specifically connected with them, were also handed down, and were incorporated in suitable places in the larger discourses, the more effectually to secure their preservation and transmission. Such may have been the case in the passage before us; *e. g.*, xi., 49, for example, which is given, in its original form, in Christ's last anti-Pharisaic discourse, Matt., xxiii., 34.

† We do not know how far the leaven of the Pharisees *did* succeed in poisoning the heart of an *Iscariot*. The caution in the text was obviously occasioned by the pretended friendship of the Pharisee who invited Christ to breakfast, and by the captious questions

After this note of warning, which probably perturbed their minds, he allowed them, for their comfort, to catch a glimpse of the coming triumphs of the kingdom of GOD, and of the victories which his truth should achieve. The craft of men, he told them, should not check its progress; it should make its way by the power of GOD. His truth, as yet veiled and covered, was to be brought to the knowledge of all men. "*For there is nothing covered that shall not be revealed; and hid, that shall not be known. What I tell you in darkness, that speak ye in light: and what ye hear in the ear, that preach ye upon the house-tops* (the flat roofs of Eastern dwellings)."* And with this promise, too, is connected an exhortation to firmness and steadfastness in their struggles for the truth: "*Be not afraid of them that kill the body,*"† &c.

put to him under pretence of securing his opinions on important points. We do not find the passage in as original a form in Matt., xvi., 6; the Pharisees are connected (as is often done in Matt.) with the *Sadducees;* a connexion, as we have remarked before, not natural or probable. It is difficult to conceive how Christ could have connected the *doctrine* of the Pharisees with that of the Sadducees; or how he could have warned his disciples against the influence of the latter, to which, from their own religious stand-point, and the circle of society in which they moved, they certainly were not exposed. *Schneckenburger* (Stud. d. Geist. Würtemb., vi., 1, 48), indeed, says that the *doctrine* of the Pharisees could not have been alluded to either, because Christ recommends the latter himself (Matt., xxiii., 3). But we cannot agree with him; Christ's object, in the passage quoted, is to contrast the rigid *precepts* of the Pharisees with their practice. It was the example of their *life* that the disciples were to guard against; but as *their* righteousness was to exceed that of the Pharisees, they were enjoined to live up even to the strict precepts of that sect, so that none might be able to accuse them of violating the law. But surely there was nothing in this inconsistent with opposition, on Christ's part, to the *doctrines* of the Pharisees in other respects; and proofs of such opposition abound in the Evangelists. It is *possible,* from the connexion in Matt., that Christ may have given his warning in view of Pharisaic ideas of the kingdom of God and of the signs of its appearance, and that the figure of the leaven may have been intended to apply to this; but yet it is more natural to explain it as alluding (in Luke's sense) to the *hypocrisy* of the sect, which Christ had just before condemned. In Mark, viii., 15, indeed, no other sense is admissible; the disciples might be warned against the *hypocrisy* of Herod Antipas, but not against his *doctrine.* It may, indeed, be said that *Luke's* version is the original one; that *Matthew,* as was usual with him, added *Sadducees* to Pharisees; and that *Mark,* finding this unsuitable, substituted *Herod.* In answer to this, Christ may have employed the phrase more than once. In the case of Herod, the caution was not uncalled for; the disciples might have been deceived by his wish to see Jesus, although he wished it with no good intentions. Mark probably employed a different and original account; and, in the nature of the case, the substitution of the Sadducees for Herod was unlikely: it is not known that Herod was a Pharisee.

* In Matt., x., 26, 27, these words are incorporated into the discourse at the mission of the Apostles, in which several other passages are out of place. Their *form* is probably more accurately given in Matt. than in Luke; in the former, it is what they *hear* that is to be proclaimed; in the latter, what they *speak;* for at that time the disciples themselves did not fully understand and utter the truth among themselves. It was only *to become* plain to them at a later period.

† Other things are added, after Luke, xii., 5, probably out of their proper connexion; especially the "blasphemy against the Holy Ghost," of which we have spoken before (p. 243). I cannot adopt the interpretation of *Schleiermacher,* which is adapted to the passage as if this were its proper place.

§ 168. *Christ Heals a Paralytic at Capernaum, and the Pharisees accuse him of Blasphemy.—The Accusation Repelled.* (Matt., ix., 1; Mark, ii., 1; Luke, v. 17.)

The attack made upon Christ at Jerusalem involved, as we have seen, two charges, viz., that he violated the law, and that he assumed a power and dignity to which no man could have a right. The Pharisees continued their persecutions, on the same grounds, in Galilee also, where his labours offered them many points of assault. But against all such attacks his Divine greatness only displayed itself the more conspicuously.

On one occasion he returned to Capernaum from one of his preaching tours, and when his arrival was known many gathered around him. Some sought him to hear the words of life from his lips; to obtain help for their bodies or their souls; others, doubtless, with hostile intent, to put captious questions, and act as spies upon his words and actions; and curiosity, too, had done its part; so that the door of the house was beset with people. The Saviour was interrupted in his teaching by a great noise without. A man palsied in all his limbs, tormented by pain of body and anguish of heart, had caused himself to be carried thither. His disease may have been caused by sinful excesses; or it may have so awakened his sense of guilt as that he felt it to be a punishment for his sins; but, be this as it may, the disease of his body and the distress of his soul seem to have been closely connected, and to have reacted upon each other.* Both required to be healed, in order to a radical cure. Though the bodily ailment was a real one, and not due to a psychical cause, still, such was the reciprocal action of spirit and body, that the spiritual anguish had first to be remedied. And, on the other hand, as the disease seemed to be a punishment for sin, he needed, for the healing of his soul, a *sensible* pledge of the pardon of his sins; and such a pledge he was to find in the cure of his palsy.

Four men carried the couch on which the sick man lay; but the throng was so great that they could not make their way through. The palsied man was anxious to see the Saviour, by whom he hoped to be relieved. Entrance by the door was impossible; but the Oriental mode of building afforded a means of access, to which they at once had recourse. Passing up the stairs, which led from the outside to the flat roof of the house,† they made an opening by removing part of the tiles, and let the couch down into an upper chamber.

* *Schleiermacher* concluded, from the great pains that were taken, and the unusual means that were resorted to to bring the sick man to Christ, that the Saviour was about to depart immediately from the city. But Mark's account shows that he had just returned, and that a vast crowd had gathered about him. A momentary exacerbation of the sick man's sufferings may have caused the haste; but we do not know enough about his case to decide this.

† The accounts of Mark and Luke bear throughout the vivid stamp of eye-witnesses.

Christ's first words to the sick man, addressed to his longing and faith, were, "*Son, thy sins be forgiven thee;*" and this balm, poured into the wounded spirit, prepared the way for the healing of his corporeal malady.

The Pharisees, always on the watch, seized upon this opportunity to renew their accusations; he had claimed a fulness of power which belonged to God alone; the power, namely, to forgive sins. Perceiving their irritation, he appealed to a *fact* which could not be denied, as proof that he claimed no power which he could not fully exercise. ["*Whether is it easier to say, Thy sins be forgiven thee; or to say, Arise and walk? But that ye may know that the Son of Man hath power on earth to forgive sins** (*then saith he to the sick of the palsy*), *Arise, take up thy bed, and go unto thy house. And he arose, and departed to his house.*"] "It is easy to say, Thy sins be forgiven thee; for if these words really produce any result, it could not be perceptible to the senses, and, for that reason, the lack of the result could not convict an impostor;† but he who says Arise and walk must really possess the power which his words claim, or his untruth will be immediately exposed."

And the *fact* that the Divine power of his words revivified the dead

The unusual feature of the event is related in the simplest possible way, without a trace of exaggeration; and it is all in perfect keeping with Oriental life. *Strauss* assumes, without the slightest ground, that these accounts are exaggerated copies of Matthew's (ix., 1), which is much the most simple. We have far more reason to take it the other way, and consider Matthew's as an *abridged* statement, the main object of which was to report what *Christ said*, and not to give a full detail of the circumstances. *Strauss* says, further, that the words, "*when he saw their faith*," gave occasion for the invention of the story of the letting down of the bier through the roof, &c. Let us look at this. If Jesus set so high a value upon the faith of the men, he did it, either because he saw their faith by that glance of his which searched men's hearts, or because they gave some *outward sign* of it. [*Strauss* would not be likely to admit the first, and the second] is precisely met by the statement of Luke. Moreover, an invention of this kind would have been utterly inconsistent with the spirit of early Christianity, which had too high a conception of Christ's power to pierce the thoughts of men to suppose that he needed any outward sign of a really existing faith. Again, if it be agreed that admittance could be had by a *door* in the roof, it may be questioned whether such a door would be large enough to admit a *couch* But, probably, no such door existed in Eastern houses. Joseph., Archæol., l. xiv., xv., § 12, confirms this. Herod I. had taken a village, in which there were many of the enemy's soldiers; part of them were taken on the roofs, and then, it is said, "*τοὺς ὀρόφους τῶν οἴκων κατασκάπτων, ἔμπλεα τὰ κάτω τῶν στρατιωτῶν ἑώρα ἀθρόως ἀπειλλημμένων.*" Even those who suppose Mark's account to be an imitation of Luke's, or of the *ἀπομνημόνευμα* which Luke followed, must still admit that it implies an intimate acquaintance with the construction of Eastern houses. Had there been a way of getting through the roof otherwise, he would not have said that they *broke* it. As I have said before, Mark's details, in many places, imply that he used a separate authority; although I cannot believe, with some, that his Gospel was the *original* basis of Matthew and Luke.

* God forgives the sins in heaven, but Christ, as Man, announces the Divine forgiveness. "*Son of Man*" and "*in earth*" are correlative conceptions.

† It was only in *this* sense, and not with reference to the act of power in itself, that Christ said, "*It is easier*" &c.

limbs of the paralytic proved that he had the power, by granting forgiveness of sins, to awaken the dead soul to a new spiritual life. In this case the two were bound together.

§ 109. *The Withered Hand healed on the Sabbath.—The Objections of the Pharisees anticipated and refuted.* (Mark, iii., 1–6; Luke, vi., 6–8; Matt., xii., 10.)

A man with a withered hand appeared in the synagogue on a certain Sabbath while Christ was teaching, probably at Capernaum. The Pharisees, perhaps, had brought him there, as they stood by and watched eagerly to see what Christ would do; but the latter saw their purpose, and acted with his characteristic calmness and confidence. Taking no notice whatever of his crafty foes until he had called the sufferer forth into the midst of the synagogue, he then, by putting an unavoidable dilemma to the Pharisees, anticipated all that they could say: "*Is it lawful to do good on the Sabbath days, or to do evil; to save life, or to kill?*" This question did not offer a choice between doing or not doing a specific good, but between doing the good or its opposite evil; and even the Pharisees could not pretend to hesitate as to the reply. It was precisely for this reason that Christ so put it.

But was he justified in this? Let us see. The point assumed was, that a sin of *omission* is also a sin of *commission*. Whoever omits to do a good act which he has the power and, therefore, the calling to do, is responsible for all the evil that may flow from his omission; *e.g.*, if he *can* save a neighbour's life, he *ought;* and if he does not, he is guilty of his death.* So with the case of this lame man; there he was; Christ could cure him; Christ *ought* to cure him; and, if he did not, would be responsible for the continuance of his impotency. That it was a duty to save *life* on the Sabbath was taught even by the Pharisees themselves; and, as the *spirit* of the law required, Christ extended the principle further. The exception allowed by the Pharisees showed that the law could not, unconditionally, be literally fulfilled.

After putting his question, he looked around to see if any of them would venture a reply. All were silent. Then, with Divine word of power, he said to the lame man, "*Stretch forth thine hand;*" and it was done.†

* *Wilke's* objections (*Urevangelisten,* p. 191) to the word ἀποκτεῖναι are not decisive. A strong word would naturally be used by Christ to give emphasis to the declaration that, in such a case, not to *save* life, is to *kill.*

† It is obvious that the accounts of this event in Matthew, Mark, and Luke were written independently of each other, from independent sources; and this seems to confirm their truth. Immediate originality, and the vivacity of an eye-witness, are strikingly exhibited in *Luke's* account; *e.g.*, before the Pharisees open their lips, Christ anticipates them both by word and deed; which is much more characteristic than Matthew's statement. And as for Christ's words, as given by Luke, being due to a later revision of the original, it is the less likely, because the striking application of which they admit does not lie upon the sur

§ 170. *Cure of the Infirm Woman on the Sabbath ; the Pharisees disconcerted.* (Luke, xiii., 10.)—*Of the Dropsical Man.* (Luke, xiv.)

On another Sabbath, while Christ was teaching in the synagogue, his attention was arrested by a woman who had gone for eighteen years bowed together and unable to erect herself. He called her to him and laid his hands upon her; she was healed, and thanked God.

The ruler of the synagogue, not venturing to attack Christ directly, turned and reproached the people with, *There are six days in which men ought to work ; in them, therefore, come and be healed, and not on the Sabbath day.* Christ saw that the reproach was intended for himself; and exposed to the man (who only illustrated the spirit of his whole party) the hypocrisy of his language, and the contrast between Pharisaic *actions* and a Pharisaic show of zeal for the law, by the question, *Doth not each of you, on the Sabbath, loose his ox or his ass from the stall, and lead him away to watering ? And shall not this daughter of Abraham, whom Satan hath bound, lo ! these eighteen years, be loosed from this bond on the Sabbath day !**

Often the hidden aims of the Pharisees were veiled in the garb of friendliness ; but the Saviour anticipated their attacks before they were uttered, and thus often prevented their utterance at all. An illustration of this is to be found in the account given by Luke (xiv.) of a meal taken at the house of a Pharisee, by whom he had been invited on the Sabbath. Whether by accident, or by the contrivance of the Pharisees, a dropsical man was there, seeking to be healed. Jesus first turned and asked them, *Is it lawful to heal on the Sabbath day ?* When they made no reply, he touched the man and cured him. When he had left the house, the Saviour saw that the Pharisees were disposed to put an ill construction on what he had done; and appealed, as he had done before, to the testimony of their own conduct: *Which of you shall have an ox or an ass fallen into a pit, and will not straightway pull him out on the Sabbath day ?*

face at all. The clause in Matt., xii., 12, *ἔξεστι τοῖς Σάββασι καλῶς ποιεῖν*, gives a hint of the thought more fully developed in Luke. As to Matt., xii., 11, it *may* be out of place ; and, in that case, may be the same as Luke, xiv., 5, in a different form, the latter being supposed to give the true occasion on which the words were uttered. But it is just as possible that Christ uttered the same thought on two occasions ; or that he appended both illustrations to his answer to the question given in Luke, vi., 9.

* The expression "whom Satan hath bound" may imply a demoniacal possession, a state, perhaps, of melancholy imbecility ; and the words *πνεῦμα ἀσθενείας* appear to confirm this. But they may also be referred to the connexion between sin and evil in general, or in this particular case ; and so a demoniacal possession, in the full sense, need not be presupposed. The terms may have been used in view of prevalent opinions, or because of the peculiar form in which Christ wished to express himself in this case.

§ 171. *The Strife for Precedence at Feasts.—The Poor, not the Rich, to be invited.—Parable of the Great Supper.* (Luke, xiv.)

When the time of sitting down to the meal arrived, there was a strife for precedence among the Pharisees, forming an apt display of their vanity and pride of rank; and illustrating, in the lower sphere of life, the arrogant and evil disposition which they carried into the higher, and which totally unfitted them for the kingdom of God. Christ took the occasion to contrast this haughty spirit of theirs with spiritual prudence, the true wisdom of the kingdom, by giving them, in a parabolic form, a rule of prudence for the lower sphere of life.

This rule was, that, instead of appropriating the highest seat, and thus exposing one's self to the shame of being bidden to leave it, one should rather seek the lowest place, and thus have the chance of being honoured, before all the guests, by an invitation to a higher. It is obvious enough, on the face of this, that Christ did not intend it merely as a rule of social courtesy; he himself (v. 11) sets forth the prominent thought illustrated, viz.: that, to be exalted by God, we must humble ourselves; that all self-exaltation can only deprive us of that humility which constitutes true elevation.

During the repast, the Saviour turned to the host and attacked the prevailing selfishness that ruled all the conduct of the Pharisees. He illustrated this by contrasting that selfish hospitality which looks to a recompense with the genuine love that does good and asks no return. The heart that is fit for the kingdom of Heaven looks to no earthly reward, but will receive, in their stead, the heavenly riches (v. 12–14) of that kingdom.

One of the guests, probably wishing to turn the conversation from a disagreeable subject, seized upon the words uttered by Christ, to allude to the blessedness of the kingdom of God. "*Blessed,*" said he, "*is he that shall eat bread in the kingdom of God.*" He may have borrowed the figure from the scene around him; or, perhaps, employed it from a tendency to Chiliastic ideas of heaven. On this, Christ took occasion to show the Pharisees, who deemed themselves secure of a share in the Messianic kingdom, how utterly destitute they were of its moral requisites, and how far those whom they most despised were superior to them in this respect. He demanded a disposition of heart ready to appreciate the true nature of the kingdom of God as manifested and proclaimed, and willing to forsake all things else in order to lay hold of it.

To set this vividly before their minds, he made use of the figure of a *supper*, suggested, doubtless, by the circumstances around him. The *first* invited—those to whom the servant is sent to say, "*Come, for all things are now ready*"—are the Pharisees, who, on account of their life-long devotion to the study of the law, and their legal piety, deemed themselves certain of a call to share in the Divine kingdom. They are not accused, in the parable, of decided hostility, but of *indifference* to that which ought to be their highest interest. Not knowing how to value the invitation, they excuse themselves from accepting it under various pretexts. The character of all persons, indeed, who are *too busy* to give heed to Christ's words, is here illustrated.

When the invited guests refused to come, a call was sent forth for "*the poor, the maimed, the halt, and the blind;*" guests uninvited, indeed, and not expecting such an honour. By these we understand the despised ones, the publicans and sinners, whom Christ took to his embrace.

Still there is room; the *highways* must be ransacked; that is, the *heathen*, strangers to the Theocratic kingdom, are to be summoned to Christ's kingdom.

§ 172. *The Pharisees attack the Disciples for plucking Corn on the Sabbath.—Christ defends them.* (Luke, vi., 1; Matt., xii., 18.)

During the first or second year of Christ's labours in Galilee, he walked, on the first Sabbath after the Passover,* through a corn-field with his disciples. The corn was ripe; and the disciples, urged by hunger, plucked a few ears, rubbed them in their hands,† and ate them. Some of the Pharisees (always on the alert) reproached them for doing such a thing on the Sabbath day. As the charge was, in fact, meant for Christ himself, he replied to and refuted it; and, not content with bare refutation, he *intimated* a higher truth, which could not be brought out clearly and fully until a later period.

First, he showed to the Pharisees, on their own ground, the falsity of their slavish adherence to the letter of the law. David, he told them, violated their principle in satisfying his hunger with the sacred bread, when no other could be had.‡ The Mosaic law itself opposed it, inasmuch as the priests were necessarily compelled, in the Temple-service, to infringe upon the Sabbath rest; clearly showing that not *all* labour was inconsistent with that rest, so that the true aim of the law was kept in view. But (he proceeded, *intimating* the higher truth) if a deviation from the letter of the law was justifiable in the priests, because engaged in the *Temple-service*, how much more in men who were engaged in the service of *that which was greater than the Temple*, the highest manifestation that had been made to mankind.§

* Σάββατον δευτερόπρωτον, Luke, vi., 1. Meaning, if the reading be correct, the first Sabbath after the second Easter-day, when the first sheaf of corn was presented in the Temple

† A customary way of appeasing hunger in those lands, even to this day; cf. *Robinson*, Palestine, ii., 429 and 430.

‡ 1 Sam., xx.

§ Cf. p. 89

Having thus vindicated the disciples, he opposed Hosea, vi., 6, to that idea of religion which rests in outward forms and lacks the inward life; which, in this as in other cases, was the root of error from which the conduct of the Pharisees proceeded. Had they known that *love* is greater than all ceremonial service, they would not have been so forward to condemn the innocent.* For *innocent* the disciples were, who had acted as they did for the sake of the Son of Man, who is greater than the Sabbath, and who, as Lord over all things, is Lord also† of the Sabbath.‡ The Sabbath was only a means of religious developement up to a certain period. That period had arrived in the manifestation of the Son of Man, the aim of all preparatory things, in whom the original dignity of man was restored, the ideal of humanity realized, and the interior life of man made independent of time and place.§

§ 173. *Christ's Discourse against the merely outward Cleanliness of the Pharisees.—He explains the Discourse to his Disciples.* (Matt., xv., 1–20.)

The free mode of life pursued by Christ's disciples was always an object of scrutiny to the Pharisees, who were constantly looking for signs of heresy. It could not fail to give them opportunities of fixing suspicion on the Master himself. Once, when he was surrounded by inquiring throngs, they put the question, involving, also, an accusation, why his disciples so despised the ancient traditions as to neglect the ordinary ablutions before eating.

His reply was, in fact, an accusation against their whole system. He told them, in effect, that all their piety was outward and hypocritical; that they justified, by their own arbitrary statutes, their actual violation of God's holy law, and thought to escape its observance by their sophistical casuistry. Having thus repulsed the Pharisees, he turned to the multitude, and warned them against the Pharisaical tendency so destructive to Jewish piety, the tendency to smother true religion under a mass of outward forms. "*Hear and understand; not that which goeth into the mouth defileth a man; but that which cometh out of the mouth, this defileth a man.*" Here Christ displays the same conscious, lofty superiority so often manifested in his disputes with the Pharisees (as recorded in John, as well as in the synoptical Gospels); instead of softening down the offensive doctrine, he presents it more and more forcibly in proportion as they take offence. The words just quoted *might* be interpreted as an attack upon the Mosaical law in re-

* The γὰρ in Matt., xii., 8, may refer either to v. 7 or v. 6; in either case it has a connexion of thought with v. 6.

† The καὶ, in Luke, vi., 5, agrees well with this.

‡ Mark, ii., 27, joins well to this. The "man" of v. 27, refers to "Son of Man" in v. 28; a reference that cannot be conceived as the work of a later hand.

§ I consider myself justified in finding all this in the passage, by taking the words in their full meaning, and comparing them with other expressions of Christ's.

spect to food, &c., and thus could afford the Pharisees a clear opportunity to fix a charge of heresy upon him.

When the disciples called his attention to the offence which the Pharisees had taken, he gave them to understand that this caused him no uneasiness: *Every plant which my heavenly Father hath not planted shall be rooted up; let them alone; they be blind leaders of the blind; both shall fall into the ditch.* ("All merely human growths—every thing not planted by God—must fall; the whole Pharisaic system shall come to the ground. Let not their talk trouble you; blind are they, and those that follow them; both leaders and led are going on to destruction.")

The disciples probably expected a different explanation; they were still too much ruled by Jewish views to apprehend correctly the full force of Christ's figurative language. The form of expression was simple enough in itself; it was the strange *thought* which made it difficult. It was only at a later period that even Peter could learn, and that, too, by the illumination of the Holy Ghost, that every thing is pure, for men, which comes pure from the Creator's hand. In the case before us, Peter, as spokesman for the disciples, asked an explanation of the obscure point. In reply, Christ first expressed his surprise that, after having so long enjoyed his society and teaching, they had made so little progress in religious knowledge; that such a saying should awake *their* scruples as well as the Pharisees'. "Do ye not yet understand," said he, "that what enters a man's mouth from without cannot defile the interior life? It is the product of the *heart*, it is that which comes from *within* that makes a man unclean." This truth was then immediately applied only to the case in point, viz.: eating with unwashed hands; the wider application of which it was capable could not be unfolded to them until a much later period.*

§ 174. *Trial Mission of the Apostles in Galilee.* (Luke, ix.; Matt., x.)

(1.) Objects of the Mission.—Powers of the Missionaries.

The extended period of time which Christ spent in Galilee was employed, also, in the education of the men who were to carry on his work upon earth. The disciples, at first, accompanied him as witnesses of his ministry; but, in order to accustom them to independent labours, and to test their qualifications for the work, he sent them forth on a trial mission. An additional object was to spread, by their agency, through all the towns and villages of Galilee, the announcement that the kingdom of God had appeared. He by no means sent them to proclaim the whole truth of salvation; they were as yet incapable of this; and it was at a later period only that he promised the gift of the

* Cf. p. 88.

Spirit to qualify them for it. So long as HE remained upon the earth, HE was the sole teacher. *They* were only to proclaim every where that the kingdom of GOD, the object of all men's desire, had come; to point out to the people of Galilee the great grace of GOD in calling the Founder of that kingdom from their midst. Their present work was to be a type of their future one, when the great work *within* them should be accomplished. As they were to become bearers of the word, the Spirit, and the powers of Christ, so preparation was already to be made for this, though as yet incompletely.

" *Then he called his twelve disciples together, and gave them power and authority over all devils, and to cure diseases. And he sent them to proclaim the kingdom of God, and to heal the sick.*" We see that Christ could communicate certain of the supernatural powers that dwelt in him to those who devoted themselves to serve him as organs. But as these powers emanated from the *source* of Divine life in him, so we conclude that the degree in which they were imparted to others depended upon the degree in which they had imbibed that life from him.

(2.) Instructions to the Missionaries.—Reasons for the Exclusion of the Samaritans and Heathen. (Matt., x., 5–6; Luke, ix., 1, &c.)

The disciples thus sent forth were to confirm the truth of their announcement by miraculous acts, pointing to Him who gave the power to perform them. At first, the general attention of the people was only to be called to the great epoch that had dawned; the developement of the *doctrine* of the kingdom was to be left to Christ's own teaching, and to the subsequent operations of his Spirit. This explains why he did not further direct the Apostles as to what they should teach. Their mission was to *Galilee* alone; and the exclusion of the Samaritans and heathen* is, therefore, not at all inconsistent with what we have said of Christ's plan for the universal establishment of his kingdom. All the difficulties that have been found in this restriction flow from considering it apart from the proper period of Christ's life to which it belongs. During his life on earth, *His* ministry was to be confined to the Jews. Before the kingdom of GOD could be planted among the *heathen* by the proclamation of his truth in this new form, it was necessary that the knowledge of it should be fully developed in the disciples; and this could only be done, after his departure, by the enlightening power of the higher Spirit that was to be imparted to them. The links of the chain of internal and external progress, by which this last great event was to be brought about, were closely bound to each other; a

* Matthew evidently connects many things with the instructions given to the Apostles in view of their *first* journey, which, chronologically, belong later, viz.: to those given at the mission of the Seventy, which he omits. But it is likely that Luke, ix., 1, seq. gives but an abridgment, and we may fill it out from Matthew

premature developement would only hinder instead of hastening the result. Before the Apostles could teach the heathen, or find access to their hearts, they had to learn the peculiarities of the Gospel itself, as well as its relations to the religion of the Old Testament. Even had they succeeded in reaching the mind of the heathen with their defective apprehension of Christ's doctrine, and thus making Jews of them, it would only have been the more difficult afterward to eradicate the laboriously-planted errors, and impart a pure form of Christianity. But this knowledge was among the things of which Christ himself said to his disciples, "*Ye cannot bear them now;*" it was bound up with many truths that were as yet veiled from them. Nor could he, consistently with his plan, as we have above unfolded it,* impart these truths as separate and *ready-made;* the fruit of knowledge had to grow up in their religious consciousness from the seeds of knowledge sown there by the Spirit of God.

The direction, therefore, given to the Apostles, *not* to go to the heathen in Galilee and on the border, necessarily followed from the plan of Jesus. "But," it may be asked, "why did he not explain to them the grounds of this restriction?" It might be enough to reply to this, that it is not likely that the full instructions, with the reasons in detail, are preserved to us, but only an extract containing the most essential features. But, apart from this, Christ *could* not at that time have given them all his reasons; for, in that case, he must have imparted to them what they could not as yet comprehend. They were *then* unconscious organs for the execution of his commands.

But their relation to the *Jews* was quite a different thing. To the latter they were to impart no entirely new doctrine; and there was, therefore, no fear, as in the case of the heathen, that they would plant seeds of error which would have to be uprooted afterward. The Apostles were to take hold of expectations already cherished among the Jews, and to proclaim that the object of desire had come. The errors which yet biassed their own minds were shared by the Jews as a body; errors from which nothing but the spirit of the Gospel could free either them or the Jews. And, besides, they must have received many seeds of the higher life from the society and teaching of Christ; and, in scattering these, they could aid in preparing the ground for subsequent culture.

Perhaps, also, the Saviour, in pointing out "*the lost sheep of the house of Israel*" as the first objects of their toil, had in view, also, "*other sheep, not of this fold,*"† belonging to those whom he had come to collect into one flock, under one shepherd. There was sufficient ground, moreover, for excluding Samaria from the sphere of this trial-mission, in the brief duration to which it had to be limited; apart from the fact that the

* Book iv., pt. i., chap. ii.

† John, x., 16.

Apostles did not stand in the same relation to the Samaritans as to the Galilean Jews. They were not prepared to adapt themselves to the feelings of the Samaritans, nor to meet the controversies into which they must inevitably be led among them; the way in which the two sons of Zebedee treated that people at a later period is proof of this. There was no danger, however, that the disciples would so misunderstand Christ as to infer that the Samaritans were to be excluded from the kingdom of God; what they had seen of his personal intercourse with that people, and of the love which he cherished for them, sufficiently guarded against that.

And so, too, they could not but infer that the exclusion of the heathen must not be extended too far. Besides, the Jews themselves* admitted that the heathen were to obtain a certain share in the kingdom of God, on condition of observing the Jewish law; and the disciples could hardly think *less* would be granted by *their* Master, whose words and actions breathed so very different a spirit.

(3.) The Instructions continued; the Apostles enjoined to rely on Providence

Christ sought to train his ministers to perform the duties of their calling without anxious care for the future. He bade them make no provision for their journey,† but to trust in God, who would not see them want while faithfully doing their duty; to be content with what was offered them; to abide in the first house that was hospitably opened to them; and thus, having made *one* family their home, to extend their labours around it as a centre. The issue satisfied them that their Master had predicted rightly; they found, as he had promised, all their wants supplied.‡ At that time the fame of Christ's miracles had rendered the dispositions of the Galileans favourable; they had to fight no battles with fanatical enemies. Moreover, the substance of their teaching was not as yet so inconsistent with the prevailing modes of thought as to excite hatred and opposition.

§ 175. *Various Opinions entertained of Jesus.* (Luke, ix., 7–9.)

In the mean time Christ's fame was spreading through all the land, and various opinions existed in regard to the character of the powers which could not be denied. A very small minority of the people recognized him as the Messiah; but the greater number expected that when Messiah *should* come, he would prove himself such by founding an earthly kingdom in visible glory; and that his power would be displayed, not in a corner of Galilee, but in the Theocratic metropolis. But those who had been impressed by the labours of John the Baptis

* Cf. p. 88, 89.

† This is the essential part of the instruction; differences of detail are of no moment.

‡ Luke, xxii., 35.

could hardly realize his total disappearance; and such, seeing greater works done so soon after his death, explained them thus: "*He is risen from the dead, and therefore mighty works do show forth themselves in him*" (Matt., xiv., 2). Others said that Elias, or one of the ancient prophets, had reappeared, to prepare the way for Messiah's kingdom.

It is obvious that the impression produced by Christ's works caused him to be generally regarded as higher than John—as the highest, indeed, next to Messiah; but not as Messiah *himself*, on account of the false expectation above mentioned. It is no matter of surprise that there should have been inconsistent and contradictory opinions at a time so disturbed and uneasy.

§ 176. *Return of the Apostles.—Miraculous Feeding of the Five Thousand.* (Matt., xiv.; Mark, vi.; Luke, ix.)—*Object and Significance of the Miracle.—Its Effect upon the Multitude.*

Christ had now spent a whole year in Galilee. The time of the Passover approached, and the Apostles returned from their missionary journey. Multitudes still thronged about him, seeking aid for soul and body; the caravans, gathering to the Passover, increased the press. The Saviour did not wish at once to expose himself to the dangers that threatened him at Jerusalem; moreover, he desired, for a time, to prolong both his ministry in Galilee, and his intercourse with the Apostles, whose training for the work was now his first object. He sought a season of undisturbed society with them; to receive the report of their first independent labours, and to give them advice and instruction for the future (Mark, vi., 30, 31). For this purpose, he departed, with the disciples, from the neighbourhood of Capernaum, on the western shore of Genesareth, to a mountain on the eastern shore, at the head of the lake, near *Bethsaida Julias.** But the multitude took care to see whither he accompanied his disciples, and immediately hastened after him.†

And here followed the *feeding of the five thousand.* This miracle formed the very acme of Christ's miraculous power;‡ in it creative

* Luke, ix., 10. The tetrarch Philip, who raised the village of Bethsaida (on the east side) to the dignity of a city, distinguished it from the village of the same name on the west side, by adding the name *Julias*, from the emperor's daughter (Joseph., Archæol., xviii., 2, § 1). It is not strange that the name בֵּית־צַיְדָה (meaning a *place of fish*, a *fishing-town*), should be applied to two places on different sides of a lake abounding in fish.—*Robinson's* Palestine, vol. iii., p. 566.

† It appears possible, from John, vi., 5, that Christ only withdrew to the east shore after spending a great part of the day with the multitude on the west side. In this case it would be natural for Christ to express, first, a care for their corporeal wants, when he saw them, after spending nearly the whole day without food, follow him at a late hour. What was done upon the two shores, therefore, may perhaps have been blended together in the synoptical accounts.

‡ Cf. p 152.

agency was most strikingly prominent, although it was not purely creation out of nothing, but a multiplication of an existing substance, or a strengthening of its properties. For this very reason, there is more excuse in regard to this than some other of the miracles for inquiring whether the subjective element of the account can be so separated from the objective as to offer a different view of the nature of the act.

A theory has accordingly been constructed to do away with the miraculous character of the act, and explain it as a result of Christ's spiritual agency, brought about in a natural way. It amounts to this: the feeding of the vast multitude with five loaves and two fishes was accomplished by the example and moral influence of Christ, which induced the better-provided to share their food with the rest, Christ's spirit of love bringing rich and poor to an equality, as it has often done in later Christian times. So, then, the result was rightly judged to have been brought about by the Spirit of Christ; but the spiritual influence was translated into a material one; Christ's power over men's hearts into a power exerted by him over nature; and the intermediate link in the chain was thus omitted.

Now, although it is *possible* that an account of the miracle might have originated in some such way as this—examples of the like are not wanting in the Middle Ages—the details of the narrative, in all the different versions of it, are irreconcilable with the hypothesis. Had part of the people been supplied with provisions, the disciples must have known it; on the contrary, according to the narrative, they had no such thought; nothing remained for them but to "*send the multitude away into the villages to buy victuals.*" Had they supposed that the caravans were partly supplied with food for their journey to Jerusalem, it would have been most natural for them to say to Christ, "Thou who canst so control the hearts of men, speak the word, that they may share with the needy." But there is no plausibility in the hypothesis that there were provisions on the ground; the multitudes had not come from a great distance; and there were villages at hand where food could be bought; so that there was no inducement to carry it with them. Moreover, had Christ seen such a misunderstanding of his act arise, he would, instead of turning the self-deception of the people to his own advantage, have taken occasion, by setting the case truly before them, to illustrate, by so striking an illustration, what the spirit of love could do. Finally, the narrative, as given by John (vi., 15), puts this theory wholly out of the question. So powerfully were the multitude impressed by what Christ had done, that they wished to take Jesus as Messiah, and make him king. The act must have been extraordinary indeed that could produce such an effect as this upon a people under the dominion of the senses, and not at all susceptible of any immediately *spiritual* agency which Christ might have employed.

The miracle was not wrought without reason; the circumstances which demanded it may be thus stated: A multitude of persons, travelling to Jerusalem for the Passover, followed Christ from the western to the eastern shore; he had spoken the words of Life to them, and healed the sick. They were chained the whole day to his presence, and evening came upon them. The sick who had just been healed were without food; they could not go, fasting, to the villages to obtain it.* Here, then, was a call for his assisting love; and, natural sustenance failing, his miracle-working power must supply the lack.

The effect of the miracle illustrates for us the mode of Christ's working in all ages; both in temporal and spiritual things, the spirit that proceeds from him makes the greatest results possible to the smallest means; that which appears, as to *quantity*, most trifling, multiplies it self, by his Divine power, so as to supply the wants of thousands. The physical miracle is for us a type of the spiritual one which the power of his words works in the life of mankind in all time.†

* John's Gospel, however, differs from others in this point (vi., 5), in stating that Christ himself asked the question, "*Whence shall we buy bread?*" &c., before any thing else was done. We find, therefore, by comparison with the other Gospels, that John has omitted part of the details. Christ would not make this the *first* question, when a multitude stood before him in want of spiritual as well as bodily relief; nor is it likely that he meant to prepare the way for the miracle from the beginning. From John, vi., 17, also, we gather that the event took place towards evening, leaving room for the inference [apart from the accounts in the other Gospels] that the multitude had been about Christ some time. In this statement, then, John plunges at once into the midst of the account, without the vividness of detail which usually marks his Gospel. On the other hand (cf. Matt., xv., 32), it is not likely that Christ waited for an intimation from the disciples before manifesting his ever-watchful love and compassion; nor was it his custom to work a miracle *suddenly*, but in a naturally-suggested and prepared way. All difficulties disappear if we adopt the view of note †, p. 261.

† The question arises, whether the miracle recorded in Matt., xv., 32, seq., and Mark, viii., 1–8, is different from the one of which we have just treated, or whether it is the same, differently stated. The fact that the narratives are *substantially* alike, and differ in matters comparatively unimportant, may be urged in favour of the latter view; but the *relative* differences of measure (4000 instead of 5000, with *seven* loaves instead of *five*, and the multitude spending *three* days with Christ) favour the former. The resemblances may be ascribed to the one account's having been modelled after the other. Matt., xvi., 9, 10, would not prove them different; that passage may have been modified at a later period, when the facts were presupposed to be different, without affecting its veracity. The *localities* might help to decide the question. The first miracle took place, as we have said, on the *eastern* side of Genesareth, near a mountain. The locality which we assign to the second will depend upon our answer to a question still debated, viz., where *Magdala,* to which Christ passed over (Matt., xvi., 39), was situated, According to the Talmudical accounts (*Lightfoot*, Chorograph., c. 76; *Wetstein*, in loc.), it was near *Gadara*, consequently, on the eastern side of the sea. If this be so, the *second* miracle must have been wrought upon a mountain on the *western* shore; thus assigning a locality to it different from that of the first. But, on the other hand, there is shown to this day, south of Capernaum, on the road to Tiberias, a village called *el-Mejdel* (Robinson), a name corresponding to the ancient *Magdala* (*Burckhardt*, Germ. trans., ii., 559; cf. *Rosenmüller*, Handbuch der Biblischen Alterthumskunde, ii., 73). This agrees with the Talmudic accounts that place the site near Tiberias; but not so well with the one quoted above, namely, that it was near *Gadara*, but cannot the *Migdal Gadar*, therein mentioned, be otherwise explained? Cf. *Gesenius's*

Up to this time Christ had only impressed the multitude with the belief that he was a mighty Prophet, whose appearance was preparatory to the Messianic era. But this climax of his miracle-working power produced one, also, in their opinions. "He that can do *such* a miracle can be no other than Messiah; we must do homage to him as Theocratic king, and urge him to establish his kingdom among us." Plans of this sort Christ had to evade; and he returned alone to the mountain.

§ 177. *Christ Walks upon the Waters.* (John, vi., 16; Matt., xiv., 22; Mark, vi., 45.)

Dismissing the disciples at evening, he commanded them to sail across to the western shore, in the direction of Bethsaida and Capernaum. They departed, but sailed for a while slowly along the shore, expecting Christ to come to them after he had dismissed the multitude; but they waited in vain. It was now dark; they became aware that their expectations would not be fulfilled, and took their way for the other shore. But the wind was against them; they had to contend with storm and waves. After struggling with the elements in great anxiety for more than an hour and a half in the open sea, they strove again to reach the shore which they had left. While they were toiling to accomplish this, suddenly, between three and six in the morning, Christ appeared to them walking on the waters, and approaching the vessel.*

remark on the passage cited; *Burckhardt*, ii., 1056; *Robinson*, iii., 529; Matt., xvi., i. (Pharisees meeting Christ), agrees better with the supposition of the *western* shore. If, then, Magdala was on the *western* shore, the second miracle, like the first, must have occurred on the *eastern;* the direction of their subsequent passage across the lake would agree pretty well. Then the *general* geographical course (indicated in Matt., xvi., 13) would accord very well with Matt., xv., 21; and all this favours the opinion that we have *two* reports of one and the same miracle. There is an important difference between Matt., xv., 39, and xiv., 22; the latter stating that Christ *sent* his disciples away first by ship; the former, that he went immediately himself; but this might have arisen from an omission in the former passage; just as we find Luke, also, saying nothing of it. The probability of the miracle having been wrought twice is lessened by the view that we have taken of it as constituting the climax of his miraculous works. We recognize in Matt., xv., 29; xvi., 12, a break in the historical and local connexion; and, in fact, we frequently find in this document, although an original and evangelical one, the same expressions and events narrated more than once; sometimes in longer, sometimes in shorter forms.

* If it were even *grammatically* possible to translate ἐπὶ τῆς θαλάσσης "*along the sea,*" and ἐπὶ τὴν θάλασσαν "*towards the sea,*" although the connexion be unnatural (thus supposing that Christ *had gone* in a half circle to the other side of the shore, and so reached the disciples, who had slowly toiled *along* the shore); if this, I say, were grammatically possible, such a construction is directly opposed to the tenor and intention of the narrative. This is most obvious in John's account, which is the most direct and simple, and has least of the miraculous about it. Suppose the disciples to have sailed 25 or 30 furlongs, not *across*, but *along* the sea, and then, seeing Jesus on the shore, to have taken him in; how will this agree with John's statement (vi., 21), "*immediately the ship was at the land, whither they went?*" If they saw Jesus, then, *on* the shore, it must have been the *western* shore; and what meaning could there be, in that case, in their taking him into the vessel? Cf. *Lücke's* excellent remarks, *in loc.*

Bewildered with fear, they did not recognize the Saviour amid the storm and darkness, but thought they saw "*a spirit.*"* But Christ called to them, "*It is I;* be not afraid." The well-known voice turned their fear into joy. They sought, longingly, to take him into the vessel; but, before they could succeed in it, they were wafted to the shore by a favourable wind. This, too, was full of import to them; as soon as Christ made himself known, every thing took a joyful turn.†

§ 178. *Christ in the Synagogue at Capernaum.* (John, vi.)

(1.) The Carnal Mind of the Multitude rebuked.

Christ met certain of the eye-witnesses of the miraculous feeding of the five thousand in the synagogue at Capernaum, either on the Sabbath, or on some other day.‡ They were surprised, and, therefore, the more gratified, at his sudden appearance, since they had left him on the eastern shore; and their pleasure was shared by others whom they had told of the miracle. Doubtless they were full of expectation that he would work new wonders to confirm his Messiahship, and gratify their carnal longings. But the higher their hopes of this kind were, the deeper was their disappointment, and the greater their rage, when he offered them something entirely different from what they sought. The miracle could produce no faith in those who were destitute of a spiritual mind; their enthusiasm, carnally excited, was soon to pass over into opposition. A process of sifting was to take place, and the discourse which Christ uttered was intended to bring it on.

They questioned him; but, instead of replying, he entered at once upon a rebuke of their carnal temper: "*Ye seek me, not because ye saw the miracles, but because ye did eat of the loaves, and were filled. Labour not for the meat which perisheth, but for that meat which endureth unto everlasting life, which the Son of Man shall give unto you; for him hath God the Father sealed.*" "Ye seek me, not because the sign of my Divine working, which ye saw, has led you to me as the Son of God, who alone can supply your *spiritual* wants; but only because I have appeased your *bodily* appetite; and so you look to me only for *sensible* gifts, which I come not to bestow (*i. e.*, such was the carnal hue of their expectations of Messiah). Strive not for perishable, but eternal food, imparting eternal life, which the Son of Man will bestow; God has sealed him to this by miracles wrought before your eyes, in attestation of his Divine calling."

* Not a likely thought, if Jesus was walking *on the shore*; it could have been nothing strange, especially towards Easter, when so many were travelling towards Jerusalem, to see a man walking on the lake-side towards morning.

† I follow John's account, as most naturally explaining itself.

‡ Part of what occurred would have been a violation of the Sabbath; in later times there were assemblies in the synagogue on the second and fifth days of the week (*Winer,* Realwörterbuch, 2d ed. vol. ii., p. 637).

Upon this, the purer-minded among them asked him, "What must we do, then, to become worthy of the Divine favour?" They expected him to prescribe new religious duties; but, instead of this, he led them back to the one work: "*Believe on him whom God hath sent.*" With *this* faith every thing is given.

(2.) A greater Sign demanded.—The Answer: "Christ the Bread of Life."

Then others* came out; either eye-witnesses of the miracle, who (according to the nature of the unspiritual mind), still unsatisfied, and seeking greater signs, were liable, from their want of faith, to be soon perplexed even in regard to what they had already experienced;† or persons who had only heard of the miracle from others, and who had decided from the first to see for themselves before they would believe. These demanded of Christ (v. 30) a new miraculous attestation;‡ and, as the Messiah was to be a *Moses* with new powers, they asked that he should give them bread from heaven—celestial manna—angels' food, according to their fancies of the millennial bliss.

Christ took the opportunity (v. 32–42) thus naturally offered to lead them from the material to the spiritual and Divine, and declared *himself* to be the true bread from heaven, at the same time seeking to awaken in them a desire for it. But their carnal feelings were susceptible of no such desire; and, still regarding only the earthly appearance, they took offence that the *carpenter's son* should say, "*I came down from heaven.*" He did not attempt to reason them out of their scruples, but laid bare the *source* of them, *i. e.*, their dispositions of heart and mind; of these they had first to be rid, before they could recognize the Divinity in his human manifestation (v. 43–47). "*Murmur not among yourselves; no man can come unto me, except the Father, which hath sent me, draw him.*" Seek *within* you, not without you, for the cause of your surprise; it lies in this: you came to me carnally, with no sense of spiritual need; and, therefore, have not the *drawing* of the Father, which all must follow who would come unto me aright." It is among the prophecies that are to be fulfilled in the Messianic age that "*they shall all be taught of God;*"§ and so,

* It is part of John's manner not to distinguish individuals or classes closely in his narrations.

† For the miracle *in* the miracle, the Supernatural, as such, can only be apprehended by the Sense for the Supernatural. The reaction of the senses on the critical understanding can soon uproot a conviction growing only in the soil of the senses. One reasons away what he thinks he has seen; "it could not have happened so."

‡ It is to be noted, in comparing the accounts of the *two* instances in which the multitude were miraculously fed, that the *second* is followed (Matt., xvi., 1) by a demand made upon Christ for *a sign from heaven*.

§ John, vi., 45. This cannot be understood of the *subsequent* teaching of all by the bestowing of the Holy Ghost, or of the general teaching of Christianity; the thing in view in the passage was, the Divine voice in men, preceding faith, to lead them to Christ as Saviour, which was not to be restrained by any human statutes.

every one that follows the Father's call, comes to me. (The voice of GOD, which testifies of the Redeemer in all needy souls and calls them, will be heard every where.) But this must not be understood as if any one could know the Father, or be united with him, except through the Son; the Son alone, derived from the Father, knows him perfectly, and can impart this knowledge to others [" *Not that any man hath seen the Father, save he which is of God; he hath seen the Father*"]. This preventing operation of the Holy Spirit was only intended to lead them to the Son, as their Redeemer: " *He that believeth on me hath everlasting life.*" Again (v. 48–51) he repeats the assertion, " *I am that bread of life from heaven,*" confirmed by the proof that none could attain a share in the Divine life, or communion with the Father, except through him; and describes himself as the true *manna* from heaven.

He then proceeds to tell them (v. 51) that he would give them *a* bread which was to impart life to the world; hence, that the bread which he *was about* to *give* was, in a certain sense, different from the bread which he *was;* different, that is, from his whole self-communication. "*And the bread which I will give is my flesh.*" This bread was to be the self-sacrifice of his bodily life for the salvation of mankind.* The life-giving power, *as such,* was his Divine-human existence; the life-giving power, *in its special act,* was his self-sacrifice. The two are inseparable; the latter being the essential *means* of realizing the former; only by his self-sacrifice could his Divine-human life become the bread of life for men.†

(3.) Eating Christ's Flesh and drinking his Blood.—His own Explanation of this (John, vi., 53, seq.)

The Jews wilfully perverted these words of Christ (v. 52) into a carnal meaning; and therefore he repeated and *strengthened* them. " *Except ye eat the flesh of the Son of Man,*" &c. (v. 53–58). "Except ye receive my Divine-human life within you, make it as your own flesh and blood, and become thoroughly penetrated by the Divine principle of life, which Christ has imparted to human nature and himself *realized* in it, ye cannot partake of eternal life."

* *Lachmann's* text omits the words ἣν ἐγὼ δώσω in v. 51, a reading which is supported by considerable authority. Omitting these words, only the general idea (the σάρξ to be devoted for the salvation of men) would be made prominent in the passage; not, however, to the exclusion of his self-sacrifice as the culminating-point of his life devoted to God and to man's salvation. But the omission would make the passage harsh, and unlike John's style: the words may have slipped out of some of the MSS., from their similarity to the preceding ὃν ἐγὼ δώσω.

† I am well aware of what *Kling* says against *Lücke* (Stud. u. Krit., 1836, 1) in regard to this division of the discourse, but my views remain unaffected. I cannot find in the words of Christ the Lutheran *Realism,* so called.

To make the sense of his figurative expressions perfectly clear, he changed the figure again to the "bread from heaven;" *as the living Father hath sent me, and I live by the Father;* so he that *eateth me,** *even he shall live by me.*† *This is the bread that came down from heaven.* But most of his disciples still lacked the capacity to understand how his words mutually explained each other. Adhering to the outward and material sense, they seized upon those expressions which were most striking, without catching their connexion, or taking the trouble to understand his figures by comparing them with each other and with the unfigurative expressions; a process which could not have been difficult even to those among them who were incapable of profound thought, accustomed as they were to the figurative style of Oriental language, and to Christ's peculiar manner of speaking. Fastening only upon the expression, "eating his flesh and drinking his blood," in this sense, they found it "a hard saying which they could not bear" (v. 60).

And this was true not merely of the mass of hearers in the synagogue, but also of many who had become his followers during his protracted labours in Galilee, without, however, in heart and spirit, really belonging to the circle of disciples. The foreign elements had to be separated from the kindred ones; and the very same impressions which served to attach really kindred souls more closely to the person of Christ were now to drive off others, who, though previously attracted, were not decided within themselves as to their relations to him (v. 61–66).

When he had left the synagogue, and was standing among persons who, up to that time, had been his constant attendants, he said, in view of the state of feeling above described, "I have spoken to you of eating my flesh; *doth this offend you?* What, then, will you say, when the Son of Man will ascend into heaven? You will *then* see me no more with your bodily eyes;‡ but *yet* it will be necessary for you to eat my flesh and drink my blood, which then, in a carnal sense, will be plainly impossible." It is obvious, therefore, that Christ meant no material participation in his flesh and blood, but one which would have its fullest import and extent at the time specified.

He then naturally passes on to explain the spiritual import of his life-streaming words: "*It is the Spirit that quickeneth, the flesh profiteth nothing; the words that I speak unto you, they are spirit and they are*

* To "eat him" and "to eat his flesh and blood" have the same meaning.

† The way in which Christ himself explains his meaning by changing his words is enough to show how far removed these words are from any reference to a communication of the body of Christ in the Lord's Supper.

‡ The removal of Christ's bodily presence from the earth, and his exaltation to heaven, are united together by him. Unbelievers see only the negative side, the removal; the eye of faith in seeing the one, sees the other

life. It is the Spirit that giveth life; the flesh is nothing; hence I could not have meant a sensible eating of my flesh and blood, but the appropriation of my Spirit, as the life-giving principle, as this communicates itself through my manifestation in flesh and blood. As my words are only the medium through which the Spirit of life that gushes forth from me is imparted, they can be rightly understood only so far as the Spirit is perceived in them." But this was precisely what those who misunderstood him were deficient in; and, "*therefore*," said he, "*I said unto you, that no man can come unto me, except it were given unto him of my Father.* Only those that hear His call, and come with a susceptibility for Divine things, can apprehend my words and obtain faith in me. As I said unto you, your carnal sense is the source of your misunderstanding and unbelief."

(4.) Sifting of the Disciples.—Peter's Confession.

Then followed a sifting of the disciples. [*From that time many of his disciples went back, and walked no more with him.*] As this was the natural result of his relations to them, he rather furthered than checked it; it was time that the crisis that had been preparing in their hearts should manifest itself outwardly. And the departure of the unworthy was to test the genuine disciples, and make them conscious of the true relation in which they stood to Christ. He wished them, therefore, in that critical moment, to prove their own selves; for there was *one* among them already upon the point of turning away, who might yet, by heeding Christ's injunction, have saved himself from the destruction that awaited him.

He said to the twelve, "*Will ye also go away?*" Peter, speaking, as usual, for the rest, bore testimony to their experience in his fellowship: "*Lord, to whom can we go?*" and confirmed Christ's words by his own consciousness, in whose depths he had felt the flow of their life-giving fountain: "*Thou hast the words of eternal life.*" And, there fore, he was able to confess in the name of all the rest, from a conviction founded in personal knowledge and experience, that Jesus was Messiah (v. 69). But Christ warned them that there was one among them who did not share this conviction, although included in Peter's confession. He had chosen them—drawn them to himself—he said, and yet one of them had the heart of an enemy. These words, showing to Judas that his inmost thoughts lay bare before Christ, might, had he been at all open to impression, have brought him to repent and open his heart to the Saviour, seeking forgiveness. Failing this, they could only strengthen his enmity.

CHAPTER X.

JESUS IN NORTH GALILEE, AND ON THE WAY TO CESAREA PHILIPPI.

§ 179. *Reasons for the Journey.*

WE have said that Christ desired to obtain an opportunity for private intercourse with the disciples, in order to hear the report of their mission journey, and to prepare their minds for the stormy times that were approaching. As it seemed impossible to secure this in the neighbourhood of Tiberias, he determined to go to some distance from that region of country, a purpose which other circumstances soon hastened.

Herod Antipas, who then reigned in Galilee, hearing of the fame of Jesus, became personally desirous to see him. This wish was probably dictated by mere curiosity, or by a desire to test Christ's power to work miracles;* certainly it arose from no sense of spiritual need. As such a meeting could lead to no good result, Christ must have desired to avoid it. This formed an additional motive for withdrawing himself into North Galilee; and perhaps beyond, into *Paneas*, or Cesarea Philippi, the domain of the Tetrarch Philip.† The first stage of the journey took him to Bethsaida Julias, on the west side of the Sea of Genesareth.

§ 180. *Cure of the Blind Man at Bethsaida.—Peter's Second Confession.—The Power of the Keys.* (Mark, viii.; Matt., xvi.)

At Bethsaida a blind man was brought to Christ, who took him out of the town to avoid public notice; and then performed on him the cure whose successive steps are so graphically described by Mark. He then forbade him for the time being to tell of what had been done as notoriety would have been inconsistent with his purpose above mentioned.‡

When left alone with the disciples, he questioned them about their travels, and concerning the opinions generally prevalent in regard to himself. Peter renewed, in a different form, the confession which he had before made on a similar occasion.§ In contrast with those who

* Cf. Luke, xxiii., 8. In view of the character of Herod, there is more internal probability in Luke, ix., 7, than Matt., xiv., 1, 2.

† We infer the direction which Christ took with his disciples from comparing Matt., xv., 21; xvi., 13; Mark, vii., 24; viii., 27; Luke, ix., 10–18.

‡ This suits well with the point of time here assigned to it.

§ In all the Gospels this event is closely connected with the miraculous feeding, which confirms our view of the historical connexion of the facts. True, it is *possible* that Peter's

saw in Jesus only a Prophet, he said, "Thou art the Messiah;" certainly implying more than was included in the ordinary Jewish sense; although he must have *felt* more than he could unfold in definite thought when he added, "*the Son of the living God.*"

Thus had Peter, on two distinct occasions, given utterance to the same confession, drawn from the depths of his inward experience; in the first instance, in opposition to those whose hearts were wholly estranged from Christ; and in the second, to those who had obtained only an inferior intuition of the person of Christ. The Saviour, therefore, thought him worthy of the following high praise: "*Blessed art thou, for flesh and blood hath not revealed it unto thee, but my Father which is in heaven.*" Peter's conviction was the result of no human teaching, no sensible impression or outward authority; but of an inward revelation from God, whose drawing he had always followed—a Divine *fact*, which comes not to men from without; which no education or science, how lofty soever, can either make or stand in stead of.*

In view of this conviction of Peter, thus twice confessed, in regard to that great fact and truth which forms the unchangeable and immovable basis of the eternal kingdom of God, Christ called him by the name which at an early period, with prophetic glance, he had applied to him (John, i., 42), *the man of rock*, on whom he declared that he would build his Church, that should triumph over all the powers of death,† and stand to all eternity.

This promise was not made to Peter as a *person*, but as a faithful organ of the Spirit of Christ, and his steadfast witness. Christ might have said the same to any one, who, at such a moment, and in such a sense, had made the same confession; although Peter's uttering it in the name of all the twelve accorded with his peculiar *χάρισμα*, which conditioned the post that Christ assigned to him.

In the same sense he confided to Peter the "keys of the kingdom of Heaven," which was to be revealed and spread abroad among men by the community founded by him; inasmuch as men were to gain admittance into that kingdom by appropriating the truth to which he had first testified, and which he was afterward to proclaim. This was

confession, as recorded by John, is the same as that recorded by Matthew, and nothing *essential* would be lost if it were so. But we may certainly suppose that, at so critical a period, Christ could have questioned his disciples thus closely on two different occasions in regard to their personal convictions, which were soon to undergo so severe a trial.

* Cf. p. 139.

† The "*Gates of Hades,*" in Matt., xvi., 18 (cf. Isa., xxxviii., 10; 1 Cor., xv., 55), designate rather the kingdom of *death* than of Satan. In this view the passage means, that "the Church should stand forever, and that its members, partakers of the Divine life, should fear death no more—of course implying, however, that she should be victorious over all hostile powers.

to be the key by which the kingdom was to be opened to all men. And with it was entrusted to him the power, on earth, "to bind and loose" for heaven; since he was called to announce forgiveness of sins to all who should rightly receive the Gospel he was to proclaim, and the announcement of pardon to such as received the offered grace had necessarily to be accompanied by the condemnation of those who rejected it.*

§ 181. *The Disciples prohibited to reveal Christ's Messianic Dignity.—The Weakness of Peter rebuked.* (Matt., xvi., 20–28; Mark, viii., 30.)

Thus Christ confirmed the Apostles in their confession of his Messianic dignity. But he knew, at the same time, that their minds were still tinctured with the ordinary ideas and expectations of a visible kingdom to be founded by Messiah; and he, therefore, gradually taught them that it was by *his own sufferings* that the kingdom of God was to be established. [*Then charged he his disciples that they should tell no man that he was Jesus the Christ. From that time he began to show to his disciples how that he must go to Jerusalem and suffer many things, &c.*]

The prohibition was doubtless given with a view to prevent them from diffusing the expectations of Messiah which they *then* entertained, and thus leading the people to political undertakings, and the like, in opposition to the objects of Christ. The words that immediately follow the prohibition confirm this view of it. But Christ's declarations that *sufferings* lay before him was too far opposed to the disciples' opinions and wishes to find easy entrance to their minds. "*Be it far from thee, Lord,*" said Peter; an exclamation inspired, indeed, by love, but a love attaching itself rather to the earthly manifestation of Christ's person, than to its higher one; a love in which natural and human feelings were not as yet made sufficiently subordinate to God and his kingdom. And as the Saviour had just before exalted Peter so highly, when he testified to that which had *not* been revealed to him by flesh and blood, but by the Father in heaven; so now he reproved him as severely for an utterance inspired by a love too much debased by flesh and blood. Human considerations were more to him than the cause of God; he sought, by presenting them, as far as in him lay, to pre

* This view of the "binding and loosing" power is sustained by John, xx., 23. The same thing is expressed in other words in Matt., x., 13; 2 Cor., ii., 15, 16. The difference between the figure of "the keys" and that of "binding and loosing" need cause no difficulty; they refer to different conceptions; the former, to reception into, and exclusion from, the kingdom of Heaven; the latter, to the *means* of reception and exclusion, viz., the pardon of sin and the withholding of pardon.

vent Christ from offering the sacrifice which his Divine calling demanded;* and his disposition was rebuked with holy indignation.†

Christ then turned to his disciples, and gave them a lesson directly opposed to Peter's weak unwillingness to sacrifice every thing to the *one* holy interest. He impressed upon them a truth pre-eminently necessary to the fulfilment of their calling, viz., that none but those who were prepared for every species of self-denial‡ could become his disciples, and enter into the kingdom of GOD, whose foundations he was about to lay. Finally, he announced to them that many among them would live to see the kingdom of GOD come forth in glorious victory over all its foes. It is true, they were not at that time able fully to comprehend this; only at a later period, by the illumination of the Holy Ghost, and by the course of events, the best commentary on prophecy, were they to be brought completely to understand it.

§ 182. *Monitions of Christ to the Apostles in regard to Prudence in their Ministry.*—(1.) *The Wisdom of Serpents and Harmlessness of Doves.* (Matt., x., 16.)—(2.) *The Parable of the Unjust Steward* (Luke, xvi., 1–13.)—(3.) "*Make to yourselves friends of the Mammon of Unrighteousness,*" &c.

(1.)

To this period, in which Christ conversed with his disciples in regard to their first missionary tour, and gave them cautions for their future and more difficult labours, doubtless belong many advices of the same tenor, found in different places in the Gospels. We, therefore, join together several sayings of this kind here; if not chronologically at least according to the substantial connexion.

As he sent the disciples forth like defenceless sheep among wolves, he bade them, in the struggles through which they must pass, to combine childlike innocence and purity of heart, symbolized by the harmless dove, with prudence and sagacity, whose symbol was the serpent.§

* The alternations in Peter's feelings, and his consequent desert of praise or blame from the Master, within so short a time, are so easily explained from the stand-point which he then occupied, that I cannot find any thing strange in Christ's expressing himself thus oppositely to him, as *Schleiermacher* does (Werke, ii., 107). And, therefore, I see no internal ground for believing that the passage is not properly connected with the narrative here.

† This helps to fix the right point of view for understanding Christ's previous declaration and promise to Peter; and the two addresses to him, taken together, attest the fidelity of the narrative as uncorrupted by a later ecclesiastical interest.

‡ It was naturally necessary for Christ to impress this truth *frequently* upon the disciples; Matt., xvi., 24; Mark, viii., 34, 35; Luke ix., 23, 24; and, therefore, the occurrence of similar passages, *e. g.*, Matt., x., 38; John, xii., 25, 26, proves nothing against the originality of the discourses there recorded; although it is possible that his sayings to this effect on one occasion may have been combined with those uttered on another to the same tenor.

§ Paul, who frequently alludes to Christ's sayings, does so several times to this one, Rom., xvi., 19; 1 Cor., xiv., 20. I place the passage in this connexion as better adapted to it than to the first Apostolical missionary journey.

They were, indeed, to labour as organs of the Divine Spirit, and to be furnished with Divine powers for their ministry; but he did not wish them, on that account, to neglect all proper human means for overcoming the difficulties they should meet with, but rather to apply that *wisdom* which knows how to use circumstances prudently. No such rule would have been given had he expected his kingdom soon to be established by a sudden interference of Omnipotence; it was prescribed in view of a gradual developement by the use of means provided in the general course of nature.

Yet the attempt to exercise prudence for the kingdom of God might (he taught) easily beguile them from purity and simplicity of heart. The wisdom of the serpent was, therefore, limited by the innocence of the dove; their prudence was to be defined by purity. They were to use none but pure and truthful means for the advancement of the holy objects of the kingdom. On the other hand, the combination of *wisdom* with innocence showed that the childlike simplicity of discipleship was perfectly consistent with the culture and use of the understanding, and with a judicious share in the manifold and diversified relations of life; the one thing needful was, that *purity* should inspire their wisdom. Here, as always, Christ brings into their higher unity things which elsewhere oppose and contradict each other.

(2.)

The parable of the *Unjust Steward* illustrates this combination of simplicity with *prudence.** We find the main point of comparison not, as some do, in the proper management of earthly possessions, but in the words emphasized by Christ himself: "*The children of this world are wiser in their generation than the children of light*" (v. 8). The children of the world, using more wisdom than the children of light, often succeed in carrying out their purposes against the latter; as, on the other hand, the children of light fail of ends connected with the Divine kingdom, because they lack wisdom in the choice of the means. That wisdom, therefore, which characterizes the children of the world is to be recommended to the children of light. This is the *main* thought; the proper use of earthly goods, subordinating every thing to the kingdom of God, is a minor one. Keeping this in view, the difficulties of the parable vanish; the special feature in it which forms a stumbling block to some will be found precisely adapted to this thought, and necessary to its illustration.

The example of the unjust steward is to be imitated, not in regard to

* It is to be noted that this parable, according to Luke, xvi., 1, was addressed to the *disciples*, even though we apply the word to the larger circle of disciples, and not specifically to the Apostles. We need not suppose, from v. 14, that it was directed against the avarice of the Pharisees.

the disposition that impelled him, but to his undivided attention to every thing which could serve as a means to his ends. As the children of the world aim steadily at their selfish objects, and, with ever-watchful prudence, seize upon all the means necessary to secure them, so the children of light are to keep constantly before their eyes the relations of life to the Divine kingdom, and to press every thing into their service in its behalf. It is, indeed, a difficult task to combine the singleness of aim and simplicity of heart which the Gospel requires with that shrewd sagacity which can bend all earthly things to its holy purposes. Yet if the aim to serve God's kingdom be the ruling power of one's life, and all the manifold interests of life are made subordinate thereto; if the holy *decision* be once made and never swerved from, it will bring forth, as one of its necessary fruits, this true sagacity and moral presence of mind. It is precisely this connexion of prudence with a single, steadfast aim, though a bad one, that is illustrated in the conduct of the unjust steward. A *bad* man was necessarily chosen for the example; its very object was to show how much the children of light might do for the kingdom of God, if they would, in this respect, imitate the children of the world.

(3.)

The subordinate point of the parable is the *special application* of this prudence to the use of earthly goods. We must take care, in interpreting the verses which follow, not to lose sight of the *parable* itself. As the unjust steward secures the favour of the debtors by gratuities, in order to make sure of a home for himself when his office is taken away; so the children of light, by the right use of earthly possessions, are to make for themselves friends who will receive them into everlasting mansions when they are called away from this life.

It is plain that charities to the pious are meant here, as none can "receive into everlasting habitations" unless they themselves dwell there. But it would be inconsistent with Christ's general teaching to suppose that he meant to say that pious souls in heaven would have the *power* to receive those who had done kindness to them on earth into a share of their blessedness; or that the merely outward act of almsgiving to the pious could atone for past sins and secure eternal joy. The persons addressed are presupposed as *already* "children of light;" and they are required to manifest their inward feelings in outward acts. The active love of Christians is to show itself such, in the use of earthly goods, by sharing them with fellow-Christians. "Fit yourselves, by your labours of love, to become fellow-inmates of the heavenly mansions with those whose wants you have willingly alleviated during their earthly wayfaring." The form of expression is adapted to the parable; *there* the debtors of the rich man were made friends by the unjust steward to secure a home on earth; *here* the pious poor are made friends by the Christian to secure an eternal mansion in heaven.

Christ annexes to this application of the parable certain directions for the use of property by the children of God. He designates worldly goods *μαμμωνᾶς τῆς ἀδικίας, ἄδικος μαμμωνᾶς*; because they are usually unjustly obtained, and employed in the service of the devil, who is, and will be, the ruler of this world (and thus called *κοσμοκράτωρ*) until the consummation of the kingdom of God. And this evil mammon is contrasted with the true *riches*, which cannot be possessed except by the children of light.* The wealth of this world belongs to the children of this world, who devote it to the service of Evil; it is *another man's*, and not the Christian's own; while he dwells in a world of strangers, *he* knows of higher riches, of which the worldling is totally ignorant.†

The summary, then, of precepts annexed to the parable by Christ, and illustrating its import, is as follows (v. 10–13): "Be faithful in managing your earthly property, that you may be found worthy to be intrusted with the higher riches. 'He that is faithful in the least, is faithful also in much;' the fidelity which is proved by the right use of wealth may be trusted with the riches of the kingdom. The latter will be granted in proportion to the former. 'But he that is unjust in the least, will be unjust also in much.' Who will trust you with the true riches, if you misapply the unrighteous mammon? 'And if ye have not been faithful in that which is *another's*, who shall give you that which is your own?' Who will give you that which properly belongs to your higher nature, if you mismanaged what was not your own, but only intrusted to you?"

The concluding thought is: "No servant can serve two masters at once, the servant, in the strictest sense, being wholly dependent upon the master, and, in fact, his instrument; so no man can have two mas-

* The antithesis of *ἄδικον* and *ἀληθινόν*, in v. 11, might lead us to interpret the first as "what is, in itself, not good;" but the phrase *μαμμωνᾶς τῆς ἀδικίας*, and the implied allusion to the parable, favour the sense given in the text.

† Here is illustrated the difference between the Ebionitish idea of worldly goods and the true Christian view. According to the first, Satan is Lord and Master of this world in a *physical* sense; and the possession of property, beyond the bare necessaries, is considered as sinful in itself, as sharing in a domain which ought to be left exclusively to the servants of Satan. According to the latter, earthly goods are not the *true* riches, which the Christian alone can possess, and shall possess forever, in greater and greater fulness; they belong to Satan in the same sense as the whole world belongs to him. But as the world, from a kingdom of Satan, is to become the kingdom of God, so worldly goods are to be employed by the children of light to advance the latter, with a wisdom (illustrated in the parable) not to be surpassed by the wisdom of the world. It is to be remarked that Christ, instead of presenting the principle in its abstract generality, applied it *specifically* to acts of benevolence; the disciples, at that period, had no opportunity of employing their property to further the other objects of the kingdom of God, such as have been abundantly furnished in the later course of its developement. Cf. *De Wette*, Matt., xix., 21.

ters spiritually; the one only who rules the whole life is *the* master.' No man's life can depend, at the same time, upon both God and Mammon. To find one's true good in Mammon, and to serve God as Master, these things are incompatible. The true child of God applies his earthly wealth to His service, and therein proves himself a faithful servant; regarding it not as a good *in itself*, but only in its bearing upon the kingdom of God—the highest good.

It is clear that this passage (placed out of its connexion in Matt., vi., 24) stands properly here, closely joined to the parable; and, indeed, requisite to set the idea of the parable in its proper light. The principal scope of the latter, as we have seen, is to show the connexion between *wisdom* and a *steadfast aim* of life; and the passage in question (v. 13) contains precisely the same thought; as it teaches that we cannot rightly use our earthly goods unless we make our choice decidedly between God and the world, and then, with undivided aim, refer all things to the *one* Master to whom we have consecrated our whole life.

Thus the parable illustrates the precept, "*Be wise as serpents, and harmless as doves.*" It exhibits the unjust steward as a model of serpent wisdom, which, imitated by Christians, becomes the wisdom of innocence. The concluding words of Christ, above explained (v. 13), teach that the *true* simplicity, *i. e.*, singleness of aim, generates that controlling presence of mind which is the element of wisdom. What, at a later period, was the chief source of Paul's Apostolical wisdom but this, that his heart was *not* divided between God and the world; that he had but one aim, and served but one Master?

§ 183. *Caution against imprudent Zeal in Preaching the Gospel.*

Akin to the wisdom thus recommended to the Apostles is the rule of preaching the truth given in Matt., vii., 6, *Give not that which is holy unto the dogs, neither cast ye your pearls before swine, lest they trample them under their feet, and turn again and rend you.* "Valuable as pearls are to men, they would only enrage hungry swine, who would trample them, and rush upon him that had so deceived their hunger." Under this vivid illustration, Christ enjoined his disciples to guard against hastily offering the sacred truths of the kingdom to minds carnally unfit for them, and destitute of a sense of spiritual need; the holy pearls would be valueless in the eyes of such. To meet them on their own ground, and yet offer them nothing to satisfy their carnal desires, would only rouse their evil passions, and expose valuable lives, which ought to be preserved for the kingdom of God, without doing any good. The witness for the truth must needs be zealous and courageous, but he need *not* be imprudent or indiscreet.

The Apostles, then, were cautioned against the error into which some later missionaries have fallen, of offering the Gospel, under the impulse of inconsiderate zeal, without regard to the proprieties of time and place. Still, it by no means followed that they were not to preach under circumstances in which the Word might prove a stone of offence to some, while it pricked others to the heart; the Word was destined, of necessity, to *sift* the various classes of men that should hear it. Nor was the caution neglected by Christ himself, when he refused to allow the rage of carnal and narrow-minded hearers to hinder him from uttering his truths boldly, and without regard to consequences, revealing a spiritual power that defied all opposition; or when he punished their obduracy by ceasing to condescend to their weakness and prejudice, and by offering the truth in its sharp and naked outlines, even although it excited the wrath of some, while it led others to reflection.

The apophthegm that we have just considered was in itself a judgment and a prediction. The more immediate application of such sayings depended upon the circumstances under which they were uttered; to interpret them, it is not sufficient to have their *letter* only, but also the life-giving Spirit which originally inspired them.

An ancient and wide-spread tradition ascribes to Christ the following saying: "*γίνεσθε τραπεζῖται δόκιμοι: become approved money-changers.*' This expression bears the stamp of Christ's figurative manner of speech; and the external and internal evidence is in favour of its genuineness.* If this expression be deemed akin to the parable of the *Talents*, its sense could be given thus: "*Be like acute money-changers; adding daily to the capital intrusted to you.*" But the principal figure in the parable of the talents is not the money-changer, but the person who puts money at interest with him; and, besides, the money-changers did not gain money with borrowed capital, but with their own. We must, therefore, look for an interpretation more in accordance with the business of the broker. Ecclesiastical antiquity, which perhaps first received these words of Christ in connexion with others that explained them, affords us such an interpretation. It was part of the business of the money-changer to distinguish genuine from counterfeit coin. So Christ might have given this rule, capable of manifold application in the labours of the Apostles; to imply a careful circumspection in order to distinguish the true from the apparent, the genuine from the counterfeit, the pure

* See *Fabricii, Cod. Apocryph. N. T.*, i., 330; iii., 524. We find this saying in apocryphal writings, both heretical and Catholic; and many imitations of it seem to have been made by the ecclesiastical teachers of the first century, which could not have happened at that time had it not been uttered by Christ or one of the Apostles. Paul (whose writings contained many allusions to Christ's words, and sentiments taking their hue from them) perhaps had this saying in mind in 1 Thess., v., 21, as has been supposed by *Hänsel*, with whose view of the apophthegm I agree.—(*Stud. u. Krit.*, 1836, I.)

from the alloyed; not to condemn hastily, but, on the other hand, not to trust lightly.

§ 184. *The Syro-Phœnician Woman.* (Matt., xv., 21; Mark, vii., 24.) —(1.) *Her Prayer.*—(2.) *Her Repulse.*—(3.) *Her Faith.*—(4.) *The Result.*

(1.)

Christ, having passed beyond the northern border of Galilee, reached a place where he wished to remain unknown. But the fame of his miracles had preceded his arrival. A heathen woman of the neighbourhood (a Canaanite or Phœnician), whose daughter was a demoniac, hastened to seek help from the Saviour. As he went out with the disciples, she ran and cried to him, "*Have mercy on me, O Lord! thou Son of David; my daughter is grievously vexed with a devil.*"

(2.)

"*But he answered and said, I am not sent but unto the lost sheep of the house of Israel. . . . It is not meet to take the children's bread and to cast it to dogs.*" Taking this reply *alone*, apart from the circumstances under which Christ uttered it, it appears mysterious, indeed, that he should so emphatically restrict his mission to the Jews, that he should speak of the heathen in such a tone of contempt, and repel the prayer of the woman with so much severity. But although we may not be able, from the close and abridged narrative, to obtain a clear view of the matter, we can yet remove its difficulties to a great extent by considering it in its proper historical connexion.*

We have before said that the restriction of Christ's mission to the lost sheep of the house of Israel was not inconsistent with his purpose of establishing a universal kingdom. This restriction referred to his *personal* agency, which in fact belonged to the Jewish people; not, however (as he himself said), but that he had "other sheep not belonging to this fold," which were at some time to be brought into the same fold, and under the same shepherd, with the lost sheep of the house of Israel. But in other cases, also (as we have seen), he afforded his *personal* assistance to individual heathens. We must, therefore, seek the reasons of Christ's conduct in the peculiar circumstances of the case, and of the time at which it occurred.

In the first place, it is clear that he wished, at that juncture, to remain hidden, and therefore to avoid public labours (Mark, vii., 24). In

* The attempt to remove these difficulties by the theory that Christ altered his plan at different periods cannot be made to harmonize with the attendant circumstances of this case, as related by Mark as well as Matthew; for these circumstances (the journey into North Galilee, &c.) prove that this case must be placed chronologically *after* other cases in which Christ had assisted individual heathens.

the previous cases in which he had assisted individual pagans, no further consequences were likely to follow; but his agency in *this* case was likely to draw multitudes around him, and to extend his ministry among the heathen, in opposition to his general plan. His action, therefore, was directed only to the Apostles and to the woman; the latter he wished to relieve after she had proved her faith and poured out her whole heart before him; to the former the case afforded an example of pagan faith that might shame the Jews, and teach the Apostles that the heathen would yet believe in him, and share, through their faith, in the blessings of his kingdom. It may be a question whether this was Christ's intention from the beginning, or whether the woman's fervent prayer and believing importunity overcame his first purpose to send her away. There is nothing in the latter supposition inconsistent with the character of Jesus, since, in his purely human being, he was differently determined by different circumstances.

And again, hard as the words "*one ought not to cast the children's bread to the dogs*" may sound to *us*, we must remember that it was a figurative expression, meaning nothing more than that the mercies destined for the Theocratic people could not as yet be extended to a people at that time far from the kingdom of God, and by no means excluding the expectation that this relation should be so changed as that *all* should become "children."

(3.)

The woman doubtless felt that these words, severe as they were, came from a heart overflowing with love, and she continued her prayer with trustful importunity, herself entering into the words of Christ and acknowledging their truth. "*Yes, Lord; yet the dogs eat of the crumbs which fall from their master's table.*"

Now if this total abasement before a *man* of another nation be regarded merely as an outward and human submission for the sake of a bodily blessing, it must appear abject indeed; nor could Christ have praised it and granted the favour so earnestly yet basely sought. But it was not of such a character; the pagan woman felt herself unworthy of the kingdom of God, and *therefore* was not degraded by her sense of inferiority to the Theocratic nation; she humbled herself, not before a *man*, but before one in whom (whatever conception she had of his person) *God revealed himself to her heart;* it was to a Divine power, not a human, that she gave so lowly a submission. It is precisely this sense of unworthiness and unconditional submission to God, when revealed in his omnipotence and mercy; it is precisely Faith, in this peculiarly *Christian* sense, which is made, throughout the New Testament, the condition of all manifestations of the grace of God. The act of Christ in the case illustrated his own saying, "*He that humbleth himself shall be exalted;*" he answered the woman, commending her as he would not commend the Jews, "*O woman, great is thy faith; be it unto thee even as thou wilt.*" He set up the believing woman as a pattern of *that* faith which was to become, among the pagans, the foundation of the kingdom of GOD.

Thus, again and again, under the most varied circumstances, did Christ set forth the value in which he held a spirit of humble, self-denying devotion to GOD and submission to his revelation in Christ; this spirit, so irreconcilably opposed to the pride of natural Reason which, in the ancient world, was held to be man's highest dignity, was made by Christ the essential condition of participation in his kingdom. Idle, indeed, and vain, therefore, must be all attempts to make Christianity, in this sense, a religion of reason, or to make Christian ethics a morality of reason.

The transaction affords another lesson, also. The Christian may comfort himself under the hardest trials and severest struggles—nay, even when his most ardent prayers appear to be unheard and unanswered—with the consoling belief that behind the veil of harshness the Father's love conceals itself:

[Behind the frowning Providence
He hides a smiling face.]

§ 185. *The Transfiguration of Christ.* (Luke, ix., 29–36.)

Six days* after the conversation in which Christ first unfolded to the Apostles the sufferings and the fate that awaited him, *he took Peter, James, and John up into a mountain apart, and was transfigured before them.*

The Transfiguration may be considered either (1) as an objective fact, a real communication with the world of spirits; or (2) as a subjective psychological phenomenon. The account of Luke bears indubitable marks of originality and historical truth; the attempts that have been made to resolve it into a mythical narrative are absurd But it certainly appears to favour the second view above stated rather than the first.

If we adopt the first view, and assume that the narrative is intended to relate an objective fact, it affords us a partial exhibition of the intercourse of *Christ himself* with the world of spirits. It could not have been intended merely for the Apostles to witness; for, during its

* Luke says *eight* days; Matthew *six;* involving no discrepancy, however, for it is easy to show that they employed different modes of computation. Statements of time thus agreeing in fact but differing in form, are among the surest signs of veracity in historical narratives.

progress, they were "*heavy with sleep*," and, therefore, unfit to apprehend it, or to transmit an account of it as matter of fact. We cannot, however, deny the possibility of such an occurrence, and of some unknown object for it, in the connexion of a history which is entirely out of the ordinary course of events. Once admitting the event as such, all that we should have to do would be to confess our ignorance, instead of losing ourselves in arbitrary hypotheses and speculative dreams.

But, on the other hand, by following the indications given in Luke, we may arrive at the following view of the narrative: Jesus retired in the evening with three of his dearest disciples, apart, into a mountain,* to pray in their presence. We may readily imagine that his prayer referred to the subjects on which he had spoken so largely with the disciples on the preceding days, viz., the coming developement of his kingdom, and the conflicts he was to enter into at Jerusalem in its behalf. They were deeply impressed by his prayer; his countenance beamed with radiance, and he appeared to them glorified and transfigured with celestial light. At last, worn out with fatigue, they fell asleep; and the impressions of the Saviour's prayer and of their conversation with him were reflected in a vision† thus: Beside Him, who was the end of the Law and the Prophets, appeared Moses and Elias in celestial splendour; for the glory that streamed forth from Him was reflected back upon the Law, and the Prophets foretold the fate that awaited him at Jerusalem. In the mean time they awoke, and, in a half-waking condition,‡ saw and heard what followed. Viewed in this light, the most striking feature of the event is the deep impression which Christ's words had made upon them, and the conflict between the new views thus received and their old ideas, showing itself thus while they were in a state of unconsciousness.

Still the difficulty remains, that the phenomena, if simply psychological, should have appeared to all the three Apostles precisely in the same form. It is, perhaps, not improbable, that the account came from the lips of Peter, who is the prominent figure in the narrative.§

* We do not know whether this was Mount *Hermon*, or the mountain from which Cesarea Philippi took the name *Paneas*. The old tradition, which makes Mount *Tabor* the site of the transfiguration, cannot be relied on.

† Cf. Matt., xvii., 9.

‡ Cf. Luke, ix., 33, last clause.

§ We have several times remarked that too much importance is not to be attached to the *omission* of any event by John that is recorded by the other Evangelists. Still his silence in regard to the transfiguration is remarkable, seeing that he himself was an eye-witness, and that the event itself, if an objective reality, was calculated to display the grandeur of Christ in a very high degree. Two reasons may be supposed for this: (1.) That he did not deem himself prepared, from the circumstances of the event, to give a distinct representation of it; or, (2.) That he did not view it as an objective reality, and, therefore, did not attach so much importance to it. *Dr. Schneckenburger* (Beiträgen zur Einleitung in das Neue Testament) thinks that John omitted the transfiguration because of the Gnostics and Docetics, who might have used it to support their views of the person of Christ; but to us it

The disciples did not, at first, dwell upon this phenomenon. The turn of Christ's conversations with them, and the pressure of events, withdrew their attention from it until after the resurrection, when, as the several traits of their later intercourse with Christ were brought to mind, this transfiguration was vividly recalled, and assigned to its proper connexion in the epoch which preceded and prepared the way for the sufferings of the Saviour.*

§ 186. *Elias a Forerunner of Messiah.* (Matt., xvii., 10–13.)

The relations of Elias to Christ at that time greatly occupied the minds of the disciples, as is obvious from the portions of one of their conversations with him that are preserved to us.†

As we have seen [Matt., xvi., 21], he was at this period unfolding to his disciples his approaching appearance at Jerusalem as Messiah, and his impending fate. They presented to him in connexion with this, as a difficulty in their minds, the prediction taught by the scribes, and the very one which they arrayed against the Messiahship of Jesus—that *Elias must first appear*, to introduce the Messiah among the Theocratic people. He answered that the scribes were right in saying that Elias must first come and make smooth the way for the coming of Messiah; but that they were wrong in the carnal and literal sense which they put upon the saying, as if Elias were to appear in person. Elias, he told them, was spiritually represented by John the Baptist; he "*is come already, and they knew him not, but have done unto him whatsoever they listed.‡ Likewise, also, shall the Son of Man suffer of them.*" The same selfish spirit, the same adherence to the *letter*, which hindered them from seeing Elias in John, and induced them to get rid of so troublesome a witness, would prevent them from recognizing Messiah in the Son of Man, and lead them to treat him as they had done the Baptist.

§ 187. *Christ Cures a Demoniacal Youth after the Disciples had attempted it in vain.* (Mark, ix., 14; Matt., xvii., 14; Luke, ix., 37.) —*He Reproves the unbelieving Multitude.*

On descending from the mountain with Peter, James and John, Christ found the rest of the disciples surrounded by a multitude of per

appears that this would have been, on the contrary, a reason why he *should* mention it, to guard, by a full and clear statement, against misinterpretation on that side.

* Luke, ix., 36, is most simple: *they kept it close, and told no man in those days any of those things which they had seen.* The statement in Matthew and Mark, that Christ forbade it, gives a reason for this silence, in accordance more with the view that the event was purely objective.

† We think we are justified in considering Matt., xvii., 10–13, as one of these; the οὖν with which the question commences shows that it has a connexion elsewhere.

‡ These words prove that Christ attributed John's fate to the machinations of the Pharisees.

sons, some well, and others ill disposed. A man in great distress on account of a deeply-afflicted son* had gone thither, attracted by the fame of Christ's agency in healing similar cases. The youth appears to have been subject to epileptic fits, with a state of imbecility or melancholy, in which last condition he was incapable of utterance. He frequently attempted to kill himself during these attacks, by throwing himself into the fire or into the water. The unhappy father had first met the disciples who remained at the foot of the mountain, and these last attempted to make use, in this case, of the powers of healing conveyed to them by Christ. But the result satisfied them that they were yet far from being able to act as organs for his Divine powers. They could not cure the demoniac; and some unfriendly scribes who were present took advantage of the failure, and of the excitement which it caused among the people, to *question* the disciples; probably disputing the miracles and the calling of their Master.†

In the mean time, Christ suddenly appeared amid the throng, to their great surprise.‡ Part of the multitude were full of hope that *He* would do what his disciples had failed to accomplish; others, doubtless, as anxiously hoped that his efforts would be as impotent as theirs. In this, as in other cases, the Saviour combined earnest reproof with condescending love. He reproved them because his long labours had not yet satisfied them; because they still felt no higher than corporeal wants; because their unbelief still demanded sensible miracles. "*O faithless generation! how long shall I be with you and suffer you.*"§

The demoniac was brought in; and, as usual in such cases, the Divine manifestation appears to have produced a crisis, attraction and repulsion. His convulsions came on with new power. To prepare the mind of the father, Christ listened patiently to his history of the disease, which he closed, as if oppressed by the sight of his suffering son, with the prayer, "*But if thou canst do any thing, have compassion on us and help us.*" Fervent as the prayer was, the words, "*If thou canst do any thing,*" implying a distant doubt, led Christ to reprove him gently,

* Nothing could be a stronger proof of historical veracity than the three separate but agreeing accounts of this event, all from different sources. Mark's narrative is obviously due to an eye-witness; it is marked by simplicity and naturalness, without a trace of the exaggeration which *Strauss* would see in it.

† The presence of the scribes would fix the site rather at some mountain of Galilee than at Mount Hermon or Paneas.

‡ ἐξεθαμβήθη, Mark, ix., 15, appears entirely natural; any thing but *exaggerated*, as *Strauss* will have it.

§ It by no means follows that Christ's exclamation refers to the disciples: much more probably to all that had preceded; the spirit in which his aid had been sought, and his miraculous power doubted. The word γενεά is too general for the Apostles; nor would the Lord, who generally bore with their weaknesses so benignantly, have so severely reproved them in this case. Nor would they, in that case, have put the question in ver. 28

and encourage him to believe, not by saying, "*Doubt not; I can do all things*," but by pointing out to him the defect *within himself:* "Can *I* do any thing? Know that *if thou canst believe, all things are possible to him that believeth*" (thou thyself canst do all things, if thou only believest; faith can do all).* The gentle reproof had its full effect; the father, full of feeling, cried out in tears, "*Yes, Lord, I believe* (yet I feel as yet that I do not believe sufficiently); *help thou my unbelief*." Christ then spoke in tones of confident command; and the demoniac suffered a new and intense paroxysm, which exhausted all his strength. He lay like a corpse; "*but Jesus took him by the hand and lifted him up, and he arose.*"

§ 188. *Christ tells the Disciples the Cause of their Failure.—The Power of Faith.—Prayer and Fasting.* (Matt., xvii., 20, 21.)

After this experience, so important in view of the coming independent labours of the disciples, they asked of Christ, "*Why could not we cast him out?*" and thus gave him occasion to point out to them a twofold ground in their own selves, viz.: (1) a want of perfectly confiding faith, and (2) a want of that complete devotion to God and renunciation of the world which is implied in *prayer* and *fasting*. The former presupposes the latter, and the latter reacts upon the former. "*Because of your unbelief;*† *for verily I say unto you, If ye have faith as a grain of mustard seed,*‡ *ye shall say unto this mountain, Remove hence to yonder place, and it shall remove,*§ *and nothing shall be impossible unto you.*"‖ And then he adds (probably after some intermediate sentences not reported in this brief but substantial account): "Such a power of the Evil Spirit as is in this form of demoniacal disease can only be overcome by prayer *and fasting*." That is, by that ardent

* I give a free translation of that very difficult passage, Mark, ix., 23; such as the connexion appears to me to demand. Εἰ δύνασαι, in v. 23, I think, refers to the words spoken by the man, v. 22: τό = "*that*," which had been said: πιστεῦσαι is wanting in *Cod. Vatican.*, according to Bentley's collation, and in *Cod. Ephraëm. Rescript.* (see *Tischendorf's* reprint); and I think it is a gloss. *Knatchbull* considers it as *middle*, but without ground.

† *I. e.*, want of lively confidence in the promises they had received of Divine Power, through Christ, to work miracles, and in their Divine calling and communion with God through Christ; in general, a want of religious conviction and confidence, as practically displayed in subduing all doubts and difficulties; *e. g.*, such as Paul's.

‡ The same figure as in the parables of the kingdom of God, probably intended to illustrate the growth of faith, once rooted in the heart, by the power of God that dwells in it: like the growth of the mighty tree from the diminutive seed-corn.

§ In Oriental manner, Christ takes a concrete figure from the visible creation before him, to set forth the general thought: "You will be able to remove all difficulties; apparent impossibilities will become possible."

‖ The right limitation of this (not to extend it to an indefinite generality) lies in its reference, in the context, to *men working as organs of the Spirit of God;* it excludes, therefore, all self-will, refusing to submit to the Divine order, which is, indeed, antagonistic to faith itself.

prayer* which is offered in humiliation before God, and abstraction from the world, in still collectedness of soul, undisturbed by corporeal feelings. Doubtless, by this whole statement, Christ intended to satisfy the disciples that they were not spiritually prepared fully to discharge the duties of their ministry.†

§ 189. *Return to Capernaum.—Dispute among the Disciples for Precedence.—The Child a Pattern.—Acting in the Name of Christ.* (Luke, ix., 46 ; Mark, ix., 33 ; Matt., xviii.)

We have seen that on a certain occasion‡ Christ replied to those who asked "why his disciples did not fast," &c., that "the time had not yet come." But a new epoch was now approaching; and he himself gave his disciples another rule, and taught them what they lacked to fit them, by further abstraction from the world and earnest collectedness of heart, for their high calling.

Although Christ had directly discountenanced, in his conversations after the return of the Apostles from their trial mission, the *sensuous* expectations which they entertained from his Messiahship, still the ideas on which their hopes were founded were too deeply rooted in their hearts and minds to be readily eradicated. With these was connected, partly as cause and partly as effect, the *self-seeking* which tinged their relations to the kingdom of God. This same feeling was manifest in

* The Jews and early Christians, in times of special prayer, retired from social intercourse and bodily enjoyments, restraining the bodily appetites; and the mention of *prayer and fasting* together implies this state of entire collectedness and devotion.

† There are some discrepancies in the Evangelists as to the collocation of the passages here referred to. The two verses in Matt. (xvii., 20, 21) harmonize well with each other and with the connexion. But in Mark, xi, 23, the saying of Christ in regard to *the power of faith* is given in a connexion not homogeneous to it, especially the withering of the fig-tree, which was not adapted to illustrate the *positive* efficiency of faith. In Luke, xvii., 6, a different figure is used, viz., the uprooting of a sycamore; and this passage was probably uttered in a different locality; as it is most likely that the Saviour, in view of his approaching separation from the disciples, took many occasions, and employed various figures, to encourage and strengthen their believing confidence.

A more striking difference is, that in Mark's account of Christ's reply to the question of the disciples (ix., 28, 29) the *first* sentence (the power of faith) is left out, and the *second* only (prayer and fasting) given. As this last is given by both Matthew and Mark, it is more certain that it was spoken in that connexion. But then, again, Mark, ix., 23, *contains* a statement of the power of faith, addressed, not to the disciples, but to the father of the demoniac, in so natural a connexion, too, that it would be impossible to deny the aptness of the collocation; but in *Matthew* this is entirely wanting. This last omission, and the mistaken interpretation put upon γενεὰ ἄπιστος (Matt., xvii., 17), may have given occasion for referring διὰ τὴν ἀπιστίαν (v. 20) to that phrase in v. 17, and for here transferring the passage on the power of faith to this place from some other. Yet it is also possible that Christ uttered both expressions (viz., Mark, ix., 23, and Matt., xvii., 20), and that their similarity of thought induced each writer to retain but one. In confirmation of this, Luke does not mention (xvii., 5, 6) the historical connexion in which the thought was uttered; the disciples would not have asked, "*Lord, increase our faith,*" but for an experience of their want of it; and precisely such an experience is given in the accounts of Matthew and Mark.

‡ Cf. p. 203.

their conversation on the way back to Capernaum from their northern tour; they disputed among themselves on the journey about their relative activity in the service of their Master, and who among them should hold the first place in the kingdom of GOD.*

After their arrival at Capernaum, Christ asked them the subject on which they had disputed by the way, intending that the very shame of answering his question might make them conscious how unworthy of disciples such a dispute had been. This end being answered, he did not directly reprove them further; but in a few words, made impressive by a vivid illustration, he set before them the worthlessness of their contention, and its utter antagonism to the spirit which must rule in the kingdom of GOD. Taking a little child, he placed him in their midst, and said, "Let this child, in its unassuming ingenuousness, be your model; he among you that is most child-like and unassuming, that thinks least of himself and his own worth, *he* shall be greatest (shall be of most importance to the kingdom of God)."† Then, embracing the child, he added, "Whosoever shall receive one such little child in my name, receiveth me; and whosoever receiveth me, receiveth him that sent me."‡

The truth herein expressed, though different from the other, is yet akin to it; and both rebuke the strife for precedence, the disposition to dwell upon one's own merits, and set a false value upon actions as *great* or *small*. It is not merely *what* a man does that makes his action worthy, but the spirit in which he does it. The deed in itself may be great or small; its *worth* depends upon its being done in the *name*

* This is not to be confounded with a later dispute of the same character; in the instance before us the question referred to the *present*, not to the *future*, who *is* the greatest in his personal qualities and performances? Christ's reply was directed to *this* question; not, as in the subsequent case (Luke, xxii., 24, &c.), to one concerning precedence in the Messianic kingdom. Matthew's account, therefore (xviii., i.), seems to be less original than those of Luke, ix., 46; Mark, ix., 33. The former is less homogeneous; and, besides, in it the *disciples* propose the question; in the others Christ anticipates them; which seems the more likely, as they might readily feel that their dispute was foreign to Christ's spirit, and, therefore, be ashamed to put the question. It is also easier to explain the origin of Matthew's statement from this, as the original form, than that of the latter from the former. It must always be a debatable question, so far as Luke, ix., 46, is concerned, whether the disciples only *thought* this, or expressed their thoughts to each other.

† Luke's report of the sayings of Christ upon this occasion, although more simple and homogeneous than those of Matthew and Mark, does not seem to retain the *order* of the two expressions so well. This is evident, both from the γάρ in the last clause of v. 48, and from John's question in v. 49, which was evidently occasioned by the words *immediately* before spoken by Christ, but *not* by those in the last clause referred to.

‡ In Matt., x., 42, we find another saying to the same effect as that which has been placed here in its connexion. "Even a drink of water given to the most insignificant person as a disciple of *Christ*, and in *his* name, will not lose its reward." It is the disposition to act in Christ's name which gives value to the most unimportant act. The *form* in which the disposition shall reveal itself is conditioned by circumstances which are not under the control of man; but the disposition itself, which is stamped as Christian from its reference to the name of Christ, is independently rooted in the heart

of Christ and for his sake. And this spirit is pleasing to GOD, for our actions can only be referred to HIM by means of our relation to Christ.

The principle thus announced by Christ struck at the root of the contention among the disciples. Their false emulation could have no place, if their actions, whether great or small, were alike in value, if alike done in the name of Christ; and to magnify themselves, or their claims, would have been absurd in view of such a rule of action.

§ 190. *Christ's two Sayings: "He that is not against you is for you, and, "He that is not for me is against me."* (Mark, ix., 40.)

It is hardly probable that the disciples at once understood the profound meaning of Christ's words on the occasion referred to in the preceding section; and thus it was that John (Mark, ix., 38) brought forward an instance which appeared to him inconsistent with the rule just laid down.*

It appears that the miracles of Christ, and those wrought by the Apostles by *calling upon his name,* had induced others, not belonging to the immediate circle of the disciples, to call upon the name of Jesus for the healing of demoniacs.† The disciples, displeased that one out of their circle, and unauthorized by Christ, should try in this way to make himself equal with them, had forbidden him to do so. Even here, selfish motives appear to have intruded; only those who belonged to *them* were to be allowed to make use of Christ's name. In view of what Christ now said, however, of the value of even the smallest actions, if done *in His name,* John seems to have thought within himself: "If *every thing* that is done in His name be so worthy, have we not done wrong in forbidding him who was thus working in his name?"

It is true Christ's words referred to the disposition of the heart, and a mere external calling upon his name would not necessarily involve all that he meant. And had the disciples fully understood his meaning, they would probably not have alluded to such an instance. But the instance itself may have been allied to that which has the aim of Christ's words; a man who thought so highly of Christ's name as to believe that by using it he could do such great works, even though he enjoyed no intimate relations with the Saviour, might have been on the way to higher attainments, and, by obtaining higher knowledge and a purer faith, might have reached the stand-point designated by Christ; and so his outward calling upon the name might have led the

* *Strauss* objects to *Schleiermacher's* view (which accords in substance with mine), that "it presupposes a readiness of thought in the disciples *of which they were by no means possessed.*" It is just the reverse; it seems to have been precisely the want of clear apprehension at the time which led John, without further thought upon the sense and bearing of Christ's remarks, to seize upon the words, "*In my name.*"

† As (though with another motive) in Acts, xix., 13.

way to a true acting in that name. He, therefore, reproved them; they should let this stand-point pass as a preparatory one: "*Forbid him not [for there is no man which can do a miracle in my name which can lightly speak evil of me]; for he that is not against you is for you.*" The explanation (in brackets) is given by Mark, but not by Luke; it aids the interpretation of the latter clause, but does not exhaust its meaning.

These words of Christ allow us to suppose that the man in question, perhaps, only used His name by way of conjuration, and was far from him in heart; but they imply, also, that the very fact of his giving credit to the Name for so great power might lead him to inquire who and what Christ was, and to attach himself to him. His procedure, also, might call the attention of others to Christ's power, and bring them nearer to his communion. Jesus here taught the disciples (and the lesson was a most weighty one for their coming labours) that they were not to require a perfect faith and an immediate attachment to their communion from men *at once;* that they were to recognize preparatory and intermediate stages; to drive back no one whose face was turned in the right direction; to hinder none who might wish to confess or glorify Christ among men in any way; in a word, to oppose no one who, instead of offering himself, in this sense, to them, sought the same end, and thus advanced the object of their ministry, even though out of their own communion, and not seeking to glorify Christ precisely in the same sense and by the same methods as themselves.

Comparing this saying of Christ with the other and opposite one, to which we have before referred,* viz., "*He that is not for me is against me,*" we must, in order to harmonize them, seek the precise objects which He had in view in the two cases. In the latter, an action was treated of which seemed to agree perfectly with Christ in its *results*—the expulsion of evil spirits—but yet not done in the Spirit of Christ at all, but just the opposite; apparently done *for* the kingdom of GOD, but, in fact, *against* it; outwardly like Christ's acts, but inwardly and essentially antagonistic to them. In the former there was an act, again, agreeing in result, and also in the mode, viz., by *calling upon the name of Christ;* not, it is true, entirely in the right way, but in a way preparatory to the right one, and which might lead to it, if not disturbed by an impatient zeal. In the former the outward coincidences concealed an inward and essential *opposition*, but in the latter an inward *affinity*, which might possibly be ripened into full communion.

The common feature, therefore, of these two sayings is this: Every thing depends upon the relation in which the outward act and its results stand to the spirit and the heart from which they proceed.

* Cf. p. 241.

§ 191. *The Stater in the Fish.* (Matt., xvii., 27.)

Christ's previous visit to Capernaum probably took place at the time set apart for collecting the Temple tribute of half an ounce of silver, *i. e.*, the month *Adar*, corresponding nearly to our March. It is likely that the great commotion which we have before described as occurring just before his departure had prevented him at that time from paying it. On his return, the collectors came to Peter, who was regarded as the spokesman of the little society, and asked why his Master did not pay the tribute. Christ and his disciples were known to perform all duties arising from the natural relations of life faithfully; but *this* tribute belonged to the religious constitution, and implied a relation of dependence upon the Theocracy; and, as it became constantly more evident that he claimed to be the Messiah, they perhaps doubted whether he would recognize its obligation. Peter, as we have seen, was at that time full of the idea of Messiah, which he saw realized in Jesus; and he might, therefore, naturally conclude that the latter, as Head of the Theocracy, was not subject to the tribute. But, on the other hand, he had just heard from the lips of Jesus that his kingdom was not to be an outward one, and that he should *suffer* before his dominion could be seen; and, in this view, he might be subject to the tax. With his usual promptness, he answered the question in the affirmative, without knowing where the tribute was to come from; for, perhaps because as they had just returned from a long journey, they were out of money.*

Christ decided to pay the tax, and showed Peter that the act formed part of the self-abasement to which, conscious of his own dignity, he submitted himself during his earthly life. He illustrated this by a comparison drawn from human relations. As kings do not tax their own children, so the Messiah, the Son of God and Theocratic King, for whose appearance the whole Temple discipline was but preparatory, was not bound to pay this purely ecclesiastical tax; his relations to the Theocracy were against it. Had the Jews known him for what he was, viz., the Messiah, they would not have asked him to pay it.† But since they did not, he wished to afford them no occasion, even from their own stand-point, to accuse him as a violator of the law. He places himself on a footing with them, as to the duties devolving upon

* This account suits well to the historical connexion in which it occurs, Matt., xvii., 24, but then we cannot take the month *Adar* strictly. If this last cannot be allowed, we must place the occurrence immediately after the feeding of the 5000; as the multitude then wished to proclaim Jesus as Messiah, the collectors might well doubt of his paying the tax. We cannot think, with *Wieseler*, that the tax was due to the Empire, for the whole import of the narrative turns upon its being a Temple tax, and not a political one.

† *De Wette's* remarks on the duty of obedience to magistrates, referring to Rom., xiii., 6 are not applicable here; the relation involved in this case was the Theocratic-political relation, which was to be abolished by Christ, with the whole form of that Theocracy.

subordinate members of the Theocracy. Nor did he work a miracle to procure the tribute-money, but directed Peter to make use of the means which his trade supplied. In a place where fishing was the common trade of the people, it was not likely that the first fish caught would be worth the whole sum needed; but an unusual blessing of Providence, as Christ well knew, attended the effort. The very first fish caught was to supply the means; a stater, which it had swallowed, was found within it.

By his procedure in this case, Christ taught the Apostles that they were not to claim all their rights, but to submit in all cases where regard to the needs of others required it; and, further, that they might look with confidence for the blessing of God upon the means employed by them to comply with such demands. It is worthy of note that this lesson was given to *Peter*, in whose name a course of conduct precisely opposed to that which it conveyed was often practiced in after ages.

CHAPTER XI.

CHRIST'S JOURNEY TO JERUSALEM TO ATTEND THE FEAST OF TABERNACLES.

§ 192. *His Precautions against the Persecutions of the Sanhedrim.* (John, vii.)

FOR nearly eighteen months Christ had been employed in scattering the seed of the kingdom of God in Galilee, and in training the Apostles for their calling. During all this time he had kept away from the metropolis, to which he had before been used to go at the time of the three chief feasts.

The Feast of Tabernacles occurred during the month of October; and he determined to attend it, in order to confirm the faith of such as had received Divine impressions from his former labours in Jerusalem, and to avoid the imputation, likely otherwise to be cast on him, that he feared to give public testimony to his Divine calling in presence of his enemies and the Sanhedrim. It was his rule of conduct to avoid, by prudent choice of time and place, all such dangers as were not necessarily to be met in the course of duty; he determined, therefore, to appear suddenly in the city, after the body of visitors to the feast had arrived, before the Sanhedrim could take measures to seize upon his person.*

* John, vii., 8. The mention of this circumstance by John proves his veracity as an eye-witness. A merely traditional or invented narrative would have said nothing about it, as tending to lower the estimate of Christ's divinity and supernatural power.

The minds of his own brothers were not fully made up as to his character.* When they were about to set out for the feast, they could not understand why he remained behind. They expressed their surprise that he kept his ministry so concealed. If he wrought such great works† (they told him), he should not confine himself to such a corner as Galilee, but should make his followers, gathered from different quarters to the feast at Jerusalem, witnesses of his miracles, and accredit himself as Messiah publicly, before the assembled nation. Imbued with such sentiments, and incapable of apprehending the reasons of Christ's conduct, they did not deserve his confidence, and needed to be made conscious that they did not. He, therefore, only told them that *his* relations to the world were different from theirs; that his movements were not to be judged by theirs; that his motives must be unknown to them, as *they* were engaged in no struggle with the world, and had nothing to fear at Jerusalem. He did not say, however, but that there *would* be, subsequently, a proper time for himself to go: "*My time is not yet come* to show myself publicly at Jerusalem; but *you* need not wait to choose the favourable moment, for *your time is always ready;* you have nothing to fear; *the world cannot hate you*, for it looks upon you as its own; *but me it hateth, because I testify of it that the works thereof are evil. Go ye up unto this feast; I go not yet up, because my time is not yet full come.*"

He afterward set out unnoticed, and arrived at Jerusalem about the middle of the eight-days' feast. Great anxiety for his arrival had been felt, and the most opposite opinions had been expressed concerning him. We need not be surprised to find the charge of Sabbath-breaking still fresh, though eighteen months had elapsed; for this was always the favourite starting-point of the Pharisees in their accusations against him, both in the city and through their agents in Galilee.

§ 193. *He explains the Nature of his Doctrine as Divine Revelation* (John, vii., 16–19.)

Anew the power of Christ's words over the hearts of the people displayed itself. Even those who were prepossessed against him had to wonder that one who had not been taught in the schools of the scribes could thus expound the Scriptures; yet they could not, from the force of prejudice, admit that his knowledge was derived from any higher source. Their conclusion was soon made up that nothing could be true that had *not* been learned in the schools; and that one not educated in them had no right to set up for a teacher. In view of this, Christ said publicly, in the Temple, "Wonder not that I, all uneduca

* Cf. p. 244.

† Little as John relates of Christ's labours in Galilee, he implies them in vii., 3, 4. This passage obviously alludes to a chasm filled up by the other Evangelists.

ted in your schools, appear to teach you; *my teaching is not mine, but his that sent me;* not invented by me as a man, but revealed by GOD. But for your lack of the *right will*, you might be convinced of this.* Whoever in *heart* desires to do the will of GOD, will, by means of that disposition, be able to decide whether my teaching is Divine or human. Such a one may see that no human self-will is mixed up with my labours, but that in them all I seek only to glorify HIM that sent me. But (v. 19) that ye lack the spirit essential to this, is shown by your deeds; pretending to zeal for the Mosaic law, and using that pretence to persecute one who seeks only to honour God, you care not, in reality, to keep that law."

It astonished the people to find that Jesus could testify thus openly against his opponents, and yet no hand be laid upon him; and they asked, "Can it be possible that the members of the Sanhedrim know this man to be the Messiah?" (v. 26). But they continued, still held in the prejudice and bondage of sense, "How can it be so, when we know him to be the son of the Nazarene carpenter? while the Messiah is to reveal himself suddenly in all his glory, so that all must acknowledge him" (v. 27). To expose the vanity of these expressions, Christ said, "It is true, ye *both know me, and ye know whence I am;* and yet ye know *not;* for ye know not the heavenly Father who hath sent me, and therefore ye cannot know *me*." Thus does he ever return to the principle that "only those who know GOD, and belong to him in heart (*i. e.*, who really endeavour to do his will), can be in a condition to recognize the Son of GOD in his self-manifestation, and to acknowledge that he is from heaven. Those who are estranged from GOD and slaves to sense, *think* they know him, but in fact do not."

§ 194. *The Pharisees attempt to arrest Christ.—He warns them that they should seek Him, but should not find Him.* (John, vii., 30, seq.)

The increasing influence of Christ's words and works naturally ex

* John, vii., 17. With *Schott* and *Lücke*, I deviate from the old exegesis which refers this passage to the testimony of inward experience, the *testimonium Spiritus Sancti.* Not the will of God, as *revealed by Christ*, was the aim of discourse here, but the will of God, as far as the *Pharisees* themselves might have known it; so that, "to do the will of God"="to make the glory of God the object of one's actions," as opposed to "following one's own will, and seeking one's own honour." When Christ had to do with such as did not fully believe, but were on the way to faith, he could say, "Try only to follow the drawing within you, to submit to my teaching and practice it, and all your doubts will be *practically* solved. Your hearts will feel the Divine power of my teaching, and this experience will remove the difficulties from which you cannot free yourselves." But the persons to whom he was speaking in this instance were far removed from faith; and to such he had to point out objective tests by which they might judge of the Divinity of his mission; but, as they were destitute of the dispositions requisite to apply these tests properly, he had to show them distinctly that they lacked the *will to be convinced*, the earnest of which is obedience to the will of God. He was justified in making this demand for a proper disposition *universal*, as without it all argument and proof must be in vain.

cited the fears and jealousy of the heads of the Pharisaical party; their domination was in danger from a spiritual power directly opposed to their spirit and statutes. He had so often, both in Jerusalem and Galilee, overcome their machinations by the power of truth, and frustrated their charges of heresy by his words and works, that no course was left but to withdraw him from his sphere of labour by actual force.

They sought, therefore, to lay hold of his person; but Christ, perceiving their plans, declared in words of prophetic warning, "*Yet a little while I am with you*, and then will I go back unto him that sent me. *Ye shall seek me, and shall not find me; and where I am, thither ye cannot come.*" He thus warned the Jews, that if they did not use the time that was rapidly passing, they would not be able to escape the distress that was to come upon them by their own fault. In that time of trouble they would long the more earnestly for the Deliverer and Messiah—whom they *might* have known—but in vain; they could then find no Redeemer, nor obtain the fellowship of Him who would have been raised into heaven. The Jews maliciously interpreted this dark saying to mean that he intended to go forth as a teacher of the heathen (v. 35); a point worthy of note, from the inference it allows, that their anxiety to make him a heretic was founded upon a dawning presentiment that his teaching was destined to be a universal one.

§ 195. *Christ a Spring of Living Water, and the Light of the World.* (John, vii., 38, seq.)—*The Validity of His Testimony of Himself.* (John, viii., 13, seq.)—*He foretels the subsequent Relations of the Jews to Him.* (John, viii., 21.)

It was the last chief feast of the last year of Christ's labours upon earth; and he could not let it pass without, at its conclusion, giving a special message to the multitudes who were soon to be scattered through the country, and many of whom would never see him more. Under various figures he represented himself to them as the source of true riches and unfailing contentment, and thus stimulated their longing for him.

Thus did he cry out to the congregation in the Temple (probably alluding to the ceremony in which the priests, in great pomp, brought water from the spring of Siloa to the altar), "Here is the true spring of living water; *if any man thirst, let him come unto me and drink.* Whosoever believeth on me, his inward life shall become a well-spring, whence shall flow streams of living water."* And in another figure

* These words were not uttered by Christ as a *prediction*, but as a declaration of the power of faith in developing the Divine life. But as it was not fully realized until the outpouring of the Holy Ghost, that stream of living water which flows without ceasing through the communion of believers in all ages, John justly applied them to this (v. 39), as illustrated in the progress of the Church before his eyes when he wrote.

(viii., 12) he declared that he was to be in the spiritual world what the sun is in the material. "*I am the light of the world; he that followeth me shall not walk in darkness, but shall have the light* which beams forth from life and leads to life."*

The Pharisees objected (viii., 13) that Christ s testimony was worthless, because it was given of himself. Christ, in reply, admitted that self-witness is not generally valid, but declared that in his case it was, because he testified of himself with the confidence and clearness of a consciousness founded in Divinity. "*Though I bear witness of myself, my testimony is true; for I know whence I came and whither I go*" (a higher self-consciousness, transcending, in its confidence, all doubt and self-deception; the eternal Light beaming through the human consciousness). Judging merely by outward appearance, and incapable of apprehending the Divine in him, they were deceived (v. 15). But his testimony and judgment were true, because not given by himself as a man of himself, but by him *with* the Father (v. 19). Thus there were two witnesses: his own subjective testimony, infallible because of his communion with the Father; and the objective testimony of the Father himself, given in his manifestation and ministry as a whole.

But these carnal-minded men, unsusceptible for this spiritual revela tion of the Father in the manifestation and works of his son, still asked, "Where is this witness? let us hear the Father's voice, and behold his appearance." He showed them, in turn, that the knowledge of *Him* and of the *Father* were interdependent; that they could not know him as he was, because they knew not the Father; and that they could not know the Father, because they knew not the Son in whom he revealed himself.

Again, with reference to the continued persecutions of the Sanhedrim, Christ repeated the saying, "*I go, and you will seek me;*" adding, also, the reason why they should seek in vain (v. 21), "Because ye will not believe in the Redeemer, but die in your sins, and there fore be excluded from heaven;" because (as he himself explained it, v. 23) there was an impassable gulf between those that belong to this world and Him who did not. But the prophetic words in v. 28 were not spoken with reference to these, but to others: "*When ye have lifted*

* Cf. these words, "*the light of life, the light which giveth life,*" with "*the bread of life,*" p. 266. The "light" precedes; as Christ enlightens the darkened world, and thus leads it from death unto life. He appears first to the dark soul as the enlightening teacher of truth, in order to raise it to communion with himself, and so to partake of the Divine life. The relation of "light" and "life" is not outward and indirect, but inward and direct. The light and the life are from the same Giver; sometimes the one is made more prominent, sometimes the other, according to the bearings in which he is spoken of; the life *as* light (John, i., 4), or the light *of* life.

up the Son of Man, then shall ye know that I am He, and that I do nothing of myself; but as my Father hath taught me, I speak these things." This was spoken of such as then mistook the Son of Man in his human appearance (who might have fallen into the *pardonable* sin of blasphemy against the Son of Man, Matt., xii., 32), but who, still possessing a dormant susceptibility kept down by prejudice, would be led to believe, by the invisible workings of his Divine Spirit, when they should see that work which was believed to be suppressed by his death, spreading abroad with irresistible power.

§ 196. *The Connexion between Steadfastness, Truth, and Freedom.* (John, viii., 30–32.) *Freedom and Servitude; their typical Meaning* (33–38).

The Divine superiority with which Christ silenced his opponents completed the impressions of his previous ministry in the minds of many of the people: "*As he spake these words, many believed on him.*" But he did not suffer himself to be carried away by the enthusiasm of the multitude. He says that many of them lacked true, spiritual faith, and knew that they would easily be turned aside, if he should not, as Messiah, satisfy their expectations. In order, therefore, to point out the requisites of true discipleship, and to show what they *might*, and what they *might not*, expect of him, he said (v. 31, 32), "Only by holding fast my doctrine can ye be my disciples *indeed;* and then only (when you shall have incorporated the truth with your life) will you *know the truth* (the knowledge, therefore, springing from the life), and the power of the truth, thus rightly known, shall make you partakers of true freedom."

Judas of Gamala and the Zelotists had incited the people to expect in Messiah a deliverer from the temporal yoke of the Romans. In the words above cited, Christ contrasted his own aims with such as these. Those who were inclined to look upon him as a temporal Messiah were to be taught that the *true* freedom, without which there can be no other, is inward and spiritual; and that this alone was the freedom which he had come to bestow, a liberty not to be communicated from without, but to spring up from within, through the interpenetration of His truth with the practical life. The fact that his words were perverted or misunderstood (v. 33), *even* if not by those who had attached themselves to him with some degree of susceptibility, gave him occasion to develope their import still further.

The *same persons* who were wont to sigh under the Roman yoke as a disgraceful servitude, now felt their Theocratic pride offended because Christ described them as "servants, who had to be made free," a disgrace for descendants of Abraham (v. 33). In view of this pride of the Theocratic people, and the carnal confidence which they indulged in their outward dignity, a dignity unaccompanied by proper dispositions, Jesus said, "*Whosoever committeth sin is the* servant *of sin.* The servant *abideth not in the house forever;* he may be expelled for his faults; but the *Son* of the house abideth in it ever. And the *Son* of the house may obtain liberty for the servant, and make him a free member of the household. Think not, therefore, that ye have an inalienable claim to the kingdom of God; you may, for your unfaithfulness, like disobedient servants, be excluded from it. Only when the Son of God, who guides the Theocracy in the name of the Father, shall make you free, will you be free indeed; no more as *servants* of the kingdom of God, but as free members thereof, as children."

They boasted without reason, he told them, of being Abraham's children. By attempting the life of one who was offering them the truth, and thus acting as enemies to the truth, they showed themselves children of Satan* rather than of Abraham; their disposition and actions savoured more of the Father of lies than the Father of the faithful (v. 37–44). The cause of their unbelief, therefore, was precisely this, that their disposition of heart was the reverse of Abraham's. Him, whom Abraham longed for, they sought to destroy. He employed thus the misunderstanding of the Jews to bring anew before them the idea of Messiah as Son of God in the higher sense, an idea always a stumbling-block† to those who entertained carnal conceptions of Messiah. This excited their rage anew, and drew upon him the accusation of blasphemy.‡

§ 197. *Vain Attempts of the Sanhedrim against Christ.* (John, vii., 40–53.)—*Dispute in the Sanhedrim.—First Decision against Christ.*

Christ continued his labours in Jerusalem for a time after the close of the feast. The Sanhedrim gradually assumed a more hostile attitude, and would have taken violent measures at once, had not a division ensued between the fanatical zealots who held that *any* means were justifiable, and those who, with various degrees of hostility, were more moderate in their opinions and feelings. Even during the continuance of the feast they had sought to seize his person, but part of

* Cf. p. 148. † Cf. p. 266.

‡ As interpreters have often remarked on John, viii., 57, the expression of the Jews was not inconsistent with the fact of Christ's being just *thirty* years old. "*Thou art not yet fifty, and hast thou seen Abraham,* who lived so many centuries ago?" (Christ was at the beginning of the middle period of life, ending with *fifty,* in which year the Levites were freed from the regular service of the Temple, Numb., iv., 3; viii., 25.) Nothing but wilfulness could lead *Weisse* and *Gförer* to conclude, in contradiction to all the accounts and to internal probability, that Jesus was much older than is generally supposed when he entered on his public ministry. On the tradition that Jesus was nearly fifty, which arose from a misunderstanding of these words, cf. my *Geschichte des Apostol. Zeitalters,* 3d. ed., vol. ii., p 539

the multitude were on his side; and even the officers of the Sanhedrim that were sent to take him, unable to resist the impression of his appearance and words, returned with the exclamation. "*Never man spake like this man.*"

The dominant party sought to secure the immediate condemnation of Jesus as a violator of the law and a blasphemer; but there were others who felt the power of his words and works more than they openly confessed; as, for instance, Nicodemus, who said, "*Doth our law judge any man before it hear him?*" This had to be admitted even by the rest; but, as is usual in such cases, the more moderate party incurred the suspicion of the zealots. And when the latter found that they could not succeed in condemning Christ personally, they proposed, to lessen his influence at least in some degree, that every one who acknowledged him as Messiah should be excommunicated. In this they presupposed that the Sanhedrim was the highest legislative and executive authority in religious affairs; and that no recognition but its own, of any Divine calling, and especially of the highest, the Messiahship, would be valid. The result was, that, although no decisive judgment was pronounced against the person of Christ, it was made punishable for any one to recognize him apart from the authority of the Sanhedrim. This, then, was the *first decree* pronounced against Christ. (John, ix., 22.)

198. *A Man, born Blind, healed on the Sabbath.—Christ's Conversation at the Time.—Individual Sufferings not to be judged as Punishment for Sins.—Christ the Light of the World.* (John, ix.)

If the charge of heresy brought against Christ, on account of the pretended violation of the Sabbath, produced such striking results, he gave a new stimulus to the rage, and, at the same time, to the jealousy, of the hierarchical party, by a miraculous cure performed on the Sabbath.

As the disciples were leaving the Temple with their Master, his attention was drawn, in passing, to a beggar who had been blind from his birth. Their first thought, suggested by their contracted Jewish ideas of the government of God,* was, how far the necessary connexion between sin and evil might be supposed in the case: "*Master, who did sin, this man or his parents, that he was born blind?*" An untenable theory drove them to this dilemma; even if, as it is hardly to be supposed that the *pre-existence* of souls was presupposed by the questioner, he either had no definite idea in referring to "*this man,*" or did not know certainly at the time that he was born blind. Christ, not admitting such a precise connexion between special sins and special evils, re

* Cf. p. 143, 144.

plied, at first, concisely, "*Neither hath this man sinned, nor his parents;** *but that the works of God should be made manifest in him;*" that his sufferings might seem the higher objects of God's love both to himself and others, and God's works of saving power and mercy be displayed in him. And for himself, apart from others, the cure of his physical blindness was to lead to that of his spiritual darkness; and then his experience was to become, also, the means of saving others. Passing over directly to the remark that through *himself* the works of God were revealed, Christ said, "*I must work the works of him that sent me while it is day;*† *the night cometh, when* the work of the day cannot be done.‡ *As long as I am in the world, I am the light of the world.*"§

The cure for which he thus prepared them was probably gradual (as in the case mentioned p. 270); the patient, perhaps, began to see when Christ anointed his eyes, and, after bathing in Siloam,‖ was completely healed.¶

* An apocryphal writer would have made Christ contradict this view more fully.

† The day, *the time for labour;* its fleeting hours must be improved. "I cannot let the opportunity pass without doing what I only upon earth can do. My stay here will soon end. Nothing, therefore, must hinder me from that which I (as the shining Sun) have now to work upon the earth."

‡ The *day* = the time allotted to Christ's ministry on earth; the *night*, therefore, = the approaching end of his earthly labours.

§ So long as Christ remained on earth, he must remain, according to his nature, the Sun of the world; so long, therefore, he must shed light around him, dispense bodily and spiritual blessings; no opportunity of doing this must pass. The cure of this blind man, bodily and spiritually, was part of his work as "light of the world." Not, indeed, that he has ever *ceased* to be "the light of the world;" but his personal and visible manifestation was here in question; the Sun of the world, visible upon the earth itself.

‖ Would any one have invented *this*, which tends to diminish, instead of magnifying the miracle? "But it was invented for the sake of the mystical allusion to Siloam." Were this so, a longer explanation than the sentence, "*which is, by interpretation,* 'sent'" (v. 7), would have been given. If ὃ ἑρμηνεύεται ἀπεσταλμένος is genuine, and a mystical meaning is assumed, it is needless to insist strictly upon grammatical accuracy in the translator, especially as the word שִׁילוֹחַ, *sending out*, could be applied by metonymy to one of the canals from the spring of Siloam; and the form שֶׁלַח (Neh., iii., 15) comes, in fact, near to this translation. As has been said, a *later* writer, intending to give a mystical interpretation, would have coloured it more deeply. But, on the other hand, if we do not arbitrarily assume that the operations of the Holy Ghost rudely tore asunder peculiarities that were rooted in the culture of the people and the times, we may readily imagine that John, who eagerly caught at all allusions to the object of his love, would be inclined to find a mystical and higher meaning in the sending of the blind man to wash in the pool, and that the more, because the act in itself was comparatively unimportant: and that he thus made Siloam the symbol of the heavenly ἀπόστολος, by whom the diseased man was to be healed.

¶ John's omission to mention *expressly* that the cure was gradual does not militate against our view. If it were not gradual, we should have to supply some other points omitted by the narrative, *e. g.*, that some one led the blind man to the pool, or, that he was so accustomed to the way as to need no guidance. Such omissions as this are no proof that the account was not due to an eye-witness; especially as, on the theory that the account was an *invention*, it would be impossible to account satisfactorily for the mention of the subsidiary features at all. In all the rest of the narrative—the conduct of the blind man and of the Pharisees—the stamp of eye-witness is indubitable; and the want of minute-

§ 199. *Attempts of the Sanhedrim to corrupt and alarm the restored Blind Man.—Christ's Conversation with him.—The Sight of the Blind, and the Blindness of the Seeing.*

A great sensation must have ensued among the multitude at sight of a man so well known as the blind beggar walking about completely restored. John gives a graphic description (ch. ix) of the arts employed by the Sanhedrim to deny or explain away a fact which so publicly testified to the power of Christ. Their craft was used in vain. Nothing could be extorted from the lips of the man or of his parents to further their designs. The beggar's incorruptible love of truth was shown in his indignation at their attempts to explain away his own experience and force him to a lie. Their spiritual arrogance was wounded by his firmness, and their rage soon turned against himself.

His heart was prepared by this conflict with the foes of Christ to receive from the latter a revelation of his character. This was given (v. 35–37) probably at some public place where Jesus found him; and since he was already convinced that the man who had cured him was endowed with Divine power, he could the more readily recognize him as Messiah, when announced by himself as such.

The conduct of this poor man on the one hand, and the Pharisees on the other, represented the tendencies of two opposite classes of mankind; and Christ set this opposition forth vividly thus: "*For judgment I am come into this world, that they which see not might see; and that they which see might be made blind.*" The spiritual was here figured by the corporeal; the blind man had been made to see, while the Pharisees, who would not see the fact before them, became blind with their eyes open. The same thing occurred in a spiritual sense; the beggar, spiritually blinded by involuntary ignorance, but conscious of it, humbly accepted the spiritual light that was offered him, and became a seeing man. The Pharisees, on the other hand, had knowledge enough, but would not use it; and, in their pride of knowledge, shutting out the Divine light, they became more culpably blind.

And this judgment avails for all ages. Wherever the Spirit of Christ operates among men, the blind are made to see, the seeing become blind. The work of Christ, in enlightening and blessing mankind, cannot be accomplished without this "sifting;" it flows necessarily from the opposite moral tendencies of men. The grace and the condemnation go hand in hand; the offer of the one involves the infliction of the other.

The Pharisees who stood around knew well that these words were directed against themselves, and asked him, in offended pride, "*Are*

ness in the detail of the fact itself was probably caused by the narrator's hastening from the miracle itself to that in which he was most interested, viz., its result.

we, then, blind also?" Christ had not said that they *were* blind, but that they *would* become so by their own guilt; and he replied: "*If ye were blind, ye should have no sin; but now ye say, we see; therefore your sin remaineth.*" (Ignorance would have excused them, as in the case of the sin against the Son of Man. But their boast of knowledge was a witness against themselves. Able to see, but not willing, their blindness was their guilt.)

§ 200. *Parable of the Good Shepherd.—The Parable extended.—Christ the Door.—Intimation of Mercy to the Heathen.* (John, x.)

Christ proceeded to characterize the Pharisees, with just severity, as false guides of the people; doubtless having in view at the time the conduct of the tyrannical hierarchs towards the poor blind man, and his bearing, in turn, towards them. He first describes himself, in contrast with the Pharisees, as the genuine and divinely-called leader of the people. The blind man whom he had healed was the representative of all such oppressed souls as were repelled by the selfish judges, and drawn to Christ. It may have been the case (although the supposition is not necessary) that the sight of a flock of sheep at hand suggested the parabolic* illustration that he employed.

The thief who leaps over the wall, instead of entering the fold by the door, represents those who become teachers and guides of the people of their own mere will. The Shepherd, entering in at the door, represents Christ, who offers himself, divinely called, to guide seeking souls to the kingdom of God. His voice harmonizes with the Divine drawing within them; they know it, and admit him; *he* knows them all, and all their wants. He goes before them, and leads the way to the pasture where their wants can be satisfied. But the voice of the selfish leaders is strange to them, and they flee with repugnance; knowing well that such guides have other aims than the salvation of the souls of those that hear them.

To present the thought still more strikingly, he extended the figure, adding several new traits.† The first outline of the parable simply contrasted a lawful with an unlawful entering into the fold; in the extended form of it, the door assumes a new significance. He himself is not only the good shepherd, but also the door of the fold, inasmuch as through him alone can longing souls find entrance into the kingdom of God. This very fact, that he is at once both shepherd and door, distinguishes him from all other shepherds; it is the peculiar feature of Christ's teaching, as distinct from all teachers, that he is himself the revealer, and all his revelations refer back to himself; he can point

* Cf., on the parables of John, p. 111.

† Examples of the same mode of extending a parable are to be found in the Synoptical Gospels.

out no other door to the kingdom but himself. He represents himself as the door both for the sheep and the shepherds; the latter more prominently here. In the simple outline of the parable he had contrasted himself, as shepherd, with the thieves; he now further contrasts *other* shepherds with the thieves. All who sought to gather followers and form parties in the Theocratic community, and, instead of turning men's hearts to Messiah, turned them rather to themselves, were thieves and robbers; but such could find no access to hearts really seeking salvation. But those shepherds that enter in by him as the door have nothing to fear; they can go in and out, and find pasture for the sheep. The true teacher who leads souls to Christ will not only be saved himself, but will be able to satisfy the wants of the souls intrusted to his care.

In this form of the parable Christ contrasts himself (as the shepherd who alone seeks the welfare of the sheep) not only with the thieves, but also with the *hirelings*. These two classes corresponded to two different classes of Pharisees, viz., those who sacrificed the welfare of the people to their wholly selfish aims; and those who, with better feelings, had not love enough, and therefore not courage enough, to risk every thing for the good of souls. The latter, afraid of the power of the former, gave the poor people up to the power of the Evil One (the wolf, v. 12), to scatter and divide. Standing between Christ and the Sanhedrim, this party, with all their good intentions, had neither the steadiness of purpose nor the self-sacrificing love which were needed in such a position. In contrast with such, Christ declares, "*I am the good shepherd, and know my sheep, and am known of mine* (thus betokening the inward sympathy between himself and those that belonged to him by the Divine drawing within them), *and I lay down my life for the sheep.*"

With this view of his coming self-sacrifice for the salvation of men before him, his eye glances forward to the greater developement of his work that was to follow that sacrifice, and *there* he sees "*other sheep not of this fold*"—souls ready for the kingdom among other nations, who were also to have their place before its consummation: "*Them, also, I must bring, and they shall hear my voice; and there shall be one fold and one shepherd.*"

§ 201. *Divisions among the People.—Christ's return into Galilee.*

The worldly-minded and fanatical portion of the people were incapable of understanding these words of Christ; instead of inspiration they saw nothing but extravagance. But others were irresistibly attracted; *words*, such as no other could utter, seemed to them in perfect harmony with *works*, such as no other could do. New divisions arose and the power of the Sanhedrim, of course, was upon the side of Christ's enemies.

The life of Jesus was more and more endangered every day at Jerusalem, and his ministry more and more disturbed. He, therefore, withdrew from the metropolis and returned to Capernaum, now, indeed, for the last time.*

CHAPTER XII.

CHRIST'S RETURN FROM CAPERNAUM TO JERUSALEM THROUGH SAMARIA.

§ 202. *Reasons for the Journey through Samaria.* (Luke, ix., 51, seq.)

AFTER a short abode at Capernaum Christ determined to take a final leave of that place, so long the centre of his labours. He

* From the statements of John, taken alone, we should infer that Christ did not leave the city immediately after the Feast of Tabernacles, but remained until that of the Dedication. It is true that John does not expressly *say* (x., 22) that he remained, which deviation from the ordinary rule we might expect him to have mentioned; but this omission can be explained more readily than the omission of the journey back to Galilee. Moreover, it would be easier to trace the connexion of the history by supposing the previous journey to have been the last, than by admitting the one adopted in our text (chap. xi.). The course of preparation for his death to which he subjected his disciples (as already related) would suit much better to this hypothesis, as taking place just before the *last* journey than before the next to the last.

Thus far we agree with *B. Jacobi* (Dissertation on the Chronology of the Life of Jesus, before cited). But we learn from Luke, ix., 51, that Jesus made his last journey *through Samaria;* that he travelled slowly, in order to scatter the seeds of the kingdom in the towns and villages as he passed, and to make wholesome impressions upon the people. Against John's *testimony* such an authority as this would not avail; and it may be admitted, too, that the accounts of *two* journeys are blended together in it, with other foreign matter. Cf. Luke, xiii., 22; xvii., 11, in which passages a beginning is made towards accounts of *two* journeys, though they, perhaps, refer to the same one. But it is clear, in any case, that many things recited here *must* belong to a *last* journey; for instance, xiii., 31–33. Now it cannot be for a moment supposed that this journey, so described, was the one that Christ took in order to attend the Feast of Tabernacles (John, viii., 2, seq.); for John tells us that in that case he remained behind the rest, and, avoiding all publicity, came into the city unexpectedly after the feast had gone on for some days; all utterly in conflict with Luke's account of the journey through Samaria. Nor is it internally probable that Christ would have remained in the city after the feast at a time when his labours must have suffered so many hindrances from the persecutions of the Pharisees; the last period of his stay on earth was to be more actively employed. Nor does this view of the case *contradict* John's statements; it only presupposes a blank necessary to be filled.

We have thus drawn attention to the arguments advanced on both sides; not intending, however, to preclude further inquiry of our own. Cannot John's statement, that Jesus went up to the feast "not openly, but, *as it were, in secret*" (vii., 10), be explained by supposing that he did not take the usual caravan road, nor journey with a caravan, but took an unusual route through *Samaria*, a province that held no connexion whatever with Judea? May not his late arrival at Jerusalem, in the middle of the feast, be explained on the ground that he intentionally took the longer route? Admitting this, it will be easy (as *Krabbe* and *Wieseler* allow) to reconcile John's account with Luke's.

wished to visit Jerusalem again at the Feast of the Dedication which occurred towards the end of December. Many had believed on him during his last stay in the city, and he had been compelled to leave them to the arts of the hierarchy; it was now necessary to strengthen and confirm their faith by his personal presence. He chose to make this journey by way of Samaria, rather than through Peræa, in order to scatter the seed of truth as widely as possible among the towns and villages on the road. A longer time than ordinary was, therefore, required for the journey; and he left Capernaum sooner than was absolutely necessary had he intended to go directly to Jerusalem.

§ 203. *Choice of the Seventy.* (Luke, x.)—*Import of the Number "Seventy."*

The prospect of the spread of the Gospel among all nations, after his own sufferings should have prepared its way, lay before him as he left Capernaum never to return; and he said to his disciples, in view of so vast a work, in which, as yet, there were so few labourers, "*The harvest, truly, is great, but the labourers are few; pray ye, therefore, the Lord of the harvest that he would send forth labourers into his harvest.*" He then chose a number of his followers as his special and devoted organs for proclaiming the kingdom, and sent them before to announce and explain his coming, and prepare the minds of the people, that the short time of his visits among them might be more successfully employed.

Some definite number of disciples had to be selected, and he chose (as in the selection of the *Twelve*, p. 116) a number at that time in common currency. The round number *seventy* may have had general reference either to the seventy elders, or to the seventy members of the Great Sanhedrim; or it may have had special reference to the opinion prevalent among the Jewish theologians that there were seventy languages and nations upon the face of the earth. If this last were the case, it was an instance of *formal* accommodation. Without confirming this opinion, Christ might have employed *seventy* to indicate symbolically that his organs were not to reach the Jewish people only, but all the nations of the earth.*

* The fact that Luke alone mentions the choice of the Seventy is no reason for questioning the account. We attach no importance to the narratives in regard to the Seventy current in the first centuries (as in the account (mixed up with legends) of the conversion of King Abgarus, written in Syriac, and kept in the archives at Edessa (Eus., Eccl. Hist., i., 13); and in the fifth book of the Hypotyposes of Clement of Alexandria (Eus., i., 12), which also contains evident falsehoods) as confirmatory of Luke's statement. But its perfect aptness in the historical connexion, and the entire and characteristic coherency of every thing spoken by Christ, according to Luke, with the circumstances (so superior to the collocation in Matthew), strengthen the argument in its favour. How appropriate is the language of Luke, x., 2, in view of the approaching new developement of the kingdom of God; whereas in Matthew (ix., 37, 38) the same words are connected with the account

§ 204. *Instructions to the Seventy on their Mission.* (Luke, x.) *The Wo to the Unbelieving Cities.*

The Spirit of Christ, and of the communion which he founded and inspired, demanded that his organs should not labour as isolated instruments, but in union with each other, reciprocally assisting each other; just as he promised, "*Where two or three are gathered together in my name, there am I in the midst of them.*" Therefore, in sending out his disciples in various directions before him, he sent them not singly, but two and two.

The instructions given to them were similar to those which he had previously impressed upon the Twelve;* but, as the opposition of the Pharisees had greatly increased in violence, he foretold that they would meet with many enemies: "*I send you forth as lambs among wolves.*" This may either imply that they were to go forth defenceless among the most fierce and cruel foes; or because the Pharisees, as selfish leaders who sacrificed the welfare of their flocks, were *wolves in sheep's clothing*, the disciples were contrasted with them as *lambs* in innocence of heart and gentleness. Or both thoughts together may have been intended. But unfavourable as was the field of their labour, he bade them take no uneasy care for the future, and to trust confidently that all their wants would be supplied. They were told, as the Apostles had been (ix., 3), to "*carry neither purse, nor scrip, nor shoes;*" but with the view, in addition to the trust in Providence, which the rule implied in both cases, to expedite their journey, as its immediate objects required haste: ["*Salute no man by the way.*"]

of the preaching in Galilee and the choice of the Twelve Apostles. So, in Matt., x., the continuation of Christ's discourse to the Seventy (as given in Luke, x.) is connected with the *Twelve*, with many passages that must have been addressed to the Apostles at a later and more hostile period. In Luke, the instructions to the Seventy are distinguished from those to the Twelve in this, that the former contain allusions to the difficulties in which the missionaries would be involved; but no definite references to the subsequent mission of the disciples to the heathen. The rebukes of Chorazim, Capernaum, etc., suit exactly to the time when Christ was taking his final leave of the neighbourhood which had been the centre of his labours, and so Luke assigns them; but in Matt., xi., they are given in connexion with the reply to John Baptist's messengers.

It is clear that Christ called upon others than the Twelve to join themselves closely to him; and we find that, after he left the earth, others *did* belong to the narrower circle of the disciples.* All this indicates that such a circle was formed by himself; for the *whole* number of disciples must have amounted not only to 120 (Acts, i., 15), but to 500 (1 Cor., xv., 6).

But it may be said [as it has been] that this story of the definite number *seventy* was invented at a later period. Even if this were so, it would not discredit Luke's statement, so precisely fitting to the history, of the way in which the circle was formed. But there is no reason to doubt that Christ, who was accustomed to adopt and use existing forms, should not have appropriated such a one as this in forming the second narrower circle of disciples.

* That is, indeed, an arrogant and presumptuous criticism which decides that the whole account of the mission of the Seventy is a mere imitation of that of the Twelve, simply because the two sets of instructions are not accurately distinguished from each other.

After declaring to them (v. 5–12) that the destiny of the towns into which they entered would be fixed by the reception they gave to the preaching of the kingdom of GOD, Christ pronounced a wo upon those towns of Galilee* which had been so greatly favoured by his labours, and had (the little flock of believers excepted) given them so unworthy a reception. "Had such miracles† been wrought in Tyre and Sidon, they had a long while ago repented. And thou, Capernaum, which art exalted to heaven, shalt be cast down to Hades."‡ The higher one may rise by rightly using the grace bestowed upon him, the deeper will be his fall if he neglects it. He who was the humblest of men here betokened himself as one whose ministry in a city could exalt it to heaven; and in the mouth of any other the expression would have been the height of arrogance. Vainly, indeed, do some attempt to flatten down this language of Christ's into *Oriental hyperbole;* an attempt, too, which is utterly unjustifiable in regard to *his* language, in which the figures of the East were so imbued with the sobriety of the West as to stamp them with fitness for all times and all countries.

§ 205. *Exultation of the Disciples on their Return.—The Overthrow of Satan's Kingdom.—Christ warns the Disciples against Vanity.* (Luke, x., 17–20.)

When the disciples, at a later period, returned from their mission to meet Christ, they related to him with child-like joy§ the great things they had achieved in his name: "*Even the devils are subject to us in thy name.*".

As Christ had previously designated the cure of demoniacs wrought by himself as a sign that the kingdom of GOD had come upon the earth,|| so now he considered what the disciples reported as a token of the conquering power of that kingdom, before which every evil thing must yield: "*I beheld*¶ *Satan as lightning fall from heaven;*" *i. e.,*

* Many miracles are here presupposed as wrought in Western Bethsaida and in the neighbouring and obscure village, Chorazin, which have not been transmitted to us.

† Such sayings from Christ's own lips prove that he himself was conscious of performing acts out of the ordinary course of the material world, by which even the dullest might have been awakened had they possessed proper religious susceptibilities; as, indeed, without these, the stimulus of miracles could have been but transient.

‡ The word ὑψωθεῖσα (v. 15) may be understood objectively or subjectively. In the first sense, it would imply that the town was exalted by the lot which had fallen to it; certainly not in reference to worldly wealth, although it was a prosperous place; but to the presence and the ministry of Christ which it had enjoyed. Taken subjectively, it would refer to the arrogance of the city, as preventing it from rightly appreciating the grace which had been bestowed upon it. The connexion favours the first.

§ This does not seem to me to justify *De Wette's* conclusion that Christ had not as yet conferred on them the same powers as on the Apostles. Even in possession of this power, they might have been surprised, conscious of what they were, to find such great things done by *them;* just as in other cases, a man who, while conscious of his own weakness, serves as an organ for the objectively Divine, may be surprised at what he *does,* in comparison with what he *is.*

|| Cf. p. 150.

¶ Beholding in the spirit is here undoubtedly meant; Christ designates by a symbolical

from the pinnacle of power which he had thus far held among men. Before the intuitive glance of his spirit lay open the results which were to flow from his redemptive work after his ascension into heaven; he saw, in spirit, the kingdom of God advancing in triumph over the king dom of Satan. He does not say "I see now," but "*I saw.*" He *saw* it before the disciples brought the report of their accomplished wonders. While they were doing these isolated works, he saw the *one* great work—of which theirs were only particular and individual signs —the victory over the mighty power of evil which had ruled mankind,* completely achieved. And, therefore (v. 19), he promised, in consequence of this general victory, that in their coming labours they should do still greater things. They were to trample the power of the enemy under foot; they were to walk unharmed over every obstacle that opposed the kingdom of God.

But at the same time he warned them against a tendency, dangerous to their ministry, which might possibly attach to their joy at its brilliant and extraordinary results. "*Notwithstanding, in this rejoice not, that the spirits are subject unto you.*" They were liable to *vanity*, glorying in the means, viz., the individual brilliant results of their ministry, rather than in the Divine end, the triumph of the kingdom, to which all single results were but subsidiary elements; a vanity which might deceive itself, and take the appearance for the reality. And many great and successful labourers have yielded to this temptation; their very works becoming the means of corrupting their interior life; and *this* having become impure, the impurity passes over into their works also. "*But rather rejoice that your names are written in heaven.*" They were to do wonderful works in the future; but these were not to be the source of their joy; the kingdom of God, the aim of all their labours, was to be the object of their rejoicing; and all else subordinate to it. "Your great deeds are to be as nothing in comparison to the grace given you, the pardon of your sins, and life everlasting."

§ 206. *The Kingdom of God revealed to Babes.—The Blessedness of the Disciples in beholding it.* (Luke, x., 21, 24.)

Thus piercing the future, and seeing that these simple, child-like men, who had nothing but what was given them, were to be organs of

figure what the glance of his Spirit foresaw in the progress of the future. There is no reason to suppose here a vision like that of the prophets, in which the truth was presented in a symbolical veil or covering. Nowhere in the history of Christ do we find an intuition in the form of a vision; indeed, such seem to have been precluded by the proper indwelling of God in Him, distinguishing him from all prophets to whom a *transient* Divine illumination is imparted; in Him the Divine and the Human were completely *one*, in Him was shown the calmness, clearness, and steadiness of a mind bearing within itself the *source* of Divine light; in His unbroken consciousness as God-Man, we dare not distinguish moments of light and moments of darkness.

* Cf. John, xii. 31.

the power of God to renovate humanity, that by their preaching men were to learn what human wisdom could never have discovered, he poured forth the holy joy of his heart before God in fervent thankfulness: "*I thank thee, O Father, Lord of heaven and earth,** *that thou hast hid these things from the wise and prudent, and hast revealed them unto babes*:† *even so, Father; for so it seemed good in thy sight.*‡ *All things are delivered to me of my Father*;§ *and no man knoweth who the Son is*|| (the true nature of the Son) *but the Father; and who the Father is, but the Son, and he to whom the Son will reveal him.*"¶

After he had thus poured out his soul before God, he turned to his disciples, and pronounced them *blessed*, because their eyes had beheld that which the prophets and the pious had waited and longed for **

The "seeing" and "hearing" are not to be taken, as Hugo à St. Victor long ago remarked, in an outward sense, but spiritually, with reference to the truth revealed to them, which had been veiled and, to some extent, hidden from those who occupied even the highest place in

* The Omnipotent Creator, who manifests himself as Father in condescending to the wants of men, and in his self-revealing love.

† The *hiding* from the wise and the *revealing* unto babes are closely connected together; it required child-like submission and devotion to receive the communications of the higher source, and therefore none could receive it but such as, like children, in need of higher light, yielded themselves up to the Divine illumination; and for the same reason, those whose imagined wisdom satisfied them, because they were devoid of child-like submission, could not receive the Divine communications.

‡ I think that ἐξομολογοῦμαι is not to be repeated after ναί in v. 21; the latter (like ἀμήν) is a confirmation of the preceding passage, and a reason is assigned—"*so it seemed good in thy sight*;" a higher necessity, viz., the pleasure of God, made it so. These words form the point of transition to the following verse, which contains the ground of the preceding; viz., that the Son receives all by communication from God, but none can know the Son except it be revealed to him by the Father.

§ That is, according to the connexion, all power to carry on and develope the kingdom of God victoriously, and to give eternal life to believers (John, xvii., 2). Christ had previously said that the Divine power given to him should show itself in the efficiency of his organs in spreading the kingdom of God.

|| For this mighty power was granted to him in view of his *original* relations to God.

¶ This entire passage, which in Luke connects itself so naturally and closely with the narrative, is placed by Matthew (xi., 25–27) in connexion with the woes pronounced upon the unbelieving towns of Galilee.

** The passage in v. 23, 24, forms an apt and fitting conclusion to what had gone before, both in form and substance. The κατ' ἰδίαν fits with the supposition that the disciples, on their return, found Christ surrounded by one of those groups that frequently gathered about him. The same words stand, also, in a clear connexion in Matt. (xiii., 16, 17), but not so close as Luke's. Even the *form* of the words is closely adapted to the occasion and the context. It is a question whether the words "*kings*" or "*righteous men*" (as Matt. gives it) were the original one. The exchange may have taken place because "kings" appeared foreign; or *vice versâ*, because "righteous men" appeared too indefinite. By the word "kings," then, we must understand "the pious kings;" and the instance of a David might have led Jesus to connect "kings" with "prophets." Thus the apparently insignificant disciples are contrasted with men of the highest importance in the developement of the Theocracy. There is no difficulty in supposing that Christ passed over from "prophets" to "righteous men," and then the adjective "many" (Matt., xiii., 17) would be the more applicable

the Old Dispensation. A conscious or unconscious longing for the future revelation was their highest attainment.

§ 207. *The Signs of Discipleship.* (Matt., vii., 22.)—*Requisites,* viz. *Self-Denial and Resignation* (Luke, ix., 56, 62): *Taking up the Cross.* (Luke, xiv., 25–35; Matt., x., 38; xvi., 24.)

If we were correct in our remarks upon the Sermon on the Mount, p. 237, we must assign to this period the following words of Christ (Matt., vii., 22): "*Many will say to me in that day, Lord, Lord, have we not prophesied in thy name? and in thy name have cast out devils? and in thy name done many wonderful works? And then will I profess unto them, I never knew you; depart from me, ye that work iniquity.*"* Words referring to that period in which Christ had already imparted miraculous powers to the disciples, and had to warn them against the danger of losing sight of the sole object of their works, in the splendour and notoriety of the works themselves. Christ then, with his piercing glance into the future, announces that not the doing great works in his name, but holy dispositions and aims alone, would be an infallible sign of discipleship. He, who recognized as his own such as gave a cup of cold water to the least *in his name,* repulsed, as aliens, those who pretended to do great works in his name; the disposition shown in their lives made it manifest that, although his name was upon their lips, it was not in their hearts. To such, also, might be applied his saying, "*He that is not with me is against me.*"

An attempt at a nearer definition of the relation in which such persons and their works stood to Christ may be made as follows: They were perhaps really, at first, in communion with him, and thus participated in the Divine life from which these miraculous powers went forth; but afterward—rejoicing more that they were able to cast out devils than that their names were written in the Book of Life—their very works became a snare to destroy them, and their higher life was lost in outward appearance. After the principle of life was gone, single and separate impulses may yet have remained. Isolated efforts may continue after the prime cause is destroyed; there may be life-like convulsions when life has departed forever. Compare what Paul says in 1 Cor., xiii., 1–3, about such separate good deeds when uninspired by the life of love.

It may be objected, however, that Christ betokens these as persons whom *he had never known* as his own. As such, we must believe that the new birth had never been fully realized in them; that they had

* There is internal proof that this passage was not (as some suppose) ascribed to Christ as a *post factum* prediction. Those who suppose this must conceive that the passage was invented to oppose the heretics, who boasted of miraculous powers. But in that case *false doctrine* would have been made more prominent than *bad actions;* and even the appearance of recognizing their works as real miracles would have been avoided.

been predominantly selfish from the first; that none but isolated impulses of the higher life, mere exaltations of the natural feelings or imagination, had ever found place in them. We must remember well that stimulated natural powers may do many things apparently resembling the work of Divine power, but, in fact, very different from it.

Many persons, in the places to which Christ came, were so powerfully affected by his preaching as to wish earnestly to attach themselves to him forever; but he did not receive all. Some, carried away by transient emotions, felt willing to promise more than they could perform; and he took pains to lay before such the sufferings and struggles they must undergo as his followers, the sacrifices and self-denial which devotion to him must cost.

One of these, who probably went with him a little distance from a village where he had stayed a short time,* said unto him, "*Lord, I will follow thee whithersoever thou goest.*" Christ bade him reflect well before taking such a step: "*Foxes have holes, and the birds of the air have nests, but the Son of Man hath not where to lay his head;*" expressing the privations and necessities to which all who followed him thereafter would expose themselves. Another whom he invited to follow him, as he was about departing, said, "*Suffer me first to go and bury my father.*" Under other circumstances Christ would not have hindered the indulgence of such a filial love; but he made use of this case to show, by a striking *example*, that those who sought to follow him must deny natural feelings that were otherwise entirely sacred, when the interests of the kingdom of God required it. "*Let the dead bury their dead, but go thou and preach the kingdom of God.*" (Let those who are themselves dead, who know nothing of the higher interests of the kingdom of God or the Divine life, attend to the lifeless clay. But thou, upon whom the Divine life, which conquers all death, is opened, *thou* must devote thyself wholly to propagate it by preaching the Gospel. It is for the dead to care for the dead; the living for the living.) So in answer to another, who said, "*Let me first go and bid them farewell which are at home at my house,*" Christ expressed a similar thought: "*No one having put his hand to the plough, and looking back, is fit for the kingdom of God*"† (no one can become a proper organ of the kingdom who does not give himself up to it with undivided soul, suffering no earthly cares to distract him).

At a certain point of this journey, whole hosts of people, attracted by Christ's appearance and preaching, followed after him (Luke, xiv.,

* If stress is to be laid upon Luke, ix., 56, 57, these little narratives, which fit so aptly to this part of the history, stand in a much clearer chronological and pragmatical connexion in Luke, ix., than in Matt., viii.

† Wetstein adduces, in illustration of this passage, the beautiful Pythagorean sentiment of *Simplicius*, in his Commentary on Epictetus: εἰς τὸ ἵερον ἀπεοχόμενος μὴ ἐπιστρέφου.

25). He took pains to impress upon the minds of this multitude the necessary conditions of fellowship with him; that they were not to expect the appearance of Messiah's kingdom in its glory upon the earth, and, therefore, to look for nothing but ease and enjoyment in his communion; nay, on the other hand, said he, "*If any man come to me, and hate not his father and mother, &c., yea, and his own life also, he cannot be my disciple.*" (The nearest and dearest earthly ties must not stand in the way of the kingdom of God.) "*And whosoever doth not bear his cross, and come after me, cannot be my disciple.*"* (As Christ, condemned to death upon the cross, must himself carry the instrument of his sufferings and ignominy, so his true followers must be prepared to undergo, of their own accord, all sufferings and shame.)

§ 208. *Self-Denial and Self-Sacrifice further illustrated.—Parable of the building of the Tower.—Of the Warring King.* (Luke, xiv., 28–33.)—*The Sacrificial Salt.* (Mark, ix., 49, 50.)—*The Treasure hid in the Field.—The Pearl of Great Price.* (Matt., xiii., 44–46.)

Christ then made use of various comparisons to set still more clearly before his hearers the necessity of counting the cost, of fairly contemplating the sacrifices and self-denial which his service required, before entering upon it. Those who heedlessly neglected this, and are afterward disgraced by shrinking from the sacrifices demanded of them, are compared to a man that sets about building a tower without calculating the expense, and is laughed at when his inability to finish it is manifested. Or to a king, who rashly goes to war with another of superior power. And then, again, he repeated the main thought: "*None of you, that forsaketh not all that he hath, can be my disciple. Salt is good, but if the salt have lost its savour, wherewith shall it be seasoned?*" The disciples of Christ, the salt of mankind, become lifeless—a mere appearance—without self-sacrifice; the salt becomes stale and worthless.†

Kindred to this is the passage in Mark, ix., 49, 50, which, con-

* It is involved in the very idea of following Christ, that he who does it decides to "bear his own cross." The sense of this phrase is well illustrated in *Plutarch* (de Sera Numinis Vindicta, c. ix.), who says, that "As wickedness bears its own punishment along with it, so the wicked man bears his own cross." *Καὶ τῷ μὲν σώματι τῶν κολαζομένων ἕκαστος κακούργων ἐκφέρει τὸν αὐτοῦ σταυρόν· ἡ δὲ κακία τῶν κολαστηρίων ἐφ' ἑαυτὴν ἕκαστον ἐξ αὐτῆς τεκταίνεται, δεινή τις οὖσα βίου δημιουργὸς οἰκτροῦ καὶ σὺν αἰσχύνῃ φόβους τε πολλοὺς καὶ πάθη χαλεπὰ καὶ μεταμελείας καὶ ταραχὰς ἀπαύστους ἔχοντος.* This passage shows that Christ *might* have employed the phrase without any known reference to his death; the form of the expression is, therefore, no proof that the passage was modified *after* his death upon the cross. But John tells us that Christ *did* allude to his impending death upon the cross in the use of the word ὑψοῦν (xii., 32); and this may have been, and probably was, before his mind, in connexion with his being delivered over to the heathen, when he used the phrase in John. The passage in Matthew, therefore, may be taken as affording a similar sense; and thus John and the Synoptical Gospels agree in stating that Christ intimated the *mode* of his death.

† Cf. p. 228.

sidered as an isolated saying, is quite obscure. But it probably formed part of one of Christ's exhortations to his disciples during this latter period of his stay with them. The thought which it contains appears to me to be this. The persecutions, struggles, and sufferings of the disciples were to be as salt to preserve and freshen the Divine life in them; to make them more and more fit sacrifices to be consecrated to God. But (v. 50) no external influences could thus operate unless the element of the inner life, in truth, exists; the *salt* must be there, the spirit of self-sacrifice, springing from the Divine life within, before outward trials can serve to purify the heart. The disciples were, therefore, exhorted to keep it within them; and, as an aid thereto, to strengthen each other in the Divine life by fellowship of heart. "*Have salt in yourselves, and have peace one with another.*"

The same thought, viz., that his followers must be prepared to sacrifice every thing to the kingdom of God as their highest good, was also illustrated by the parables of the *treasure hid in the field*, and *the pearl of great price.*

The single aim of the first parable is to show that whoever will obtain this treasure must give up all that he has in order to secure it, and must consider all other possessions valueless in comparison with this, his highest good. All the rest is the colouring of the picture to give impressiveness to this one thought. The same thought is presented, under another figure, in the parable of the costly pearl. It is probable, however, that these varying forms of illustration were used to describe the different ways by which men reach the kingdom of God; the accidental finder of the treasure in the field corresponding to those to whom the proclamation of the kingdom comes unsought and unexpected; but whom, nevertheless, it finds ready to receive it, and to sacrifice every thing when its revealed glory rouses the slumbering Divine consciousness within them. On the other hand, as the merchant seeks for precious pearls, and, after repeated search, finds one of surpassing beauty and value; so some, impelled by anxious longings, pursue the kingdom of God with restless earnestness, and find in it at last, to the joy of their hearts, that precious treasure which transcends all others, however valuable, in a lower sense, they may be.

§ 209. *Christ refuses to interfere in Civil Disputes.* (Luke, xii., 13–15.)—*His Decision in the Case of the Adulteress.*

It was natural that there should be some, among the number who came under the powerful influence of Christ, to seek from his authority the decision of questions foreign to his calling. In such cases he refused to interfere; *his* kingdom was to rule the *hearts* of men; not to establish outward law or equity. On a certain occasion, one* of the listening crowd asked him to decide a dispute between himself and his brother in regard to an inheritance. The Saviour repelled him, declining to fix the limits of civil property and decide in questions of civil right; so important did he consider it to avoid even the appearance of intermeddling with the affairs of human law and government. And in the light of his conduct in this case, we see that Christianity is not directly to order the relations of civil society; this *outward* Divine authority is foreign to its calling. Christ worked only in his own sphere, the sphere of men's hearts; although, indeed, by operating upon the heart, he meant to operate upon every thing else; for all human relations grow out of it. He made use of this opportunity (v. 15) to rebuke covetousness, the source of such contentions; to show the vanity of earthly wealth; and to point out the heavenly treasures as the only object worth men's striving after

The case which follows undoubtedly belongs, chronologically, to an earlier period, not precisely determinable; but we place it here because of its affinity, in a certain sense, with that just mentioned, inasmuch as it involved a question of outward law.†

At a period before the open and decided manifestation of hostility on the part of the Pharisees, while they were seeking privately to attach suspicion to Christ as the friend of publicans and sinners, they brought to him a woman taken in adultery, and asked whether she ought not to suffer the penalty of death prescribed by the Mosaic law. Had he ventured to pronounce her free, as they perhaps expected from his well-known gentleness to sinners, their object would have been gained; they might have involved him in a dispute with the law of Moses. As the question was foreign to his sphere, he at first paid no at

* I cannot agree in *Schleiermacher's* opinion that this was one of those whom Christ had asked to follow him. Had it been so, Christ would doubtless have replied to him, as he did to others, that *his* followers must be prepared to renounce all earthly possessions. It was not at all wonderful that a man who recognized in Jesus a teacher of Divine authority should ask him to arbitrate a dispute between himself and his brother, who may have also admitted Christ's authority.

† [There has been much dispute about the authenticity of the account of the adulterous woman; John, viii., 1–11.] We think, both from internal and external grounds, that it does not belong to John's Gospel (see Lücke on the passage); perhaps its insertion there was suggested by viii., 15. But in all essential features it bears the stamp of truth and originality. If invented at all, it must have been by the Marcionites; but in that case it would have been coloured more highly with opposition to the Mosaic law; nor could an invention of theirs have found such general currency in the Catholic Church. The difficulties consist more in the form than in the substance of the narrative; and even these can be readily overcome. As to the account in *Evang. ad Hebræos* (Eus., iii., 39) of a woman accused of many sins before the Saviour, we know too little about it to decide whether it was true and original, or a mere exaggeration either of the one before us in John, or of the other account of the sinful woman who anointed the feet of Jesus (p. 211); or whether it arose from a blending of the two together.

tention, but stooped and wrote upon the ground. They pressed the point, however, and he then drew the question out of the sphere of *law* into that of *morality*, which was properly his own. Looking round upon them with all his majesty of mien, he said, "*He that is without sin among you, let him first cast a stone at her.*"

It is true, that from the stand-point of *law* the moral character of the judge is of no account; it is the *law* alone that judges. But from the stand-point of *morality*, he that condemns another (*i. e.*, the *sinner*, not merely the sin) while conscious of sin himself, though of another kind, pronounces his own condemnation (Rom., ii., 1). His own conscience bears witness against him. In this case, therefore, Christ appealed to the consciences of the accusers, not only to dispose them to leniency, but also to awaken in them a common sense of sin, and need of pardon and redemption. To the woman, who was bowed down under the burden of sin, he said, "*Neither do I condemn thee;*" cautioning her, at the same time, to guard against falling again into transgression

§ 210. *Christ's Intimations of the Future.*

The discourses of Christ in the course of this journey reveal to us the topic on which his thoughts were chiefly occupied at this critical period. In the spiritual results of his preaching he saw the earnest of that *new creation* which was to follow his death. Knowing all that lay before him at Jerusalem, he went on to meet his death in conflict with the representatives of the depraved spirit of the world at Jerusalem; yet contemplating with joy the progress of his kingdom, for which this self-sacrifice was to pave the way. At the same time commenced those vehement emotions of soul which afterward, under various and painful excitements from without, grew stronger and stronger, until his final and triumphant "*It is finished!*"

§ 211. *Parables of the Mustard Seed and of the Leaven.* (Luke, xiii. 18–21.)—*Points of Agreement and Difference.—Compared with the Parable of the Ripening Grain.* (Mark, iv., 26.)

Christ recognized in the little circle that gathered around him the germ of a community which was to embrace all nations. Piercing the veil which obscured the future from ordinary eyes, he saw the spiritual life of mankind in all its relations revolutionized by the power of his word. A total change in the disciples' mode of thinking was in preparation; the truth they had received was to be freed from the many foreign elements that yet encumbered it. Thus the Divine word was to work both *extensively* and *intensively*. These forms of its operation he illustrated by the parables of the *mustard seed* and *the leaven.**

* Luke gives these parables in the connexion we have assigned to them. In Matthew they are placed along with others of a very different character, only agreeing in the one

The point in which the two parables agree is, the designating of the power with which the kingdom of GOD, where the truth has once been received, developes itself outwardly from within; the greatest results proceeding from apparently the most insignificant beginnings. The point in which they differ is, that the developement illustrated in the parable of the mustard seed is more *extensive*, in that of the leaven more *intensive;* in the former is shown the power with which the Church, so feeble in its beginning, spreads over all the earth; in the latter, the principle of Divine life in Christianity renews human nature, in all its parts and powers, after its own image, to become its own organ; thus illustrating the growth of religion not only in the race, but also in individual men.

Here we notice, also, a parable* preserved to us by Mark alone (iv., 26). "*So is the kingdom of God, as if a man should cast seed into the ground; and should sleep, and rise night and day, and the seed should spring and grow up, he knoweth not how. For the earth bringeth forth fruit of herself; first the blade, then the ear, after that the full corn in the ear. But when the grain is ripe, immediately he putteth in the sickle, because the harvest is come.*" Christ obviously intended by this parable to impress upon the disciples that *their* duty was to preach the word [not to make it fruitful]; that where the truth was once implanted in the heart, its growth was independent of human agency; unfolding itself by its own inherent Divine power, it would gradually accomplish the transformation of human nature into that perfection for which GOD designed it [the *full corn* in the ear]. The preachers of truth are instruments of a power whose effects they cannot measure. If they only preach the word, and do nothing further to it, it will by its own efficacy produce in men a new creation, which they must behold with amazement (v. 27). No words could have more pointedly opposed the prevalent carnal notions of the Jews in regard to the nature of Messiah's kingdom, or have more effectually rebuked the tendency to ascribe too much to human agencies and too little to the substantive power of the word itself.

§ 212. *The Fire to be Kindled.—The Baptism of Sufferings.—Christianity not Peace, but a Sword.* (Luke, xii., 49–53.)

"*I am come to send fire upon the earth; and what will I* (more), *if*

point of general bearing upon the kingdom of God. On the arrangement of the parables, cf. p. 108.

* This parable bears the undeniable stamp of originality both in its matter and form; so that we cannot consider it as a variation of one of the other parables of the growing seed. It is worthy of note that, just as in the different narratives of the same discourse given in the first three Gospels, one Evangelist preserves one portion and another another, so in regard to these parables illustrative of the *intensive* operation of the kingdom of God, Mark alone has preserved the one of the *ripening corn*, omitting the *leaven*; while Matthew and Luke give the latter, omitting the former.

it be already kindled?" As he had compared the pervading and renewing power of the word of truth to the leaven, so here, as that word sends forth a holy flame which is to seize upon human nature and burn out all its dross and impurity—inextinguishable until it has enveloped all mankind—he compares it to a fire kindled by himself, whose unquenchable flames he already sees bursting forth. "What will I more?" says he; "the object of my ministry on earth is so far accomplished."

But after speaking thus of what had been already done, he passed on to what remained for the fulfilment of his work, viz., the sufferings that were awaiting him. These he betokens by a baptism which he must undergo; partly, perhaps, in view of the multitude of afflictions that were to overwhelm him,* and partly in view of baptism as a religious symbol, and of the baptism of *suffering* as his last and perfect consecration as Messiah and Redeemer; just as John's baptism was the first and preparatory one. "*I have yet a baptism* [of suffering] *to be baptized with, and how sorely am I pained until it be accomplished.*"†

In this saying, also, Christ contradicted the prevailing idea that the Messiah was to work an outward revolution. The preached word itself was the mighty flame which was to produce such wonderful effects among mankind. He was not to end his labours by coming forward to subdue his foes and glorify his reign by miraculous power; *his* victory consisted in his being overcome by suffering and death. And he warned his disciples, in addition (v. 51, 52), not to imagine that he would leave them to enjoy outward peace; far from it; the truth of God was to be a separating power, to cause the sharpest strifes in nations and in families. The dearest natural ties were to be sundered by his true disciples (v. 53), for the sake of the kingdom of God.‡ The higher unity of Christianity was to shape itself out of the midst of discords and contradictions. So clearly had Christ at that time before

* To "immerse himself in sufferings."

† The common interpretation of these two verses (which is certainly a possible one) considers the two members as co-ordinate—τί θέλω as corresponding to πῶς συνέχομαι; and εἰ ἤδη ἀνήφθη to ἕως οὗ τελεσθῇ: "I am come to send a fire on the earth, and how do I wish it were already kindled! but I have still the baptism of suffering to undergo, and how am I pained until it be fulfilled." This places the whole in the future. And in a certain sense, indeed, Christ *might* have said that the fire which he came to light among men was not as yet kindled; for the great crisis which Christianity was to produce in humanity had not as yet come. In this sense of the passage, it expresses Christ's longing for this crisis; for the accomplishment of his work as Saviour by the consecration of his sufferings. But we think, in view of the parables of the mustard seed, the leaven, and the ripening corn, that he alluded in the first clause to what *had* been done; the fire burned already, though but glimmering in secret, in the hearts of those that received his preaching as the word of eternal life. The words τί θέλω are thus interpreted more naturally; though, as we have said, the other rendering is not impossible (Matt., vii., 14, cannot decide the question, as the reading of that passage is doubtful). The δέ in v. 50 is adversative, according to our view, which, by the way, was adopted (among the ancients) by *Euthymius Zigabenus* The word συνέχομαι, thus apprehended, was Christ's first expression of his struggles of soul in view of the approach of death.

‡ Cf. Matt., x., 34 seq.

his eyes the effects subsequently produced every where by Christianity in the life of nations and of families.

§ 213. *The Kingdom of God cometh not with Observation.* (Luke, xvii., 20.)

When the Pharisees demanded of him when the kingdom of God should appear, he assured them, "*The kingdom of God cometh not with outward show*" (cannot be outwardly seen by human eyes);* "*neither shall they say, Lo here! or, Lo there! for, behold, the kingdom of God is among you.*"†

§ 214. *The personal Return of Christ to the Earth, and the Day of Judgment.* (Luke, xvii., 22–37.)

Having thus pointed out that the kingdom of God was manifested in his own appearance, Christ turned directly to the disciples, and told them (v. 22) that the time would come when they should look back longingly upon the days of their personal intercourse with him, and wish, though in vain, to have him even for one day in their midst. But (v. 23, 24) as this longing might lay them open to deception (as, in fact, at a later period, their anxious yearnings did lead them to expect his personal return too soon), he warned them against this danger. "Do not suffer yourselves to be deceived by false reports of my return; when it comes, it will be as the lightning that flashes suddenly from one end of the sky to another, dazzling all men's eyes; none need point it out to others; none can fail to see it, or deny its approach."‡

To obviate all carnal expectations, he then told them (v. 25) that "*He must first suffer many things, and be rejected of this generation;*"

* The antithesis is, that it reveals itself invisibly, so as to be seen only by the eye of faith.

† The words ἐντὸς ὑμῶν may, indeed, mean "within you," as they are commonly interpreted; but this would not suit the persons addressed, for they were as yet strangers to the kingdom of God, the foundation of faith not having been laid in their hearts. The passage, thus understood, would have been applicable only to believers. Christ would not have expressed himself in a way so liable to misconstruction and perversion on the part of the Pharisees. Had he meant to tell them that the kingdom of God *must* be prepared within their hearts, he would have warned them, instead of looking for its outward appearance, to strive to fit themselves for it by laying the only basis of which it admitted, in the dispositions of their hearts. Every thing is clear and natural if we take the words in the sense that we have assigned to them: "The kingdom of God is in your midst, if you will only recognize it. You must not seek at a distance what is already near; the kingdom of God *has* come in my ministry; and all that believe on me belong to it." This agrees also with his usual mode of treating the Pharisees; he always pointed out to them the true meaning of his appearance. Cf. Matt., xii., 28; and p. 241, seq.

‡ Christ here declares that his actual coming would not follow the analogy of earthly manifestations; and this ought to have been enough to hinder believing dogmatists from seeking to define its character too accurately, and from adhering too closely to the letter of some of the expressions of the Apostles, who could themselves as yet have had no adequate intuition of its precise nature.

and that, when the glorified Son of Man should appear to judge a corrupt world (v. 26–32), in that day of trial and sifting that was to precede the consummation of the kingdom, he would take men unawares, and surprise sinners in their lusts. He presented the whole in one view before them, without distinguishing the separate moments.* His object was to guard them against both premature expectations and arbitrary calculations upon the character of the final decision; to impress them with the importance of being *always* prepared, both in heart and in life, by that self-denial and renunciation of the world (v. 33) which he always made the necessary condition of entering into his kingdom. He then pointed out (v. 34–36) the fanning process by which the distinctive characters of men in the same relations of life would be revealed; "one shall be taken (saved and received into the kingdom) and another left" (to the judgment of GOD; not removed from it). As this last expression (though intelligible enough from the connexion) was somewhat obscure, the disciples asked him, "Left? where, Lord?" He replied, "*Wheresoever the carcase is, thither will the eagles be gathered together*"† (condemnation will fall upon those that have deserved it).

§ 215. *Exhortation to Watch for Christ's Coming* (Luke, xii., 36–48): *to Confidence in the Divine Justice.—The importunate Widow.* (Luke, xviii., 1.)

On another occasion, when surrounded by a larger circle of disciples, Christ exhorted the faithful to watch for the time when he would return from his glory in heaven and demand an account of their stewardship. How earnestly he sought to guard them against all attempts to determine the precise *time* of his coming, is manifest from his declaring that it was just as uncertain as the moment when a thief would break into the house at night. It might be deferred, he told them, until the night was far spent—even to the third watch.‡ Very naturally Peter (conscious of his position and that of the other Apostles) here interrupted Jesus with the question, whether the parable was spoken in reference to the narrower circle of disciples in particular, or to all that were present. The reply of Christ (v. 47, 48) was, in effect, that the greater one's knowledge, the greater his guilt, if that knowledge be not improved. On this principle the Apostles could decide for themselves the relation in which they stood to others.

Christ exhorted his followers, in all their struggles with the sins of mankind, to trust in the justice of their heavenly Father, who would

* See below, where we speak of Christ's last discourses.

† Luke, xvii., 37, gives the natural connexion of these words; in Matt., xxiv., 28, they are placed with many other similar passages referring to this last crisis.

‡ It is clear that Paul had these words of Christ in view in 1 Thess., v., 1.

judge between them and a persecuting world (Luke, xviii., 1, seq.); and to seek support and encouragement in prayer. If a judge to whom nothing is sacred does justice to the persevering widow, simply to get rid of her importunity, how could God leave unheard the continued prayers of his chosen ones invoking his justice? Though His forbearance may seem like delay, his justice will not fail; "*He will avenge them speedily.*"* The decision of the Divine justice between the degenerate Theocratic nation and the new and genuine congregation of God was, indeed, to prepare its course more and more rapidly.

To long for a revelation of Divine justice before all the world, and for the time when He shall judge between the good and the bad, is not at all inconsistent with prayer for the salvation of the enemies of his kingdom, as enjoined both by Christ's teaching and example. The combination of the two is a thoroughly Christian one.

The Saviour finally put the question whether, under the delays of Divine justice, all that believed on him would hold fast their integrity; whether the Son of Man would find faith remaining in them all when he should reveal himself to his Church a second time.†

§ 216. *Call to entire Devotion.—The Strait Gate and the Narrow Way.—Heathen admitted to the Kingdom of Heaven.* (Luke, xiii., 24–28.)

The hosts that gathered about the Saviour at this period were exhorted to make good use of the short time remaining to them to repent and believe, in order to escape the Divine judgments that were so soon to break upon the Jewish people. Such as were not hostile, and even rejoiced in his society, were told not to rest upon his personal presence (v. 26), or upon their superficial interest in him. All this would do no good (he told them) unless his word were truly received and applied; unless they sought earnestly, by self-denial and self-sacrifice, to enter the kingdom to which no road leads but this narrow

* We cannot see a clear correspondence between Luke, xviii., 1, and what follows. The whole passage exhorts to confidence in God's justice, no matter what wrong we may see done; not to praying *always*; for constant prayer has another aim and object. It is presupposed that those who are addressed pray, like children, to their heavenly Father; but they are exhorted not to waver, if the answer to their prayers be delayed.

† Luke, xviii., 8. This was probably the sense of the words in this connexion; we must remember the various applications of which the phrase "the coming of the Son of Man" admits, and in the intentional indefiniteness in which it was left. It may be applied either to his spiritual or his personal self-manifestation in the progress of human affairs and of the Church. At all events, we find no ground to suppose (as some do) that the passage was modified at a later period, when men were running to and fro in perplexity of opinion about the second advent of Christ. The prophetic description of the last days given by Paul presupposes that intimations of the same had been thrown out by Jesus. It is more likely that the words were transferred from some other connexion in which Christ really spoke of his second advent, than that they were thus modified at an after period.

and toilsome way.* "*Many will seek to enter in, and shall not be able.*" Not those who seek aright; but those who seek, without the heart or the will, to fulfil the essential condition of entire self-denial.

Thus the one truth proclaimed by Christ presents opposite aspects under opposite circumstances. To oppressed and weary souls, groaning under the heavy burdens imposed by the Pharisees, he describes his yoke as mild and easy—easy to those that love—in comparison with the yoke of the law;† while to those who are yet in bondage to the world of sense, and expect to find his service easy, he represents it as painful and laborious. Every thing depends upon the heart and the motives; what is hard to one is easy to another

In further contrast with the disposition to look merely at outward relations, he announced prophetically (v. 28), that while many who gloried in their personal intercourse with him might be excluded from the kingdom for want of fellowship of *spirit* with him, many, on the other hand, from all quarters of the world, should be called to enter in

§ 217. *The Signs of the Times.* (Luke, xii., 54.)

Others, again, were referred by Christ to the *signs of the times* to learn the import of his appearance, and what awaited them if they neglected it. As they could know from a cloud in the west that a storm was approaching, and from the blowing of the south wind that there would be heat; so (he told them), if they would observe the signs of history as carefully as those of nature, they could discern the approaching judgments of God from the phenomena of the times. But this was precisely their guilt (v. 56), that in their heedless folly they gave no thought to these indications of the evil that was nigh. He called them *hypocrites*, either because they affected to plead ignorance while the means of knowledge were within their reach, and lacked the disposition to see, not the ability; or because, while the *present* was serious, and the *future* threatening, they were utterly unconscious of the value of intercourse with him from their folly in neglecting the signs of the times, and now sought him under the impulse of a merely transient excitement.‡

* Cf. p. 236. † Cf. p. 202.

‡ Cf. Matt., xvi., 1. In a very similar discourse the Pharisees demanded a sign from heaven to accredit his calling; he told them severely, that if they would only consider the sign of his *whole manifestation*, in connexion with the signs given by God in the events *of the times*, they would make no such demand. They could foretel the weather from the clouds and sky; but would not see in the events around them the signs of the coming crisis, the approach of the kingdom and judgment of God. 'This fallen generation seeks a sign from heaven, but no sign shall be given to it but the sign of the Prophet Jonah; the whole appearance of Christ, which announces to them, as Jonah did to the Ninevites, the Divine judgments over their corrupt city, calling them to repent.' His manifestation was above all other signs of the times, and they might discern what was coming from it. He

"*Yea, and why even of yourselves judge ye not what is right! When thou goest with thine adversary,*" &c. (v. 58). (Why must another point out to them what they ought to know themselves, viz., that they should agree with the Messiah while he was yet with them on earth; since he would otherwise become their accuser before God,† and make it impossible to escape the penalty they so justly deserved‡—an allusion to the terrible lot which the Jewish people procured for themselves.)

§ 218. *The contracted Jewish Theodicy Rejected.* (Luke, xiii., 1–5.)

Certain sad events of the times were employed by Christ as types and warnings of the future. It was reported to him that Pilate had caused several Galileans to be slain while offering sacrifices in the Temple. The details of the case are unknown to us; whether it was carelessly reported by persons who did not know its connexion with the whole sad and terrible course of events into which the guilt of the nation was hurrying it; or whether they considered, according to the contracted notions of the Jews in regard to the avenging justice of God, that these Galileans deserved this wretched fate.§ In answering them, Christ declared that guilt was common to the whole people, and that unless they became convinced of it and repented, they might all expect destruction. A tower, also, had fallen upon several persons in Jerusalem and killed them; but this, he told them, did not prove any marked guilt on the part of the unfortunate sufferers, but was rather a sign of the universal wretchedness which the guilt of the whole people was to bring upon them.

§ 219. *The Parable of Dives and Lazarus.* (Luke, xvi., 19–31.)

The worldly spirit, suppressing all sense of higher interests, was the chief cause of the unbelief or inattention of the eye-witnesses of Christ's

calls them *hypocrites* because, for want of a right spirit, they *would* not see the signs before their eyes; which very fact was the cause of their seeking a sign from heaven. This is very similar to the discourse in Luke, and Christ might very well have uttered both in separate but similar connexions. The connexion is entirely apt in both Evangelists, though not so obvious in Luke. To be sure, the one in Matthew follows immediately after the unhistorical *second* feeding of 4000, but the question in xvi., 1, afforded a very suitable occasion for it; whether the occasion was the same as that mentioned on p. 245, or a different one. It is very possible that the question and answer occurred twice.

* It is true that v. 57 will *admit* of *Schleiermacher's* interpretation, viz., "That which they might know of themselves from within in contrast to the signs of the times without." But does not what follows presuppose that they had already learned from the signs of the times the true import of Christ's appearance, and *therefore* could easily decide for them selves what line of conduct to pursue in order to escape the impending judgments of God.

† In so far, namely, that their guilt lay in their conduct towards him.

‡ The parabolic comparison in its complete form is given in Luke, xii., 58, 59, and in its proper connexion; but not in Matt., v., 25, 26. Cf. p. 233. It is obvious that the passage has no reference, as has been erroneously supposed, to the state of man after death

§ See p. 298

labours. In the parable of *Dives and Lazarus* Christ showed that no miracles or revelations could lead a thoroughly worldly mind to repentance and faith; that change of *nature* was indispensably necessary. Impressions made upon such minds from without could be but transient and superficial. The disposition with which a given grace is used is the one important element; and their bearing towards Christ's revelations ought to correspond to the regard which they professed to entertain for those of the Old Testament.

The prominent thought in the parable is this: "He that could not be awakened to repentance by Moses and the prophets could not be by the reappearance of the dead."* The subordinate point is the contrast between the rich man and Lazarus; the former, representing those who seek their highest good in the pleasures of the world, and are thereby excluded from the kingdom of God, forming the principal figure. Lazarus serves as a foil to the worldly rich man; but it must yet be remembered that the kingdom found the hearts of rich men far less accessible than those of the humbly poor like Lazarus; for the very reason that their feelings and dispositions were precisely those of the Dives of the parable.†

* There is no allusion in Luke, xvi., 31, to Christ's resurrection; a proof that it has been transmitted pure, especially as such a bearing could easily have been given to it, as was done in Matthew on the "Sign of the Prophet Jonah." *De Wette* has remarked this. Still the passage contains a reason for Christ's non-appearance after his resurrection to those who could not be brought to believe on him during the period of his public ministry on earth.

† The assertion has been made (especially by *Strauss*) that this parable does not treat at all of the dispositions of the heart, and of their consequences in another world, but only of the opposite conditions of human life, poverty and wealth; and of the removal of such inequalities in the next life. It is pretended that the parable is founded on the Ebionitish doctrine that wealth is intrinsically sinful, and poverty intrinsically meritorious; and, accordingly, that the conditions of men in the future life will be inversely as their conditions here. In support of this view, it is remarked that the parable says nothing of the spirit in which Lazarus bore his sufferings; that it does not ascribe a sinful life to the rich man; and that the rebuke of the latter says, not that he deserved to suffer for his sins, but that it was now his *turn* to suffer, because he had enjoyed his good things in this life. But (1.) Is not the description of Lazarus, sick and starving, waiting at the rich man's door for a morsel from his table, and receiving from dogs the tendance which man refused—is not this the strongest possible indictment of Dives's selfishness and want of love? Misery lay at his door; but instead of sympathizing with it, he sated himself with sensual enjoyments (2.) The sentence, "*Thou in thy lifetime hadst thy good things, and now . . thou art tormented,*" implies the *cause* of his torment; he had sought his highest good in earthly things and stifled all the higher wants of his soul; and *now*, when torn from his illusions, the sense of want, the thirst for what alone could refresh his spirit, arose of necessity more powerfully within him. The figures, as figures, are not accidental; they contain the truth in a symbolical form, although we must not look for it in all the subordinate details of the picture; and although it is altogether foreign to the scope of the parable to give a clue to the *nature* of the future life. (3.) The very expression of a desire on the part of Dives to send Lazarus to warn his brothers by describing his sufferings to them, implies that he drew those sufferings upon himself, and might have escaped them by a change of heart and life. *Moses and the prophets* would not have taught them to throw away riches as sinful in themselves the expression could only apply to the rich man's pursuit of pleasure, and want of love for his neighbour. (4.) It is true, nothing is said of Lazarus's state of heart; but then he is

§ 220. *Persecutions of Herod Antipas.* (Luke, xiii., 31.)

Before Christ had passed the border of Galilee, certain Pharisees came and advised him, with pretended anxiety for his safety, to leave that region as quickly as possible, because the king, Herod Antipas, had resolved to slay him. It is a question whether this were really the case, or whether it was a mere invention of the Pharisees to rid themselves of Christ's troublesome presence. The latter would have been perfectly in keeping with their character. Herod's previous conduct certainly afforded no substantial ground for suspicion; at first he seems to have been actuated by mere curiosity to see a man of whose deeds so much was said, and to witness one of his miracles (Luke, ix., 9); and at a later period, he was rejoiced at finding an opportunity of the kind (Luke, xxiii., 8). But, on the other hand, had the Pharisees invented the story, Jesus would have levelled his reproof at them, and not against Herod. It would not have been in harmony with his character to rebuke them over Herod's shoulders by calling him a crafty "fox," when the epithet was intended for themselves, instead of telling them directly that he knew their cunning aim to drive him out of the country. Nor is it to be supposed that the feelings and dispositions of a man like Herod Antipas would not fluctuate under different influences. The protracted travels of Christ in Galilee, and the striking effects of his labours, might very naturally excite the fears and suspicions of Herod, especially in view of the relation in which Christ stood to John the Baptist. Even if he did not really intend to kill him, he may have circulated such a report, and thus sought to gain his end by getting him out of Galilee. This would have been characteristic of the "fox," as Jesus styled him.

But since Herod's relations with the Pharisees were not the most friendly, and since he must have known their hostility to Jesus, it is not likely that they were *his* instruments in approaching the Saviour. They probably acted from motives of their own; whether they belonged to the less hostile party, and gave him the warning in good faith, or whether, without inventing the report, they used it to get rid of one who so troubled them by his reproofs, and threatened to injure their authority with the people so seriously.

§ 221. *Christ's Words of his Death.*

Christ answered the Pharisees that there was no occasion for such

only a foil to the rich man, not the chief figure. Moreover, the contrast that is drawn between him and Dives, and the relation in which he is made to stand to Abraham, indicate that he was intended to represent a pious man, suffering during his life on earth, and bearing his afflictions with religious resignation. Perhaps, in the original form of the parable, several points were more prominently brought out than they are in the account of it which has been transmitted to us.

craft and stratagem; he should stay in Galilee a few days, but would not leave it sooner; he had nothing to fear during the time fixed by God for his labours there; at *Jerusalem* was his career to terminate, and thither he should go to meet his fate. "*Go tell that fox, behold, I cast out devils, and I do cures to-day and to-morrow* (*i. e.*, but a short time), *and the third day* (shortly) *I shall be perfected* (find the end of my labours). *Nevertheless, I must go on with my labours* to-day and to-morrow;† and the day following I go away, for it cannot be that a prophet perish out of Jerusalem.*"‡

The extent of this last declaration may appear strange, as John the Baptist, whom Christ called the greatest of prophets, *did* perish out of Jerusalem. But obviously he did not mean to express a general and inevitable law, but only to characterize strikingly the persecuting spirit of the hierarchical party in the metropolis, to which the witnesses of the truth must always fall victims. And although Jerusalem itself was not the seat of John's labours, still the city—*i. e.*, the ruling party there—was the cause of his death.§

§ 221. *Journey continued through Samaria.* (Luke, xvii., 11, seq.)—*Inhospitality of certain Samaritans.—Displeasure of the Disciples.* (Luke, ix., 54.)—*Ingratitude of Nine Jewish Lepers that were Healed.—Gratitude of the Samaritan Leper.* (Luke, xvii., 15, 16.)

Christ determined, in this his last journey, to pass through Samaria,‖ as he had done on his first return from the Feast of Passover. The seventy disciples prepared his way among the Samaritans. A few of them met with a bad reception at a certain place; the people refused

* To give a complete sense to v. 33, we must (with the *Peschito*) insert ἐργάζεσθαι, or some like word, after αὔριον.

† This is by no means a mere repetition; the preceding verse says what *is* done; this, what *must* be done: δεῖ με—implying a ruling Providence. "Do not think that any human power can shorten my ministry; it is the Divine will that I work here a short time, and then go to end my earthly career at Jerusalem."

‡ The verses following (34, 35) are found, also, in Matt., xxiii., 37–39. The question is, to which place do they *originally* belong? Both the place and time given by Matthew appear entirely suitable, and the connexion between verses 34, 35 (Luke), appears to prove that the words were spoken *at* Jerusalem. It may be said that ὁ οἶκος ὑμῶν does not necessarily designate the Temple; and hence that Jesus might have used the words when leaving *Galilee*; but, in fact, he was *not* leaving that country, but said expressly that he would remain a little time longer. On the whole, therefore, we adopt the connexion in Matthew as the original one. The affinity between verses 33 and 34 in Luke may have led to the insertion of the passage in this place.

§ Cf. p. 179.

‖ As all that is found in this part of Luke's Gospel does not refer to *one* journey, it is possible that Luke, ix., 52, belongs to a separate one. We place it in this later period from the "*messengers*" (v. 52), which we take to allude to the Seventy, and from the confidence of the Apostles in the efficacy of their prayer (v. 54), which implies that they were at that time organs of miraculous power. The mention in verse 52 of the sending out of messengers, without express allusion to the Seventy, taken in connexion with the fact that this is a fragmentary account, separate from the narrative of the mission of the Seventy, serves to confirm the veracity of the latter.

to entertain them and their Master because they were going to the Feast *at Jerusalem*. James and John, the sons of Zebedee, with a zeal not yet sufficiently tempered by love—probably relying on the miraculous powers intrusted to them by Christ—said to him, "*Lord, wilt thou that we command fire from heaven and consume them, even as Elias did?*" But he rebuked them with the question, "Know ye not with what temper of mind* ye ought, as representatives of my spirit, to be actuated?" And they went to another village.

In the case just mentioned the *Samaritans* were in fault, and their conduct tended to strengthen the Jewish prejudice of the disciples against them.† But another soon occurred in which Samaritan *gratitude* was made use of by the Saviour to counteract that prejudice.‡

On the outskirts of a village ten lepers met him, nine of whom were Jews, and the tenth a Samaritan. Shut out in common from the fellowship of men, they forgot their national hatred in their sufferings, and banded together. Not daring, as lepers, to approach the Saviour, they stood afar off and called for help. They were healed, but not immediately; Christ telling them to show themselves to the priests for inspection. Of all the ten, only the Samaritan came back to thank Christ, and in him God, for the grace of healing.§

The Saviour drew the attention of the disciples to the susceptible mind of the thankful Samaritan, in contrast with the dulness of heart

* Namely, not to call judgments down upon the enemies of the kingdom, but to seek their salvation; the spirit of love and mercy, sympathizing with those that err from mistaken zeal; as Jesus himself had distinguished the sin against the Son of Man from that against the Holy Ghost. Cf. p. 227, 243. They should have known that his miracles were designed to bless, not to punish. Cf. p. 134.

† The absence of any allusion here to Christ's former reception among the Samaritans proves nothing against the veracity of the narrative; it only illustrates the manner in which the synoptical Gospels were compiled.

‡ Of course we do not pretend to *prove* that this event (Luke, xvii., 11) necessarily falls in the chronological place in which we give it.

§ There are several obscurities in the narrative. At what point did the Samaritan *turn back* (v. 15)? *Schleiermacher* supposes that it was not until after the lepers had been declared to be healed by the priest, and had brought the usual sacrifices; that the *Jews* might have expected to meet Christ at the feast in Jerusalem and thank him there; but the other, following the Samaritan sense of the Mosaic law, went to the Temple of Gerizim, and therefore could not expect to meet him again. Had this been the case, Christ would not have praised him to the disadvantage of the others, merely because his gratitude, without being *greater*, was sooner expressed. This being inadmissible, let us suppose the case thus: the Samaritan, from intercourse with Jews, had imbibed Jewish opinions, and admitted the authority of their prophets, so far, at least, as to apply the law in their sense, in fact, it appears from the account that all the ten went together. But his ardent gratitude could not wait for Christ's arrival at Jerusalem; and as soon as he had the priest's certificate, he hurried back to meet Jesus—who travelled slowly—on the way, and express his thanks. But the sense which naturally flows from Luke's words is also the most probable in itself; the lepers found themselves healed soon after leaving the village, and the Samaritan, full of gratitude, hastened back to give utterance to it.

shown by the Jews. This simple example was, in fact, a type of the conduct of multitudes.*

CHAPTER XIII.

CHRIST'S STAY AT JERUSALEM DURING THE FEAST OF THE DEDICATION.

§ 223. *His Statement of the Proof of his Messiahship.—His Oneness with the Father.—He defends his Words from the Old Testament.* (John, x., 22–39.)

IN the month of December Christ arrived at Jerusalem to attend the Feast of the Dedication. As he had not always alike openly declared himself to be Messiah, he was asked, while walking in Solomon's Porch, by certain Jews, "*How long wilt thou hold us in suspense? If thou be the Christ, tell us plainly.*" We do not know by whom, or in what spirit, this question was asked. In view of the prevalent notions of the Jews in respect to the nature of Messiah's kingdom, we may readily imagine that persons not entirely hostile might complain of the uncertainty in which they were held. Probably, however, among those who put the question were some that had no other object than to use his answer to his disadvantage. Whoever they were, it is clear that they had no just ideas of Christ's ministry or of his relations to mankind; and, therefore, no further explanation than that which his words and deeds had already afforded could have been of use to them.

He, therefore, replied, "I told you, and ye believed not. What use to repeat it? There is no need of telling you in express terms. You might have known it from the (objective) testimony of my works, had you been so disposed. The works that I do in my Father's name, they bear witness of me. But you lack faith; and you lack it because you are not of my sheep (your spirit excludes you from my fellowship). *My* sheep† hear my voice, and I know them, and they follow me; and

* In the narrative the miracle holds a subordinate place; the prominent feature is the contrast between the thankfulness of the Samaritan and the ingratitude of the Jews; and this fact alone testifies to its veracity in respect to the miracle itself. The attempts that have been made to impugn it, or to show that it was originally a parable, are futile; it bears no mark of improbability, and its position in the historical account of the journey is perfectly natural. A narrator of events naturally gives prominence to those points in which his own mind is most interested, and throws others comparatively into the background; so that many things may appear wanting in his statements to readers who wish to form for themselves a perfect image of the transactions. But this certainly is no ground for supposing all the rest to be mere *invention*. This much against *Hase*, who expresses himself, however, with uncertainty, and opposes *Strauss*.

† If this alludes to the parable of the Good Shepherd, and the words καθὼς εἶπον ὑμῖν (v.

I grant unto them eternal life; and they shall never perish, neither shall any man pluck them out of my hand (*i. e.*, my protecting care, under which they will reach, in safety, the full enjoyment of eternal life). My Father, who gave them to me, is the Almighty; and no power of the world can pluck them from the hand of Omnipotence. Through me, they are united with the Almighty Father; *I and the Father are one.*"

We understand by the "oneness" here spoken of the oneness of Christ with the Father in will and works, in virtue of which his work is the work of the Father; but this was founded on the consciousness of his original and essential oneness with the Father, as is clear from his testimonies in other places as to his relations to God. In and of itself the language of Christ contained nothing that might not have been said from the stand-point of the Jewish idea of the Messiah. But the hostile spirits gladly seized the occasion to accuse him of blasphemy, and preparations were made to stone him.

The rigid, legal Monotheism of the Jews placed an infinite and impassable gulf between God and the creature; and they, therefore, took offence at Christ's words, especially at the higher sense in which he was accustomed to call himself the Son of God. He then sought to prove to them, on their own ground, that Messiah might call himself in that higher sense the Son of God, and appropriate the titles founded thereon, without the slightest prejudice to the honour of God. "If," said he, "in your own law (Ps. lxxxii., 6) persons who, in specific relations, represent God (*e. g.*, judges and kings), are called gods (אֱלֹהִים); how much more, and in how far higher a sense, is the highest Theocratic King entitled to call himself the *Son of God.*" The Jews had not directly taken offence at his calling himself the Son of God, but at his saying, "*I am one with the Father;*" but Christ considered the latter claim as a necessary result of the former.* He concluded by say-

26) are genuine, it might be inferred that this conversation took place shortly after the other, and, therefore, that the journey to Galilee and back could not have occurred between them. But it would not be at all decisive to that effect; Christ may have alluded to the parable frequently, and thus kept it fresh in the memory of his hearers.

* I cannot agree with the views of this argument which *Strauss* (3te. Aufl., i., 536) has adopted from *Kern* (Tübinger Zeitschrift, 1836, ii., 89): "Jesus used this line of argument to prove his right to style himself the Son of God to persons who did not admit *his Messiahship*, and who could not be convinced by passages in which *Messiah* was so called, that *he* had a right to apply the title to himself." This is totally foreign to the connexion in which the argument is handed down to us. The Jews were not offended because Christ had appropriated a title to which none but Messiah had a right, but because they believed him to claim more than any *creature* could. It was not his Messiahship that was in question, but whether any human being could place himself in such relations to God without prejudice to the Divine honour. Christ's concluding sentence (v. 36) implied that if any one could appropriate such a title, it was much more the privilege of one hallowed by God, and sent by him into the world, *i. e.*, of the Messiah; thus presupposing his own Messiah

ing, that, if they would not believe his words, they might, from his *works*, know and believe that He was in the Father, and the Father in Him.

CHAPTER XIV.

JESUS IN PERÆA (BETHABARA).

§ 224. *His Decision on the Question of Divorce.—Celibacy.* (Matt., xix, 2–12; Mark, x., 3–12.)

AS Jesus could remain no longer at Jerusalem with safety, he retired for a while into the vicinity of Bethabara, in Peræa,* where he had first appeared publicly, and where he had always found, in the results of the Baptist's labours, a point of departure for his own. Many in that neighbourhood were prepared to recognize Jesus as higher than John, because the latter had done no such Divine works as the former daily performed.

In view of his admitted authority, weighty questions in theology—at least some which were much debated in the schools of the time—were proposed to him for solution. These questions were put either to test his wisdom, or because of the confidence men had already acquired in his illumination as a prophet. One of them concerned the interpretation of the Mosaic law of divorce, and was chiefly disputed between the schools of Hillel and of Schammai. Both schools erred in confounding the political and juridical with the moral elements of the question.† The school of Hillel held that the *moral* law of marriage was satisfied in the Theocratico-political law of Moses; that of Schammai understood the demands of morality better, but erred in interpreting the Mosaic law, and in their idea of the stand-point from which it was given.

When the question was presented to Christ for decision, he separated the two stand-points—the moral and the legal—which had been confounded by the schools; in substance, however, in the notion of marriage itself, he agreed most with the school of Schammai. He declared (as he had before done in the Sermon on the Mount‡) that mar-

ship. The argument is, therefore, rather a *conclusio a minori ad majus* than, as *Kern* thinks, an apagogic one.

* John, x., 40. This brief stay in Peræa is intimated also in Matt., xix., 1; for whatever sense is put upon the words *εἰς τὰ ὅρια τῆς Ἰουδαίας*, it is expressly said that Christ went *πέραν τοῦ Ἰορδάνου*. What is said in Mark, x., 1, *i. e.*, that he went through Peræa to Judea, appears to conflict with the original account of the journey, as given in Luke. Comparing Matt., xix., 1, seq., and Mark, x., 1, seq., we infer that what is here related took place partly during Christ's stay in Peræa, and partly when he had retired from Jerusalem into Judea.

† Cf. Michaelis on the Law of Moses, ii., § 120.

‡ Cf. p. 233.

riage is, according to its idea, an indissoluble union, by which man and wife are joined into one whole, constituting but one life ["*they twain are one flesh*"]. As it was his work every where to lead back all human relations to their original intention, so he decided that the idea of marriage represented in Genesis, as originally the basis of its institution by God, should be realized in life.

This idea of marriage is not an isolated thing, separate from the system of life that emanated from Christ, but belongs to its organism as a whole. As Christ has restored in human nature the image of God in its totality, so the two-fold ground-form for its exhibition, denoted by the opposite sexes, must be reinstated in its rights—its *ideal* must be *realized*. It is essential to this that these two ground-forms fulfil their destiny, and become mutually complementary to each other in a higher unity of life, binding two personalities together; and this is *marriage*. It was by Christ, therefore, that the true import of this relation had to be unfolded.

Having derived from Gen., ii., 24, the higher unity into which two persons of different sexes should be joined by marriage, he drew the following conclusion: "*What, therefore, God* (by the original institution of marriage, by the inward relation of the two persons to each other, and by the leadings through which he makes them conscious of it) *hath joined together, let not man put asunder.*" Upon this they asked, "How, then, does this bear upon the Mosaic law, which admits of divorce?" He replied, "*Moses, because of the hardness of your hearts* (your rude and carnal condition), *suffered you to put away your wives* (as state laws do not aim to realize moral ideas or to create a moral sense, but to bring about *outward* civilization, the laws being adapted to the stand-point of the nature); *but from the beginning it was not so.*"

But Christianity, from its very nature, can make no such condescensions. It is her problem every where to realize the *ideals* of the creation; a task which the new life imparted by God makes possible to her. In fact, Christ's decision in this particular case illustrates the entire relation of Judaism to Christianity; *there*, condescension to a rude condition of the natural man, which could not be removed by outward means; *here*, the restoration of that which *was in the beginning*. Judaism, in a word, stood midway between the *original* and the *renewal* (Gal., iii., 19.)

This high idea of marriage was at that time beyond the reach of the disciples; its indissolubility appeared so hard, and the responsibility (if every separation were adultery) so great, that they said, in alarm, "If the case be so, it is better not to marry at all."

Now it is not to be imagined that Christ would reply to this only by praising those who were incapable of realizing the Christian idea of marriage and exalting the superiority (even though a conditional one) of a single life. We should have expected, in accordance with his usual mode of teaching, that he would point out the *ground* of their alarm in the state of their hearts, and show that what appeared so difficult would be made easy by the power of the Divine life. Moreover, if he intended to answer them only by recommending celibacy, he omitted precisely that which the occasion demanded, viz., the mention of celibacy arising from conscious inability to come up to the moral standard of marriage. This sudden leap, from a lofty definition of the idea of marriage to a laudation of celibacy, appears certainly unaccountable; we must, therefore, suppose that some intermediate part of the conversation has been omitted. The disciples might have inferred, from his placing marriage so high, that it was to be *indispensable*, under the new covenant, to the manifestation of the kingdom of God. In this respect, however, Christ stood directly opposed to the Jewish standpoint, which absolutely required marriage; he was far from prescribing an unconditional form, binding under all the manifold and diversified circumstances of life; the kingdom of God could be served under various relations and conditions, and all was to bend to this object.

We must presume, therefore, either that (as is often the case in Matthew's Gospel) the passage has been transferred from some other connexion to this; or, if it really belongs here, that the intermediate portions of the conversation have not been transmitted to us.

Christ's doctrine on celibacy here is, that, if it aim at the glory of God, it must, like true marriage, be connected with the power of controlling nature. Such celibacy, and such only, does he recognize, as implies the sacrifice of human feelings from love to the kingdom of God, and for the sake of rendering it more efficient service. Only in this sense could he have spoken of celibacy "*for the kingdom of Heaven's sake;*" he never used this expression to denote fitting one's self for the kingdom by a contemplative life, &c., but always to denote a holy activity in its service. He condemns those who bury their talents in order to preserve them. But at a time when the outward spread of the kingdom of God was the chief object of religious effort, celibacy, for its sake especially, might find place.

It is to be carefully noted that Christ by no means says "Blessed are those who abstain from marriage for the sake of the kingdom," &c., as if this, in itself, was pre-eminently excellent; but simply describes an existing state of facts: "*There are some eunuchs*," &c.; distinguishing such as adopt this mode of life for the sake of the kingdom from those that either have no choice in the matter, or are actuated by other motives. His decision, therefore, was opposed not only to the old Hebrew notion that celibacy was *per se* ignominious, but also to the ascetic doctrine which made it *per se* a superior condition of life; a doctrine so widely diffused in later times. It involves his great principle, that the heart and disposition must be devoted to the interests of the kingdom of God, and for it must voluntarily modify all the relations of life as necessity may require.

§ 225. *The Blessing of Little Children.* (Luke, xviii. 15–17; Matt., xix., 13–15; Mark, x., 13–16.)

As the Saviour was leaving a certain place in Peræa, where he had deeply impressed the people, they brought their little children to receive his blessing. The disciples, unwilling to have him annoyed, turned them away. But Jesus called them back, and said, "*Suffer the little children to come unto me, and forbid them not; for of such is the kingdom of Heaven.*" He then took them up in his arms, laid his hand upon them, and blessed them; adding, "*Whosoever shall not receive the kingdom of* God *as a little child, shall not enter therein.*" These words were opposed partly to the idea still entertained by the disciples (manifested in their deeming the approach of the children inconsistent with his dignity), that the glory of Messiah and his kingdom would be outward; and partly to the self-willed and self-seeking spirit which debased their religious conceptions; a spirit strikingly exhibited in many of their expressions during this last period of Christ's labours.

In fact, this single saying expressed the whole nature of the Gospel proclaimed by Christ. It implied that he viewed the kingdom of God as an invisible and spiritual one, to enter which a certain disposition of heart was essential, viz., a child-like spirit, free from pride and self-will, receiving Divine impressions in humble submission and conscious dependence: in a word, all the qualities of the child, suffering itself to be guided by the developed reason of the adult, are to be illustrated in the relations between man and God.* Without this child-like spirit there can be no religious faith, no religious life. On the one hand, Christ rebuked that self-confidence which expects a share in the kingdom on the ground of intellectual or moral worth;† but on the other, by making *children* a model, he recognized in them not only the undeveloped spirit of self, but also the undeveloped consciousness of God, striving after its original. The whole transaction illustrates the love with which Christ goes to meet the dawning sense of God in human nature.

* Precisely the same spirit as was demanded in the sayings of Christ alluded to on p 225, seq.

† The belief that *reason* is self-sufficient would utterly unhinge the Christian world, and cause its life to assume forms directly the reverse of those which Christian principles have created. It would, indeed, cause a contest of life and death.

§ 226. *Christ's Conversation with the rich Ruler of the Synagogue (young man?).* (Matt., xix., 16–24; Mark, x., 17, seq.; Luke, xviii., 18, seq.)

Christ was followed from the place above mentioned by a ruler* of the synagogue whose mind had been impressed by his words, and who came to ask what remained for him to do that he might inherit eternal life. It is clear that he was one of the self-righteous, and had as yet no just sense of his legal deficiencies and need of redemption. He probably expected to hear from the lips of the great Teacher himself that he had already done all that was requisite to secure eternal life; or merely that some additional exercises of piety were necessary; he himself being all the time perfectly content with his own moral condition. And in this spirit he asked the question, "*Good Master, what shall I do to inherit eternal life?*"

Christ replied, "*Why callest thou me good?*† *none is good save one, that is, God.*" The difficulty which appears to lie in these words, when compared with other declarations of Christ in regard to his person, will vanish if we keep in view the general sense in which the antithesis is expressed. God is good in a sense which can be predicated of *no creature*. He alone is the primal source and cause of all good in rational beings, who are created to be free organs of his revelations of himself. (It is the high import of true morality that the glory of God, the only good and holy one, is revealed in it.) Christ would not have exhibited, in his character as man, a model of perfect humility, had he not traced back to God all the good that was in him. But in the instance before us he doubtless had a special reason for answering thus; in any other case he might have allowed the title to be applied

* According to Luke an ἄρχων, which might also mean "a member of the Sanhedrim;" but as Christ was at Peræa, it was more probably "a ruler of the synagogue." According to Matthew, he was a "young man," which does not suit very well with his arrogant language "All these have I kept from my youth up." It is true, the words ἐκ νεότητός μου are wanting in *Cod. Vatic.*, but the authorities for retaining them preponderate; their omission may have been caused by the very discrepancy to which we allude. Although it cannot be said to be entirely improbable that he was a youth, yet the whole tone of discourse appears to imply that he was advanced in years, and had a self-righteous confidence founded on a life blameless from his youth up.

† *Lachmann* reads, τί με ἐρωτᾶς περὶ τοῦ ἀγαθοῦ: εἷς ἐστὶν ὁ αγαθός. Even if this be the true reading, *De Wette's* explanation, which seems to me to conflict with the whole teaching of Christ, by no means follows from it. It may be thus interpreted: "Why do you ask me about what is good? There is one who is good, and to him thou must go to learn what is good; and he has, in fact, revealed it to thee." (*Müller*, Lehre v. d. Sünde, p. 80, gives, as the thought expressed in the passage, "that only from communion with him who alone is good can the created spirit receive the good;" thus making the sense about the same as in the common reading.) "Thou couldst then answer the question for thyself. But since thou askest me, then know," &c. But Lachmann's reading of the reply has not the air of originality, it was, perhaps, invented because Christ's declining the epithet "good" was a stumbling-block.

to him without incurring the charge of self-deification. We infer this from the fact of the answer itself, and also from the conduct of the questioner. The Saviour, looking into his heart, saw that he was vainly trusting in his own morality, and was most of all lacking in humility; and it was precisely these defects which Christ suggested to him, by declining for *himself* the epithet "good."

In regard to the subsequent words of Christ two suppositions are possible. (1.) The first would run as follows: Jesus did not at once answer the ruler's question, but put to him another, viz., whether he had kept the commandments, *i. e.*, in their literal and outward sense,* without special reference to the law of love. He could not, of course, mean that *this* would secure eternal life; the Sermon on the Mount had already demanded a higher and purer obedience. Thus far he only described the lower stand-point—that of a *justitia civilis;* with the *intention* to follow it up with the declaration (contained in v. 22) that *such* a fulfilment would not suffice to gain eternal life; that one thing higher was still lacking. (2.) The second interpretation, and the one to which our own opinions incline, is as follows: Christ answers (Matt., xix., 17), "*If thou wilt enter into life, keep the commandments;*" implying, doubtless, a *true* fulfilment of the law as representing the holiness of God, and, therefore, presupposing the existence of the all-essential love in the specific duties mentioned (v. 18, 19). But it is clear that Christ did not presuppose that the ruler *had* kept the commandments in this sense; on the contrary, seeing his wilful self-righteousness, he adapted his answers thereto, to make him conscious how far he was from that true obedience which is requisite for inheriting the kingdom. He thus gives the man occasion himself to *express* his self-righteousness: "*All these have I kept from my youth up.*" When he adds, "*What lack I yet?*" Jesus tells him the one thing necessary:† "Exchange thine earthly wealth for heavenly treasure (the highest treasure, a share in the kingdom of God, which none can secure but those who hold all other treasures as valueless in comparison with it); *give thy goods to the poor, and come and follow me.*"

* As quoted Luke, xviii., 20.

† It is a question whether the form given by Luke is not that which most accurately expresses Christ's meaning. Matthew has it, "If thou wilt be *perfect;*" but even here could not be intended a perfection superior to the *fulfilment* of the law; for, according to the Sermon on the Mount, there can be no higher perfection; and, moreover, the subsequent expressions of the disciples show that they understood Christ to specify a state of heart which *all* must possess in order to secure eternal life. A misunderstanding of this conversation of Christ gave rise to a distinction between the fulfilment of the law, *i. e.*, *the performance of duty*, and *moral perfection;* which has been a fruitful source of error ever since the first ages of Christianity. *Clement* of Alexandria understood and explained the passage more correctly; not so much in his beautiful treatise "*Quis Dives Salv.*," as in his *Strom.*, iii., 449. He says on Matt., xix., 21: *ἐλέγχει τὸν καυχώμενον ἐπὶ τῷ πάσας τὰς ἐντολὰς ἐκ νεότητος τετηρηκέναι, οὐ γὰρ πεπληρώκει το· ἀγαπήσεις τὸν πλησίον ὡς ἑαυτόν· τότε δὲ ὑπὸ τοῦ κυρίου συντελειούμενος, ἐδιδάσκετο δι' ἀγάπην μεταδιδόναι.*

Christ commands him to follow, just as he was, without delaying to care for his possessions; expressing, in this particular command, the general thought: "The one thing which thou lackest, and without which none can enter into eternal life, is the denial of thyself and of the world, making every thing subordinate to the interests of the Divine kingdom." He chose the particular form, instead of the general rule, in order to convince the rich man of his lack the more strikingly, by pointing out his weakest side; for he clung to his wealth with his whole heart; to teach him, from his own *experience* of his love of the world, how far he was from possessing that love which is the *essence* of obedience to the law.*

§ 227. *The Danger of Wealth.* (Matt., xix., 22, seq.; Mark, x., 22, seq.; Luke, xviii., 23, seq.)

The rich man, incapable of the sacrifice demanded of him, went away in perplexity; and Christ said to the disciples, "By this example you may see how hard it is for the rich to enter the kingdom of Heaven;" and then he employed a figure by which, indeed, it appears to be impossible: "*It is easier for a camel,*" &c. Nor is this to be interpreted as a hyperbole; the words of v. 26, "*With men this is impossible* (*i. e.*, to unassisted human nature); *but with God all things are possible,*" show that Christ meant to say that it *is* impossible to the unaided powers of man, before he has partaken of that higher life which alone can destroy the love of self and of the world. Some of the hearers were amazed at Christ's saying, and exclaimed, in alarm, "*Who, then, can be saved?*"

If this exclamation were made by any of the Apostles, it must appear strange; *they* had no wealth to absorb their affections; and had, in fact, made the very sacrifice demanded. But if we suppose that they *did* make it, they probably took Christ's words in a general sense—in which they would be as applicable to the poor as to the rich—as implying

* If we compare with this narrative, as given in our Gospels, that form of it which appears in the *Evang. ad Hebræos,* we can see that the latter is a later revision, from the way in which some points are contracted and others unhistorically dilated; *e. g.,* Christ, instead of throwing out a single thought to excite the man's mind, gives him at once a full explanation (though a correct one). "*Dixit ad eum alter divitum* (whether *several* rich men were mentioned in the original tradition, or this was a piece of invention) *magister,* quid bonum faciens vivam? Dixit ei: Homo, leges et prophetas fac (an imitation of Christ's saying that 'in love both the law and the prophets are fulfilled'). *Respondit ad eum: feci. Dixit ei: vade, vende omnia quæ possides, et divide pauperibus et veni, sequere me. Cœpit autem dives scalpere caput suum* (clearly enough a little colouring matter thrown in; although such graphic features are not always a mark of spuriousness; their character will generally decide the point. In this instance the fancy is apparent). *Et dixit ad eum Dominus: Quomodo dicis: legem feci et prophetas, quoniam scriptum est in lege: diliges proximum tuum sicut te ipsum, et ecce, multi fratres tui, filii Abrahæ, amiciti sunt stercore, morientes præ fame et domus tua plena est multis bonis et non egreditur omnino aliquid ex ea ad eos.*"

total renunciation of earthly things. Yet Peter's question, v. 27, does not accord very well with this supposition. It is also very possible that the persons referred to in the passage did not belong to the number of the Apostles.*

"*The things*," said Christ, "*which are impossible with men are possible with God.*" What man cannot do by his unaided powers, he *can* accomplish by the power of God. By enunciating this truth as the result of his whole course of remark, he showed its point of departure and its aim. While the rest stood, as it were, stupified, Peter ventured to say, "Does what you have said apply to us? *Lo, we have left all and followed thee.*"† Then uttered the Saviour those words, so full of consoling promise: "*There is no man that hath left house, or parents, or brethren, or wife, or children for the kingdom of God's sake, who shall not receive manifold more in this present time, and in the world to come life everlasting.*" The first part of the promise (referring to *this life*) was enough to show even those whose minds were filled with carnal and Chiliastic expectations, that the whole was to be taken, not literally, but spiritually; Christians were to receive back all that they had sacrificed, increased and glorified, in the communion of the higher life on earth. The second part expressed the common inheritance of believers—everlasting life in heaven.

§ 228. *Believers are to Reign with Christ.*

Matthew mentions in this connexion (xix., 28) the promise of Christ to his disciples, that, when the Son of Man should appear with dominion corresponding to his glory in the renewed and glorified world, they should "*sit upon twelve thrones, judging the twelve tribes of Israel.*" The word "judging" includes the idea of "governing," according to its ancient acceptation. The collocation of this passage may be one of those instances in which Matthew arranges his matter more according to the connexion of thought than of time; but there is no reason to question its originality. The idea of a participation of believers with Christ in the government and judgment of the future world is bound up with the whole mode of representing the kingdom of God in the New Testament;‡ our duty must be to separate the idea from its symbolical form derived from the old Theocratic mode of thought, and to recognize the new Spirit that was to be developed from it. The passage (like the other promises in the context) recognizes *degrees* in the share of government and judgment allotted to believers. Not only

* Luke, xviii., 26, supports this.

† The form of the question of Peter given by Matthew (xix., 27) implies a looking for *reward* on his part. But had this been his object in putting it, Christ would have more emphatically reproved it.

‡ Cf. p. 225. Various passages of Paul (1 Cor., vi., 2, &c.) presuppose such sayings of Christ

the Head, but also all the organs of the kingdom of God are to share in its dominion; because its dominion is to be universal. This is an important idea for Christian ethics. There are to be "judges" and "judged," "rulers" and "ruled"—but in an exalted sense—in the new form of the Theocracy as well as in the old

---

CHAPTER XV.

JESUS IN BETHANY.

§ 229. *The Family of Lazarus.—Martha and Mary; their different Tendencies.* (Luke, x., 38, seq.)

A PRESSING call induced Christ to leave Peræa, where he found so susceptible a soil, perhaps sooner than he would otherwise have done.

About a mile and a half from Jerusalem, at the foot of the Mount of Olives, lay the village of *Bethany*, where dwelt a family, two sisters and a brother, with whom Christ had formed, during his repeated and protracted visits to the city, a close and affectionate intimacy. Luke has left us a description of this family agreeing perfectly (without design or concert) with that given by John* (xi., 1–5). On one occasion when Christ was partaking of their hospitality, one of the sisters, Martha, showed more anxiety to provide for the bodily comforts of her exalted guest, and to give him a worthy reception, than to secure the blessings for her soul which his presence so richly offered; while her more spiritual sister, Mary, gave herself wholly to listening to the words of life from the lips of the Saviour. Martha, finding all the cares of the family thrown upon her, complained to Jesus thereof; and he made use of the occasion to impress upon her mind the general

* The passage in John probably refers to the earlier period of this intimacy. It is true, Luke (x., 38) does not mention the *name* of the village; the account transmitted to him probably did not contain it, and here, as in other cases, he would not insert the name merely for the sake of giving definiteness to the narrative. The event itself, as a very significant one, had been faithfully kept and transmitted; the locality, being unimportant to the interest of the event, was probably forgotten. It is true, the position of the passage, in the account of Christ's last journey to Jerusalem, might lead to the inference that the place was at some distance from the city; but, as we have already said, the account itself mingles two journeys together, as is especially evident in the single case before us. *De Wette* has remarked this. Luke simply adhered to the account he had received, which gave him no information about the locality; this last we must learn from John. The probabilities, in regard to time, are favourable to our supposition. The undesigned coincidence, therefore, of John with Luke, in the description of the family, &c., is a strong proof of credibility. *Strauss*, however, adduces Luke's silence in regard to Lazarus as invalidating John's credibility, but without the slightest reason; Luke's object was to make prominent the relation of the *two sisters* to Christ, and the mention of Lazarus was, therefore, not at all necessary.

truth which he so often, and under so many diversified forms, taught to his hearers: "*Martha, thou art careful and troubled about many things, but one thing is needful;* and Mary hath chosen that good part* (that which is good *in itself;* the only worthy aim of human effort), *which shall not be taken from her* (a possession that shall be everlasting, not perishable, like these worldly things)."

It is wholly contrary to the sense of history to interpret this narrative [as some do] so as to make Martha represent the *practical* and Mary the *contemplative* tendency, and thence to infer that Christ ascribes superiority to the latter. The antithesis is between that turn of mind which forgets, in a multiplicity of objects, the one fundamental aim; and that, on the other hand, which devotes itself solely to the one object from which all others should proceed. Christ demands of his followers constant activity in his service, and therefore could not have approved an entirely contemplative spirit. What he honours in Mary is the spirit which ought to be the centre and animating principle of all activity. It is true, Martha is more practical and worldly; Mary more contemplative and spiritual; but these manifestations do not *necessarily* indicate character; although in this instance (and, indeed, commonly) the manifestation corresponds to the character. It was not *necessary* that Martha's multiplied cares should distract her from the one thing needful; Christ blamed her, not for her cares, but for not making them subordinate: for so surrendering herself to them as to put the greater interest in the back-ground.

§ 230. *The Sickness of Lazarus; Christ's Reply to the Messengers who informed him of it.* (John, xi., 1–4.)

While Christ was in Peræa, about a day's journey from Bethany, LAZARUS, the brother of Martha and Mary, was taken sick, and the sisters sent to inform the Saviour of it, doubtless in the hope of obtaining his assistance. His reply gave *this* consolation, at least, to the sisters—that their brother should not be *separated* from them by death; although its true import was not obvious until afterward: "*This sickness is not unto death, but for the glory of God, that the Son of God might be glorified thereby.*"

Now, as Lazarus actually *died*, these words appear to need explanation. Did Christ, in view of the symptoms that were reported to him, really think that Lazarus would not die? and was the object of his message simply to console the sisters with the assurance that the mercy

* This clause is wanting in *Cod. Cantab.*, and other Latin authorities; but nothing would be lost to the sense even if it were left out; for "that good part which cannot be lost" is the "one thing" to which life should be supremely devoted, in contrast with the "many things" which waste and dissipate a divided mind.

and power of God would be glorified in themselves and their brother, by saving the latter from death? Was the latter part of the message, "That the *Son* might be glorified," added by the Evangelist himself, incorporating his own explanation with Christ's words?

Certainly we shall not assert that Christ *could* not but foreknow, infallibly, in the exercise of his superhuman knowledge, the result of the disease; it *may* have been the case that he described it, in view of the symptoms at the time, as not necessarily fatal, although it afterward took another turn. But if all this were granted, there is something else to be considered. Christ *could* not, consistently with his character, have given so positive a prediction on the deceptive evidence of mere symptoms; he could not have mocked his friends with baseless hopes, so soon to be scattered. We must take it for granted, therefore, that his confidence was founded on a far surer basis; it was the Divine nature, dwelling in him, that illuminated his *human* mind. To be sure, it is *possible* that his confident conviction that Lazarus would be saved may have been coupled with uncertainty as to whether he should be saved from *sickness*, or from *death;* but the language of his reply, although it might admit this construction, is not at all inconsistent with absolute certainty on his part that Lazarus would die. The reply was intended to comfort the sisters, and to them it could make no difference whether their brother was saved from apparent or real death, in case the latter were of short duration; and Christ may, therefore, have wished to avoid presenting the naked idea of death in his words. And the partial ambiguity of his language may also have been designed to test the faith of the sisters. It is possible that with this view he uttered the words "ὑπὲρ τῆς δόξης τοῦ θεοῦ," and stopped there, the rest being (possibly) added by the Evangelist.

§ 231. *The Death of Lazarus; Christ's Conversation with the Disciples in regard to it.* (John, xi., 11, seq.)

The affliction of Lazarus determined Jesus to leave Peræa, where his labours had been so fruitful. Still, he remained there two days (v. 6), continuing his ministry. But although his course was thus decided by circumstances, he very well knew that the result would produce the happiest religious effects upon the sisters.

It was probably on the very evening of the return of the messengers that Lazarus died. What comfort could Christ's encouraging language now afford them! The word of promise seemed to be broken; *his* word, whom they had always known as the Faithful and True; *his* word, which they had never seen come to naught. What conflicting feelings must have struggled for the mastery in their hearts! Either they sent a second messenger to the Saviour,* or the latter became

* John's not mentioning a second messenger (v. 11) does not prove that none was sent.

aware of the event by his own supernatural knowledge. When he announced to his disciples that Lazarus "slept," they thought at first that he had heard it in some way, and took it as a sign of recovery.* Thereupon he said to them in express terms, "*Lazarus is dead; and I am glad for your sakes that I was not there, to the intent ye may believe*" (still further). Not, however, by any means asserting that he had purposely stayed away, that Lazarus might die and their faith be confirmed by his resurrection; but, in fact, implying that although his delay had been caused by other reasons, he rejoiced at the means it would afford of strengthening their faith at a time when such rude shocks were at hand. His words imply, also, that if he had been in Bethany, he would not have suffered the family to reach such a pitch of anguish merely for the sake of relieving them, and displaying the highest degree of miraculous power afterward; in compassion to their grief he would not have suffered the sick man to die. Just as a merciful man employs natural means to relieve suffering according to the circumstances, so Christ made use of his *super*-natural power; with this difference, however, that the aims of his Divine calling were always kept in view in the exercise of those powers. For this reason, too, he did not cure *all* the sick around him.

His decision to go to Bethany astonished and alarmed the disciples to such an extent that they lost sight of their higher expectations from him as Messiah, and of their higher view of his person. It was characteristic of Thomas, who was more in bondage to sense than the others, to give utterance to his anxiety more prominently (v. 16); and, in fact, this anxiety must have appeared out of place to the disciples had they kept in view their ordinary conceptions of Messiah.

The Saviour now set himself to dispel the clouds which their fears had created; to revive their higher intuition of his person and their just sense of communion with him; and to remind them that, in the few remaining days in which they were to enjoy his personal guidance, they should submit to it implicitly and trustfully. They were accustomed to hear him compare himself with the natural sun, shedding its beams upon the earth during certain fixed hours;† and it was, perhaps,

Moreover, when John is giving any instance of the exercise of Christ's supernatural knowledge, he generally intimates it in some way; here he gives no such intimation. When Christ told the disciples that Lazarus "slept," they understood his words in a natural sense; and it appears most probable that they thought he had received a message from the sisters. Be the case decided as it may, John's language is not such as would be used by a man who wished to give special *prominence* to the supernatural.

* The disciples knew, at least, that persons believed to be dead had been restored by Christ; they knew, also, that "sleep" was a common image of death; yet their misunderstanding is by no means inexplicable, as some suppose; nor does it throw the least shade upon the credibility of the Evangelist.

† John, ix., 5; cf. p. 294, 299. A similar figure, Luke, xi., 33: The light that cannot but shine. Cf. p 228, 246.

in allusion to this symbol that he now said,* "*Are there not twelve hours in the day? If any man walk in the day he stumbleth not, because he seeth the light of this world.*" So the disciples, so long as they had the Sun of the spiritual world to guide them with his light, were to follow him without fear or care. "*But if a man walk in the night he stumbleth, because their is no light in him.*" So, in the time then rapidly approaching, when they should lose this light, they were to choose their way with caution, lest they should stumble. Yet, in the mean time, the higher life was to become independent within them, so far that they should not need this *sensible* guidance; inward communion with the Light of the World was to supply the place of his visible presence, as Christ afterward told them in his last discourses. In this spiritual sense, it is always true that CHRIST IS THE LIGHT OF THE WORLD.

§ 232. *The Death of Lazarus.—Christ's Conversation with Martha* (John, xi., 21–28) *and with Mary* (v. 33, 34).—*Jesus Weeps* (v. 35).

The intelligence of Christ's approach to Bethany reached Martha sooner than her less practical sister. Mary, lost in grief, gave no heed to the busy world about her. The former went out to meet the Saviour; and when she saw him who had done so many mighty works, and whom she believed to be Messiah, a ray of hope beamed into her soul, but she hardly dared to cherish it. "*Lord, hadst thou been here, my brother had not died; but I know that even now, whatsoever thou wilt ask of God, God will give it thee.*" Jesus replied, "*Thy brother shall rise again;*" referring directly to her own words, and not to the future resurrection; for had he wished to give her *that* consolation, he would not have done it in such bare and naked terms. He wished to confirm her hope, but yet did it in rather indefinite language, either designedly, or because her impatience interrupted him. His language was too general to satisfy her feelings; she wished a definite assurance that Lazarus should be raised; and, therefore, said, "*I know that he shall rise again in the resurrection of the last day;*" intimating what she did not venture to express, viz., her wish first mentioned. Christ made use of her misunderstanding (as was his wont) to lead her mind to the great central truth of religion—the ground of all the believer's hopes—as the source of a new hope in her brother's case. He points to himself as the true life, the source of all life, the author of all resurrection: "*I am the resurrection and the life; he that believeth in me, though he were dead, yet shall he live; and whosoever liveth and believeth in me shall never die.*" He then asked her the direct question, "*Believest thou this?*" He intended to teach her that the faith of Lazarus had been rewarded by a life beyond the power of death; and that He,

* The words are enigmatical without this allusion; with it, they are plain.

the author of the resurrection and of a life which death could not even interrupt, could now also call her dead brother back again to life.

Although she did not fully comprehend his words, they gave her new hopes; and, after expressing anew her faith in him as the Messiah—which included for her all things else—she hastened away to call her broken-hearted sister, who had not even yet heard of the Saviour's approach. Nothing could rouse her from her profound and passive grief but her love for Him to whose words of life she had so often surrendered herself, as passively and humbly. She hastened toward Jesus. The Jews that were condoling with her in the house, fearing that she was going to her brother's grave to give up to an excess of sorrow, followed after. She saw Jesus, but offered no such request as her sister had done; falling at his feet, she only cried, "*Lord, if thou hadst been here, my brother had not died.*" Tears choked her further utterance; nor, indeed, was it her wont to anticipate Him whom her soul so revered and loved. The Jews around, sympathizing in her sorrow, could not refrain from tears.

And Jesus wept in the depth of his compassion. It has been inferred from this, that although he hoped to restore Lazarus, he was not, as yet, *sure* of it; had he been so (it is said), the consciousness that he was soon to turn the mourning into joy would have banished all grief from his mind. But surely the expressions of bitter lamentation, the tears and agony of all around, were enough to stir the compassionate heart of Him who sympathized so deeply with all human feelings, even though he knew that he should soon remove the cause of grief itself. A physician (though the analogy is utterly inadequate), standing by the bedside of a patient surrounded by weeping friends, may well be affected by their grief, though he may be sure, so far as human skill can give surety, that he will heal the disease. And we must bear in mind, too, that Christ was Man as well as God; and that the blending of the Godhead and the manhood, the Divine infallibility with the human hesitancy, must, in the very nature of the case, offer many enigmas for our contemplation.

The Evangelist gives a graphic description of the effects produced upon the Jews around by the sight of the tears of Jesus. The better disposed saw in them only a manifestation of his love for Lazarus. Others affected to doubt the truth of his miracles; he loved Lazarus and his family; why did he not save him? "*Could not this man, which opened the eyes of the blind,** *have caused that even this man should not have died?*"

* *Strauss* finds a contradiction here between John and the other Evangelists: "The Jews quote only the *curing of the blind;* why did they not quote the *raising of the dead,*

§ 233. *The Resurrection of Lazarus.—The Prayer of Christ.* (John, xi., 38–44.)

When the store was about to be lifted from the grave, Martha,* whose heart fluctuated between hope and fear, gave new utterance to her doubts: "*Lord, by this time he stinketh;*† *for he hath been dead four days.*" Jesus said unto her, "*Said I not unto thee, that if thou wouldst believe, thou shouldst see the glory of God?*"‡ (see God glorify himself in the effects of his Almighty mercy).

Then looking down into the grave, and assured that Lazarus would rise, as though the miracle were already wrought, he offers first his thanksgiving to the Father: "*Father, I thank thee that thou hast heard me; and I knew that thou hearest me always; but because of the people which stand by, I said it, that they may believe that thou hast sent me.*" Meaning that his utterance of thanks did not imply that he only *then* became conscious of power to raise up Lazarus. Prayer and thanksgiving were not isolated fragments of Christ's life; his whole life was one prayer and one thanksgiving; for he knew that the heavenly Father heard him in all things, and always granted the powers needful to his calling. He made this public, individual thanksgiving, to testify to those around that he did this, like all his other acts, as the messenger of the Father, and considered it, as all things else, his Father's gift.

This prayer has led some to distinguish this miracle from others as one not accomplished by Christ's indwelling Divine power, but by God for him; to class it, in fact, among answers to prayer. But as Christ's whole life was one prayer, in the sense just mentioned, as he always acted in unity with God, in the form of dependence, he could have expressed himself in the same terms in regard to any of his miracles. And although Lazarus did not rise until the voice of Jesus called him

of which the other Evangelists give several instances?" But how do we know that these Jews at the city were acquainted with what had occurred in Galilee? Was it not natural for them to recur to the miraculous act performed by Christ in the city itself so short a time before, and which had excited such virulent opposition against him? If John's Gospel were an *invention*, the inventor must have heard other narratives of Christ's raising the dead; and had he wished, as must have been the case, to invent a stronger example than any of those recorded, he would surely have alluded to them. The question, then, is just as applicable if the narrative be fictitious as if it be true.

* The conduct of Martha and Mary is in entire harmony with their characters; the former doubts, and expresses her doubt; the latter looks on in silence.

† We must grant that those are right who say that this expression of Martha's is no *proof* that corruption had commenced in the corpse.

‡ The reference of the words ὄψει τὴν δόξαν τοῦ θεοῦ is doubtful. Some refer them to the reply to the messengers, John, xi., 4. In that reply nothing is said of "believing," but faith is silently presupposed. Others refer them to Christ's words addressed *directly* to Martha (v. 25), in which faith is expressly required. It is true, the words "ὄψει," &c., are not given in that verse expressly, but it contains, as we have already remarked, the basis of a promise of the kind, only not announced.

forth, he could thank God for it as an act achieved, in his certainty of at once accomplishing it; and, in so doing, testify that the power to do it was from God.*

§ 234. *Measures taken against Christ by the Sanhedrim.* (John, xi., 47, seq.)

The raising of Lazarus exerted an important influence in bringing about the final catastrophe of Christ's life. On the one hand, it led many to believe in his Divine calling, and, on the other, it decided the ruling Pharisaic party to adopt more violent measures against him. They were now satisfied that their sentence of excommunication† had not counteracted the impressions which his ministry had made upon the minds of the people; and feared that, if they let him alone, all men would believe on him as Messiah In view of the threatened danger, a council of the Sanhedrim was summoned. Men who were in the habit of sacrificing the peace of the state to their own passions now made it a plea for vigorous steps against Christ. "If the thing is allowed to go on, all will believe on him. The people will proclaim him king; and the Romans will come and take away what power and nationality they have left us." Caiaphas, the high-priest, adopting the view thus presented, said, "It is, at any rate, better that one should die for all, than that the whole nation should perish." And without any legal investigation of the criminality of Jesus, it was resolved, on pretext of the safety of the state, by the majority (against whose vehemence a few more moderate members could do nothing), that he must

* The omission of the raising of Lazarus in the first three Gospels has been adduced as an argument against its credibility. Were it not that other events are omitted in the same way, and were we not able to account for it by the peculiar character, origin, and aims of John's Gospel, the argument might have more weight. To seek a *special* reason for the omission in this case could lead to nothing but arbitrary hypotheses. But it is sufficiently explained by the *general* reason, viz., that the former Gospels contain only traditions of the ministry of Christ at Jerusalem, followed by an account of his last stay in that city. In this outline there is no point at which the raising of Lazarus would naturally and necessarily be joined. It has been said that the *intention* to exaggerate is obvious in John's Gospel, which always sets forth the miracles which it records as the highest possible, *e. g.*, the cure of the palsy of 38 years' standing; of the man that was *born* blind; the raising of Lazarus, &c. In reply to this, we might admit that John, having an apologetic object, only selected, from the abundant materials furnished by the Evangelical history, a few events illustrating in the highest degree the δόξα of Christ; but this admission would not affect the veracity of his narratives in the slightest degree. But the *healing of the lepers*, one of the most marked displays of miraculous power, is omitted by John; while the *feeding of the five thousand*, the very highest of them all, is given by the other Evangelists as well as by him. A high degree of miraculous power, therefore, was not the sole ground on which John selected the miracles that he recorded; he had regard, also, partly to their connexion with Christ's discourses, and partly to their connexion with the course of the facts in his history. This last holds good especially of the narrative in question—that of the raising of Lazarus. It connects with the course of his life the triumphal entry into Jerusalem, and the enthusiasm of the people in his favour; and it also explains the resolution soon taken by the Sanhedrim to put him out of the way. And this, in turn, confirms the veracity of the narrative itself.

† Cf. p. 298.

die. The mode of his death was to be subsequently decided on, according to circumstances. An order was issued for the seizure of his person, in case he should attend the Feast of the Passover at Jerusalem.

CHAPTER XVI.

JESUS IN EPHRAIM.

§ 235. *The Necessity for Christ's Death.*

TO avoid the snares of his enemies, and secure a short season of undisturbed intercourse with the disciples before the close of his career on earth, Jesus retired into the obscure village of *Ephraim*,* in the desert of Judea, several miles† north of Jerusalem. He knew that in travelling to the Passover at the city he should be overcome by the machinations of the Pharisees, and be put to death. The question may be asked, Why, then, did he not keep himself concealed still longer? He might then have carried on the still defective religious training of his disciples, and might, also, have prepared a greater number of agents to disseminate his truth.

So, indeed, it might be said if he had been a *mere* teacher of truth, like other men. Even though at last he had to fall a victim to the hierarchical party, he might thus have gained *some* time, at least, for the training of his followers; a work of the highest possible importance, as every thing, in the developement of his work, depended upon the way in which they apprehended his doctrine. But the doctrine of Jesus was not a system of general conceptions; it was founded upon a fact, viz., that in *Him* had been manifested the end to which all previous revelations to the Jewish people had been but preparatory; that *He* was the aim of the prophecies of the Old Testament; that in *Him* the kingdom of GOD was realized. Of this fact, to which his whole previous ministry had borne witness, he had now to testify openly before the face of his enemies. Moreover, his labours in Galilee, and the raising of Lazarus at Bethany, had raised the expectations of the people to the highest pitch (John, xi., 56); and many who had gone up to the city before the Passover to purify themselves were anxious to know whether he would venture to come in spite of the hostile intentions of the Sanhedrim. To stay away *then*, would have been to lose the most favourable juncture; and to manifest both fear of his enemies and distrust of his own Divine calling to the Messiahship. Now was the time, when the rage of the Pharisees was at its highest, in the face of their sentence and their threats, to bear witness to himself openly as Messiah. He did not *seek* death, but went to meet it in the execution

* John, xi., 54.

† According to Jerome, 20 Roman miles.

of his calling, in obedience to the Divine will, and with a love to God and man that was ready for any sacrifice.* And he was assured that precisely by his *death* was the great object, to which in holy love he had devoted his whole life, to be fully realized.

As for the imperfect training of his disciples, it must have caused him uneasiness had he not been able to rely (as no human teacher could do) upon his own continued operation, and that of the Divine Spirit, in their hearts and minds, to complete their culture. With *this* presupposition he could not but be confident that his separation from them would further their independent developement, as he himself told them afterward in his closing conversations with them.

CHAPTER XVII.

CHRIST'S LAST PASSOVER JOURNEY TO JERUSALEM.

§ 236. *Journey to Jericho.—The Healing of Blind Bartimeus.* (Matt., xx., 30, seq.; Luke, xviii., 35, seq.; Mark, x., 46, seq.)

CHRIST did not go directly from Ephraim to Jerusalem, but passed first eastwardly towards the Jordan, to the vicinity of Jericho, a small town about six hours† distant from the metropolis. Here he could meet the caravan coming from Galilee to the feast.‡ Various reasons may be assigned for this course on the part of Christ: a wish not to fall at once into the hands of the Sanhedrim; or to meet the Galilean multitudes on whom his ministry had produced such powerful effects; or, by means of the festal caravans, to carry out his plan of a solemn Messianic entry into Jerusalem. And as this last might excite false hopes in the disciples, it was the more necessary to impress upon them anew the fact that his kingdom was to be glorified by his *sufferings*, and not to be established in earthly and visible splendour.§

As the Saviour entered Jericho attended by the festal caravans, honouring him as Theocratic king, there sat, not far from the gate of

* There must be a right conception of Christ's self-sacrifice as a moral act, in connexion with his whole calling, in order to any just *doctrinal* view of his sufferings.

† According to Josephus, 150 stadia.

‡ Perhaps, also, he took his way through Jericho in order to extend his ministry in Judea. As the raising of Lazarus is not mentioned by the three first Evangelists, so the retirement into Ephraim, nearly connected with the former event, is only to be found in John. Apart from the latter, we should be led to suppose that he passed through Jericho on his direct way from Galilee to Jerusalem.

§ The departure from Ephraim connects itself naturally with Luke, xviii., 31; why, otherwise, should it be said there that *before* they came to Jericho he "took his disciples apart, and said unto them?" &c.

the town, a blind beggar named *Bartimeus*,* who heard the noise of the procession, and inquiring its cause, was told that Jesus of Nazareth was passing by. He then cried to the Messiah for mercy. The rebukes of many, who did not wish him to disturb the Theocratic king with his clamour, had no effect upon him. Jesus stood, and told him to come near. Then the people, knowing that the Saviour called none whom he did not mean to help, said to the blind man, "*Be of good comfort; he calleth thee.*" He cast off his garment to run the faster, and hastened towards Jesus. He was healed, and followed the procession, joining in the general Hosannah!

§ 237. *Christ Lodges with Zaccheus.* (Luke, xix., 2, seq.)

The healing of the blind man heightened the rejoicing of the multitude. But Jesus went with them no further; perhaps the caravan wished to reach Jerusalem on the same day.† In the suburbs of Jericho lived a rich publican, named *Zaccheus*, who probably knew Christ by the reports of other publicans. Being of short stature, he climbed a tree, in order to see Christ when the procession passed by. Ever ready to welcome the dawning of better feelings in the hearts of sinners, the Saviour looked up, and said, "*Zaccheus,‡ make haste and come down, for to-day I must abide at thy house.*" The love with which Christ met his desire affected him more deeply than any thing else could have done; his heart was won; and in the fulness of his joy he vowed to prove his repentance by dividing half of his property among the poor, and remunerating four-fold all whom he had overreached. It surprised many that HE, who was recognized as Theocratic king,

* According to Luke, Christ met the blind man on *entering* the town; according to Matthew and Mark, on *leaving* it; and Matthew, besides, speaks of *two* blind men. It is easy to conceive how these different representations of the same event could arise; the only question is, which has the more internal probability? Mark not only gives the name of the blind man, but his whole account is so graphic and circumstantial, that it must have been derived from the report of an eye-witness. But in Luke the connexion of events is so close that we cannot drop a single link: the entry, the blind man's joining the procession, its passage through the town, its halt at the house of Zaccheus; all hang together and bear the evident stamp of truth. In this particular, then, we follow Luke. The account used by Mark, perhaps, stated that the blind man joined the procession at the gate and went forth with it; and this might naturally lead to the supposition that the event occurred on the passage out. The statement of Matthew, that *two* were cured, is more difficult. It may be explained either on the ground that two accounts were blended together, or that two blind men were cured, one at the entrance, the other at the outlet, of the town. (It was a common thing for blind beggars to sit at the gates.) This supposition, and a subsequent blending of the two narratives, would account not only for Matthew's mentioning *two* blind men, but also for the discrepancy in Mark and Luke as to the spot of the cure.

† It was but a short distance from Jericho to Jerusalem; and we know neither at what point Christ joined the caravan, nor how far it had journeyed that day, nor what time of the day it was.

‡ Whether he had known Zaccheus before, or was informed of his name by the bystanders, is of no moment. The Evangelist does not intimate that he made use of his supernatural knowledge in calling the man by name.

should go to "be guest with a man that was a sinner." With reference to this feeling Christ said, "*This day is salvation* come to this house, forasmuch as he also is a son of Abraham; for the Son of Man is come to seek and to save that which was lost.*"† And this was only an application to a particular case of the general truth, that it was his mission to restore again the image of God that had been defaced in humanity.

§ 238. *The Request of Salome.—The Ambition of the Disciples rebuked.* (Matt., xx., 20–28; Mark, x., 35–45.)

The worldly views of Christ's Messiahship which had been revived in the minds of the disciples by the reception he had met with from the festal caravan, could hardly fail to be strengthened by what occurred in Jericho. His own teachings had not yet fully convinced them; and these impressions upon their senses were stronger, for the moment, than those which he had made upon their souls.

The sons of Salome, James and John, enjoyed Christ's closest intimacy; the latter, indeed, always sat at his right hand. In view of this intimate relation, and not without the knowledge of her sons,‡ she came to Christ and prayed him, that when Messiah's kingdom should be outwardly realized, her two sons might sit, the one on his right hand, the other on his left.

As usual, Christ did not combat these ideas of his kingdom directly and at length; he wished to destroy the *root* in the hearts of his followers. He taught them anew that they were to share with him, not places of honour, but pains and sufferings. "*Ye know not what ye ask. Can ye drink of the cup* (of suffering) *that I shall drink of?*" To this they replied, probably without duly weighing the import of his words, "*We are able.*" And he answered: "I can, indeed, impart to you the fellowship of my sufferings; but *rank* in the kingdom of God depends not upon my will, but upon the allotment of the Father" (it was not to be an arbitrary allotment, but the highest necessity of Divine wisdom and justice).

The disciples were indignant at the ambition of James and John; but Christ called them all about him, and showed them how inconsistent such strifes were with their relations to each other and the spirit

* He had become convinced of sin, and received the bringer of salvation with repentance and love.

† *Schleiermacher* thinks (ii., 174) that this occurred on the second day, after the affair had become generally known. We see no sufficient ground for this supposition. It appears from the whole narrative that the murmurs of the people, and the words of Zaccheus. arose from an immediate impression. The word σήμερον (Luke, xix., 9), and its relation to σήμερον (v. 5), speaks in favour of our view. *Schleiermacher* seems to lay too much stress on ἀκούοντων (v. 11).

‡ According to Mark, the brothers presented the request directly to Christ; according to Matthew (which seems the more likely), they did it through their mother. Christ's address to them (Matt., xx., 22) presupposes that really *they* made the request.

that ought to animate them. There could not be (he told them) among them such relations of superiority and subordination as existed in civil communities; the communion of the Divine kingdom could know of none such. They were to emulate each other only in serving each other with self-sacrificing love; like their Lord and Master, who had come, not to be ministered unto, but to minister, and to sacrifice his life for the ransom of many. Whosoever was greatest in *this* was the greatest among them.*

§ 239. *Parable of the Pounds.* (Luke, xix., 11, seq.)

Christ made use of several parables during this last period of his life, while his disciples were still expecting that he would establish a visible kingdom, to give them purer ideas of the process by which it was to be founded and developed. Among these is the parable of the *Pounds*, which was given, according to Luke, just as they left Jericho, expressly because "he was nigh to Jerusalem, and they thought that the kingdom of God should immediately appear."

There were three points on which he specially sought to fix their attention, viz., the opposition he was to encounter at Jerusalem; his departure from them, and return at a later period to subdue his foes and establish his kingdom in triumph; and, finally, their duty to labour actively in the interval, and not to await in indolence the achievement of victory by other means, without their co-operation. He particularly aimed to show them that the position they should occupy in the developement of the kingdom of God would depend upon their zeal and activity in the use of the means intrusted to them. This he illustrated under the figure of a capital, loaned on interest; the same amount, viz., one *mina*, is committed to each of ten servants, and in proportion to the gain of this, whether more or less, is the station assigned to them by their master. One only is wholly rejected—he that guards carefully the sum committed to him and loses nothing, but *gains* nothing. The apology which he makes assists us to determine the particular character which Christ has in view. He excuses himself on the ground of fear; the lord is a hard master. He represents those, therefore, whose mistaken apprehensions of the account they will have to render keep them in inactivity, and who retire from the active labours of the world in order to avoid contamination from its unholy atmosphere. In many of the disciples, indeed, the prospect of the approaching struggle with the world may have suggested the thought of such a retirement.

* Luke does not give this narrative, but mentions (xxii., 24) a similar dispute for rank among the disciples, and recites these similar expressions of our Lord. It is probably out of place, as such a contention could hardly have arisen at the last meal, after the institution of the Sacrament. The collocation may have arisen from the fact that the symbolical washing of feet, so striking a rebuke of this ambitious spirit, was connected with the last meal.

And not without reason is the capital which the unfaithful servant failed to employ appropriated to him who made the most of his. Indeed, the key to the whole parable is given by Christ himself in that memorable saying, repeated so often and in such various connexions:* "*Unto every one that hath* (*i. e.*, hath as real and productive capital) *shall* (more, and ever more) *be given* (and most to him that gaineth most); *and from him that hath not* (*i. e.*, does not truly *possess* what he has, but buries it) *shall be taken away even that which he hath.*"

In this parable, in view of the circumstances under which it was uttered, and of the approaching catastrophe, special intimations are given of Christ's departure from the earth, of his ascension, and return to judge the rebellious Theocratic nation and consummate his dominion. It describes a great man, who travels to the distant court of the mighty emperor, to receive from him authority over his countrymen, and to return with royal power. So Christ was not immediately recognized in his kingly office, but first had to depart from the earth and leave his agents to advance his kingdom, to ascend into heaven and be appointed Theocratic King, and return again to exercise his contested power.

§ 240. *Parable of the Labourers in the Vineyard.* (Matt., xx., 1–16.)

Here, also, belongs the parable of the *labourers in the vineyard*, which opposes all assertion of one's own merits, and all anxiety for rank and rewards among the servants of the kingdom of God. This parable admits of many and various applications; but, in order to understand it correctly, we must consider it by itself, apart from the introductory and concluding passages.†

* Cf. p. 105, 190.

† The words "*The last shall be first, and the first last*" (v. 16), cannot possibly denote the *punctum saliens* of the parable; in it the last are not *preferred* to the first; the latter simply fail to receive more than the former, as they had expected. Nor do they complain of receiving their wages last, but only that they do not get more than the others. It is something merely accidental, necessary only for the consistency of the representation, and arising merely from its form, that the turn of the first comes last; they *had* to see the last receive equally as much as themselves before they could complain of it, and thus give occasion for the utterance of the truth which it is the main object of the parable to set forth. In Luke, xiii., 30, the same words occur ("there are last," &c.), but in a totally different sense. Here the "last" are those who are wholly shut out from the kingdom of God; and the passage teaches that many from among the nations, estranged from God, should be called to share in his kingdom; while, on the other hand, many should be excluded from it who had held high places among the ancient people. Taken in this sense, these words would be foreign to the scope of the parable. The latter clause of the verse, "many are called, but few chosen," mean (according to Matt., xxii., 14) that many are outwardly called, and belong by profession to the kingdom of God. Nor is this relevant to the parable; which draws no contrast between the few and the many, the called and the chosen; and, in fact, makes no mention at all of such as are entirely excluded from the kingdom. We, therefore, cannot but suppose that this parable, so faithfully preserved, and bearing so indubitably the stamp of Christ, is joined to the words that precede and follow by a merely accidental link of connexion. (In this supposition, which, indeed, has long been a certainty

The prominent idea of the parable is, that all who faithfully obey their call, who are truly converted, and labour diligently after their conversion, whether it occur at an earlier or later period, whether the term of their new life is long or short, are made partakers of the same blessedness in the kingdom of GOD. The question is not what they were before their conversion, but what they become after it. All who have reached this point have the same thing in common; for all receive the principle of the higher life, with which, where it really exists, is also presupposed the entire new moral creation that proceeds from it; although this latter may yet be far from complete, and can only be fully realized in the future. No one is entitled to ask more than his fellow receives; there being no human merit in the case, *all* that is given is of GOD's free grace and mercy in redemption. And it applies not only to the relations of nations (*e. g.*, the later called heathen, to the Jews), but also of individuals.

But how important a thing it is for us that a parable exhibiting the doctrine of free and unmerited grace, so strongly put forth by Paul, has been preserved to us! Taken in connexion with that of the talents (pounds), it forms a complete *whole* (the two parables being mutually complementary to each other) of Christ's truth; on the one hand, that the gifts of grace are equally bestowed, and are to be received by all alike in humility of heart; and, on the other, that there are various stages of Christian progress, depending upon the use that is made of the grace given: on the one hand, the humble receiving of grace is contrasted with the asserting of one's own merits; and, on the other a self-active zeal is opposed to slothful inactivity

§ 241. *The Passion for Rewards rebuked.* (Luke, xvii., 7.)

Akin to the foregoing parable, though not chronologically connected with it, is the following fragment of a conversation* in which Christ rebuked the prevalent longing of his disciples for ease and reward. "*Which of you, having a servant ploughing, or feeding cattle, will say unto him, when he is come from the field, Come and sit down to meat?*

with me, I agree with *Strauss* and *De Wette.*) The most elaborate efforts to harmonize the passages in question with the parable only result in destroying its sense, so pregnant with characteristic Christian truth. Among these elaborate attempts must be reckoned the interpretation recently given by *Wilke* (Urevangelist, s. 372). The collocation of the parable in Matthew may afford a clue to its interpretation. Peter appears (xix., 27; although we prefer Luke, xviii., 28) to have a passion for rewards, and the parable bears upon such a disposition, which, by-the-way, prevailed at that time. In this connexion, also, the words "Many that are last shall be first," &c., might bear against measuring by merit, judging by appearance, &c. Christ may, perhaps, have spoken the words in this sense; though, as we have seen, he gave them another; but they cannot be made to fit the parable.

* Luke, xvii., 7, shortly before the account of the last journey to Jerusalem. It is plain that the 17th chapter begins with portions of unconnected conversations. We have already seen that v. 5, 6, belong to the period now before us.

and will not rather say unto him, Make ready wherewith I may sup, and gird thyself, and serve me, till I have eaten and drunken; and afterward thou shalt eat and drink? Doth he thank that servant for having done the things that were commanded him? I trow not. So likewise ye, when ye shall have done all those things that are commanded you, say, We are unprofitable servants; we have done that which was our duty to do."

Two thoughts are here presented: First, the disciples were not to expect at once in the kingdom of God, for whose appearance they were looking, a reward for their efforts to do Christ's will. Their Master was first to enter into his glory, and they were to remain upon earth and labour for him. Then for them, too, would come the time of rest and refreshment. Secondly, the servant who only fulfils his master's commands has no reason to boast, and no claim to his master's thanks; he has only rendered the duty owed by a servant to his lord. It is only when he goes beyond express commands, and does all that his master's advantage demands out of pure love, that he can look for thanks; he acts then, not as the servant, but as the friend. So the Apostles, acting simply as servants to Christ, were to call themselves unprofitable servants after they had fulfilled his express commands; they lacked as yet the all-prevailing love that would of itself, without such commands, impel them to every service which his cause required. This disposition obtained, they would be no more servants, but friends; and all disputes for rank, all mercenary longing for rewards, would fall away. They would then never think that they had done enough for the Master. To *this* spirit, the essence of genuine Christianity, they were to be exalted.*

§ 242. *Christ Anointed by Mary in Bethany.* (John, xii., 1, seq.)

After Christ had thus prepared the minds of the disciples for the great events that were approaching, he departed, accompanied by them only, from Jericho on the Friday. The journey thence to Bethany could easily be accomplished before the Sabbath, which he intended to spend in the latter place with the family of Lazarus.

He sat at the Sabbath-meal with the man whom he had raised from the dead. Again did the two sisters manifest their differences of character in their way of evincing their love and gratitude to the Saviour.†

* My view of the moral import of this passage agrees with that of my dear friend *Julius Müller* (Von der Sünde, 2te. Aufl., i., 48), although he gives it a somewhat different turn. I differ from him, however, in regard to the bearing of the passage; he applies it to the Pharisees rather than to the Apostles.

† The narrative of this remarkable incident is not only given by John, but preserved also by Matthew and Mark, though with variations. Luke alone says nothing about it; but then he mentions nothing of Christ's stay in Bethany at this interval. Even if [as some suppose] the account which he gives (vii., 38, seq.) of the anointing at the house of Simon

The industrious Martha waited upon him at table; but Mary, indulging her feelings, and laying aside all ordinary calculations, anointed the feet of Jesus with costly balsam of spikenard, and wiped them with the hair of her head.* The disciples knew that Jesus rather declined than sought demonstrations of honour for his person; and perhaps Judas, who could not understand or appreciate Mary's feelings, meant to enter into his views in this respect when he said, "*Why was not this ointment sold for three hundred pence, and given to the poor?*"†

(cf. p. 211, seq.) gave occasion for the omission of this, it would not follow that both accounts record but one and the same fact. Matthew and Mark differ from John in fixing the time at *two* days before Easter, instead of *six;* and in placing its scene, not in the house of Lazarus, but of Simon the leper. But since Matthew and Mark omit entirely the history of Lazarus, and connect the narrative directly from Jericho to Jerusalem, it is easy to explain their placing this anointing where they do, seeing that its nature was such as to secure its preservation, and its reference to Christ's approaching death necessarily assigned its chronological position. John introduces it in the connexion of *facts.* We see in his account the *occasion* of the festive meal, and of Mary's demonstration of love Whether the transfer of the scene to the house of Simon (in Matthew and Mark) was occasioned by blending this narrative with that of the other banquet that took place at Simon's house, or by some other cause, can not be decided; nor has it any bearing whatever upon the veracity of their narratives.

* In the other Gospels the "washing of the head" is mentioned; that of the feet accords more with Eastern usages. It was customary for servants to bring water to wash the feet of the guests; but Mary bathed them *herself,* not with *water,* but with a costly unguent. *Strauss* thinks it inexplicable that the *name* should have been lost in the other Gospels if the woman was so eminent in Gospel history, and especially as Christ said the incident should be kept in memorial of her wherever his Gospel was preached (Matt., xxvi., 13); and, on the other hand, he supposes that "this very saying of Christ might have occasioned the ascribing of the act to a definite person." To be sure, it is as *possible* that the tradition itself gave name to the unknown person at a later period, as that the name originally given should be lost. But that the one is more probable than the other cannot be proved in any way. Omitting Lazarus's history, they had no occasion to mention Mary. The commonness of the name (it belonged to several noted women in the New Testament) may have led to the omission. So in Luke, x., 38, as we have seen, the description of Martha and Mary in their family circumstances, the place of their abode, &c., is omitted, although the very gist of the anecdote turns upon their marked differences of character. But the connexion of the narrative now before us, with the approaching death of Jesus, also tended to preserve the locality. And as John mentions the *name,* without the promise given by Matthew (xxvi., 13), it is the more evident that the latter did not cause him to invent the former. His graphic description is that of an eye-witness; and it would even be easier to believe that Matt., xxvi., 13, was itself a later invention than that John was led by it to invent the name.

† None of the Evangelists but John mention the name of Judas. *Strauss* thinks that "if Judas had really been named in the original tradition, the name would not have been lost;" and, on the other hand, that "his bad character would easily lead to the ascription of this bad trait to him." But *care for the poor* was not a likely trait to ascribe to Judas, and John expressly assigns a motive of his own for his language (v. 6); and the very inaptness of this plea to Judas may have caused its transfer to others. We certainly cannot suppose that all, or many, of the Apostles made use of it, but the one who said it may have expressed the thought of others; though Christ's words do not necessarily presuppose this. Little as we may be surprised by various defects in their views and feelings at that time, there are two points of view in this plea that can hardly be conceived as used by any other than Judas: (1.) If their minds were then full of anticipations of Christ's glory, the anointing, as a demonstration of reverence for his person, could not appear improper to them; (2.) Or if their thoughts were turned to his approaching sufferings (which is not so

But Christ, who looks only at the heart, saw in Mary's act an exhibition of that overflowing love which is the spring and source of true holiness, and rebuked the vulgar tendency that wished to measure every thing by its own standard. "*Let her alone; against the day of my burying hath she kept this* (she has preserved it for my embalming); she has shown me the last tokens of honour and affection, not to be measured by vulgar standards; she knows that you will soon have *me* no more among you, while the *poor* ye shall have always."

probable), they could still less disapprove an expression of love for him whom they were so soon to lose. Neither of these remarks would apply to Judas.

PART II.

FROM THE TRIUMPHAL ENTRY INTO JERUSALEM TO THE ASCENSION.

CHAPTER I.

FROM THE TRIUMPHAL ENTRY TO THE LAST SUPPER.

§ 243. *The Entry into Jerusalem.**

THE fame of Christ's acts had been diffused among the thousands of Jews† that had gathered from all quarters for the Passover. The resurrection of Lazarus, in particular, had created a great sensation. As soon as the Sabbath law allowed,‡ they flocked in crowds to Bethany to see Jesus, and especially to convince themselves of the resurrection of Lazarus by ocular evidence and inquiry on the spot. Perhaps on Sunday morning, too, before Christ went to Jerusalem, many had gone out.§

* We must here account for the chronology that we adopt. We set out with the presupposition (for which reasons will be given hereafter) that the beginning of the Passover, 14th Nisan, occurred in that year on a Friday. Now John, xii., 1, gives a fixed mark—Christ's arrival at Bethany *six* days before the Passover; which six days may include that which forms the *terminus a quo*, and also the *terminus ad quem*. If he included the first, Christ reached Bethany on the Sabbath; not very likely, as he was wont to avoid the charge of violating the Mosaic law except in cases of urgent necessity. If he included both days, Christ reached Bethany on the *first* day of the week. But then the Passover caravan must have reached Jericho on Sabbath, or on Friday, remaining there on Sabbath, which is not probable, from the general tenor of the separate accounts. The only supposition that avoids these difficulties is that John included neither of the two days, and that Christ arrived in Bethany on Friday. (Cf. note, p. 281.) *B. Jacobi* supposes that Christ arrived so late on Friday that the Sabbath had begun, and John, therefore, regarded Friday as past; this supposition would remove the difficulty without altering the chronology.

† By a census taken under Nero, 2,700,000 men gathered at Jerusalem to the Passover Joseph., B. J., vi., 9, § 3.

‡ The Sabbath-day's journey allowed by the law was 1000 paces; but Bethany was twice that far from Jerusalem. The habit was to walk the first 1000 on Sabbath before sunset; the others afterward.

§ John, xii., 9, 13. According to the other Evangelists, Jesus came on the same day with the multitude from Jericho. The difficulty is not wholly inexplicable; nor does it affect the substance of the narrative. It is possible to distinguish (as *Schleiermacher* and others do) *two* entries of Christ into the city; the first being described in the first three Gospels, the second in John. According to this view, he entered first with the caravan towards evening, and a great sensation was produced; thence he went immediately to Bethany, and on the next morning (according to our view, the *second* day after) returned to the city, the fame of his works having, in the mean time, been still more widely bruited among the people; the second entry, expected and prepared for, causing much greater excitement than the first unannounced and unexpected one. But in this case we should have to admit that

The question may arise whether the triumphal entry into Jerusalem was part of Christ's plan, or not. It is certainly possible, from the circumstances just mentioned, that it was unsought on his part. But had such really been the case, he would have avoided the multitude, and entered the city quietly and privately, as he could easily have done. Had he not had higher interests in view, he must have avoided a mode of entry which confirmed the opinion that he claimed to be more than a mere teacher, and which would afford so excellent a handle to his enemies. We do not, indeed, look upon it as brought about by any management on his part, but as a natural result of the circumstances, as a final and necessary link in a chain of consecutive events. We regard it, therefore, as foreseen and embraced in his plan; and his plan was nothing else but the will of his Father, which he fulfilled as a free organ. He wished to yield to the enthusiasm of the people, transient as he knew it would be in most of them, and thus to testify, in the face of the nation and of mankind, that the kingdom of GOD had come, and that he was the promised Theocratic King. And this was the result of his previous labours, brought about by the Divine guidance. If he had not before, in the same direct and public way, proclaimed himself Messiah, he *now* did it before the eyes of all, most publicly and strikingly. This triumphant entry was the reply to many questions; a reply which shut out all doubt; it was, in a word, a world-historical event.*

the two narratives had been blended; parts that belonged to the second, as given by John, being transferred to the first. As the other Gospels (Mark especially) relate that he arrived late in the evening at the city, and went directly thence to Bethany, there appears good ground for the supposition. The statement of the other Evangelists (his going to Bethany) suits exactly John's account of his relations with the family of Lazarus.

But yet, if our mode of viewing the Gospels be correct, it may very well have been inferred—the narrative of the entry being separately transmitted, and the supposition naturally arising that he came directly with the caravan from Jericho—that the Messianic entry took place immediately on his arrival.

* It may be matter of question what features of the entry belonged to Christ's plan, and what were brought about entirely by the circumstances. To admit that any of them belonged to the latter class would not deprive them of significance; the developement of the circumstances themselves, apart from Christ's immediate intention, or in connexion therewith, might adapt them to symbolize the appearance of the kingdom of God. From John, xii., 14, we learn that Christ, finding the throng so great, seated himself upon an ass found just at hand, which act was subsequently referred to Zach., ix., 9, and the narrative somewhat modified accordingly, as, indeed, is seen in Matthew (xxi., 2–7), where *two* beasts are mentioned, from a misapprehension of the passage in Zachariah, following the Alexandrian version. It is to be carefully observed that John, xii., 16, makes a clear distinction between the view of this event taken by the disciples at the time, from that in which they regarded it at a later period, when all had been fulfilled, and they had seen Jesus as the glorified Messiah; showing that what at first appeared to be only accidental afterward gained a higher significance. None but an eye-witness would have made such a distinction at the time when this Gospel was written. If this should be taken as implying that the ass was accidentally there (though it by no means necessarily implies this), the use of the animal is not thereby rendered the less significant, or a less apt fulfilment of the Messianic prophecy. But, on the other hand, the other Gospels represent the act as *intentional* on Christ's part; not, however, as *Strauss* will have it, *miraculous*. It is

Attended by his disciples and the host that had gathered into Bethany, Christ set out for Jerusalem. Many more advanced to meet him from the city, and were hailed by those who had been with Christ with the assurance that Lazarus had indeed been raised from the dead. In the increasing throng, Christ mounted an ass which he found at hand, for his own convenience, and that the people might see him. And thus the natural course of circumstances aptly symbolized the peaceable character of the kingdom of GOD, and its total rejection of worldly pomp and display, as typified by the Prophet Zachariah (ix., 9). With joyous songs and shoutings he was introduced into the city as Messiah, while on all sides was heard the loud acclaim, "Hosanna! Jehovah prosper him! Blessed is he that cometh in the name of Jehovah" (Ps. cxviii., 25, 26). Some Pharisees among the multitude, who were perhaps not fully decided in their opinions, though recognizing Jesus as a great teacher, were displeased that he was thus proclaimed Messiah on entering the city, and asked him to silence his followers. He answered, "*I tell you, if these should hold their peace, the stones would cry out.*"* An event had occurred, so lofty and so pregnant with the best interests of mankind, that it might rouse even the dullest to rejoice. In the mouth of any other, even the greatest of *men*, these words would have been an unjustifiable self-exaltation; uttered by *Him*, they show the weighty import which he gave to his manifestation. Christ's conduct in this respect, moreover, shows that such an entry into Jerusalem formed part of his plan.

§ 244. *Sadness of Christ at Sight of Jerusalem.* (Luke, xix., 41–44.)

With what sorrow must that heart, so full of love, so overflowing with pity for the misery of men, have been wrung as he approached for the last time the CITY whose people he had so often summoned in vain to repent, the metropolis of the earthly Theocracy—soon to be left to deserved destruction, from which he *could* not save it, because His voice was not listened to! With tears he cried, "*If thou hadst known, even thou, at least in this thy day, the things which belong unto thy peace! but now they are hid from thine eyes.*" And then he uttered prophecy (v. 43 44) which the destruction of Jerusalem afterward abundantly verified.

Although Christ, doubtless, went immediately on his entry to the

not at all impossible to harmonize John's account with that of the other Evangelists; the word εὑρών in v. 14 does not of necessity define the way in which Christ obtained the ass; and John states many points very concisely. In the mean time, it is a question which account is the most simple.

* Luke, xix., 39. If we suppose there were *two* entries (which this passage appears, though not necessarily, to favour), these words would refer to the first; and the Pharisees probably accompanied the Passover caravan from Galilee.

Temple to thank GOD, it does not follow that we must place here the expulsion of the buyers and sellers.*

During the few remaining days of his ministry on earth, he made use of the favourable temper of the people to impress their minds with his teaching. In the mornings he taught in the Temple; the rest of the day was given to the disciples, with whom, in the evening, he was wont to retire to Bethany.

§ 245. *The Fig-tree Cursed.* (Matt., xxi., 18; Mark, xi., 12.)—*Parable of the Fig-tree.* (Luke, xiii., 6–9.)

A remarkable occurrence in this part of the history must now be examined somewhat closely. Christ, returning with his disciples in the morning from Bethany to Jerusalem, became hungry, and saw at a distance a fig-tree in full leaf. At that season of the year such a tree might be expected, in full foliage, to bear fruit;† and he walked towards it to pluck off the figs. Finding none, he said, "*No man eat fruit of thee hereafter forever.*" On the second morning,‡ the disciples, coming the same way, were astonished to find the fig-tree withered.

In what light is this fact to be regarded? Shall we see in it the immediate result of Christ's words; in fact, a miracle, as Matthew's statement appears to imply? All his other miracles were acts of love, acts of giving and creation; this would be a punitive and destroying miracle, falling, too, upon a natural object, to which no guilt could cling. It would certainly be at variance with all other peculiar operations of Christ, who came, in every respect, "not to destroy, but to fulfil." Shall we conceive that the coincidence with Christ's words was merely accidental—a view which suits Mark's statement better than Matthew's? If so, we shall find it impossible to extract from Christ's words, twist them as we may, a sense worthy of him.

The proper medium is to be found in the symbolical meaning of the act. If the miracles generally have a symbolical import (and we have shown that in some it is particularly prominent), we have in this case one that is *entirely* symbolical. The fig-tree, rich in foliage, but destitute of fruit, represents the Jewish people, so abundant in outward

* According to Matt., xxi., 15, 16, the displeasure of the priests was kindled when the children cried "Hosanna!" in the Temple. Jesus said to them, "Have ye never read, Out of the mouths of babes and sucklings hast thou ordained praise?" (Ps. viii., 3). This incident might be confounded with the one before quoted from Luke; but it has features essentially different. The haughty scribes are here offended because *children* rejoice, and Christ replies, in effect, "The glory of God is revealed to children, while the chiefs of the hierarchy, in the pride of their imagined wisdom, receive no impressions into their cold and unsusceptible hearts."

† See article "Feige," in *Winer's* Realwörterbuch. The remark in Mark, xi., 13, "The time of figs was not yet," presents a difficulty; the whole significance of the narrative lies in the fact that the tree might be expected to bear fruit, but was destitute of it.

‡ I follow here Mark's statement, which seems to me to be the most original in this particular.

shows of piety, but destitute of its reality. Their vital sap was squandered upon leaves. And as the fruitless tree, failing to realize the aim of its being, was destroyed; so the Theocratic nation, for the same reason, was to be overtaken, after long forbearance, by the judgments of God, and shut out from his kingdom.

The prophets were accustomed to convey both instructions and warnings by symbolical acts; and the purport of this act, as both warning and prediction, was precisely suited to the time. But to understand Christ's act aright, we must not conceive that he at once caused a *sound* tree to wither. This would not, as we have said, be in harmony with the general aim of his miracles; nor would it correspond to the idea which he designed to set vividly before the disciples. A sound tree, suddenly destroyed, would certainly be no fitting type of the Jewish people. We must rather believe that the same cause which made the tree barren had already prepared the way for its destruction, and that Christ only hastened a crisis which had to come in the course of nature. In this view it would correspond precisely to the great event in the world's history which it was designed to prefigure: the moral character of the Jewish nation had long been fitting it for destruction; and the Divine government of the world only brought on the crisis.

It is true, no explanation on the part of Christ is added in the account of the event above related, although we may readily believe that the disciples were not so capable of apprehending his meaning, or so inclined to do it, as to stand in need of no explanation. But we find such an explanation in the parable of the *barren fig-tree* (Luke, xiii., 6–9), which evidently corresponds to the fact that we just unfolded. As the *fact* is wanting in Luke, and the *parable* in Matthew and Mark, we have additional reason to infer such a correspondence. We cannot conclude, with some, that the narrative of the fact was merely framed from an embodiment of the parable; nor that the fact itself, so definitely related, was purely ideal; but we find in the correspondence of the two an intimation that idea and history go here together; and that, according to the prevailing tendencies of the persons who transmitted the accounts, the one or the other was thrown into the background.

It may be a question whether the words of Christ (Matt., xxi., 21; Mark, xi., 23) on the power of faith to "remove mountains" really belong in this connexion. Against it is the fact that the miracle proper was really subordinate, and that the faith of the disciples was to show its power in modes very different from that illustrated by the fact. But if the words *are* to be taken in this connexion, we must suppose that, after the attention of the disciples had been drawn to the subordinate feature (the withering of the tree), Christ made use of their astonishment for a purpose very important in this last period of his stay with them, viz., to incite them to act of themselves by the power of God; not to be so amazed at what *He* wrought with that power, but to remember that in communion with him *they* would be able to do the same, and even greater things. The sense of his words then would be: "You need not wonder at a result like this; the result was the least of it; *you* shall do still greater things by the power of God, if you only possess the great essential, Faith."

If we adopted this view, we should be disposed to consider Luke, xvii., 6, as the original form of Christ's language with regard to the fig-tree; and to suppose that in Matthew and Mark different expressions, conveying similar thoughts, had been blended together. Yet it cannot be asserted that the view itself is altogether well supported. Perhaps it may have been the case that the original form of Christ's words in explanation of the miracle was lost; its symbolical import, which is really its chief import, was made subordinate to the miracle itself; and another expression of Christ, better adapted to this conception of the fact, was brought into connexion with it.

§ 246. *Machinations of the Pharisees.*

The sensation created by the raising of Lazarus had, as we have seen, quickened the resolution to which the more hasty portion of the Sanhedrim had long been inclined, to put Jesus out of the way. The time and mode of its execution depended upon the fact and the manner of his entering the city; and men of all classes waited anxiously to see whether he would dare openly to face his enemies. Before his arrival, the Sanhedrim ordered that any one who should ascertain his place of abode should inform them of it, that measures might be taken for his arrest.*

The triumphant Messianic entry of Christ, amid the shouts of the enthusiastic multitude, was an unexpected blow to the hierarchical party. "See," said they in anger, "*how ye prevail nothing!* behold, the world is gone after him!"† They now determined to make use of craft. We cannot decide, from the brief intimations of the Evangelists, whether they first intended to make use of the *Sicarii*,‡ who at that time were employed frequently by the unprincipled heads of parties; or whether it was their plan from the beginning to get him into their power by stratagem, and then have him condemned under the forms of law. This last would be more in consonance with their usual hypocrisy.

* John, xi., 56, 57. † Ibid., xii., 19.

‡ Matt., xxvi., 4. It cannot be well decided whether ἀποκτείνειν refers to assassination or to legal murder.

Doubtless the pleas and accusations to be employed were all ready; abundant material had been gathered from Christ's labours both in Galilee and Jerusalem. Still, they must have welcomed any new developements which might serve to justify his condemnation on the ground of Jewish law, or to present him to the Roman authorities as a culprit.*

§ 247. *Combination of the Pharisees and Herodians.—Christ's Decision on paying Tribute to Cæsar.*

Besides the Pharisaical party, there was another among the Jews at that time, the Herodians, a political rather than religious party, whose greatest care was to preserve the public quiet, and avoid all occasions of offence to the Romans. These two parties now combined against Christ;† not the first or the last instance in history in which priests have made use of politicians, even otherwise opposed to them, to crush a reformer whose zeal might be inimical to both.

A question was proposed to Christ, apparently out of respect to his authority, but really with a view to draw such an answer from him as would offend either the hierarchs or politicians: "*Master, we know that thou art true; for thou regardest not the person of men, but teachest the way of God in truth: is it lawful to give tribute to Cæsar, or not?*"‡ A denial of the obligation would subject him to accusation before the Roman authorities as a man politically dangerous, and a ringleader of rebellion. To acknowledge it, might lay him open to the charge of degrading the dignity of the Theocratic nation. Asking for a Roman

* In order to obtain an exact view of the events that preceded and contributed to the death of Christ, we must compare the synoptical accounts with that of John. The former, however, collecting into the space of a few days events which, according to John, occurred at various points of time, leave many gaps and obscurities. Pharisaical plots and schemes that were, perhaps, going on for years, are all transferred to this period. According to the synoptical accounts, the Sanhedrim sent a deputation to Christ while he taught publicly in the Temple, asking his authority for so doing. Christ, seeing that they only meant to ensnare him, replied by a question that was rather dangerous for them: "The baptism of John, whence was it? from heaven, or of men?" (Matt., xxi., 25). Their interests would be prejudiced by admitting it to be "from heaven;" their fear of alienating the people, who revered John as a prophet, forbade them to say it was "of men." They therefore evaded the question, and Christ declared himself to be thereby justified in refusing to answer theirs. In this statement itself there is nothing improbable; the only possible doubt is as to its chronological connexion. Could the Sanhedrim have sent such a deputation to Christ at a time when matters had gone so far as John's account represents them? The question proposed cannot but remind us of that offered to Christ (John, ii., 18) at the beginning of his ministry; the answer reminds us, also, of Christ's appeal, at an earlier period, to the testimony of John the Baptist. Without venturing to decide the point, we may suggest that the chronology is at fault. And, at any rate, the obscurity in the connexion of events in the synoptical Gospels, arising from the omission of Christ's previous labours in Jerusalem, makes it necessary for us to fill them up from John's definite historical outline. Matt., xxi., 46, recalls forcibly John's statements of similar facts before occurring in the city.

† Mark, iii., 6, perhaps implies that this union was formed at an earlier period.

‡ Mark, xii., 14, 15.

denarius, he inquired. "*Whose is this image and superscription?*" "Cæsar's." The very currency of the coin implied an acknowledgment of the political dependence of the nation upon the Roman Empire, and of the obligations that flowed from such dependence. This conclusion he uttered in very few words: "*Render unto Cæsar the things that are Cæsar's, and to God the things that are God's.*"

These words imply that it was not Christ's calling to alter the relations and duties of civil society. Had he meant to represent himself as Messiah in the sense of Messiahship held by the Pharisees, he must have given a different reply; but his answer taught them that their obligations to Cæsar were not inconsistent with their duties to God; on the contrary, that the latter constituted the basis of the former. At the same time, it reminded them of a duty to which they were most unfaithful, viz., *to give truly to God what is God's; as man, bearing the stamp of his image, belongs to him, and should be dedicated to him.* And the "giving to God what is God's" not only affords the basis, but also fixes the just limitations of the civil obligations growing out of relations brought about by Divine Providence.

§ 248. *Christ's Reply to the Sadducees about the Resurrection.* (Matt., xxii., 23, seq.; Mark, xii., 18; Luke, xx., 27.)

Between the spirit of Christ and that of the Sadducees there was, as we have already seen,* nothing in common. But although that party generally paid little heed to popular religious movements, and had as yet hardly noticed Christ, their attention, and even their favour, was drawn to him by the opposition of the Pharisees. His happy defeat of the schemes of the latter induced the Sadducees to tempt him with a question in regard to marriage in the resurrection, which might, perhaps, embarrass him on the ground that he occupied. But with them, as with the Pharisees, he struck at the root, and traced their errors to ignorance of the Scriptures and of the omnipotence of God. Had they known the Scriptures, he showed them (even the *law*, which they acknowledged, for he quoted out of Exodus), not only in the letter, but the spirit, they could not fail to see a necessary connexion between the faith revealed there and the doctrine of an eternal, individual life for man (v. 31, 32). Had they known the omnipotence of God, they would not have supposed that the forms and relations of the present life must be preserved in the future; God could bestow the new existence in a far different, nay, in a glorified form (v. 29, 30).

He thus refuted the Sadducees, both negatively and positively. Negatively, by showing that their question went on the false hypothesis that the forms and relations of the present sensible life would be transferred to the future spiritual one; and positively, by showing the es-

* Cf. p. 3[illegible].

sential import of the declaration in the Pentateuch, "*I am the God of Abraham, and the God of Isaac, and the God of Jacob.*" How could God place himself in so near a relation to individual men, and ascribe to them so high a dignity, if they were mere perishable appearances; if they had not an essence akin to his own, and destined for immortality?

We must bear in mind here the emphatic sense in which Christ contrasts the "dead" and the "living;" a sense which is evident (apart from John's Gospel) in the passage, "*Let the dead bury their dead.*"* It is in this emphatic sense that he says, "*God is not the God of the dead, but of the living*"† (v. 32). The living God can only be conceived as the God of the living. And this argument, derived from the Theocratic basis of the Old Testament, is founded upon a more general one, viz., the connexion between the consciousness of God and that of immortality. Man could not become conscious of God as his God, if he were not a personal spirit, divinely allied, and destined for eternity, an eternal object (as an individual) of God; and thereby far above all natural and perishable beings, whose perpetuity is that of the species, not the individual.

It is worthy of remark, that Christ does not enter further into the faith of immortality as defined in the belief of the resurrection; his opponents could not appreciate the latter until they had been made to feel the need of the former.

§ 249. *Christ's Exposition of the First and Great Commandment.*— (Mark, xii., 28–34.)

The promptness with which Christ silenced the Pharisees and Sadducees inclined towards him many of the better-minded.‡ One of these, who felt himself compelled to acknowledge Jesus as a witness of truth, if not as Messiah, put a question to him in good faith, in order to make known his agreement of sentiment with him:§ "*Which is the first commandment of all?*" And when Christ replied that all the commandments were implied in two "the supreme love of God, and the love of one's neighbour as one's self," he assented with all his heart, declaring that this was, indeed, more than "all whole burnt-offerings and sacrifices." Jesus, whose loving heart always welcomed the germs of

* Cf. p. 310.

† The quibbles of the Rabbinical writers on this passage, compared with Christ's profound saying, illustrate the proverb, "*Duo cum dicunt idem, non est idem.*"

‡ So, at the council of Costnitz, when John Huss, the witness for Christ and truth, was condemned by a majority of scribes and priests, there were yet a few among the multitude of better spirit, who were moved by the power of truth in his replies and conduct, and manifested their sympathy.

§ We follow Mark rather than Matthew, who represents the question as put in a hostile spirit. Mark's description coincides with Luke, xx., 39, where certain of the scribes are represented as expressing their assent to the Saviour's answers.

truth and goodness, praised the spirit of the man's reply, saying, "*Thou art not far from the kingdom of God.*" And in this he intended no more and no less than the words themselves conveyed. Had he considered an earnest moral striving, such as this man expressed, to be sufficient, he would have acknowledged him as not only *near*, but *in* the kingdom of God. He tells him, however, that he is on the way to it, because he was freed from the Pharisaic delusion of the righteousness of works, and knew the nature of genuine piety; and could, therefore, more readily be convinced of what he still lacked of the *spirit* of the law, which he so well understood. The conscious need of redemption, thus awakened, would lead him to the only source whence his wants could be supplied.

§ 250. *The Parable of the Good Samaritan.* (Luke, x., 25, seq.)

We here deviate a moment from chronological order, to introduce a similitude germane to the conversation just set forth. It is remarkable that Luke omits that conversation and gives the parable *of the good Samaritan*,* which is obviously akin to it in import, and is, in turn, omitted by the other Evangelists. Perhaps in this, as in other cases already mentioned,† the Evangelists divided the matter among them, in view of this very congeniality of meaning.

The parable introduces a man asking Christ what he must do to inherit eternal life. We might infer from Luke's statement that his motives were bad; but the narrative does not confirm this view, although Christ's reply does not place him beside the man who was "near" the kingdom of God. He was one of the νομικοί (lawyers), who, as we have said (p. 247, note), differed from the Pharisees in occupying themselves more with the original writings of Scripture than with the traditions. In this respect they stood nearer to Christ than the Pharisees. The Saviour does not prescribe, as the lawyer, perhaps, expected, any new and special command, but refers him to the law itself, which he had made his particular study: "*What is written in the law? How readest thou?*" The lawyer quoted in reply (as did the scribe referred to in the last section) the all-embracing commandment to love God and one's neighbour. "*Do this,*" said Christ, "*and thou shalt live;*" implying, what, indeed, is the doctrine of the whole New Testament, that if a man were really capable of a life wholly pervaded by this love, he would lack nothing to justify him before God.

The lawyer was probably ill-disposed to dwell upon the requisites of this perfect law; and Christ, therefore, sets vividly before him in the

* This parable, like that mentioned p. 216, note, is peculiar in this, that the truth of the higher sphere is not illustrated by a fact from the lower, but the general truth, by a special case from the same sphere, which may in itself have been matter of fact.

† Cf. p. 315, note, and p. 358.

parable the nature of a genuine and practical love, shown in the Samaritan, in contrast with that obedience to the law which goes no further than the lips, illustrated by the priest and the Levite. And in conclusion, he told him, "*Go thou and do likewise*, and thou shalt fulfil the law." The contrast between true and pretended love is thus made prominent in the parable in opposition (1) to the hypocrisy, and (2) to the narrow exclusiveness of the Pharisees.*

§ 251. *Christ's Interpretation of Psalm* cx., 1. (Mark, xii., 35–37.)

We return now to the order of the narrative. We are informed by the Evangelists that in the course of these controversies with his opponents Christ put to them the question, how it could be that Messiah was to be the Son of David, and yet that David called him "Lord" (Ps. cx., 1). We are not precisely told with what view he proposed the question; though it might, perhaps, be inferred from Matthew's statement, that after he had so answered their captious queries as to put them to shame, he sought in turn to embarrass them. But was it consistent with the dignity of his character to put questions merely for such a purpose? Nothing like it, at all events, is to be found in his words or actions. Nor can we well imagine that the shrewd Pharisees could have been much embarrassed by such an interrogatory. Their views would naturally have suggested the reply that Messiah was alluded to in respect to his bodily descent, when called the "Son of David;" and to his Divine authority as Theocratic King when called "Lord." In this case, then, as in a recent one, we follow in preference the statement of Mark; according to which, Christ put the question while teaching in the Temple, perhaps in answer to something said in hostility to him.†

But for what purpose of instruction did he quote the Psalm? Shutting out every thing but what Mark says, we should have to suppose that he used it to combat the opinion that Messiah must come of the line of David; in order, perhaps, to make good his claim to the Messiahship against those who questioned his own descent from David (John, vii., 42). But Paul could not have presupposed it as a settled fact‡ that Christ was of the seed of David, had He ever expressed himself according to the supposition just given. Nor would his argument, in this case, be as striking as we commonly see in his disputes; for, as we have said, he might be David's Lord, in one sense, and his

* It has been supposed, since Christ's reply is not precisely an answer to the question in v. 29, that the parable may have been separately transmitted, and at a later period put into this connexion, a connexion imitated from Mark, xii., 28, seq.; the two verses of this passage (29–31) being transferred in Luke from Christ's mouth to the lawyer's. But even if we admit that the connecting link in the dialogue is not fully given in Luke, x., 29, the historical order is so obvious, that we are thrown upon no such forced explanations.

† The word ἀποκριθείς favours this conclusion.

‡ Cf. p. 17, and Heb. vii., 14

Son in another. Our view, then, is that Christ quoted the Psalm in order to unfold the higher idea of the Messiah as the Son of God, and to oppose, *not* the idea that he was to be Son of David, but a one-sided adherence to this, at the expense of the other and higher one. Perhaps offence had been taken at the higher titles which he assumed to himself; and he may have been thereby led to adopt this course of argument. As he had before used Ps. lxxxii., 6,* to convince the Jews on their own ground that it was no blasphemy for him to claim the title "Son of God" in the highest sense; so now he used Ps. cx. to convince them that the two elements were blended together in the Messianic idea.† Still, the passage may only have preserved to us the head or beginning of a fuller exposition.

Even though it be proved that David was not the author of the Psalm quoted, Christ's argument is not invalidated thereby. Its principal point is precisely that of the Psalm; the idea of the Theocratic King, King and Priest at once, the one founded upon the other, raised up to God, and looking, with calm assurance, for the end of the conflict with his foes, and the triumphant establishment of his kingdom. This idea could never be realized in any *man;* it was a prophecy of Christ, and in Him it was fulfilled. This idea went forth necessarily from the Spirit of the Old Dispensation, and from the organic connexion of events in the old Theocracy; it was the blossom of a history and a religion that were, in their very essence, prophetical. In this regard it is matter of no moment whether David uttered the Psalm or not. History and interpretation, perhaps, may show that he did not. But whether it was a conscious prediction of the royal poet, or whether some other, in poetic but holy inspiration, seized upon this idea, the natural blossom and off-shoot of Judaism, and assigned it to an earthly monarch, although in its true sense it could never take shape and form in such a one—still it was *the* idea by which the Spirit, of which the inspired seer, whoever he may have been, was but the organ, pointed to Jesus. The only difference is that between conscious and unconscious prophecy. And if Christ really named David as the author of the Psalm, we are not reduced to the alternative of detracting from his infallibility and unconditional truthfulness, or else of admitting that David really wrote it. The question of the authorship was immaterial to his purpose; it was no part of his Divine calling to enter into such investigations; his

* Cf. p. 327.

† We see here a mark of that higher unity in which the lineaments of Christ's picture as given by the first three Gospels, harmonize with those given by John. Although at a later period the view which conceived Christ, as to his calling, person, and authority, wholly or mainly as "the Son of David," was opposed by another equally one-sided theory which recognized him only as "Son of God," and thrust out the "Son of David" entirely it would be a most arbitrary procedure, indeed, to infer [as some have done] that the prevalence of the latter doctrine alone gave rise to the invention of this passage.

teachings and his revelation lay in a very different sphere. Here [as often elsewhere] he doubtless employed the ordinary title of the Psalm—the one to which his hearers were accustomed.

What we have said in another place* in regard to the place assigned by Christ to the Old Testament and to the prophecies is enough, we think, to show that he regarded it as a revelation not fully developed, but veiled; not brought out entirely into clear consciousness, but containing also a circle of unconscious prophecies. Let us be careful that we are not again brought into bondage to a Rabbinical theology of the *letter*, than which nothing can be more at variance with the spirit of Christ.

§ 252. *The Widow's Mite.* (Luke, xxi., 1–4; Mark, xii., 41–44.)

Christ had warned the disciples against the mock-holiness of the Pharisees. A poor widow cast two mites, all her wealth, into the treasury of the Temple. He made use of this incident to impress them again with the truth, so often and so variously illustrated by him, that it is the *heart* which fixes the character of pious actions; that the greatest gifts are valueless without pure motives; the smallest, worthy, with them. The same principle was set forth in his saying that great and small acts were alike in moral worth, if done *in his name*.†

§ 253. *Christ predicts the Divine Judgments upon Jerusalem.* (Matt., xxiii.)

Before leaving the Temple, Christ delivered a discourse‡ full of severity against the heads of the hierarchy, through whom destruction was soon to be brought upon the nation. He then announced the judgments of God, in a series of prophecies that were afterward fulfilled in the destruction of Jerusalem. Regarding himself as already removed from the earth, he says nothing further of what was to befall his own person, but predicts that the agents by whose labours his work was to be extended would be persecuted, like the witnesses for the truth of old; and that the Jews, thus partaking of the wicked spirit of their fathers, would fill up the measure of their sins, and bring upon themselves the wrath which the accumulated guilt of ages had been gathering. Glancing with Divine confidence at the developement of his work, he says: "*Behold! I send unto you prophets, and wise men, and scribes;*§ *and some of them ye shall scourge in your*

* Cf. p. 200. † Cf. p. 288.

‡ This discourse, as given in Matt., xxiii., contains many passages uttered on other occasions.

§ The application of these Old Testament designations to Christ's organs is not strange; he intended by it an analogy to the Theocratic developement. There were *prophets* in the early Christian Church; and the term "*scribes*" is applied, in Matt., xiii., 52, to teachers in the "kingdom of heaven" on earth. As this last discourse, as given by Matthew, con-

synagogues, and persecute them from city to city; and some of them ye shall kill and crucify." He concludes with a mournful allusion to the catastrophe which was to be so big with interest to the kingdom of GOD, to the judgment over Jerusalem, and to his second advent to judge the earth and complete his work. "*O Jerusalem, Jerusalem, thou that killest the prophets, and stonest them which are sent unto thee, how often would I have gathered thy children together, even as a hen gathereth her chickens under her wings, and ye would not.* Behold! your house is left unto you desolate;† for I say unto you, that ye shall not see me henceforth, till ye shall say, Blessed is he that cometh in the name of the Lord.*" He obviously, in this last clause, betokens his second and triumphal advent as Theocratic King. Other persons, however, are implied than those to whom the discourse was directed: *they* were least likely ever to welcome him with praises, and the words denote a willing, not a forced submission. We take them as referring to the Jews in general, as the previous verse refers to the inhabitants of Jerusalem in general; the particular generation intended being left undefined.

§ 254. *Christ's Prediction of the Coming of the Kingdom of God, and of his Second Advent.* (Mark, xiii.; Matt., xxiv.)

Christ had left the Temple with the disciples. They were admiring the external splendour of the edifice, and he, still full of prophecy, took advantage of it to tell them that all this magnificence should be swept away in the general ruin of the city. These intimations kindled an anxious curiosity in their minds, and when they were alone with him, upon the Mount of Olives, they questioned him closely as to the signs by which the approaching catastrophe could be known, and the time when it should take place.

tains various passages given by Luke in the table-conversation (ch. xi.), so Luke inserts *there* this prophetic announcement, whose proper position is found in Matthew. In opposition to Dr. *Schneckenburger* (Stud. d. Evang. Geistl. Würtemb., vi., 1, p. 35), I must think that the form of Christ's words given by Luke is the less original. It shows the traces of Christian language. In Luke, xi., 49, this prophecy is introduced as coming from "the wisdom of God" (cf. Wisdom of Solomon, vii., 27). The origin of this form of citation is accounted for very naturally by my dear colleague and friend, Dr. *Twesten*, on the ground that so notable a prediction could readily be transmitted as a separate one; that it was so transmitted as an utterance of the Divine wisdom manifested in Christ; and that Luke, receiving it in this form, so incorporated it in his collection.

* We have already remarked that these words necessarily presuppose previous and repeated labours of Christ at Jerusalem. Cf. p. 157, 324, note.

† He withdraws from them his blessing, saving presence, and "leaves" them, since they *will* not be saved, to the desolation and destruction they have brought upon themselves. By the word "house" we need not necessarily understand "temple" (cf. *De Wette*, in loc.); but it is yet a question whether Christ did not really mean the Temple, which he was just leaving. If so, he calls it "their" house, not the house of God, because their depravity had desecrated the holy place. His leaving it was a sign that God's presence should dwell in it no more.

It was certainly far from Christ's intention to give them a complete view of the course of developement of the kingdom of Gor up to its final consummation. He imparted only so much as was necessary to guard them against deception, to stimulate their watchfulness, and confirm their confidence that the end would come at last. Much, indeed, was at that time beyond their comprehension, and could only be made clear by the enlightening influence of the Spirit, and by the progress of events. Indeed, if they had fully understood the intimations he had previously given, they might have spared themselves many questions. It was always Christ's method to cast into their minds the seeds of truth, that were only to spring up into full consciousness at a later period. This was especially the case in his prophecies of the future progress and prospects of the kingdom of God. A clear and connected knowledge on that point was not essential to the preachers of his Gospel. Many predictions had necessarily to remain obscure until the time of their fulfilment. He himself says (Matt., xxiv., 36; Mark, xiii., 32) that the day and hour of the final decision are known only to the counsels of the Father; and, as it would be trifling to refer this to the *precise* "day and hour," rather than to the *time* in general, it could not have been his purpose to give definite information on the subject. To know the *time*, presupposed a knowledge of the hidden causes of events, of the actions and reactions of free beings—a prescience which none but the Father could have; unless we suppose, what Christ expressly denies, that He had received it by a special Divine revelation. Not that he could err, but that his knowledge was conscious of its limits; although he knew the progress of events, and saw the slow course of their developement,* as no mortal could.

When, therefore, Christ speaks in this discourse of the great import of his coming for the history of the world, of his triumphant self-manifestation, and of the beginning of his kingdom, he betokens thereby partly his triumph in the destruction of the visible Theocracy, and its results in the freer and wider diffusion of his kingdom, and partly his second advent for its consummation. The judgment over the degenerate Theocracy, and the final judgment of the world; the first free developement of the kingdom of God, and its final and glorious consummation, correspond to each other: the former, in each case, prefiguring the latter. And so, in general, all great epochs of the world's history, in which God reveals himself as Judge, condemning a creation ripe for destruction, and calling a new one into being; all critical and creative epochs of the world's history correspond to each other, and collectively prefigure the *last* judgment and the *last* creation—the consummation of the kingdom of God.

If Christ had been but a *prophet*, we might indeed suppose that the

* Cf. p 80, on the Plan of Jesus, and 189. seq., on the Parables of the Kingdom of God.

image of the glorious future which unveiled itself to his *seeing* glance in moments of inspiration, was involuntarily blended in his mind with the realities of the present; and that events, separated by long intervals of time, presented themselves as closely joined together. But we must here distinguish between the conscious truth and the defective forms in which it was apprehended; between the revelation of the Divine Spirit in itself, and the hues which it took from the narrowness of human apprehension, and the forms of the time in which it was delivered. In Christ, however, we can recognize no blending of truth with error, no alloy of the truth as it appeared to his own mind.* What we have already said is enough to show that this could not coexist with the expositions given by him of the kingdom of GOD. But it is easy to explain how points of time which He kept apart, although he presented them as counterparts of each other, without assigning any express duration to either, were blended together in the apprehension of his hearers, or in their subsequent repetitions of his language.†

§ 255. *Parable of the Marriage Feast of the King's Son.* (Matt., xxii., 1–14.)

Matthew assigns to this period several parables in which Christ illustrated the course of developement of the kingdom of GOD. Some of them are allied to those mentioned by us before in following Luke's account. But their affinity does not justify us in concluding, with some modern writers, that they were originally one and the same, and that the variations in their form are due to their more or less faithful transmission. We hope to be able to show, as we have done in other cases, that the allied parables are alike original, and were alike uttered by Christ himself.

* Cf. p. 80.

† It was peculiar as we have seen, to the editor of our Greek Matthew to arrange together congenial sayings of Christ, though uttered at different times and in different relations; and we have remarked this (p. 318, note †) in reference to the discourse in Matt., xxiv. We need not, therefore, wonder if we find it impossible to draw the lines of distinction in this discourse with entire accuracy; nor need such a result lead us to forced interpretations, inconsistent with truth and with the love of truth. It is much easier to make such distinctions in Luke's account (ch. xxi.), though even that is not without its difficulties. In comparing Matthew and Luke together, however, we can trace the origin of most of these difficulties to the blending of different portions together, when the discourses of Christ were arranged in collections. It is true, *Strauss* and *De Wette* assert that the form of the discourses in Matthew is much more original than in Luke; that the latter bears marks of a date subsequent to the destruction of Jerusalem; and, therefore, that it was remodelled *after* the event had given its light to the prediction, and shown the falsity of some of the expectations entertained by the disciples. But does the character of the discourse confirm this hypothesis? Would the narrator, in such a case, have left such passages unaltered as xxi., 10, also 18, compared with 16 and 28? It is impossible to carry the hypothesis through consistently with itself; and the natural conclusion is, that Luke has, as usual, given us Christ's discourses in the most faithful and original way.

We take up first the parable of the *Marriage of the King's Son* (Matt., xxii). The kingdom of God is here represented under the figure of a marriage feast given by the King (God) to his Son (Christ). The guests invited are the members of the old Theocratic nation. When the banquet is prepared (*i. e.*, when the kingdom of God is to be established upon earth), the king sends his servants out at different times to call in the guests that were before bidden. Some follow their business without the least regard to the invitation; corresponding to those men who are wholly devoted to earthly things, and indifferent to the Divine. Others, going still further, seize, abuse, and finally kill the servants; representing men decidedly hostile to the Gospel, and persecutors of its preachers. It is not strange that Christ does not in this, as in another parable, add another point of gradation, by sending out the son to be maltreated also; it would not harmonize with the plan of the parable for the king's son, in whose honour the feast was given, to go about like a servant and invite his guests. Moreover, the parable refers to Christ's agents, not to himself; as he speaks of a time when he shall no more be present on the earth.

When the king learns what has passed, he sends his armies, seizes the murderers, and burns their city; corresponding to the prophecy of the judgment over the Jews and the destruction of Jerusalem. As the city is destroyed, new guests cannot be invited from thence; the king sends his servants out into the highways, frequented by many travellers, with orders to invite every body to the wedding; a prophetic intimation, obviously, that, after the destruction of Jerusalem and of the old Theocratic nation, the doors of the kingdom would be thrown wide open, and all the heathen nations be invited to come in. The servants, in execution of the command, bring in all whom they meet, both good and bad.

A second prominent feature of the parable now appears: the sifting of the guests. Those who have a just sense of the honour done them by the invitation, and come in a wedding-garment, represent such as fit themselves for membership of the kingdom of God by proper dispositions of heart; while those who come in the garb in which the invitation happens to find them correspond to such as accept the calls of the Gospel without any change of heart. Christ himself gives prominence to this feature of the parable in the words, "*Many are called, but few are chosen;*" distinguishing the great mass of outward professors who obey the external call from the few who are "chosen," because their hearts are right.*

* Many interpreters think the case should be conceived thus: The *caftan*, or wedding-dress, was offered to the guests, according to Oriental custom, by the king himself, and their disrespect was shown in refusing to accept it at his hands; thus representing justification by faith as the offered gift of Divine grace. This conception would help us to explain how the guests taken upon the road might have secured the wedding-garment, had

This parable is certainly similar to that in Luke, xiv., 16–24, before treated of;* but the new and different features which it presents indicate that it was uttered at a different period. In Luke's parable the hostility of the invited guests is not so decided; they offer *excuses* for not coming. The contrast, in fact, is limited to the Jewish nation; the poor and despised Jewish *people* being opposed to the Pharisees. And as no general Jewish enmity is alluded to, so the destruction of Jerusalem is not mentioned at all, and the calling of the heathen only by the way.

§ 256. *Parable of the Wicked Husbandman.* (Matt., xxi., 33–44; Mark, xii., 1–12; Luke, xx., 9–18.)

The gradations of guilt in the conduct of the Jews towards the Divine messengers, and, finally, towards the Son himself, are set forth more prominently in the parable of the *vineyard and the wicked vine-dressers* (Matt., xxi., 33). The *enjoyment* of the kingdom of God is the point contemplated in the parable of the marriage of the king's son; the *labour* done for it is that of the parable now before us. The former represents the kingdom in its consummation in the fellowship of the redeemed; the latter, in its gradual developement on earth, demanding the activity of men for its advancement. The lord of the vineyard had done every thing necessary for its cultivation; so had God ordained all things wisely for the prosperity of his kingdom among the Jews; all that was wanting was that they should rightly use the means instituted by him. The lord of the vineyard had a right to demand of his tenants a due proportion of fruit at the vintage; so God required of the Jews to whom he had intrusted the Theocracy to be cultivated, the fruits of a corresponding life. When the earlier messengers sent to call them to repentance had been evilly entreated and slain, he sends his Son, the destined heir of the vineyard, the King of the Theocracy. But as they show like dishonour to him, and kill him to secure themselves entire independence—to turn the kingdom of God into anarchy—his judgments break forth; the Theocratic relation is broken, and

they chosen to do so; nor is it a sufficient objection to it to say that such a usage cannot be proved to have prevailed in *ancient* times; for the similarity of modern to ancient customs in the East is so great, that we can infer from such as exist now, or at late periods, that like ones prevailed in the earliest ages. But if a thought so important to the whole parable had been intended, Christ would not have failed to express it definitely; he would have expressly reprimanded the delinquent guests with, "The garment was offered as a gift, and ye would not accept it; so much the greater your guilt." In short, if this conception be the right one, we must infer either that the parable has not been faithfully transmitted, or that the usage referred to was so general in the East that no particular reference to it was necessary. At all events, the mode by which the wedding-dress could be obtained was not important to Christ's purpose; and the absence of any allusion to it does not justify *Strauss's* conclusion that there is a foreign trait in the parable, [illegible] that it is composed of several heterogeneous parts.

* Cf. p. 254.

the kingdom is transferred to other nations that shall bring forth fruits corresponding to it.*

§ 257. *Parable of the Talents* (Matt., xxv., 14–30) *compared with that of the Pounds* (Luke, xix., 12).

The parable of the *talents* (Matt., xxv.) is evidently allied to that of the *pounds*† (Luke, xix., 12); but there are points of difference too striking to be ascribed to alterations in transmission. In the latter, each of the servants receives the same sum, one pound, and their position in the kingdom is assigned according to their gains. In the former, different sums are intrusted to the servants in proportion to their ability, and those who bring gains in the *same* proportion are rewarded accordingly. The aim, therefore, of Luke's parable is to represent different degrees of zeal in the management of one and the same thing, granted to all alike; of Matthew's, to show that one's acceptance does not depend upon his powers, or the extent of his sphere of labour, but upon faithfulness of heart, which is independent of both. If the different number of *talents* in the latter parable represents different spheres of labour, greater or less, corresponding to different measures of power, then the one *pound* in the former must represent the *one* common endowment of Christians—the one Divine life or the one Divine truth received into the life in all believers—the one Divine power, proving itself by its fruits in all who partake of it—but yet admitting of different degrees of fruitfulness according to the completeness with which it is willingly received and appropriated. These points of difference in the two parables presuppose that they had different objects. That of the *talents* aimed to intimate that the reward depends upon the motives, not upon the amount of one's labours, except so far as this might be affected by the disposition of the heart; and perhaps, also, to rebuke ambition and jealousy among the disciples themselves. That of the *pound*, on the other hand, was designed to stimulate the zeal of the Apostles in their labours for the kingdom of God, and encourage them to a holy emulation.

In both parables the servant who makes no use of the capital intrusted to him is condemned. But in Matthew this servant is precisely the one to whom only *one* talent is given; representing, perhaps, those who, with inferior powers, have insufficient confidence, and make the smallness of their gifts and the narrowness of their sphere of labour a plea for inactivity; such as say, comparing their talents and opportunities with those of others, "What can be expected of me, to whom so little has been given?" Here again, then, faithfulness and zeal, not the

* It is to be observ[illegible]hat the judgment of the Jewish nation is here represented as a "coming of the Lord:" intimating that we are to see in that judgment a "coming" of his in a spiritual sense

† Cf. p. 348.

measure of gifts, are made prominent. In the parable of the *pounds*, the one pound is taken away from the negligent servant and given to him that gained most; in harmony with the scope of the parable, that which the negligent one never truly possessed (because he never used it) is transferred to him who proved himself worthy of the trust by gaining *most*. It is not so in the parable of the talents; here equality in motive and disposition is the main point, so that the *quantitative* differences disappear, and he who with five talents gains other five deserves no pre-eminence on that account. The feature, therefore, given in Matt. xxv., 28, is not so appropriate to his parable as to Luke's; at all events, it belongs only to the filling up of the picture in the former, while in the latter it is a prominent feature.

§ 258. *Parable of the Wise and Foolish Virgins.* (Matt., xxv., 1–13.)

The parable of the *virgins* was designed to set vividly before the disciples the necessity of constant preparation for the uncertain time of Christ's second advent, without at all clearing up the uncertainty of the time itself; thus harmonizing exactly with all his teachings on the subject. It is certainly, also, the representation (so often made by Christ) of the idea of Christian virtue under the form of prudence; and illustrates the connexion between Christian prudence and that ever-vigilant presence of mind which springs from one constant and predominant aim of life. But we must distinguish between the fundamental thought of the parable and its supplementary features. It may be that one of these latter is the fruitless application of the foolish virgins to the wise for a supply which they might have secured for themselves by adequate care and forethought; yet, perhaps, Christ, piercing the recesses of the human heart, and seeing its tendency to trust in the vicarious services and merits of others, may have intended, by this feature of the parable, to warn his disciples against such a fatal error.

§ 259. *Christ teaches that Faith must prove itself by Works.* (Matt. xxv., 31–46.)

At the close of the twenty-fifth chapter of Matthew there is given a representation of the final judgment. There has been, and may be, much debate as to both the form and the substance of this representation. In regard to the latter it may be asked, "What judgment is alluded to, and who are to be judged?" One reply is, that the judgment of unbelievers alone is meant;* because, according to Christ's own words (John, iii., 18), believers are freed from judgment; and because the objects of the judgment are designated by the term ἔθνη, גוֹים, a term applied exclusively to that portion of mankind which does not belong to the kingdom of God.

* Advocated particularly by *Keil* (Opuscula) and *Olshausen* (Commentar.).

It is true, the Scriptures teach (Rom., ii., 12, seq.) that even among these nations there are degrees of moral character which will certainly be recognized by the just judge; but the distinctions drawn by the judge in the passage before us are not of this character. Further, the theory alluded to will not explain why sympathy and assistance rendered to believers are made the sole standard, and all other moral tests thrown out. All that it can offer is one or the other of the following suppositions: either that this sympathy is a *general* love for mankind, and its manifestation to proclaimers of the Gospel merely an accidental feature; or that it springs from a direct interest in the cause of Christ and the Gospel itself. But the first supposition would make the ascription of *special* value to these acts inconsistent with the standard set up by Christ himself; for the acts are (according to the hypothesis) outward and accidental. The second does, indeed, afford a ground for preference in the motive, viz., love of Christ's cause; but, then, it does away the theory itself, for the developement of such a sentiment in the minds of those who entertain it would inevitably make them Christians.

This theory, therefore, is untenable on either side. It is further refuted by the fact that, in the passage, Christ bestows upon those to whom he awards his praise the very titles which belong exclusively to believers: as the "*righteous;*" the "*blessed of the Father, for whom the kingdom was prepared from the foundation of the world.*" We conclude, therefore, that the judgment will include the trial and sifting of professors of the faith themselves. As before that final decision the faith of the Gospel will have been spread among all nations, so all nations are represented as brought to the bar; but, among these, genuine believers will be separated from those whose fidelity has not been proved by their lives. Indeed, we have already treated of several parables which presuppose such a final sifting of believers; nor is it at all inconsistent with the conscious assurance of the faithful that they are free from judgment through the redemption of Christ.

It is every where taught by him that brotherly love is a peculiar fruit of faith, the very test of its genuineness; and we cannot wonder, therefore, to find it made so prominent in this passage. The pious are represented in it as following the impulses of a true brotherly love, founded upon love to Christ, and as manifesting this love in kind acts to their brethren without respect to persons. Yet they attach no merit to their works, and are amazed to find the Lord value them so highly as to consider them *done unto himself.* But those whose faith is lifeless and loveless, and who rely upon their outward confessions of the Lord for their acceptance, are amazed, on the other hand, at their rejection. Never conscious of the intimate connexion between faith and love, or of genuine Christian feelings referring every thing to Christ, and seeing him in all things, they cannot understand why he interprets their lack of love for the brethren into lack of love for himself. The mere fact that faith is not expressly mentioned in connexion with the judgment does not affect our view; it is taken for granted that all have already professed the faith, and the genuine believers are to be separated from the spurious.

On the whole, then, we are not to look upon this representation as a *picture* of the final judgment. Its aim is to set forth, most vividly and impressively, the great and fundamental truth, that no faith but that which proves itself by works can secure a title to the kingdom of Heaven. We cannot fail to see in the "throne," the "right hand," the "left hand," &c., a figurative drapery, attending and setting off the one fundamental thought. Moreover, it was not Christ's usage to speak of himself *directly* under the title of "King." The form of the description, then, we suppose to have been parabolical; and its character in this respect was probably still more obvious when Christ delivered it.

§ 260. *The Heathens with Christ.* (John, xii., 20, seq.)

Among the hosts of visiters at the feast there were not a few *heathens* who had come to the knowledge of Jehovah as the true God, and were accustomed to worship statedly at Jerusalem; perhaps proselytes of the gate.* Christ's triumphal entry† and ministry attracted their attention, and all that they heard found a point of contact in their awakened religious longings. Not venturing to address him personally, they sought the mediation of one of his disciples.‡ Seeing in these individual cases a prefiguring of the great results, in the moral regeneration of mankind and the diffusion of the kingdom of God, that

* This may be inferred from the use of ἀναβαινόντων (v. 20).

† There appears to be a discrepancy between John and the other Evangelists, if the facts related by him in xii., 20, seq., took place after Christ's entry, on the same day, and if Christ retired from the public immediately after his last warning to the Jews. On this supposition time could not have been afforded for the transactions we have already introduced in this interval from the synoptical Gospels. But it is evident from John's own narrative that Christ found many followers just after his entry, and that this led even his enemies to be cautious. It may be inferred, therefore, that Christ made use of the great impression produced by his appearance, and did *not* immediately withdraw himself. The chasm in John is well filled by the other Gospels, and with matter precisely suited to the time. John's main object was to give (as he alone could) the last discourses of Jesus with his disciples; and for this reason, probably, he omitted several features of Christ's public labours. Two hypotheses are possible: (1) Christ's conversation with the Greeks took place *several days* after his entry, and just before the end of his public labours; thereby leaving ample space for the transactions recorded in the synoptical Gospels; (2) or it took place on the *day* of his entry, and was occasioned by the sensation produced by that event; leaving a few days before his retirement, in which interval the events recorded in the synoptical Gospels occurred. These John did not mention; but, after giving a brief summary of Christ's final warning to the Jews, hastened on to his last discourses with the disciples.

‡ Philip does not take at once the bold step of presenting the heathen to Christ: he tells Andrew, and then both together tell Jesus. Thus naturally does John relate it.

were to flow from his own sufferings, he said, "*The hour is come that the Son of Man should be glorified.*" (The *man* Jesus, exalted to glory in heaven by his sufferings; the glorified one, who was to reveal himself in his influences upon mankind; especially in the invisible workings of his Divine power for the spread of the Divine kingdom.) The necessity of his death is next set forth. The seed-corn "abideth alone" unless it is thrown into the earth; but when it dies, it brings forth fruit: so the Divine life, so long as Jesus remained upon earth in personal form, was confined to himself; but when the earthly shell was cast off, the way was open for the diffusion of the Divine life among all mankind. As yet the disciples themselves were wholly dependent upon his personal appearance; and, therefore, he said that He alone, as the Son of Man, was yet in possession of this Divine life. And as He was to be glorified through sufferings, so he told his disciples that the happiness and glory destined for them was to be secured only by self-denial. "*He that loveth his life* (makes the earthly life his chief good) *shall lose it* (the true life); *but he that hateth his life in this world* (*i. e.*, deems it valueless in comparison with the interests of His kingdom), *shall keep it unto life eternal.*"

§ 261. *Christ's Struggles of Soul, and Submission to the Divine Will. —The Voice from Heaven.* (John, xii., 27–29.)

At the same time that the great creation to proceed from his sufferings was expanding before his eyes, the struggles of soul to which we have before alluded were renewed within him. The life of God in him did not exclude the uprising of human feelings, in view of the sufferings and death that lay before him, but only kept them in their proper limits. Not by *unhumanizing* himself, but by subordinating the human to the Divine, was he to realize the ideal of pure human virtue; he was to be a perfect example for men, even in the struggles of human weakness.

"*Now is my soul troubled!*" But, sorely as the terrors of his dying struggle pressed upon him, they could not shake his will, strong in God, or disturb the steadfast calmness of his mind. He does not, in obedience to the voice of nature, pray to be exempted from the dying hour: "I cannot say, *Father, save me from this hour;* for this cause have I been brought to this hour, not to escape, but to suffer it."* In full consciousness he had looked forward to it from the beginning, as essential to the fulfilment of his work. Therefore all his feelings and wishes are concentrated upon the one central aim of his whole life, that God may be glorified in mankind by his sufferings: "*Father glorify thy name!*"

* John, xii., 27. Cf. *Kling*, Stud. u. Krit., 1836, iii., 676.

As he uttered this fervent prayer, the very breathing of unselfish holiness. there came a voice* from heaven, heard by the believing souls who stood by as witnesses, saying, "*I have both glorified* my name in thee, *and will* continue to *glorify it.*" All his previous life, in which human nature had been made the organ of the perfect manifestation of God in the glory of His holy law, had *glorified the name of God;* and now his sufferings, and their results, were more and more to glorify that Name, in the establishment of His kingdom among men. The Saviour himself, however, needed no assurance† that his prayer was accepted: "*This voice came not because of me, but for your sakes.*"

* Some interpret this account as a mythus, founded upon the Jewish idea of the *Bath-Col.* But the difficulties in the account are not of a nature to justify this view, or to impeach the veracity of the narrator. On the contrary, the very point on which the mythical theory seizes, viz., that in this case a natural phenomenon conveyed a special import to the religious consciousness, and the very difficulty itself of defining the relation between the subjective and the objective, tend to confirm the narrative as a statement of fact. Would the writer have said that the multitude heard only the *thunder,* and not the *words,* if he meant to describe a voice sounding in majesty amid the thunder, or a voice sounding with a noise like thunder? Certainly he would have represented it as heard by *all,* and thus have avoided the possible interpretation that the whole phenomenon was merely subjective. Only on the supposition that it was a real *fact,* related by an eye-witness, can we account for the clear distinction made by the writer between his own experience in the case and that of others, difficult as it may be for us to discover the common ground of these diverse experiences.

It is supposed by some that the *Bath-Col* was nothing else but a subjective interpretation of the Divine voice in thunder, considered as an omen or Divine sign of answer to prayer. Even if this theory be correct, it is clear that *John* did not mean to record such an omen and interpretation; *he* really heard the words, and the natural phenomenon must have only been a connecting link for the actual apprehension in his religious consciousness. The matter would have to be thus conceived: The impression made upon John by Christ's words, and the natural phenomena that attended them, conspired so to affect the susceptible by-standers, that the word of God within them re-echoed the words of Christ. They were assured that His prayer was answered; receiving, in fact, the same impression as that reported in the narrative, though in a different form. And, as the natural phenomenon coincided with the inward operation of the Divine Spirit—a word from the Omnipresent God, who works alike in nature and in spirit—so Christ, who knew that His work was the Father's, and always recognized God's omnipresent working, both in nature and in the hearts of men, allowed it to be interpreted as a voice from Heaven.

But the conception of the Bath-Col, on which this whole interpretation is founded, cannot be sustained. In the Rabbinical passages collected by *Meuschen* and *Vitringa* there are no traces of it: they interpret the Bath-Col as a *real* voice, accompanied by thunder. In the Old Testament, thunder often appears as a *sign,* indeed, but as a sign of God's anger or majesty, not of his grace. Still there are difficulties in the way of supposing that in the case before us this voice was audible simply to the *senses.* In every place in the New Testament in which such a voice is mentioned, it can be traced back to an inward fact and, in the case in question, the voice was heard only by a part, the susceptible minds The hearing, then, depended upon the spiritual condition of the hearer.

Two points are clearly obvious: (1) there was *thunder,* and this alone was heard by the unsusceptible multitude; (2) there was a *voice from God,* heard by the susceptible; and these last, again, lost to outward and sensible impressions, did not hear the thunder.

In my view of this event, I agree for the most part (and gladly) with my worthy friend *Kling;* and I agree with him, also, that it is better to acknowledge the existence of inexplicable difficulties, than to twist the text and history, in order to carry out some theory which may suit our own notions (Stud. u. Krit., loc. cit., 676, 677).

† Cf. p. 342

He interpreted the voice, and showed them how God was to be glorified in him: "*Now is the judgment of this world; now shall the prince of this world be cast out. And I, if I am lifted up from the earth, will draw all men unto me.*" His sufferings are his triumph. He finishes his work in them; and they form the sentence of condemnation to the ungodly world. The baselessness of Satan's kingdom is laid bare. The Evil One is cast down from his throne among men. And Christ's triumph will still go forward; the power of evil will be more and more diminished; and the Glorified One will not only free his followers from that evil power, but will exalt them to communion with himself in heaven.

§ 262. *Christ closes his Public Ministry.—Final Words of warning to the Multitude.*

The public ministry of Jesus was closed with these warning words addressed to the assembled multitude: "*Yet a little while is the light with you; walk while ye have the light* (receive it by faith, and become, by communion with it, children of the light), *lest darkness come upon you* (lest, lost in darkness, ye hasten headlong to your own destruction); *for he that walketh in darkness knoweth not whither he goeth.*"

§ 263. *Machinations of Christ's Enemies.*

The few hours that intervened between the end of Christ's public ministry and his arrest were devoted to instructing and comforting his disciples in view of his approaching departure, and the severe conflicts they were to undergo. In these conversations he displayed all his heavenly love and calmness of soul; his loftiness and his humility. In order that our contemplation of these sweet scenes may not be interrupted, we shall, before entering upon them, glance at the machinations of his enemies which brought about his capture and his death.

As we have seen, the Sanhedrim had resolved upon his death; all that remained was to decide how and when it should be brought about. The time of the feast itself would have been unpropitious for the attempt;* it must be made, therefore, either before or after. The for-

* Matt., xxvi., 5, implies that Jesus was arrested *before* the commencement of the Jewish Passover. I do not see the justice of *Weisse's* (i., 444) assertion, that this view of the passage is opposed to its natural sense. The passage certainly implies (what is most important for my purpose) that he was *not* apprehended on the *feast-day*; whether *before* or *after* is left undecided. But this information is not sufficient to show an inaccuracy in the chronology of the first three Gospels. For we might suppose that the Sanhedrim were led, by the opportunity afforded by the treachery of Judas, to seize Jesus quietly at night, abandoning their original design. It would therefore follow, at any rate, that they had not decided to effect their purpose *during* the feast; and they may have made up their minds to wait until its close, when the unexpected proposition of Judas led them to attempt it *during* the feast. But it is not probable that they would allow Christ, unmolested, to make use of the time of the feast to increase his followers among the multitude. We shall see

mer was the safest, and therefore the favorite plan. An unexpected and most favourable opening was afforded, by the proposition of *Judas Iscariot*, to deliver him into their hands.*

§ 264. *The Motives of Judas in betraying Jesus.*

It is difficult to decide upon the motives that impelled Judas to the outrage which he perpetrated. How could one that had daily enjoyed the influences of Christ's Divine life, had been a witness of his mighty works, and received so many proofs of his love, have been driven to such a fatal step? It cannot be supposed, as we have before remarked,† that he originally attached himself to Jesus for the purpose of betraying him; it rather appears that his motives were at first as pure as those of the rest of the disciples. Had not Christ seen in him capacities which, with proper cultivation, might have made him an efficient Apostle, he would not have received him into his narrower circle on the same footing with the others, and sent him out along with them on the first trial mission.§ Nor does this view deny either that the evil germ which, when fully developed, led him to his great crime, lay in his heart at the time; or that Christ saw the evil as well as the good.§ But the Saviour may have hoped to make the latter preponderate over the former.

Among the possible motives for the crime of Judas are, (1.) His alleged avarice; (2.) Jewish views of Christ's Messiahship on his part; and, (3.) A gradual growth of hostile feelings in his heart. These we shall now examine in order.

hereafter that there are strong objections to the opinion that Christ was crucified on the first day of the feast; and these, if valid, will confirm our supposition that he was arrested on the day before its commencement. Cf. *Gförer*, iii, 198.

* Matt., xxvi., 14–16; Mark, xiv., 10, 11; Luke, xxii., 3–6. These passages agree in showing that Judas made his bargain with the Sanhedrim *before* the night on which he consummated his treachery. It might be inferred from John, xiii., 26, that he only imbibed the Satanic thought on rising from the Last Supper; but how could he have negotiated with the Sanhedrim so late in the night, and just before the fatal act? John himself says (xiii., 2) that the devil had before put it in his heart to do it. We conclude, therefore, that v. 26 refers to the *last* step—the execution of his evil purpose; and this agrees very well with the supposition that he had previously arranged all the preliminaries. A favourable moment only was wanting; and this he found during that last interview with Jesus.

† Cf. p. 118. ‡ Cf. p. 257, seq.

§ John, vi., 64, teaches that Jesus knew at once the motives of all that attached themselves to him. No mock faith, founded on carnal inclinations, could deceive him, and therefore he knew at once the spiritual character of the one that should betray him. The passage does not necessarily imply that he marked at first the *person* of the traitor; but only that he noticed in Judas, from the very beginning, the disposition of heart that finally led him to become a traitor. But it need not appear strange to us if John, after so many proofs of the superhuman prescience of Jesus, attributed to the indefinite intimations of Christ, given by him to Judas in order to make him *know himself*, more than was really expressed by them at the time.

(1.)

Was Judas impelled by avarice?

There are certain intimations in the Evangelists that appear to favour the hypothesis that *avarice* was his leading motive. In John, xii., 6, this vice is ascribed to him, and he is charged with embezzling money from the common purse, committed to his charge as treasurer. Moreover, according to the synoptical Gospels, he bargained for a certain sum of money, as the price of his treachery. It might be inferred, therefore, that a love of money, which sought to gratify itself by any means, even by the violation of a sacred trust, grew upon him to such an extent as finally to induce the commission of his awful crime.

But there are many and strong objections to this view of the case. If Judas's avarice were so intense, it is difficult to conceive how Christ, whose piercing glance penetrated the recesses of men's hearts, could have received him into the number of the disciples. Could He, who knew so well how to adapt the special duties which he assigned his followers to their individual peculiarities, have allowed precisely this most *avaricious* disciple to keep charge of the common purse? And, had he attributed Judas's reproof of Mary* (John, xii., 5) to this motive, would he not have noticed it in his reply?† It must be remembered, John's explanation (v. 6) was added *after* Judas was known to have bargained to betray his Master for money. Had such an accusation been made at an earlier period, he would doubtless have been removed from the treasurership. In all *Christ's* allusions to the character of Judas that have come down to us, there is not the slightest indication that He thought it necessary to warn him against this sin. There may, indeed, have been indications in John's memory which he believed to afford sufficient ground for such a charge;‡ and, after attributing the treachery of Judas in betraying Christ to avarice, he might have been led to look for traces of the same vice in his previous management of the common funds.

Again, it is difficult to understand, if the crime was committed for the sake of money alone, how so small a sum as *thirty shekels*§ could

* Cf. p. 352.

† Dr. *G. Schollmeyer*, a young but promising theologian, remarks this in his "Jesus and Judas," Lüneburg, 1836.

‡ *Strauss* (iii., 422, 3te Aufl.) thinks this is inconsistent with my fundamental principle, since I acknowledge the *Apostle John* as the author of this Gospel; just as if I accused the Apostle of a groundless slander. The black deed of Judas justified John in ascribing this vice to him, as many of his recollections seemed to indicate it. He certainly could not be expected to exercise a cool impartiality towards the traitor. In the mean time, I think I am justified in saying that John's allusions are not to be taken *unconditionally* as proof. But the single trait of avarice suits well the general character of Judas, in whom earthly aims were all-controlling.

§ Between 25 and 26 rix dollars. Twenty shekels = 120 denarii, and one denarius was at that time the ordinary wages for a day's labour (Matt., xx., 2); so that the whole sum

have satisfied the traitor.* Would not the Sanhedrim, in view of the importance of getting hold of Jesus quietly, before the feast began, freely have given Judas more if he had asked it? True, that body may have relied upon the surety of seizing him in some way, and upon the impression, gathered from his character, that he would cause no rescue to be attempted; and, therefore, so far as their *offer* is concerned, thirty pieces is likely enough.

On the whole, then, we conclude that to gain so small a sum of money could not have been Judas's *chief* motive. And, even had the sum been a large one, it remains almost impossible to conceive that avarice *alone* could lead him to deliver Jesus over to his foes, if he really were impressed with a sense of his Divinity and Messiahship. It must be presupposed that he had stood for some time in a spiritual relation to Christ different from that of the other Apostles; and when this is once admitted, avarice is a superfluous motive.

(2.)

Was Judas impelled by Jewish views of Christ's Messiahship?

Did Judas foresee and intend to bring about the result which followed Christ's arrest? The answer to this question will obviously go a great way in fixing our opinion of his character and motives. It is connected with another, viz., in what way did the traitor himself die? If, according to Matthew's account, he committed suicide immediately after Christ's condemnation, we might infer that he did *not* intend this result, and was thrown into despair by it.

This inference has led some to the opinion† that Judas expected Christ's arrest only to bring about the triumph of his cause by com-

amounted to about four months' wages of a day-labourer. (Cf. *Paulus* on Matt., xxvi., 16.) Thirty shekels, it is to be noticed, was the value set upon a single slave, according to Exod., xxi., 32.

* It is questioned, with some plausibility, by *Strauss* and *De Wette*, whether the precise sum, *thirty shekels*, is correctly given. Their arguments are that Matthew alone mentions it (xxvi., 15), while in Mark and Luke only the general term ἀργύριον is given; and that the tendency of Matthew to find types of Christ's history in the Old Testament induced him to fix this precise sum, in view of Zech., xi., 12 (cf. Matt., xxvii., 9).

Without making any positive assertion, we must observe on this (1) that, although Mark and Luke do not expressly mention the small sum, they would not have used the indefinite term ἀργύριον, if the sum had been known to be large; (2) although there is a discrepancy between Matt., xxvii., 7, and Acts, i., 18, yet this discrepancy seems to presuppose that the money was just sufficient to purchase a field, which certainly could not have required a *large* sum; (3) the passage in the Old Testament *alone* would not have been enough to induce the assignment of so small a sum, in the face of the probability, on the other side, that the Sanhedrim would give a large amount to secure so important an end; (4) it could not have been invented to blacken the character of Judas still further: his deed must have been black enough at any price; (5) there is no great improbability in the Sanhedrim's offering so small a reward: people of this stamp would give Judas no more than the lowest possible price for which he would do the deed; and their fanatical hatred of Christ may have led them to offer exactly the price of a *slave*, in order to degrade the character of Jesus.

† See, especially, *Schollmeyer's* Treatise, above cited.

pelling him to establish his visible Messianic kingdom. If this were the case, the traitor must have expected either (1) that the enthusiastic multitude would rescue Christ by force and make him king; or (2) that Christ himself, by an exertion of his miraculous power, would overthrow his foes and establish his kingdom. But the *first* is utterly untenable; little as Judas may have known of Christ's spirit, he *must* have known that He would not make use of worldly power to accomplish his purposes; nor could he himself have supposed such power to be needed, if (according to the hypothesis) he acknowledged Jesus as Messiah.

The *second* view may be more fully stated thus: Holding the same Messianic expectations as the other Apostles, he only gave way more entirely to a wilful impatience; Christ delayed too long for him; he planned the arrest to hasten his decision, surely expecting a display of his miraculous power, and the establishment of his visible kingdom. Terrible was his consternation when he saw the Saviour, whom he loved, condemned to death! Not, however, that his act is in the slightest degree justified. It was sinful wilfulness to seek to control the actions of Him whose wise guidance, as Lord and Master, he ought to have followed in all things. He sacrificed all other considerations to his own arbitrarily-conceived idea, and acted upon that vile principle which has given birth to the most destructive deeds recorded in history—that the end sanctifies the means. Still his decision of character and energy of will, if sacrificed in obedience to Christ's spirit, would have made him a most efficient agent in propagating the Gospel, and prove that Christ had good reasons for receiving him into the number of the Apostles.

Such is the second hypothesis. But if Judas acted on such principles, would Jesus have abandoned him to his delusion, and allowed him to rush blindly on destruction? The authority of Christ as Prophet and Messiah (and, according to the hypothesis, Judas recognized him as such) could easily have removed the scales from the eyes of the deluded Apostle. Could the Saviour possibly have uttered a word at the Last Supper (John, xiii., 27) that might be interpreted into an approval of his undertaking?

The hypothesis, then, must at least be modified into the view that Judas's faith wavered because Christ was making no preparations for a visible kingdom; the result alone could solve his doubts; and therefore he brought about the arrest, reasoning on this wise: "If Jesus is really Messiah, no power of the world can harm him, and all opposition will only serve to glorify him; if, on the other hand, he succumbs, it must be taken as a judgment of God against him." His subsequent repentance is not inconsistent with this view; his conclusions *after* the result, when, perhaps, the full power of Christ's image stood before him, may have been very different from what he had expected. As a general thing, the impressions made upon a man by the results of his actions testify but little as to the character of his motives; none can tell how an evil deed, even when deliberately planned and perpetrated, will react upon the conscience.

(3.)

Was Judas impelled by a gradually developed hostility?

The mode of Judas's death,* as we have seen, is not sufficient to prove that his purpose in delivering Christ to the Sanhedrim was not a decidedly hostile one.

The final view before mentioned may be stated thus: The first feelings of Judas, in attaching himself to Christ, were the same as those of the other Apostles. He had a practical and administrative talent, which caused him to be made treasurer; and which may have been usefully employed in organizing the first Christian congregations. But the element of carnal selfishness, although it affected the other Apostles more or less, was in him deeply rooted; the Spirit and love of Christ could not gain the same power over him as over the other more spiritually-minded disciples. As he gradually found that his expectations were to be disappointed, his attachment turned more and more into aversion. When the manifestation of Christ ceased to be attractive, it became *repulsive;* and more and more so every day. The miracles alone could not revive his faith, so long as he lacked the disposition to perceive Divinity in them. If Christ showed striking proofs of Divine power, so, also, he gave evident signs of human weakness; and the sight of the latter could easily cause an estranged heart to doubt and hesitate in regard to the former. A man's view even of facts depends upon the tendencies of his mind and heart; these necessarily give their own hue to his interpretations even of what his eyes behold.† Nor do

* Matthew's account of the death of Judas stands in (at least) partial contradiction to Acts, i., 18, which states that Judas bought a field with the money, and met his death by falling from a height. This may, indeed, possibly mean suicide; but it is doubtful. The wild and fabulous narrative of *Papias* (first published by *Cramer*, Catena in Acta S. Apost., Oxon., 1838, p. 12) presupposes that Judas did not die by his own hand. "Μέγα δὲ ἀσεβείας ὑπόδειγμα ἐν τούτῳ τῷ κόσμῳ περιεπάτησεν ὁ Ἰούδας· πρησθεὶς ἐπιτοσοῦτον τὴν σάρκα, ὥστε μηδὲ ὁπόθεν ἅμαξα διέρχεται ῥαδίως ἐκεῖνον δυνασθαι διελθεῖν· ἀλλὰ μηδὲ αὐτὸν μόνον τὸν τῆς κεφαλῆς ὄγκον αὐτοῦ· τὰ μὲν γὰρ βλέφαρα τῶν ὀφθαλμῶν αὐτοῦ φασὶ τοσοῦτον ἐξοιδῆσαι, ὡς αὐτὸν μὲν καθόλου τὸ φῶς μὴ βλέπειν· τοὺς ὀφθαλμοὺς δὲ αὐτοῦ μηδὲ ὑπὸ ἰατροῦ διόπτρας ὀφθῆναι δύνασθαι· τοσοῦτον βάθος εἶχον ἀπὸ τῆς ἔξωθεν ἐπιφανείας· τὸ δὲ αἰδοῖον αὐτοῦ πάσης μεν ἀσχημοσύνης ἀηδέστερον καὶ μεῖζον φαίνεσθαι· φέρεσθαι δὲ δι' αὐτοῦ ἐκ παντὸς τοῦ σώματος συρρέοντας ἰχῶρας τε καὶ σκώληκας εἰς ὕβριν δι' αὐτῶν μόνον τῶν ἀναγκαίων· μετὰ πολλὰς δὲ βασάνους καὶ τιμωρίας, ἐν ἰδίω φασὶ χωρίῳ τελευτήσαντα· καὶ τοῦτο ἀπὸ τῆς ὀδοῦ ἔρημον καὶ ἀοίκητον τὸ χωρίον μέχρι τῆς νῦν γενέσθαι· ἀλλ' οὐδὲ μέχρι τῆς σήμερον δύνασθαί τινα ἐκεῖνον τὸν τόπον παρελθεῖν, ἐὰν μὴ τὰς ῥῖνας ταῖς χερσὶν ἐπιφράξῃ· τοσάυτη διὰ τῆς σαρκὸς αὐτοῦ καὶ επὶ γῆς κρίσις ἐχώρησεν." It is easy to see how the expressions in Acts could give rise to this extravagant legend.

† The following profound thought of Pascal, abundantly verified in history, may be applied to the scientific treatment of the Life of Christ, and to those who boast a cold impar

we know how far the crafty Pharisees understood Judas and tampered with him. It was just at the time of the sifting, before alluded to,* among the masses that had followed Christ, that the spirit of enmity seems to have germinated in the heart of Judas, and Christ noticed and intimated it (John, vi., 70); although it could not, *all at once*, have become predominant in him: there were, doubtless, inward struggles before the fatal tendency acquired full sway.†

The life of man furnishes many analogies that may help to clear up the enigmatical conduct of Judas. He who does not follow the impulses of good which he receives from within and without, but rather gives himself up to the selfish propensities which those impulses are meant to counteract, becomes finally and irrecoverably enslaved to them; all things that ought to work together for his good serve for his harm; the healing balm becomes for him a poison. This is the severe judgment upon which our free agency is conditioned; and to it may we apply the saying of our Lord: "*From him that hath not, shall be taken away even that which he hath.*"

CHAPTER II.

THE LAST SUPPER OF JESUS WITH THE DISCIPLES.

§ 265. *Object of Christ in the Last Supper.*

JESUS looked forward without fear, nay, with confidence, to the fate that awaited him. We need not necessarily presuppose that he was supernaturally informed of it; for it may be said that his friends in the Sanhedrim (and he had such) informed him of the negotiations of Judas. He foresaw that he would have to leave his disciples before the proper Passover,‡ and determined to give a peculiar

tiality in regard to it: "La volonté est un des principaux organes de la créance, non qu'elle forme la créance, mais parce que les choses paraissent vrayes on fausses, selon la face, par où on les regarde. La volonté, qui se plaist à l'une plus qu'a l'autre, détourne l'esprit. de considérer les qualitéz de celle, qu'elle n'aime pas, et ainsi l'esprit marchant d'une pièce avec la volonté, s'arreste à regarder la face qu'elle aime, et en jugeant parce qu'il y voit, il régle insensiblement sà créance suivant l'inclination de la volonté."

* P. 268, 269.

† We do not wish to be understood as attempting a full explanation of the conduct of Judas, so enigmatical in itself, and so little explained by the accounts that are left to us. We have only sought to present the theory which seems to us most probable from the data before us.

‡ I presuppose, with *Ideler, Lücke, Sieffert, De Wette*, and *Bleek*, that the Last Supper was held, not on the 14th Nisan, the holy Passover eve, but on the 13th, and that the Friday of his passion was that holy evening. (a.) A candid interpretation of John's Gospel confirms this supposition. We cannot infer much from xiii., 1, 2, although that passage seems to imply that the supper occurred before the beginning of the feast. But xviii., 28, tells us that the deputies of the Sanhedrim would not enter the Prætorium for fear of defile-

import to his *last* meal with them, to place it in a peculiar relation to the Jewish Passover, as the Christian covenant-meal was to take the

ment, as they had to eat the Passover on that evening. The words ἵνα φάγωσι τὸ πάσχα *must* be applied, according to prevailing usage, both among Jews and Christians, to the feast of Passover. It is objected that this care was needless, as, if a defilement were thus incurred, it would not, on account of the טְבוּל יוֹם, last until the *evening, i. e.,* until the beginning of the following day; but this is easily answered; many things had to be done as preparatory to the feast, which would trench upon both days. In xix., 31, the day of the crucifixion is treated as an ordinary Friday. No scruples were entertained about the crucifixion on that day, but only about leaving the bodies on the cross on the *Sabbath,* which was a *fixed* feast-day. But how could the Friday, if it were the first day of the principal feast, be treated as an ordinary Friday? All difficulties are removed by supposing that it *was* only a common Friday, and that the next day was at once the Sabbath and the first day of the Passover feast. Even if the Sanhedrim were compelled to expedite the crucifixion of *Christ,* and were impelled, in their fanatical hatred, to violate the sanctity of the feast by it, yet is it likely that they would have waited just to the holiest feast-day for the crucifixion of the *malefactors,* or that the pardon of a condemned criminal (granted by the Romans in honour of the feast) would have been delayed until the feast had begun? But the haste and the pardon would harmonize well with the view that the crucifixion took place *before* the feast, on the 13th Nisan. (b.) *Lücke* has called attention to two passages in 1 Corinthians, though without deeming them perfectly conclusive (Götting. Anzeig.): (1.) The first passage is 1 Cor., v., 7, 8, in which Paul seems to contrast the Christian with the Jewish Passover as held at the same time (Christ, as the spiritual Passover, as sacrificed simultaneously with the Jewish Paschal lamb; (2.) 1 Cor., xi., 23, speaks indefinitely of the night of Christ's *betrayal,* not of his partaking of the Passover. (c.) It may, perhaps, be the case that in Matt., xxvi., 18, the writer presupposed that Christ really partook of the Passover with his disciples; but may not the passage mean, "My time for leaving the world is at hand; and therefore I will celebrate the Passover *to-day* with my disciples, in anticipation?" (d.) In Luke, xxiii., 54, the day of the crucifixion is mentioned as a common Friday (the day of preparation), a day on which there could be no scruples about any kind of business; but would it have been so mentioned if it had been the first day of Passover, the greatest feast-day in all the year? (e.) The general diffusion of the belief that Christ held a proper Passover with his disciples may be explained on the ground that Christ really did hold his *last* supper with reference and allusion to the Passover supper and the ceremonies that accompanied it; that the first Christians, intent upon the substance, paid little heed to chronological niceties; that the Jewish-Christians kept up the Jewish usage of the Passover, giving it, however, a Christian import; while the purely Gentile converts kept no such festal seasons. The interchange of *the first day of unleavened bread* (as the day of Christ's passion) with the *first day of the Passover feast* may also have contributed to it. These grounds might suffice to explain the admission into the synoptical Gospels of the idea that the Passion occurred on the *first* day of the Passover; but are utterly inconsistent with the hypothesis that the author of *John's* Gospel (whether it be admitted as genuine or not) could have inserted and got into circulation a statement invented by himself, and conflicting with the general stream of tradition. John's chronology, as we have said, is consistent throughout; but that of the synoptical Gospels presents discrepancies that appear irreconcilable.

Little use can be made of the ancient disputes about the Passover; from such mere fragments we cannot decide how far the Evangelical accounts were appealed to. The advocates of the occidental usage, Apollinaris of Hierapolis, Clement of Alexandria, and Hippolytus, appealed to John's Gospel (if the fragments in *Chronicon paschale Alexandrinum,* ed. Niebuhr, Dindorf, i., 13, are genuine) to prove that the Last Supper was *not* a Passover proper. Polycrates, bishop of Ephesus (Eus., Hist. Eccl., v., 24) appealed to "*the Gospel*" in behalf of the opposite usage; but whether he appealed, under the title "the Gospel," to one, or all of the Evangelists, we cannot conceive how he could reconcile the declarations in John with the Passover usages of Asia Minor (cf. Dr. *Rettberg's* Abhandl. üb. d Paschastreit, Ilgen's Zeitschrift für Histor. Theol., ii., 2, 119). What is the meaning of

place of that of the Old Testament. Perhaps, as the Sanhedrim had determined to carry out their plans against him before the feast, he spent Thursday, 13th Nisan, in Bethany, in order to employ these last hours with the disciples undisturbed. In the morning he sent Peter and John into the city, to make the necessary preparations for the Passover supper. To preserve secrecy, and avoid all hazard of surprise by the Sanhedrim, he designated the house at which the supper was to be held by a sign understood by its owner, without specifying the name of the latter.*

Two prominent acts of Christ marked this last meal with the disciples, viz., the *washing of feet* and the institution of the *Lord's Supper*.†

§ 266. *Christ washes the Disciples' Feet. Conversation with Peter in regard to it.* (John, xiii., 2–16.)

In washing the disciples' feet, Christ obviously intended to impress vividly and permanently upon their minds, by means of a specific act, a general truth; and to remove those carnal expectations of a secular kingdom, and the selfishness necessarily connected therewith, which were not yet wholly banished from their minds.‡

Such an act, on the part of the Divine Master, must doubtless have surprised more than one of the disciples. That HE, the object of their deepest reverence and love, should do for them so lowly a service, may well have been a surprise and a contradiction to their feelings. Yet that same reverence prevented them from resisting his will. But the fiery and impetuous Peter could not so command his feelings: "Lord,

the words of Polycrates, *ἄγειν, τηρεῖν τὴν ἡμέραν*? Not, certainly, the keeping of the Paschal supper; nor the Jewish Passover, assisted at by Christians; for the added words *πάντοτε τὴν ἡμέραν ἤγαγον οἱ συγγενεῖς μου, ὅταν τῶν Ἰουδαίων ὁ λαὸς ἤρνυε τὴν ζύμην*, would then be sheer tautology. He must have meant, then, "the day for commemorating the passion of Christ." If, then, it is in *this* sense that Polycrates says of "all the bishops of Lesser Asia since the time of St. John," that they *πάντες ἐτήρησαν τὴν ἡμέραν τῆς τεσσαρεσκαιδεκάτης τοῦ πάσχα κατὰ τὸ εὐαγγέλιον*, he obviously means that they "all celebrated the 14th Nisan," on which the Jewish Passover began, in commemoration of our Lord's Passion; and for confirmation of *this* he might very well appeal to the Gospel of John.

We must also allude to a remarkable passage in Hippolytus (in his first book upon the Feast of Passover, l. c. p. 13), there reported as coming from the lips of Christ: *οὐκέτι φάγομαι τὸ πασχα* (surely Luke, xxii., 16, cannot be meant); as if Christ had predicted that he "would no more eat of the Paschal lamb, and hence not live to see another Feast of Passover."

* I cannot see a miracle in this; it cannot be shown that Luke (xxii., 13) means to narrate it as miraculous.

† John does not describe the institution of the Eucharist: it was known and commemorated in the Church regularly; but the *washing of feet*, not preserved by any such commemoration, he gives in detail, as an especially marked incident.

‡ Cf. p. 352, on Luke, xxii., 26, 27. I cannot assert, with *Gförer*, that this passage is unmeaning, unless interpreted in view of the symbolic act: the word *διακονεῖν*, might apply to his *whole life*, as devoted to the service of others (cf. Matt., xx., 28). But the form of the passage in Luke certainly appears to imply an allusion to the symbolic act which John records. The thought contained in it is the same as that in John, xiii., 13–16.

dost thou wash *my* feet?" Even when Christ told him, in view of this reluctance, that he should know the import of the act thereafter, he was not satisfied; until, at last, the Saviour rebuked his self-will with the declaration, "*If I wash thee not, thou hast no part in me:*" And this was to be taken *literally*, for this single case was a test of the state of heart essential for union with Christ: it was necessary for Peter to show forth a complete renunciation of his own will, and absolute subjection to that of Jesus. But the *spiritual* meaning afterward set forth by Christ, viz., that none could enter or remain in his communion unless spiritually purified through him, was probably implied also in these words. Peter, alarmed, cries out, "Yea, if it be so, Lord, *not my feet alone, but also my hands and my head.*" To this Christ replied: "That is too much: *he that is washed* (bathed) *needeth not save to wash his feet, but is clean every whit.*" (A figure taken from Eastern usage: he that is already bathed, need only, on coming in from the road, wash off the soil that may have gathered on his feet.) The spiritual import, then, of the symbolical act, and of Christ's language in regard to it, probably is: Whosoever, through faith in me, has received the purifying principle of *life*, who is pure in heart and motives, needs only thereafter continued purification from sins cleaving to him outwardly; just as the Apostles, though inspired by pure love to Christ, still stood in need of the power of this animating love, to cleanse and purify their mode of thought.

§ 267. *The Words of Christ with and concerning his Betrayer.* (John, xiii., 11, 21, seq.)

To the Apostles he said, in the sense above defined, "*Ye are clean;*" but, as this could not be applied to Judas, he added, "*yet not all.*" Intimations of this kind he threw out more and more frequently, partly, as he himself said (v. 19), to prepare them for the act of treachery, that it might not take them unawares, and lead them to infer that He, too, had been deceived; and partly, perhaps, in order to rouse, if possible, the conscience of Judas himself. But his foresight of the awful deed—that one who had been a special object of his love should disarm him and become a tool of his enemies—and of the conflict with depravity that he must go through, even up to his last hour, moved him most deeply; and he now spoke more plainly, "*Verily I say unto you, that one of you shall betray me.*"

The disciples, not yet able to understand him, looked upon each other, surprised and confounded. All were anxious to know *whom* he alluded to; but Peter alone, as usual, gave expression to the wish. Even he did not venture to ask aloud, but beckoned to John, who was leaning upon the Saviour's breast, as they surrounded the table, that *he* should put the question. In answer to John, Christ said, in a low tone, that it was he whose turn it just then was to receive from his hands the morsel of the lamb dipped in the sauce. And this was Judas.*

This occurrence could not fail either to awaken the slumbering conscience of Judas, or to make him anxious to leave such a fellowship and take the last step of his crime. When he arose, Christ said to him, "*That thou doest* (hast resolved to do), *do quickly*." Not implying a command to commit the deed, but rather calculated to move his conscience, had it been still susceptible of impression. But he had decided upon the act: so far as his *intentions* could go, it was as good as done; and therefore Christ asked him to hasten the crisis.†

The departure of Judas to inform the Sanhedrim how they might most readily seize the person of Jesus, decided his death; and, in view of it, he said, "*Now is the Son of Man glorified* (in reference to the sacrifice of his earthly life, because the ideal of holiness is realized in Him under the last struggles, because human nature attains therein its highest moral perfection), *and God is glorified in him* (as the moral glorifying of human nature is the perfect glorifying of God in it; the perfect manifestation of God in his holiness and love). *If God be glorified in him, God shall also glorify him in himself*‡ (shall raise him to Himself, and glorify him), *and shall straightway glorify him.*"§

§ 268. *The Institution of the Eucharist.* (Luke, xxii., 17–20.)‖

The description of the institution of the Eucharist given by Luke, harmonizing with that of Paul (1 Cor., xi., 23, seq.), seems to afford

* According to Matthew, Judas also asked, "Is it I?" and Jesus answered in the affirmative. This incident would come in most naturally at this point. Judas, noticing the alarmed countenances of the disciples, seeing Peter whisper to John, John to Jesus, and Jesus reply, felt that he was discovered, and was led to ask the question directly. This must certainly have been done in an under tone, if Judas could have had a position near enough.

† An allusion to the severer struggles that yet awaited Christ: not expressly mentioned by John, but related by the other Evangelists.

‡ The expressions ἐν αὐτῷ and ἐν ἑαυτῷ (John, xiii., 32) obviously correspond to each other. As the first betokens the glorifying of God in Jesus, as the Son of Man, so the second denotes the glorifying of the Son of Man in God, by his being raised up unto God in heaven.

§ We presuppose that Jesus wished Judas to depart before he should institute the Lord's Supper. As the words in verses 31, 32 were directly connected with the departure of the betrayer, they too must have been uttered before the institution.

‖ As John does not give an account of the institution of the Eucharist, there is some difficulty in deciding precisely at what point of his narrative (ch. xiii.) it should be inserted. It was stated in the last note that v. 31, 32 were connected directly with the departure of Judas, and it seems to us that the proper point of juncture for the account in question is between v. 32 and 33. The words ἐντολὴ καινή, commencing v. 34, connect very well, it is true, with the objects of the institution; but still, if v. 33 was uttered *before* the institution, it seems strange that Peter's question (v. 36), obviously referring to v. 33, should have been

us the most clear and natural view of the transaction. It is distinguished from those of Matthew and Mark in stating definitely that the giving of the bread was separated by a certain interval from that of the wine; the former occurring during the supper, the latter after it.

It is introduced by the following words of Christ: "*I have heartily desired to eat this Passover with you before I suffer; for I say unto you, I will not any more eat thereof until it be fulfilled in the kingdom of God*" (*i. e.*, until, in the consummation of the kingdom, he should celebrate with them the higher and true Passover Supper). After these words of farewell, he takes the cup of red wine, blesses it, sends it round, and reminds them that he should no more drink of the fruit of the vine until he should partake with them of a higher wine in the kingdom of God. After thus vividly impressing them with his departure, and preparing them for the institution of a rite in its commemoration, he breaks one of the loaves, and divides it among them, showing them that the broken bread was to represent his body, given up for them; and this they were to repeat in remembrance of him. Then, after the conclusion of the meal, he sends round the cup again, and tells them that the wine is to represent his blood, about to be shed for them. Each of these acts, therefore—the giving of the bread and

put after the intervention of that solemn act, which must have drawn the attention of the disciples so strongly. We consider, then, that v. 33 was spoken *after* the institution. *Strauss* (3te. Aufl., p. 449) objects to this collocation, as arbitrarily severing the words εὐθὺς δοξάσει αὐτόν (v. 32) from ἔτι μικρὸν μεθ' ὑμῶν εἰμι (v. 33). I cannot see the force of the objection. The pause after v. 32 is natural; and then follows the solemn symbolical act, in which Christ sets before the disciples his departure from the earth, and gives them a pledge of communion with him—a communion to endure after his ascension to his glory. Then v. 33 opens a new beginning precisely adapted to the import of the symbolical act.

The aptness with which the account of the institution can be here fitted to John's narrative, and its admirable adaptation to the last discourses of Christ, as recorded by him, shows that was one of the links, and a most important one, in the chain of Christ's last acts. *Gfrörer* seeks to prove, however, from John's omission to mention the institution, that although Christ may have spoken at the Last Supper the words ascribed to him, they were words spoken by the way, and not intended to establish such a commemorative rite as that which was afterward founded upon them; just as a deeper signification was found in other expressions of Christ after his departure than was manifest before; and that, therefore, John omitted them, as he did so many other things comparatively unimportant. This hypothesis contradicts itself. Even *Gfrörer* must presuppose that John personally knew and partook of the Eucharist before writing his Gospel; and it must be presupposed just as certainly, that it was at that time connected with these words of Christ; and that John, who certainly was not inclined to attribute a less meaning than others to Christ's sayings at the Last Supper, must have conceived the words to be so connected. On purely psychological grounds, therefore, John's omission cannot be explained in this way. In a word, no one having an intuition of Christ, and conceiving his solemn state of mind at that Last Supper, can believe that he uttered those solemn words without a deeper and more earnest meaning. As for the hypothesis, recently revived, of an influence exerted by *Essenism* upon Christian culture, it is wholly destitute of historical foundation (cf. p. 37, seq.); the derivation of the *Agapæ* from the common repasts of the Essenes is wholly an invention of fancy. It is altogether unhistorical to seek an *external* origin for a usage that can be naturally explained from *internal* grounds, as the origin of the celebration of the Eucharist from an imitation of Christ's Last Supper with his disciples.

the giving of the wine—denotes the same thing, viz., the remembrance of the Last Supper. Each had its signification separately; but the repetition, during the meal and after it, served to impress the symbolical meaning of the act still more deeply upon the minds of the disciples.

The *giving of thanks* before the distribution of the bread and wine corresponds to a similar act on the part of the head of the family in the Jewish Passover feast, in which thanksgiving was offered for the gifts of nature, and also for the deliverance of the fathers out of Egypt and the founding of the old covenant; we may infer, therefore, that Christ's thanksgiving had reference partly to the creation of all material things for man (bread and wine symbolizing all God's gifts in nature); partly, and indeed chiefly, to his own death, in order to deliver men from the bondage of sin, and, by his redemptive act, to establish the *new* covenant between God and man.*

As to the *words* used in the distribution, "This is my body;" and, "This is my blood," it is impossible that any of the recipients at that time could have supposed them to be *literally* meant; as he was then before them in his corporeal presence. Had he intended to present so new and extraordinary a sense to their minds, he could not but have stated it more definitely; and had they so understood him, the difficulty would assuredly have led them to question him further. But as the whole transaction—the institution, at the close of a farewell supper, of a visible sign of communion to endure after his departure—had a symbolical character, they would have interpreted these *words* also unnaturally, if they had understood them literally, and not symbolically. "This is, for you, my body and blood; *i. e.*, represents to you my body and blood." The breaking of the bread was a natural symbol of the breaking of his body; the pouring out of the *red* wine (the ordinary wine of Palestine) was a natural symbol of the pouring out of his blood. "I offer up my life for your redemption; and when, in remembrance thereof, you meet again to partake of this supper, be assured that I shall then be with you as truly as now I am with you, visibly and corporeally, in body and blood. The bread and wine, which I now divide among you as symbols of my body and blood, will then stand in stead of my corporeal presence."

It may be added, that this symbol was not an entirely new one to the disciples: it had been used substantially, in the conversation before referred to (p. 267, seq.) between Christ and the Jews, in the syna-

* The gifts of nature and of redemption are inseparable; redemption alone has re established the original relation between man and nature. Only when man is restored to communion with God is he assured that all nature exists for his good, to be used by him for the glory of God.

gogue at Capernaum. To "eat his flesh and drink his blood" was an understood sign of the closest spiritual communion with his Divine-human nature. And therefore he said, in giving the wine, "This is my blood, the seal of the new covenant, *which is given for many for the remission of sins.*"*

CHAPTER III.

CHRIST'S LAST DISCOURSES WITH HIS DISCIPLES.

§ 269. *The New Commandment.* (John, xiii., 33–35.)

AFTER Christ, in taking leave of his own, had given them the symbol and pledge of continued communion, he said to them, in the familiar style of a father to his family, "*Little children, yet a little while I am with you, and, as I said unto the Jews,* 'whither I go ye cannot come,' *so now I say unto you.*† *A new commandment give I unto you, that ye love one another; as I have loved you, that ye also love one another. By this shall all men know that ye are my disciples, if ye love one another.*" The commandment of love is here called a *new* one, because it was the characteristic of the new covenant, in view of which the Lord's Supper had just been instituted, and which he was then about to seal with his sufferings. It is true, the all-comprehending commandment, to "love God supremely, and one's neighbour as one's self," was contained in the old covenant; but it became a *new* one, by its reference to the sacrifice of Christ, which expressed its essence: it demanded a love, willing, after His example, to sacrifice every thing for the brethren—the spirit of love, in a word, which was to be the soul of the new congregation of God, proceeding, of itself, from communion with him and intuition of his image. It was *new*,

* It has been disputed whether the words "*for the remission of sins*" were really added by Christ. But the import of the words of consecration is fully complete without them. The founding of the *new covenant* (which none will deny to have been embraced in the words of consecration; Paul gives it so, as well as Luke, and they must have received them from ear-witnesses) covers the whole ground. The "new covenant," founded upon the self-offering of Christ, could only refer to the new relation between man and God, secured by that self-sacrifice; viz., the pardon of sin through his sufferings, and the restoration of communion with God, which the old covenant *could* not restore. The whole import of Christianity, in relation to the old covenant, is clearly set forth in that of the Lord's Supper, as given by Christ himself.

† In a different sense, however, from that in which it was said to the Jews: the latter were to remain separated from him in spirit and disposition, but to the disciples he had given a pledge of continued communion—the Supper of the new covenant. He then proceeds to give them the *commandment* of the new covenant, the law of love, embracing all others, by which the inward and spiritual communion was to be outwardly manifested.

also, with respect to the earlier stages of the disciples' association with him: it was only when his death was at hand that he could set it vividly before them in this sense.

§ 270. *The Request of Peter.—Christ predicts Peter's Denial of Him.* (John, xiii., 36–38.)

So strongly were the disciples wedded to their earlier ideas and expectations, that it seemed impossible to make them realize the approaching departure of Christ. Peter, alarmed at his words, inquired, "*Lord, whither goest thou?*" Jesus, in reply, explained the sense of his words, at the same time intimating that Peter should be able, at a later period, though he then was not, to follow the Master through suffering: "*Whither I go thou canst not follow me now, but thou shalt follow me afterward.*" Peter, ever rash and self-confident, was not satisfied to wait for the future: believing himself *then* able, he asked, "*Lord, why can I not follow thee now? I will lay down my life for thy sake.*"

Christ then predicted his three-fold denial—the punishment of his froward self-confidence: "*Wilt thou lay down thy life for my sake? The cock shall not crow till thou hast denied me thrice.*"*

§ 271. *Christ predicts the Danger of the Disciples in their new Relations to the People.* (Luke, xxii., 35–38.)†

Certain fragments of Christ's conversation at the table are preserved to us in the first three Gospels, not given by John, whose object was to record those profound and connected discourses which so strikingly exhibited the loftiness of his Divinity, his heavenly calmness and serenity of soul. Among these fragments are contained intimations, in a variety of forms, of the great change in their condition that was at hand. Reiteration and emphasis were necessary to break away their stubborn prejudices.

Reminding them of the first trial mission‡ on which he had sent them, with express directions to provide nothing for their journey, he asked whether they had then lacked any thing; and they said, Nothing. In

* The agreement of three independent accounts—Matthew, Luke, and John—in stating this remarkable incident, confirms its credibility. In John's Gospel, it is presented in an obvious connexion; in the other two, as an isolated fact.

† *Gfrörer* asserts (Heilig. Sage, i., 336) that this passage was of later origin, and supports his assertion on the ground that the connexion of thought between verses 36 and 37 is false. Not so: verse 37 contains the *ground* of the change in the disciples' condition, recited in verse 36; the execution of Christ as a transgressor, making him an object of aversion and disgust, was to react upon the condition of his followers. It is said, further, that the passage was inserted here because men stumbled at Peter's conduct, as recited in verse 50. But it would be a strange way to get rid of *this* difficulty, to introduce a greater one, viz., an advice on the part of Jesus himself to his disciples, to provide swords above all things.

‡ Cf. p. 257, seq.

that mission, they found the people of Galilee favourably disposed; no open hostility had been excited against Jesus; on the contrary, the fame of his actions inclined the people to acknowledge him, at least, as a man endowed with Divine powers. But *now* his own fate, and the consequent change of popular feeling, was about to react upon the disciples. Accordingly, he gave them—not rules for a new mode of life and conduct, but—a striking illustration, in figurative terms, not only of his own sufferings, but of the dangers that awaited *them*, from the sudden reflux of the popular feeling. The figures chosen were directly antithetical to those employed on the former occasion. "If I formerly bade you travel without purse, or scrip, or shoes (without provisions for the journey, as your wants would all be supplied); so now, on the contrary, I tell you that you shall find men differently disposed towards you. He that hath a purse, let him take it, and likewise his scrip (all the necessaries of travel); and he that hath no purse* (money), let him sell his garment and buy a sword" (or knife). As if he had said, "You will hereafter need to care more for the safety of your lives than of your garments; you will need, more than all things else, means to carry you safely through the difficulties that will surround you."

The whole connexion of these words taught the disciples that they were to be taken, not literally, but as the symbolical veil of a general thought. And they could easily have gathered from Christ's example, from the spirit of his whole life, and from his teaching, in the Sermon on the Mount and elsewhere (if they were not utterly thoughtless hearers), that he could not really intend to bid them furnish themselves with swords.

From this change in the feelings of the world towards his disciples Christ naturally passed to his own fate, which was to cause that change itself. He told them that he was "to be reckoned among transgressors" as an object of hatred and abhorrence. Then said two of the disciples, "Behold, Lord! two of us are already provided with swords."† Language implying an utter misunderstanding of what he had said; a misunderstanding hardly to be expected in men who had so long enjoyed the Saviour's personal society. But, perhaps, in justice to the disciples, we ought to suppose that their words were uttered in the confusion and distress of mind which his declarations occasioned. Perhaps Peter, the most hasty and headlong of the Apostles, who carried a sword, was one of the speakers. It was well that this misunderstanding was expressed, to be checked and done away. "*It is enough*," said Christ, plainly showing that he had not the slightest in-

* The antithesis is between ὁ ἔχων βαλάντιον and ὁ μὴ ἔχων.

† The word may be rendered "knives;" and these were in common use among travellers in those regions for a variety of purposes

tention to advise the use of weapons of defence, as *two* swords among them would have been nothing for that purpose. Perhaps, however, the phrase might be more correctly rendered, "*enough of it;*" *i. e.*, a sign to drop the subject; as if a reproof of their tendency to stick to the words and literal features of his language, rather than to its spirit and sense.

§ 272. *Christ consoles the Disciples with the Promise of his Return.* (John, xiv.)

The last connected discourses of Christ are given at length in John's Gospel.* In these he made use of a different turn of thought from that above referred to, to prepare the minds and hearts of the disciples for the struggles that awaited them. In view of their evident distress, while yet sitting at the table, he said, "Let not your hearts be troubled; trust in God, and confide in Me." Even when his visible presence should be removed, they were to trust in him as the Mediator of their communion with God; nor, in grief for his departure, to think that he had left them alone in the world. There would be mansions

* It is charged by some that John could not possibly have remembered these discourses thus amid the thousand painful and tumultuous emotions that must have immediately followed. Little do such objectors conceive of the nature of the human soul, and of the might of deep impressions upon it. Such impressions these discourses must have made upon a mind and heart like John's, and what was once received thus into the depths of the soul no concussions could cast out. Moreover, these emotions, how powerful soever they may have been, lasted but for a few days, and were followed by a reunion with Christ, by a new epoch of the interior life of the disciples which developed itself more and more gloriously. How, in these few days, could John have forgotten discourses so weighty in themselves, and affecting his own soul so powerfully? And, when the spiritual life of the disciples, sunken for a moment, emerged again after the resurrection of their Master, how brilliantly must the image of these last discourses have shone forth from the depths of their memories and their hearts! How precious must each word have been to them! With what intense interest must they have turned them over and dwelt upon their import! And how clear, in the light of their experience of the fulfilment of his predictions, must many things have appeared that were before obscure!

Equally futile is the objection that John wrote his Gospel at an advanced age, when some things must have escaped his memory, and others become blended with his own thoughts. He must have repeated these discourses, times without number, to others; how, then, can it be said that he could not commit them faithfully to writing? (we do not mean to say *verbatim et literatim*, cf. index, sub voc. *John*). The remark of Irenæus with regard to what he had heard in his youth from the lips of Polycarp will apply with vastly greater force to *John* and *Christ*: "Μᾶλλον γὰρ τὰ τότε διαμνημονεύω τῶν ἔναγχος γινομένων, αἱ γὰρ ἐκ παίδων μαθήσεις συναύξουσαι τῇ ψυχῇ, ἑνοῦνται αὐτῇ." (Comp. the entire passage, *Euseb.*, v. 20; it bears remarkably against human efforts to convert a historical period into a mythical one.)

John could not have been *John* had it been possible for him to forget such discourses of Christ.

A further proof of the originality of these discourses, as recorded by John, is the aptness with which many passages are joined into them which, in the other Gospels, are presented in isolated forms, or in inapt connexions; *e. g.*, Luke, xii., 11, 12; Matt., x., 17–20; Mark, xiii., 11. The passage in John, xvi., 32, is connected in Matt., xxvi., 31, Mark, xiv., 27 with the account of Peter's denial.

for all, he told them, in his Father's house. He was going before (it was the object of his redeeming sufferings and of his ascension to heaven), to prepare a place for them; just as a friend goes before his friend to make his dwelling ready. And then he promises them, "*If I go and prepare a place for you, I will come again and receive you unto myself; that where I am, there ye may be also.*"

This might be understood of Christ's second advent, were it not that he speaks of what was to happen *immediately* upon his return to the Father, and that his design was to comfort them in view of the *immediate* pain of separation. Nor can it be applied to his Resurrection, because his "going to the Father" was to *follow* the resurrection, and this, again, to be followed by a separation.* The only remaining interpretation is to apply it to his spiritual coming, to his revealing himself again to them, as the glorified one, in the communion of the Divine life. Not only were *they* to follow Him to the heavenly "mansions,"† where he was to "provide a place for them," but he himself was "again to come to *them*," that where He was, there they might be also, in spirit, united with him, never again to be separated. But as they could not as yet fully apprehend this spiritual coming and communion, it was only at a later period that these expressions, sufficiently within their capacity to give them consolation at the time, were understood in their full import.

§ 273. *Conversation with Philip and Thomas.—Christ the Way.* (John, xiv.)

The institution of the Eucharist also contained an allusion‡ to the promise that he would be with his disciples as truly after his departure as he had been during his corporeal presence. And as he knew that their minds were not yet entirely free from carnal and unspiritual views, he gave occasion for them to express themselves freely, in order to give them clearer ideas by means of their very misunderstandings.

"*Whither I go,*" said he, "*ye know; and the way ye know.*" Still, the death of *Messiah* was a hard conception for them; a miraculous removal from the earth would have accorded better with their feelings.

* This objection would fall away if we could believe, with *L. Kinkel* (Stud. u. Krit., 841, 3), that Christ, after leaving the grave and appearing to Mary, ascended to heaven, and only returned thence when he reappeared to the disciples. But the words under consideration do not justify this supposition. However we may conceive Christ's reappearance after his resurrection, they could not satisfy the promises, given in these discourses, of a new and higher spiritual connexion between him and his disciples. In view of this *continued* manifestation, this uninterrupted communion, his bodily reappearance was only preparatory and subordinate.

† Compare the analogy in the figure of the "everlasting mansions," p. 275.

‡ The last promise, also, Matt., xxviii., 20, presupposes such fuller explanations as those which we find recorded by John in these discourses.

Thomas,* who seems to have remained in bondage to sense more than any of the others, said to him, "*Lord, we know not whither thou goest; and how can we know the way?*" The Saviour, in his reply, inverts the order; if they had known the "*way,*" they would have known the "*whither:*" "*I am the way, the truth, and the life; no man cometh unto the Father but by me. If ye had known me, ye should have known my Father also.*" (Had they better known *Him*, through whom the Father reveals and communicates himself, they would have known better all the rest.) The three conceptions in this passage are closely connected together. He designates himself not merely as the *guide*, but as the *Way* itself; and that because he is himself, according to his nature and life, the *Truth;* the truth springing from the *Life;* because he is, in himself, the Source of the Divine Life among men, as well as the personal manifestation of the Divine Truth. He is, therefore, the *Way*, inasmuch as mankind, by communion of Divine life with him, receive the *truth*, and are brought by it into union with the Father. He that knows him, therefore, knows the Father also. "*And from henceforth ye know him, and have seen him;*" *i. e.*, after their long intercourse with Christ, they were now, at least, to see and recognize the Father in him.

But Philip, still on the stand-point of sense, applied these words to a *sensible* theophany, as a sign of the Messianic era: "*Lord, show us the Father, and it sufficeth us.*" This misunderstanding led Christ *again* to impress upon their minds the same truth, that whoever obtained a just spiritual intuition of *Him* saw the Father in Him; the Father, with whom *He* lived in inseparable communion, and who manifested himself in *His* words and works (v. 9, 10, 11). But these works, and the manifestation of God in them, were not to remain to the disciples something merely external. Whoever believed on him was, through his fellowship, to become an organ of his continued Divine working for the renewal of the life of mankind; the aim of his whole manifestation was to do yet greater things than he had done:† "*Verily, verily, I say unto you, he that believeth on me, the works that I do shall he do also; and yet greater works than these shall he do.*"‡

And the source of all this power was to be, in his own words, "*Because I go unto my Father;*" they were to gain it precisely by that separation, the prospect of which then filled them with grief and sorrow. When he should go to the Father, and remove from them the visible, human, and, therefore, limited form of his manifestation, as a source of dependance, *then* would he, as the glorified one, work invisibly from

* Thomas displays the same character here as in his subsequent doubts concerning Christ's resurrection. It is wholly incredible that the author of John's Gospel, who obviously was little capable of assuming different characters, should have invented such a one

† Cf. the excellent remarks of *Kling*, Stud. u. Krit., 1836, iii., 684.

‡ Cf. p. 184, 358

heaven in them, and among them, with Divine power. And therefore it was that, through communion of the Divine life with him, they were to "do yet greater things than these."

§ 274. *Of Prayer in the Name of Christ. He promises the Spirit of Truth, the Comforter; and His own Return.* (John, xiv., 13–26.)

The disciples were to enter into new relations with Christ. He, therefore, specially taught them to pray *in his name.* As they had before, during his bodily presence, expressed their wants to him personally, so now, trusting in him, and conscious of the new relations in which, through him, they stood to the Father, they were to apply to the Father in his name. "*And whatsoever ye shall ask of the Father in my name* (*i. e.*, through his mediation), *that will I do, that the Father may be glorified in the Son*" (by what the Son should work among men to the glory of the Father, by the spread of the kingdom of God through him). At the same time, certain conditions were essential on their part: "*If ye love me, keep my commandments.*"

And this forms the transition to the promise which follows: "*And I will pray the Father, and he shall give you another Comforter, that he may abide with you forever.*" Through his mediation, the Father would send them, instead of Him who had, up to that time, been their help in all things, *another* Helper, who should not leave them, as He was about to do. "*Even the Spirit of Truth:*" and he calls the Spirit so, because it alone can unfold the meaning of *his* truth, and because union with the Holy Spirit can only be obtained by appropriating that truth. This Spirit, he told them, the world could not receive, because it was totally foreign to the world; but *they* were to know it, in the only way in which it could be known, by inward and personal experience: "*He dwelleth with you, and shall be in you.*"

His description of the Spirit makes it, in relation to his own previous personal presence among them, something different from himself. This prepared them to apprehend, in a more spiritual way than before, the announcement of his own return, which he now repeated. *With this Spirit it was that he himself was to come to them:* "*I will not leave you orphans; I will come to you.*" He speaks now of himself, just as he had before spoken of the Spirit: "*Yet a little while, and the world seeth me no more, but ye see me;* because I live, and ye live; I reveal myself, as the Living, to the living." The world, cut off from the Divine life, and therefore dead, knows nothing of Christ, as the Living it holds him dead; but to those who are susceptible of Divine communion of life with him, he will reveal himself as the Living one.

He then tells them that only at the period when they should reach this higher communion with him, would they be able fully to understand his relation to the Father and to them: "*At that day shall ye know that I am in my Father, and ye in me, and I in you.*" Throughout these final discourses, *promises* alternate with *duties;* so now he points out an essential requisite on their part—love, proved in keeping his commandments: "*He that hath* (knows and preserves) *my commandments, and also keepeth* (faithfully observes) *them, he it is that loveth me; and he that loveth me shall be loved of my Father, and I will love him* (including an *active demonstration* of love), *and will manifest myself to him.*" One of the disciples, yet blinded by carnal expectations, said to him, "*Lord, how is it that thou wilt manifest thyself unto us, and not unto the world?*" This led Christ to say that this manifestation spoken of would be made only to those who should be spiritually susceptible of it, thereby implying that it would be entirely a spiritual manifestation (v. 23, 24).

Finally, he referred them again (v. 26) to the Holy Ghost, to be sent through his mediation, who should teach them rightly to understand his own (Christ's) doctrine; and should call back to their memories any thing which might, through misunderstanding, become darkened in their minds.

§ 275. *Christ's Salutation of Peace; its Import.* (John, xiv., 27, seq.)

When about to rise from the table, the Saviour pronounced a blessing, as was usual at salutation and leave-taking: "*Peace I leave with you, my peace I give unto you.*" A fitting conclusion to the promises of comfort was this farewell word of peace. But, after all that he had promised, he could, even in view of the approaching separation, and the conflicts and strifes to which he was about to leave the disciples, promise them the enjoyment of peace. And he told them that his salutation implied another peace than that of the world: "*Not as the world giveth, give I unto you.*" This peace the world has not, and therefore cannot give. It was peace in itself, a real peace, that he left behind unto his own; a peace which none but He possesses, and none can find but in communion with him. No room in *them*, therefore, for fear or disquiet: "*Let not your heart be troubled, neither let it be afraid.*"

Again he recurs to his departure, and reminds them of the promise which ought to remove all the sting of separation: "*Ye have heard how I said unto you, I go away, and come again unto you. If ye loved me, ye would rejoice because I said, I go unto the Father, for the Father is greater than I.*" He went; but it was to return in greater glory. They could not love him, if they did not rejoice at the glorious change that he was to leave the limits of his earthly and visible human nature, and ascend to the Father Almighty, in order to operate, thenceforward, in union with Him, in the power of God, invisible and infinite.* He had foretold to them what would happen, that their faith might not waver in the evil hour (v. 29). He could speak but a few words more as the Prince of this World was coming (in his agents); though that Prince had no power over him, and He could, if he chose, escape the power of his foes (v. 30); but he did *not* choose. Voluntarily he would go to meet death, to prove, in the face of the world, his love to the Father, by completing the work committed to him by the Father (v. 31).

And then he called them to arise from table, and go with him to the final conflict.

CHAPTER IV.

DISCOURSES OF CHRIST AFTER RISING FROM TABLE AT THE LAST SUPPER.

§ 276. *Similitude of the Vine and Branches.— The Law of Love.* (John, xv.)

THERE were many thoughts which his mind and heart yet laboured to pour forth. After leaving the table he began to discourse anew, and called their attention specially to two thoughts: (1.) That the relation which had subsisted between them was to remain, with this difference only, that, instead of *external* dependence and connexion, they would be *internally* allied to and dependent on him; (2.) That they must now become self-active agents for the spread of the kingdom of God, but that they could only become such by continued communion and fellowship with him.

To illustrate these points, he made use of the similitude of a *Vine*: God, the vine-dresser; Christ, the vine; his followers, the branches. The fructifying sap flows from the vine-stock through all the branches, and without it they can produce no fruit; so the followers of Christ can only obtain, by inward and inseparable communion with him, the Divine life which can fit them to be productive labourers in the kingdom of God. The branches wither when torn from the vine, and deprived of its vital sap; so, also, the disciples of Christ live and prosper only in continuous communion with him. But as the branches show, by bearing fruit, that they have shared in the fructifying power from the vine-stock; so the disciples of Christ must show their participation in the Divine life through communion with Him, by abundant and fruitful

* As *Lücke* and *Kling* (loc. cit.) have remarked, this passage can only be applied to the relation between God, as the Almighty, and Jesus, as man, standing then before his disciples, in the narrow form of humanity.

labours in the kingdom of God. The vine-dresser cuts off all useless branches, which, like mere excrescences, consume the vital power of the vine without bearing fruit; so will all those who do not manifest the Divine life in fruitful works, proving, by this deficiency, that their communion with Christ is not real, but apparent, be cut off from the kingdom of God.* But even the productive branches stand in constant need of the vine-dresser's care; all exuberant growth must be trimmed; all excrescences hindering the course of the vital sap must be pared away; so, also, the disciples, even those who enjoy the Divine life in communion with Christ, must be purified constantly from foreign elements, that there may be no obstacles to the developement of the Divine life within them, or of the outward activity corresponding to it.

It was only by this activity in communion with him that they could prove themselves to be his genuine disciples (v. 8);† by activity in observing all his commandments;‡ and again he condenses all "the commandments" into love (v. 9–14). Such love they were to show to each other as he, laying down his life, had shown to them. In thus communicating to the disciples the whole counsel of the Father in regard to the plan of salvation through their agency, and in calling upon them to devote themselves to this service as organs of the Divine kingdom, with clear consciousness and free self-determination, he removes them from the stand-point of "servants" and takes them up to that of "friends" (v. 15).§

United to each other in love, they must also be hated in common by the world; the world must feel to them as to their Master. He predicts the persecutions that await them. He sees before him the conflict of Christianity with all existing institutions (v. 18–23).||

§ 277. *Promise of the Holy Ghost.—Concluding Words of Comfort to the Disciples.* (John, xvi., 7–33.)

But he further promises¶ that in all their conflicts they shall have the Holy Ghost for a helper.** The Holy Ghost was to accomplish, through them, all things necessary for the spread of the Divine kingdom. The

* The same thought as "He who hath, to him shall be given," &c., p. 105, 189.

† Mark the inner connexion between these discourses and those recorded in the first three Gospels. The same demand is implied in the parables of the *talents* and the *pound* (p. 347, 348) as in this similitude of the vine.

‡ Hence "the commandments" are not "the *letter* of the law;" where there is life, rooted in communion with Christ, it *cannot*, according to its very essence, manifest itself otherwise except in works corresponding to the law.

§ Cf. p. 120.

|| Not "peace," but a "sword," as in the synoptical Gospels; cf. p. 315.

¶ Cf. p. 396, 397.

** Cf. p. 117, on the two-fold relation of the disciples, (1.) As individual witnesses of Christ's ministry; (2.) As organs of the spirit, like believers in general.

process he states as follows: The Holy Ghost will convince the world of *sin*, and show that unbelief is the ground of sin; and further, will convince the world that Christ did not die as a sinner, but, as the Holy One, ascended to his Father in heaven, most perfectly manifesting His *righteousness* in his death, and in the exaltation to God which followed it; indeed, all that are convinced of sin will recognize him as the Holy One, and the source of all holiness in men. So he will gradually convince the world of *judgment;* that Satan, so long ruler of the world, has been judged; that evil has lost its sway, and therefore can cause no fear to such as hold communion with Christ. These, then, are the three great elements of the process: the consciousness of *sin;* of the *righteousness* of Christ, the Redeemer from sin; of the impotency of evil (*judgment*) in opposition to the kingdom of God. And to be conscious of sin; to know Christ as the Holy Redeemer; and the kingdom of God as the conqueror of evil, which shall finally subdue all things to itself: *this* is the whole essence of Christianity.

Christ had many things to say of his doctrine which the disciples were not then in a condition to understand. But he was just about to leave them; and therefore he pointed them to the Spirit of Truth, which was to unfold all the truth he had proclaimed. It was not to announce any *new* doctrine; but to open the truth of *his* doctrine; to glorify Him (v. 14) in them, by developing the full sense of what He had taught them. Again he passes from the giving of the Holy Ghost to his own communion with them; repeating what he had before said: "*A little while, and ye shall not see me, and again a little while, and ye shall see me, because I go to the Father*" (inasmuch as his "going to the Father" was to be the ground of the new spiritual communion).* And, again, some of them expressed the surprise of their contracted minds at his words (v. 17). Jesus, seeing their uncertainty, developed the thought still further. He told them they should be sorrowful for a season, but their sorrow would be turned into permanent joy. Their transient pains, like those of a woman in travail, would be the birth-throes of a new creation within them. "And ye now, therefore, have sorrow; but I will see you again, and your heart shall rejoice, and your joy no man taketh from you."

"*And in that day ye shall ask me nothing;*" they would no more need his *sensible* presence to ask of him as they had been wont. "Whatsoever ye shall ask the Father *in my name* (in conscious communion through Christ's mediation), *he will give it you.*" (The Father would reveal all things needful to them through Christ's mediation; clearing up all obscurities, and supplying the place of his corporeal presence.)

* But the promise certainly contains an allusion to his resurrection, inasmuch as his reappearance was to the disciples the point of transition to the state of new spiritual communion.

Up to that time (v. 24), not having yet obtained confidence of communion with the Father through Christ, they had asked nothing of HIM; but *then* they should ask, and receive, that their joy might be full. Then, too, would Christ no more speak unto them in figures or parables, but would openly unveil all he had to say to them of the Father. "But," says he, "I say *not* unto you that I will pray the Father for you;" in their conscious communion with Him they would be *sure* of the Father's love, and in His name would address themselves directly to the Father.

At last a ray of light beamed into the souls of the disciples. They felt the impression of the high things which Christ, in confident Divinity, had just announced to them. Yet, as their language shows* that they did not fully understand him, it was rather a feeling than a clearly developed consciousness. Christ cautioned them against trusting it too far; that the hour was at hand when a faith of this kind would give way to a powerful impression of another nature; that they should be scattered, and leave him alone: "*Yet not alone*," said he, "*because the Father is with me.*"

The aim of the whole discourse had been to impart to the minds of the disciples a spring of Divine comfort amid their struggles with a hostile world for the advancement of the kingdom of GOD. He closed it with a few words of farewell, embracing its whole scope: "*These things have I spoken to you, that in* (communion with) *me ye might have peace.*† *In the world ye shall have tribulations; be of good cheer; I have overcome the world.*"‡

§ 278. *Christ's Prayer as High-priest.* (John, xvii.)

With a prayer Christ concludes this last interview with his disciples; with a prayer he prepares himself for the separation and the final conflict.

The import of the prayer is the same as that of the discourse. Conscious that his work (viz., to glorify GOD in man) on earth is finished, he prays the Father to take him to himself, and glorify him with himself. Not, however, with a selfish aim or selfish longings; it was to glorify the Father, and, what was inseparable therefrom, to impart the Divine life to mankind: "*Glorify thy Son, that thy Son also may glorify*

* It appears clear from v. 29, 30 that they understood the phrase, "Ye shall ask me nothing," in a sense different from that which he intended. It may readily be imagined that John's subsequent better comprehension of Christ's meaning caused this misapprehension to appear remarkable, and served to impress it the more upon his memory.

† Inward peace; Divine calmness amid the struggle with the world.

‡ The relation is two-fold: (1) The inward life in communion with Christ, who has overcome the Power of Evil, and gives his own to share in his victory; (2) The outward life in contact with the world, possibly harming, indeed, the outward man, but incapable of subduing, or disturbing the peace of, the inner man, rooted in Christ's fellowship

thee; as thou hast given him power over all flesh, that he should give eternal life to as many as thou hast given him."* But as eternal life is only to be obtained by knowing the true God, revealed in Christ, he prays that this knowledge may be diffused among all men, and so eternal life be given to all.

Then, first, he prays for those who had already received this knowledge, and were to become instruments of its diffusion among men. As he is about to leave the world, and to leave the disciples alone in it, he commends them to the protecting care of the Father, to whom they are consecrated through him; that the Divine communion of life, which he had established, might be preserved among them. He commends them to His care, because the world, in whose midst they are, will hate them, since they are not of it. He does not ask their removal *from* the world; that would subvert the very work he had assigned them, the work of regenerating the world through the knowledge of God in Christ; he only prays that they may be inwardly separated from the world and its evil powers, and sanctified through the truth he had revealed; that his life, sanctified to God, and given up for them, might become the ground of their sanctification.

He then extends his prayer to all that may be brought to faith by their preaching (v. 20). He prays that they may be united in the communion of life with God which he had established; that by it they may testify of him; that thereby they might show forth the glory of the inner life given by him, and bear witness of *that* love of God (v. 23) which they had experienced through him. (The true communion of Christ's disciples shows forth His glory, and the glory which He has imparted to them; the glory, namely, of their whole relation to God as children, secured for them by Him. The outward appearance is the reflection of the glory within.†) He then prays (v. 24) that all those who are "given to him" (already united with him—his glory already revealed in them) may be raised up to be where He is, to complete communion with him, to the beholding of his Divine glory (and this implies a *share* in that glory; for *intuition* and *life* coincide in the Divine).

This incomparable prayer of consecration for his own, and for all mankind, is closed with the words, "*O Holy‡ Father, the world hath not known thee* (lost in sin, it *cannot* know the Holy One); *but I have known thee* (the Holy One knows the Holy One); *and these have known that thou hast sent me* (they are, therefore, separated from the world of sin, which is estranged from the Holy God); *and I have declared unto them thy name* (have revealed unto them Thee, as the Holy One, and

* He considers those, and those only, as truly his own who follow the inward Divine call, the "drawing" of the Father. Cf. p. 138, 360.

† In all time the spread of Christianity is *most* advanced by the power of the Christian life.

‡ I translate δίκαιε, "holy;" cf. xvi., 10; 1 John, ii., 29; iii., 7, 10

not only as the Holy God, but as the Holy Father, with whom they stand in child-like communion), *and will declare it* further (all that had been revealed was but the germ, as it were, of subsequent developements); *that the love wherewith thou hast loved me may be in them, and I in them* (that as they know Thee more and more through the revelations of my spirit, they may, in communion with me, learn more and more how thou lovest me and those that belong to me)."

Thus this prayer embraces the *whole* work of Christ, up to its final consummation; his work, upon the basis laid down by himself, continually carried on, until all that submit to him shall be brought to a share in his glory—to a complete communion of Divine life with him. What is expressed in the "Lord's Prayer" as the object of the prayer of believers is here presented as the object of his own prayer *for* believers.

CHAPTER V.

GETHSEMANE.

§ 279. *Comparison of John's Gospel with the Synoptical Gospels in regard to Jesus' Conflict of Soul.—Historical Credibility of the Synoptical Account.*

FULL of celestial serenity, Jesus went forth with the disciples, as was his wont, to the garden at the foot of the Mount of Olives, to await the coming of his captors. Various alternations of feeling ensued in his soul; and in regard to them there is an obvious difference between the synoptical Gospels and John; the former not mentioning them at all, the latter giving a partial account of them. In modern times this discrepancy has been supposed by some to be irreconcilable; so much so that one side or the other must be maintained, according to the view which we take of the whole subject.

It is argued that we cannot imagine Christ, who had just spoken with such Divine confidence, and had poured out his soul before God in a prayer of heavenly calmness and assurance, as undergoing, immediately after, such struggles of soul as are recorded in the synoptical Gospels. But, laying John's Gospel out of the case, do we not find the *same* contrast in the other Gospels? Was not all this heavenly elevation, serenity, and confidence presupposed in the institution of the Eucharist, according to its deeper sense? Was not that act, the pledge of his continuing communion with the Church, as recorded in the first three Gospels, as great a proof of those high thoughts on which his calmness was founded, as is contained in the final discourse and prayer given by John? Nay, even in these last, can we not trace alternations of feeling; subordinate, however, to the fundamental and Divine tone?

As for these alternations of feeling themselves, may we not conceive, that as, in the life of believers, who represent (imperfectly indeed) the image of Christ on earth, calmness and tumult, confidence and despondency, alternate with each other under the diverse influences of the outward world,* so too there might be similar fluctuations (unconnected, however, with the reactions of sin, which might exist in believers†) in the soul of Him who, with all his Divine elevation, was like unto man in all things but sin, and sympathized, unutterably, with all purely human feelings?‡

Even in *John's* account of the raising of Lazarus we find such alternations in the prominency of the Divinity and the humanity of Christ; would not, therefore, similar manifestations at the approach of death be in harmony with his image, as depicted by John himself? Moreover, both John and Luke alluded to the *beginnings* of this struggle of soul at different times before;§ momentary, however, and soon followed by the accustomed confidence of Divinity. In John, xiii., 21,‖ we find Jesus "troubled in spirit" in contemplating Judas. It would be contrary to all analogy, then, that such moments should *not* occur, even with increased intensity, amid the ever-accumulating pangs both of soul and body that he endured up to the moment of the final and triumphant exclamation. "But," it will perhaps be said, "according to John's account, there *was* no struggle of *soul* at last." How, then, could John record Christ's "trouble of soul" (xii., 27) in view of the last hour, and his wish¶ (xiii., 27) that the catastrophe might be hastened?

The account of the agony in the garden, taken from the other Gospels, can be aptly inserted in John's narrative. "But why, then, does *John* not record it?" It is enough to say, in reply to this, that his object was, not to give a complete biography, but to arrange a number of separate features of the great picture, according to a peculiar point of view. If John, having intimated the beginnings of this struggle in the soul of Jesus, preferred, instead of delineating all its subsequent stages, to picture forth the Divine elevation of Christ as shown in his

* Cf. *John the Baptist.* † Cf. p. 79, 82.

‡ Thus did that genuine disciple of Christ, JOHN HUSS, who had formed his life upon the intuition of Christ's example, learn from the experience of his own last struggles how to comprehend these opposite manifestations in the Saviour's life. With reference to such alternations in his own experience, he writes: "Pro certo grave est, imperturbate gaudere, et omne gaudium existimare, in variis tentationibus. Leve est loqui et illud exponere, sed grave implere. Siquidem patientissimus et fortissimus miles, sciens quod die tertia esset resurrecturus, et per mortem suam vincens inimicos, post coenam ultimam turbatus est spiritu et dixit,—tristis est anima, usque ad mortem."

§ Cf p. 314, 376. ‖ Cf. p. 387. ¶ Cf. p. 388.

last discourses, can we infer *any thing* from this, except that in his delineation certain features of Christ's picture are more prominent than others? Throughout, it is the method of John's Gospel to present connected chains of Christ's discourses and acts, rather than isolated incidents, however characteristic, such as we find in the other Evangelists. Moreover, as an eye-witness of this last struggle, he was not in a state of mind to perceive, and subsequently to describe, it as a *whole*. It must not be inferred, however, from this last remark, that the disciples could not have remembered, and faithfully recorded, *individual* features that made a deep impression upon them.

Let us now dwell for a moment upon the credibility of the synoptical account. It agrees entirely with Heb., v., 7, which was founded upon direct Apostolical tradition. How can it be conceived that such a description of Christ's agony could have arisen from an invented legend, intended to *glorify* him? Nor can it be said that it was made up by collecting and putting together the various types and prophecies of the Old Testament that prefigured such an agony; *after* the description was extant, as *history*, it was natural that these should be gathered up, and doctrinal reasons assigned for the agony itself; but *before*, its invention would have been utterly inconsistent with the idea, generally prevalent, of the glory of Messiah. In the representations of the Evangelists, particularly Matthew, we can detect no aim but a historical one; not a trace of *doctrinal* motives can be discovered; only at a later period were such *thrust* upon them by that wilfulness which can find in a narrative any thing it chooses.

It was easy, indeed, from a *natural* point of view, to find a contradiction between such expressions of human weakness on the part of Christ, and his miracle-working power, his conscious dignity as Messiah or as the Son of God, his foreknowledge of his resurrection, &c. Nor could such a contradiction ever have *naturally* arisen from an idealizing invention. It was precisely with a view to do it away as a ground of objection, that a *Docetic* Christ was afterward conceived in place of the *real* Christ; or, his human nature was sundered from the Divine. The Divinity, the Divine Logos, was recognized in the miracles and lofty discourses; but it was feigned that this Logos, the true Redeemer, withdrew from Christ during his sufferings.

Such a Christ, indeed, as the real Christ, was always a stone of stumbling for Jewish modes of thought. How much, therefore, must the author of the epistle to the Hebrews have been concerned to remove this rock of offence, and to prove that these very struggles belonged necessarily to the Messianic calling? To be sure, after the idea of Messiah had once been modified according to the real, historical Christ, and the minds of men had thereby received a new tendency, it was easy to find the higher unity for all these contradictions, and combine them all into the one idea. But we can by no means infer from this possibility its converse, viz., that the new idea, suddenly arising like a *Deus ex machina*, could have given birth to such a historical representation of Christ.

§ 280. *The Agony in the Garden.* (Matt., xxvi.; Mark, xiv.; Luke, xxii.)

In prayer and retirement Christ had prepared himself for the *beginning* of his public ministry; in prayer and retirement he now prepared to close his calling on earth. As then, so now, before entering upon the outward conflict, he passed through it in the inward struggles of his soul. *Then* he had in spirit gained the victory, before he appeared openly among men a conqueror; *now* the conquest of suffering was achieved within, before the final, outward triumph.

Arrived at the garden, he took apart Peter, James, and John, his three best-loved disciples, to be the honoured witnesses of his prayer, and to pray with him. From the nature of the case, we could not have so full an account of this as of his prayer for his disciples (John, xvii.) In the pains of suffering that are pressing upon him he prays, "*Father, if it be possible, let this cup pass from me.*" But this feeling could not for a moment shake his submission to the Divine will. All other feelings are absorbed in the fundamental longing, "*Thy will be done.*" The Divinity is distinguished from the Humanity; and by this distinction their unity, in the subordination of the one to the other, was to be made prominent. As a *man*, he might wish to be spared the sufferings that awaited him, even though from a higher point of view he saw their necessity; just as a Christian may be convinced that he ought to make a certain sacrifice in the service of God, and yet, in darker moments, his purely human feelings may rise against it, until his conviction, and his will guided by his conviction, at last prevail. It was not merely that Christ's *physical* nature had to struggle with death, and *such* a death, but his *soul* had to be moved to its depths by sympathy with the sufferings of mankind on account of sin.* Thus the wish might arise within

* By the "cup" we must understand not only his suffering of death, but all that preceded and followed it: the treason of Judas, the rage of Christ's enemies, the delusion of the multitude. It is not my object here to set forth the higher doctrinal and theological import of the death of Christ; yet I agree heartily in the following, from *Dettinger's* beautiful dissertation on Christ's agony (Tübing. Zeitschrift, 1838, i., 95, 96): "While, on the one hand, in a sinful nature, the conviction that death is a judgment for sin is blunted in proportion as the power of sin in the individual is greater, and the sense of its guilt less; in a word, in proportion as the harmonic unity of life is disturbed by sin, so much the more powerful, on the other hand, in a *sinless* human nature, in which the unity of life's harmony is undisturbed, must be the conviction that death *is* a judgment for sin, a dissolution and separation, not originally belonging to human nature, of elements which in all stages of the developement of life belong together." I can make this agree, also, with the view of the connexion between sin and death presented in my "Apostol. Zeitalter," vol ii.

him, as a man, to be spared that bitter cup; only on condition, how ever, that the will of GOD could be done in some other way. But the conviction that this *could* not be, immediately followed; he knew, from the beginning,* that, according to the plan of Divine wisdom, the kingdom of GOD was to be founded through his self-sacrifice in the struggle with the sins of the people; and he submitted to what he knew was the will of GOD and the work of his life.†

As a proof how little the higher calmness of his spirit was disturbed by these uprisings of human feeling, we find him, a moment after the first struggle, caring for his yet weak disciples. Finding them overcome with sleep, he roused them, saying, "*Could ye not watch with me one hour? Watch and pray, that ye enter not into temptation* (that the outward temptation become not an inward one‡); *for, though the spirit is willing* (as in their fulness of love, when danger was not pressing upon them, they had declared themselves ready to suffer all things with him and for him), *the flesh is weak.*" (The impressions of outward danger may affect the flesh so strongly as to bear down the spirit; there is need, therefore, of Divine power, gained by prayer, to strengthen the spirit amid these fearful impressions, that it may triumph over the weakness of the flesh.)

Again he bends in prayer. And *now* he does not say, "*If* it be possible, let—;" but, penetrated by the conviction that the counsel of Divine Wisdom demands the sacrifice, "*O my Father, if this cup may not pass away from me except I drink it, Thy will be done.*" And the third time he repeats the same words. The victory of his soul was gained; the struggle was over, until the brief conflict of the final pang. Finding the disciples still asleep, he said to them, "Sleep on now; *I* will§ rouse you no more to watch and pray with me; but your sleep shall be rudely disturbed; for behold, the hour of my suffering is at hand. Already my captors are near."

§ 281. *The Arrest of Christ.—Peter's Haste, and its Reproof.—The Power of Darkness.*

Judas approached with a band of armed servitors of the Sanhedrim and a part of a Roman cohort from the garrison, the latter as a guard against a disturbance from the sympathy of the people. Probably the traitor alone knew *who* was to be apprehended;‖ as there was good

* Cf. p. 82. † Cf. p. 344. ‡ Cf. p. 209.

§ The words τὸ λοιπόν, in Matt., xxvi., 45, compel us to take these words as a warning, or reproof; otherwise the word καθεύδετε might be taken as the indicative, with or without interrogation.

‖ We may the more expect differences in the four accounts here, from the state of mind in which the disciples must necessarily have been. Discrepancies, even if irreconcilable

reason (supposed, at least) for secrecy in the procedure. Jesus did not wait for Judas and the band to enter the garden. With majestic calmness he went to meet them, and asked, "*Whom seek ye?*" His sudden appearance in calm majesty, associated with the impressions of his life and the authority of his name as, at least, a prophet, so deeply affected a part of the band (not the Roman soldiers*) that they recoiled and fell on the ground before him. In their perplexity they then prepared to seize the disciples, perhaps because they made show of defending their Master. The rash Peter hastily gave way to impulse; without waiting to know the Master's will, he made use of the sword. Christ sharply rebuked his precipitancy: "*All that take the sword* (uncalled, as here, in resistance to authority that is to be respected as the ordinance of God) *shall perish by the sword* (as a judgment for rebellion against the order of God; a warning against the use of force to defend his cause against the state); *thinkest thou that I cannot now pray to my Father, and he shall presently give me more than twelve*† *legions of angels?* (This he could only have done had the Divine will been so.) *The cup which my Father hath given me, shall I not drink it?*‡ (not the human choice, but the higher necessity, must prevail.)"

Turning then to the band, he said to them, more than once, "I am he whom ye seek; let these go their way." And this saying—supported by that authority which had so impressed them that they would not have ventured to lay hands on him had he not given himself up—this saying caused them to let the disciples go, and to take no vengeance on Peter, exasperated as they were by his resistance.§

in points of detail, do not impeach the veracity of the essential features of a narrative; but in this case they are not so irreconcilable as has been supposed. According to John, whom we have followed, Judas and the band remained outside, and Jesus went out and gave himself up: the other Evangelists report that Judas gave the signal by a kiss. But as John's account gives no reason at all for Judas's coming, and as it could not have been to show the way to the garden, we must suppose it was impelled by pure hatred, or by a desire to see the end of the matter (this would suit the view that he did not betray Jesus with hostile intent, and expected a miracle), or that he came to point out the *person* to be seized, and this leads us directly to the statement of the other Gospels. The sign agreed upon may have been omitted, or given at the wrong moment, in the confusion of his mind, produced by a bad conscience and a reverence that he could not get rid of; so that the different accounts may entirely harmonize. In any case, John's statement is the more simple, and we rely upon it.

* Had these cared at all about the matter, they would not have served as instruments of the Jewish authorities.

† Instead of the Twelve Apostles, who made show of defending him.

‡ John, xviii., 11, referring to the prayer in the garden. The preceding words, omitted by John, are strongly characteristic of the Spirit of Christ.

§ It is mentioned by all the Evangelists that Peter cut off the ear of the high-priest's servant. It cannot but appear surprising that this arbitrary act produced no more serious consequences to the rash Apostle. The healing of the ear, mentioned by Luke, might serve as an explanation; but John says nothing about it. His narrative, however, explains all in the way given by us in the text; and its veracity, therefore, is confirmed by comparison with the other Gospels.

When the person of Jesus was secured, he said, further, "Are ye come out, as against a thief, with armed bands, to take me? When I was daily with you in the Temple, ye stretched forth no hands against me; but this is your hour, and the power of darkness."* During his public teaching none ventured to assail him. The power of darkness shuns the light of day. The Sanhedrim found the night the fitting time to execute their schemes; the policy that springs from darkness, and serves it, must not show itself in open day. Perhaps the words also allude to the brief duration of the power of evil.†

CHAPTER VI.

THE TRIAL AND CONDEMNATION.

§ 282. *Night-Examination before Annas.*

IN the mean time, the high-priest, Caiaphas, informed of what had passed, had summoned a council of the Sanhedrim at his palace for the trial of Jesus. As this could not be accomplished until daybreak, Jesus was taken before Ananos, or Annas, the former high-priest, father-in-law of Caiaphas, for a preliminary examination.‡

* Christ was always fain to point from the sensible to the spiritual; and as the time chosen to execute the work of darkness here gave occasion for such a connexion, we join the two together.

† In any event, this passage refers to the futile attempts before made to secure the arrest of Christ of which John informs us; it belongs, also, to that class of passages which can only be clearly understood in the light of John's representation of the history (cf. p. 222 294). John, xviii., 20, is certainly not so similar to the above passage as to justify the inference, which some have drawn, that the one is but a variation of the other. True, in Luke, xxii., 52, the words are addressed to the chief priests, &c., which could not be literally true; but we explain this on the ground that they were addressed through the instruments to the *real* captors, the Sanhedrim; and not on the ground of an interchange with John, xviii., 20.

‡ In Luke, xxii., 66, we find that some time elapsed between the arrest and the meeting of the Council; the latter occurring "as soon as it was day." This accounts for the arraignment before Annas, mentioned only by John (xviii., 13). As for the *invention* of such a fact as this, the idea is absurd; there could be no motive for it; and John himself only relates it by the way. The mention of such minute incidents, however, prove him to have been an eye-witness.—(Note to ed. 4th.) *Bleek's* review of *Ebrard* has led me to re-examine this subject. I cannot think John would have given such prominence to the arraignment before Caiaphas had he not meant to unfold this preparatory trial further; and, therefore, cannot suppose that, in xviii., 19–24 he records the official examination before the Council. In that case he certainly would have dwelt upon it more, and made more of it. On the other hand, it is easy to understand that he *omitted* the latter examination, because generally known by other traditions, and *gave* the one which was least known. In fact, this is presupposed in the examination before Pilate, as recorded by him, when compared with the account of the trial before the Council in the other Evangelists. In xviii., 13, express mention is made of Caiaphas as ἀρχιερεύς *"for that year,"* to distinguish him from Annas, who bore the same title. In v. 14 he cites the declaration of Caiaphas (notable as coming from the lips of the Head of Ecclesiastical affairs during the year in which Christ suffered) *in*

Annas began with questions about his followers and his doctrine. But Christ gave no satisfactory replies. And this was fully consistent with his dignity; for he knew that the questions were put not to elicit truth, but to extort something that might be used against him; that the decision was as good as made, and the investigation only intended to throw over it the forms of justice. He referred Annas, therefore, to his public discourses in the Temple and in the synagogues. One of the servitors deemed his reply an insult to the high-priest's dignity, and struck him in the face. The blow could not disturb his serenity of soul; he only asserted the justice of his cause in saying, "*If I have spoken evil, bear witness of the evil; but if well, why smitest thou me?*"

§ 283. *Morning.—Examination before Caiaphas.*

In the examination before the Sanhedrim, over which Caiaphas presided, Christ preserved the same silence as before Annas, and for similar reasons. The conflicting evidence of the witnesses afforded no ground for the condemnation on which the court had already decided. The high-priest insisted on his defending himself against the witnesses; but he still held his peace. Finally, he called upon Jesus, in the name of the Living God, to declare whether or not he was "Messiah, the Son of God." After answering in the affirmative, Christ announced the great events then approaching, which were to testify, more strongly than words, that He *was* the promised Theocratic King: "*Hereafter shall ye see the Son of Man sitting on the right hand of power* (of God), *and coming in the clouds of heaven*"* (a figurative expression, implying, "You shall see me prove my Divine power in act, spreading my kingdom, and subduing its foes in spite of all your machinations;" the actual proof of his Messianic dignity, an announcement of the impending judgment of God). Then the high-priest rent his robes, as a sign of horror at the blasphemy uttered by Christ, saying, "From his own lips ye have heard it." He was then condemned to death, either as a false prophet, and thereby incurring the punishment ordained by the law of Moses, because he had falsely proclaimed himself Messiah; or as a blasphemer, because he had attributed Divine honours to himself.

view of the omission of the full trial before him. In v. 24, *after* the examination, it is stated that Annas "sent him to Caiaphas, the actual high-priest." Perhaps the leading out of Christ occasioned one of Annas's servants to put the question (v. 25) which brought out Peter's second denial; and perhaps, also, Luke, xxii., 61, should be joined in immediately after. In this case we should make the fore-court of the house of Annas the scene of Peter's denials; and might infer that, when this preparatory examination before Annas was forgotten, or laid aside as unimportant, the denial of Peter, which was preserved on account of its intrinsic importance, was laid in the court of *Caiaphas*, in connexion with the second examination.

* Christ's "coming," "coming in the clouds," &c., not only indicate his second advent at a far-distant period, but also his spiritual, world-historical manifestation.

The latter appears more probable from Matt., xxvi. 65, 66; and, indeed, they had often before accused him of blasphemy.

After the condemnation he was given up, as one expelled from the Theocratic nation, to the rude derision and mocking of the servants in the court.

§ 284. *Double Dealing of the Sanhedrim.*

It is obvious, at first sight, that the procedure of the Sanhedrim in condemning Christ was illegal and arbitrary. It was not a regular inquiry after the truth; Christ stood in the way of the hierarchy, and his case had been prejudged; Caiaphas himself had, in fact, announced that his death was decided on. A wicked policy demanded the victim. Moreover, the necessity of putting him to death before the feast caused the sentence to be hastened as rapidly as possible under the forms of justice.

It must be borne in mind that at that time the Sanhedrim had only subordinate authority to assign penalties for violations of the religious law; it could not lawfully pronounce sentence of death without the authority of the Roman governor.* It had, therefore, to seek, in Christ's case, some plausible grounds for condemnation that would stand the scrutiny of that officer. No accusation of heresy, blasphemy, or false assumption of the prophetic character would suffice. Some political charge must, therefore, be trumped up. But in this the hierarchical party had to act in direct opposition to their own convictions; Jesus had always refused to meddle with civil affairs. It is true, he had been attended into the city by an enthusiastic multitude, acknowledging him as Messiah; but his withdrawal from them, and, indeed, all his movements on that occasion, abundantly proved that he had no intention to make use of worldly means. This is shown sufficiently by the fact that no attempt was made by the Sanhedrim to use the triumphal entry as ground for a political charge. Had it been at all suspicious in that respect, the Roman governor would have taken it up; as popular movements of the kind were generally, and with good reason, looked upon with distrust.

A charge of interference with the state, then, could not be sustained, even according to the judgment of his enemies. It was clear that he had used no other influence over men's minds than the inward power of his words and works to move their convictions; and this was

* Joseph., Archæol., xx., 9, § 1. The high-priest, Ananus (Annas), had taken advantage of the absence of the governor to inflict capital punishment on the authority of the Sanhedrim. He was accused for the act before the Prefect Albinus: "Ὡς οὐκ ἐξὸν ἦν Ἀνάνῳ χωρὶς τῆς ἐκείνου γνώμης καθίσαι συνέδριον;" obviously showing that the consent of the governor was essential in such cases. The misdemeanor was deemed so grave that Ananus was removed from office. The reading of *Synkellos*, "ἐκευνων," would give an entirely different meaning; but it is obviously incorrect.

obviously beyond the sphere of civil jurisdiction. But antiquity could not conceive of a holy sphere of conscience and conviction beyond the reach of human tribunals. It was first opened to the Old-World consciousness by the idea of the kingdom of GOD as brought to light by Christ. Before, either religion was subordinated to the state, or the state to religion (the latter being the *Theocracy* in its political form; the former being *state-religions*). In the Jewish constitution (which, however, did not exist in its original form under the Roman sway) the state was subordinate to religion. It was the crime of the Sanhedrim that it decided, arbitrarily, to retain this old stand-point, contrary to the judgment of GOD, as shown in the signs of the times pointed out by Christ; that it would not give up its selfish interests, or bow before the higher power which had come into the world to break down the old landmarks. Even if it could not fully admit Christ's claims, it was bound, on its own stand-point, to investigate the proofs which he offered in testimony of his Divine calling; and when phenomena appeared which could not be explained except as the workings of the Spirit of God, at least to leave them, as Gamaliel did afterward, to the judgment of GOD as history* should unfold it. But the *grounds* of the incapacity of the heads of the hierarchy to admit the proofs of Christ's Divine calling had often before been pointed out by himself; the inability was a moral one, founded in their dispositions of heart, and therefore it was *guilty*.†

As before remarked, the grounds on which the *Sanhedrim* condemned Christ were not sufficient to induce *Pilate*, the Roman procurator, tc inflict capital punishment upon him. Another charge was needed. To serve the purpose, recourse was had to his claim of Messiahship, on which they had professed to found their own decision, with the addition of a political element: "He has claimed to be a king;" and hence "he perverts the nation (contests the Roman authority), and for bids to give tribute to Cæsar."‡ An accusation of this sort could be the more readily admitted, as the Roman authorities were well aware that the Jews felt themselves degraded and disgraced by paying taxes to a heathen power.

§ 285. *Jesus before Pilate.—Christ's Kingdom not "of this World."*

The procurator, Pontius Pilate, a representative of the rich and coı

* To this judgment Moses refers, Deut., xviii., 20–22. † Cf. p. 293, 294.

‡ Luke, xxiii., 3. This passage is obviously presupposed in John, xviii., 33. John's account takes many things for granted that are recorded in the other Gospels; but the latter in turn, must often find their supplement in the former, as is the case in this part of Luke. None but an eye-witness could have given the account in so exact a connexion as John's. The simple reply to Pilate's question, σὺ λέγεις, as given in Luke, xxiii., 3, Matt., xxvii., 11, needs the further explanation given by John (xviii., 36, 37), to make it fully accord with the facts; for he was not, and did not claim to be, "King of the Jews," in the Roman sense of the phrase: nor could Pilate have pronounced him guiltless after such a declaration

rupt Romans of that age, acted throughout the case in accordance with his well-known character. An enemy to the Jews, he was glad of an opportunity to vex and mock them. But, on the other hand, his administration had been marked by many acts of arbitrary injustice, and his evil conscience feared an accusation from the Jews, such, indeed, as subsequently wrought his downfall. Care for his own security, therefore, led him to avoid giving them any handle against him on this occasion; and he was by no means inclined to sacrifice his own interests to those of innocence and justice. With all his disposition to save a man guiltless of political crimes, and whose zeal he perhaps himself acknowledged to be well-meant, it was no part of his character to risk personal or political objects in such a cause.

The Sanhedrim, in delivering Jesus up to Pilate as "a disturber of the public peace," expected that he would be satisfied with their recognition of the Roman authority, and lend his power, without further inquiry, to the execution of their decree. But Pilate, seeing no grounds for immediate acquiescence, demanded a more particular accusation. As he had heard of no disturbance produced by Jesus, the statement made by the deputies of the Sanhedrim appeared by no means credible; and, suspecting that religious disputes were at the bottom, he wished to get rid of the whole affair, and told them "to take him, and judge him according to their law." The deputies understood his meaning. But to treat the case as a purely ecclesiastical one, and inflict only a corresponding penalty on Jesus, was not what they desired. Their desire and wishes were distinctly expressed in their reply: "*It is not lawful for us to put any man to death.*"

The procurator thought it necessary, therefore, to enter upon the political accusation, although he believed it to be unfounded; and said to Jesus, not without mockery, "*Art thou the King of the Jews?*" To this question Christ could give neither an express affirmative nor an express negative: in the religious sense, the answer must be "Yes;" in the political, "No." He, therefore, asked Pilate, "*Sayest thou this thing of thyself* (*i. e.*, inquiring whether he asked the question in the Roman sense, and thought, with reference to the rights of the state, that Christ was liable to the accusation of claiming to be "king"), *or did others tell it thee of me?*" Pilate answered that he did nothing more than repeat the accusation brought by the Jews. And Jesus answered, "*My kingdom is not of this world*" (not worldly in its nature, its instruments, or its conflicts). He proved its unworldly character by the means he used in founding it: "*If my kingdom were of this world, then would my servants fight,*" &c.; "*but now is my kingdom not from hence.*"

The very words in which Christ denied that he was king in a worldly sense, implied that in another sense he certainly claimed to be both a king and the founder of a kingdom. He then defined more exactly the sense in which he was both: "*To this end was I born, and for this cause came I into this world, that I should bear witness unto the truth.*" It followed that He could be recognized as *King*, and the nature of his *kingdom* be understood by those only who were susceptible of receiving the truth: "*Every one that is of the truth heareth my voice.*" This was, at the same time, a summons to the conscience of Pilate himself. But the procurator—a type of the educated Roman world, especially of its higher classes, lost in worldly-mindedness, and conscious of no higher wants than those of this life—had no such sense for truth. "*What is truth?*" was his mocking question. "*Truth is an empty name,*" he meant to say.

§ 286. *Jesus sent to Herod.*

Pilate now looked upon Jesus simply as a religious enthusiast, innocent of all political crimes, and told the deputies that he "could find no fault in him at all." They then replied (Luke, xxiii., 5) that his teaching had stirred up the people every where, from Galilee to Jerusalem. As soon as Pilate heard that Jesus was of Galilee, it occurred to him to lay the case before Herod Antipas, tetrarch of Galilee and Judea, who had just then come to the feast at Jerusalem.

Herod had for long wished to see Jesus.* The fame of the miracles inspired him with curiosity to see what Christ could do. But it was no part of the Saviour's calling to satisfy an idle curiosity. To describe his doctrine fully to a man so utterly worldly, would have been, in his own language, to "cast pearls before swine."† He, therefore, answered none of Herod's questions. The disappointed king, having arrayed the Saviour, in mockery, in a gorgeous purple robe, and exposed him to the cruel sport and derision of the soldiers, sent him back to the procurator. Doubtless the latter was confirmed in his own views by the word which Herod sent him.

§ 287. *Pilate's fruitless Efforts to save Jesus.—The Dream of Pilate's Wife.*

In honour of the Passover, and as a privilege to the Jews, pardon was granted every year to a criminal condemned to death. Pilate endeavoured to make use of this privilege in favour of Jesus; hoping thus at once to admit the validity of the decree of the Sanhedrim, and yet leave it unexecuted. In order to satisfy their hatred against Jesus to some extent, he proposed, not to free him from all punishment, but to mitigate it into scourging. But the multitude, always open to the impressions of the moment—the very multitude who, a few days be-

* Cf. p. 323. † Cf. p. 247.

fore, had welcomed Jesus, with shouts of enthusiasm, as Theocratic King—were *now*, when their carnal expectations were deceived, blind instruments of the Sanhedrim, and obedient to every fanatical impulse of the Pharisees. They clamoured for the pardon of a murderer rather than of the false prophet (as they held him) who had deceived their hopes.

The procurator ordered Jesus to be scourged. It could not have cost the feelings of a *Pilate* much to inflict such violent pain and deep disgrace upon an innocent man. He thought that Jesus, as an enthusiast, who had already given so much trouble, deserved scourging; and he probably expected to appease the rage and excite the sympathy of the multitude by the infliction, and so, perhaps, to succeed in saving his life. With the cruel marks upon his body, the Saviour was brought out, in the attire which the soldiers had put upon him in derision, and set before the people; when Pilate, having declared that he found no guilt in him, said, "*Behold the man!*" ("Can it be believed that *he* would wish to make himself king?") The sight only stimulated their fanatical rage; and, with unceasing clamours, they demanded his crucifixion. Full of displeasure, Pilate said to them, "*Take ye him, and crucify him, for I find no fault in him.*" The Jews knew well how to understand this; and, as their political accusation had failed, they had recourse again to the religious one: "*We have a law, and by our law* (confirmed by the Roman state) *he ought to die, because he made himself the Son of God.*"

Unsusceptible as Pilate was of all impressions from the higher life, unable to recognize the majesty that dwelt in that lowly form, he yet found in Christ's demeanour under his sufferings something peculiar and inexplicable. Moreover, his wife,* troubled by fearful dreams, sent him a warning to "*Have nothing to do with that just man.*" And now, in addition to all this, he was told that Jesus had declared himself to be the "Son of God," a title which he interpreted according to the pagan conceptions of the "Sons of the Gods."

§ 288. *Last Conversation of Jesus with Pilate.—The* **Sentence.**

The transition is easy from *infidelity*, springing from worldliness and frivolity, to sudden emotions of *superstition*. So he who but a moment before had mockingly asked Christ, "*What is truth?*" went now, in a sudden access of superstitious fear, and inquired, "*Whence art thou?*" As the question was prompted only by superstition and curiosity, and

* According to the Apocryphal Gospel of *Nicodemus* (c. ii.), and later accounts (all of which, however, probably came from the same source), she was a proselyte of the gate, θεοσεβής, and was named *Procla* (*Thilo*, Cod. Apocryph., i., 520). Judaism had found its converts particularly among the female sex.

as the questioner was incapable of apprehending Jesus as the Son of God in the only sense in which he wished to be acknowledged as such, the Saviour made no reply. Pilate, in astonishment, renewed his questions: "*Speakest thou not unto me? Knowest thou not that I have power to crucify thee, and have power to release thee?*" To this Jesus answered: "*Thou couldst have no power at all against me, except it were given thee from above* (if God had not brought it to pass that I should be delivered to thee by the Sanhedrim); therefore is the guilt of those by whom God hath delivered me unto thee greater than thine."

Thus did Christ declare that no human will limited his life, but that his death took place in consequence of a higher necessity ordained by God, for a higher end. Pilate thereupon strove more earnestly to save him; but the Jews alarmed him with the cry, so terrible at that time, of *crimen majestatis:* "If thou let this man go, thou art not Cæsar's friend; whosoever maketh himself a king, revolts against the authority of the emperor." To this storm of clamour the procurator at last, though reluctantly, yielded: his conscience feared the charges which the Sanhedrim might prefer against him at Rome; and his personal security was more to him than the life of an innocent man.

§ 289. *Jesus led to Calvary.—Simon of Cyrene.—The Words of Christ to the Weeping Women.*

As was usual with condemned criminals, Jesus himself carried the instrument of death to the place of execution. But his severe struggles and sufferings, both of body and mind, had so exhausted his strength that he sunk under the burden. Even the rude soldiers, who had so lately mocked him, were filled with compassion, and compelled a Jew, whom they met on the way, Simon of Cyrene, to take his cross and bear it to the place of death.*

Amid all his sufferings he was moved with compassion for the

* This account, given in the first three Gospels, carries the proof of its veracity in itself It is nothing strange that Roman soldiers, in the public service, could do, unresisted, so high-handed an act (cf. *Hug's* instructive remarks on the narrative of Christ's passion, Zeitschrift für d. Geistl. d. Erzbisthums Freiburg, 1831, v., s. 12). Mark, whose account bears evidence in this, as in several other places, of peculiar sources of information, oral or written, mentions (xv., 21) that this Simon was the father of two men well known in the first Christian congregations. Notwithstanding all that *Strauss* says to the contrary, John's statement, that Jesus was led bearing his own cross, is not at variance with that given by the other sources, viz., that he was afterward relieved of the load on account of his exhaustion. John passes lightly over some things in the narrative of Christ's passion, and gives prominence to others not mentioned by the other Evangelists; there is, therefore, no ground of surprise in his omission of this particular incident. If it be supposed that the Apostle John did *not* write this Gospel, can it be imagined that its author *knew* nothing of this account (for a *doctrinal* motive to intentional silence is out of the question)? In what corner must he have written, to remain ignorant of an incident so closely interwoven with the traditional accounts of the passion? And how could a document issuing from such a corner be passed off as the production of John, the Apostle.

blinded people, over whose heads he saw impending the judgments of God, called down by their long-accumulated guilt, of which he had so often warned them. Seeing the women of Jerusalem in tears,* he said to them, "Weep not for me, but weep for yourselves and for your children." Then, after predicting the woes of the siege and destruction of Jerusalem, he said, "*If they do these things in a green tree, what shall be done in the dry?*"†

CHAPTER VII.

THE CRUCIFIXION.

§ 290. *Details of the Crucifixion.*

WHEN Jesus reached the place of execution, he was offered, as was usual, a spiced wine,‡ intended to stupify the mind and deaden the pains of death. Oppressed with burning thirst, he tasted of the wine; but when he perceived the stupifying drug, he refused to drink, that he might die in full consciousness. Stripped of nearly all his clothing,§ he was lifted up to the cross, bound, and then nailed to it by his hands and feet.|| (The chief pain of this cruel death,

* Luke, xxiii., 27–31.

† "If the Holy One, entering among sinful men, is so entreated, what must happen to those whose sufferings will be the just penalty of their own accumulated guilt?"

‡ Matt., xxvii., 34. Mark describes it exactly (xv., 23) as *οἶνος ἐσμυρνισμένος*. Cf. Acta Fructuosi Tarraconensis, where it is related of the martys, "*Cum multi ex fraterna caritate iis offerent, uti conditi permixti poculum sumerent,*" &c. (c. iii., Ruinart., Acta Martyrum, Amstel., 1713, 220). The *merum conditum* was given by the Christians to the confessors *tanquam antidotum*, that, by means of it, they might be less sensible of suffering (Tertull. de Jejuniis, c. xii.).

§ John's mention of the *χιτὼν ἄῤῥαφος* is confirmed by the statement of Isidore of Pelusium, that such garments were peculiar to Galilee. Such a garment, though somewhat common in Galilee, and worn by the lower classes, might have been a novelty to the Roman soldiers, and, therefore, an object of value in their eyes. Isidore says, "*τίς δὲ ἀγνοεῖ τὴν εὐτέλειαν τῆς ἐσθῆτος ἐκείνης, ἧπερ οἱ πτωχοὶ κέχρηνται τῶν Γαλιλαίων, καθ' οὓς καὶ μάλιστα τὸ τοιοῦτο φιλεῖ γίνεσθαι ἱμάτιον, τέχνῃ τινί, ὡς αἱ στηθοδισμίδες, ἀνακρουσιὸν ὑφαινόμενον.*"

|| There has been much dispute on this point, and many have given it undue importance; the result of the most candid inquiry is, that the *feet* were nailed as well as the *hands*. The most striking confirmation is afforded by the fact that the fathers, writing at a time when crucifixion was in use, speak of the *piercing of Jesus's feet* as a matter of course, without laying any stress upon it as necessary to fulfil Ps. xxii., 17. We cannot enter into the inquiry at length, but will only allude to the passage in Tertullian so important in reference to this question (Adv. Marcion., iii., 19). After citing "*foderunt manus meas et pedes*" from the Psalm, he undertakes to show that it was fulfilled in the crucifixion of Christ. The words immediately following, "*quæ proprie atrocitas crucis,*" can mean nothing else than that it was the piercing of the hands and feet which, on the whole, made this punishment of death so terrible. He then speaks of the *apices crucis* as belonging to the cross in general, not Christ's in particular. Further, he says that the Psalm cannot be applied to any other that had died as a martyr among the Jews; no man of God except Christ had suffered *this* mode of death, "*qui solus a populo tam insigniter crucifixus est*" (who suffered so marked a death by crucifixion—one otherwise unknown in the Old Testa

ccording to a writer who lived while it was yet known and used, onsisted in the hanging of the body while the hands and feet were ailed.)

§ 291. *Christ Prays for his Enemies.—The Two Thieves.*

When he was fastened to the cross, amid the jeers and scoffs of the arnal multitude, He did not invoke the Divine judgments upon the eads of those who had, returning evil for good, inflicted such terrible ortures upon him; on the contrary, with boundless love,* he comnended his enemies to the mercy of God, praying, "*Father, forgive hem, for they know not what they do*" (the ignorance of delusion, hough a guilty one).

Two criminals, of widely opposite dispositions, were crucified with im. While the one, hardened in sin, joined in mocking Christ, the ther rebuked him for so doing. Perhaps the men's offences had been ifferent; the one may have been a common robber, the other a criminal led away by the political passions that then excited the nation—ke the *Sicarii*,† the tools of the hierarchy; but on this question we ave no light. At any rate, one of them, roused to a sense of sin and uilt, became susceptible of higher impressions. And the deeper his onsciousness that his own punishment was justly due to his crimes, the nore deeply must he have been affected by the sufferings of the Holy One beside him. Who can reckon the power of a Divine impression pon a contrite soul—a soul freed from the bonds of sense by immeiate sufferings?

It is at once a proof as well of the Divine life manifested by Christ the very face of death, as of the religious susceptibility of the criminal himself, that he, who had perhaps before seen none of the proofs f Christ's majesty, should have anticipated the faith even of Apostles; nd this he did in trampling upon Jewish prejudices, and recognizing ne Messiah in the sufferer. "*Lord*," said he, "*remember me when hou comest into thy kingdom.*" The answer of Christ‡ is full of imort in more respects than one. In view of the sinner's faith, founded n genuine repentance, he promises him bliss; and in opposition to he expectation that His kingdom was only to be founded in the future, e promises him *immediate* bliss: "*Verily, I say unto thee, to-day shalt hou be with me in Paradise.*"§

ent—defining him, before all others, and fixing him alone as the one to whom the words the Psalm could be applied). Cf. *Hug's* Dissertation, before cited; *Hase's* Leben Jesu, 143.

* Thus illustrating *practically* his precepts in the Sermon on the Mount.

† As Barabbas, Luke, xxiii., 19.

‡ Its contradiction to ordinary Jewish notions proves its originality.

§ A symbolical name for the regions of bliss.

§ 292. *Christ's Exclamation: Psalm* xxii.—*His Last Words.*

What Divine confidence did Christ's words to the malefactor display, even in the midst of his sufferings! But he partook of all purely human feelings, and was therefore subject to the alternations which the outward circumstances tended to produce. The first struggles of death may call forth in *man* the sense of personal sin; but He, the perfectly Holy, could have no such sense. All that he could feel (and that he *did* feel) was a consciousness that his sufferings were the result of the sins of men, and a deep sympathy with the sufferings brought upon mankind by sin. Under these pangs of soul and body he sees before him the Holy One, persecuted, mocked, proved in the bitterest sufferings, yet steadfastly trusting in God, as described in the twenty-second Psalm: and the idea, as delineated by the inspired Psalmist, was realized—not only in itself, but in the minutest traits of its delineation also—in Him, who stood among men as the only Holy One, not only exhibiting the ideal of holiness in conflict and suffering, but triumphing through them.

At the acme of his pangs he cries aloud, "*My God, my God, why hast thou forsaken me?*" The form of the words, "*my God,*" implies the consciousness, in his inmost soul, of inseparable union with God. The words must also be taken as the expression of a single subordinate moment, in connexion with the whole state of soul expressed in the Psalm.

An enigma, indeed, must this exclamation appear to all who isolate it from its connexion with the state of Christ's soul up to the last expression of triumph, "*It is finished!*" an enigma, indeed, to those who forget that Christ suffered and died for mankind—for mankind laid up in his heart; an enigma to all, in a word, who are strangers to the Christian life. But the Christian sees, in this feature of his Master's history, a type of the life of individual believers and of the whole Church; for both must be led through all stages of suffering, and even through moments of apparent abandonment by God, to perfection and glorification.

Parched with inward heat, the Saviour asks, for the last time, for a cooling drink. A sponge, filled with the acid drink used by the soldiers,* was placed to his lips. Dying, he commends his mother to the care of that beloved disciple who stood nearer to him than a brother. And then he utters the word of triumph, the greatest and the weightiest that has been uttered upon the earth: "*It is finished!*" and commends his soul, separating from his bodily being, to the Father in Heaven.

* Posca.

§.293: *Phenomena accompanying the Death of Christ: the Earthquake the Darkness; the Rending of the Temple-veil.*

The wise men from the East were led to the Redeemer by the remarkable phenomena which attended his *birth;* and similar wonders accompanied his *death.* As the unity of the world as a whole [the world of nature and of spirit], is seen in natural signs accompanying epoch-making events in history, so we need not marvel to find the *greatest* event of history—shown as such by its fruits in the spiritual renovation of mankind even to those who cannot comprehend its internal import—attended by similar manifestations. At the moment of Christ's death there was an earthquake; and at the same time, and perhaps from the same cause, a darkness spread over the sky, producing effects like those of an eclipse of the sun.* The veil of the Holy of Holies in the Temple was rent asunder,† signifying that the Holy

* *Julius Africanus*, the first Christian author of a world-historical work, says that the heathen historian *Thallus* described this darkness as an ἔκλειψις τοῦ ἡλίου. Africanus rightly contradicts this, since no eclipse could possibly have taken place at the time, and infers, justly, that the darkness could only have occurred as a real miracle. (See the fragment in *Georg. Syncell. Chronograph.*, ed. Niebuhr, Dindorf, i., 610.) The Fathers of the first century refer frequently to a statement made by *Phlegon*, the author of a "Chronicle," under Hadrian. Eusebius quotes his words, Chron., under the fourth year of 202d Olymp.: "ἔκλειψις ἡλίου μεγίστη τῶν ἐγνωσμένων πρότερον, καὶ νὺξ ὥρᾳ ἕκτῃ τῆς ἡμέρας ἐγένετο, ὥστε καὶ ἀστέρας ἐν οὐρανῷ φανῆναι." A great earthquake in Bithynia had destroyed most part of Nicœa (l. c., p. 614.)

† By καταπέτασμα, Matt., xxvii., 51, it is most natural to understand the curtain before the "Holy of Holies," for this was distinctively so called; the veil before the Sanctuary was called κάλυμμα (Philo, de Vit. Mos., iii., § 5); or ναός must mean the Sanctuary in the stricter sense, which does not accord with the usage of Matthew. The latter view destroys the peculiar import of the occurrence.

It has been questioned whether the fact of the rending of the veil is well supported. It is true, it is not *so* well sustained as the other phenomena, not being mentioned by Luke and John; but there is no decisive ground for doubting its credibility. It is true that the account *may* have originated from the occurrence of *some* fact of the kind, which assumed this particular form in the narrative, from the idea, subsequently received, that access to the "Holiest" was opened by Christ. Those who presuppose this would call it a *mythical* element, blended with the historical. We use the term "mythical" purposely, having no superstitious fear of the *word* when we wish to make use of the *idea.* Although we assert that Christianity is, in its essense, not a mythical, but a historical religion, founded upon a chain of real historical facts; and although we make a broad distinction between *myths* and symbolical representations of *facts;* still we do not assert it to be *impossible* that, after religious intuition had received a new direction from the extraordinary facts of Christianity, certain mythical elements, attaching themselves to the facts, could have crept into the Christian tradition. The mythical must *predominate*, in order to make a narrative apocryphal.

But to admit this *possibility*, even in individual cases like the one before us, is not to admit its *reality.* Although it is true that none but a few priests could possibly have witnessed the rending of the veil of "the Holy of Holies," it was by no means impossible that it could be generally known afterward; since, among other reasons, many priests afterward became Christians. Nor is the *argumentum e silentio* at all decisive in this case. The authors of the New Testament had so rich a treasure of proofs at command that they did not need to run to every individual fact which they might have used. They drew from full sources (as the Apostolical epistles show), and could afford to pass by many available

of Holies in heaven is opened to all men through the finished work of Christ; the wall of partition between the Divine and the Human broken down; and a spiritual worship substituted for an outward and sensible one.

CHAPTER VIII.

THE RESURRECTION.

§ 294. *Did Christ predict his Resurrection?*

BEFORE describing the Resurrection, we must examine the question whether Christ foresaw and predicted that event as well as his sufferings.

It is true, we cannot prove, *à priori*, that he must necessarily have foreknown the Resurrection. If he had had only a confident certainty that the Holy Spirit would continue to work in his disciples, unfolding the truth He had taught them, and completing the training He had commenced, he might have left behind him his work on earth with calm assurance of the future; He need not necessarily have concluded that his corporeal reappearance to his followers in so short a time must form the link of connexion between his departure and the renewal of spiritual communion with them. Notwithstanding all this, however, the close connexion of Christ's resurrection with his whole work as Redeemer must, in the outset, make it appear altogether improbable that he should not have foreknown it.

"But if he looked forward to his resurrection with full confidence, how can we account for his conflicts at the approach of death?" Here is the same enigma of the union of Divinity and Humanity which pervade the whole life of Christ, and is especially prominent at particular moments. Phenomena somewhat analogous appear in the coexisting emotions of the Divine and the natural life in believers imbued with the Spirit of Christ. The consciousness, in Him, that death was but a passage to his glorification did not prevent the strivings of nature with sufferings; nor could the assurance of speedy resurrection save him from the struggle. All that we can do is to distinguish the separate *moments* of his consciousness; remembering that faith is not one with

things. In the *Evang. ad Hebræos*, it is related that a beam over the Temple-door broke in two (*superliminare templi infinitæ magnitudinis fractum esse atqui divisum.* See Hieron. in Matt., xxvii., 51; tom. vii., pt. 1, p. 336, ed. Vallars); which might have been caused by the earthquake. Cf., also, the statement cited from the *Gemara* (in Hug's Dissertation above mentioned), that the folding-doors of the Temple, though locked, suddenly burst open about 40 years before the destruction of Jerusalem. All these accounts hint at some *fact* lying at the bottom of them.

intuition. The sacrifice of Christ lost as little of its moral import by the assurance of resurrection as does the self-sacrifice of the believer who submits to the death-struggle in faith of a blissful life beyond.

But can it be proved that Christ *predicted* his resurrection to the disciples? May they not, at a later period, have attributed such an import to figurative expressions of his, like those in John, which, in reality, only referred to his *spiritual* manifestations to them; as was done with Matt., xii., 40, and John, ii., 19?

Even if we grant that this may have been the case with some of Christ's expressions of the kind, it by no means follows that *all* the intimations of the resurrection were applied in this way only at a later period. The very fact that some of his sayings really *did* intimate it may have led to the attributing of this meaning to others that did not. In John, xx., 8, 9, we see an indication that the disciples, soon after his death, began to call to mind what he had said concerning his resurrection, and hope began to struggle with fear in their souls. But John has preserved to us one of Christ's sayings which plainly points to his resurrection, viz., x., 17, 18. It is obvious that the declaration, "*I have power to lay down my life, and I have power to take it up again,*" was meant to imply something distinctive and peculiar to Christ; it is entirely emasculated by being applied to that immortality which is common to all men; nor can it be satisfied except by reference to his resurrection. There are passages in the synoptical Gospels (*e.g.*, Matt., xvi., 21; Luke, ix., 22) in which Christ expressly foretells his resurrection, along with his sufferings, specifying the precise interval of three days; but it is marvellous that these precise declarations should neither have been understood nor made the subject of direct inquiry, often as they were repeated. This appears unhistorical; indeed, it is a thing to be looked for that tradition would give to such expressions, *after* the event, when their bearing was better understood, a more precise form than they really had at first. In John's Gospel all Christ's intimations are distant and indefinite, as is usual in prophecy; and this is one of the proofs of its genuine Apostolic origin.

§ 295. *Dejection of the Apostles immediately after Christ's Death.—Their Joy and Activity at a later Period.—The Reappearance of Christ necessary to explain the Change.*

The death of Christ annihilated at a stroke the Messianic expectations of the Apostles. Their dejection was complete. But if, of all that they had hoped, *nothing* was ever realized, this dejection could not have passed away. It is true, we may suppose it abstractly possible that, after the first consternation was over, the deep, spiritual

* Christ is represented, Heb., xii., 2, as leading the way for *believers*, by himself reaching his glory through a perfectly tried faith.

impressions which Christ had made might have revived, and operated more powerfully, and even more purely, now that they could no longer see him with their bodily eyes. But this view could not arise except along with the recognition of a historical Christ as the personal ground and cause of such a new spiritual creation; without the presupposition of such a Christ there is no possible foundation on which to conceive of such after-workings.

And even *with* it, we cannot explain (not bare conceivable possibilities, but) the actual state of the case, viz., the dejection of the Apostles at *first*, and what they were and did *afterward*. There must be some intermediate historical fact to explain the transition; *something* must have occurred to revive, with new power, the almost effaced impression; to bring back the flow of their faith which had so far ebbed away. The reappearance, then, of Christ among his disciples is a connecting link in the chain of events which cannot possibly be spared. It acted thus: Their sunken faith in his promises received a new impulse when these promises were repeated by Him, risen from the dead; his reappearance formed the point of contact for a new spiritual communion with him, never to be dissolved, nay, thenceforward to be developed ever more and more. According to their own unvarying asseverations, it was the foundation of their immovable faith in his person, and in himself as Messiah and Son of God, as well as of their steadfast hope, in his communion, of a blissful, everlasting life, triumphing over death. Without it they never could have had that inspiring assurance of faith with which they every where testified of what they had received, and joyfully submitted to tortures and to death.

§ 296. *Was the Reappearance of Christ a Vision?*

If, then, it be the task of history to connect the course of events, the reappearance of Christ must be recognized as an essential link in the chain which brought about the spiritual renovation of the life of humanity. Without it, the historical inquirer will always have an inexplicable enigma to solve. But reason, which demands this connexion of events, feels itself—until it has obtained a higher light by faith—repelled by a *supernatural* event, not to be explained from the connexion itself. And the inquirer who does not recognize (as we felt ourselves compelled to do at the outset) the whole manifestation of Christ as supernatural, must set himself to the task of finding some natural explanation of his reappearance, in the connexion of cause and effect.

Those who attempt such an explanation on *internal* grounds suppose Christ's reappearance to have been a *vision*. Now in any vision (other than magical, and such are precluded by the hypothesis of this inquiry, which goes upon natural and historical grounds) a psychological starting-point is necessarily presupposed, even when the vision is said to be seen by one individual, much more when it is repeatedly seen, in the same way, by different individuals. But no such starting-point can be found in the mental condition of the Apostles, such as it has been described. It is precisely in order to explain the change in that condition that we need another cause. How is it possible to derive from the psychological developement itself a condition precisely its contrary? That were indeed a *petitio principii*.

Moreover, the very nature of the Evangelical narratives, bearing, as they do, the stamp of sensible reality, subverts such a hypothesis. And to these must be added the concurrent testimony of a contemporary, who himself came forward within a very few years as a witness for the reality of Christ's resurrection, whose personality lies before us, in his letters, in all the traits of undeniable historical reality, and whose convictions, founded on that resurrection, gave him power to encounter cheerfully all perils, labours, and sufferings—the Apostle PAUL. And Paul bears witness that Christ appeared to more than five hundred at one time.*

§ 297. *Was Christ's a real Death?*

If the inquirer still perseveres in rejecting every thing supernatural, he must have recourse to *external* grounds for the explanation of Christ's reappearance, and deem it a revival from apparent death, brought about by the use of natural means.

It may be admitted, inasmuch as crucifixion was not immediately fatal, that one who had endured its torture for several hours might be restored by careful medical aid; although it certainly was not an *easy* thing to do, as the examples mentioned by Josephus† testify. But let us, without inquiring for other signs of death in the case of Jesus, notice the following points. Before his crucifixion, he had endured multiplied sufferings, both of soul and body; he had been scourged; he was so worn out on the way to Golgotha that he could not carry his cross, and even the Roman soldiers had pity on him; he was nailed to the cross by his hands and feet; he had remained from noon till towards evening‡ in this painful position, under the rays of a burning

* 1 Cor., xv., 6.

† In his autobiography, § 75. He had been sent, with a troop of Roman horse, to the village of Tekoah, four or five hours distant, to reconnoitre. Jerome, living in Bethlehem, writes of this village, "Thecoam viculum esse in monte situm et duodecim millibus ab Jerosolymis separatum, *quotidie oculis cernimus*" (t. iv., pt. i., p. 882). Returning from the village to Jerusalem, Josephus saw several prisoners hanging on crosses, who must have been crucified in the interim, as he had *not* seen them in going out. On arriving at camp, he begged of Titus the lives of three, and had them at once taken down (after hanging, therefore, but a few hours), and treated, medically, with the utmost care; yet but one out of the three survived. (Cf. *Bretschneider's* remarks on this account, Stud. u. Krit., 1832, iii.; also, *Hug*, Freiburg. Zeitschrift, No. vii., 148.)

‡ A close computation of the hours cannot be arrived at from the Evangelical accounts. It is hardly to be supposed that even the disciples who were eye-witnesses were able, under the circumstances, to note the precise time.

sun; he took leave of the world in the struggles of death; his side was pierced* by the lance of a Roman soldier; and, after all this, he remained two nights and a day in a fresh grave. Yet, without medical aid or attendance, *the same man* walks about on a sudden among his disciples, apparently in sound health and full of vital power! Had he appeared among them sick and suffering, as he must have done had he been restored by natural means from apparent death, such a sight could not have revived their sunken faith, or become the foundation for all their hopes. A weak *man* would have reappeared, subject to death like any other. But, on the contrary, he seemed to them so much more like a glorified being that he had to give them sensible proofs of his humanity. He appeared to them thenceforth as one over whom death had no power; and, *therefore*, became a pledge that the life of man should conquer death and enjoy forever a glorified existence.

Even if all this could be made to agree with a restoration of Christ by natural means from apparent death, we should have further to suppose either that his life was subsequently prolonged for some time, or that he died soon after in consequence of his wounds and sufferings The former supposition is a mere fancy; there is no possible ground for it in history; the latter is contradicted by the facts of his reappearance; there was no *cause* of death apparent. And the very fact of his dying would have destroyed all the moral effect of his resurrection, which consisted solely in the conviction wrought by it that he, as Mes-

* I make the following remarks with reference to John, xix., 31, to guard against the interpolations placed in this passage by a profane vulgarity, which reads John's Gospel as it would a police report. The *suffringere crura* was indeed an ignominious punishment, particularly used as a capital punishment for slaves; but it certainly was not *immediately* fatal. (After the hands were cut off, the legs broken, and the body maimed in various ways, the criminals were thrust into a pit, still alive: Κολοβώσαντες δὲ καὶ συντρίψαντες τὰ σκέλη, ἔτι ζῶντας ἔῤῥιψαν εὖς τινα τάφρον. Polyb., i., c. 80, § 13.) The death-blow was afterward given in some other way. Hence (Ammian. Marcellin., Hist., xiv., 9) it is expressly added, "fractis cruribus, *occiduntur*." The soldiers, having completed the *effractio crurum* on the two malefactors that were crucified with Jesus, either gave them the death blow or permitted them, after being taken down, to perish slowly from their broken limbs. But, as no signs of life could be seen in Jesus, they saw no necessity to execute the command, which was given solely under the presupposition that crucifixion could not kill so soon. Nor was this at all strange; all that was demanded was that the crucifixion should have done its work effectually. They deemed it enough, therefore, to thrust the lance into his side, either to assure themselves that he was dead, or to give him the death-blow. It would have been a bad manœuvre, indeed, to do this as a mere pretence, with the intention to save him. Although the word νύττειν may denote a slight wound, its meaning (as denoting a severe wound) is fixed by the weapon employed; and, moreover, John uses it as synonymous with ἐκκεντεῖν, v. 37. The wound could not have been a small one, as Christ afterward called on the disciples to thrust their hands into it. And there are other instances in which we read of the death-blow being given by piercing the side with a lance; two martyrs, Marcus and Marcellianus, had remained a day and a night tied to a stake, to which their feet were nailed, *jussit præfectus ambos, ubi stabant, lanceis per latera perforari* (Acta Sanct., Jun., t. iii., f. 571).

siah, had conquered death, and was no more subject to its power. Moreover, if it be true that Christ's sufferings caused his death, he is chargeable with grossly deceiving the disciples to present his body to them in a higher light, and thereby give an impulse to their faith which it could not otherwise have obtained. And so that great fact which formed the immovable basis of the disciples' faith in Christ's person and work, and in his plan of salvation, on which rests the whole fabric of the Christian Church, must have gained its high import from an actual deception on the part of Christ himself, or at least from an intentional concealment of the truth!

Had the Jewish opponents of the Gospel made use of this hypothesis to invalidate the proof of Divinity which the disciples derived from Christ's reappearance, and circulated it freely, it would neither be matter of surprise nor ground of suspicion. But the fact that they did *not* make use of any such hypothesis, but employed any and every other means to invalidate the Christian faith, is a powerful proof that there was nothing in the circumstances of Christ's death to favour such an explanation. Of a totally different character was the report, so easily diffused,* that the disciples had found means to remove the body from the grave. The invention and circulation of such a report was most natural; the empty grave was a proof that *must* be invalidated. But, on the other hand, there is not a vestige of proof that the Jews, presupposing the accounts of Christ's reappearance to be true, ever reported that he had been revived from a merely apparent death: on the contrary, the *truth* of those accounts was the object of attack from the very first. The opponents of Christianity declared that the disciples either intentionally deceived others, or were themselves deceived; *e. g.*, *Celsus*, who made great use of the attacks of the Jews upon Christianity and the fables they spread abroad concerning it. And in this connexion it was that the accusation of stealing away the body was brought against the disciples; they did it, it was said, to nullify the evidence of the corpse against their *pretence*† that Christ had risen and reappeared to them. Paul did not find it necessary to prove that Christ had really died; this was taken for granted; his task was to show that he had *risen* from the dead (1 Cor., xv.).‡

* Matt., xxviii., 15. We cannot mistake the additions of tradition to the original facts. Dial. c. Tryph. Jud., f. 335, ed. Colon, and the extracts by *Eisenmenger*, i., 192.

† L. c., Justin Mart.: "πλανῶσι τοὺς ἀνθρώπους λέγοντες ἐγηγέρθαι."

‡ But I must believe, contrary to some of the latest interpreters, that John (xix., 34), as an eye-witness, meant to prove that Christ was really dead, from the nature of the blood that flowed from the wound. Ver. 35 certainly refers to ver. 34, and not to ver. 36, 37. Although John, in these last verses, referred to the Old Testament prophecy, it does not follow that he made it the seal of faith (v. 34), particularly *for his readers*, who were not such as to be led to faith from arguments founded in Judaism. These verses are added to show that what had taken place was conformed to a higher necessity. It appears, then, that John thought it necessary to prove that Christ had really died. It does not follow, however, that

§ 298. *The Resurrection intended only for Believers.*

The manifestation of the risen Saviour was only designed for those who had been brought to faith by his previous ministry. It was not one of the miracles by which unbelievers were to be convinced. Those whose dispositions of heart had made them unsusceptible of impression from his whole ministry would have received, for the same reason, but transient impressions from his reappearance. If the *living* Jesus could not lead them to repent, neither would they have been persuaded by one risen from the dead.*

The reappearance of the risen one, therefore, was designed to seal and confirm the faith of such as already believed; to form the point of transition from their sensible communion with the visible Christ to their spiritual fellowship with the invisible, but ever-present Saviour. And as *this* was the reason why Christ did not, in his last promises recorded by John, make express mention of his reappearance as a preparatory moment, so we shall find in his conversations with the disciples *after* the resurrection conspicuous allusions to the promises made before. Here, too, we find the reason why he only appeared to them occasionally, and remained among them but a short time; they were not to accustom themselves anew to cleave to his visible manifestation, but to learn that his reappearance was to mediate a higher and everlasting union.†

§ 299. *The Women, Peter, and John at the Grave.*

We now proceed to a brief statement of the details of the resurrection.

On Sunday morning, the second day of Easter, Mary of Magdalene, with certain other women, came to the tomb, and found the stone removed. They began to fear that the body had been taken away, and that they should see it no more. Mary, in alarm, ran to seek for John and Peter; the other women afterward went to other of the Apostles. Peter and John hastened to the tomb. John, in anxious haste, anticipated Peter. Looking down into the tomb, and seeing the shroud de

he had in view any definite opponents who *denied* that fact. As he intended to testify to the *resurrection*, it was necessary that he should testify to the *death*, especially for readers who were not believers; in view of the well-known fact that crucifixion, endured for a few hours, was not in itself always fatal. If he *had* definite opponents in view, they were probably (corresponding to John's sphere of labour) heathens, and not Jews.

* Luke, xvi., 31; cf. p. 136, 322.

† I agree with *De Wette*, against *Lücke*, that John, xx., 30, does not refer to other appearances of Christ after the resurrection not mentioned by John, but that it is intended as a word of conclusion to his whole Gospel. This is supported by the whole form of the expression, and by the use of the words σημεῖα ποιεῖν, which cannot mean any thing but "to work miracles." The phrase ἐνώπιον τῶν μαθητῶν proves nothing to the contrary; the Apostles were eye-witnesses of Christ's whole ministry; and John wrote his Gospel as one of these eye-witnesses.

cently disposed, but no corpse there, he started back in consternation. Peter, taking courage, descended into the tomb; John followed; and, now convinced that the body was not there, called to mind* the intimations which Christ had given† of his resurrection, and faith began to spring up in his soul.

§ 300. *Christ appears to the Women at the Tomb; to Mary; to the two Disciples on the Way to Emmaus.*

During the absence of the Apostles, Christ appeared first to the two women who had gone away; and they, filled with joy, surprise, fear and reverence, fell before him and embraced his feet. But he spoke to them encouragingly: "*Be not afraid.*" All that he said was encouraging and cheering; and in bidding them announce his resurrection to the Apostles, he spoke of them as "*brethren.*"‡

He then appeared to Mary, who had remained at the tomb oppressed with anxiety and grief. Seeing him so unexpectedly, in the morning twilight, she did not at first recognize him. But when he called her by name, she knew at once the well-accustomed voice. With an exclamation of joy she turned and (probably) stretched out her hands towards him. But Jesus bade her not to grasp him: "*Touch me not for I am not yet ascended to my Father; but go to my brethren, and say unto them, 'I ascend unto my Father and your Father, to my God and your God.'*"§ This obscure saying obviously refers to the last discourses reported by John, and cannot be understood apart from them. We know he had promised the disciples that, after ascending to the Father, he would return and remain with them forever. *Now* he had returned; and they might deem *this* to be the return which he had promised, and expect him to remain with them thenceforth in the same form. He cautioned them against so misunderstanding the promise as to cleave to him in the form in which he then appeared, because he had not "yet ascended to the Father." After that event, when he should manifest himself as the glorified one, were they to embrace him wholly; obviously not in a natural, but in a spiritual

* The word ἐπίστευσεν (John, xx., 8) must be referred to a previous fortelling of the resurrection by Christ himself, in accordance with John's usage of the idea of "belief," as *Lücke* has admitted (Commentar, 2te Aufl.). The sense of the passage is as follows: The disciples needed such an outward sign to revive their faith in Christ's predictions of his resurrection; for they were not as yet penetrated by the conviction that Jesus, as Messiah, had *necessarily* to rise in order to accomplish the Messianic work according to the prophecies of Scripture. Had they been, they would have needed no such external perception. (Cf. *Lücke's* excellent remarks on the passage.)

† Cf. p. 423.

‡ Matt., xxviii., 10.

§ The word ἅπτεσθαι (John, xx., 17) means not only a momentary touching, but to *seize*, to *grasp*. It can, also, be applied to the embracing of an object that one intends to retain hold of; and of the beginning of a continued occupation with any subject.

sense.* His stay in his then form was to be but transient; only after his ascension could he remain permanently, and that in another form.† Therefore, he did not commission Mary to announce his sensible coming, but his ascension to the Father, and his subsequent revelation to them; making no mention of the intermediate and brief manifestation that was only to prepare the way for the higher and permanent one. The words "my brethren, my Father, my God, your God," served to remind them of the promise in his last discourses, viz., that they, through Him, should enter into a special relation to the Father, whom He, in a sense peculiarly his own, could call "His Father" and "His God;" that they should, in communion with Him, recognize the Father also as "their Father" and "their God," and, therefore, have full confidence that He would come to them with the Father.

Two disciples‡ (not of the number of the Apostles§) were going in the afternoon to the village of *Emmaus*, about a mile from Jerusalem. They had heard that the body was not found in the grave, and of what the women had seen before Christ appeared to them; but had not yet learned that he had risen and appeared. As they walked they conversed, in sorrow, of what had occurred; of the expectations they had cherished that Jesus should be the Messiah to redeem the people of God; of the failure of their hopes, and their uncertainty as to the future. Absorbed in this conversation, they were joined by Jesus. He took part in their conversation, expounded the Scriptures relating to himself, and pointed out the errors into which they had fallen. Under the power of his words their hearts burned within them, and new anticipations dawned upon their souls. But still they did not recognize the speaker, either because the thoughts he uttered withdrew their attention from his person; or because they could not suppose that *He* should first appear to *them;* or, finally, because of a change in his person. Not until, as they sat at meat, he pronounced the blessing, broke the bread, and gave it to them, did they discern Him who had sat so often with them at table. Although the lateness of their recognition may appear strange, the *time* of it—just at the repetition of an accustomed habit—is entirely natural. There is not even a mystical feature about it, in itself considered; although we may perhaps trace, in the way in which he made himself known, an allusion to the promise given

* If the passage only meant, "Delay not here with me, but go," we might expect οὔπω γὰρ ἀναβαίνω instead of οὔπω γὰρ ἀνάβεβηκα.

† It is clear that the passage contains no proof that Christ ascended to heaven immediately after his conversation with Mary. Even with this view (since it cannot be supposed that he would have brought from *heaven* a body that could be physically touched) the ἅπτεσθαι, after his reappearance from heaven, would have to be taken in a higher sense.

‡ Luke, xxiv., 13.

§ And, therefore, Paul does not mention the occurrence.

at the Last Supper, that he would always be as truly with them in their common meals as he was on that occasion.

§ 301. *Christ appears to Peter; and to the rest of the Apostles, except Thomas.—The "Breathing" upon the Apostles.*

The two disciples, on returning to the city, found that Christ had appeared in the mean time to the Apostle Peter.* In the evening of the same day, the Apostles, Thomas excepted, were assembled with closed doors,† when Christ suddenly appeared in their midst, with the usual salutation, "*Peace be unto you*"—a salutation which, from *his* lips, had a peculiar significance.‡ To prove that he was present in body, he showed them the wounds in his hands, feet,§ and side. In taking leave of them, he said, "*Peace be unto you. As my Father hath sent me, even so send I you.*" Thus, while announcing to them the peace of fellowship with him, he consecrated them as messengers of peace to all mankind.

He then "breathed" upon them—a symbol of the inspiration they were to receive from heaven, to fit them to preach his Gospel and proclaim forgiveness of sins in his name.|| Here, again, he obviously intended to impress vividly upon their minds the promises given in his last discourses.

Christ, having thus given a sign of the bestowing of the Divine "breath"—the Divine life proceeding from him—added, in explanation, "*Receive ye the Holy Ghost.*" The hearts of the disciples were prepared for this by the reappearance of Christ and his words to them; and the symbolical act, recalling the predictions of his last discourses in regard to the imparting of the Spirit, must have impressed them profoundly. The higher life received from Christ had before been covered and dormant; now, perhaps, a new consciousness of it arose within them. Still the full sense of the sign and of the words was far

* Luke, xxiv., 33, 34; 1 Cor., xv., 5.

† Luke, xxiv., 36; 1 Cor., xv., 5. Paul says he "was seen of the *twelve;* but this term might be used even though one of the number were wanting; the point was, Christ's appearance to the Apostles as a *body.* The *word* "twelve" was the common designation of the Apostles; the *number* was a subordinate point. Perhaps even Paul did not recur at the time to the absence of one of the number.

‡ John, xiv., 27. Cf. p. 398.

§ It may be the case that, in Luke's account, this scene is intermingled with that which took place eight days later in presence of Thomas. He relates the proof of corporeity given by Christ in tasting food with the disciples, which John, who does not appear to give full details, may have omitted, or, perhaps, mentioned in another connexion, John, xxi., 13. But these are unimportant points.

|| In Luke, xxiv., 47, 48, we find a fuller developement—John gives it more in a symbolical form. "The promise of my Father" (Luke, xxiv., 49) seems to allude to Joel, iii., 1 but a comparison with Acts, i., 4, leads us to refer it to a promise given by Christ in the Father's name; hence to the last discourses recorded by John Cf. Luke, xii., 12; and p. 395.

from being realized. Not as yet were they the mighty organs of that Spirit for the diffusion of the kingdom of God. The act, therefore, was in part *prophetical.*

But it was something more than a sign or symbol; a Divine operation accompanied it. It formed a link of connexion between the promise of the Spirit and its fulfilment; between the impressions which Christ's personal intercourse had made upon the Apostles, and the great fact which we designate as "the outpouring of the Holy Ghost." The operation of the promised Spirit on the disciples must be considered, it is true, as a progressive, gradually increasing influence—a new inspiring principle of their whole nature, in all its powers and tendencies. But we must believe, according to the analogy of all religious historical developement, that there was a *moment,* forming an epoch, in which the consciousness of the common higher life, and of the new creation of which Christ was the origin, broke forth with peculiar power in a general inspiration of the first Christian congregations. All great religious movements set out from such actual epoch-making moments; although, indeed, gradual preparatory stages must always be presupposed.

§ 302. *Christ appears to five hundred Believers; to his Brother James; to the Apostles, Thomas included.—His Conversation with Thomas.*

Christ next appeared to more than five hundred disciples, assembled in one place; and then to his brother James.* And on Sunday, eight days after his first appearance among the living, he again showed himself to the Apostles unawares, while they were assembled with closed doors. Thomas was now among them; the same Thomas who on a former occasion had displayed his peculiar character in an expression

* 1 Cor., xv., 7. No specific description of "James" being given by Paul in this passage, it was, in all probability, James the Just, as he was called, the brother of our Lord. This appearance of Christ is mentioned in the *Evang. ad Hebræos* (translated by Jerome); but apparently as his *first* appearance; for it goes on, "After Jesus had given the shroud to the servant of the high-priest, he went to James." Perhaps this arose partly from the high rank assigned to James by the sect among whom this Gospel arose, and partly from the fabulous circumstances that are given in the account of the following sort: "James had made a vow, after partaking of the bread given by Christ at the Last Supper, that he would eat no more until he had seen Jesus risen from the dead. Jesus, coming to him, had a table with bread brought out, blessed the bread, and gave it to James, with the words, 'Eat thy bread now, my brother, since the Son of Man has risen from the dead'" (Hieron. de Viris Illust., c. ii.). Mark the contrast between the objective tone of the traditions that form the base of the synoptical Gospels, and this tradition of a party that owed its origin to an alloying doctrinal element, remodelling the facts to serve a subjective purpose. Another and striking contrast is, that our Gospels (and Paul following them) make Christ appear only to believers, for reasons explained in our text. Had they aimed to make the testimony as strong as possible, without regard to truth, they would have represented him as appearing also to his opponents. The statement above cited from *Evang. ad Hebr.,* of his appearing to a servant of the high-priest, conflicts with the whole import and object of his resurrection.

of doubt. Christ's appearance, and the way in which he reproached the doubting Thomas, impressed the latter with so powerful and overwhelming a sense of the Divinity that beamed forth in the manifestation of the risen Saviour, that he addressed him by a title which had been ascribed to him, so far as we know, by none of the disciples: "*My Lord and my God.*" We are not justified in ascribing to Thomas, whose immediate impressions impelled him to this exclamation, a fully-formed theory of doctrine; yet how mighty a cause must have been at work to induce a man trained in the common opinions of the Jews to use such a title!*

Christ then said to Thomas, "*Because thou hast seen me, thou hast believed; blessed are they who have not seen, and yet have believed.*" We must endeavour to unfold the rich import of these words. Christ does not refuse the title given to him by Thomas. He acknowledges his exclamation as an expression of the true faith. The words "believed" and "believe" cannot be confined solely to Christ's resurrection; they refer to his person and work in general, and to the resurrection only as one necessary element thereof. But the words of Christ also reproved Thomas for needing a visible sign in order to believe. It was implied in them that the long personal intercourse of Thomas with Christ, and his faith in Jesus as the Son of God and as superior to death, should have been enough to overcome his doubts—and, on this foundation, he should have found the statements of Christ's reappearance, given him by the others, any thing but incredible.† His faith should have arisen from within, not waited for a summons from without. And, on the other hand, Christ assigns a higher place to those who are led to faith, without such visible proofs, by his spiritual self-manifestation in the preaching of the Gospel—a faith arising inwardly from impressions made upon a willing mind.‡ His words implied that, in all after time, faith would be impossible, if there were no other way of passing from unbelief to belief except by sensible signs of assurance. The passage is strikingly illustrative of the process by which faith is developed. It contains the ground and reason why *the Gospel history had to be handed down precisely in a form which could not but give occasion for manifold doubts to the human understanding, when it conducts its inquiries apart from the religious consciousness and religious wants.*

* Or, are we to suppose that John involuntarily remodelled the words of Thomas, in accordance with his own views? Certainly not. Nowhere, in John's accounts, do the disciples speak out of character. Least of all could he have attributed to one like Thomas more than he uttered. On the contrary, such an expression, coming from a *Thomas*, would, for that very reason, impress itself more strikingly upon the minds of the disciples. It is not difficult, therefore, to account for the precision with which John records the expression.

† Christ's reproof, perhaps, referred also to the intimations he had given of his approaching resurrection.

‡ Cf. p. 138, 139.

§ 303. *Christ's Appearances in Galilee; to the Seven on the Sea of Genesareth.—The Draught of Fishes.—The Conversation with Peter.*

We must now briefly compare the narrative of Matthew, which reports Christ's appearances to the disciples in Galilee alone, with that of the other Gospels.*

As Matthew's Gospel records particularly the events of Christ's ministry, of which Galilee was the theatre, it might be imagined that, for that reason, the theatre of his appearances after the resurrection was also, in that Gospel, unintentionally transferred to Galilee; this view would ascribe to the tradition inaccuracy as to localities, but not as to the facts themselves. But Matthew coincides most accurately, in this particular, with the account appended to John's Gospel (ch. xxi.); in which it is stated that the disciples soon retired to Galilee, where Christ reappeared to them. As for internal probability, it is not likely that they remained in the city, in the midst of Christ's enemies, but rather that they returned to their own land, where dwelt most of Christ's followers and friends. Nor is there any thing impossible in Matthew's statement that Christ bade them return for a season to Galilee, where he could have quiet and undisturbed intercourse with them. Their return thither being once admitted as natural in itself, it would naturally follow that Christ should appear often in order to prevent them from forgetting their high calling amid the cares of life; and, what was most important, to repeat to them the promise (before given at Jerusalem) of the gift of the Holy Ghost, to fit them for the duties of that calling.

Seven of the disciples† were fishing in the Sea of Genesareth. During the whole night they caught nothing. Early in the morning Jesus appeared and asked them, kindly, as was his wont, "*Children, have ye any meat?*" When they replied in the negative, he bade them cast the net anew on the right side of the vessel. John was the first to recognize the voice of Jesus. The hasty Peter could not wait until the vessel reached the shore, but swam over.

After the repast, Christ gently reminded Peter of his promise, so precipitately made, and so soon broken: "*Lovest thou me more than these?*" Peter replied, "*Yea, Lord, thou knowest that I love thee.*"

* With regard to Paul's statements (1 Cor., xv.), it is probable that he mentioned the appearances of Christ to the Apostles (as more extensively known) up to a certain period, especially his first appearances at Jerusalem, and stopped short; it being unimportant for his purpose to give a complete enumeration, adding only the manifestation which he himself received. Another explanation, however, might be given.

† John, xxi. The account in this chapter was, in all probability, received from John's own lips, and written down, after his death, by one of his disciples. There is no ground to question its credibility as a whole.

Then said Christ, "*Feed my lambs** (prove your love by acts)." On Christ's third repetition of the question, Peter felt its force, and exclaimed, in grief, "*Lord, thou knowest all things; thou knowest that I love thee.*" The Saviour again repeated the injunction, "*Feed my lambs;*" and added, as a proof of confidence in Peter's fidelity, that at some future time he would have to sacrifice his life in the faithful discharge of his calling.

§ 304. *Christ appears in Galilee for the last Time.—The Commission of the Apostles.*

In his final appearance among the disciples in Galilee (Matt., xxviii., 18), Christ reminded them anew of their calling, viz., to preach the Gospel to all nations; and to admit the men of all nations, by baptism, into his communion and discipleship. And he assured them that all power was given to him, in heaven and in earth, to establish the kingdom of God victoriously; and that he would be with his own, even until the consummation of that kingdom.†

§ 305. *Christ appears for the last Time near Jerusalem, on the Mount of Olives.*

The minds of the disciples were eagerly directed to the feast in commemoration of the giving of the Law of the Old Covenant (Pentecost); the new relation established between God and man naturally connected itself with the idea of the old. It was a reasonable expectation that at this feast the promise of the Holy Spirit, by which they were to be

* Referring either to the preaching of the Gospel in general, or in particular to the supervision of the first congregations, inasmuch as Peter, especially, had the χάρισμα κυβερνήσεως.

† The subsequent scruples of the disciples to go among the heathen do not prove that they had not received this commission. These scruples turned upon the single point of admitting the heathen without a previous conversion to Judaism. Some suppose that the naming of "Father, Son, and Holy Ghost" in connexion with baptism (v. 19) is foreign to the passage, and was derived from later ecclesiastical language. But that expression, coming from the lips of Christ, was precisely fitted to betoken the peculiar nature of the new communion and worship, with reference to his earlier teaching, and especially to his last discourses preserved by John; for every thing there refers to the Father, as revealed by the Son; to the Spirit, proceeding from the Father and imparted by the Son; to communion with the Father, through the Son, in the Spirit of Divine life imparted by him. It is possible that these words were not at first considered as a formula to be adhered to rigidly in baptism, and that the rite was performed (the essential being made prominent) with reference to Christ's name alone; and that only at a later period it was thought that the words constituted a literal and necessary form. It is undeniable that this account does not bear so distinct a historical stamp as other narratives of Christ's reappearance; it is possible that several occurrences, on separate occasions, were taken together and transferred to Galilee. The fact that Matthew represents Christ as reappearing to his disciples *only* in Galilee, while Luke and Paul testify to the contrary, may help us to decide upon the synoptical accounts of Christ's ministry up to the time of his last journey to Jerusalem, the theatre of which, also, they place in Galilee. This is another testimony in favour of John's account.

made powerful organs of their Divine Master, would be fulfilled. They went to Jerusalem a week before the time of the feast. As they were walking to the Mount of Olives, just forty days after Christ's first appearance, they were joined by Christ, and he repeated the promise for the last time.

Still cleaving to their worldly Messianic hopes, they asked the Saviour whether he intended *then* to found his kingdom in its glory (Acts, i., 6). In reply, he declared, as he had always done during his life on earth, "*It is not for you to know the times or the seasons, which the Father hath put in his own power.*" It was enough (he told them) for them to know their own calling in reference to the kingdom of God, and how they were to obtain power to fulfil it, viz., by receiving the Holy Ghost. With this last reply, and this last promise, he was removed from their eyes.

CHAPTER IX.

THE ASCENSION.

§ 306. *Connexion of the Ascension with the Resurrection.*

WE come now to treat of the Ascension of Christ—a close of Christ's ministry on earth corresponding to its beginning.

It must not be thought that the essential feature of the ascension is vouched for only by Luke. It would rest on firm grounds, even apart from the particular form in which it is represented in Luke; nay, even if there were not a word about it either in his Gospel or in the Acts. That essential feature is, that *Christ did not pass from his earthly existence to a higher through natural death, but in a supernatural way; i. e.,* that he was removed from this globe, and from the conditions of earthly life, to a higher region of existence in a way not conformed to the ordinary laws of corporeal existence or to be explained by them. *This* fact is as certain as his resurrection; both must stand or fall together. Either the resurrection itself must be denied; or it must be considered as a mere natural recovery from a transitory suspension of the powers of life (both which hypotheses we have shown to be untenable); or such a termination of his life on earth as we have just defined, must be inevitably admitted.

Although obscurity rests,* to a great extent, upon the nature of the

* We deem it better to acknowledge a problem unsolved than to give attempts at solution, on the one side or the other, which will not satisfy a clear thinker. Certainly we over-estimate our knowledge of the laws of the creation not a little, when we deem ourselves authorized to deny the reality of a phenomenon, simply because we cannot explain it satisfactorily. *There are more things between heaven and earth than our philosophy may dream of.*

existence of Christ on earth after his resurrection, and upon the nature of the corporeal organism with which he rose from the dead; still, this much is certain, that the fundamental conception, on which all the representations of the New Testament are founded, exhibits the resurrection only as the means of transition from the form of his earthly being, whose close was his *death*, to a higher form of personal existence superior to death; as the beginning of a new life which was not to be, as the former, subject to the laws of a corporeal, earthly organism, but was destined for an imperishable developement. When Paul declared (Rom., vi., 9, 10) that Christ, risen from the dead, should die no more, because death had no dominion over him; when he opposed this resurrection (2 Cor., xiii., 4) as the commencement of a life in Divine power, to his earlier life in human weakness through which he was made subject to death, he only gave utterance to a conviction that was common to all the eye-witnesses of the resurrection. The mode of Christ's reappearance had made the same impression upon them all. And the resurrection had *necessarily* to be considered as the restoration from death, in a higher form, of his personal existence (consisting of the union of body and soul, not subject thereafter to death, but destined for an unbroken eternity of life), in order to become the foundation of belief in an eternal life of the glorified human personality, to spring out of death; in order to be the *fact* on which this faith (as a historically-grounded belief) could be established. The restoration of an earthly life from death, afterward to be developed according to ordinary laws, and to terminate in death, would, in this respect, have been of no value.

§ 307. *The Ascension necessary for the Conviction of the Apostles.*

Moreover, the resurrection of Christ, considered as a historical link in the psychological developement of the Apostles (which cannot be explained, as we have shown, unless the resurrection is taken for granted), loses its true significance in this regard, if Christ were removed from the earth in any other than a supernatural way. How could his resurrection have formed, for the disciples, the basis for belief in an eternal life, if it had been subsequently followed by death? Their faith, raised by his reappearance, would have sunk with his dissolution. Their belief in his Messiahship would have been rudely shocked; he would have been to them again an ordinary man. And how could the conviction of his exaltation, which we find every where outspoken in their writings with such strength and confidence, ever have arisen? Although, therefore, the visible fact of the ascension is only expressly mentioned by Luke, yet all that John says of his going up to his heavenly Father, and all that the Apostles preached of his elevation to God, *presupposed* their conviction that he had been supernaturally removed from the earth, to the utter exclusion of the idea that he had departed in the ordinary way of death. It was not necessary to make express mention of the outward and visible fact, as they never entertained the thought that Christ, in the form in which he appeared to them after his resurrection, could be touched again by death. When he took leave of them, and they saw him no more, they never thought of any thing else but that he had been supernaturally removed from human view to a higher region of existence.

If it be said now that "it does not follow, because the Apostles conceived the matter so, that it really *was* so; and that we must distinguish the fundamental *fact* from their subjective conceptions," we have the reply ready. Their subjective conception was founded in a *fact* which it presupposed, viz., the way in which Christ showed himself to them after his resurrection; in the impression which he made upon them by his higher and celestial appearance. And further, apart from this necessary presupposition, if Christ led the Apostles to form such a subjective conception merely by mysteriously appearing and vanishing, by keeping silence as to his abode and as to the end towards which he advanced, he must have planned a fraud, to form the basis of their religious conviction from that time on. As surely as we cannot attribute such a fraud to the Holy One, who called himself the "Truth," so certainly must we take for granted an *objective fact* as the source of the faith of the Apostles.

§ 308. *Connexion of all the Supernatural Facts in Christ's Manifestation.*

We make the same remark upon the Ascension of Christ as was before made upon his miraculous Conception.* In regard to neither is prominence given to the special and actual *fact* in the Apostolic writings; in regard to both such a fact is presupposed in the general conviction of the Apostles, and in the connexion of Christian consciousness. Thus the end of Christ's appearance on earth corresponds to its beginning. No link in its chain of supernatural facts can be lost without taking away its significance as a whole. Christianity rests upon these facts; stands or falls with them. By faith in them has the Divine life been generated from the beginning; by faith in them has that life in all ages regenerated mankind, raised them above the limits of earthly life, changed them from *glebæ adscriptis* to citizens of heaven, and formed the stage of transition from an existence chained to nature, to a free, celestial life, far raised above it. Were this faith gone, there might, indeed, remain many of the *effects* of what Christianity had been; but as for Christianity in the true sense, as for a Christian Church, there could be none.

* Cf. p. 16.

INDEX.

F.

G.

H.

I.

J.

K.

L.

M.

N.

O.

P.

PASSAGES OF SCRIPTURE

QUOTED OR ALLUDED TO.

John.

PASSAGES FROM ANCIENT WRITERS

QUOTED OR ALLUDED TO.

THE END.